murach's beginning Java with NetBeans

Joel Murach
Michael Urban

TRAINING & REFERENCE

murach's beginning Java with NetBeans

Joel Murach

Michael Urban

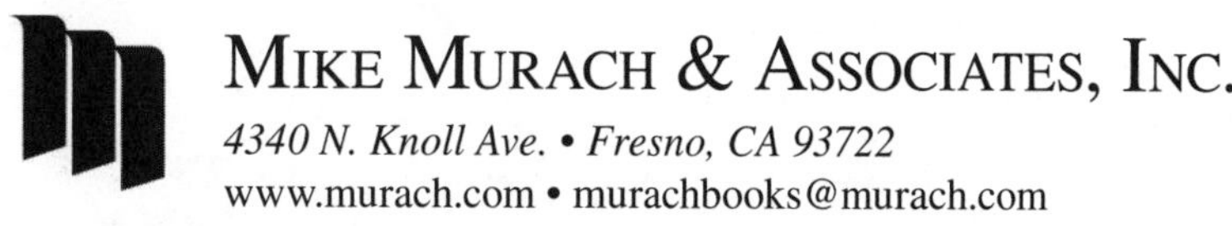
Mike Murach & Associates, Inc.

4340 N. Knoll Ave. • Fresno, CA 93722

www.murach.com • murachbooks@murach.com

Editorial team

Authors:	Joel Murach Michael Urban
Editor:	Ray Halliday
Production:	Maria Spera

Books for Java programmers

Murach's Beginning Java with Eclipse
Murach's Java Servlets and JSP (3rd Edition)
Murach's Android Programming
Murach's Java Programming (4th Edition)

Books for database programmers

Murach's MySQL (2nd Edition)
Murach's Oracle SQL and PL/SQL for Developers (2nd Edition)
Murach's SQL Server 2012 for Developers

Books for web developers

Murach's HTML5 and CSS3 (3rd Edition)
Murach's Dreamweaver CC 2014
Murach's JavaScript
Murach's jQuery
Murach's PHP and MySQL (2nd Edition)

Books for .NET programmers

Murach's C# 2012
Murach's ASP.NET 4.5 Web Programming with C# 2012

Murach's Visual Basic 2012
Murach's ASP.NET 4.5 Web Programming with VB 2012

For more on Murach books, please visit us at www.murach.com

Printed in the United States of America

10 9 8 7 6 5 4 3 2 1
ISBN: 978-1-890774-84-4

Content

Introduction xvii

Section 1 Get started right

Chapter 1	An introduction to Java and NetBeans	3
Chapter 2	How to start writing Java code	31
Chapter 3	How to use classes and methods	61
Chapter 4	How to code your own classes and methods	95
Chapter 5	How to structure an object-oriented application	131
Chapter 6	How to test and debug an application	147

Section 2 Essential skills as you need them

Chapter 7	How to work with primitive types and operators	167
Chapter 8	How to code control statements	197
Chapter 9	How to work with strings	233
Chapter 10	How to work with arrays	253

Section 3 Object-oriented programming skills

Chapter 11	How to work with inheritance	275
Chapter 12	How to work with interfaces	307
Chapter 13	How to work with inner classes, enumerations, and documentation	333

Section 4 More essential skills as you need them

Chapter 14	How to work with collections, generics, and lambdas	357
Chapter 15	How to work with dates and times	389
Chapter 16	How to work with exceptions	409
Chapter 17	How to work with file I/O	433
Chapter 18	How to work with threads	463

Section 5 Real-world skills

Chapter 19	How to work with a MySQL database	483
Chapter 20	How to use JDBC to work with a database	505
Chapter 21	How to develop a GUI with Swing (part 1)	531
Chapter 22	How to develop a GUI with Swing (part 2)	573

Appendixes

Appendix A	How to set up Windows for this book	607
Appendix B	How to set up Mac OS X for this book	617

Expanded contents

Section 1 Get started right

Chapter 1 An introduction to Java programming

An overview of Java ... 4
Java timeline ... 4
Java editions ... 4
How Java compares to C++ and C# ... 6

Types of Java applications ... 8
Two types of desktop applications ... 8
Two types of web applications ... 10
Mobile apps ... 12

An introduction to Java development ... 14
The code for a console application ... 14
How Java compiles and interprets code ... 16
Introduction to IDEs for Java development ... 18

An introduction to NetBeans ... 20
How to open a project ... 20
How to open a file in the code editor window ... 22
How to compile and run a project ... 24
How to use the Output window with a console application ... 24
How to work with two or more projects ... 26
How to close or delete a project ... 26

Chapter 2 How to start writing Java code

Basic coding skills ... 32
How to code a class ... 32
How to code a main method ... 32
How to code statements ... 34
How to code comments ... 34
How to print output to the console ... 36

How to use NetBeans to work with a new project ... 38
How to create a new project ... 38
How to work with Java source code and files ... 40
How to use the code completion feature ... 42
How to detect and correct syntax errors ... 44

How to work with numbers ... 46
How to declare and initialize variables ... 46
How to assign values to a variable ... 48
How to code arithmetic expressions ... 50

How to work with strings ... 52
How to declare and initialize String variables ... 52
How to join strings ... 52
How to include special characters in strings ... 54

The Code Tester application ... 56
The user interface ... 56
The CodeTesterApp class ... 56

Chapter 3 How to use classes and methods

How to work with classes, objects, and methods 62
How to import classes 62
How to create an object from a class 64
How to call a method from an object 64
How to call a method from a class 64
How to view the documentation for the Java API 66

How to work with the console 68
How to use the Scanner class to get input 68
How to convert strings to numbers 70
A class that reads input from the console 72
How to convert numbers to formatted strings 74
A class that prints formatted numbers to the console 76

How to code simple control statements 78
How to compare numbers 78
How to compare strings 78
How to code a while loop 80
How to code an if/else statement 82

The Line Item application 84
The user interface 84
The code 86

The Future Value application 88
The user interface 88
The code 90

Chapter 4 How to code your own classes and methods

An introduction to classes 96
How encapsulation works 96
The relationship between a class and its objects 98

How to work with a class that defines an object 100
How to use NetBeans to create a new class 100
The Product class 102
How to code instance variables 104
How to code constructors 106
How to code methods 108
How to create an object from a class 110
How to call the methods of an object 112

How to work with static fields and methods 114
The ProductDB class 114
How to code and call static fields and methods 116
When to use static fields and methods 116

The Product Viewer application 118
The user interface 118
The ProductApp class 118

More skills for working with classes and methods 120
Reference types compared to primitive types 120
How to overload methods 122
How to use the this keyword 124
The Product class with overloading 126

Chapter 5 How to structure an object-oriented application

How to use the three-tier architecture 132
How the three-tier architecture works 132
How to work with packages 134
How to use NetBeans to work with packages 136
The Line Item application 138
The user interface 138
The class diagram 138
The LineItem class 140
The LineItemApp class 142

Chapter 6 How to test and debug an application

Basic skills for testing and debugging 148
Typical test phases 148
The three types of errors 148
Common Java errors 150
How to determine the cause of an error 152
A simple way to trace code execution 154
How to use NetBeans to debug an application 156
How to set and remove breakpoints 156
How to step through code 158
How to inspect variables 158
How to inspect the stack trace 160

Section 2 Essential skills as you need them

Chapter 7 How to work with primitive types and operators

Basic skills for working with data 168
The eight primitive data types 168
How to declare and initialize variables 170
How to declare and initialize constants 172
How to code arithmetic expressions 174
How to use the binary operators 174
How to use the unary operators 176
How to use the compound assignment operators 178
How to work with the order of precedence 180
How to work with casting 182
How to use Java classes to work with numbers 184
How to use the Math class 184
How to use the BigDecimal class 186
How to fix rounding errors 188
The Invoice application 190
The user interface 190
The code 190

Chapter 8 How to code control statements

How to code Boolean expressions 198
How to compare primitive data types 198
How to use the logical operators 200

How to code if/else and switch statements 202
How to code if/else statements 202
How to code switch statements 206
A new if/else statement for the Invoice application 210

How to code loops 212
How to code while loops 212
How to code do-while loops 214
How to code for loops 216
How to code break and continue statements 218

How to code try/catch statements 220
How exceptions work 220
How to catch exceptions 222

The Future Value application 224
The user interface 224
The code 224

Chapter 9 How to work with strings

How to work with the String class 234
How to create strings 234
How to join strings 234
How to append data to a string 234
How to compare strings 236
How to work with string indexes 238
How to modify strings 240

How to work with the StringBuilder class 242
How to create a StringBuilder object 242
How to append data to a string 242
How to modify strings 244

The Product Lister application 246
The user interface 246
The StringUtil class 246
The Main class 248

Chapter 10 How to work with arrays

Essential skills for working with arrays 254
How to create an array 254
How to assign values to the elements of an array 256
How to use for loops with arrays 258
How to use enhanced for loops with arrays 260
How to work with two-dimensional arrays 262

How to use the Arrays class 264
How to fill an array 264
How to sort an array 264
How to search an array 264
How to create a reference to an array 264
How to copy an array 266
How to compare two arrays 266

The Month Selector application 268
The user interface 268
The Main class 268

Section 3 Object-oriented programming skills

Chapter 11 How to work with inheritance

An introduction to inheritance 276
How inheritance works..276
How the Object class works 278
Basic skills for working with inheritance 280
How to create a superclass 280
How to create a subclass 282
How polymorphism works 284
The Product application 286
The console 286
The Product, Book, and Software classes 288
The ProductDB class...288
The ProductApp class 292
More skills for working with inheritance 294
How to cast objects 294
How to compare objects...296
How to work with the abstract and final keywords 298
How to work with the abstract keyword...298
How to work with the final keyword..300

Chapter 12 How to work with interfaces

An introduction to interfaces... 308
A simple interface 308
Interfaces compared to abstract classes..310
Basic skills for working with interfaces 312
How to code an interface...312
How to implement an interface 314
How to inherit a class and implement an interface 316
How to use an interface as a parameter...318
How to use inheritance with interfaces 320
New features for working with interfaces 322
How to work with default methods 322
How to work with static methods..324
The Product Viewer application 326
The console 326
The ProductReader interface..326
The ProductDB class...326
The ProductApp class 328

Chapter 13 How to work with inner classes, enumerations, and documentation

How to work with inner classes.. 334
An introduction to GUI programming 334
How to code an inner class..336
How to code an anonymous class 338

How to work with enumerations 340
How to declare an enumeration 340
How to use an enumeration 340
How to enhance an enumeration 342
How to work with static imports 342

How to document a class 344
How to add javadoc comments to a class 344
How to use HTML and javadoc tags in javadoc comments 346
How to use NetBeans to generate documentation 348
How to view the documentation 348

Section 4 More essential skills as you need them

Chapter 14 How to work with collections, generics, and lambdas

An introduction to Java collections 358
A comparison of arrays and collections 358
An overview of the Java collection framework 360
An introduction to generics 362

How to use the ArrayList class 364
How to create an array list 364
How to add and get elements 366
How to replace, remove, and search for elements 368
How to store primitive types in an array list 370

The Invoice application 372
The user interface 372
The Invoice class 374
The InvoiceApp class 376

How to work with lambda expressions 378
An introduction to lambdas 378
A method that doesn't use a lambda expression 380
A method that uses a lambda expressions 382
How to use the Predicate interface 384

Chapter 15 How to work with dates and times

An introduction to date/time APIs 390
The date/time API prior to Java 8 390
The date/time API for Java 8 and later 390

How to use the new date/time API 392
How to create date and time objects 392
How to get date and time parts 394
How to compare dates and times 396
How to adjust date/time objects 398
How to add or subtract a period of time 400
How to format dates and times 402
An Invoice class that includes an invoice date 404

Chapter 16 How to handle exceptions

An introduction to exceptions 410
The exception hierarchy 410
How exceptions are propagated 412

How to work with exceptions **414**
How to use the try statement 414
How to use the try-with-resources statement 416
How to use the methods of an exception 418
How to use a multi-catch block 420
How to use the throws clause 422
How to use the throw statement 424

How to work with custom exception classes **426**
How to create your own exception class 426
How to use exception chaining 428

Chapter 17 How to work with file I/O

An introduction to directories and files **434**
A package for working with directories and files 434
Code examples that work with directories and files 436

An introduction to file input and output **438**
How files and streams work 438
A file I/O example 440
How to work with I/O exceptions 442

How to work with text files **444**
How to connect a character output stream to a file 444
How to write to a text file 446
How to connect a character input stream to a file 448
How to read from a text file 450
A class that works with a text file 452

The Product Manager application **456**
The console 456
The Main class 456

Chapter 18 How to work with threads

An introduction to threads **464**
How threads work 464
Typical uses for threads 464
Classes and interfaces for working with threads 466
The life cycle of a thread 468

Two ways to create threads **470**
Constructors and methods of the Thread class 470
How to extend the Thread class 472
How to implement the Runnable interface 474

How to synchronize threads **476**
How to use synchronized methods 476
When to use synchronized methods 476

Section 5 Real-world skills

Chapter 19 How to work with a MySQL database

How a relational database is organized **484**
How a table is organized 484
How the tables in a database are related 486
How the columns in a table are defined 488

An introduction to MySQL **490**
What MySQL provides 490
Ways to interact with MySQL 492
How to open a database connection 494
How to enter and execute a SQL statement 494

A SQL script that creates a database **496**
How to drop, create, and select a database 496
How to create a table and insert data 496
How to create a user and grant privileges 496

The SQL statements for data manipulation **498**
How to select data from a table 498
How to insert, update, and delete rows 500

Chapter 20 How to use JDBC to work with databases

How to work with JDBC **506**
An introduction to database drivers 506
How to connect to a database 508
How to return a result set and move the cursor through it 510
How to get data from a result set 512
How to insert, update, and delete data 514
How to work with prepared statements 516

Two classes for working with databases **518**
The DBUtil class 518
The ProductDB class 520
Code that uses the ProductDB class 526

Chapter 21 How to develop a GUI with Swing (part 1)

An introduction to GUI programming **532**
A summary of GUI toolkits 532
The inheritance hierarchy for Swing components 534

How to create a GUI that handles events **536**
How to display a frame 536
How to add a panel to a frame 538
How to add buttons to a panel 538
How to handle a button event 540

How to work with layout managers **542**
A summary of layout managers 542
How to use the FlowLayout manager 544
How to use the BorderLayout manager 546

How to work with tables **548**
How to create a model for a table 548
The ProductTableModel class 550
How to create a table 554
How to get the selected row or rows 554
How to add scrollbars to a table 556

How to work with built-in dialog boxes **558**
How to display a message 558
How to confirm an operation 560

The Product Manager frame **564**
The user interface 564
The ProductManagerFrame class 566

Chapter 22 How to develop a GUI with Swing (part 2)

How to work with labels and text fields 574
How to work with labels 574
How to work with text fields 576

How to use the GridBagLayout manager 578
An introduction to the GridBagLayout manager 578
How to lay out components in a grid 580
How to add padding 582
How to avoid a common pitfall 584

How to code a data entry form 586
How to create a custom dialog 586
How to pass data between a dialog and its parent 588

The Product form 590
The user interface 590
The ProductForm class 592
Two methods that use the ProductForm class 600

How to use threads with Swing 602
A common problem 602
How to solve the problem 602

Appendix A How to set up Windows for this book
How to install the JDK and NetBeans 608
How to install the source code for this book 610
How to install MySQL and MySQL Workbench 612
How to create the database for this book 614
How to restore the database for this book 614

Appendix B How to set up Mac OS X for this book
How to install the JDK and Netbeans 618
How to install the source code for this book 620
How to install the MySQL Community Server 622
How to install MySQL Workbench 624
How to create the databases for this book 626
How to restore the databases 626
How to update the password for the root user 628

Introduction

Murach's Beginning Java is especially designed for beginning programmers and programmers with limited experience who want to learn Java at a professional level. Because Java is a language that's especially difficult for beginners, we knew we needed to do something different to make this the best beginning book on the market. That's why this book isn't like any of the competing books.

Even better, this isn't just a beginning book. By the time you finish this book, you'll have all the skills that you need for moving on to Java web programming or Android programming. You'll also know the basics for building desktop applications that get their data from MySQL databases.

What this book does

Section 1 of this book presents a six-chapter Java course that gets you off to a great start. This section works for complete beginners as well as experienced programmers because it lets you set your own pace. If you're a beginner, you'll move slowly and do all the exercises. If you have some experience, you'll move more quickly and do the exercises that you choose.

From the start, you'll be using the NetBeans IDE because that will help you learn faster. Then, by chapter 3, you'll be developing applications that use classes from the Java API. By chapter 4, you'll be developing object-oriented applications that use your own classes. By chapter 5, you'll be using the 3-tier architecture to structure your object-oriented applications like a professional. And by chapter 6, you'll be using the best practices for testing and debugging your applications.

Once you've mastered the skills of section 1, the hard work is done. Then, you can add to your skills by reading the chapters in sections 2, 3, and 4. When you finish those sections, you'll have all the Java skills that you need to get started with web or mobile programming.

But that's not all! The four chapters in section 5 present real-world skills that you can use to develop desktop applications. To start, these chapters show you how to create a MySQL database for an application and how to write the Java code that works with the data in this database. Then, these chapters show how to develop a graphical user interface (GUI) for the application.

Why you'll learn faster and better

When we started writing this book, we knew we had to take a new instructional approach if we wanted to teach you everything you need to know in a way that's faster and better than the existing approaches. Here are some of the unique features of this book:

- Unlike many Java books, this book shows you how to use an IDE for developing Java applications. That's how Java programming is done in the real world, and that by itself will help you learn faster.
- Unlike many Java books, all of the examples in this book are drawn from real-world applications. This is especially apparent in the object-oriented chapters, where most competing books resort to unrealistic examples that are difficult to apply to real-world applications.
- Unlike many Java books, this one focuses on the Java features that you will use every day. As a result, it doesn't waste your time by presenting Java features that you probably won't ever need.
- Like all of our books, this book uses our unique paired-pages format where each topic is presented in a two-page spread, with code examples, diagrams, and screen captures on the right page and the text on the left page. This helps you learn more while reading less and makes this book the ideal reference after you've used it for learning.
- Like all of our books, the exercises at the end of each chapter give you a chance to apply what you've just learned. They guide you through the development of applications, challenge you to apply what you've learned in new ways, and provide the hands-on experience that builds your confidence.

What software you need

Java SE 8 is the current version of Java and the one that this book shows how to use. However, since all versions of Java are backwards compatible, the code and skills presented in this book will work with later versions too. Besides that, this book clearly identifies when Java introduced its most recent features. That way, you can avoid these features if you want your code to work with older versions of Java.

As you can tell from its title, this book shows you how to use the NetBeans IDE to code, test, and debug applications. We chose NetBeans because we think it's the best IDE for beginners and because it will help you learn faster. It's also easy to use, free, and runs on all operating systems.

If you already have experience with Eclipse and want to use it instead, please note that we have an Eclipse version of this book called *Murach's Beginning Java with Eclipse*. The only difference between that book and this one is the IDE.

How our downloadable files can help you learn

If you go to our website at www.murach.com, you can download all the files that you need for getting the most from this book. These files include:

- all of the applications in this book
- the starting code for the chapter exercises
- the solutions to the chapter exercises

These files let you test, review, and copy the code. In addition, if you have any problems with the exercises, the solutions are there to help you over the learning blocks, which is an essential part of the learning process. For more information on downloading and installing these files, please see appendix A (Windows) or appendix B (Mac OS X).

Support materials for trainers and instructors

If you're a corporate trainer or a college instructor who would like to use this book for a course, we offer an Instructor's CD that includes: (1) a complete set of PowerPoint slides that you can use to review and reinforce the content of the book; (2) instructional objectives that describe the skills a student should have upon completion of each chapter; (3) test banks that measure mastery of those skills; (4) extra exercises and projects that prove mastery; and (5) solutions to the extra exercises and projects.

To learn more about this Instructor's CD and to find out how to get it, please go to our website at www.murach.com. Then, if you're an instructor, click on the Instructors tab at the top of the page. If you're a trainer, click on the Trainers link in the navigation bar. Or, if you prefer, call Kelly at 1-800-221-5528 or send her an email at kelly@murach.com.

Companion books

When you finish this book, you'll have all of the Java skills that you need for web or mobile programming with Java. Then, if you want to move on to web programming, *Murach's Java Servlets and JSP* will show you how to use Java servlets and JavaServer Pages to develop professional web applications. Or, if you want to move on to Android programming, *Murach's Android Programming* will get you started with that.

Another Murach book that you should be aware of is *Murach's Java Programming*. This book has been one of the best-selling Java books since its first edition in 2001, but it isn't a beginning book. As a result, it is organized differently, moves faster, goes into greater depth, and presents some additional subjects, particularly on GUI programming and handling data. In general, though, you shouldn't need this book if you have *Murach's Beginning Java*.

Let us know how this book works for you

When we started this book, our goals were (1) to teach you all the skills you need to move on to web or mobile programming with Java, (2) to teach you these skills as quickly and easily as possible, and (3) to show you some of the professional skills that are needed to develop a desktop application. Now, we hope that we've succeeded.

If you have any comments about this book, we would appreciate hearing from you at murachbooks@murach.com. We thank you for buying this book. We hope you enjoy reading it. And we wish you great success with your Java programming.

Joel Murach, Author
joel@murach.com

Mike Murach
Publisher

Section 1

Get started right

This section gets you started quickly with Java programming. First, chapter 1 introduces you to some concepts and terms that apply to Java development. In addition, it shows you how to use the NetBeans IDE to open and run existing projects.

After that, chapter 2 shows you how to use NetBeans to start writing Java code. Chapter 3 shows how to develop two procedural applications by using classes and methods that are available from the Java API. Chapter 4 shows how to convert a procedural application to an object-oriented application by creating your own classes and methods. Chapter 5 shows how to structure an object-oriented application. And chapter 6 shows how to thoroughly test and debug this application. When you complete these chapters, you'll be able to write, test, and debug simple object-oriented applications of your own.

1

An introduction to Java programming

This chapter starts by presenting some background information about Java. This information isn't essential to developing Java applications, so you can skim it if you want. However, it does show how Java works and how it compares to other languages.

This chapter finishes by showing how to use the NetBeans IDE to work with an existing project. This gives you some hands-on experience using NetBeans to work with projects such as the projects for this book that you can download from our website.

An overview of Java **4**
Java timeline 4
Java editions 4
How Java compares to C++ and C# 6
Types of Java applications **8**
Two types of desktop applications 8
Two types of web applications 10
Mobile apps 12
An introduction to Java development **14**
The code for a console application 14
How Java compiles and interprets code 16
Introduction to IDEs for Java development 18
An introduction to NetBeans **20**
How to open a project 20
How to open a file in the code editor window 22
How to compile and run a project 24
How to use the Output window with a console application 24
How to work with two or more projects 26
How to close or delete a project 26
Perspective **28**

An overview of Java

In 1996, Sun Microsystems released a new programming language called Java. Today, Java is owned by Oracle and is one of the most widely used programming languages in the world.

Java timeline

Figure 1-1 starts by describing all major releases of Java starting with version 1.0 and ending with version 1.8. Throughout Java's history, the terms *Java Development Kit* (*JDK*) and *Software Development Kit* (*SDK*) have been used to describe the Java toolkit. In this book, we'll use the term *JDK* since it's the most current and commonly used term.

In addition, different numbering schemes have been used to indicate the version of Java. For example, Java SE 8 or Java 1.8 both refer to the eighth major version of Java. Similarly, Java SE 7 and Java 1.7 both refer to the seventh major version of Java. The documentation for the Java API uses the 1.x style of numbering. As a result, you should be familiar with it. However, it's also common to only use a single number such as Java 6.

This book shows how to use Java 8. However, Java is backwards compatible, so it should also work for future versions of Java. In addition, most of the skills described in this book have been a part of Java since its earliest versions. As a result, those skills should work with earlier versions of Java.

Java editions

This figure also describes the three most common editions of Java. To start, there is the Standard Edition, which is known as *Java SE*. It's designed for general purpose use on desktop computers and servers, and it's the edition that you'll learn how to work with in this book. For example, you can use Java SE to create a desktop application like the one presented at the end of chapter 22.

The Enterprise Edition is known as *Java EE*. It's designed to develop distributed applications that run on an intranet or the Internet. You can use Java EE to create web applications.

The Micro Edition is known as *Java ME*. It's designed to run on devices that have limited resources such as mobile devices, TV set-top boxes, printers, smart cards, hotel room key cards, and so on.

With some older versions of Java, Java SE was known as J2SE (Java 2 Platform, Standard Edition). Similarly, Java EE was known as J2EE (Java 2 Platform, Enterprise Edition). If you are searching for information about Java on the Internet, you may come across these terms. However, they aren't commonly used anymore.

Java timeline

Year	Month	Event
1996	January	JDK 1.0 released.
1997	February	JDK 1.1 released.
1998	December	SDK 1.2 released.
1999	August	Java 2 Platform, Standard Edition (J2SE) released.
	December	Java 2 Platform, Enterprise Edition (J2EE) released.
2000	May	J2SE with SDK 1.3.
2002	February	J2SE with SDK 1.4.
2004	September	J2SE 5.0 with JDK 1.5.
2006	December	Java SE 6 with JDK 1.6.
2010	April	Oracle buys Sun.
2011	July	Java SE 7 with JDK 1.7.
2014	March	Java SE 8 with JDK 1.8.

Java editions

Platform	Description
Java SE (Standard Edition)	For general purpose use on desktop computers and servers. Some early versions were called J2SE (Java 2 Platform, Standard Edition).
Java EE (Enterprise Edition)	For developing distributed applications that run on an intranet or the Internet. Some early versions were called J2EE (Java 2 Platform, Enterprise Edition).
Java ME (Micro Edition)	For devices with limited resources such as mobile devices, TV set-top boxes, printers, and smart cards.

Description

- The *Java Development Kit* (*JDK*) includes a compiler, a runtime environment, and other tools that you can use to develop Java applications. Some early versions were called the Software Development Kit (SDK).

Figure 1-1 Java timeline and editions

How Java compares to C++ and C#

Figure 1-2 compares Java to C++ and C#. As you can see, Java has some similarities and some differences with these languages.

When Sun's developers created Java, they tried to keep the syntax for Java similar to the syntax for C++. That way, it would be easy for C++ programmers to learn Java. In addition, they designed Java so its applications can be run on any computer platform without needing to be compiled for each platform. In contrast, C++ needs to be compiled for each platform.

Java was also designed to automatically handle many operations involving the allocation and de-allocation of memory. This is a key reason why it's easier to develop programs and write bug-free code with Java than with C++.

To provide these features, early versions of Java sacrificed some speed (or performance) when compared to C++. However, improvements in later versions of Java have greatly improved Java's speed. Now, Java runs faster than C++ in some contexts, and its performance is adequate in most contexts.

When Microsoft's developers created C#, they used many of the best ideas of Java. Like Java, C# uses a syntax that's similar to C++. In addition, C# automatically handles memory operations.

C# can run on any platform that has a runtime environment for it. However, Windows is the only operating system that fully supports runtime environment for C#. As a result, C# is primarily used for developing applications that only need to run on Windows.

Java runs faster than C# in most contexts. However, the performance of C# is adequate in most contexts.

Operating systems that support Java

- Windows
- Mac OS X
- Linux
- Most versions of UNIX.
- Most other modern operating systems

A note about Android

- The Android operating system doesn't support Java in the same way as most operating systems. However, you can use most features of Java 6 and 7 to write the code for Android apps.

Java compared to C++

Feature	Description
Syntax	Java syntax is similar to C++ syntax.
Platforms	Compiled Java code can run on any platform that has a Java runtime environment. C++ code must be compiled once for each type of system that it is going to be run on.
Speed	C++ runs faster than Java in some contexts, but Java runs faster in other contexts.
Memory	Java handles most memory operations automatically, but C++ programmers must write code that manages memory.

Java compared to C#

Feature	Description
Syntax	Java syntax is similar to C# syntax.
Platforms	Like Java, compiled C# code can run on any platform that has a runtime environment for it.
Speed	Java runs faster than C# in most contexts.
Memory	Like Java, C# handles most memory operations automatically.

Figure 1-2 Java compared to C++ and C#

Types of Java applications

You can use Java to write almost any type of application (also known as an app or a program). In this book, you'll learn how to develop desktop applications. However, you can also use Java to develop web applications and mobile apps.

Two types of desktop applications

Figure 1-3 shows two types of *desktop applications* that you can create with Java. This type of application runs directly on your computer.

The easiest type of desktop application to create is known as a *console application*. This type of application runs in the *console*, or *command prompt*, that's available from your operating system. The console provides an easy way to get input from the user and to display output to the user. In this figure, for example, the user has entered three values in the console application, and the application has performed a calculation and displayed the result. When you're learning Java, it's common to work with console applications until you have a solid understanding of the Java language.

Once you have a solid understanding of the Java language, you can create a desktop application that uses a *graphical user interface* (*GUI*). In this figure, for example, the GUI application performs the same tasks as the console application. In other words, it gets the same input from the user, performs the same calculation, and displays the same result. However, the GUI application is more user-friendly and intuitive.

Since developing the GUI for an application requires some significant Java coding skills, this book doesn't present a GUI application until the last two chapters of this book. Until then, this book uses console applications to teach the basics of Java.

A console application

```
Command Prompt - java -jar FutureValueConsole.jar
Microsoft Windows [Version 6.1.7601]
Copyright (c) 2009 Microsoft Corporation.  All rights reserved.

C:\Users\Joel>cd \murach\java_netbeans\files

C:\murach\java_netbeans\files>java -jar FutureValueConsole.jar
Welcome to the Future Value Calculator

Enter monthly investment:   100
Enter yearly interest rate: 3
Enter number of years:      3
Future value:               $3,771.46

Continue? (y/n):
```

A GUI application

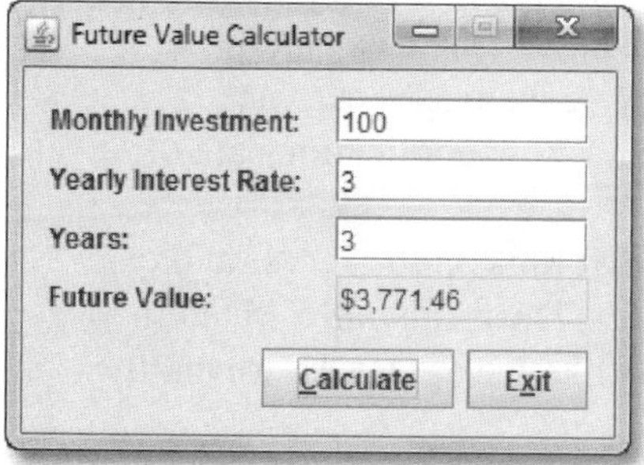

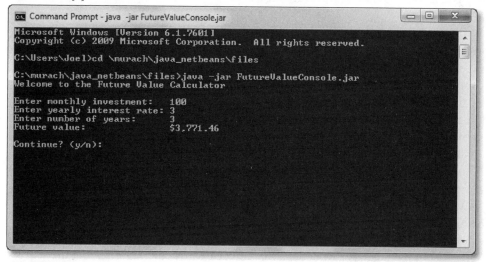

Description

- A *console application* uses the console to interact with the user.
- A *GUI application* uses a *graphical user interface* to interact with the user.

Figure 1-3 Two types of desktop applications

Two types of web applications

Figure 1-4 shows two types of *web applications* that you can develop with Java. In the early days of Java, which were also the early days of the Internet, one of the most exciting features of Java was that you could use it to create a special type of web-based application known as an *applet* like the one shown in this figure. This applet works like the GUI application presented in the previous figure. However, unlike that GUI application, an applet could be stored in an HTML page and run inside a Java-enabled browser. As a result, it was once possible to distribute applets via the Internet or an intranet.

In recent years, with tightening security restrictions, fewer and fewer browsers support applets, even if you install the plug-in that was designed to allow applets to run in browsers. That's why the applet in this figure is shown in the Applet Viewer, which comes as part of the JDK, instead of being shown in a web browser. Due to these security restrictions, applets are effectively obsolete. They are still included as part of Java SE for backwards compatibility, but they aren't used much anymore, and we don't cover them in this book.

In addition, since applets run within a browser on the client, they were never an ideal way to work with resources that run on the server, such as enterprise databases. A better way to provide access to enterprise databases is to use Java EE to create web applications that run on the server. These applications are often based on servlets.

A *servlet* is a special type of Java application that runs on the server and can be called by a client, which is usually a web browser. This is also illustrated in this figure. Here, you can see that the servlet works like the applet. However, the servlet runs on the server, not the client.

To start, the web browser on the client sends a request to the servlet that's running on the server. This request includes the user input. When the servlet receives this request, it performs the calculation and returns the result to the browser, typically in the form of an HTML page.

In this figure, the servlet doesn't access a database. However, it's common for servlets to work with a database. For example, suppose a browser requests a servlet that displays all unprocessed invoices that are stored in a database. Then, when the servlet is executed, it reads data from the database, formats that data within an HTML page, and returns the HTML page to the browser.

When you create a servlet-based application like the one shown here, all the processing takes place on the server and only HTML, CSS, and JavaScript is returned to the browser. That means that anyone with an Internet or intranet connection, a web browser, and adequate security clearance can access and run a servlet-based application.

To make it easy to store the results of a servlet within an HTML page, the Java EE specification provides for *JavaServer Pages* (JSPs). As a result, it's common to use JSPs with servlets. Although servlets and JSPs aren't presented in this book, they are present in a companion book, *Murach's Java Servlets and JSP*. For more information about this book, please visit our website at www.murach.com.

An applet

Applet Viewer: murach/ui/FutureValueA...
Applet
Monthly Investment: 100
Yearly Interest Rate: 3
Years: 3
Future Value: $3,771.46
Calculate
Applet started.

A servlet

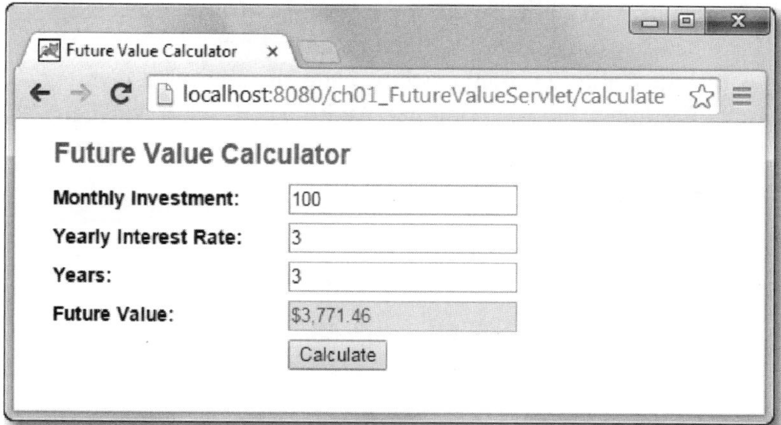

Description

- An *applet* is a type of Java application that runs within a web browser.
- In the past, it was possible to run applets in most web browsers. Today, fewer and fewer web browsers support applets. As a result, they are effectively obsolete.
- A *servlet* is a type of Java application that runs on a web server.
- A servlet accepts requests from clients and returns responses to them. Typically, the clients are web browsers.

Figure 1-4 Two types of web applications

Mobile apps

You can also use Java to develop *mobile apps*, which are applications that run on a mobile device such as a smartphone or tablet. In particular, Java is commonly used to write the code for apps that run on Android devices. For example, figure 1-5 shows a mobile app that was developed with Java. This app performs the same task as the applications presented in the previous figures.

An app works much like a traditional application. However, the user interface has to be modified so that it's appropriate for a mobile device. In this figure, for example, the user interface has been modified to work with a touch-screen device that has a small screen and no keyboard. As a result, the user can use the keypad that's displayed onscreen to enter numbers and can press the Done button on this keypad to perform the calculation.

The Android operating system includes its own virtual machine that supports a subset of Java, including most features of Java 6 and 7. As a result, if you use Java to develop Android apps, you can't use all of the features of Java, especially the newest ones. That's because the Android virtual machine is not a Java virtual machine. In other words, the Android virtual machine can't run compiled Java code, and a Java virtual machine can't run compiled Android code. Still, you can use most features of Java to write code for Android apps, and it's easy enough to compile that code so the Android virtual machine can run it.

A mobile app

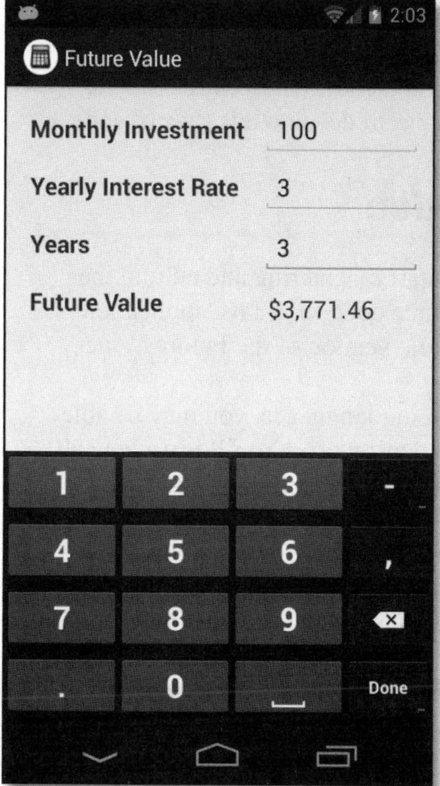

Description

- A *mobile app* uses a mobile device such as a smartphone or tablet to interface with the user.
- The Android operating system supports a subset of Java, including most features of Java 6 and 7.

Figure 1-5 Mobile apps

An introduction to Java development

At this point, you're ready to see the source code for an application. You're ready to learn how Java compiles and interprets this code. And you're ready to be introduced to some of the IDEs that you can use to develop this type of code.

The code for a console application

When you develop a Java application, you start by entering and editing the *source code*. To give you an idea of how the source code for a Java application works, figure 1-6 presents the code for the console version of the Future Value application shown in figure 1-3.

If you have experience with other programming languages, you may be able to understand much of this code already. If not, don't worry! You'll learn how all of this code works in the next few chapters. For now, here's a brief explanation of this code.

Most of the code for this application is stored in a *package* named murach.fv that corresponds with the murach/fv folder. Within this package, there is a *class* named Main that corresponds with a file named Main.java. This class begins with an opening brace ({) and ends with a closing brace (}).

Within this class, the code defines one *method* named main. This method also begins with an opening brace ({) and ends with a closing brace (}). These braces are indented to clearly show that they are contained within the class.

This is a special type of method known as the *main method* for the application. The code within this method is executed automatically when you run the application. In this case, the code prompts the user for input, gets input from the user, converts the input to appropriate data types, calculates the future value based on the user input, and displays the results to the user.

To do that, this code uses two while loops. Each loop begins with an opening brace ({) and ends with a closing brace (}). The code within these braces is also indented. This shows that the first loop is coded within the main method and the second loop is coded within the first loop.

The first while loop allows the user to continue making calculations by entering "y" or to exit by entering "n". The second while loop is executed once for each month and contains the statements that calculate the future value. To do that, these statements add the monthly investment and the monthly interest amount to the current future value.

The code for a console application

```
package murach.fv;

import java.text.NumberFormat;
import java.util.Scanner;

public class Main {

    public static void main(String[] args) {
        // displayLine a welcome message
        System.out.println("Welcome to the Future Value Calculator");
        System.out.println();

        Scanner sc = new Scanner(System.in);
        String choice = "y";
        while (choice.equalsIgnoreCase("y")) {

            // get input from user
            System.out.print("Enter monthly investment:   ");
            double monthlyInvestment = Double.parseDouble(sc.nextLine());

            System.out.print("Enter yearly interest rate: ");
            double yearlyInterestRate = Double.parseDouble(sc.nextLine());

            System.out.print("Enter number of years:      ");
            int years = Integer.parseInt(sc.nextLine());

            // convert yearly values to monthly values
            double monthlyInterestRate = yearlyInterestRate / 12 / 100;
            int months = years * 12;

            // calculate the future value
            double futureValue = 0;
            int i = 1;
            while (i <= months) {
                futureValue = futureValue + monthlyInvestment;
                double monthlyInterestAmount =
                        futureValue * monthlyInterestRate;
                futureValue = futureValue + monthlyInterestAmount;
                i = i + 1;
            }

            // format and displayLine the result
            System.out.println("Future value:               " +
                    NumberFormat.getCurrencyInstance().format(futureValue));
            System.out.println();

            // see if the user wants to continue
            System.out.print("Continue? (y/n): ");
            choice = sc.nextLine();
            System.out.println();
        }
        System.out.println("Bye!");
    }
}
```

Figure 1-6 The code for a console application

How Java compiles and interprets code

Once the source code has been written, you use the *Java compiler* to compile the source code into a format known as Java *bytecodes* as shown in figure 1-7. At this point, the bytecodes can be run on any platform that has a *Java runtime environment* (*JRE*) installed on it. A JRE includes all of the software needed to run bytecodes. Among other things, this includes an implementation of a *Java virtual machine* (*JVM*). This JVM includes a *Java interpreter* to translate the Java bytecodes into native code that can be understood by the underlying operating system.

Most modern implementations of the JVM have replaced the Java interpreter with a *just-in-time compiler* (*JIT compiler*). A JIT compiler is similar to an interpreter in some ways, but it actually compiles the most used parts of the Java bytecodes into native code and stores this code in a cache. This improves performance significantly.

Since JREs are available for all major operating systems, you can run Java on most platforms. This is what gives Java applications their *platform independence*. In contrast, C++ requires a specific compiler for each platform.

How Java compiles and interprets code

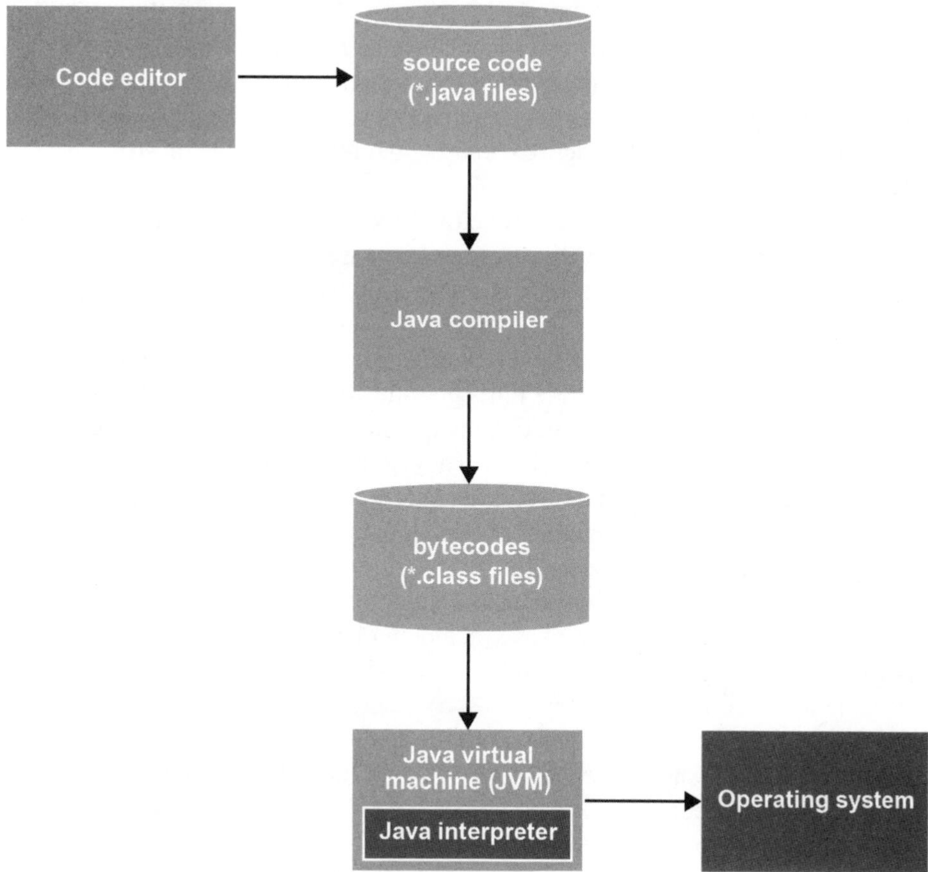

Description

- When you develop a Java application, you typically use a code editor to work with the *source code* for the application. Files that contain source code have the .java extension.
- The *Java compiler* translates Java source code into a *platform-independent* format known as Java *bytecodes*. Files that contain Java bytecodes have the .class extension.
- A *Java virtual machine* (*JVM*) includes a *Java interpreter* that executes Java bytecodes. Most modern implementations of the JVM have replaced the Java interpreter with a *just-in-time compiler* (*JIT compiler*). A JIT compiler is similar to an interpreter in some ways, but it improves performance significantly.
- A *Java runtime environment* (*JRE*) has all of the components necessary to run bytecodes including a JVM. Since JREs are available for most operating systems, Java bytecodes can be run on most operating systems.

Figure 1-7 How Java compiles and interprets code

Introduction to IDEs for Java development

To develop Java applications, you typically use an *Integrated Development Environment (IDE)*. Although you can use a simple text editor with command-line tools, an IDE provides features that can make developing Java applications considerably easier. Figure 1-8 describes some of the features of the most popular IDEs.

All of the IDEs listed in this figure are either free or have a free edition. That makes them particularly attractive to students as well as programmers who are learning on their own. Most of these IDEs also run on all modern operating systems.

The first two IDEs listed in this figure, NetBeans and Eclipse, are two of the most popular Java IDEs. Both of these IDEs provide all of the features listed in this figure. For example, both of these IDEs help you complete your code and notify you of potential compile-time errors. They both automatically compile your code before you run it. And they both include a debugger that lets you perform standard debugging functions like setting breakpoints, stepping through code, and viewing the values of variables.

The third IDE listed in this figure, IntelliJ IDEA, isn't as popular as NetBeans and Eclipse. However, we have included it here to give you an idea of the range of IDE choices that are available for Java. In addition, other Java IDEs are available that aren't included here.

The fourth IDE listed in this figure, Android Studio, is designed for developing Android apps. It was developed by Google and IntelliJ, and version 1.0 was released in December 2014.

This book shows how to use NetBeans because we think it's a great IDE. However, we also plan to publish an Eclipse version of this book because we think it's a great IDE too.

Popular Java IDEs

IDE	Description
NetBeans	A free, open-source IDE that runs on most modern operating systems. NetBeans is commonly used for most types of Java applications, but not for Android apps.
Eclipse	A free, open-source IDE that runs on most modern operating systems. Eclipse is commonly used for developing all types of Java applications including Android apps.
IntelliJ IDEA	The Community Edition of this IDE is a free, open-source IDE that runs on most modern operating systems.
Android Studio	An IDE specifically designed for Android development that's based on IntelliJ IDEA and backed by Google.

Features provided by most IDEs

- A code editor with code completion and error detection.
- Automatic compilation of classes when you run the application.
- A debugger that lets you set breakpoints, step through code, and view the values of active variables.

Description

- To develop Java applications, you typically use an *Integrated Development Environment* (*IDE*) like those listed above. All of these IDEs are either free or have free editions.

Figure 1-8 Introduction to Java IDEs

An introduction to NetBeans

In NetBeans, a *project* is a virtual folder that contains all the folders and files for an application. The easiest way to get started with NetBeans is to open an existing project. For example, you can open any of the applications for this book after you download them from our website as described in the appendixes.

How to open a project

To open a project in NetBeans, you use the Open Project dialog box shown in figure 1-9. This dialog box lets you navigate to the folder that contains the project you want to open. In this figure, for example, the Open Project dialog box shows all of the existing NetBeans projects in this folder:

```
/murach/java_netbeans/book_apps
```

To clearly indicate when a folder contains a Java project, the Open Project dialog box displays a small coffee cup icon to the left of the folder name. Then, you can open the project by selecting it and clicking the Open Project button.

The dialog box for opening a project

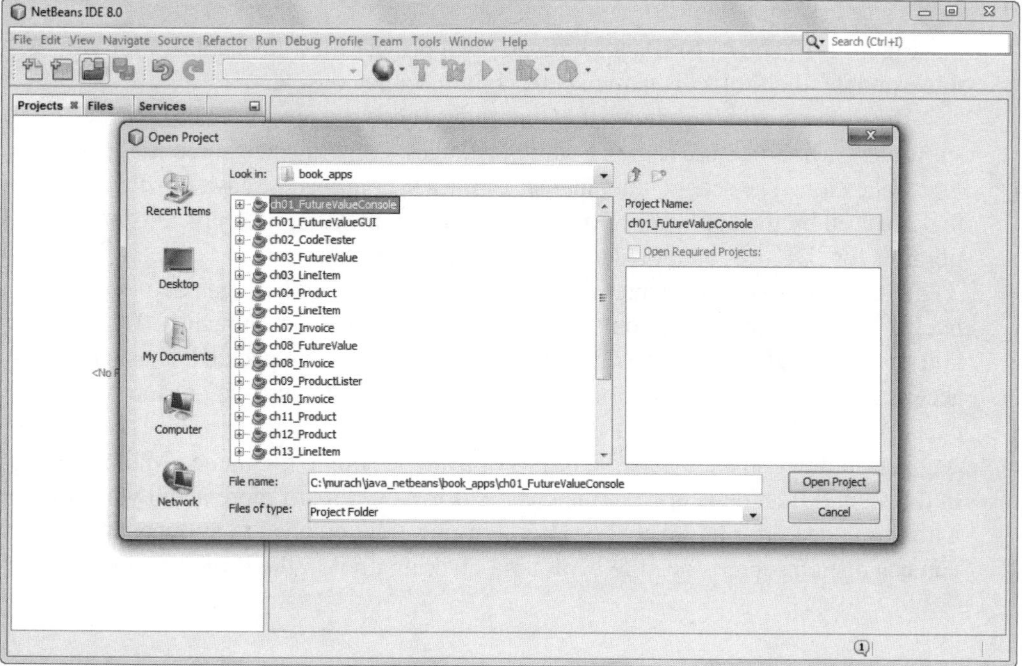

Description

- A NetBeans *project* consists of a top-level folder that contains the subfolders and files for a Java application.
- To open a project, click the Open Project button in the toolbar or select the File→Open Project command. Then, use the Open Project dialog box that's displayed to locate and select the project and click the Open Project button.
- You can also open a project by using the File→Open Recent Project command and then selecting the project from the list that's displayed.

How to open a file in the code editor window

Figure 1-10 shows NetBeans with an open project for a Java application. In this example, the project is named ch01_FutureValueConsole.

The Projects window shows that the folder for this project contains two subfolders. The first one, named Source Packages, contains the source files for the application. The second one, named Libraries, contains the Java *libraries* that are used by the application. In this case, the application uses just the default libraries for JDK 1.8, but you can add others if necessary.

Within the Source Packages folder, the source files can be organized into *packages*. Here, the project contains a single package named murach.fv. When you develop small applications like the one shown here, one package is usually acceptable. For larger applications, though, you'll want to use two or more packages as described later in this book.

The application shown here consists of a single source file named Main.java. In this figure, this file is open in the *code editor*. You'll learn more about working with this code editor in the next chapter. For now, all you need to know is that you can open a source code file by double-clicking on it in the Projects window.

The Projects window and code editor for a project

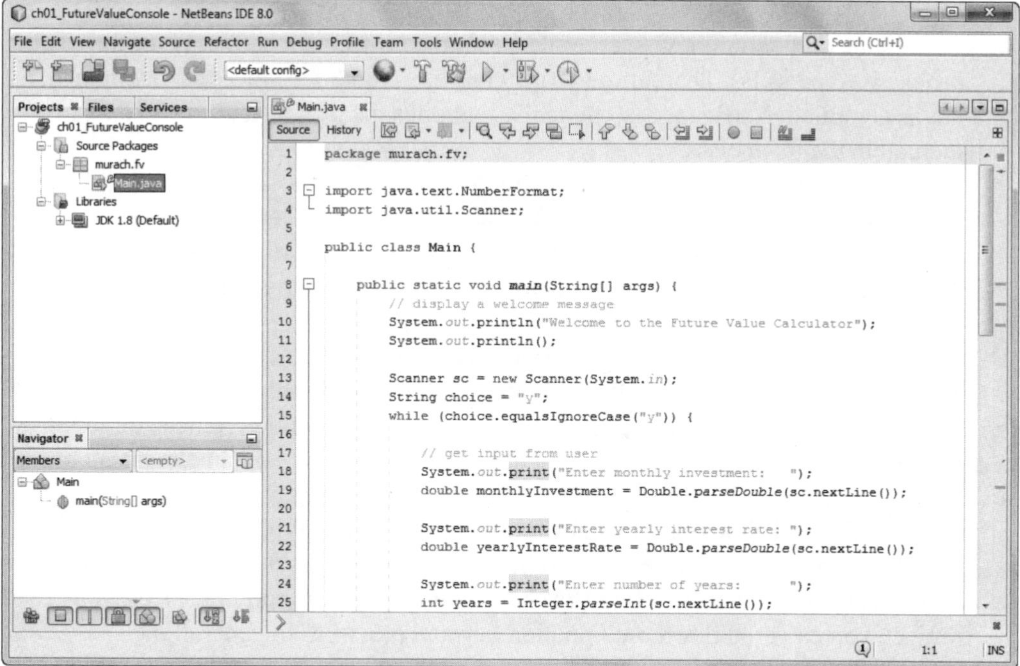

How to navigate through the Projects window

- To expand or collapse the nodes in the Projects window, click on the plus and minus signs to the left of its folders, files, and libraries.
- The Source Packages subfolder contains the .java files that make up the project. These files define the classes that store the code for your application.
- The Source Packages folder can store the .java files for your project in one or more *packages*, which are folders that store .java files.
- The Libraries subfolder contains the *libraries* that are available to your project. By default, you can use the packages and classes in the JDK libraries.
- The Projects window displays the folders, files, and libraries that make up a NetBeans project. If necessary, you can display the Projects window by selecting the Window→Projects command.

How to open a file in the code editor window

- You can use the *code editor window* to work with the source code of a .java file.
- To open a file in the code editor window, use the Project window to navigate to the .java file and then double-click on it.

Figure 1-10 How to open a file in the code editor

How to compile and run a project

Figure 1-11 shows how to compile and run a project. An easy way to run a project is to press F6. Then, if the project has been modified since the last time it was compiled, NetBeans automatically compiles the project and runs the main method in the main class.

If you want to compile a project without running it, you can use the Build command as described in this figure. You can also use the Clean and Build command to compile the project and remove any files that are no longer needed. This sometimes helps to get a project to work correctly after you have copied, moved, or renamed some of its files.

This book often instructs you to right-click because that's common in Windows. However, on Mac OS X, right-clicking is not enabled by default. Instead, you can enable right-clicking by editing the system preferences for your mouse. Or, if you prefer, you can hold down the Control key and click instead of right-clicking.

Similarly, this book presents keystrokes that work for Windows. However, with Mac OS X, you may need to modify some of these keystrokes by holding down the Command or Function (Fn) keys. For example, to run the current project, you can hold down the Function key and press F6. In general, the Mac OS X keys are clearly marked in the menus, so you can look them up if necessary.

How to use the Output window with a console application

When you run a console application in NetBeans, any data that's written to the console is displayed in the Output window. In addition, the Output window can accept input.

In this figure, for example, the application started by displaying a welcome message. Then, it prompted the user to enter a monthly investment. At this prompt, the user typed "100" and pressed Enter. After that, the application prompted the user to enter a yearly interest rate and a number of years. At both of these prompts, the user typed "3" and pressed Enter. Then, the application performed the calculation, and displayed the result. After that, the application asked the user if he or she wanted to continue. At this point, the application is still running, and the user can enter "y" to perform another calculation or "n" to end the application.

When you're learning Java, it's common to create applications that use the console to display output and get input. Because of that, the first four sections of this book teach you Java using console applications. Then, section 5 of this book teaches you how to create a graphical user interface.

A project that uses the Output window for input and output

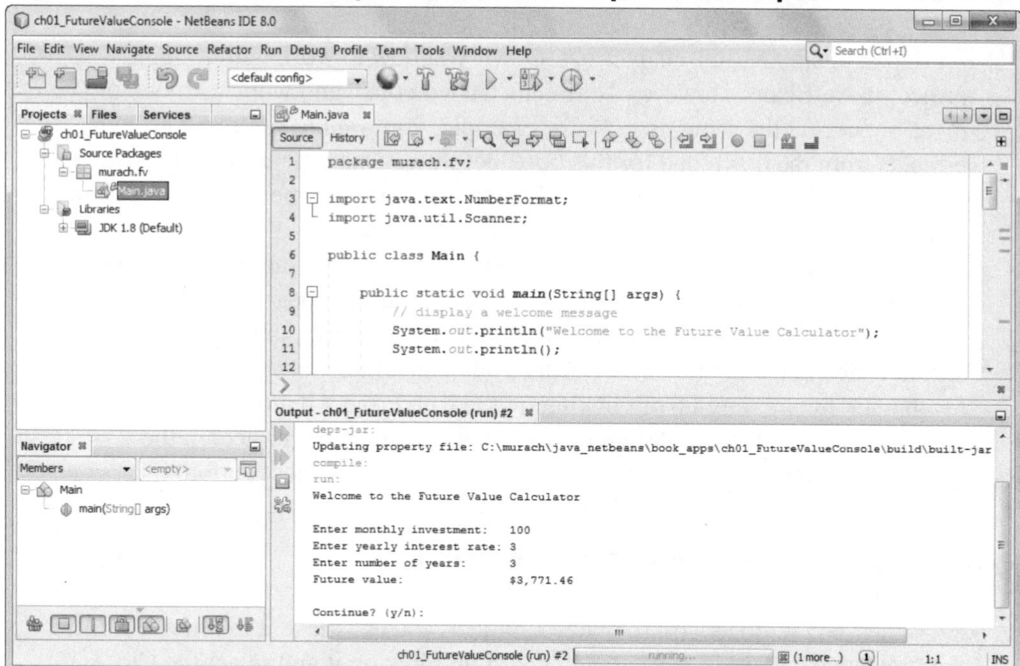

How to compile and run a project

- To run the current project, press F6 or click the Run Project button in the toolbar.
- When you run a project, NetBeans automatically compiles it. As a result, you usually don't need to compile a project separately.
- To compile a project without running it, you can right-click on the project in the Projects window and select the Build command.
- To delete all compiled files for a project and compile them again, you can right-click on the project and select the Clean and Build command.

How to work with the Output window

- When you run an application that prints data to the console, that data is displayed in the Output window.
- When you run an application that requests input from the console, the Output window pauses to accept the input. Then, you can click in the Output window, type the input, and press the Enter key.
- The Output window also displays messages when you compile an application, and it can display errors when you run an application.

Mac OS X note

- To enable right-clicking, you can edit the system preferences for the mouse.
- To use the Windows keys shown in this book, you may need to hold down the Command or Function (Fn) keys to modify those keys.

Figure 1-11 How to compile and run a project

How to work with two or more projects

Up to this point, this chapter has shown you how to work with a single project in NetBeans. However, NetBeans lets you open and work with two or more projects at the same time. If, for example, you want to run some of the projects from the download for this book before you start creating your own projects, you can open those projects in NetBeans at the same time. You'll get a chance to do that in the exercise at the end of this chapter.

Figure 1-12 presents the skills for working with two or more projects. When you open two or more projects, all of the open projects appear in the Projects window. Then, when you open any of the files for a project, they appear in separate tabs in the main window. After you open a file, you can run the project for that file by pressing F6 or clicking on the Run Project button in the toolbar. Or, if you want to run a different project, you can select the project in the Projects window and then press F6 or click on the Run Project button.

How to close or delete a project

When you're done working with a project, you can close it to remove it from the Projects window. To do that, you can right-click on it and select the Close command.

You can also delete a project if you decide that you no longer want to work with it in NetBeans. Before the project is deleted, NetBeans prompts you to confirm the deletion. Then, by default, NetBeans deletes all of the files for the project except for the source files. That way, you can work with those files outside of NetBeans if you want to. If you want to delete the source files as well, you can select the "Also Delete Sources" option in the dialog box that's displayed.

NetBeans with two open projects

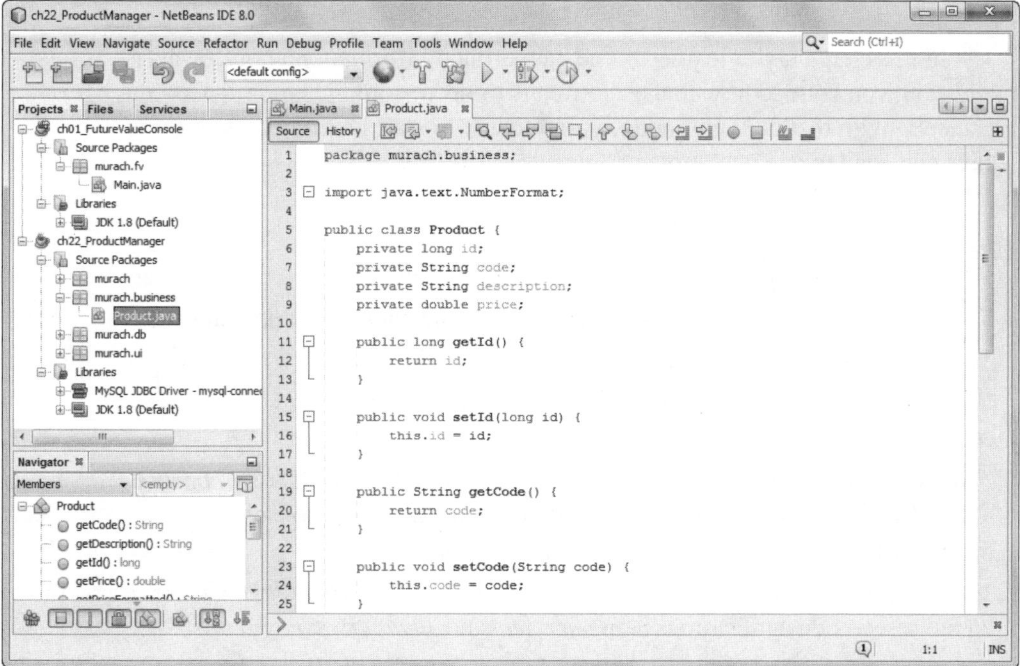

Description

- NetBeans lets you open and work with two or more projects at the same time.
- The Projects window displays all open projects.

How to change the current project

- When you open a file for a project, NetBeans opens the file in a tab in the main window and makes the project associated with that file the current project.
- To change the current project, click on the project in the Projects window.

How to close or delete a project

- To close a project, right-click on the project in the Projects window and select the Close command, or select the project and then use the File→Close Project command.
- To delete a project, right-click on the project in the Projects window and select the Delete command. When you do, you'll have the option of deleting just the files that NetBeans uses to manage the project or deleting all the folders and files for the project.

Figure 1-12 How to work with two or more projects

Perspective

In this chapter, you learned some background information about Java. In addition, you learned how to use NetBeans to open, compile, and run existing projects. With that as background, you're ready to start learning how to write Java code and create new projects.

Summary

- You can use the *Java Development Kit* (*JDK*) to develop Java applications.
- The *Standard Edition* (*SE*) of Java is called *Java SE*.
- You can use Java SE to create *desktop applications* that run on your computer.
- A desktop application can use a *graphical user interface* (*GUI*) or a *console* to display output and get user input. Applications that use a console to interact with the user are known as *console applications*.
- You can use the Enterprise Edition of Java, which is known as *Java EE*, to create server-side applications using *servlets* and *JavaServer Pages* (*JSPs*).
- The *Java compiler* translates *source code* into a *platform-independent* format known as Java *bytecodes*.
- A *Java runtime environment* (*JRE*) includes all of the software needed to run bytecodes.
- A JRE includes an implementation of a *Java virtual machine* (*JVM*).
- A JVM includes a *Java interpreter* to translate the Java bytecodes into native code that can be understood by the underlying operating system.
- Most modern JVMs have replaced the Java interpreter with a *just-in-time compiler* (*JIT compiler*). A JIT compiler is similar to an interpreter in some ways, but it improves performance significantly.
- An *Integrated Development Environment* (*IDE*) can make working with Java easier by providing code completion, error detection, automatic compilation, and a debugger.
- In NetBeans, a *project* is a folder that contains all of the files that make up an application.
- If an application prints text to the console, NetBeans displays the text in the Output window. NetBeans also allows you to enter input into the Output window.

Before you do the exercises for this chapter

Before you do any of the exercises in this book, you need to install NetBeans and the JDK. In addition, you need to install the source code for this book from our website (www.murach.com). See appendix A (PC) or B (Mac) for details.

Exercise 1-1 Open and run two projects

This exercise guides you through the process of using NetBeans to open and run two applications.

Open and run the console version of the Future Value application

1. Start NetBeans. When the Start Page is displayed, review it. Then, close this page.
2. Open the project named ch01_FutureValueConsole. This project should be stored in this folder:
   ```
   murach/java_netbeans/book_apps
   ```
3. Expand the murach.fv package.
4. Open the Main.java file in the code editor and review its code to get an idea of how this console application works.
5. Press F6 to run the application. Enter values for monthly investment, yearly interest rate, and years when you're prompted for them. Then, when you're asked if you want to continue, enter "n" to exit the application.

Open and run the GUI version of the Future Value application

6. Open the project named ch01_FutureValueGUI.
7. Expand the murach.fv package.
8. Open the .java files in the code editor and review their code. This should give you an idea of what it takes to develop a simple GUI application. For now, don't worry if you don't understand this code! You'll learn how to write code like this at the end of this book.
9. Click the Run Project button in the toolbar to run the application. Enter values in the first three text boxes, click the Calculate button, and view the result of the calculation. Then, click the Exit button to exit the application.

Set the main project and run the applications again

10. Select the ch01_FutureValueConsole project in the Projects window. Then, press F6 to run this application.
11. Select the ch01_FutureValueGUI project in the Projects window. Then, click the Run Project button to run this application.
12. Exit NetBeans. If NetBeans displays a dialog that indicates that these applications are still running, confirm that you want to exit and stop those applications.

2

How to start writing Java code

The quickest and best way to *learn* Java programming is to *do* Java programming. That's why this chapter shows you how to start writing Java code. When you finish this chapter, you should be able to write a simple application that performs a calculation and prints the result of the calculation to the console.

Basic coding skills 32
How to code a class 32
How to code a main method 32
How to code statements 34
How to code comments 34
How to print output to the console 36
How to use NetBeans to work with a new project 38
How to create a new project 38
How to work with Java source code and files 40
How to use the code completion feature 42
How to detect and correct syntax errors 44
How to work with numbers 46
How to declare and initialize variables 46
How to assign values to a variable 48
How to code arithmetic expressions 50
How to work with strings 52
How to declare and initialize String variables 52
How to join strings 52
How to include special characters in strings 54
The Code Tester application 56
The user interface 56
The CodeTesterApp class 56
Perspective 58

Basic coding skills

This chapter starts by introducing some basic coding skills. In particular, it shows how to code a class, a main method, statements, and comments.

How to code a class

Figure 2-1 shows how to write the starting code for a *class*, which is where you store Java code. To start, you typically code a package statement. This statement specifies the *package* for the class, which corresponds with the subfolder that stores the class. In this figure, for example, the package specifies a package of murach.test. This package corresponds with the murach/test subfolder of the application folder. Storing your classes in packages isn't required. However, it's highly recommended. When an application contains many classes, packages help organize the classes and prevent naming conflicts.

After coding the package statement, you declare a class by coding a *class declaration*. Typically, a class declaration begins with the public keyword, which means that other classes can access it. This keyword is an *access modifier* that controls the *scope* of a class.

After the public keyword, you code the class keyword followed by the name of the class. Here, it's a common coding convention to start the class name and every word within that name with a capital letter. In addition, it's a common convention to use letters and digits only. In this figure, for example, the class declaration specifies a class named CodeTesterApp.

The filename for the class is the same as the class name with .java added as the extension. For example, the CodeTesterApp class is stored in a file named CodeTesterApp.java.

After the class name, you code a left brace ({) that identifies the start of the class and a right brace (}) that identifies the end of the class. Typically, you code the right brace at the same indentation level as the class declaration. This clearly shows where the class ends, and it helps to prevent missing braces.

How to code a main method

Within the braces of a class, you can code one or more *methods*. Here, each method contains code that performs an action. In this figure, the class only contains one method, the *main method*. Java automatically executes this method when it runs the class that contains it. All Java applications contain at least one main method that starts the application.

To code a main method, you begin by coding a *main method declaration* within the class declaration. Later in this book, you'll learn more about the keywords used by this declaration. For now, all you need to know about the main method declaration is that you can code it exactly as shown in this figure.

The code within a pair of matching braces is called a *block* of code. In this figure, for example, there are two blocks of code: (1) the block for the class and (2) the block for the main method.

A class that has a main method

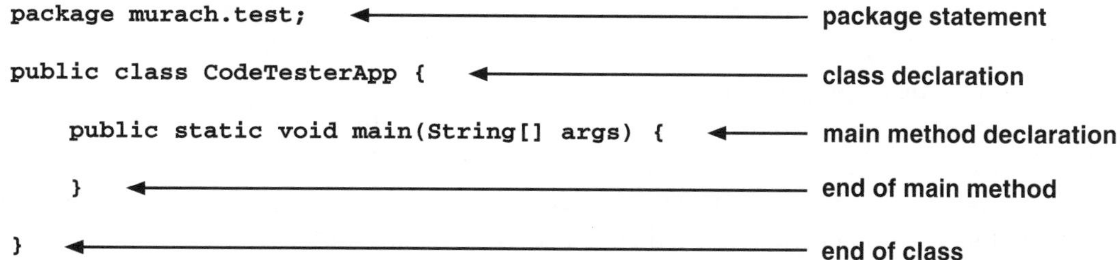

package murach.test;
package statement
public class CodeTesterApp {
class declaration
public static void main(String[] args) {
main method declaration
}
end of main method
}
end of class

The folder and filename for this class

```
murach/test/CodeTesterApp.java
```

The guidelines for naming a class

- Start the name with a capital letter.
- Start every word within a class name with an initial cap.
- Use letters and digits only.

Description

- A *class* stores Java code. Each class starts with a *class declaration*.
- A *package* is a folder that contains one or more classes. They are useful for organizing multiple classes. Most classes start with a package statement that identifies the folder that contains the class.
- A *method* is a block of code that performs a task. A class can contain one or more methods.
- A class can contain one *main method*. This method is often the starting point for an application. You can execute this method by running the class.
- Opening and closing braces identify the start and end of classes and methods. The code within the braces can be referred to as a *block* of code.
- The public keyword is an *access modifier* that allows a class or method to be used by other code.
- The file name for a class is the same as the class name with .java as the extension.

Figure 2-1 How to create a class that has a main method

How to code statements

A *statement* performs a task and ends with a semicolon. In figure 2-2, for example, the main method contains three statements. The first statement prints a welcome message to the console, the second prints a blank line, and the third prints a message that says, "Bye!"

When you code a statement, you can start it anywhere in a line, and you can continue it from one line to another. However, to make your code easier to read, you should use indentation and spacing to align statements as shown throughout this book.

How to code comments

When you write code, you can use *comments* to document what the application does and what specific blocks and lines of code do. Since the Java compiler ignores comments, you can include them anywhere in your code without degrading the performance of your code.

A *single-line comment* typically describes one or more lines of code. This type of comment starts with two slashes (//) that tell the compiler to ignore all characters until the end of the current line. This figure uses single-line comments to identify the structure of this code: the package statement, the class declaration and end, and the main method declaration and end. In addition, it uses a single-line comment to describe the statement that prints a blank line to the console. Since these comments are coded on the same line as code, they are sometimes referred to as *end-of-line comments*.

However, you can also code a single-line comment on its own line. In this figure, for example, the comment that describes the statement that prints the welcome message is coded on its own line.

A *block comment* is typically used to document information that applies to a block of code. For example, a block comment might include the author's name, the code's completion date, the purpose of the code, the files used by the code, and so on. In this figure, the code begins with a block comment that includes the author's name and the purpose of the code.

Although many programmers sprinkle their code with comments, that shouldn't be necessary if you write code that's easy to read and understand. Instead, you should use comments only to clarify code that's difficult to understand. In this figure, for example, an experienced Java programmer wouldn't need any of the single-line comments.

One problem with comments is that they may not accurately represent what the code does. This often happens when a programmer changes the code, but doesn't change the comments that go along with it. Then, it's even harder to understand the code because the comments are misleading. So if you change the code, be sure to change the comments too.

A class that includes statements and comments

```
/*
 * Author:  J. Murach
 * Purpose: This application displays some text on the console.
 *          It can be used as a starting point for testing code.
 */
package murach.test;                               // package statement

public class CodeTesterApp {                       // start CodeTesterApp class

    public static void main(String args[]) {       // start main method
        // display a welcome message
        System.out.println("Welcome to the Code Tester");
        System.out.println();                      // print a blank line
        System.out.println("Bye!");
    }                                              // end main method
}                                                  // end CodeTesterApp class
```

Description

- A *statement* performs a task and ends with a semicolon.
- You can start a statement at any point in a line and continue the statement from one line to the next. To make your code easier to read, you should use indentation and extra spaces to align statements and parts of statements.
- A *comment* typically documents what the code does. Well-written comments can be helpful to the programmer who writes the code and to other programmers who need to review or maintain the code later.
- To code a *single-line comment*, type // followed by the comment. You can code a single-line comment on a line by itself or after a statement. A comment that's coded after a statement is sometimes called an *end-of-line comment*.
- To code a *block comment*, type /* at the start of the block and */ at the end. You can also code asterisks to identify the lines in the block, but that isn't necessary.

How to print output to the console

Most applications require some type of user interaction. For example, they usually need to display output to the user and get input from the user. The easiest way to do that is to use a command-line interface known as the *console* to interact with the user. To get started, figure 2-3 shows how to display output to the user by printing it to the console.

When you use the console, its appearance may differ slightly depending on the operating system. However, the application should work the same. Also, most IDEs provide an easy way to work with the console as you're developing and testing console applications.

To print output to the console, you can use the println and print methods of the System.out object. Both the println and print methods accept an *argument* that specifies the data that's printed to the console. To code an argument, you code a set of parentheses after the name of the method. Then, you code the argument within these parentheses. In this figure, the first println method prints a *string* of characters to the console. To identify this string of characters, the code places double quotation marks around the text.

This code doesn't pass an argument to the second println statement. As a result, it just prints a blank line to the console. However, the third println method prints a string of characters to the console, just like the first println method.

The print and println methods work similarly. The main difference between the two is that the println method starts a new line after it displays the data, and the print method doesn't.

The example in this figure shows a complete class that uses the println method to display data on the console. By now, you shouldn't have much trouble understanding how this code works.

Two methods of the System.out object

Method	Description
println(data)	Prints the data argument to the console followed by a new line character.
print(data)	Prints the data argument to the console.

A class that prints output to the console

```
package murach.test;

public class CodeTesterApp {

    public static void main(String args[]) {
        // display a welcome message
        System.out.println("Welcome to the Code Tester");
        System.out.println();

        // display a goodbye message
        System.out.println("Bye!");
    }
}
```

The output displayed on the console

```
Welcome to the Code Tester

Bye!
```

Description

- Although the appearance of a console may differ from one system to another, you can always use the println and print methods of the System.out object to print data to the console.

How to use NetBeans to work with a new project

Now that you understand how to code a class that prints data to the console, you're ready to learn how to use NetBeans to create a new project that contains such a class. Then, you can use NetBeans to enter the code for this class.

How to create a new project

Figure 2-4 presents the dialog boxes for creating a Java application. To start, you can use the New Project dialog box to choose the type of project you want to create. For this book, you'll use the Java Application item to create a Java application as shown here. Then, when you click the Next button, NetBeans displays a dialog box like the second one in this figure.

The second dialog box lets you enter a name and location for the project. In this figure, for example, the project name is "ch02_CodeTester" and it will be stored in this folder:

```
/murach/java_netbeans/book_apps
```

If you install the source code for this book as described in the appendix, all of the applications presented in this book are stored within this folder.

By default, when you create a Java application in NetBeans, NetBeans generates a main class with a main method. If that's not what you want, you can remove the check mark from the "Create Main Class" option. In most cases, though, you'll leave this option checked. Then, you can enter a name for the main class. In addition, you typically want to enter a package for this class.

For the project in this figure, for example, I named the project ch02_CodeTester, I named the package murach.test, and I named the class CodeTester. As a result, NetBeans created a project named ch02_CodeTester that contains a package named murach.test that contains a class named CodeTesterApp.

When you pick the name for a package, you should pick a name that helps to avoid naming conflicts with other classes. In addition, you should pick a name that helps you organize your classes in a logical way. Here, I used "murach" as the first part of the name because it's the name of our company, and it's unlikely that anyone else would use that name. Then, I used "test" as the second part of the name because I intend to use this package to store a class that's used for testing.

To make sure that the name of a package is unique, one common naming scheme is to start package names with the company's Internet domain in reverse. For example, a company with a domain of murach.com could start its package names with com.murach.

When this dialog box is complete, you can click the Finish button to create the project and the class that contains the main method. Then, NetBeans creates a folder that corresponds with the project name, and it creates some additional files that it uses to configure the project.

The dialog boxes for creating a new project

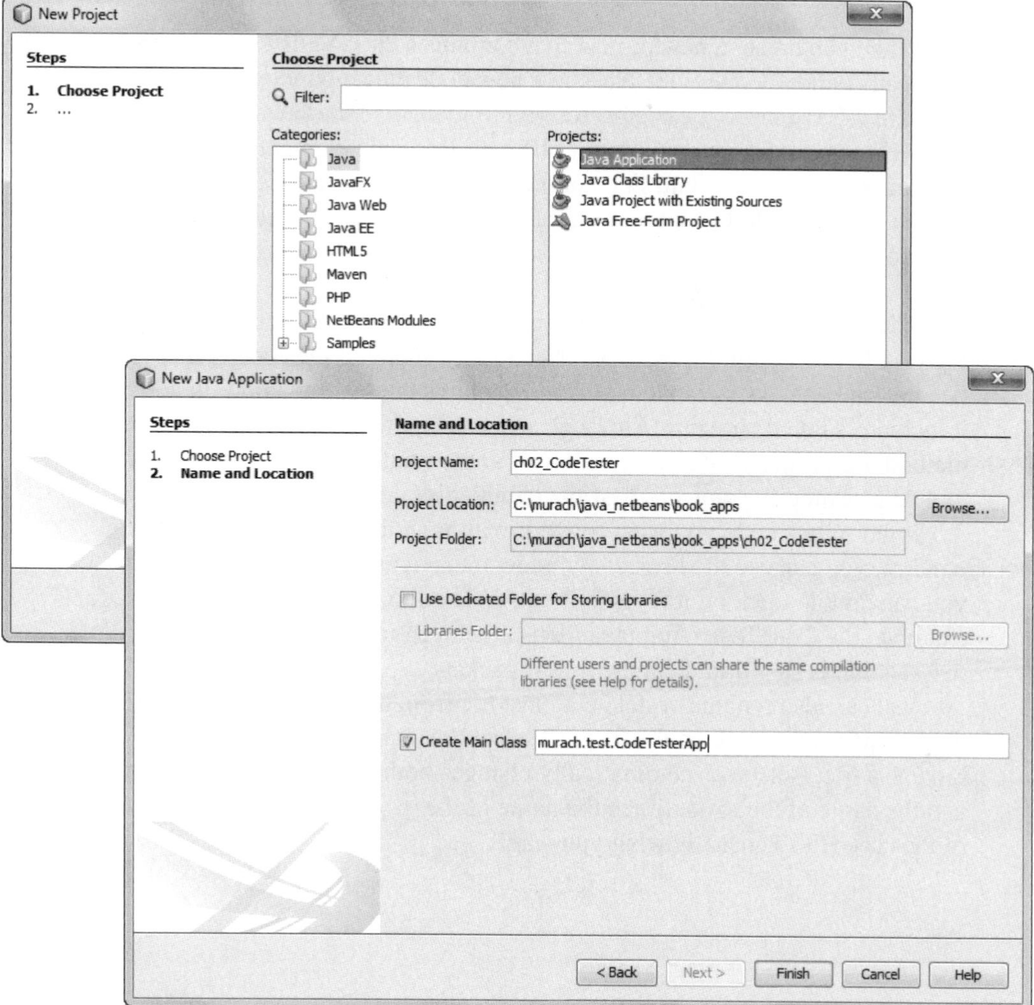

Description

- To create a new project, use the File→New Project command or click the New Project button in the toolbar to display the New Project dialog box. Then, select a project type, click the Next button, and respond to the dialog box that's displayed.
- To create a Java Application project, enter the project name and location. Then, enter the name you want to use for the main class. It's generally considered a best practice to supply a package name for this class.

How to work with Java source code and files

When you create a new project that contains a class with a main method, NetBeans typically opens the class in a new code editor window as shown in figure 2-5. To make it easier to for you to recognize the Java syntax, the code editor uses different colors for different language elements. In addition, NetBeans provides standard File and Edit menus and keystroke shortcuts that let you save and edit the source code. For example, you can press Ctrl+S to save your source code, and you can use standard commands to cut, copy, and paste code.

When you create a project with a main class, NetBeans generates some code for you. In this figure, for example, NetBeans generated the code that specifies the package, declares the class, and declares the main method. In addition, it includes some comments. Although you can delete or modify the class and method declarations, you don't usually want to do that. However, you may want to delete or modify some or all of the comments.

If the source code you want to work with isn't displayed in a code editor window, you can use the Projects window to navigate to the .java file. Then, you can double-click on it to open it in a code editor window. In this figure, for example, the CodeTesterApp.java file is displayed in the Projects window. Note that this file is stored in the murach.test package.

You can also rename or delete a .java file from the Projects window. To do that, just right-click on the file and select the appropriate command. If you rename a file, NetBeans automatically changes both the name of the .java file and the name of the class. Since the name of the .java file must match the name of the class, this is usually what you want.

The code editor with the starting source code for a project

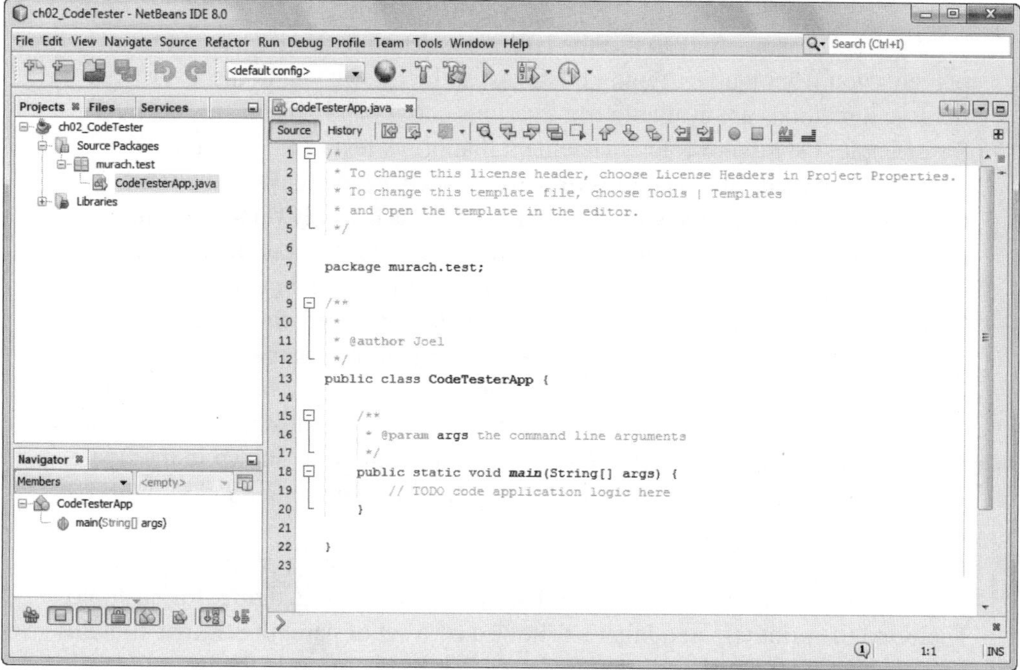

Description

- To open a .java file in the code editor, double-click on it in the Projects window. Then, you can use normal editing techniques to work with the source code.
- To collapse the code for a method or comment, click the minus sign (-) to its left. Then, a plus sign (+) appears to the left of the method or comment, and you can click the plus sign to display the code again.
- To save the source code for a file, use the File→Save command (Ctrl+S) or click the Save All Files button in the toolbar. This automatically compiles the file so it doesn't have to be compiled when the project is run.
- To rename a file, right-click on it, select the Refactor→Rename command, and enter the new name in the resulting dialog box.
- To delete a file, you can right-click on it, select the Delete command, and confirm the deletion in the resulting dialog box.

How to use the code completion feature

Figure 2-6 shows how to use the *code completion feature*. This feature prevents you from making typing mistakes, and it allows you to discover what fields and methods are available from various classes and objects. In this figure, for example, I started to enter a statement that prints text to the console.

First, I entered "sys" and pressed Ctrl+Spacebar (both keys at the same time). This displayed a list with the System class as the only option. Then, I pressed the Enter key to automatically enter the rest of the class name.

Next, I typed a period. This displayed a list of fields and methods available from the System class. Then, I used the arrow keys to select the field named out and pressed the Enter key to automatically enter that field name.

Finally, I typed another period. This displayed a long list of method names. Then, I typed "pr" to scroll down the list to the methods that start with "pr", and I used the arrow keys to select one of the println methods as shown in the figure. At this point, I could press Enter to have NetBeans enter the method into the editor for me.

When you use code completion, it automatically enters opening and closing parentheses and arguments whenever they're needed. In this figure, for example, I selected the println method that's followed by a set of parentheses that contains an argument. When I pressed the Enter key, NetBeans inserted the parentheses and argument into the code editor and highlighted the argument so I could enter a value for it.

The code completion feature can also make it easy for you to enter values for a string of text. If you type a quotation mark to identify a string, the code completion feature automatically enters both opening and closing quotation marks and places the cursor between the two. At this point, you can enter the text.

If you experiment with the code completion feature, you'll quickly see when it helps you enter code more quickly and when it makes sense to enter the code yourself. In addition, you'll see that it helps you understand the kinds of fields and methods that are available to the various classes and objects that you're working with. This will make more sense as you learn more about Java in the next few chapters, but it's extremely helpful to most programmers, especially to those who are new to Java.

The code editor with a code completion list

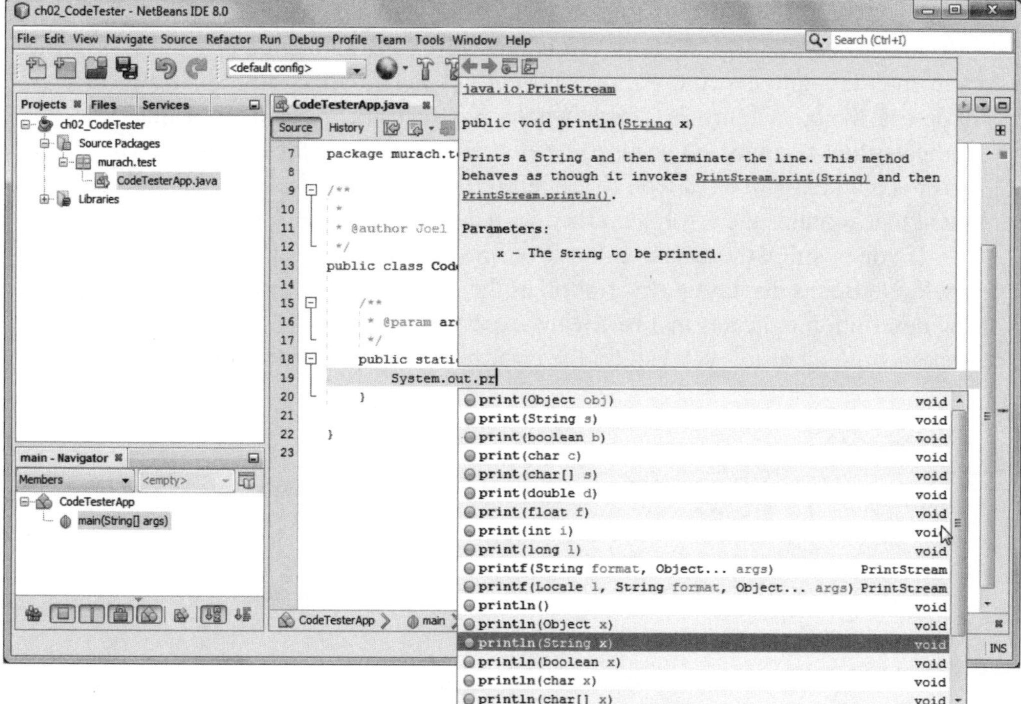

Description

- You can use the *code completion feature* to help you enter the names of classes and objects and select from the methods and fields that are available for a class or object.
- To activate the code completion feature for entering a class or object name, press Ctrl+Spacebar after entering one or more letters of the class or object name. Then, a list of all the classes and objects that start with those letters is displayed.
- To activate the code completion feature for a method or field of a class or object, enter a period after a class or object name. Then, a list of all the methods and fields for that class or object is displayed.
- To insert an item from a code completion list, use the arrow keys to select the item and press the Enter key. If the item requires parentheses, they're added automatically. If the item requires one or more arguments, default values are added for those arguments and the first argument is highlighted so you can enter its value. Then, you can press the Tab key and enter the values for any remaining arguments.
- If you enter the opening quote for a string of text, the code completion feature automatically adds the closing quote and places the cursor between the two quotes so you can enter the text.

Figure 2-6 How to use the code completion feature

How to detect and correct syntax errors

In NetBeans, a statement that won't compile causes a *syntax error*. As you enter text into the code editor, NetBeans displays syntax errors whenever it detects them. In figure 2-7, for example, NetBeans displays an error that indicates that a semicolon needs to be entered to complete the statement. This error is marked with a red icon to the left of the statement. In addition, the statement that contains the error is marked with a wavy red underline.

If you position the mouse cursor over the red error icon or over the statement itself, NetBeans displays a description of the error. In this figure, for example, the description indicates that NetBeans expects a semicolon at the end of the statement. As a result, you can fix the error by typing the semicolon.

The code editor with an error displayed

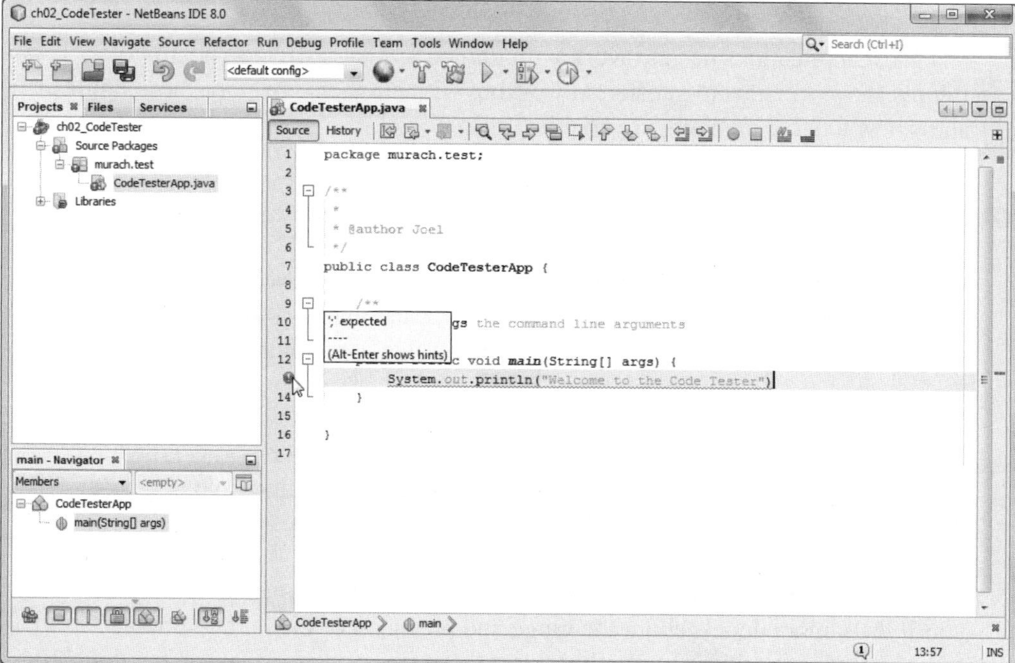

Description

- NetBeans often detects *syntax errors* as you enter code into the code editor.
- When NetBeans detects a syntax error, it displays a red error icon to the left of the statement in error and it places a red wavy line under the statement.
- To get more information about a syntax error, you can position the mouse pointer over the error icon. Or, you can move the cursor to the line that contains the error and press Alt+Enter.

How to work with numbers

Most applications need to work with numbers. That's why the next two figures show you how to get started working with numbers. To start, these figures show how to store numbers in variables.

How to declare and initialize variables

A *variable* stores a value that can change as your code executes. Before you can use a variable, you must *declare* its data type and name. When you do that, you often *initialize* the variable by assigning a value to it. Figure 2-8 shows how to do that.

But first, this figure summarizes two of the eight *primitive data types* that are available in Java. To start, you can use the int data type to store *integers*, which are whole numbers that don't contain decimal places. In addition, you can use the double data type to store numbers that can contain decimal places. For now, that's all you need to know about primitive data types.

In chapter 7, you'll learn about the other six primitive types. In addition, you'll learn more details about the range and precision of the int and double types, including a common rounding error that often occurs if you use the double type to work with financial calculations.

The first example shows how to declare and initialize a variable in two statements. Here, the first statement declares a variable of the double type named productPrice. Then, the second statement uses an equals sign (=) to assign a value of 14.95 to this variable. Since this statement assigns a value to the variable, it's known as an *assignment statement*.

The second example shows how to declare and initialize a variable in one statement. Here, the statement declares a double variable named productPrice and uses the equals sign (=) to assign a value of 14.95 to it. This accomplishes the same task as the first example.

When naming variables, it's a common Java coding convention to begin the variable with a lowercase letter and to capitalize the first letter in each subsequent word in the name as in productPrice or maxQuantity. This is commonly referred to as *camel notation*.

When you create a name, you should try to make the name both meaningful and easy to remember. To make a name meaningful, you should use as many characters as you need, so it's easy for other programmers to read and understand your code. For instance, netPrice is more meaningful than nPrice, and nPrice is more meaningful than np.

To make a name easy to remember, you should avoid abbreviations. If, for example, you use nwCst as a name, you may have difficulty remembering whether it was nCust, nwCust, or nwCst later on. If you code the name as newCustomer, though, you won't have any trouble remembering what it was. Yes, you type more characters when you create names that are meaningful and easy to remember, but that's usually justified by the time you save when you test, debug, and maintain the application.

Two of the primitive data types

Type	Description
`int`	Integers (whole numbers) that range from -2,147,483,648 to 2,147,483,647.
`double`	Double-precision floating-point numbers (decimal numbers).

How to declare and initialize a variable in two statements

Syntax

```
type variableName;
variableName = value;
```

Example

```
double productPrice;            // declaration statement
productPrice = 14.95;           // assignment statement
```

How to declare and initialize a variable in one statement

Syntax

```
type variableName = value;
```

Example

```
double productPrice = 14.95;    // initialize a double variable
```

Naming recommendations for variables

- Start variable names with a lowercase letter and capitalize the first letter in all words after the first word.
- Each variable name should be a noun or a noun preceded by one or more adjectives.
- Try to use meaningful names that are easy to remember.

Java keywords

```
boolean    if          interface   class        true
char       else        package     volatile     false
byte       final       switch      while        throws
float      private     case        return       native
void       protected   break       throw        implements
short      public      default     try          import
double     static      for         catch        synchronized
int        new         continue    finally      const
long       this        do          transient    goto
abstract   super       extends     instanceof   null
```

Description

- Java provides for eight *primitive data types* that you can use for storing values in memory. The two most common are the int and double data types.
- A *variable* stores a value that can change as an application executes.
- To create a variable, you can start by *declaring* its data type and name. Then, you can *assign* a value to the variable to *initialize* it. It's common to initialize integer variables to 0 and double variables to 0.0.
- A *keyword* is a word that's reserved by the Java language such as int and double. As a result, you can't use a keyword as the name for a variable.

Figure 2-8 How to declare and initialize variables

For some common variable names, programmers typically use just one or two lowercase letters. For instance, they often use i as the name of an int variable that's used as a counter variable. This is acceptable in short blocks of code where it's easy to understand what the variable does.

When naming a variable, you can't use a Java *keyword* as the name of the variable. There are 50 keywords reserved by the Java language that are shown in figure 2-8. To help you identify keywords in your code, most Java IDEs display these keywords in a different color than the rest of the Java code. As you progress through this book, you'll learn how to use most of these keywords.

How to assign values to a variable

Figure 2-9 shows how to assign a value to a variable that has already been declared. To start, the first code example declares and initializes two variables. These variables are used by the other examples in this figure. The first variable is named quantity and is initialized to an int value of 0. The second variable is named maxQuantity and is initialized to an int value of 100.

The second example begins by changing the quantity variable by assigning it a value of 10. Then, it changes the quantity variable again by assigning it the value that's stored in the maxQuantity variable. This shows that the value of a variable can change. It shows that you can assign a *literal* value like 100 or 10 to a variable. And it shows that you can assign another variable such as maxQuantity to a variable.

The third example shows a common coding error that occurs if you attempt to declare a variable again after it has already been declared. In that case, you'll get a syntax error. That's because this statement unnecessarily declares the type for the variable. To fix this, you can remove the type declaration from the statement. In this figure, for example, you can remove the int keyword from the beginning of the statement.

The fourth example shows another common coding error that occurs if you use the wrong case to refer to a variable. This error occurs because Java is *case-sensitive*. As a result, you need to be careful when you create and use variable names. In this figure, for example, the first example names the variable maxQuantity. As a result, the fourth example can't refer to it as maxquantity.

The syntax for an assignment statement

```
variableName = value;
```

Code that declares and initializes two variables

```
int quantity = 0;                    // quantity is 0
int maxQuantity = 100;
```

Code that assigns new values to the quantity variable

```
quantity = 10;                       // quantity is now 10
quantity = maxQuantity;              // quantity is now 100
```

Code that attempts to declare a variable a second time

```
int quantity = 99;     // ERROR: the quantity variable is already declared
```

Code that uses incorrect case to refer to a variable

```
maxquantity = 200;     // ERROR: can't find variable due to incorrect case
```

Description

- An *assignment statement* assigns a value to a variable that's already declared. This value can be a literal value, another variable, or an expression like the arithmetic expressions shown in the next figure.
- If you attempt to declare a variable a second time, it causes an error.
- Java is a *case-sensitive* language. As a result, make sure to use the correct case when referring to the names of variables.

Figure 2-9 How to assign values to a variable

How to code arithmetic expressions

To code simple *arithmetic expressions*, you can use the four *arithmetic operators* summarized in figure 2-10 to work on *operands*, which are the primitive values or variables that the operators work with. These operators work the way you would expect them to with one exception: If you divide one integer by another integer, any decimal places are truncated.

The first example shows how to calculate the total amount for a line item. Here, the first two statements declare and initialize a double variable named productPrice and an int variable named quantity. Then, the third statement declares a double variable named total and assigns the result of an arithmetic expression to that variable. This arithmetic expression uses the multiplication operator (*) to multiply the productPrice variable by the quantity variable. Since this expression mixes int and double variables, Java *casts* (converts) the int variable to a double variable before it performs the calculation. Then, it returns the result as a double value.

The second example shows how to calculate sales tax. Here, the third statement uses the multiplication operator (*) to calculate the sales tax amount. Then, the fourth example uses the addition operator (+) to add the sales tax amount to the subtotal.

The third example shows how to calculate an average. Here, the third statement includes an expression that uses the division operator (/) to divide the double variable named sum by the int variable named count. As a result, Java casts the int value to a double variable before performing the calculation and returns a double value as the result of the expression.

The fourth example shows what happens if you divide one int value by another int value. In that case, since all of the variables are of the int type, the result of the calculation is 4. This makes sense as 2 goes into 9 four times with a remainder of 1. However, if the data types for this example were changed from the int type to the double type, the result would be 4.5. This makes sense as 4.5 goes into 9 twice.

The fifth example shows how to code an expression that uses multiple operators. Here, the third statement multiplies the length by 2, multiplies the width by 2, and adds the results together.

When you use more than one operator in an arithmetic expression, you sometimes need to use parentheses to control the sequence of the operations. In the fifth example, Java happens to perform the operations in the sequence that you want. However, if necessary, you could use parentheses to control the sequence of operations. Then, Java performs the operation in the innermost set of parentheses first. For example, if you wanted to clarify the sequence or operations in this example, you could code the third statement like this:

```
double perimeter = (2 * width) + (2 * length);
```

This clearly shows that Java should perform the multiplication operations before the addition operation.

The basic operators that you can use in arithmetic expressions

Operator	Name	Description
+	Addition	Adds two operands.
-	Subtraction	Subtracts the right operand from the left operand.
*	Multiplication	Multiplies the right operand and the left operand.
/	Division	Divides the right operand into the left operand. If both operands are integers, then the result is an integer.

Code that calculates a total amount

```
double productPrice = 9.99;
int quantity = 2;
double total = productPrice * quantity;        // 19.98
```

Code that calculates sales tax

```
double subtotal = 250.00;
double taxPercent = .075;                      // 7.5%
double taxAmount = subtotal * taxPercent;      // 18.75
double grandTotal = subtotal + taxAmount;      // 268.75
```

Code that calculates an average

```
double sum = 206.75;
int count = 3;
double average = sum / count;                  // 68.91666666666667
```

Code that divides two int values

```
int miles = 9;
int hour = 2;
int milesPerHour = miles / hour;               // 4
```

Code that uses multiple operators in one expression

```
double width = 4.25;
double length = 8.5;
double perimeter = 2 * width + 2 * length;     // 25.5
```

Description

- An *arithmetic expression* consists of one or more *operands* and *arithmetic operators*.
- When an expression mixes the use of int and double variables, Java automatically *casts* the int types to double types. To retain the decimal places, the variable that receives the result must be a double.
- If you use multiple operators in one expression, you can use parentheses to specify the sequence of operations. Then, Java performs the operations in the innermost set of parentheses first, followed by the operations in the next set, and so on.

Figure 2-10 How to code arithmetic expressions

How to work with strings

Most applications need to work with text. That's why the next two figures show you how to get started with strings. A *string* is a sequence of characters such as letters, numbers, and punctuation marks.

How to declare and initialize String variables

To declare a String variable, you use the syntax shown in figure 2-11. Although this is much like the syntax for declaring an int or double variable, a string is an *object* that's created from the String class. When you declare a String variable, you must capitalize the String keyword because it is the name of a class, not a primitive data type.

When you create an object, you can think of the class as the template for the object. That's why the object can be called an *instance* of the class, and the process of creating the object can be called *instantiation*. Whenever necessary, you can create more than one object or instance from the class. For instance, you often use several String objects in a single application.

When you declare a String object, you can assign a *string literal* to it by enclosing the characters for the literal value within double quotes. You can also assign an *empty string* to a string by coding a set of quotation marks with nothing between them. Finally, you can use the null keyword to assign a *null* to a String object. This indicates that the String variable doesn't point to a String object.

How to join strings

If you want to *join* two or more strings, you can use the + operator. For instance, the second example joins a first name, a space, and a last name. This is also known as *concatenating* a string. Then, you can assign that string to a String variable like the name variable shown in the second example. When concatenating strings, it's common to mix string literals (the space) with String variables (firstName and lastName) as shown in this example.

You can also join a string with a primitive data type as shown in the third example. Here, the second statement appends a variable that's defined with the double type to a literal of the String type. When you use this technique, Java automatically converts the double type to the String type.

When you code string literals, they mostly work as you would expect. However, you can't split a string literal over multiple lines like this:

```
String name = "Bob
               Smith";
```

Instead, you have to close the string literal at the end of the first line and join a second string literal on the second line like this:

```
String name = "Bob "
            + "Smith";
```

How to declare and initialize a String variable

Syntax

```
String variableName = value;
```

Examples

```
String message1 = "Invalid data entry.";
String message2 = "";                        // an empty string
String message3 = null;                      // a null string
```

How to join strings

```
String firstName = "Bob";                    // firstName is Bob
String lastName = "Smith";                   // lastName is Smith
String name = firstName + " " + lastName;    // name is Bob Smith
```

How to join a string and a number

```
double price = 14.95;
String message = "Price: " + price;          // message is Price: 14.95
```

Description

- A *string* can consist of one or more characters including letters, numbers, and special characters like *, &, and #.
- In Java, a string is actually a String object that's created from the String class that's part of the Java *API* (*Application Programming Interface*). This API provides all the classes that are included as part of the JDK.
- Since a string is an object created from the String class, you start the declaration for a string by coding String with a capital S. By contrast, you don't use any capital letters when declaring primitive types such as the int and double types.
- To specify the value of a string, you can enclose text in double quotation marks. This is known as a *string literal*.
- To assign a *null* to a string, you can use the null keyword. This means that the String variable doesn't point to a String object that's allocated in memory.
- To assign an *empty string* to a String object, you can code a set of quotation marks with nothing between them. This means that the string doesn't contain any characters.
- To *join* (or *concatenate*) a string with another string or a data type, use a plus sign (+). Whenever possible, Java automatically converts the data type and joins it with the string.

Figure 2-11 How to create and join strings

How to include special characters in strings

Figure 2-12 shows how to include special characters within a string. In particular, this figure shows how to include backslashes, quotation marks, and control characters such as new lines, tabs, and returns in a string. To do that, you can use *escape sequences*, which are a sequence of characters that begin with a backslash.

Some escape sequences let you insert special characters such as new line characters. For example, if you code a backslash followed by the letter *n*, the compiler includes a new line character in the string. The first example in this figure shows how this works. If you omitted the backslash, of course, the compiler would just include the letter *n* in the string.

The escape sequences for the tab and return characters work similarly. The second example shows how this works. This example includes two tabs, one return character, and one new line character in the string literal. In most cases, the return character returns to the beginning of the current line without advancing to the new line. As a result, in most cases, the return character is followed by the new line character as shown in this example.

Other escape sequences let you include characters that are part of the Java syntax. For example, it's part of the Java syntax to code a string literal within double quotes. As a result, if you attempt to code a double quote within a string literal, the compiler thinks you are attempting to end the string literal, which results in a syntax error like the one in the third example. To fix this error, you can use an escape sequence as shown in the fourth example. This example includes two double quotes within the string literal.

The escape sequence for a backslash works similarly. When you code a backslash, the compiler thinks you are coding an escape sequence. As a result, if you follow the backslash with a character that doesn't complete a valid escape sequence, it results in a syntax error like the one shown in the fifth example. To fix this error, you need to use an escape sequence as shown in the sixth example. This example includes two backslashes within the string literal.

Common escape sequences

Sequence	Character
`\n`	New line
`\t`	Tab
`\r`	Return
`\"`	Quotation mark
`\\`	Backslash

The new line character

```
"Code:  JSP\nPrice: $49.50"
```

Displayed on the console

```
Code:  JSP
Price: $49.50
```

The new line, return, and tab characters

```
"Code:\tJSP\r\nPrice:\t$49.50"
```

Displayed on the console

```
Code:  JSP
Price: $49.50
```

A syntax error due to quotation marks

```
"Type "x" to exit"     // syntax error - ')' expected
```

Quotation marks

```
"Type \"x\" to exit"
```

Displayed on the console

```
Type "x" to exit
```

A syntax error due to backslashes

```
"C:\java\files"         // syntax error - illegal escape character
```

Backslashes

```
"C:\\java\\files"
```

Displayed on the console

```
C:\java\files
```

Description

- Within a string, you can use *escape sequences* to include certain types of special characters such as new lines and tabs. You can also use escape sequences to include characters that are part of the Java syntax such as quotation marks and backslashes.

Figure 2-12 How to include special characters in strings

The Code Tester application

This chapter finishes by presenting the Code Tester application. You can modify this application to get some hands-on practice declaring variables, making calculations, and displaying the results of those calculations on the console.

The user interface

Figure 2-13 shows the console for this application. To start, it displays a weclome message. Then, it displays the values of four variables. Finally, it displays a goodbye message.

The CodeTesterApp class

This figure also presents the code for the Code Tester application. All of this code is stored in the CodeTesterApp class. If you read this chapter, you should already understand most of this code.

Within the main method, the first statement uses the println method to print a message to the console that says, "Welcome to the Code Tester". Then, the second statement prints a blank line to the console.

After these first two statements, this code declares and initializes three variables: one String variable, one double variable, and one int variable. Then, it performs a calculation and assigns the result to a fourth variable. Next, it builds a string that includes the data for these four variables. To do that, this string uses string literals to label and align the data. In addition, this string uses the new line escape sequence (\n) to start a new line after each variable.

After this code builds the string, it prints this string to the console. Then, it prints a message to the console that says, "Bye!"

The console

```
Welcome to the Code Tester

Code:     java
Price:    49.5
Quantity: 2
Total:    99.0

Bye!
```

The CodeTesterApp class

```
package murach.test;

public class CodeTesterApp {

    public static void main(String args[]) {
        // display a welcome message
        System.out.println("Welcome to the Code Tester");
        System.out.println();

        // hard code three values
        String productCode = "java";
        double price = 49.50;
        int quantity = 2;

        // perform a calculation
        double total = price * quantity;

        // display the output
        String message =
            "Code:     " + productCode + "\n" +
            "Price:    " + price + "\n" +
            "Quantity: " + quantity + "\n" +
            "Total:    " + total + "\n";
        System.out.println(message);

        // display a goodbye message
        System.out.println("Bye!");
    }
}
```

Figure 2-13 The Code Tester application

Perspective

The goal of this chapter is to get you started with Java programming. Now, if you understand how the Code Tester application works, you can get some hands-on experience coding variables and arithmetic expressions of your own. However, this application doesn't get input from the user or format the output that's displayed to the user. To do that, you can use some of the classes that are available from the Java API as described in the next chapter.

Also, keep in mind that this chapter is just an introduction to Java programming. In chapter 7, you'll learn more about working with primitive data types, including how to work with the other six primitive data types. And in chapter 9, you'll learn more about working with strings.

Summary

- A *class* stores Java code. A *package* is a folder that can store one or more Java classes. Packages are used to organize classes.
- A class can contain one or more *methods*. A method is a block of code that performs a task.
- A *main method* is a special type of method that's executed when you run the class that contains it.
- A *statement* performs a task and ends with a semicolon.
- *Comments* typically document what code does.
- You can use the NetBeans *code editor* to enter and edit code. As you enter code, you can use the *code completion feature* to help you enter the names of classes and objects and select from fields and methods.
- Java provides for eight *primitive data types*. Two of the most common are the int and double types.
- *Variables* store data that changes as an application runs. An *assignment statement* can assign a value to a variable.
- A *string* can consist of one or more characters including letters, numbers, and special characters. You can use the plus sign to *join* a string with another string or primitive type.
- You can use *escape sequences* to include special characters in strings.

Exercise 2-1 Experiment with the Code Tester application

In this exercise, you can experiment with the Code Tester application that's presented at the end of this chapter.

Test the application

1. Start the NetBeans IDE and open the project named ch02_ex1_CodeTester. This project should be in this folder:
   ```
   /murach/java_netbeans/ex_starts
   ```
2. Expand the murach.test package, open the file named CodeTesterApp.java, and review the code for this file.
3. Run this application. It should work as described at the end of this chapter.

Initialize and print more variables

4. Within the main method, initialize String variables for your first and last name. Then, print these String variables to the console in this format:
   ```
   Name: Lastname, Firstname
   ```
5. Run the application to make sure it works correctly.
6. Add an assignment statement that changes the value of the variable for the first name.
7. Run the application again to make sure this changes the first name that's printed to the console.

Work with arithmetic expressions

8. Declare and initialize a double variable that stores a sum and an int variable that stores a count.
9. Calculate an average by dividing the sum variable by the count variable. Then, assign the result of the calculation to the average variable and print it to the console. When you're done, the console should look like this:
   ```
   Sum:      301.75
   Count:    6
   Average:  50.291666666666664
   ```
10. Run the application to make sure it works correctly.
11. Add an assignment statement that changes the value for the sum variable.
12. Run the application again to make sure it changes the data that's printed to the console for the sum and average.

Calculate tax and grand total

13. Modify the starting code as described in the following steps so it includes a product description, tax, and grand total. When you're done modifying this code, it should print this data to the console:

```
Code:         android
Description:  Murach's Android Programming
Price:        57.5
Quantity:     2
Total:        115.0
Tax Percent:  7.5
Tax Amount:   8.625
Grand Total:  123.625
```

14. Declare and initialize a String variable for the product description.
15. Declare and initialize a double variable for the tax percent. For now, you can assign a value of .075, which is 7.5%.
16. Declare and initialize a double variable for the tax amount. Then, calculate the amount by multiplying the total by the tax percent and assign the result to this variable.
17. Declare and initialize a double variable for the grand total. Then, calculate the grand total by adding the total and tax amounts and assign the result to this variable.
18. Modify the string that displays the data so the application prints it to the console as shown above. To get the tax percent to display correctly, you can multiply it by 100.
19. Run the application to make sure it works correctly.

Continue to test and experiment!

20. Add code to test any Java features described in this chapter.
21. Experiment with any NetBeans features described in this chapter.

3

How to use classes and methods

This chapter shows you how to write a complete Java application that gets input from a user, makes a calculation, formats the output, and displays it to the user. This teaches you how to use some of the classes and methods that are available from the Java API. When you finish this chapter, you should be able to write comparable applications of your own.

How to work with classes, objects, and methods 62
How to import classes 62
How to create an object from a class 64
How to call a method from an object 64
How to call a method from a class 64
How to view the documentation for the Java API 66
How to work with the console 68
How to use the Scanner class to get input 68
How to convert strings to numbers 70
A class that reads input from the console 72
How to convert numbers to formatted strings 74
A class that prints formatted numbers to the console 76
How to code simple control statements 78
How to compare numbers 78
How to compare strings 78
How to code a while loop 80
How to code an if/else statement 82
The Line Item application 84
The user interface 84
The code 86
The Future Value application 88
The user interface 88
The code 90
Perspective 92

How to work with classes, objects, and methods

In the previous chapter, you learned how to create String objects from the String class in the Java API. As you develop Java applications, though, you need to use dozens of different Java classes. To do that, you need to know how to create objects from Java classes, how to call Java methods, and how to import Java classes.

How to import classes

The Java SE API stores related classes in packages. Figure 3-1 begins by summarizing three commonly used packages. The java.lang package contains the classes (such as the String class) that are fundamental to the Java language. As a result, this package is automatically available to all Java code.

However, if you want to use a class from a package other than java.lang, you can include an import statement for that class at the beginning of the current class. If you don't, you can still use the class, but you have to qualify it with the name of the package that contains it each time you refer to it. Since that can lead to a lot of unnecessary typing, most programmers code import statements for the classes they use.

When you code an import statement, you can import a single class by specifying the class name, or you can import all of the classes in the package by typing an asterisk (*) in place of the class name. In this figure, for example, the first import statement imports the Scanner class that's in the java.util package. On the other hand, the second import statement imports all of the classes in the java.util package including the Scanner class. However, this only imports all classes in the java.util package, not any classes from other packages that begin with java.util such as java.util.regex.

Although it requires less code to import all of the classes in a package at once, importing one class at a time provides a couple benefits. First, it clearly identifies the classes that your code uses, which can be helpful to other programmers who review your code. Second, it helps avoid ambiguous references to classes. For example, the Date class exists in both the java.util and java.sql packages. As a result, if you import all classes from both packages and attempt to use the Date class, the compiler doesn't know which Date class you want to use.

Common packages

Package name	Description
`java.lang`	Classes that are fundamental to the Java language, including classes that work with primitive data types and strings.
`java.util`	Utility classes, including those for getting input from the console.
`java.text`	Classes that handle text, including those that format numbers and dates.

Common classes

```
java.lang.String
java.lang.Integer
java.lang.Double
java.util.Scanner
java.text.NumberFormat
```

The syntax of the import statement

For a single class

```
import packagename.ClassName;
```

For all classes in the package

```
import packagename.*;
```

How to import the Scanner class

For the Scanner class only

```
import java.util.Scanner;
```

For all classes in the java.util package

```
import java.util.*;
```

Code that uses the Scanner class

If it has been imported

```
Scanner sc = new Scanner(System.in);
```

If it has not been imported

```
java.util.Scanner sc = new java.util.Scanner(System.in);
```

Description

- The API for the Java SE provides a large library of classes that are organized into packages.
- All classes stored in the java.lang package are automatically available to all Java code.
- To use classes that aren't in the java.lang package, you can code an import statement. To import one class, specify the package name followed by the class name. To import all classes in a package, specify the package name followed by an asterisk (*).

Figure 3-1 How to import classes

How to create an object from a class

To use a Java class, you typically start by creating an *object* from a Java *class*. As the syntax in figure 3-2 shows, you do that by coding the new keyword, and the name of the Java class followed by a set of parentheses. These parentheses *call* the *constructor* of the class, which is a special block of code that creates the object from the class and initializes it. Within the parentheses, you code any *arguments* that are required by the constructor. In most cases, you assign the object that's created by the constructor to a variable. That way, you can use it later.

In the first example, the code assigns the Scanner object that's created to a Scanner variable named sc. Here, the constructor for this object requires one argument, the System.in object. This object represents console input and is created by Java automatically. As a result, you can use this object to get console input. Although this constructor requires only one argument, some constructors require zero arguments and some require two or more arguments. You'll learn more about how this works as you go through this book.

When you create an object, you can think of the class as the template for the object. That's why the object can be called an *instance* of the class, and the process of creating the object can be called *instantiation*. Whenever necessary, you can create multiple objects from a class. For instance, you often use multiple String objects in a single block of code even though there is only one String class.

How to call a method from an object

Once you create an object from a class, you can call the *methods* of the object. A method is a block of code that performs an action. In addition, a method typically returns a value or object that you can assign to a variable. To call a method from an object, you code the object name, a dot (.), and the method name followed by a set of parentheses. Within the parentheses, you code the arguments that are required by the method.

In the second example, the statement calls the nextLine method of the Scanner object named sc to get the current line of text from the console. This method doesn't require an argument. As a result, it's followed by an empty set of parentheses. This method returns a String object, and this example assigns it to the String variable named line.

How to call a method from a class

Besides the regular methods that you can call from an object, some classes provide *static methods*. Static methods are similar to regular methods, but you can call them directly from the class without creating an object from the class.

In the third example, the statement calls the static parseDouble method of the Double class. This method requires one argument. As a result, this example specifies the argument within the parentheses that come after the method name.

How to create an object from a class

Syntax

```
new ClassName(arguments);
```

Example

```
Scanner sc = new Scanner(System.in);    // creates a Scanner object named sc
```

How to call a method from an object

Syntax

```
objectName.methodName(arguments)
```

Example

```
String line = sc.nextLine();          // get a String object from the console
```

How to call a static method from a class

Syntax

```
ClassName.methodName(arguments)
```

Example

```
double price = Double.parseDouble(line);    // convert a String to a double
```

Description

- When you create an *object* from a Java class, you are creating an *instance* of the *class*. Then, you can use the *methods* of the class by *calling* them from the object.
- Some Java classes contain *static methods*. You can call these methods directly from the class without creating an object.
- When you create an object from a class, the *constructor* may require one or more *arguments*. These arguments must have the required data types. If there are multiple arguments, you must code them in the correct sequence, and you must separate each argument with a comma.
- When you call a method from an object or a class, the method may require one or more arguments. Here again, these arguments must have the required data types. If there are multiple arguments, you must code them in the correct sequence, and you must separate each argument with a comma.
- When you call a method from an object or a class, the method may return a primitive value or an object. If you want to use this data, you can assign the primitive value or object to a variable.

Figure 3-2 How to work with classes, objects, and methods

Here, the argument is the String variable named line created in the second example. This method returns a double value, and this example assigns it to the double variable named price.

As you read this book, you'll learn how to use dozens of classes and methods. For now, though, you just need to focus on the syntax for creating an object from a class, for calling a method from an object, and for calling a static method from a class.

How to view the documentation for the Java API

One of the most difficult aspects of using Java is learning how to use the classes and methods that your applications require. To do that, you frequently need to study the API documentation that comes with Java.

Figure 3-3 summarizes some of the basic techniques for navigating through the API documentation. This figure shows the start of the documentation for the Scanner class, which goes on for many pages. To display the documentation for a class, you can click the package name in the upper left frame. Then, you can click the class name in the lower left frame.

If you scroll through the documentation for the Scanner class, you'll get an idea of the amount of the documentation that's available. After a few pages of descriptive information, you come to a summary of the eight constructors for the class. After that, you come to a summary of dozens of methods of the class. That's followed by more detail about the constructors, which is followed by more detail about the methods.

For a beginning programmer, this is too much information. That's why one of the goals of this book is to introduce you to a subset of classes and methods that you'll use in most of the applications that you develop. Once you've learned how to use those classes and methods, the API documentation should make more sense to you, and you should be able to use that documentation to research classes and methods that aren't presented in this book.

However, it's never too early to start using the documentation. So, feel free to use the documentation to learn more about the classes and methods presented in this book. After you learn how to use the Scanner class, for example, use the API documentation to learn more about that class.

The documentation for the Scanner class

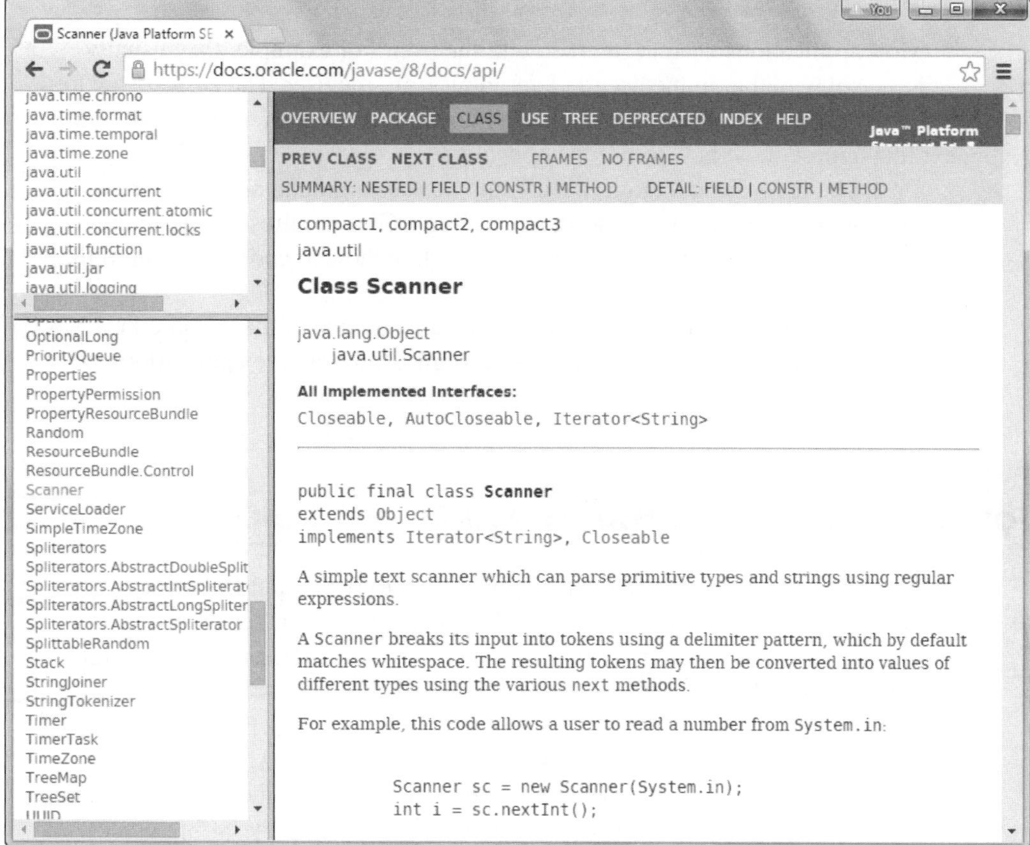

Description

- The Java SE API contains thousands of classes and methods that can help you do most of the tasks that your applications require.
- You can use a browser to view the Java SE API on the Internet by going to this address:

  `http://docs.oracle.com/javase/8/docs/api`
- You can select the name of the package in the top left frame to display information about the package and the classes it contains. Then, you can select a class in the lower left frame to display the documentation for that class in the right frame.
- Once you display the documentation for a class, you can scroll through it or click a link to get more information.

Figure 3-3 How to use the API documentation to research Java classes

How to work with the console

Most applications need to interact with the user. For example, they usually need to display output to the user and get input from the user. The easiest way to do that is to use a command-line interface known as the *console*. That's why the next few figures show how to use the console.

Once you learn Java, though, it's common to use a graphical user interface (GUI) to interact with the user. However, coding a GUI requires a solid understanding of Java. As a result, this book doesn't show how to code a GUI until the last two chapters.

When you create console applications, the appearance of the console may differ slightly depending on the operating system. However, the application should work the same. Also, most IDEs provide an easy way to work with the console as you're developing and testing console applications.

How to use the Scanner class to get input

Figure 3-4 shows how to use the Scanner class to read input from the console. To start, the first example shows how to create a Scanner object named sc. This works as described in figure 3-2. Then, the next three examples use this object to get input from the user.

In the second example, the first statement uses the print method of the System.out object to prompt the user to enter a product code. After the user presses the Enter key, the second statement uses the nextLine method to read the line of text that the user entered. Then, this statement assigns the String object that's returned for the line of text to the String variable named productCode.

The third and fourth examples use the print method to prompt the user to enter numeric data. For example, the third example prompts the user to enter a quantity, and the fourth example prompts the user to enter a price. However, since the nextLine method returns a String object, this code stores the data entered by the user in String objects named quantityLine and priceLine. In the next figure, you'll learn how to convert these String objects into int and double values.

The Scanner class

```
java.util.Scanner
```

How to create a Scanner object

```
Scanner sc = new Scanner(System.in);
```

A method of the Scanner object

Method	Description
`nextLine()`	Returns all text on the current line as a String object.

How to get a String object for a product code

```
System.out.print("Enter product code: ");
String productCode = sc.nextLine();
```

How to get a String object for a quantity

```
System.out.print("Enter quantity: ");
String quantityLine = sc.nextLine();
```

How to get a String object for a price

```
System.out.print("Enter price: ");
String priceLine = sc.nextLine();
```

Description

- To create a Scanner object that gets input from the *console*, specify System.in in the parentheses.
- When the nextLine method of the Scanner class runs, the application waits for the user to enter text with the keyboard. To complete the entry, the user presses the Enter key.
- Since the Scanner class is not in the java.lang package, you typically include an import statement whenever you use this class.

Figure 3-4 How to get input from the console

How to convert strings to numbers

When you get input from a user, you typically get a String object that contains the text that the user entered. In some applications, you may want to convert that text to a number. Then, you can use that number in arithmetic calculations. For example, you may want to convert the quantityLine variable from the previous figure to an int value. Similarly, you may want to convert the priceLine variable to a double value. Then, you can use these variables in arithmetic calculations.

Figure 3-5 shows how to use the Integer and Double classes to convert strings to numbers. To do that, you can use static methods that are available from these classes. In the first example, for instance, you can use the static parseInt method of the Integer class to convert a String object to an int value. The second example works similarly to the first. However, it uses the static parseDouble method of the Double class to convert the String variable named priceLine to a double value named price.

But what happens if the string contains a non-numeric value like "ten" that can't be parsed to an int or double type? In that case, the parseInt or parseDouble method causes a runtime error known as an exception. Using Java terminology, you can say that the method *throws an exception*. In chapter 8, you'll learn how to *catch* the exceptions that are thrown by these methods.

The Integer class

```
java.lang.Integer
```

A static method of the Integer class

Method	Description
parseInt(stringName)	Attempts to convert the String object that's supplied as an argument to an int type. If successful, it returns the int value. If unsuccessful, it throws an exception.

The Double class

```
java.lang.Double
```

A static method of the Double class

Method	Description
parseDouble(stringName)	Attempts to convert the String object that's supplied as an argument to a double type. If successful, it returns the double value. If unsuccessful, it throws an exception.

How to convert a String object to an int value

```
int quantity = Integer.parseInt(quantityLine);
```

How to convert a String object to a double value

```
double price = Double.parseDouble(priceLine);
```

Description

- The Integer and Double classes provide static methods that you can use for converting values from a String object to an int or double value.
- If the parseInt and parseDouble methods can't successfully parse the string, they will cause an error to occur. In Java terminology, this is known as *throwing an exception*. Later in this book, you'll learn how to *handle* exceptions by *catching* them.

Figure 3-5 How to convert strings to numbers

A class that reads input from the console

Figure 3-6 puts the last few figures into context by presenting all of the skills together in a single class named LineItemApp. This class reads input from the console and displays output to the console.

To start, this class imports the Scanner class. This makes it easy to refer to the Scanner class within the LineItemApp class.

Within the main method, the first statement creates a Scanner object named sc. The second statement prompts the user to enter a price. The third statement gets the text entered by the user and stores it in a String object named priceLine. The fourth statement converts the String object named priceLine to a double value named price. And the fifth statement prints a label and the value of the price variable to the console.

After this class, the second example shows the two statements from the LineItemApp class that get the double value named price. Then, the third example shows how to get the double value named price in a single statement. To do that, you supply the call to the nextLine method as the argument for the parseDouble method. When you use this approach, you don't have to provide a name for the variable for the String object. This is helpful because it can be difficult to provide meaningful names for multiple variables that are related.

The first console shows what happens if the user enters 49.50. In this case, the second line doesn't include the zero that the user entered. That's because this zero is no longer needed when the String object is converted to a double value.

The second console shows what happens if the user enters 123.45. Here, all of the digits are needed. As a result, none of them are lost when the String object is converted to a double value.

The third console shows what happens when the user enters a non-numeric value such as "ten". Here, the parseDouble method throws an exception and Java prints data about the exception to the console.

A class that reads an entry from the console

```
package murach.lineitem;

import java.util.Scanner;    // import the Scanner class

public class LineItemApp {

    public static void main(String[] args) {

        // create a Scanner object named sc from the Scanner class
        Scanner sc = new Scanner(System.in);

        // prompt the user to enter a price
        System.out.print("Enter price: ");

        // get the text entered by the user
        String priceLine = sc.nextLine();

        // convert the String object to a double value
        double price = Double.parseDouble(priceLine);

        // display the price
        System.out.println("Price:        " + price);
    }
}
```

How to get a double value from the user with two statements

```
String priceLine = sc.nextLine();
double price = Double.parseDouble(priceLine);
```

How to get a double value from the user with one statement

```
double price = Double.parseDouble(sc.nextLine());
```

The console if the user enters 49.50

```
Enter price: 49.50
Price:       49.5
```

The console if the user enters 123.45

```
Enter price: 123.45
Price:       123.45
```

The console if the user enters “ten”

```
Enter price: ten
Exception in thread "main" java.lang.NumberFormatException: For
input string: "ten"
    at sun.misc.FloatingDecimal.readJavaFormatString(
        FloatingDecimal.java:2043)
    at sun.misc.FloatingDecimal.parseDouble(
        FloatingDecimal.java:110)
    at java.lang.Double.parseDouble(Double.java:538)
    at murach.lineitem.LineItemApp.main(LineItemApp.java:17)
```

Figure 3-6 A class that reads an entry from the console

How to convert numbers to formatted strings

When you use numeric values in your code, you often need to format them. For example, you may want to apply a standard currency format to a double value. To do that, you need to add a dollar sign and commas. In addition, you only need to display two decimal places. Similarly, you may want to display a double value in a standard percent format. To do that, you need to add a percent sign and move the decimal point two digits to the right.

To do this type of formatting, you typically use the NumberFormat class that's summarized in figure 3-7 to convert numeric types back to String objects. Since the NumberFormat class is part of the java.text package, you usually want to include an import statement for this class before you begin working with it.

Once you import this class, you can call one of its static methods to return a NumberFormat object. For instance, the first example calls the static getCurrencyInstance method directly from the NumberFormat class.

Once you use a static method to return a NumberFormat object, you can call regular methods from that object. For instance, the second example calls the regular format method from the NumberFormat object named currency. This returns a String object that consists of a dollar sign plus the value of the price variable with two decimal places. In this format, negative numbers are enclosed in parentheses.

This example also shows how you can use a single statement to create a NumberFormat object and use its format method. To do that, you call the format method directly from the getCurrencyInstance method. Since this code calls one method directly from another, it's known as *method chaining*. This accomplishes the same task as the previous code. However, it doesn't create a variable for the NumberFormat object that you can use later in your code. This can be inefficient if your code creates a large number of NumberFormat objects. As a result, you typically use code like this when you only need to format one number.

The third example shows how to format numbers with the percent format. The main difference between the second and third examples is that you use the getPercentInstance method to create a NumberFormat object that has the default percent format. Then, you can use the format method of this object to format a number as a percent. In this format, negative numbers have a leading minus sign.

The fourth example shows how to format numbers without applying currency or percent formatting. This example shows how you can add commas to separate thousands without adding a currency or percent symbol. In addition, it shows how to set the number of decimal places for a NumberFormat object. To do that, you call the setMaximumFractionDigits method from the NumberFormat object and specify the number of decimal places. This example changes the number of decimal places from the default of three decimal places to just one decimal place. In this format, negative numbers also have a leading minus sign.

The NumberFormat class

```
java.text.NumberFormat
```

Three static methods of the NumberFormat class

Method	Returns a NumberFormat object that ...
`getCurrencyInstance()`	Has the default currency format ($99,999.99).
`getPercentInstance()`	Has the default percent format (99%).
`getNumberInstance()`	Has the default number format (99,999.999).

How to create a NumberFormat object

```
NumberFormat currency = NumberFormat.getCurrencyInstance();
```

Three methods of a NumberFormat object

Method	Description
`format(anyNumberType)`	Returns a String object that has the format specified by the NumberFormat object.
`setMinimumFractionDigits(int)`	Sets the minimum number of decimal places.
`setMaximumFractionDigits(int)`	Sets the maximum number of decimal places.

How to format a number as currency

```
double price = 49.5;
```

Without method chaining

```
NumberFormat currency = NumberFormat.getCurrencyInstance();
String priceFormatted = currency.format(price);     // $49.50
```

With method chaining

```
String priceFormatted = NumberFormat.getCurrencyInstance().format(price);
```

How to format a number as a percent

```
double discountPercent = .2;
NumberFormat percent = NumberFormat.getPercentInstance();
String discountPercentFormatted = percent.format(discountPercent);    // 20%
```

How to format a number with one decimal place

```
double miles = 15341.253;
NumberFormat number = NumberFormat.getNumberInstance();
number.setMaximumFractionDigits(1);
String milesFormatted = number.format(miles);      // 15,341.3
```

Description

- When you use the format method, the result is automatically rounded by using a rounding technique called half-even. This means that the number is rounded up if the preceding digit is odd, but the extra decimal places are truncated if the preceding digit is even.
- Since the NumberFormat class is in the java.text package, you typically include an import statement when you use this class.

Figure 3-7 How to format numbers

The examples in figure 3-7 use the default currency, percent, and number formats for the United States. If you want to use the default format for the current locale, you can modify the method that gets the NumberFormat object by passing it this argument:

```
Locale.getDefault()
```

For example, you can call the getCurrencyInstance method like this:

```
NumberFormat.getCurrencyInstance(Locale.getDefault());
```

Then, the NumberFormat object that's created uses the currency format for the current locale. For example, if you're in Europe, it uses the symbol for the Euro instead of the symbol for the U.S. dollar.

A class that prints formatted numbers to the console

Figure 3-8 puts the last figure into context by showing a class that performs a calculation, formats the numbers used in the calculation, and prints those formatted numbers to the console. To start, the first shaded statement imports the NumberFormat class since it's stored in the java.text package. This makes it easy to refer to the NumberFormat class within the LineItemApp class.

Within the main method, the second shaded statement creates a NumberFormat object named currency. The third shaded statement formats the double variable named price and stores the result in a String variable named priceFormatted. The fourth shaded statement formats the double variable named total and stores the result in a String variable named totalFormatted. And the remaining code prints the formatted numbers to the console.

A class that prints formatted output to the console

```
package murach.lineitem;

import java.text.NumberFormat;

public class LineItemApp {

    public static void main(String args[]) {
        // display a welcome message
        System.out.println("Welcome to the Line Item Calculator");
        System.out.println();

        // hard code three values
        String productCode = "java";
        double price = 49.50;
        int quantity = 2;

        // perform a calculation
        double total = price * quantity;

        // apply currency formatting
        NumberFormat currency = NumberFormat.getCurrencyInstance();
        String priceFormatted = currency.format(price);
        String totalFormatted = currency.format(total);

        // display the output
        String message =
            "Code:     " + productCode + "\n" +
            "Price:    " + priceFormatted + "\n" +
            "Quantity: " + quantity + "\n" +
            "Total:    " + totalFormatted + "\n";
        System.out.println(message);

        // display a goodbye message
        System.out.println("Bye!");
    }
}
```

The console

```
Welcome to the Line Item Calculator

Code:     java
Price:    $49.50
Quantity: 2
Total:    $99.00

Bye!
```

Description

- Although the appearance of a console may differ from one system to another, you can always use the print and println methods to print data to the console.

How to code simple control statements

As you write applications, you need to determine when to perform certain operations and how long to continue repetitive operations. To do that, you code *control statements* like the while loops and if/else statements that you'll learn about in a moment. But first, you need to learn how to compare numbers and strings.

How to compare numbers

Figure 3-9 shows how to code *Boolean expressions* that use *relational operators* to compare int and double data types. This type of expression evaluates to either true or false, and the operands in the expression can be either variables or literals.

In the first group of examples, the first expression evaluates to true if the variable named months is equal to a literal value of 3. The second expression is true if the variable named years is not equal to a literal value of zero. The third expression is true if the variable named discountPercent is greater than a literal value of 2.3. The fourth expression is true if the variable named i is less than the variable named months. The fifth example is true if the variable named subtotal is greater than or equal to 500. And the sixth example is true if the variable named quantity is less than or equal to the variable named reorderPoint.

Although you shouldn't have any trouble coding simple expressions like these, you must remember to code two equals signs instead of a single equals sign for the equality comparison. That's because a single equals sign is used for assignment statements. As a result, if you code a Boolean expression with a single equals sign, your code won't compile as shown in the second example.

When you compare numeric values, you usually compare values of the same data type. However, if you compare different types of numeric values, Java automatically casts the less precise numeric type to the more precise type. For example, if you compare an int type to a double type, Java casts the int type to the double type before it makes the comparison.

How to compare strings

Unlike many programming languages, you can't use the equals sign (=) or two equals signs (==) to test two strings for equality. Instead, you must use the equals or equalsIgnoreCase methods of the String class. Both of these methods require an argument that provides the String object that you want to compare with the current String object.

For instance, in the third group of examples, the first expression evaluates to true if the String variable named choice is equal to "y". The second expression evaluates to true if the String variable named choice is equal to "y" or "Y". The third expression evaluates to true if the String variable named lastName is not equal to "Jones". The fourth expression evaluates to true if the String variable named code is equal to the String variable named productCode.

Relational operators

Operator	Name	Description
`==`	Equality	Returns a true value if both operands are equal.
`!=`	Inequality	Returns a true value if left and right operands are not equal.
`>`	Greater Than	Returns a true value if left operand is greater than right operand.
`<`	Less Than	Returns a true value if left operand is less than the right operand.
`>=`	Greater Than Or Equal	Returns a true value if left operand is greater than or equal to right operand.
`<=`	Less Than Or Equal	Returns a true value if left operand is less than or equal to right operand.

Code that uses relational operators

```
months == 3                    // equal to a numeric literal
years != 0                     // not equal to a numeric literal
discountPercent > 2.3          // greater than a numeric literal
i < months                     // less than a numeric variable
subtotal >= 500                // greater than or equal to a numeric literal
quantity <= reorderPoint       // less than or equal to a numeric variable
```

A common error when testing numbers for equality

```
months = 3                     // this does not test for equality!
```

Two methods of the String class

Method	Description
`equals(String)`	Compares the value of the String object with a String argument and returns a true value if they are equal or a false value if they are not equal. This method makes a case-sensitive comparison.
`equalsIgnoreCase(String)`	Works like the equals method but is not case-sensitive.

Code that uses the methods of the String class

```
choice.equals("y")                       // equal to a string literal
choice.equalsIgnoreCase("y")             // equal to a string literal
(!lastName.equals("Jones"))              // not equal to a string literal
code.equalsIgnoreCase(productCode)       // equal to another String variable
```

Two common errors when testing strings for equality

```
choice = "y"                   // this does not test for equality!
choice == "y"                  // this does not test for equality!
```

Description

- A *Boolean expression* is an expression that evaluates to either true or false.
- You can use the *relational operators* to compare two numeric operands and return a Boolean value that is either true or false.
- To test two strings for equality, you must call one of the methods of the String class. The equality operator (==) does not test two strings for equality.

Figure 3-9 How to compare numbers and strings

How to code a while loop

Figure 3-10 shows how to code a *while loop*. This is one way that Java implements a control structure known as the *iteration structure*. This structure lets you repeat a block of statements.

When a while loop is executed, Java executes the statements within the braces of the loop *while* the Boolean expression at the beginning of the statement is true. In other words, the loop ends when the expression becomes false. As a result, if the expression is false when the statement starts, Java never executes any of the statements within the loop.

In the first example, the Boolean expression for the while loop uses the equalsIgnoreCase method to check whether the String variable named choice is equal to "y" or "Y". If so, the statements within this loop do some processing. Then, the statements within the loop prompt the user to enter a "y" to continue or an "n" to exit. As a result, if the user enters "y" or "Y", the loop executes again. Otherwise, the loop ends.

The braces of the loop define a block of code. As a result, any variables that are defined within this block of code have *block scope*. In other words, these variables can't be accessed outside the loop. That's why the String variable named choice is defined before the loop. That way, it can be accessed by the loop's Boolean expression and by the statements coded within the loop.

The second example shows how to code a loop that prints the numbers 1 through 4 to the console. Here, a *counter variable* (or just *counter*) named i is initialized to 1 before the loop starts. Within the loop, the first statement prints the counter variable to the console. Then, the second statement adds 1 to the counter variable. When the value of the counter variable becomes 5, the Boolean expression for the while loop is no longer true. As a result, the loop ends. When coding loops, it's common to use a counter variable, and it's common to use a single letter like *i* as the name of a counter variable.

If you don't code a loop correctly, the loop might never end. For instance, if you forget to code the statement that adds 1 to the counter variable in the second example, the loop never ends because the counter never gets to 5. This is known as an *infinite loop*. Then, you have to cancel the application so you can debug your code. In NetBeans, you can do that by clicking on the Stop button that's available from the Output window when a console application is running.

The syntax of the while loop

```
while (booleanExpression) {
    statements
}
```

A loop that continues while choice is "y" or "Y"

```
String choice = "y";
while (choice.equalsIgnoreCase("y")) {

     // get input from the user, process it, and display output here

     // see if the user wants to continue
     System.out.print("Continue? (y/n): ");
     choice = sc.nextLine();
     System.out.println();
}
```

A loop that prints 1 through 4 to the console

```
int i = 1;
while (i < 5) {
     System.out.println("Loop " + i);
     i = i + 1;
}
```

The console

```
Loop 1
Loop 2
Loop 3
Loop 4
```

Description

- A *while loop* executes the block of statements within its braces as long as the Boolean expression is true. When the expression becomes false, the while loop skips its block of statements so execution continues with the next statement in sequence.
- Any variables that are declared in the block of statements for a while loop have *block scope*. As a result, you can only access them within that block.
- If the Boolean expression in a while loop never becomes false, the loop never ends. Then, the application goes into an *infinite loop*. In NetBeans, you can cancel an infinite loop by clicking on the Stop button in the Output window.

Figure 3-10 How to code a while loop

How to code an if/else statement

Figure 3-11 shows how to use the *if/else statement* (or just *if statement*) to control the logic of your applications. This statement is the Java implementation of a control structure known as the *selection structure* because it lets you select different actions based on the results of a Boolean expression.

The syntax summary shows that you can code an if statement with just an if clause, you can code it with one or more else if clauses, and you can code it with a final else clause. Here, the ellipsis (...) means that the preceding element (in this case the else if clause) can be repeated as many times as it is needed. And the brackets [ ] mean that the element is optional.

When an if/else statement is executed, Java begins by evaluating the Boolean expression in the if clause. If it's true, Java executes the statements within this clause and skips the rest of the if/else statement. If it's false, Java evaluates the first else if clause (if there is one). Then, if its Boolean expression is true, Java executes the statements within this else if clause and skips the rest of the if/else statement. Otherwise, Java evaluates the next else if clause.

This continues with any remaining else if clauses. Finally, if none of the clauses contains a Boolean expression that evaluates to true, Java executes the statements in the else clause (if there is one). However, if none of the Boolean expressions are true and there is no else clause, Java doesn't execute any statements.

If you want to code two or more statements within a clause, you must use braces to identify the block of code for the clause as shown in the first three examples. Then, if you declare a variable within a block, that variable has block scope, which means that it can only be accessed within that block. That's why the price variable used in these examples is declared before the if statement. That way, it can be accessed by any clause in the if/else statement.

If a clause only contains one statement, you aren't required to enclose that statement in braces. However, it's generally considered a good practice to always use braces for the clauses of an if/else statement for two reasons. First, the braces clearly identify the start and end of the clause. Second, the braces make it easy to add additional statements to the clause later.

The examples in this figure set the price variable depending on the value that's stored in a String variable named productCode. For example, the third example sets the price to 57.50 if the productCode variable is equal to "java". It sets the price to 57.50 if the productCode variable is equal to "jsp". It sets the price to 54.50 if the productCode variable is equal to "mysql". And it sets the price to 49.50 if the productCode variable isn't equal to "java", "jsp", or "mysql".

The syntax of the if/else statement

```
if (booleanExpression) {statements}
[else if (booleanExpression) {statements}] ...
[else {statements}]
```

Examples of if/else statements

Without an else if or else clause

```
double price = 49.50;
if (productCode.equalsIgnoreCase("java")) {
    price = 57.50;
}
```

With an else clause

```
double price;
if (productCode.equalsIgnoreCase("java")) {
    price = 57.50;
} else {
    price = 49.50;
}
```

With two else if clauses and an else clause

```
double price;
if (productCode.equalsIgnoreCase("java")) {
    price = 57.50;
} else if (productCode.equalsIgnoreCase("jsp")) {
    price = 57.50;
} else if (productCode.equalsIgnoreCase("mysql")) {
    price = 54.50;
} else {
    price = 49.50;
}
```

Description

- An *if/else statement*, or just *if statement*, always contains an if clause. In addition, it can contain one or more else if clauses, and a final else clause.
- Any variables that are declared within a block for an if/else clause have block scope. As a result, they can only be accessed within that block.
- If a clause requires just one statement, you don't have to enclose the statement in braces. However, it's generally considered a good practice to always include braces. That way, if you decide to add more statements to a clause later, you won't accidentally introduce a bug.

Figure 3-11 How to code if/else statements

The Line Item application

To put the skills in this chapter into the context of an application, the next two figures present the Line Item application. If you understand the code presented in this chapter, you should be able to write comparable Java applications of your own.

The user interface

Figure 3-12 shows the console for the Line Item application. This application starts by displaying a welcome message on the console. Then, it prompts the user to enter a product code and a quantity. Next, it displays the data for the line item. To get that data, the application retrieves the price based on the product code entered by the user, and it calculates the total by multiplying the price and quantity.

After displaying the data for the line item, the application prompts the user to enter a "y" to continue or an "n" to exit. If the user enters a "y" or "Y", he or she can enter another line item. If the user enters "n" or any other character, the application ends and displays an exit message.

The console after two calculations

```
Welcome to the Line Item Calculator

Enter product code: java
Enter quantity:     2

LINE ITEM
Code:        java
Price:       $57.50
Quantity:    2
Total:       $115.00

Continue? (y/n): y

Enter product code: jsp
Enter quantity:     1

LINE ITEM
Code:        jsp
Price:       $57.50
Quantity:    1
Total:       $57.50

Continue? (y/n): n

Bye!
```

Description

- When the application starts, the user can enter a product code that identifies a product and the quantity for that product. The application determines the product price based on the product code. Then, it calculates the total amount for the line item and displays the line item.
- After calculating the total for the invoice, the user can enter "y" or "Y" at the prompt to continue. Or, the user can enter "n" or any other character to end the application.

Figure 3-12 The user interface for the LineItem application

The code

Figure 3-13 shows the code for the Line Item application. Although this application is simple, it gets input from the user, performs a calculation that uses this input, and displays the result of the calculation.

This code begins with a package statement that declares that it is stored in the murach.lineitem package. As a result, this code is stored in the murach/lineitem subfolder of the application folder.

The two import statements import the NumberFormat and Scanner classes. As a result, the rest of this code can use these classes without having to prefix the class name with the package name.

The class declaration specifies a name of LineItemApp. As a result, this code is stored in a file named LineItemApp.java.

The main method is coded within the braces of the LineItemApp class. This method is executed when you run the LineItemApp class.

The main method begins by printing a welcome message to the console. Then, it creates a Scanner object named sc. Although this object could be created within the while loop, that would mean that the object would be recreated each time through the loop, which would be inefficient.

Before the while loop, the code declares a String variable named choice and initializes it to "y". Then, the loop checks whether the choice variable is equal to "y". If so, it starts by getting the product code from the user and storing it in a String variable named productCode. Then, it gets a quantity from the user, converts it from a String object to an int value, and stores it in a variable named quantity.

After getting this data, an if/else statement sets the double variable named price based on the value of product code. If, for example, the productCode is equal to "java", the price is set to 57.50.

When the if/else statement is finished, this code calculates the line item total by multiplying the price and quantity. Then, it stores the result of that calculation in a double variable named total.

After this calculation, this code uses the NumberFormat class to apply currency formatting to the price and total variables. In addition, it creates a String variable named message that contains string literals, variables, and escape sequences for new line characters. Then, it prints that string to the console.

After printing this data to the console, this code displays a message that asks the user if he or she wants to continue. If the user enters "y" or "Y", the loop is repeated. Otherwise, the application ends.

If you're new to programming, you can learn a lot by writing simple applications like the Line Item application. This gives you a chance to become comfortable with getting input, performing calculations, and displaying output. In addition, it gives you a chance to get comfortable with control statements such as while loops and if/else statements.

The code for the LineItem application

```
package murach.lineitem;

import java.text.NumberFormat;
import java.util.Scanner;

public class LineItemApp {

    public static void main(String args[]) {
        System.out.println("Welcome to the Line Item Calculator");
        System.out.println();

        Scanner sc = new Scanner(System.in);
        String choice = "y";
        while (choice.equalsIgnoreCase("y")) {
            // get input from user
            System.out.print("Enter product code: ");
            String productCode = sc.nextLine();

            System.out.print("Enter quantity:     ");
            int quantity = Integer.parseInt(sc.nextLine());

            // set product price based on product code
            double price;
            if (productCode.equalsIgnoreCase("java")) {
                price = 57.50;
            } else if (productCode.equalsIgnoreCase("jsp")) {
                price = 57.50;
            } else if (productCode.equalsIgnoreCase("mysql")) {
                price = 54.50;
            } else {
                price = 0;
            }

            // calculate total
            double total = price * quantity;

            // format and display output
            NumberFormat currency = NumberFormat.getCurrencyInstance();
            String priceFormatted = currency.format(price);
            String totalFormatted = currency.format(total);
            String message = "\nLINE ITEM\n" +
                "Code:         " + productCode + "\n" +
                "Price:        " + priceFormatted + "\n" +
                "Quantity:     " + quantity + "\n" +
                "Total:        " + totalFormatted + "\n";
            System.out.println(message);

            // see if the user wants to continue
            System.out.print("Continue? (y/n): ");
            choice = sc.next();
            System.out.println();
        }
        System.out.println("Bye!");
    }
}
```

Figure 3-13 The code for the LineItem application

The Future Value application

This chapter finishes by presenting another application, the Future Value application. This application is similar in some ways to the Line Item application. However, it uses a loop to calculate the future value of a monthly investment that's made over a series of years.

The user interface

Figure 3-14 shows the console for this application. Here, the user starts by entering the monthly investment, the yearly interest rate, and the number of years for the investment. Then, the application calculates and displays the future value, and it prompts the user to see if he or she wants to continue. At that point, the user can enter a "y" to continue or an "n" to exit.

The console after two calculations

```
Welcome to the Future Value Calculator

Enter monthly investment:    100
Enter yearly interest rate:  3
Enter number of years:       3
Future value:                $3,771.46

Continue? (y/n): y

Enter monthly investment:    120
Enter yearly interest rate:  3
Enter number of years:       3
Future value:                $4,525.75

Continue? (y/n): n

Bye!
```

Description

- When the application starts, the user can enter a monthly investment, yearly interest rate, and number of years. Then, it calculates the future value of the investment at the end of the specified number of years and displays that value to the user.
- After calculating the future value, the user can enter "y" or "Y" at the prompt to continue. Or, the user can enter "n" or any other character to end the application.

Figure 3-14 The user interface for the Future Value application

The code

Figure 3-15 shows the code for this application. This code uses a while loop to determine when the application ends. Within this loop, the code gets the three entries from the user. Then, it converts these entries to the same time unit, which is months. To do that, it multiplies the number of years by 12 and divides the yearly interest rate by 12. In addition, it divides the yearly interest rate by 100 so it calculates the interest correctly.

Once those variables are prepared, a second while loop calculates the future value. This loop executes one time for each month. Within this loop, the first statement adds the monthly investment to the future value. The second statement calculates the amount of monthly interest. The third statement adds the monthly interest to the future value. And the fourth statement increments the counter variable.

When this loop finishes, the code displays the result. To do that, it uses the NumberFormat class to apply currency formatting to the future value. Then, it asks whether the user wants to continue.

The code for the Future Value application

```
package murach.fv;

import java.text.NumberFormat;
import java.util.Scanner;

public class Main {

    public static void main(String[] args) {
        // display a welcome message
        System.out.println("Welcome to the Future Value Calculator");
        System.out.println();

        Scanner sc = new Scanner(System.in);
        String choice = "y";
        while (choice.equalsIgnoreCase("y")) {

            // get input from user
            System.out.print("Enter monthly investment:   ");
            double monthlyInvestment = Double.parseDouble(sc.nextLine());

            System.out.print("Enter yearly interest rate: ");
            double yearlyInterestRate = Double.parseDouble(sc.nextLine());

            System.out.print("Enter number of years:      ");
            int years = Integer.parseInt(sc.nextLine());

            // convert yearly values to monthly values
            double monthlyInterestRate = yearlyInterestRate / 12 / 100;
            int months = years * 12;

            // calculate the future value
            double futureValue = 0;
            int i = 1;
            while (i <= months) {
                futureValue = futureValue + monthlyInvestment;
                double monthlyInterestAmount =
                        futureValue * monthlyInterestRate;
                futureValue = futureValue + monthlyInterestAmount;
                i = i + 1;
            }

            // format and display the result
            System.out.println("Future value:               " +
                    NumberFormat.getCurrencyInstance().format(futureValue));
            System.out.println();

            // see if the user wants to continue
            System.out.print("Continue? (y/n): ");
            choice = sc.nextLine();
            System.out.println();
        }
        System.out.println("Bye!");
    }
}
```

Figure 3-15 The code for the Future Value application

Perspective

The goal of this chapter has been to show you how to create a console application that uses classes and methods from the Java API to get input from the user and display output to the user. Now, if you understand how the Line Item and Future Value applications work, you've come a long way. However, these applications don't use objects in a professional way. That's why the next two chapters show you how to convert the Line Item application into an object-oriented application that uses objects in a professional way.

Also, keep in mind that this chapter is just an introduction to Java programming. As a result, you'll learn more details about writing Java code as you progress through this book. For example, you'll learn more about coding control statements in chapter 8.

Summary

- You *call* a *method* from an object and you call a *static method* from a class. A method may require one or more *arguments*.
- Before you use a class from the Java SE API that isn't in the java.lang package, you typically code an import statement for the class.
- When you use a *constructor* to create an *object* from a Java class, you are creating an *instance* of the class.
- You can use the static methods of the Integer and Double classes to convert strings to int and double values.
- You can use the NumberFormat class to apply standard currency, percent, and number formats to any of the primitive numeric types.
- You can code a *while loop* that executes a block of statements repeatedly when its *Boolean expression* returns a true value and skips that block of statements when its Boolean expression returns a false value.
- You can code an *if statement* to control the logic of an application based on the true or false values of Boolean expressions.

Exercise 3-1 Modify the Line Item application

In this exercise, you can test and modify the Line Item application presented at the end of this chapter.

Test the application

1. Start the NetBeans IDE and open the project named ch03_ex1_LineItem. This project should be in this folder:

   `C:\murach\java_netbeans\ex_starts`

2. Open the file named LineItemApp.java. Then, review the code for this file.
3. Run this application and test it with valid product codes like "java" and valid quantities like 2, 10, and 1000 that make it easy to see whether or not the calculations are correct.
4. Run the application again and test it with an invalid quantity value like "two". This should cause the application to crash. Study the error message and determine which line of source code was running when the error occurred.
5. Run the application again and enter "x" when the application asks you whether you want to continue. What happens and why?

Modify the application

6. Modify the if/else statement so it sets a description for the product. Then, modify the code that displays the data for the line item so it includes the description. When you're done, the application should look like this:

```
Welcome to the Line Item Calculator

Enter product code: java
Enter quantity:     2

LINE ITEM
Code:         java
Description: Murach's Java Programming
Price:        $57.50
Quantity:     2
Total:        $115.00

Continue? (y/n):
```

7. Modify the if/else statement so it includes another product code named "android". Make up a description and price that correspond with this code.
8. Modify the code that displays the data for the line item so that it doesn't declare the priceFormatted and totalFormatted variables. To do that, replace these variables with a call to the format method of the NumberFormat object named currency. This should cut two lines of code.

Exercise 3-2 Create the Area and Perimeter application

In this exercise, you can create a new application that calculates the area and perimeter of a rectangle. When you're done, a test run should look something like this:

```
Welcome to the Area and Perimeter Calculator

Enter length: 100
Enter width:  200
Area:         20,000.000
Perimeter:    600.000

Continue? (y/n): y

Enter length: 8.25
Enter width:  4.30
Area:         35.475
Perimeter:    25.100

Continue? (y/n): n

Bye!
```

1. Create a project named ch03_ex2_AreaAndPerimeter that contains a class named Main that contains the main method.
2. Write the code that displays the welcome and the exit message. Then, run the application to make sure this works.
3. Write the code that prompts the user for the length and width of a rectangle and converts these entries to double values.
4. Write the code that calculates and displays the area and perimeter. The formulas for calculating area and perimeter are:
   ```
   area = width * length
   perimeter = 2 * width + 2 * length
   ```
   Run the application and test it with valid data. This application should perform one calculation and end.
5. Write the while loop that allows the user to perform multiple calculations. The end of this loop should ask the user if he or she wants to continue. Then, run this application and test it with valid data to make sure it works correctly.

4

How to code your own classes and methods

In the previous chapter, you learned how to code two procedural applications. However, most professional Java applications are object-oriented. That's why this chapter shows how to develop an object-oriented application. To do that, it starts by showing how to create and use classes that define objects. Then, it shows how to create and use classes that contain static fields and methods.

An introduction to classes 96
How encapsulation works 96
The relationship between a class and its objects 98
How to work with a class that defines an object 100
How to use NetBeans to create a new class 100
The Product class 102
How to code instance variables 104
How to code constructors 106
How to code methods 108
How to create an object from a class 110
How to call the methods of an object 112
How to work with static fields and methods 114
The ProductDB class 114
How to code and call static fields and methods 116
When to use static fields and methods 116
The Product Viewer application 118
The user interface 118
The ProductApp class 118
More skills for working with classes and methods 120
Reference types compared to primitive types 120
How to overload methods 122
How to use the this keyword 124
The Product class with overloading 126
Perspective 128

An introduction to classes

The first two figures in this chapter introduce you to some concepts that apply to classes. That includes how encapsulation works and how a class relates to its objects.

How encapsulation works

Figure 4-1 shows a *class diagram* for a class named Product. This diagram uses *Unified Modeling Language* (*UML*), a modeling language that is the industry standard for working with all object-oriented programming languages including Java.

In this class diagram, the class contains three *fields* and seven *methods*. Here, the minus sign (-) identifies *private* fields and methods that are available only within the current class, and the plus sign (+) identifies *public* fields and methods that are available to other classes.

In this case, all of the methods are public, and all of the fields are private. As a result, other classes can't access the fields directly. However, the methods make the data stored by the fields available to other classes. For instance, the getCode method returns the data that's stored in the code field, and the setCode method assigns new data to the code field.

This illustrates the concept of *encapsulation*, a fundamental concept of object-oriented programming. This means that the programmer can *hide*, or encapsulate, some fields and methods of a class, while *exposing* others. Since the fields (or data) of a class are typically encapsulated within a class, encapsulation is sometimes referred to as *data hiding*.

Encapsulation lets you change the code for a method within a class without affecting any code that uses the method. For instance, you can change the code for the getPrice method without changing any code in other classes that use that method. This is possible because the code in other classes can't directly access the price field. The result is that encapsulation makes it easier for you to modify or improve the methods of a class later.

If a method accepts arguments, it must include *parameters* that define the data types for its arguments. In a class diagram, the diagram specifies the data types for the parameters within the parentheses of the method. After these parentheses, a class diagram includes a colon followed by the data type that's returned by the method.

A class diagram for the Product class

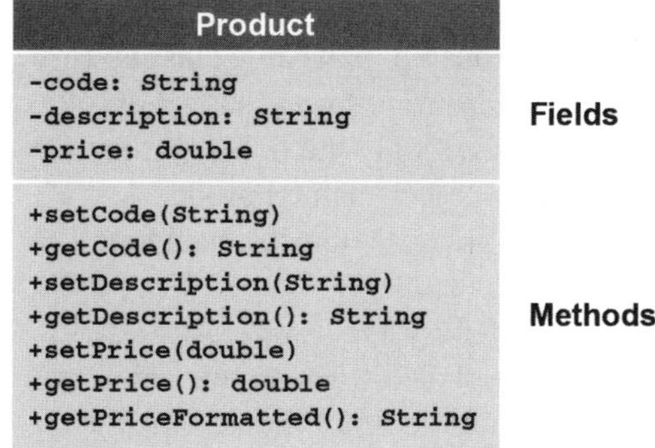

Description

- The *fields* of a class store the data of a class.
- The *methods* of a class define the tasks that a class can perform. Often, these methods provide a way to work with the fields of a class.
- *Encapsulation* is one of the fundamental concepts of object-oriented programming. This means that the class controls which of its fields and methods can be accessed by other classes. As a result, the fields in the class can be hidden from other classes, and the methods in a class can be modified or improved without changing the way that other classes use them.

UML diagramming notes

- *UML* (*Unified Modeling Language*) is the industry standard used to describe the classes and objects of an object-oriented application.
- A UML *class diagram* describes the fields and methods of one or more classes.
- The minus sign (-) marks the fields and methods that are *private*. This means that other classes can't access them.
- The plus sign (+) marks the fields and methods that are *public*. This means that other classes can access them.
- For each field, the diagram gives the name of the field, followed by a colon, followed by the data type.
- For each method, the diagram gives the name of the method, followed by a set of parentheses. If a method accepts arguments, it must define *parameters* that correspond with the arguments. To do that, the diagram lists the data type of each parameter in the parentheses. After the parentheses, the diagram includes a colon, followed by the data type that's returned by the method.

Figure 4-1 How encapsulation works

The relationship between a class and its objects

Figure 4-2 uses UML diagrams to show the relationship between a class and its objects. In this figure, one class diagram and two *object diagrams* show how objects are created from a class. Here, the diagrams show only the fields, not the methods, of the class and its objects. In this case, two objects named product1 and product2 are created from the Product class. Within these objects, each field contains some data.

Once an *instance* of a class is created, it has an *identity* and a *state*. An object's identity is its address in internal memory, which is always unique. An object's state refers to its data. For example, the state of the first Product object is different than the state of the second Product object because these objects store different data. As an application executes, the state of an object may change.

The relationship between a class and its objects

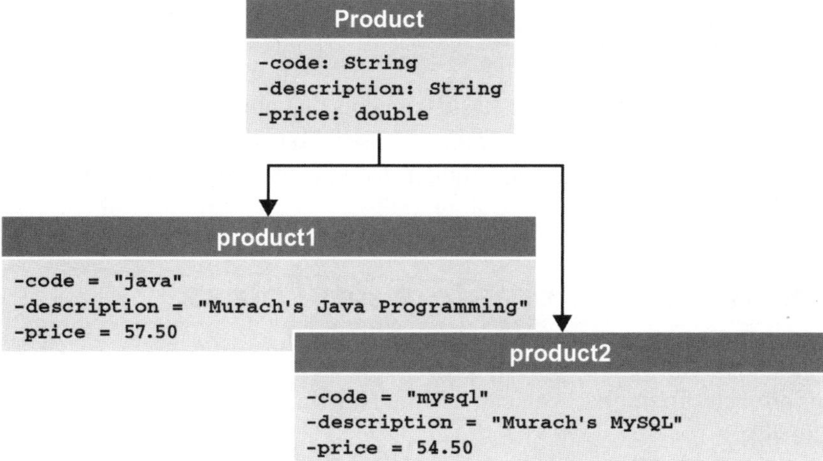

Description

- A *class* can be thought of as a template from which *objects* are made.
- Once an *instance* of a class is created, it has an *identity* (a unique address) and a *state* (the data that it stores). As an application runs, an object's state may change.

Figure 4-2 The relationship between a class and its objects

How to work with a class that defines an object

Now that you've learned some of the basic concepts that apply to classes, you're ready to learn the basic skills for creating classes. To start, the next few figures show how to create a class named Product that you can use to store data about a product.

How to use NetBeans to create a new class

When you develop object-oriented applications, you often need to add new classes to your projects. To do that, you can use the New Java Class dialog box shown in figure 4-3.

The dialog box in this figure creates a class named Product, and it specifies a package named murach.product that corresponds with the murach/product folder that's shown in the dialog. If this folder doesn't already exist, NetBeans automatically creates it.

When you complete the New Java Class dialog box, NetBeans creates a file to store the code for the class. For the Product class, that file is named Product.java. NetBeans also generates the starting code for the class as shown in this figure. Here, the package statement specifies the name of the package. In addition, the name of the class matches the name of the file, which is required. Finally, the public *access modifier* specifies that other classes (including classes in other packages) can access this class, which is usually what you want.

The dialog box for creating a new Java class

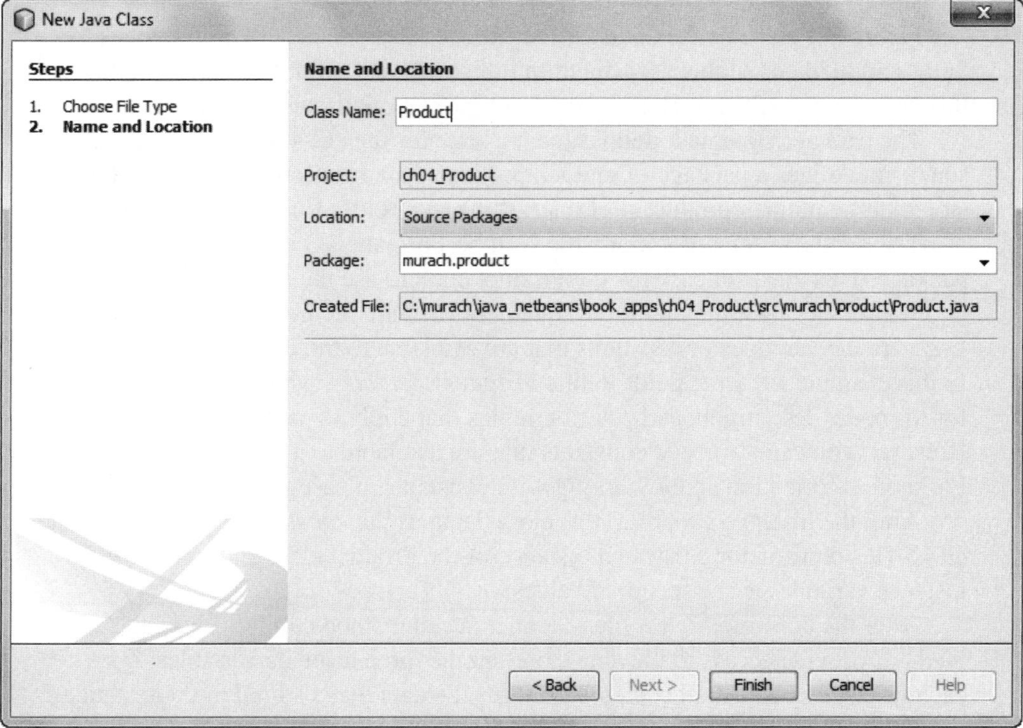

The code that's generated for the Product class

```
package murach.product;

public class Product {

}
```

Description

- To create a new class, right-click on the package where you want to add the class, select the New→Java Class command, and respond to the resulting dialog box. At the least, you should enter a name for the class in the Class Name text box.
- Although this dialog box encourages you to select a package for the class, this isn't required. If you don't select a package for the class, NetBeans stores the class in the default package.
- When you store a class in a package, the first statement of the class must be a package statement that specifies the name of the package.
- If you specify a package when you add a new class and that package doesn't already exist, NetBeans automatically creates it for you.
- If you add a new class to a package, NetBeans automatically adds the necessary package statement to the class.

Figure 4-3 How to create a new class

The Product class

Figure 4-4 presents the code for the Product class. This code implements the fields and methods of the class diagram in figure 4-1. If you don't understand this code now, don't worry! The next few figures explain this code in detail.

The package statement defines the package for the class. In this figure, this statement defines a package of murach.product. As a result, this class must be stored in the murach/product subfolder of the root folder for the application.

The import statement imports the NumberFormat class of the java.text package. This makes it easy for the Product class to use the NumberFormat class.

Within the class, the first three statements declare the fields of the class. The *fields* are the variables or constants that are available to the class and its objects. In this example, all three fields define *instance variables*, which store the data for the code, description, and price variables that apply to each Product object. However, you can also code constants that are available to a class and its objects. For more information about working with constants, please see chapter 7.

After the instance variables, this class declares the *constructor* of the Product class. This constructor creates an instance of the Product class and initializes its instance variables to the specified values.

After the constructor, this class defines seven methods. In this class, the methods provide access to the data stored in the three instance variables. For each instance variable, a *get method* returns the data that's stored in the instance variable, and a *set method* assigns a new data to the instance variable. Of these methods, the getPriceFormatted method is the only method that does any work beyond getting or setting the data of the instance variable. This method applies the standard currency format to the price variable and returns the resulting string.

Although the Product class includes both a get and a set method for each field, you don't always have to code both of these methods for a field. In particular, it's common to code just a get method for a field so that its data can be retrieved but not changed.

The private and public keywords determine which *members* of a class are available to other classes. Here, all of the instance variables of the Product class have been declared as private. As a result, these members are only available within that class. On the other hand, the constructor and the methods have been declared as public. As a result, these members are available to all classes.

Now that you've seen the code for the Product class, you might want to consider how it uses encapsulation. To start, the three fields are hidden from other classes because they're declared with the private keyword. In addition, all of the code contained within the constructor and methods is hidden.

Because of that, you can change any of the code within the constructors and methods of this class without having to change the way other classes call these constructors and methods. For example, if you want to modify the getPriceFormatted method so it uses the current locale when it formats the price, you can modify the code within this method so it does that. However, when you change the data that's returned by a method like this, it's possible that the code that calls this method won't work correctly after this change. As a result, you should take care when modifying a method that's used by other classes.

The Product class

```
package murach.product;

import java.text.NumberFormat;

public class Product {

    // the instance variables
    private String code;
    private String description;
    private double price;

    // the constructor
    public Product() {
        code = "";
        description = "";
        price = 0;
    }

    // the set and get methods for the code variable
    public void setCode(String code) {
        this.code = code;
    }

    public String getCode() {
        return code;
    }

    // the set and get methods for the description variable
    public void setDescription(String description) {
        this.description = description;
    }

    public String getDescription() {
        return description;
    }

    // the set and get methods for the price variable
    public void setPrice(double price) {
        this.price = price;
    }

    public double getPrice() {
        return price;
    }

    // a custom get method for the price variable
    public String getPriceFormatted() {
        NumberFormat currency = NumberFormat.getCurrencyInstance();
        String priceFormatted = currency.format(price);
        return priceFormatted;
    }
}
```

Figure 4-4 The Product class

How to code instance variables

Figure 4-5 shows how to code the instance variables that define the data that's stored in the objects that are created from a class. When you declare an instance variable, you typically use an access modifier to control its accessibility. If you use the private keyword, the instance variable can't be directly accessed by other classes. In other words, it can only be directly accessed from within the current class. In contrast, if you use the public keyword, the instance variable can be directly accessed by other classes.

This figure shows four examples of declaring an instance variable. The first example declares a variable of the double type. The second one declares a variable of the int type. The third one declares a variable of the String type. And the last one declares a variable of the Product type, which is the class that you're learning how to code right now.

Although instance variables work like regular variables, you must declare them within the body of the class, but not within methods or constructors. That way, they'll be available throughout the entire class. In this book, all of the examples declare instance variables at the beginning of the class. However, when you review code from other sources, you may find code that declares the instance variables at the end of the class or at other locations within the class. In this figure, for example, the code declares an instance variable named test at the end of the class, after the getPriceFormatted method.

The syntax for declaring instance variables

```
public|private primitiveType|ClassName variableName;
```

Examples

```
private double price;
private int quantity;
private String code;
private Product product;
```

Where you can declare instance variables

```
public class Product {
    // typical to code instance variables here
    private String code;
    private String description;
    private double price;

    //the constructor and methods of the class
    public Product(){}
    public void setCode(String code){}
    public String getCode(){ return code; }
    public void setDescription(String description){}
    public String getDescription(){ return description; }
    public void setPrice(double price){}
    public double getPrice(){ return price; }
    public String getPriceFormatted(){ return priceFormatted; }

    // possible to code instance variables here
    private int test;
}
```

Description

- A *field* of a class defines the data that's available to the entire class. A field can be an instance variable or a constant. To learn how to work with constants, see chapter 7.
- An *instance variable* stores data that's available to the entire object. In other words, an instance variable stores data that's available to an instance of a class.
- An instance variable may be a primitive data type, an object created from a Java class such as the String class, or an object created from a user-defined class such as the Product class.
- Typically, instance variables are declared with the private keyword. This helps to prevent other classes from directly accessing instance variables.
- You can declare the instance variables for a class anywhere outside the constructors and methods of the class.

Figure 4-5 How to code instance variables

How to code constructors

Figure 4-6 shows how to code a constructor for a class. When you code one, it's a good coding practice to initialize all of the instance variables of the class as shown in the examples. You can also include any additional statements that you want to execute within the constructor.

When you code a constructor, you typically use the public access modifier. In addition, you must use the same name, including capitalization, as the name of the class. Then, if you don't want to accept arguments, you code an empty set of parentheses as shown in the first example. On the other hand, if you want to accept arguments, you code the parameters for the constructor as shown in the next two examples. When you code the parameters for a constructor, you must code a data type and a name for each parameter. For the data type, you can code a primitive data type or the class name for any class that defines an object.

The second example shows a constructor with three parameters. Here, the first parameter is a String object named code, the second parameter is a String object named description, and the third parameter is a double type named price. Then, the three statements within the constructor use these parameters to initialize the three instance variables of the class.

In this example, the names of the parameters are the same as the names of the instance variables. As a result, the constructor must distinguish between the two. To do that, it uses the keyword named *this* to refer to the instance variables of the current object.

The third example works the same as the second example. However, it doesn't need to use the this keyword because the parameter names aren't the same as the names of the instance variables. In addition, the parameter names are more descriptive since they indicate that the code, description, and price are for a product. As a result, this code might be slightly easier for other programmers to read and understand than the code in the second example.

When you code a constructor, the number of parameters and the data type for each parameter form the *signature* of the constructor. You can code more than one constructor per class as long as each constructor has a unique signature. For example, the first two constructors shown in this figure have different signatures. As a result, they can both be coded within the Product class. This is known as *overloading* a constructor.

If you don't code a constructor, the compiler automatically creates a *default constructor* that doesn't accept any parameters. However, if you code a constructor that accepts parameters, the compiler doesn't create this default constructor. In that case, if you need a default constructor, you need to code it yourself.

The syntax for coding constructors

```
public|private ClassName([parameterList]) {
    // the statements of the constructor
}
```

A default constructor that explicitly initializes three instance variables

```
public Product() {
   code = "";
   description = "";
   price = 0.0;
}
```

A constructor with three parameters

```
public Product(String code, String description, double price) {
    this.code = code;
    this.description = description;
    this.price = price;
}
```

Another way to code the constructor shown above

```
public Product(String productCode, String productDescription,
               double productPrice) {
    code = productCode;
    description = productDescription;
    price = productPrice;
}
```

Description

- A *constructor* can be used to create, or construct, an object from a class.
- The constructor must use the same name and capitalization as the name of the class.
- To code a constructor that has parameters, code a data type and name for each parameter within the parentheses that follow the class name.
- The name of a constructor combined with the parameter list forms the *signature* of the constructor. Although you can code multiple constructors for a class, each constructor must have a unique signature. This is known as *overloading* a constructor.
- You can use the keyword named *this* to refer to an instance variable of the current object. This is required if an instance variable has the same name as a parameter of the constructor. Otherwise, it's optional.
- If you don't explicitly initialize an instance variable, Java automatically initializes it for you by setting numeric variables to zero, boolean variables to false, and variables for objects to null.

Default constructor rules

- A *default constructor* has zero parameters.
- If you don't code any constructors in your class, the Java compiler automatically creates a default constructor for your class.
- If you code a constructor that has parameters, and you don't code a default constructor, the Java compiler doesn't automatically create a default constructor for your class.

Figure 4-6 How to code constructors

How to code methods

Figure 4-7 shows how to code the methods of a class. To start, you code an access modifier. Most of the time, you can use the public keyword to declare the method so it can be used by other classes. However, you can also use the private keyword to hide the method from other classes.

After the access modifier, you code the return type for the method. This specifies the data type that the method returns. After the return type, you code the name of the method followed by a set of parentheses. Within the parentheses, you code the parameter list for the method. Last, you code the opening and closing braces that contain the statements of the method.

Since a method name should describe the action that the method performs, it's a common coding practice to start each method name with a verb. For example, methods that set the data of an instance variable usually begin with *set*. Conversely, methods that get the data of an instance variable usually begin with *get*. These types of methods are typically referred to as *accessors* because they let you access the data that's stored in the instance variables. Methods that perform other types of tasks also begin with verbs such as print, read, and format.

The first example shows how to code a method that doesn't accept any parameters or return any data. To do that, it uses the void keyword for the return type and it ends with a set of empty parentheses. When this method is called, it prints the instance variables of the Product object to the console, separating each instance variable with a pipe character (|).

The next three examples show how to code methods that return data. To do that, these methods specify a return type, and they include a return statement to return the appropriate data. When coding a method like this, you must make sure that the return type that you specify matches the type of the data that you return. Otherwise, your code won't compile.

In the fourth example, the getPriceFormatted method uses a NumberFormat object to apply standard currency formatting to the double variable named price. This converts the double variable to a String object. Then, the return statement returns the String object to the calling method.

The fifth and sixth examples show two possible ways to code a set method. In the fifth example, the method accepts a parameter that has the same name as the instance variable. As a result, the assignment statement within this method uses the this keyword to identify the instance variable. In the sixth example, the parameter has a different name than the instance variable. As a result, the assignment statement doesn't need to use the this keyword.

The syntax for coding a method

```
public|private returnType methodName([parameterList]) {
    // the statements of the method
}
```

A method that doesn't accept parameters or return data

```
public void printToConsole() {
    System.out.println(code + "|" + description +  "|" + price);
}
```

A get method that returns a string

```
public String getCode() {
    return code;
}
```

A get method that returns a double value

```
public double getPrice() {
    return price;
}
```

A custom get method

```
public String getPriceFormatted() {
    NumberFormat currency = NumberFormat.getCurrencyInstance();
    String priceFormatted = currency.format(price);
    return priceFormatted;
}
```

A set method

```
public void setCode(String code) {
    this.code = code;
}
```

Another way to code a set method

```
public void setCode(String productCode) {
    code = productCode;
}
```

Description

- To allow other classes to access a method, use the public keyword. To prevent other classes from accessing a method, use the private keyword.
- When you name a method, you should start each name with a verb. It's a Java standard to use the verb *set* for methods that set the values of instance variables and to use the verb *get* for methods that return the values of instance variables. These methods are typically referred to as set and get *accessors*.
- To code a method that doesn't return data, use the void keyword for the return type.
- To code a method that returns data, code a return type in the method declaration. Then, code a return statement in the body of the method to return the data.
- To code a method that has a parameter, code the data type and name of the parameter between the parentheses of the method.

Figure 4-7 How to code methods

How to create an object from a class

Figure 4-8 shows how to create an object with one or two statements. Most of the time, you can use one statement to create an object. However, in some situations, you need to use two statements to create an object.

When you use two statements to create an object, the first statement declares the class and the name of the variable. However, the object isn't created until the second statement is executed. This statement uses the new keyword to call the constructor for the object. This creates the object by initializing its instance variables, and it stores the object in memory. Then, the assignment operator (=) assigns a *reference* to this object to the variable. That's why objects are known as *reference types*.

When you send arguments to the constructor of a class, you must make sure that the constructor can accept the arguments. To do that, you must send the correct number of arguments, in the correct sequence, and with compatible data types. When a class contains more than one constructor, Java executes the constructor that matches the arguments.

The two-statement example in this figure creates a new Product object without passing any arguments to the constructor of the Product class. The first one-statement example accomplishes the same task. Then, the second one-statement example shows how to send three arguments to the constructor. Of course, this assumes that the Product class has a constructor with three parameters that are compatible with these three arguments.

How to create an object in two statements

Syntax

```
ClassName variableName;
variableName = new ClassName(argumentList);
```

No arguments

```
Product product;
product = new Product();
```

How to create an object in one statement

Syntax

```
ClassName variableName = new ClassName(argumentList);
```

No arguments

```
Product product = new Product();
```

Three arguments

```
Product product = new Product("java", "Murach's Java Programming", 57.50);
```

Description

- To create an object, you use the new keyword to create a new instance of a class. Each time the new keyword creates an object, Java calls the constructor for the object, which initializes the instance variables for the object and stores the object in memory.
- After you create an object, you assign it to a variable. When you do, a reference to the object is stored in the variable. Then, you can use the variable to refer to the object. As a result, objects are known as reference types.
- The variable for a *reference type* stores a *reference* to an object.
- To send arguments to the constructor, code the arguments between the parentheses that follow the class name. To send more than one argument, separate the arguments with commas.
- When you send arguments to the constructor, the arguments must be in the sequence called for by the constructor and they must have data types that are compatible with the data types of the parameters for the constructor.

Figure 4-8 How to create an object

How to call the methods of an object

In the last chapter, you learned how to call methods from objects created from some of the classes in the Java API such as the String, Scanner, and NumberFormat classes. Figure 4-9 shows that the same skills apply to calling methods from your own classes such as the Product class. In short, you type the object name, followed by the dot operator, followed by the method name, followed by a set of parentheses. Then, if the method requires arguments, you code the argument list between the parentheses, separating multiple arguments with commas.

The first two examples show two ways to call methods that don't return any data. The first example doesn't send an argument, but the second example sends a String variable named productCode. However, this argument could also be a String literal such as "java". Either way, when you call a method that accepts arguments, you need to send the correct number of arguments, and the data types of those arguments must be compatible with the data types specified in the parameter list of the method.

The third and fourth examples show how to call a method that returns data and how to assign that data to a variable. In the third example, the getPrice method returns a double value, and the code assigns that value to a double variable named price. In the fourth example, the getPriceFormatted method returns a String object, and the code assigns that object to a String variable named priceFormatted.

The fifth example shows how to call a method within an expression. Here, the expression includes a call to the getCode method. This returns a String object. Then, the code joins that String object with two String literals, and assigns the result to another String object named message.

The syntax for calling a method

```
objectName.methodName(argumentList)
```

A statement that sends no arguments and returns nothing

```
product.printToConsole();
```

A statement that sends one argument and returns nothing

```
product.setCode(productCode);
```

A statement that sends no arguments and returns a double value

```
double price = product.getPrice();
```

A statement that sends one argument and returns a String object

```
String priceFormatted = product.getPriceFormatted();
```

A statement that calls a method within an expression

```
String message = "Code: " + product.getCode() + "\n";
```

Description

- To call a method that doesn't accept arguments, type an empty set of parentheses after the method name.
- To call a method that accepts arguments, enter the arguments between the parentheses that follow the method name. Here, the data type of each argument must be compatible with the data type that's specified by the method's parameters.
- To code more than one argument, separate the arguments with commas.
- If a method returns data, you can code an assignment statement to assign the data that's returned to a variable. Here, the data type of the variable must be compatible with the return type of the method.

Figure 4-9 How to call the methods of an object

How to work with static fields and methods

In the last chapter, you learned how to call static methods from some of the classes in the Java API such as the Integer and Double classes. Now, you'll learn how to code and call static fields and methods.

The ProductDB class

Figure 4-10 presents a class named ProductDB. This class consists of a single static method named getProduct that returns a Product object based on the product code parameter.

To start, the package statement indicates that the ProductDB class is stored in the package named murach.product, which corresponds with the folder named murach/product. Since this is the same package as the Product class described earlier in this chapter, the ProductDB class can access the Product class without importing it.

The getProduct method accepts a String parameter for the product code, and it returns a Product object that matches the product code parameter. In addition, the declaration for this method includes the static keyword. As a result, the getProduct method is a static method that you can call directly from the ProductDB class.

Within the getProduct method, the code starts by creating a Product object. This causes the code and description fields to be set to empty strings and the price to be set to zero.

After this code creates the Product object, it sets the product's code to the productCode parameter of the method. To do that, it uses the setCode method of the Product object. Then, the getProduct method uses an if/else statement to set a description and price for the product that correspond with the code for the product. To do that, the clauses of the if/else statement use the setDescription and setPrice methods of the Product object. However, if the product code doesn't match any of the specified products, the else clause sets the description to "Unknown" and it leaves the price at its default value of zero. Finally, this method returns the Product object.

Because this class doesn't get the data for a product from a database, it isn't realistic. However, it does simulate the processing that's done by a class that retrieves product data from a database. To keep things simple, the early chapters of this book use this class as a way to get product data. Then, in section 5, this book shows how to code a ProductDB class that gets product data from a database.

The ProductDB class

```
package murach.product;

public class ProductDB {

    public static Product getProduct(String productCode) {  // static method

        // create the Product object
        Product product = new Product();

        // fill the Product object with data
        product.setCode(productCode);
        if (productCode.equalsIgnoreCase("java")) {
            product.setDescription("Murach's Java Programming");
            product.setPrice(57.50);
        } else if (productCode.equalsIgnoreCase("jsp")) {
            product.setDescription("Murach's Java Servlets and JSP");
            product.setPrice(57.50);
        } else if (productCode.equalsIgnoreCase("mysql")) {
            product.setDescription("Murach's MySQL");
            product.setPrice(54.50);
        } else {
            product.setDescription("Unknown");
        }
        return product;
    }
}
```

Description

- You can use the static keyword to identify a method as a static method.
- A more realistic ProductDB class would get the data for the Product object from a database.

Figure 4-10 The ProductDB class

How to code and call static fields and methods

As you learned earlier in this chapter, instance variables and regular methods belong to an object that's created from a class. In contrast, *static fields* and *static methods* belong to the class itself. As a result, they're sometimes called *class fields* and *class methods*. To code static fields and static methods, you can use the static keyword as shown in figure 4-11.

In this figure, all of the static fields are static variables. However, you can also define static constants. For more information about working with constants, please see chapter 7.

The first example shows how to code a class that contains two static fields and a static method. To start, this class declares two static fields. The first static field is a private field for a Scanner object named sc. As a result, no other class can access it. The second static field is a public field for a String object named message. As a result, other classes can access it.

After the static fields, this class defines a static method named getString. This method accepts a prompt parameter and returns a String object. Within this method, the first statement prints the prompt parameter to the console. The second statement calls the nextLine method of the static Scanner object to get the line of text that's entered by the user. And the third statement returns that line of text to the calling code.

This example shows that the static variable for the Scanner object is available to the static methods of the class such as the getProduct method. However, if any instance variables were declared in this class, they would not be available to the static getProduct method.

The second example shows how to call the static method defined in the first example. This works much like calling a regular method. However, you start by coding the name of the class instead of the name of the variable for the object. In this example, the code supplies an argument that specifies a string literal for the prompt parameter.

Typically, the static fields of a class are declared with private access. As a result, they are only available to static methods within the current class. However, it's possible to declare a static field with public access. That way, other classes can access and use the field. In this figure, for example, the third example shows how to set and get the data that's stored in the static variable named message. To do that, you can refer to this variable by coding the class name, followed by the dot operator, followed by the name of the variable.

When to use static fields and methods

Now that you know how to code static fields and methods, you may wonder when to use them and when to use regular fields and methods. In general, if you need to perform a single task like a calculation, you can use a static method. Then, the method performs the task and returns the data you need. However, if you need to create an object that stores data, you need to use instance variables and regular methods to define and process the data that's stored in the object.

How to code static methods and fields

```
package murach.product;

import java.util.Scanner;

public class Console {

    private static Scanner sc = new Scanner(System.in);
    public static String message;

    public static String getString(String prompt) {
        System.out.print(prompt);
        String s = sc.nextLine();
        return s;
    }
}
```

How to call static methods

Syntax

```
ClassName.methodName(argumentList)
```

A static method of the Console class

```
String productCode = Console.getString("Enter the product code: ");
```

How to call static fields

Syntax

```
ClassName.fieldName
```

A static field of the Console class

```
Console.message = "This is a test.";     // set the field
String message = Console.message;        // get the field
```

Description

- You can use the static keyword to code *static methods* and *static fields*. Since static methods and static fields belong to the class, not to an object created from the class, they are sometimes called *class methods* and *class fields*.
- There are two types of fields: variables and constants. To learn how to code constants, see chapter 7.
- When you code a static method, you can only use static fields and fields that are defined in the method. In other words, you can't use instance variables in a static method.
- To call a static method, type the name of the class, followed by the dot operator, followed by the name of the static method, followed by a set of parentheses. If the method requires arguments, code the arguments within the parentheses, separating multiple arguments with commas.
- To call a static field, type the name of the class, followed by the dot operator, followed by the name of the static field.

Figure 4-11 How to code and call static methods and fields

The Product Viewer application

Figure 4-12 presents an object-oriented application that lets you view the data for the product with the specified code. This application uses the Product and ProductDB classes shown earlier in this chapter.

The user interface

This figure starts by showing the console for the Product Viewer application. When this application starts, it displays a welcome message. Then, it prompts the user to enter a product code. Next, it displays the data for the product that matches the product code entered by the user. Finally, it displays a prompt that allows the user to continue or exit the application.

The ProductApp class

This figure also shows the code for the ProductApp class. This class contains the main method that gets input and displays output to the user.

To start, the package statement specifies the package for the class. In this figure, this statement defines a package of murach.product. This is the same package as the Product and ProductDB classes shown earlier in this chapter. As a result, the ProductApp class can easily refer to the Product and ProductDB classes without needing to import them.

After the package statement, the import statement imports the Scanner class of the java.util package. As a result, it's easy to refer to this class in the rest of the ProductApp class.

Within the main method of this class, the first two statements display a welcome message. Then, the third statement declares a Scanner object named sc and creates a new Scanner object that this class uses to get input from the user. Next, the fourth statement declares a String object named choice and sets it to a string literal of "y".

The while loop begins by checking whether the choice variable is equal to "y" or "Y". If so, it executes the loop. Within the while loop, the first two statements get the product code from the user. Then, this code calls the getProduct method of the ProductDB class to get a Product object that corresponds to the product code.

After getting the Product object, this application creates a String object named message that stores the data that's displayed. To get this data, this code uses the get methods of the Product object. Then, this code displays the data for the Product object.

After displaying the data, this code checks whether the user wants to continue. If the user enters "y" or "Y", this code executes the while loop again. Otherwise, this code exits the while loop. This displays a goodbye message, and exits the main method, which causes the application to end.

The console

```
Welcome to the Product Viewer

Enter product code: java

PRODUCT
Code:        java
Description: Murach's Beginning Java
Price:       $49.50

Continue? (y/n): n

Bye!
```

The ProductApp class

```
package murach.product;

import java.util.Scanner;

public class ProductApp {

    public static void main(String args[]) {
        // display a welcome message
        System.out.println("Welcome to the Product Viewer");
        System.out.println();

        // create 1 or more line items
        Scanner sc = new Scanner(System.in);
        String choice = "y";
        while (choice.equalsIgnoreCase("y")) {
            // get input from user
            System.out.print("Enter product code: ");
            String productCode = sc.nextLine();

            // get the Product object
            Product product = ProductDB.getProduct(productCode);

            // display the output
            String message = "\nPRODUCT\n" +
                "Code:        " + product.getCode() + "\n" +
                "Description: " + product.getDescription() + "\n" +
                "Price:       " + product.getPriceFormatted() + "\n";
            System.out.println(message);

            // see if the user wants to continue
            System.out.print("Continue? (y/n): ");
            choice = sc.nextLine();
            System.out.println();
        }
        System.out.println("Bye!");
    }
}
```

Figure 4-12 The Product Viewer application

More skills for working with classes and methods

If you understand the Product Viewer application, you understand the basic concepts and skills for coding classes and methods. Now, this chapter finishes by presenting some additional concepts and skills that you may need when you're working with classes and methods.

Reference types compared to primitive types

By now, you should know that a class such as the Product class defines a reference type. In addition, you should know that reference types such as the Product type work differently than primitive types such as the double and int types. That's because a primitive type stores a value. However, a reference type refers to an object. Figure 4-13 summarizes a few important differences between reference types and primitive types.

The first example shows how assignment statements work. With primitive types, the assignment statement makes a copy of the double value. As a result, the third statement changes the double value that's stored in the variable named p2, but not the double value that's stored in the variable named p1.

With reference types, the assignment statement does *not* store a copy of the object. Instead, it causes both variables to refer to the same Product object. As a result, when the third statement uses the variable named p2 to change the double value that's stored in that Product object, this change is also reflected in the variable named p1. That's because both variables refer to the same Product object. As a result, if you have multiple variables that refer to the same object, you need to be careful about changing its data.

The second example shows how the parameters of a method work. This example uses a method named increasePrice that increases the price by 10%. With a primitive type, the price parameter stores a copy of the double value. Then, the first statement increases the price parameter by 10%. However, this doesn't change the price in the calling code. As a result, the second statement returns the price to the calling code so it can access the new price.

With a reference type, the product parameter refers to the same Product object as the calling code. As a result, this method doesn't need to return the Product object to the calling code. Instead, its second statement can set the new price in the Product object. This changes the price in the calling code.

The third example shows the code that calls the methods in the second example. With a primitive type, the code that calls the increasePrice method assigns the return value to the variable named price to change it. With a reference type, the code just calls the increasePrice method. This increases the price that's stored in the product variable in this example.

Most of the time, you can write your code without thinking too much about the differences between reference types and primitive types. Occasionally, though, you do need to be aware of these differences. When you do, you can refer back to this figure to refresh your memory.

How assignment statements work

For primitive types

```
double p1 = 54.50;
double p2 = p1;                  // p1 and p2 store copies of 54.50
p2 = 57.50;                      // only changes p2
```

For reference types

```
Product p1 = new Product("mysql", "Murach's MySQL", 54.50);
Product p2 = p1;                 // p1 and p2 refer to the same object
p2.setPrice(57.50);              // changes p1 and p2
```

How parameters work

For primitive types

```
public static double increasePrice(double price) {
    // the price parameter is a copy of the double value
    price = price * 1.1;         // does not change price in calling code
    return price;                // returns changed price to calling code
}
```

For reference types

```
public static void increasePrice(Product product) {
    // the product parameter refers to the Product object
    double price = product.getPrice() * 1.1;
    product.setPrice(price);     // changes price in calling code
}
```

How method calls work

For primitive types

```
double price = 54.50;
price = increasePrice(price);    // assignment necessary
```

For reference types

```
Product product = new Product();
product.setPrice(54.50);
increasePrice(product);          // assignment not necessary
```

Description

- A variable for a primitive type always stores its own copy of the primitive value. As a result, changing the value for one primitive type variable doesn't change the value of any other primitive type variables.
- A variable for a reference type stores a *reference* to the object. This allows multiple reference type variables to *refer* to the same object. As a result, changing the data for one object also changes the data for any other variables that refer to that object.
- When you code a method that has a primitive type parameter, the parameter gets its own copy of the value that's passed to the method. As a result, if the method changes the value of the parameter, that change doesn't affect any variables outside the method.
- When you code a method that has a reference type parameter, the parameter refers to the object that's passed to the method. As a result, if the method uses the parameter to change the data in the object, these changes are reflected by any other variables outside the method that refer to the same object.

Figure 4-13 Reference types compared to primitive types

How to overload methods

Figure 4-14 shows how to *overload* a method, which is similar to overloading a constructor. When you overload a method, you code two or more methods with the same name, but with unique combinations of parameters. Here, the number of parameters and the data types of those parameters form the *signature* of the method, and each method signature must be unique.

For a method signature to be unique, the method must have a different number of parameters than the other methods with the same name. Or, at least one of the parameters must have a different data type. Here, the names of the parameters aren't part of the signature. Similarly, the return type isn't part of the signature. As a result, using different parameter names or return types doesn't make the signatures unique.

Overloading allows you to provide more than one way to invoke a given method. This can make the method more flexible and useful. For example, this figure shows three signatures of a printToConsole method that can be added to the Product class presented in this chapter. Each signature provides functionality that might be useful to another programmer.

The first signature accepts a String parameter named separator that's used to separate the code, price, and description of a Product object. Then, it prints the resulting string to the console.

The second signature doesn't accept any parameters. Instead, it separates the code, price, and description with the pipe character (|). In other words, it provides a default separator for the first signature. To do that, it calls the first printToConsole method and passes the pipe character to it. Note that this code doesn't qualilfy this method call with an object name since both of these methods are coded in the same class.

You could also code the statement for the second method like this:

```
System.out.println(code + "|" + description + "|" + price);
```

However, passing the pipe character the first printToConsole method reduces code duplication and makes this code easier to maintain. For example, if the code in the first signature was modified to include another instance variable, the code in the second signature would still work correctly.

The third signature accepts two parameters: (1) a String object for the separator and (2) a String object that provides a label that's printed before the product data. This method begins by printing the label specified by the second parameter. Then, it calls the printToConsole method and passes the separator parameter to it.

When you refer to an overloaded method, the number of arguments you specify and their types determine which signature of the method is executed. The three statements in this figure that call the printToConsole method show how this works. The first statement doesn't specify an argument. As a result, it executes the second signature shown in this figure. The second statement specifies a single String argument. As a result, it executes the first signature. And the third statement specifies two String arguments. As a result, it executes the third signature.

A signature that has one parameter

```
public void printToConsole(String separator) {
    System.out.println(code + separator + description + separator + price);
}
```

A signature that doesn't have any parameters

```
public void printToConsole() {
    printToConsole("|");                  // call the method in the first example
}
```

A signature that has two parameters

```
public void printToConsole(String separator, String label) {
    System.out.print(label);              // print label to console
    printToConsole(separator);            // call the method in the first example
}
```

Code that calls this method

```
Product p = new Product("java", "Murach's Java Programming", 57.50);

p.printToConsole();                       // use the default separator
p.printToConsole("/");                    // use a non-default separator
p.printToConsole("|", "Product: ");       // include a label
```

The console

```
java|Murach's Java Programming|57.5
java/Murach's Java Programming/57.5
Product: java|Murach's Java Programming|57.5
```

Description

- When you create two or more methods with the same name but with different parameter lists, the methods are *overloaded*. It's common to use overloaded methods to provide two or more versions of a method that work with different data types or that supply default values for omitted parameters.
- The name of the method combined with the parameter list forms the *signature* of the method. Although you can use the same name for multiple methods, each method must have a unique signature.
- Within a class, you can call one regular method from another regular method by coding the method name and its arguments. In other words, you don't need to prefix the method name with the object name.

How to use the this keyword

In figures 4-6 and 4-7, you saw how to use the this keyword to refer to an instance variable from a constructor or a method. Now, figure 4-15 reviews this skill. In addition, it shows how to use the this keyword to call another constructor of the current class, to call methods of the current object, or to pass the current object to another method.

The first example shows how to use the this keyword to refer to instance variables. If the parameters of a constructor or method have the same names as the instance variables of the class, you need to use the this keyword to explicitly identify the instance variables. Of course, another approach would be to change the parameter names so they aren't the same as the instance variable names.

The second example shows how to call one constructor from another constructor in the same class. In this example, the constructor uses the this keyword to call the constructor in the first example that accepts three parameters, and it passes three arguments to it. This is an easy way to overload a constructor so it provides default data for missing parameters.

The third example shows how to call the getPrice method of the current object. In this case, the this keyword isn't necessary because it would be added implicitly. However, it does make it clear that the getPrice method is a method of the current object.

The fourth example shows how to use the this keyword to pass the current object to a method. In this example, a method named printCurrentObject passes the current object to the println method of the System.out object. If this printCurrentObject method was added to the Product class shown in this chapter, you could call this method from a Product object to print that object to the console.

How to refer to instance variables of the current object

Syntax

```
this.variableName
```

A constructor that refers to three instance variables

```
public Product(String code, String description, double price) {
    this.code = code;
    this.description = description;
    this.price = price;
}
```

How to call a constructor of the current object

Syntax

```
this(argumentList);
```

A constructor that calls another constructor of the current object

```
public Product() {
    this("", "", 0.0);
}
```

How to call a method of the current object

Syntax

```
this.methodName(argumentList)
```

A method that calls another method of the current object

```
public String getPriceFormatted() {
    NumberFormat currency = NumberFormat.getCurrencyInstance();
    String priceFormatted = currency.format(this.getPrice());
    return priceFormatted;
}
```

How to pass the current object to a method

Syntax

```
methodName(this)
```

A method that passes the current object to another method

```
public void printCurrentObject() {
    System.out.println(this);
}
```

Description

- Java implicitly uses the this keyword for instance variables and methods. As a result, you don't need to explicitly code it unless a method parameter or a variable that's declared within a method has the same name as an instance variable. Then, you need to use the this keyword to identify the instance variable.
- If you use the this keyword to call one constructor from another constructor in the same class, the statement that uses the this keyword must be the first statement in the constructor.

Figure 4-15 How to use the this keyword

The Product class with overloading

To put the skills in the last two figures into context, figure 4-16 shows an enhanced version of the Product class that was shown earlier in this chapter. This Product class begins by coding two overloaded constructors. Since these constructors were described in the previous figure, you shouldn't have much trouble understanding how they work. In short, these constructors are overloaded, and the first constructor uses the this keyword to call the second constructor and pass it some arguments.

After the constructors, this class contains all of the same get and set methods as the Product class shown earlier in this chapter. However, to save space, these methods aren't shown again here.

Instead, this class only shows the three overloaded printToConsole methods. Since these methods were described earlier figure 4-14, you shouldn't have much trouble understanding how they work. In short, the first printToConsole method calls the second one and passes it the pipe character as the separator. The second printToConsole method prints the instance variables to the console using the specified separator. And the third printToConsole method prints the specified label before calling the second printToConsole method.

The Product class with overloading

```
package murach.product;

import java.text.NumberFormat;

public class Product {

    private String code;
    private String description;
    private double price;

    public Product() {
        this("", "", 0);
    }

    public Product(String code, String description, double price) {
        this.code = code;
        this.description = description;
        this.price = price;
    }

    // all get and set methods are the same as the Product class
    // shown earlier in this chapter

    public void printToConsole() {
        printToConsole("|");
    }

    public void printToConsole(String separator) {
        System.out.println(code + separator + description + separator +
            price);
    }

    public void printToConsole(String separator, String label) {
        System.out.print(label);
        printToConsole(separator);
    }
}
```

Figure 4-16 The Product class with overloading

Perspective

At this point, you may be wondering why you should take the time to create an object-oriented application like the one shown in this chapter. After all, you could accomplish the same task with less code by coding a procedural application like the one shown in chapter 3.

Although there are many advantages to the object-oriented approach, I'll just mention two for now. First, dividing the code into classes makes it easier to reuse code. For example, any application that needs to work with products can use the Product and ProductDB classes. Second, using classes helps you separate the different layers of an application. That can simplify the development of the application and make the application easier to maintain and enhance later on. In the next chapter, you'll learn how to use classes to structure an application so it has three layers.

Summary

- The *Unified Modeling Language* (*UML*) is the standard modeling language for working with object-oriented languages. You can use UML *class diagrams* to identify the *fields* and *methods* of a class.
- *Encapsulation* lets you control the fields and methods within a class that are *exposed* to other classes. When fields are encapsulated within a class, it's called *data hiding*.
- Multiple *objects* can be created from a single *class*. Each object can be referred to as an *instance* of the class.
- The data that makes up an object can be referred to as its *state*. Each object is a separate entity with its own state.
- A *field* is a variable or constant that's defined at the class level. An *instance variable* stores data that's available to an object (instance) of a class.
- You can use a *constructor* to create, or construct, an object from a class.
- When you code the methods of a class, you often code public *get* and *set methods*, called *accessors*, that provide access to its instance variables.
- If you want to code a method or constructor that accepts arguments, you code a list of *parameters* between the parentheses for the constructor or method. For each parameter, you must include a data type and a name.
- You can use the static keyword to define *static fields* and *static methods*. Then, you can call those fields and methods directly from the class, not from an object created from the class.
- The name of a method combined with the list of parameter types is known as the *signature* of the method. You can *overload* a method by coding different parameter lists for methods that have the same name.
- When coding a class, you can use the this keyword to refer to the current object.

Exercise 4-1 Modify the Product Viewer application

This exercise guides you through the process of testing and modifying the Product Viewer application that's presented in this chapter.

Review and test the project

1. Open the project named ch04_ex1_Product that's in the ex_starts folder. Then, open the Product, ProductDB, and ProductApp classes and review their code.
2. Run the project and test it with valid product codes like "java", "jsp", and "mysql" to make sure that this application works correctly. Then, test it with an invalid code to see how that works.

Modify the ProductDB class

3. In the ProductDB class, modify the if/else statement so it includes another product.
4. Run the project and test it to make sure the new product code works. This shows that you can modify the code for a class without needing to modify the other classes that use it.

Add a constructor to the Product class

5. In the Product class, add a constructor that defines three parameters and uses them to set the values of the three instance variables.
6. In the ProductDB class, modify the code so it uses the new constructor to set the data in the Product object instead of using the setCode, setDescription, and setPrice methods. To do that, you can assign a new Product object to the Product variable within each if/else clause.
7. Run the project to make sure it still works correctly.

Add a method to the Product class

8. In the Product class, add a method named getPriceNumberFormat that returns the price with number formatting (not currency formatting). This method should return the number with 2 decimal places but no currency symbol.
9. In the ProductApp class, modify the code so it uses this method.
10. Run the project to make sure it still works correctly.

Modify the ProductDB class so it defines an object

11. In the ProductDB class, modify the getProduct method so it's a regular method instead of a static method.
12. In the ProductApp class, modify the code so it creates a ProductDB object named db. Then, use this object to call the getProduct method of the ProductDB class.
13. Run the project to make sure it still works correctly.

Exercise 4-2 Use objects in the Area and Perimeter application

This exercise guides you through the process of converting an Area and Perimeter application from a procedural application to an object-oriented application.

Create and use an object

1. Open the project named ch04_ex2_AreaAndPerimeter that's stored in the ex_starts folder. Then, review the code for the Main class.
2. Create a class named Rectangle and store it in the murach.rectangle package.
3. In the Rectangle class, add instance variables for length and width. Then, code the get and set methods for these instance variables. If possible, use your IDE to generate the get and set methods. With NetBeans, you can get started by selecting the RefactorEncapsulate Fields command.
4. Add a zero-argument constructor that initializes the length and width to 0.
5. Add a get method that calculates the area of the rectangle and returns a double value for the result. If you want, you can copy the code that performs this calculation from the Main class.
6. Add a get method that returns the area as a String object with standard numeric formatting and a minimum of three decimal places. To make it easy to refer to the NumberFormat class, you should add an import statement for it.
7. Repeat the previous two steps for the perimeter.
8. Open the Main class. Then, add code that creates a Rectangle object and sets its length and width.
9. Modify the code that displays the calculations so it uses the methods of the Rectangle object to get the area and perimeter of the rectangle.
10. Remove any leftover code from the Main class that's unnecessary including any unnecessary import statements.
11. Run the application and test it with valid data. It should calculate the area and perimeter for a rectangle.

Overload the constructor

12. Open the Rectangle class. Then, overload the constructor by supplying a second constructor that accepts two arguments: length and width. This constructor should set the length and width of the rectangle to the values supplied by these arguments.
13. Open the Main class. Then, modify its code so it uses this constructor instead of the zero-argument constructor.
14. Run the application and test it to make sure it still works correctly.

5

How to structure an object-oriented application

When you create an object-oriented application like the one shown in the previous chapter, you typically want to structure it so that it's divided into multiple layers. To help show this structure, you can use packages to organize your classes.

To show how this works, this chapter presents an object-oriented version of the Line Item application described in chapter 3. This application also works much like the Product Viewer application presented in the previous chapter. In fact, it uses the Product and ProductDB classes described in the previous chapter. However, it also uses a LineItem class.

How to use the three-tier architecture 132

How the three-tier architecture works 132

How to work with packages 134

How to use NetBeans to work with packages 136

The Line Item application 138

The user interface 138

The class diagram 138

The LineItem class 140

The LineItemApp class 142

Perspective 144

How to use the three-tier architecture

Now that you know how to define your own classes, you're ready to learn how to use those classes to structure an application.

How the three-tier architecture works

Figure 5-1 shows how you can use classes to simplify the design of a business application using a *multi-tier architecture*. In a multi-tier application, the developer separates the classes that perform different functions of the application into two or more layers, or *tiers*.

A *three-tier* application architecture like the one shown in this figure consists of a presentation tier, a business tier, and a database tier. This is the most common architecture for structuring applications.

The classes in the *presentation tier* handle the details of the application's user interface. So far, all of the applications presented in this book have been console applications. In these applications, the main method contains most of the code for the presentation tier, though it may call methods of other classes. However, the last two chapters of this book show how to write Java applications that display a graphical user interface (GUI). In these applications, the developer typically uses multiple classes to define the windows and other components of the presentation tier.

The classes of the *database tier* are responsible for all of the database access that's required by the application. These classes typically include methods that retrieve, add, update, and delete the data in a database. Then, the other tiers can call these methods to work with the database, leaving the details of how this is done to the database classes. Although we refer to this tier as the database tier, it can also contain classes that work with data that's stored in files.

The *business tier* provides an interface between the database tier and the presentation tier. This tier often includes classes that correspond to business entities such as products and customers. It may also include classes that implement business rules, such as discount or credit policies. The classes in this tier are often referred to as business classes, and the objects that are created from these classes are often called business objects.

One advantage of developing applications with a multi-tier architecture is that you should be able to swap out one tier without having to modify the other tiers. For example, you should be able to swap out the presentation tier so it uses a GUI instead of using the console without having to modify any classes in the business or database tiers.

A second advantage of developing applications with a multi-tier architecture is that it allows programmers to divide work among members of a development team. For example, one group of developers might work on the database tier, another group on the business tier, and still another group on the presentation tier.

A third advantage is that it allows developers of an application to share classes. In particular, developers working on different parts of an application can all use the classes that make up the business tier.

The three-tier architecture of an application

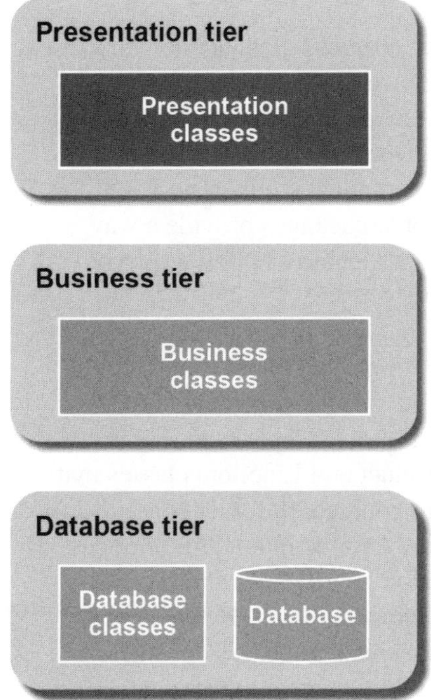

Description

- To simplify development and maintenance, many applications use a *three-tier architecture* to separate the application's user interface, business rules, and database processing. Each tier of the architecture may consist of one or more classes.
- The classes in the *presentation tier* control the application's user interface. For a console application, the presentation tier typically consists of a class with a main method and any other classes related to console input and output. For a GUI application, the user interface typically consists of one class for each window of the GUI.
- The classes in the *database tier* handle all of the application's data processing.
- The classes in the *business tier* define the *business objects* and rules for the application. These classes act as an interface between the classes in the presentation and database tiers.

Figure 5-1 How the three-tier architecture works

How to work with packages

In chapter 3, you learned how the Java API organizes its classes into *packages*. Now, you'll learn how to organize your own classes into packages. Often, these packages help to divide the classes of an application into tiers.

Packages provide two main advantages. First, when a project contains a large number of classes, packages can provide some logical structure to your application and make it easier to find classes. Second, packages provide a way to avoid naming conflicts between classes. This is particularly important if you make your classes available to other programmers.

Figure 5-2 shows the folders and files of the Line Item application presented in this chapter after packages have been used to organize the classes in that application. Here, the ch05_LineItem/src folder contains the subfolders for each package. Then, each subfolder contains the classes for a package. For example, the murach/business folder stores the Product and LineItem classes that define the business objects for this application. The murach/db folder contains the ProductDB class that defines the database class. And the murach/ui folder contains the LineItemApp class that provides the code for the user interface.

When you name a package, you can use any name you want. However, if you want to make sure that the name of your package is unique, it's considered a best practice to start the name with your Internet domain name in reverse. For example, since our Internet domain name is murach.com, all packages created by our company would begin with com.murach.

Even if you don't follow this convention, you should avoid using a generic name that might be used by someone else. For example, a package name of business is too generic. However, murach.business is specific enough that it's unlikely to conflict with any other package names. This book uses murach as the first level of the package name to clearly identify the company that created this code. Then, you can use the second level to organize the packages within the first level.

Once you store a class in the correct folder, you must code a package statement at the beginning of the class. This statement consists of the package keyword followed by the name of the package. In this figure, for example, each class begins with a package statement that corresponds with the folder that contains the class.

If a class is stored in a package, it can't be accessed from classes in other packages without qualifying it with the package name. As a result, you typically import the class to make it easier to refer to that class. This works the same for the packages and classes that you create as it does for the classes of the Java API. In this figure, for example, the ProductDB class imports the Product class in the murach.business package. This makes it easy for the ProductDB class to use the Product class.

The folders and files for an application that uses packages

```
ch05_LineItem/src
    murach
        business
            LineItem.java
            Product.java
        db
            ProductDB.java
        ui
            LineItemApp.java
```

The LineItem class

```
package murach.business;

import java.text.NumberFormat;

public class LineItem {...}
```

The Product class

```
package murach.business;

import java.text.NumberFormat;

public class Product {...}
```

The ProductDB class

```
package murach.database;

import murach.business.Product;

public class ProductDB {...}
```

The LineItemApp class

```
package murach.ui;

import java.util.Scanner;

import murach.db.ProductDB;
import murach.business.LineItem;
import murach.business.Product;

public class LineItem {...}
```

Description

- A *package* can store one or more classes.
- Each package name corresponds with a folder that has the same name. The names you use should be unique to prevent conflicts with other packages.
- When you store a class in a package, the first statement of the class must be a package statement that specifies the name of the package.
- After the package statement, you can code the import statements for the class. These statements work the same for the packages and classes that you create as they do for the packages and classes of the Java API.

Figure 5-2 How to work with packages

How to use NetBeans to work with packages

When you work with packages, you need to make sure that the name of the package corresponds with the name of the folder for the package. If you have to do this manually, it can quickly become a tedious task. Fortunately, NetBeans handles this for you automatically.

When a project contains packages, you can use the Projects window to navigate through the packages for the project. To do that, you can click on the plus and minus signs to the left of the packages to expand or collapse them.

In figure 5-3, the Projects window displays the three packages for the Line Item application that's presented in this chapter. The package named murach.business stores the business classes, the package named murach.db stores the database classes, and the package named murach.ui stores the user interface classes.

To get started with packages, you can add a new package to a project as described in this figure. As you do that, remember that package names correspond to the folders and subfolders that are used to store the source code for the packages. If these folders and subfolders don't already exist, they're created when you create the packages.

Once you've created packages for your application, NetBeans automatically adds the necessary package statement to any new class that you add to a package. In addition, if you rename a package, NetBeans automatically renames the corresponding folders and updates any package or import statements in the project that need it. Similarly, if you move a class from one package to another, NetBeans updates the package statement for that class and any import statements that need it. In short, when you use NetBeans to work with packages, it automatically takes care of most of the details for you.

A NetBeans project that contains multiple packages

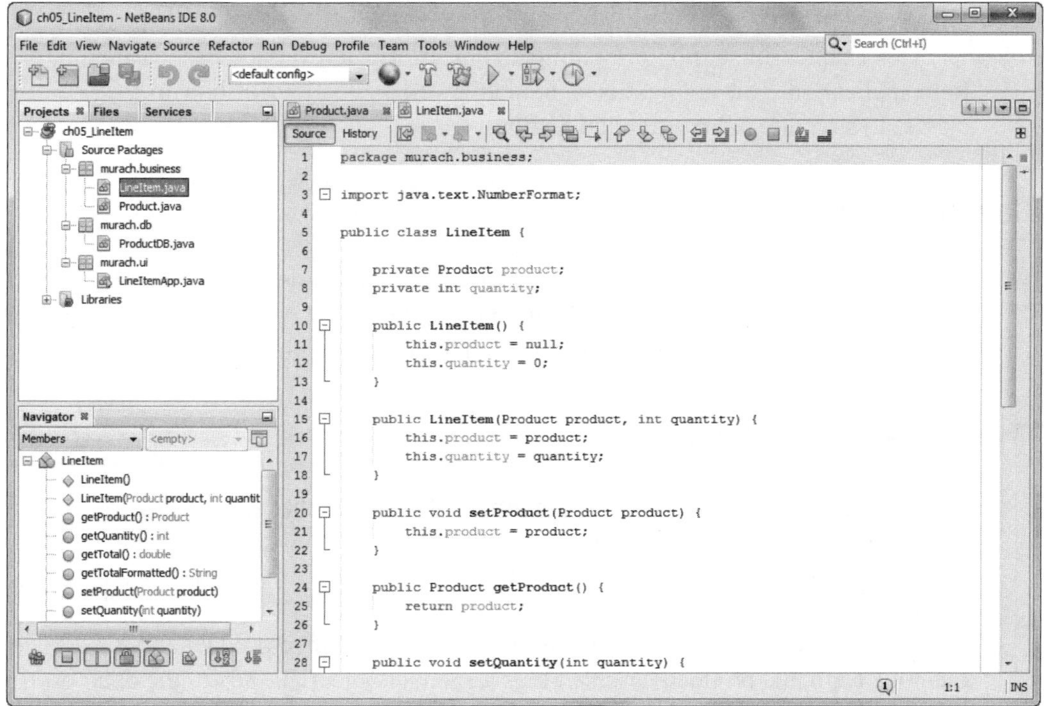

Description

- To navigate through existing packages, use the Projects window to expand or collapse the packages within a project.
- To add a new package to a project, right-click on the project name or the Source Packages folder in the Projects window, select the New→Java Package command, and enter the name of the package in the resulting dialog box.
- To rename a package, select the Refactor→Rename command and use the resulting dialog box to specify the new name.
- To move a class from one package to another, drag it in the Projects window. Then, click the Refactor button in the resulting dialog box.
- To delete a package from a project, right-click on the package and select the Delete command from the resulting menu. If the package contains classes, this also deletes those classes.
- When you use NetBeans to work with packages, it automatically updates the corresponding folders. In addition, it automatically updates any package or import statements in the project that need it.

Figure 5-3 How to use NetBeans to work with packages

The Line Item application

This chapter finishes by presenting an object-oriented version of the Line Item application. This application should give you a good idea of how to use classes to structure a three-tier application.

The user interface

Figure 5-4 shows the console for the Line Item application. This console works much like the Line Item application presented in chapter 3. However, it displays all of the data for a Product object, including the product description.

The class diagram

This figure also shows a class diagram for the classes that are used by the Line Item application. Here, the Product and ProductDB classes are the classes presented in the previous chapter. By now, you should be familiar with these classes.

The LineItem class defines two instance variables named product and quantity. Here, the product variable holds a Product object that stores the data for the product, and the quantity variable holds an int value for the quantity.

The LineItem class also defines six methods. The first four are the get and set methods that provide access to the instance variables. In contrast, the getTotal method returns a double value for the line item total. Similarly, the getTotalFormatted method returns a String object that represents the total after currency formatting has been applied. This works similarly to the getPriceFormatted method of the Product class.

The arrows between the ProductDB and Product classes and the LineItem and Product classes indicate that one class uses another class. In this diagram, both the ProductDB and LineItem classes use the Product class. That's because the getProduct method of the ProductDB class returns a Product object, and the LineItem class declares an instance variable of the Product type. However, the Product class doesn't use either of the other classes. Instead, it only uses the String class and primitive types.

The console

```
Welcome to the Line Item Calculator

Enter product code: java
Enter quantity:     2

LINE ITEM
Code:        java
Description: Murach's Beginning Java
Price:       $49.50
Quantity:    2
Total:       $99.00

Continue? (y/n):
```

The class diagrams

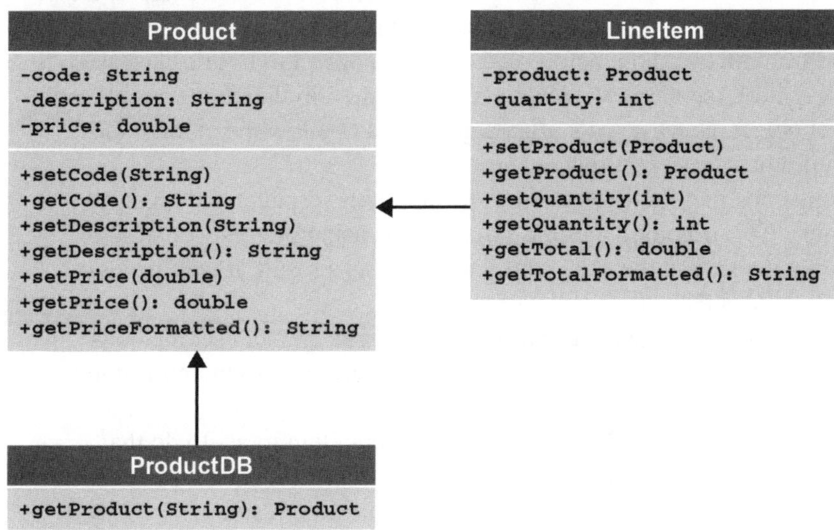

Description

- The Line Item application accepts a product code and quantity from the user, creates a line item using that information, and displays the result to the user.
- The two instance variables of the LineItem class store a Product object and an int value for the quantity. The first four methods of the LineItem class access the values of these variables. The getTotal method calculates the line item total. And the getTotalFormatted method formats the total as a currency value.

Figure 5-4 The user interface and the class diagram for the Line Item application

The LineItem class

Figure 5-5 shows the LineItem class. This class defines a line item for an invoice. Like the Product class, the LineItem class defines a business object in the application's business tier.

The package statement defines the package for the class. In this figure, this statement defines a package of murach.business, the same package that stores the Product class.

The import statement imports the NumberFormat class of the java.text package. As a result, the getTotalFormatted method can use this class without needing to qualify it with its package name.

Within the class, the first two statements define the instance variables of the class. Here, the first instance variable stores a Product object for the product, and the second instance variable stores an int value for the quantity.

The first constructor of this class initializes the instance variables. Here, the first statement initializes the product variable to a null. As a result, if you try to call a method from this variable before you assign an object to it, this class will throw a NullPointerException. To solve this, you could initialize this variable to a new Product object. However, it's often a good idea to allow the class to throw an exception if it hasn't been initialized correctly.

The second constructor allows the user to supply the product and quantity for the line item. This accomplishes the same task as using the first constructor, the setProduct method, and the setQuantity method. As a result, it isn't necessary. However, it does make the class easier to use.

After the constructors, the next four methods provide get and set methods for the two instance variables. These methods access the corresponding instance variables.

The fifth method returns a double value for the line item total. To do that, this method calls the getPrice method of the Product object to get the price of the product, multiplies the price by the quantity, and returns the result.

The sixth method returns a String object for the line item total after currency formatting has been applied to it. To do that, this method calls the getTotal method to return a double value for the total. Then, it uses the NumberFormat class to apply currency formatting to this double value, and it returns the resulting String object.

The LineItem class

```
package murach.business;

import java.text.NumberFormat;

public class LineItem {

    private Product product;
    private int quantity;

    public LineItem() {
        this.product = null;
        this.quantity = 0;
    }

    public LineItem(Product product, int quantity) {
        this.product = product;
        this.quantity = quantity;
    }

    public void setProduct(Product product) {
        this.product = product;
    }

    public Product getProduct() {
        return product;
    }

    public void setQuantity(int quantity) {
        this.quantity = quantity;
    }

    public int getQuantity() {
        return quantity;
    }

    public double getTotal() {
        double total = quantity * product.getPrice();
        return total;
    }

    public String getTotalFormatted() {
        double total = this.getTotal();
        NumberFormat currency = NumberFormat.getCurrencyInstance();
        String totalFormatted = currency.format(total);
        return totalFormatted;
    }
}
```

Figure 5-5 The LineItem class

The LineItemApp class

Figure 5-6 shows the code for the LineItemApp class. This class contains the main method for the application. This method gets the input from the user and displays the output to the user.

The package statement defines the package for the class. In this figure, this statement defines a package of murach.ui. This indicates that this class contains the code for the user interface of this application.

The import statement imports the Scanner class of the java.util package. In addition, it imports the Product, LineItem, and ProductDB classes from the murach.business and murach.db packages. As a result, it's easy to refer to any of these classes for the rest of the LineItemApp class.

Within the main method of this class, the first two statements print a welcome message. Then, the third statement declares a Scanner object named sc and creates a new Scanner object that this class uses to get input from the user. Next, the fourth statement declares a String variable named choice and sets it to a String literal of "y".

The while loop begins by checking whether the choice variable is equal to "y" or "Y". If so, it executes the loop.

Within the while loop, the first four statements get the product code and quantity from the user. However, if the user enters a quantity that the parseInt method of the Integer class can't convert to an int value, this code throws an exception, and the application crashes.

If the user enters a valid product code and quantity, this code calls the getProduct method of the ProductDB class to get a Product object that corresponds with the product code. Then, it creates a new LineItem object from the LineItem class and sets the Product object and the quantity in the LineItem object.

After creating the LineItem object and setting its data, this application creates a String object named message that stores the data that's displayed. To get this data, this code uses the get methods of the Product and LineItem objects. Then, this code prints this data to the console.

After displaying the data for the LineItem object, this code checks whether the user wants to continue. If the user enters "y" or "Y", this code executes the while loop again. Otherwise, this code exits the while loop. This prints a goodbye message to the console and exits the main method, which causes the application to end.

The LineItemApp class

```
package murach.ui;

import java.util.Scanner;

import murach.db.ProductDB;
import murach.business.LineItem;
import murach.business.Product;

public class LineItemApp {

    public static void main(String args[]) {
        // display a welcome message
        System.out.println("Welcome to the Line Item Calculator");
        System.out.println();

        // create 1 or more line items
        Scanner sc = new Scanner(System.in);
        String choice = "y";
        while (choice.equalsIgnoreCase("y")) {
            // get input from user
            System.out.print("Enter product code: ");
            String productCode = sc.nextLine();

            System.out.print("Enter quantity:     ");
            int quantity = Integer.parseInt(sc.nextLine());

            // get the Product object
            Product product = ProductDB.getProduct(productCode);

            // create the LineItem object
            LineItem lineItem = new LineItem(product, quantity);

            // display the output
            String message = "\nLINE ITEM\n" +
                "Code:        " + product.getCode() + "\n" +
                "Description: " + product.getDescription() + "\n" +
                "Price:       " + product.getPriceFormatted() + "\n" +
                "Quantity:    " + lineItem.getQuantity() + "\n" +
                "Total:       " + lineItem.getTotalFormatted() + "\n";
            System.out.println(message);

            // see if the user wants to continue
            System.out.print("Continue? (y/n): ");
            choice = sc.nextLine();
            System.out.println();
        }
        System.out.println("Bye!");
    }
}
```

Figure 5-6 The LineItemApp class

Perspective

If you understand the Line Item application presented in this chapter, you understand a lot about Java programming, including how to use packages and classes to create a three-tier structure. With that as background, you're ready to learn more details about using Java. And that's what you'll learn in the rest of this book.

But first, the next chapter shows how to test and debug the Line Item application presented in this chapter. That way, whenever your code doesn't work correctly, you'll have some skills that you can use to fix it.

Summary

- A *three-tier architecture* separates an application into three layers, or *tiers*.
- The *presentation tier* consists of the user interface.
- The *database tier* consists of the database and the database classes that work with it.
- The *business tier* consists of the business classes that define the *business objects* and rules of the application.

Exercise 5-1 Modify the Line Item application

This exercise guides you through the process of testing and modifying the Line Item application that's presented in this chapter.

Review and test the project

1. Open the project named ch05_ex1_LineItem that's in the ex_starts folder. Then, review the code for the LineItem and LineItemApp classes.
2. Run the project and test it with valid product codes like "java", "jsp", and "mysql" to make sure that this application works correctly.

Rename a package

3. In the Project window of NetBeans, navigate to the murach.db package. Then, rename this package to murach.database.
4. Open the ProductDB class and note that NetBeans also changed the package statement for this class to correspond with the new package name.
5. Open the LineItemApp class and note that NetBeans also changed the import statement for the ProductDB class to correspond with the new package name.
6. Run the project and make sure it still works correctly.

Exercise 5-2 Use objects in the Area and Perimeter application

This exercise guides you through the process of converting the Area and Perimeter application so it uses object-oriented approach.

Review and test the project

1. Open the project named ch05_ex2_AreaAndPerimeter that's stored in the ex_starts folder. Then, review the code for the Main and Rectangle classes. Note that they are both stored in the murach.rectangle package.
2. Run the project and make sure this application works correctly.

Work with packages

3. Create a package named murach.ui. Then, move the Main class into that package.
4. Create a package named murach.business. Then, move the Rectangle class into that package.
5. Open the Rectangle class. Then, note that NetBeans has modified its package statement.
6. Open the Main class. Then, note that NetBeans has modified its package statement and added an import statement for the Rectangle class.
7. Delete the murach.rectangle package.
8. Run the project and make sure it still works correctly.

6

How to test and debug an application

As you develop a Java application, you need to test it to make sure that it performs as expected. Then, if you encounter any problems, you need to debug the application. To do that, you need to find the cause of each problem, and you need to fix each problem.

Basic skills for testing and debugging 148
Typical test phases 148
The three types of errors 148
Common Java errors 150
How to determine the cause of an error 152
A simple way to trace code execution 154
How to use NetBeans to debug an application 156
How to set and remove breakpoints 156
How to step through code 158
How to inspect variables 158
How to inspect the stack trace 160
Perspective 162

Basic skills for testing and debugging

When you *test* an application, you run it to make sure that it works correctly. As you test the application, you try every possible combination of input data and user actions to be certain that the application works in every case. In other words, the goal of testing is to make an application fail.

When you *debug* an application, you fix the errors (*bugs*) that you discover during testing. Each time you fix a bug, you test again to make sure that the change that you made didn't affect any other aspect of the application. This process is known as *debugging*.

Typical test phases

When you test an application, you typically do so in phases. Figure 6-1 lists three common test phases you can use for small applications like the ones in this book. However, for large applications, developers sometimes test the business classes before they even develop the user interface or database classes.

In the first phase, you test the user interface. For a console application, that means you should make sure that the console displays the correct text and prompts the user for the correct data. For an application with a graphical user interface, that means you should visually check the controls to make sure they're displayed properly with the correct text. Then, you should make sure that all the keys and controls work correctly. For instance, you should test the Tab and Enter keys as well as the operation of check boxes and drop-down lists.

In the second phase, you test the application with valid data. To start, you can enter data that you would expect a user to enter. Then, you should enter valid data that tests all of the limits of the application.

In the third phase, you try to make the application fail by testing every combination of invalid data and user action that you can think of. That should include random actions like pressing the Enter key or clicking the mouse at the wrong time.

The three types of errors

Three types of errors can occur as you test an application. These errors are described in figure 6-1.

Compile-time errors occur when the Java compiler attempts to compile the code. This type of error prevents your application from compiling and running and is the easiest to find and fix. Most Java IDEs automatically detect syntax errors as you type and give you suggestions for how to fix them.

Unfortunately, some errors can't be detected until you run an application. These errors are known as *runtime errors*, and they often throw *exceptions* that stop the execution of an application.

Even if an application runs without throwing exceptions, it may contain *logic errors* that prevent the application from working correctly. This type of error is often the most difficult to find and correct. For example, the Line Item application in figure 6-1 has a logic error. Can you tell what it is?

The Line Item application with a logic error

```
Welcome to the Line Item Calculator

Enter product code: java
Enter quantity:     2

LINE ITEM
Code:         java
Description: Murach's Java Programming
Price:        $57.50
Quantity:     2
Total:        $59.50

Continue? (y/n):
```

The goal of testing

- To find all errors before the application is put into production.

The goal of debugging

- To fix all errors before the application is put into production.

Three test phases

- Check the user interface to make sure that it works correctly.
- Test the application with valid input data to make sure the results are correct.
- Test the application with invalid data or unexpected user actions. Try everything you can think of to make the application fail.

Three types of errors that can occur

- *Compile-time errors* occur when the Java compiler compiles the code. This occurs before the Java Runtime Environment (JRE) runs the code. These types of errors often violate the syntax for how Java statements must be written.
- *Runtime errors* occur when the Java Runtime Environment (JRE) runs the code. This occurs after the Java compiler compiles the code. These types of errors often throw *exceptions* that stop the execution of the application.
- *Logic errors* occur when the application runs without throwing any errors but still produces the wrong results such as displaying incorrect data.

Description

- To *test* a Java application, you run it to make sure that it works properly no matter what combinations of valid or invalid data you enter.
- When you *debug* an application, you find the cause of all the errors (*bugs*) that you find when you test the application. Then, you fix those errors. This process is known as *debugging*.

Figure 6-1 An introduction to testing and debugging

Common Java errors

Figure 6-2 presents some of the coding errors that are commonly made as you write a Java application. If you did the exercises for the last two chapters, you've probably encountered some of these errors already. The code at the top of this figure is from the main method of the Line Item application, but with four errors introduced.

The first error is a missing semicolon at the end of the statement that declares the variable named choice. As you know, Java requires a semicolon at the end of every statement unless the statement contains of a block of code that's enclosed in braces.

The second error is a missing closing parenthesis at the end of the condition for the while statement. As you code, you need to remember that every opening parenthesis, brace, or quotation mark must have a closing parenthesis, brace, or quotation mark.

The third error is that a data type has not been declared for the variable named productCode. Unlike some other languages, Java requires that you declare the data type for all variables.

The fourth error is that the statement that calls the nextLine method from the Scanner object named sc uses improper capitalization. For this statement, "NextLine" should be "nextLine" since Java is case-sensitive.

Code that contains errors

```
Scanner sc = new Scanner(System.in);
String choice = "y"                         // missing semicolon
while (choice.equalsIgnoreCase("y") {       // missing closing parenthesis
    // get the input from the user
    System.out.print("Enter product code: ");
    productCode = sc.nextLine();            // no data type declared

    System.out.print("Enter quantity:     ");
    String quantity = sc.NextLine();        // improper capitalization

    // see if the user wants to continue
    System.out.print("Continue? (y/n): ");
    choice = sc.next();
    System.out.println();
}
```

Common syntax errors

- Forgetting to code a semicolon at the end of a statement.
- Forgetting an opening or closing parenthesis, brace, or quotation mark.
- Forgetting to declare a data type for a variable.
- Using incorrect case for an identifier.
- Misspelling an identifier.

Description

- An *identifier* is a name that refers to a piece of Java code such as a variable, method, class, or package.

Figure 6-2 Common Java errors

How to determine the cause of an error

Figure 6-3 shows how to find the cause of an error. Once you find the cause of an error, it's usually easy to fix the error. The way you find the cause of an error depends on what type of error you encountered.

If you get a compile-time error, the error message usually shows the line or lines of code that prevented the code from compiling. In addition, the error message typically includes a description that should help you determine why the code didn't compile. In this figure, for example, the compile-time error specifies the line of the LineItemApp class that prevented the code from compiling. In addition, the message for this error indicates that the compiler expected a semicolon (;) at the end of this line.

If you get a runtime error, the error message usually shows the line of code that was running when the application crashed. In addition, the error message typically includes a description that should help you determine why the application crashed. In this figure, for example, the error shows the line of the main method of the LineItemApp class that was running when the application crashed. This line is the statement that uses the parseInt method of the Integer class to convert the data that was entered by the user to an int value. In addition, the message for this exception indicates that this method was attempting to format an input string of "x". That's because the user entered "x" instead of entering a valid number such as "2". You'll learn how to handle this type of error in chapter 8.

If you have a logic error, you can start by figuring out why the application produced the output that it did. In this figure, for example, you can start by asking why the application didn't calculate the correct total. Once you figure that out, you're well on your way to fixing the bug.

For compile-time and runtime errors, most IDEs include links that you can click to jump directly to the line of code that caused the error. This makes it easy to fix the error. For logic errors, it may be helpful to trace code execution as shown in the next two figures.

A compile-time error

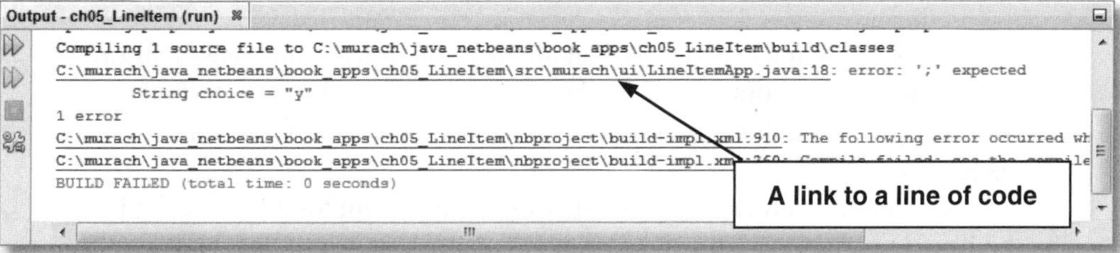

Output - ch05_LineItem (run)
Compiling 1 source file to C:\murach\java_netbeans\book_apps\ch05_LineItem\build\classes
C:\murach\java_netbeans\book_apps\ch05_LineItem\src\murach\ui\LineItemApp.java:18: error: ';' expected
String choice = "y"
1 error
BUILD FAILED (total time: 0 seconds)
A link to a line of code

A runtime error

```
Output - ch05_LineItem (run)
Welcome to the Line Item Calculator

Enter product code: java
Enter quantity:     x
Exception in thread "main" java.lang.NumberFormatException: For input string: "x"
        at java.lang.NumberFormatException.forInputString(NumberFormatException.java:65)
        at java.lang.Integer.parseInt(Integer.java:580)
        at java.lang.Integer.parseInt(Integer.java:615)
        at murach.ui.LineItemApp.main(LineItemApp.java:25)
Java Result: 1
BUILD SUCCESSFUL (total time: 6 seconds)
```

A link to a line of code

A logic error

```
Output - ch05_LineItem (run)
Welcome to the Line Item Calculator

Enter product code: java
Enter quantity:     2

LINE ITEM
Code:        java
Description: Murach's Java Programming
Price:       $57.50
Quantity:    2
Total:       $59.50

Continue? (y/n):
```

Description

- The first step in fixing an error is to determine the cause of the error. Once you know the cause of the error, it's often easy to fix the error.
- For a compile-time error, go to the line in the source code that won't compile. In NetBeans, you can do that by clicking on the link to the line of source code. That should give you a strong indication of what caused the error.
- For a runtime error, go to the line in the source code that was running when the application crashed. In NetBeans, you can do that by clicking on the link to the line of source code. That should give you a strong indication of what caused the error.
- For a logic error, review the output, review the source code, and try to figure out how the source code produced that output. It's often difficult to determine what caused the error, but some of the techniques presented later in this chapter can help.

Figure 6-3 How to determine the cause of an error

A simple way to trace code execution

When you *trace* the execution of an application, you display messages or variable values at key points in the code. You typically do this to help find the cause of a logic error. One simple way to trace code execution is to add statements to your code.

If, for example, you can't figure out why the line item total that's calculated by the Line Item application is incorrect, you can insert println statements into the code for the application as shown in figure 6-4. Here, the first println statement prints a message that indicates that the getTotal method is starting. Then, the next three println statements print the values of the price, quantity, and total variables. Finally, the last println statement prints a message that indicates that the getTotal method is ending.

When you use this technique, you typically start by adding just a few println statements to the code. Then, if that doesn't help you solve the problem, you can add more. This works well for simple applications, but it creates extra work for you because you have to add statements to your code and remove them later.

In the next few figures, you'll learn how to use NetBeans to debug an application without having to add or remove statements. Since this is usually easier than adding and removing statements, you'll rarely need to use the technique shown in this figure. However, it can be useful in some cases.

Code that uses println statements to trace execution

```
public double getTotal() {
    System.out.println("start getTotal() method");

    double total = quantity + product.getPrice();
    System.out.println("price: " + product.getPrice());
    System.out.println("quantity: " + quantity);
    System.out.println("total: " + total);

    System.out.println("end getTotal() method");
    return total;
}
```

The data that's printed to the console

```
start getTotal() method
price: 57.5
quantity: 2
total: 59.5
end getTotal() method
```

Description

- A simple way to *trace* the execution of an application is to insert println statements at key points in the code that print messages to the console.
- The messages that are printed to the console can indicate what code is being executed, or they can display the values of variables.
- When you see an incorrect value displayed, there is a good chance that the application contains a logic error between the current println statement and the previous one.

Figure 6-4 A simple way to trace code execution

How to use NetBeans to debug an application

Debugging is one of the most difficult and frustrating parts of programming. Fortunately, NetBeans includes a powerful tool called a *debugger* that can help you find and fix these errors.

How to set and remove breakpoints

The first step in debugging an application is to figure out what is causing the bug. To do that, it's often helpful to view the values of the variables at different points in the application's execution. This often helps you determine the cause of the bug, which is critical to debugging the application.

The easiest way to view the variable values as an application is executing is to set a *breakpoint* as shown in figure 6-5. To do that, you click on the line number to the left of the line of code. Then, the breakpoint is marked by a red square. Later, when you run the application with the debugger, execution will stop just prior to the statement at the breakpoint. Then, you will be able to view the variables that are in scope at that point in the application. You'll learn more about that in the next figure.

When debugging, it's important to set the breakpoint before the line in the application that's causing the bug. Often, you can figure out where to set a breakpoint by reading the runtime exception that's displayed when your application crashes. Sometimes, though, you have to experiment before finding a good location to set a breakpoint.

After you set the breakpoint, you need to run the current application with the debugger. To do that, you can use the Debug Project button that's available from the toolbar (just to the right of the Run Project button). If you encounter any problems, try right-clicking on the project in the Projects window and selecting the Debug command.

Once you set a breakpoint, it remains set until you remove it. That's true even if you close the project and exit from NetBeans. As a result, when you want to remove a breakpoint, you must do it yourself. One way to do that is to click on its icon.

A code editor window with a breakpoint

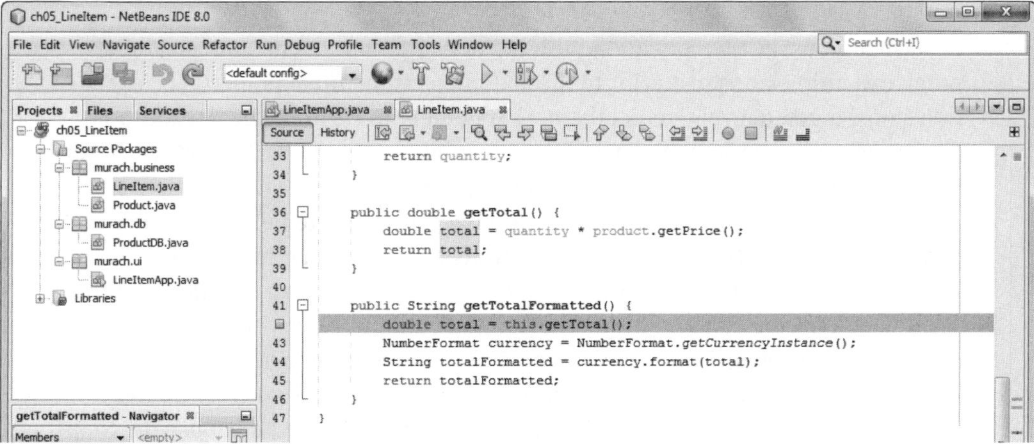

Description

- When debugging, you need to stop application execution before the line of code that caused the error. Then, you can examine variables and step through code as described in the next few figures.
- To stop application execution, you can set a *breakpoint*. Then, when you run the application, execution stops when it reaches the breakpoint.
- To set a breakpoint for a line, open the code editor for the class and click on the line number. The breakpoint is identified by a small red square that's placed to the left of the line of code.
- To remove a breakpoint, click on the breakpoint icon.
- You can set and remove breakpoints either before you start debugging or while you're debugging. In most cases, you'll set at least one breakpoint before you start debugging.
- To start debugging for the main project, click the Debug Main Project button on the toolbar. If a single project is open and it's not set as the main project, the name of this button is Debug Project.
- You can also start debugging by right-clicking on a project and selecting the Debug command or by right-clicking on the file that contains the main method you want to run and selecting the Debug File command.

How to step through code

When you run an application with the debugger and it encounters a breakpoint, execution stops just prior to the statement at the breakpoint. Once execution stops, a green arrow marks the next statement to be executed. In addition, NetBeans opens the Variables window shown in figure 6-6. This window shows the values of the variables that are in scope at the current point of execution.

NetBeans also displays the Debug toolbar while you're debugging. You can click the Step Over and Step Into buttons on this toolbar repeatedly to step through an application one statement at a time. Then, you can use the Variables window to observe exactly how and when the variable values change as the application executes. That can help you determine the cause of a bug.

As you step through an application, you can click the Step Over button if you want to execute a method without stepping into it. Or, you can use the Step Out button to step out of any method that you don't want to step through. When you want to continue normal execution, you can click the Continue button. Then, the application will run until the next breakpoint is reached. Or, you can use the Finish Debugger Session button to end the application's execution.

These are powerful debugging features that can help you find the cause of serious programming problems. Stepping through an application is also a good way to understand how the code in an existing application works. If, for example, you step through the Line Item application presented in the previous chapter, you'll get a better idea of how that application works.

How to inspect variables

When you set breakpoints and step through code, the Variables window automatically displays the values of the variables that are in scope. In figure 6-6, the execution point is in the getTotalFormatted method of the LineItem class. Here, the Variables window shows the values of three local variables that are declared within the method (total, currency, and totalFormatted).

When the Variables window displays variables for numbers and strings, it shows the value. In this figure, for example, the variable named total has a value of 115.0 and the variable named totalFormatted has a value of "$115.00".

However, when the Variables window displays a variable that refers to an object, it doesn't display the values of its variables automatically. Instead, it displays a plus sign to the left of the object's name. Then, you can view the values for the object by clicking on that plus sign to expand it. In this figure, for example, the variable named currency refers to an object that's created from the NumberFormat class.

Similarly, when you are examining the code from within an object that's executing, the Variables window begins by displaying a variable named *this* that refers to the current object. As a result, you can expand this variable to view the values of the instance variables that are defined by the current object. In this figure, for example, you can expand the variable named this to view the values of the instance variables for the current LineItem object.

A debugging session

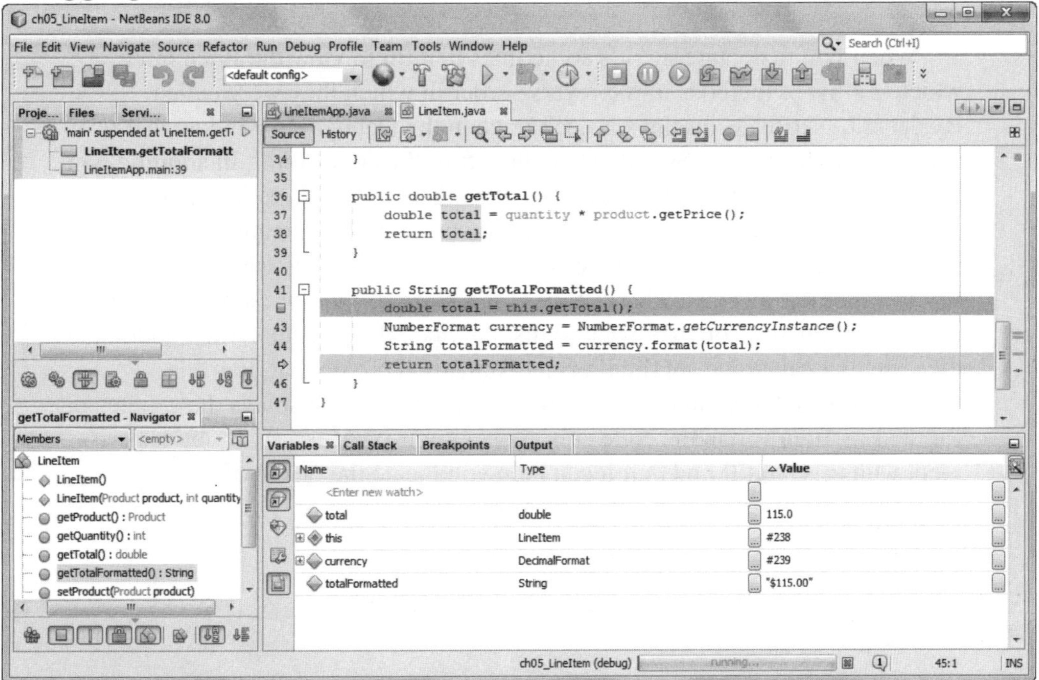

Some of the buttons on the Debug toolbar

Button	Keyboard shortcut	Description
Step Over	F8	Steps through the code one statement at a time, skipping over called methods.
Step Into	F7	Steps through the code one statement at a time, including statements in called methods.
Step Out	Ctrl+F7	Finishes executing the code in the current method and returns to the calling method.
Continue	F5	Continues execution until the next breakpoint.
Finish Debugger Session	Shift+F5	Ends the application's execution.

Description

- When a breakpoint is reached, execution is stopped before the line is executed.
- The arrow in the bar at the left side of the code editor window shows the line that will be executed next.
- The Variables window shows the values of the variables that are in scope for the current method. This window is displayed by default when you start a debugging session. If you close it, you can open it again using the Window→Debugging→Variables command.
- If a variable in the Variables window refers to an object, you can view the values for that object by clicking the plus sign to the left of the object name to expand it.
- You can use the buttons on the Debug toolbar to control the execution of an application.

Figure 6-6 How to step through code and inspect variables

How to inspect the stack trace

When you're debugging, it's sometimes helpful to view the *stack trace*, which is a list of methods in the reverse order in which they were called. By default, NetBeans displays a stack trace in the Debugging window that's displayed in the group of windows to the left of the code editor. In addition, you can display a stack trace in the Call Stack window as shown in figure 6-7.

The Call Stack window in this figure shows that code execution is on line 45 of the getTotalFormatted method of the LineItem class. This window also shows that this method was called by line 39 of the main method of the LineItemApp class. At this point, you may want to display line 39 of the main method to view the code that called the getTotalFormatted method. To do that, you can double-click on the main method in the stack trace. This displays the source code for the LineItemApp in the code editor, opening it if necessary. If you experiment with this, you'll find that it can help you locate the origin of a bug.

A debugging session with the Call Stack window displayed

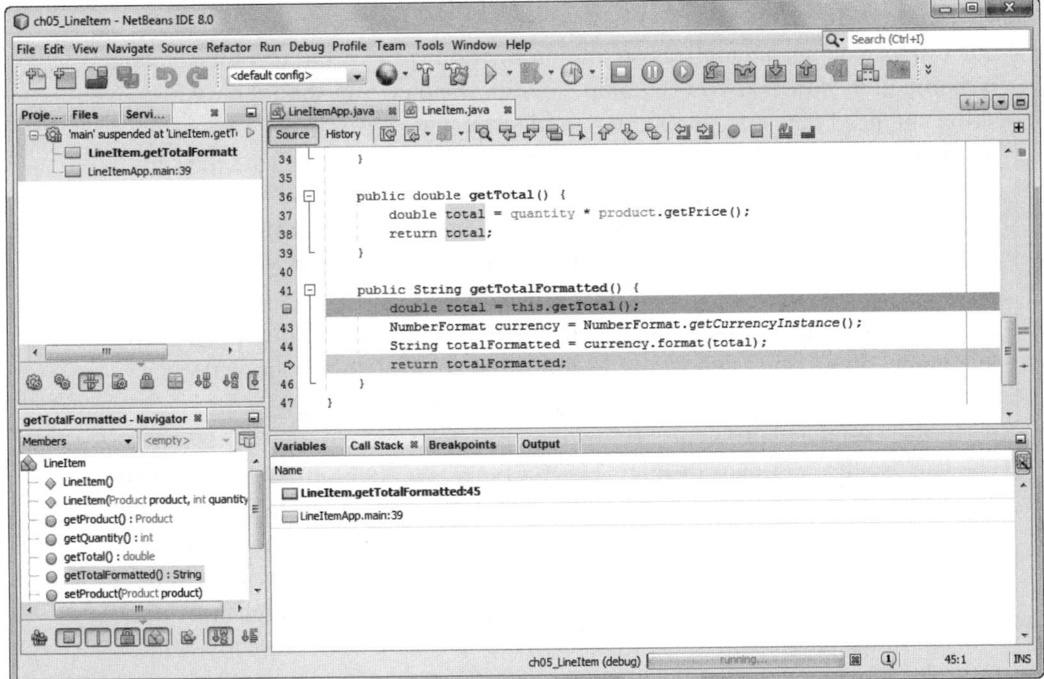

Description

- A *stack trace* is a list of the methods that have been called in the reverse order in which they were called.
- By default, NetBeans displays a stack trace in the Debugging window that's included in the group of windows at the left side of the IDE.
- You can also display a stack trace in the Call Stack window, which appears in the group of windows below the code editor. You can display this window by selecting the Window→Debugging→Call Stack command.
- To jump to a line of code in the code editor that's displayed in the stack trace, double-click on that line in the stack trace.

Figure 6-7 How to inspect the stack trace

Perspective

Before you put an application into production, you should test it and debug it thoroughly. Now that you've completed this chapter, you should have the skills you need to test an application to identify any bugs it may contain. In addition, you should be able to use the NetBeans debugger to locate the cause of those bugs.

The skills presented in this chapter should give you a solid foundation for testing and debugging any application that you develop. However, NetBeans provides some additional features that you can use to test and debug your applications. After reading this chapter, you should have the background you need to learn more about other debugging features that are available from NetBeans.

As you test an application, you may also run into memory or performance-related problems. To help identify the source of these problems, you can use the NetBeans Profiler. This tool lets you monitor the performance of an application. Then, you can use the data it provides to locate code in your application that can be optimized so the application will run more efficiently.

As you begin to develop more complex applications, you may also want to learn about unit testing. Unit testing is a way of creating tests for individual units of source code such as methods to make sure they work correctly. Unit tests can automate much of the application testing you would normally have to do manually. By automating the testing, it's more likely that the testing will actually be done each time an application is updated. This makes it easier to find and fix a bug since it's easier to determine what new code introduced the bug.

Summary

- To *test* an application, you run it to make sure that it works properly no matter what combinations of valid or invalid data you enter.
- When you *debug* an application, you find and fix all of the errors (*bugs*) that you find when you test the application. This process is known as *debugging*.
- *Compile-time errors* violate the rules for how Java statements must be written. These errors are detected by the Java compiler before you can run the application.
- *Runtime errors* occur while you are running an application. These types of errors throw *exceptions* that stop the execution of the application.
- *Logic errors* don't cause the application to crash, but they prevent it from working correctly.
- A simple way to *trace* the execution of an application is to insert println statements at key points in the code.
- NetBeans includes a powerful tool known as a *debugger* that can help you find and fix these errors.

- You can set a *breakpoint* on a line of code to stop code execution just before that line of code. Then, you can step through the code and view the values of the variables as the code executes.
- A *stack trace* is a list of methods in the reverse order in which they were called.

Exercise 6-1 Test and debug the LineItem application

This exercise guides you through the process of using NetBeans to test and debug an application. This should give you some idea of how useful the NetBeans debugger can be.

Introduce and correct a compile-time error

1. Open the ch06_ex1_LineItem project. Then, open the LineItemApp.java file that's in the murach.ui package.
2. Delete the semicolon at the end of the statement that prints the welcome message and save the file. This should display an error in the code editor window.
3. Replace the semicolon at the end of this statement. This should fix this error.

Introduce and examine a runtime error

4. Run the Line Item application and test it with a value product code of "java" and an invalid quantity of "ten". This should cause the application to crash and print an error message to the Output window.
5. Study the error message and note the line number of the statement in the LineItemApp class that caused the crash. Then, click on the link to jump to that line of code. This should open the LineItemApp.java file and highlight the line of code that caused the crash. Based on this information, you should be able to figure out that the application crashed because "ten" isn't a valid integer value. In chapter 8, you'll learn how to handle this type of problem.

Set a breakpoint and step through a method

6. Open the LineItem class and set a breakpoint on the first line of code in the getTotalFormatted method.
7. Click on the Debug Project button in the toolbar. This runs the project with the debugger on.
8. Click the Output tab to display the Output window and enter a value of "java" for the product code and a value of 3 for the quantity. When you do, the application runs to the breakpoint and stops.
9. Click the Variables tab to display the Variables window.
10. Expand the variable named this. This allows you to view the instance variables for the current LineItem object. Note the value of the quantity instance variable and expand the instance variable named product. This allows you to view the instance variables for the Product object that's stored within the LineItem object.

11. Click the Step Over button in the toolbar repeatedly to step through the statements in this method. After each step, review the values in the Variables window to see how they have changed.
12. Click the Continue button in the toolbar to continue the execution of the application.
13. Display the Output window again. Then, enter "n" to exit the application and end the debugging session.

Set a breakpoint and step through the application

14. Open the LineItemApp class and set a breakpoint on the first line of code in the main method.
15. Click on the Debug Project button in the toolbar.
16. Use the Step Over and Step Into buttons to step through each line of the application. To do that, use the Step Over button for most statements and the Step Into button for any statements that call constructors and methods from the LineItem, Product, and ProductDB classes. As you do this, use the Output window to enter data and the Variables window to inspect the variables. This should give you a good idea of how this code works.

Stop the debugger and remove the breakpoints

17. Once you have the hang of stepping through this application, click the Finish Debugger Session button to end the application.
18. Remove the breakpoints that you set earlier in this exercise. To do that, you can click on the red square icon for the breakpoint.

Section 2

Essential skills as you need them

This section consists of four chapters that show you how to use more of the core Java features. Chapter 7 presents the most important skills for working with data types and operators. Chapter 8 presents the most important skills for working with control statements. Chapter 9 presents the most important skills for working with strings. And chapter 10 presents the concepts and techniques you need to know to work with arrays.

We have designed each chapter in this section as an independent unit. As a result, you can read these chapters in any sequence you like. If, for example, you want to learn more about control structures, you can read chapter 7 next. Or, if you want to learn about arrays, you can read chapter 9 next.

7

How to work with primitive types and operators

In chapter 2, you learned how to use two of the eight primitive data types. In addition, you learned how to use operators to perform some simple arithmetic calculations. Now, you'll learn about the other six primitive data types. In addition, you'll learn the details for using operators to work with these data types at a professional level.

Basic skills for working with data 168

The eight primitive data types 168

How to declare and initialize variables 170

How to declare and initialize constants 172

How to code arithmetic expressions 174

How to use the binary operators 174

How to use the unary operators 176

How to use the compound assignment operators 178

How to work with the order of precedence 180

How to work with casting 182

How to use Java classes to work with numbers 184

How to use the Math class 184

How to use the BigDecimal class 186

How to fix rounding errors 188

The Invoice application 190

The user interface 190

The code 190

Perspective 194

Basic skills for working with data

The next three figures review some of the skills presented in chapter 2 for working with data. In addition, these figures present some new skills that are related to this topic.

The eight primitive data types

Figure 7-1 shows the eight *primitive data types* provided by Java. You can use these eight data types to store numbers, characters, and true or false values.

In chapter 2, you learned how to use the int data type to store *integers* (whole numbers). However, Java provides three other data types for integers. For example, if a value is too big for the int type, you can use the long type. Conversely, if you only need store small integer values and you want to save system resources, you can use the short and byte types.

In chapter 2, you also learned how to use the double data type for storing numbers with decimal places. However, if you want to save system resources, you can use the float data type. The values in both of these data types are stored as *floating-point numbers* that can hold very large and very small values, but with a limited number of *significant digits*. For instance, the double type has 16 significant digits. As a result, it supports numbers like 12,345,678,901,234.56 or 12,345,678.90123456 or 12.34567890123456. However, the float type only has 7 significant digits. However, it can still support very large and small numbers such as 1234567000000000 and .0000000001234567.

To express the value of a floating-point number, you can use *scientific notation*. This lets you express very large and very small numbers in a sort of shorthand. To use this notation, you type the letter *e* or *E* followed by a power of 10. For instance, 3.65e+9 is equal to 3.65 times 10^9 (3,650,000,000). Similarly, 3.65e-9 is equal to 3.65 times 10^{-9} (.00000000365).

You can use the *char* type to store one character. Since Java uses the two-byte *Unicode character set*, it can store practically any character from any language around the world. As a result, you can use Java to create applications that read and print Greek or Chinese characters. In practice, though, you'll usually work with the characters that are stored in the older one-byte *ASCII character set*. These characters are the first 256 characters of the Unicode character set.

Last, you can use the boolean type to store a true or false value. This data type is typically used to represent a condition in a control statement that can be true or false.

The eight primitive data types

Type	Bytes	Use
byte	1	Very short integers from -128 to 127.
short	2	Short integers from -32,768 to 32,767.
int	4	Integers from -2,147,483,648 to 2,147,483,647.
long	8	Long integers from -9,223,372,036,854,775,808 to 9,223,372,036,854,775,807.
float	4	Single-precision, floating-point numbers from -3.4E38 to 3.4E38 with up to 7 significant digits.
double	8	Double-precision, floating-point numbers from -1.7E308 to 1.7E308 with up to 16 significant digits.
char	2	A single Unicode character that's stored in two bytes.
boolean	1	A *true* or *false* value.

Description

- *Integers* are whole numbers.
- *Floating-point numbers* provide for very large and very small numbers that require decimal positions, but with a limited number of *significant digits*. A *single-precision number* provides for numbers with up to 7 significant digits. A *double-precision number* provides for numbers with up to 16 significant digits.
- The *Unicode character set* provides for over 65,000 characters with two bytes used for each character. The *ASCII character set* provides characters for the English language. These characters are the first 256 characters of the Unicode character set.
- A *Boolean value* can be true or false. In Java, the boolean data type provides for Boolean values. Like the other primitive types, it uses all lowercase letters.

Technical notes

- To express the value of a floating-point number, you can use *scientific notation*. For example, 2.382E+5 means 2.382 times 10^5, which is a value of 238,200. Conversely, 3.25E-8 means 3.25 times 10^{-8}, which is a value of .0000000325. Java sometimes uses this notation to display the value of a floating-point number.
- Because of the way floating-point numbers are stored internally, they can't represent the exact value of the decimal places in some numbers. This can cause a rounding problem. Later in this chapter, you'll learn how to use the BigDecimal class to solve these rounding problems.
- By default, Java uses Intel 80-bit extended precision floating-point when it is available from the CPU. As a result, code that uses floating-point numbers may produce slightly different results on different systems.

Figure 7-1 The eight primitive data types

How to declare and initialize variables

In chapter 2, you learned how to *declare* and *initialize* a *variable*. Figure 7-2 reviews this skill, and it presents some new information. In particular, it shows how to declare and initialize some of the data types that weren't presented in chapter 2.

Although you usually declare and initialize a variable in one statement, it occasionally makes sense to do it in two. For instance, you may want to declare a variable at the start of a coding routine without giving it a starting value because its value won't be set until later on.

The one-statement examples in this figure show how to declare and initialize various types of variables. Here, the third and fourth examples show how to assign values to the float and long types. To do that, you can add a letter after the value. For a float type, you must add an *f* or *F* after the value. Otherwise, the code won't compile. For a long type, you can add an *L*. However, this isn't necessary for the code to compile. You can also use a lowercase *l*, but that letter can easily be mistaken for the number 1. As a result, it's generally considered a better practice to use an uppercase *L*.

The fifth and sixth statements show how to assign an integer value that has seven digits. Although these statements assign the same value, the second statement uses underscores to separate each group of three digits. Since you can't use commas in numeric literals, you'll want to use underscores whenever that improves the readability of your code. And you can use this technique with all types of numeric literals including double, float, and long values. However, since this feature was introduced with Java 7, you should only use it if you're sure your code will be run by Java 7 or later.

The seventh statement shows how you can use scientific notation as you assign a value to a variable. Then, the eighth and ninth examples show that you can assign a character to the char type by enclosing a character in single quotes or by supplying the integer that corresponds to the character in the Unicode character set. And the tenth example shows how to initialize a variable named valid as a boolean type with a false value.

The last example shows that you can declare and initialize two or more variables in a single statement. Although you may occasionally want to do this, it's usually better to declare and initialize one variable per statement since it usually results in code that's easier to read and modify later.

The assignment operator

Operator	Name	Description
=	Assignment	Assigns a new value to the variable.

How to declare a variable and assign a value to it in two statements

Syntax

```
type variableName;
variableName = value;
```

Example

```
int counter;                   // declaration statement
counter = 1;                   // assignment statement
```

How to declare a variable and assign a value to it in one statement

Syntax

```
type variableName = value;
```

Examples

```
int counter = 1;               // initialize an int variable
double price = 14.95;          // initialize a double variable
float interestRate = 8.125F;   // F indicates a floating-point value
long numberOfBytes = 20000L;   // L indicates a long integer
int population1 = 1734323;     // initialize an int variable
int population2 = 1_734_323;   // improve readability - Java 7 and later
double distance = 3.65e+9;     // scientific notation
char letter1 = 'A';            // stored as a two-digit Unicode character
char letter2 = 65;             // integer value for a Unicode character
boolean valid = false;         // where false is a keyword
int x = 0, y = 0;              // initialize 2 variables with 1 statement
```

Description

- A *variable* stores a value that changes as an application executes. In other words, a variable varies as an application executes.
- Before you can use a variable, you must *declare* its data type and its name.
- After you declare a variable, you can *assign* a value to the variable. To do that, you use the *assignment operator* (=).
- You can *initialize* a variable by declaring it and assigning a value to it. To do that, you can use two statements, but it's common to use one statement.
- To declare and initialize more than one variable for a single data type in a single statement, use commas to separate the assignments.
- To identify float values, you must type an *f* or *F* after the number.
- To identify long values, you can type an *l* or *L* after the number.

Naming conventions

- Start variable names with a lowercase letter and capitalize the first letter in all words after the first word. This naming convention is known as *camel case*.
- Try to use meaningful names that are easy to remember as you code.

Figure 7-2 How to declare variables and assign values to them

How to declare and initialize constants

In chapter 2, you learned that a variable stores a value that changes as an application executes. In other words, a variable varies as an application executes. However, a *constant* stores a value that does not change as an application executes. In other words, a constant remains constant as an application executes.

Most of the skills for declaring and initializing variables also apply to declaring and initializing constants. However, when you declare a constant, you begin the statement with the *final* keyword. As a result, constants are sometimes called *final variables*. In addition, it's a common coding convention to use all uppercase letters for the name of a constant and to separate the words in the name with an underscore as shown in figure 7-3.

How to declare and initialize a constant

Syntax

```
final type CONSTANT_NAME = value;
```

Examples

```
final int DAYS_IN_NOVEMBER = 30;
final float SALES_TAX = .075F;
final double LIGHT_YEAR_MILES = 5.879e+12
```

Description

- A *constant* stores a value that does not change as an application executes. In other words, a constant remains constant as an application executes.
- To declare a constant, you begin the declaration statement with the final keyword. After that, the skills for initializing variables also apply to constants.
- To make it easy to distinguish between variables and constants, most Java developers use camel case for variables and all caps for constants.

Naming conventions

- Capitalize all of the letters in constants and separate words with underscores.
- Try to use meaningful names that are easy to remember.

Figure 7-3 How to declare and initialize constants

How to code arithmetic expressions

In chapter 2, you learned how to code simple *arithmetic expressions*. These expressions used the first four *arithmetic operators* in figure 7-4. Now, the next three figures show how to use more of the operators that Java provides for working with arithmetic expressions. These operators perform operations on the *operands* in the expression, which can be either literal values or variables.

How to use the binary operators

In figure 7-4, the first five operators work on two operands. As a result, they're referred to as *binary operators*. For example, when you use the subtraction operator (-), you subtract one operand from another.

The addition (+), subtraction (-), and multiplication (*) operators are self-explanatory. However, the division (/) and modulus (%) operators require some explanation.

If you're working with integer types, the division operator returns an integer value that represents the number of times the right operand fits into the left operand. Then, if necessary, you can use the modulus operator to return an integer value that represents the remainder (which is the amount that's left over after dividing the left operand by the right operand).

If you're working with floating-point types, the division operator returns a floating-point value. This value uses decimal places to indicate the result of the division. In most cases, that's what you want.

The arithmetic binary operators

Operator	Name	Description
+	Addition	Adds two operands.
-	Subtraction	Subtracts the right operand from the left operand.
*	Multiplication	Multiplies the right operand and the left operand.
/	Division	Divides the right operand into the left operand. If both operands are integers, then the result is an integer.
%	Modulus	Returns the value that is left over after dividing the right operand into the left operand.

Code that initializes two integer values

```
int x = 14;
int y = 8;
```

How to perform addition and subtraction

```
int result1 = x + y;          // result1 = 22
int result2 = x - y;          // result2 = 6
```

How to perform multiplication

```
int result3 = x * y;          // result3 = 112
```

How to perform integer division

```
int result4 = x / y;          // result4 = 1
int result5 = x % y;          // result5 = 6
```

Code that initializes two double values

```
double a = 8.5;
double b = 3.4;
```

How to perform decimal division

```
double result6 = a / b;      // result6 = 2.5
```

Description

- An *arithmetic expression* consists of *arithmetic operators* that operate on one or more numbers known as *operands*.
- *Binary operators* operate on two operands.
- An assignment statement can assign the value of an expression to a variable. Then, when Java executes the assignment statement, it determines the value of the expression and stores the result in the variable.

Figure 7-4 How to use the arithmetic binary operators

How to use the unary operators

Figure 7-5 shows four operators that work on one operand. As a result, they're referred to as *unary operators*. For example, you can code the increment operator (++) after an operand to increase the value of the operand by 1.

When you code an increment (++) or decrement (--) operator, you can *prefix* the operand by coding the operator before the variable. Then, the increment or decrement operation is performed before the rest of the statement is executed. Conversely, you can *postfix* the operand by coding the operator after the variable. Then, the increment or decrement operation isn't performed until after the statement is executed.

Often, an entire statement does nothing more than increment a variable as shown in the first two examples. Then, both the prefix and postfix forms yield the same result. However, if you use the increment and decrement operators as part of a larger statement, you can use the prefix and postfix forms of these operators to control when the operation is performed. This is shown by the third and fourth examples.

If necessary, you can code the negative sign operator (-) in front of an operand to reverse the value of the operand as shown in the fifth example. Although you can also code the positive sign operator (+) in front of an operand, it doesn't change the value of the operand. As a result, this unary operator is rarely used.

Since each char type is a Unicode character that has a numeric code that maps to an integer, you can perform some integer operations on char types. For instance, the sixth example shows how you can use the increment operator to change the numeric value for a char variable from 67 to 68, which changes the character from *C* to *D*.

The arithmetic unary operators

Operator	Name	Description
++	Increment	Adds 1 to the operand (x = x + 1).
--	Decrement	Subtracts 1 from the operand (x = x - 1).
+	Positive sign	Indicates that the value is positive.
-	Negative sign	Changes a positive value to negative, and vice versa.

A typical statement that uses the increment operator

```
int i = 1;
i++;                    // after execution, i = 2
```

A typical statement that uses the decrement operator

```
int i = 10;
i--;                    // after execution, i = 9
```

How to postfix an increment operator

```
int x = 14;
int result = x++;       // after execution, x = 15, result = 14
```

How to prefix an increment operator

```
int x = 14;
int result = ++x;       // after execution, x = 15, result = 15
```

How to reverse the value of a number

```
int x = 14;
int result = -x;        // result = -14
```

How to perform an arithmetic operation on a character

```
char letter1 = 'C';           // letter1 = 'C'  Unicode integer is 67
char letter2 = ++letter1;     // letter2 = 'D'  Unicode integer is 68
```

Description

- *Unary operators* operate on just one operand.
- When you use an increment or decrement operator as a *postfix* to a variable, Java performs the increment or decrement operation after other operations.
- When you use an increment or decrement operator as a *prefix* to a variable, Java performs the increment or decrement operation before other operations.
- If you code an increment or decrement operation as a single statement, not as part of an expression, it doesn't matter whether the operator is prefixed or postfixed.

Figure 7-5 How to use the arithmetic unary operators

How to use the compound assignment operators

When coding assignment statements, it's common to code the same variable on both sides of the equals sign as shown by the first example in figure 7-6. That way, you can use the current value of the variable in an expression and update the variable by assigning the result of the expression to it.

Since it's common to write statements like this, the Java language provides the five *compound assignment operators* shown in this figure. Although these operators don't provide any new functionality, you can use them to write shorter code that doesn't require you to code the same variable on both sides of the equals sign. This is shown by the second example.

If, for example, you need to increment or decrement a variable by a value of 1, you can use a shortcut operator. For example:

```
month = month + 1;
```

can be coded with a shortcut operator as

```
month += 1;
```

which is equivalent to

```
month++;
```

Similarly, if you want to add the value of a variable named nextNumber to a summary field named sum, you can do it like this:

```
sum += nextNumber;
```

which is equivalent to

```
sum = sum + nextNumber;
```

The technique that you use is mostly a matter of preference because both techniques are easy to read and maintain.

The compound assignment operators

Operator	Name	Description
`+=`	Addition	Adds the operand to the starting value of the variable and assigns the result to the variable.
`-=`	Subtraction	Subtracts the operand from the starting value of the variable and assigns the result to the variable.
`*=`	Multiplication	Multiplies the operand by the starting value of the variable and assigns the result to the variable.
`/=`	Division	Divides the starting value of the variable by the operand and assigns the result to the variable. If the operand and the value of the variable are both integers, the result is an integer.
`%=`	Modulus	Derives the value that is left over after dividing the right operand by the value in the variable, and then assigns this value to the variable.

Statements that use the same variable on both sides of the equals sign

```
count = count + 1;          // count is increased by 1
count = count - 1;          // count is decreased by 1
total = total + 100.0;      // total is increased by 100.0
total = total - 100.0;      // total is decreased by 100.0
price = price * .8;         // price is multiplied by .8
sum = sum + nextNumber;     // sum is increased by the value of nextNumber
```

Statements that use the compound assignment operators

```
count += 1;                 // count is increased by 1
count -= 1;                 // count is decreased by 1
total += 100.0;             // total is increased by 100.0
total -= 100.0;             // total is decreased by 100.0
price *= .8;                // price is multipled by .8
sum += nextNumber;          // sum is increased by the value of nextNumber
```

Description

- Besides the assignment operator (=), Java provides for five *compound assignment operators*. These operators provide a shorthand way to code common assignment operations.
- The compound assignment operators are also referred to as the *augmented assignment operators*.

Figure 7-6 How to use the compound assignment operators

How to work with the order of precedence

Figure 7-7 gives more information about coding arithmetic expressions. In particular, it gives the *order of precedence* of the arithmetic operations. This means that all of the prefixed increment and decrement operations in an expression are done first, followed by all of the positive and negative operations, and so on. If there are two or more operations at the same order of precedence, the operations are done from left to right.

This sequence of operations doesn't always work the way you want it to. As a result, you sometimes need to override the sequence by using parentheses. Then, the expressions in the innermost sets of parentheses are done first, followed by the next sets of parentheses, and so on. Within the parentheses, though, the operations are done left to right by the order of precedence. In general, you should use parentheses to specify the sequence of operations whenever there's any doubt about it.

The first example shows why you sometimes need use parentheses to specify the order of precedence. Here, the first expression that calculates price doesn't use parentheses. As a result, Java uses the default order of precedence and performs the multiplication operation before the subtraction operation, which gives an incorrect result. In contrast, the second expression that calculates price encloses the subtraction operation in parentheses. As a result, Java performs the subtraction operation before the multiplication operation, which gives a correct result.

The second example shows how you can use parentheses in a more complicated expression. Here, the first expression uses three sets of parentheses to calculate the current value of an investment account after a monthly investment amount is added to it, monthly interest is calculated, and the interest is added to it. If you have trouble following this, you can plug the initial values into the expression and evaluate it one set of parentheses at a time:

```
(5000 + 100) * (1 + (.12 / 12))
(5000 + 100) * (1 + .01)
5100 * 1.01
5151
```

If you have trouble creating an expression like this for a difficult calculation, you can often break the expression down into a series of statements as shown in the last four lines of code. Here, the first statement adds the monthly investment amount to the current value. The second statement calculates the monthly interest rate. The third statement calculates the monthly interest amount. And the fourth statement adds the interest to the current value. This takes away the need for parentheses. In addition, it makes the code easier to read and debug.

The order of precedence for arithmetic operations

1. Increment and decrement
2. Positive and negative
3. Multiplication, division, and remainder
4. Addition and subtraction

Code that calculates a discounted price

Using the default order of precedence

```
double discountPercent = .2;            // 20% discount
double price = 100;                     // $100 price
price = price * 1 - discountPercent;    // price = $99.8
```

Using parentheses to specify the order of precedence

```
price = price * (1 - discountPercent);  // price = $80
```

Code that calculates the current value of a monthly investment

```
double currentValue = 5000;          // current value of investment account
double monthlyInvestment = 100;      // amount added each month
double yearlyInterestRate = .12;     // yearly interest rate
```

Using parentheses to specify the order of precedence

```
currentValue = (currentValue + monthlyInvestment) *
               (1 + (yearlyInterestRate/12));
```

Using separate statements to control the order of precedence

```
currentValue += monthlyInvestment;                      // add investment
double monthlyInterestRate = yearlyInterestRate / 12;
double monthlyInterest = currentValue * monthlyInterestRate;
currentValue += monthlyInterest;                        // add interest
```

Description

- Unless parentheses are used, the operations in an expression takes place from left to right in the *order of precedence*.
- To specify the sequence of operations, you can use parentheses. Then, the operations in the innermost set of parentheses are done first, followed by the operations in the next set, and so on.

Figure 7-7 How to work with the order of precedence

How to work with casting

As you develop Java applications, you'll frequently need to convert data from one data type to another. To do that, you use a technique called *casting* as shown in figure 7-8.

Java provides for two types of casting. *Implicit casts* are performed automatically and can be used to convert data with a less precise type such as the float type to a more precise type such as the double type. Similarly, implicit casts can be used to convert data from a smaller type such as the int type to a larger type such as the long type. This is called a *widening conversion* because the new type is always wide enough to hold the original value. For instance, the first statement in this figure converts an integer value of 93 to a double value.

Java also performs an implicit cast on the values in an arithmetic expression if some of the values have more precise data types than other values as shown by the next three statements. Here, the variable named d is declared with the double type, and the variables named i and j are declared with the int type. Then, when these variables are used together in an expression, Java converts both i and j to double values when it evaluates this expression.

A *narrowing conversion* is one that casts data from a more precise data type to a less precise data type. With this type of conversion, the less precise data type may not be wide enough to hold the original value, which may result in the loss of some data. In that case, you must use an *explicit cast*.

To perform an explicit cast, you code the data type in parentheses before the variable that you want to convert. For instance, the first example that performs an explicit cast converts a double value of 93.75 to an int value of 93. Here, an explicit cast is required because Java won't perform an implicit cast for a narrowing conversion that may result in the loss of data. In this case, the conversion results in the loss of the decimal digits.

When you use explicit casting in an arithmetic expression, Java performs the casting before the arithmetic operations as shown by the last two examples of explicit casts. In the last example, Java casts two integer types to double types before the division is done so the result has decimal places if necessary. Without explicit casting, the expression would return an integer value that Java would then cast to a double.

When you code an explicit cast, an exception may occur at runtime if the JRE isn't able to perform the cast. As a result, you should use an explicit cast only when you're sure that the JRE is able to perform the cast.

Although you typically cast between numeric data types, you can also cast between the int and char types as shown by the third example. That's because every char value corresponds to an int value that identifies it in the Unicode character set. Since there's no possible loss of data, you can implicitly cast between these data types. However, if you prefer, you can also code these casts explicitly.

If you use a compound assignment operator such as +=, an explicit cast is implied. This can result in the loss of data as shown in the fourth example. As a result, you should be careful when using the compound assignment operators and mixing data types.

How implicit casting works

Data types

byte→short→int→long→float→double

Examples

```
double grade = 93;                  // convert int to double

double d = 95.0;
int i = 86, j = 91;
double average = (d+i+j)/3;         // convert i and j to double values
                                    // average = 90.666666...
```

How to code an explicit cast

Syntax

```
(type) expression
```

Examples

```
int grade = (int) 93.75;            // convert double to int (grade = 93)

double d = 95.0;
int i = 86, j = 91;
int average = ((int)d+i+j)/3;       // convert d to int value (average = 90)
int remainder = ((int)d+i+j)%3;     // convert d to int value (remainer = 2)

double result = (double) i / (double) j;    // result has decimal places
```

How to cast between char and int types

```
char letterChar = 65;               // convert int to char (letterChar = 'A')
char letterChar2 = (char) 65;       // this works too
int letterInt = 'A';                // convert char to int (letterInt = 65)
int letterInt2 = (int) 'A';         // this works too
```

How the compound assignment operator can cause an explicit cast

```
int i = 4;
double d = 4.5;
i += d;                             // i = 8 (4.5 is cast to the int type)
```

Description

- If you assign a less precise data type to a more precise data type, or you assign a smaller data type to a larger data type, Java automatically performs the cast and makes the conversion. This can be referred to as an *implicit cast* or a *widening conversion.*
- When you code an arithmetic expression, Java implicitly casts the less precise data types to the most precise data type.
- To code an assignment statement that assigns a more precise data type to a less precise data type, you must use parentheses to specify the less precise data type. This can be referred to as an *explicit cast* or a *narrowing conversion.*
- When you code an explicit cast in an arithmetic expression, Java performs the cast before any arithmetic operations.
- Since each char value has a corresponding int value, you can implicitly or explicitly cast between these types.

Figure 7-8 How to work with casting

How to use Java classes to work with numbers

As you learned in chapter 3, Java provides hundreds of classes that include methods that you can use in your code. The next few figures present two classes that are designed to work with the numeric data types. In addition, they show how to use the BigDecimal class to fix rounding errors that sometimes occur with the floating-point types.

How to use the Math class

The Math class provides a few dozen methods for working with numeric data types. Figure 7-9 presents some of the most useful ones.

The first example shows how to use the round method. Here, the first statement rounds a double type to a long type, and the second statement rounds a float type to an int type. However, this method only rounds to an integer value. As a result, it's not that useful. In the next figure, you'll learn how to use the BigDecimal class to round to the specified number of decimal places, which is much more useful.

The second example shows how to use the pow method to raise the first argument to the power of the second argument. This method returns a double value and accepts two double arguments. However, since Java automatically converts any arguments of a less precise numeric type to a double, the pow method accepts all of the numeric types. In this example, the first statement is equal to 2^2, the second statement is equal to 2^3, and the third and fourth statements are equal to 5^2.

In general, the methods of the Math class work the way you would expect. However, you may need to cast numeric types to get the methods to work the way you want them to. For example, the pow method returns a double type. So if you want to return an int type, you need to cast the double type to an int type as shown in the fourth example of the pow method.

The third example shows how to use the sqrt method to get the square root of a number. Then, the fourth example shows how to use the max and min methods to return the greater or lesser of two values. If you study these examples, you shouldn't have any trouble understanding how they work.

The fifth example shows how to use the random method to generate random numbers. Since this method returns a random double value greater than or equal to 0.0 and less than 1.0, you can return any range of values by multiplying the random number by another number. In this example, the first statement returns a random double value greater than or equal to 0.0 and less than 100.0. Then, the second statement casts this double value to a long data type. If you want, you can use code like this to generate random values for an application.

If you have the right mathematical background, you shouldn't have any trouble using these or any of the other Math methods. For example, if you've taken a course in trigonometry, you should be able to understand the trigonometric methods that the Math class provides.

The Math class

```
java.lang.Math
```

Common static methods of the Math class

Method	Description
`round(number)`	Returns the closest long value to a double value or the closest int value to a float value. The result has no decimal places.
`pow(number, power)`	Returns a double value of a double argument (number) that is raised to the power of another double argument (power).
`sqrt(number)`	Returns a double value that's the square root of the double argument.
`max(a, b)`	Returns the greater of two float, double, int, or long arguments.
`min(a, b)`	Returns the lesser of two float, double, int, or long arguments.
`random()`	Returns a random double value greater than or equal to 0.0 and less than 1.0.

The round method

```
long result = Math.round(1.667);        // result is 2
int result = Math.round(1.49F);         // result is 1
```

The pow method

```
double result = Math.pow(2, 2);         // result is 4.0 (2*2)
double result = Math.pow(2, 3);         // result is 8.0 (2*2*2)
double result = Math.pow(5, 2);         // result is 25.0 (5 squared)
int result = (int) Math.pow(5, 2);      // result is 25 (5 squared)
```

The sqrt method

```
double result = Math.sqrt(20.25);       // result is 4.5
```

The max and min methods

```
int x = 67;
int y = 23;
int max = Math.max(x, y);               // max is 67
int min = Math.min(x, y);               // min is 23
```

The random method

```
double x = Math.random() * 100;  // result is a value >= 0.0 and < 100.0
long result = (long) x;          // converts the result from double to long
```

Description

- You can use the static methods of the Math class to perform common arithmetic operations. This figure summarizes the methods that are the most useful for business applications.
- When a method requires one or more arguments, you code them between the parentheses, separating multiple arguments with commas.
- In some cases, you need to cast the result to the data type that you want.

Figure 7-9 How to use the Math class

How to use the BigDecimal class

The BigDecimal class is designed to solve two types of problems that are associated with floating-point numbers. First, this class allows you to create an exact representation of a decimal number. Second, this class allows you to work with decimal numbers that have more than 16 significant digits.

Figure 7-10 summarizes a few of the constructors that you can use with the BigDecimal class. These constructors accept an int, double, long, or String argument and create a BigDecimal object from it. Because floating-point numbers are limited to 16 significant digits and because these numbers don't always represent decimal numbers exactly, it's often best to create BigDecimal objects from strings rather than doubles.

Once you create a BigDecimal object, you can use its methods to work with the data. For example, the add, subtract, multiply, and divide methods let you perform those operations as shown in the next figure.

The setScale method lets you set the number of decimal places (*scale*) for the value in a BigDecimal object as well as the rounding mode. For example, you can use the setScale method to return a number that's rounded to two decimal places like this:

```
salesTax = salesTax.setScale(2, RoundingMode.HALF_UP);
```

In this example, RoundingMode.HALF_UP is a value in the RoundingMode enumeration that's summarized in this figure.

An *enumeration* contains a set of related constants and is similar to a class in some ways. For example, you typically import an enumeration at the start of a class so you don't have to fully qualify its name when you use it. For now, you can code the rounding mode as HALF_UP because it provides the type of rounding that's normal for business applications.

If you want to round a double value so it includes decimal places, you can create a BigDecimal object from the double value. Then, you can use the setScale method to specify the number of decimal places and the rounding mode. Finally, you can call the doubleValue method to get a double value. In this figure, for example, the last code example rounds the double variable named discountAmount so it has 2 decimal places. To do that, this code uses method chaining. In other words, it calls the setScale method directly from the BigDecimal constructor, and it calls the doubleValue method directly from the setScale method. This is possible because the setScale method returns the BigDecimal object.

When working with BigDecimal objects, you may sometimes need to create one BigDecimal object from another BigDecimal object. However, you can't supply a BigDecimal object to the constructor of the BigDecimal class. Instead, you need to call the toString method from the BigDecimal object to convert the BigDecimal object to a String object.

If you look at the API documentation for the BigDecimal class, you'll see that it provides several other methods that you may want to use. This class also provides many other features that you may want to learn more about.

The BigDecimal class

```
java.math.BigDecimal
```

Constructors of the BigDecimal class

Constructor	Description
`BigDecimal(int)`	Creates a new BigDecimal object with the specified int value.
`BigDecimal(double)`	Creates a new BigDecimal object with the specified double value.
`BigDecimal(long)`	Creates a new BigDecimal object with the specified long value.
`BigDecimal(String)`	Creates a new BigDecimal object with the specified String object. Because of the limitations of floating-point numbers, it's often best to create BigDecimal objects from strings.

Methods of the BigDecimal class

Methods	Description
`add(value)`	Returns the value of this BigDecimal object after the specified BigDecimal value has been added to it.
`subtract(value)`	Returns the value of this BigDecimal object after the specified BigDecimal value has been subtracted from it.
`multiply(value)`	Returns the value of this BigDecimal object multiplied by the specified BigDecimal value.
`divide(value, scale, roundingMode)`	Returns the value of this BigDecimal object divided by the value of the specified BigDecimal object, sets the specified scale, and uses the specified rounding mode.
`setScale(scale, roundingMode)`	Sets the scale and rounding mode for the BigDecimal object.
`doubleValue()`	Converts the BigDecimal value to a double value.
`toString()`	Converts the BigDecimal value to a String object.

The RoundingMode enumeration

```
java.math.RoundingMode
```

Two of the values in the RoundingMode enumeration

Values	Description
`HALF_UP`	Round halfway values up to nearest neighbor.
`HALF_DOWN`	Round halfway values down to nearest neighbor.
`HALF_EVEN`	Round halfway values toward the nearest even neighbor.

How to round a double value to 2 decimal places

```
discountAmount = new BigDecimal(discountAmount)
    .setScale(2, RoundingMode.HALF_UP).doubleValue();
```

Description

- The BigDecimal class provides a way to perform accurate decimal calculations in Java. It also provides a way to store numbers with more than 16 significant digits.

Figure 7-10 How to use the BigDecimal class

How to fix rounding errors

Figure 7-11 shows how you can use the BigDecimal class to fix rounding errors that often occur when using the double type. To start, the first example uses the double type to store monetary values for the subtotal, discount amount, and total before tax. In addition, it uses the double type to store a percent for the discount.

The second example creates two NumberFormat objects and uses them to format the values of the first example. Then, it prints these formatted values to the console. Unfortunately, this displays results that aren't correct. If the discount amount is $10.01, the total before tax should be $90.04. However, it's $90.05.

What's causing the error? Well, because of the way NumberFormat class works, the discount amount value of 10.005 is rounded up to 10.01, and the total before tax value of 90.045 is also rounded up to 90.05. Although an error like this may be acceptable in some types of applications, it is unacceptable in most business applications. For those applications, you need to provide solutions that deliver the results that you want. Imagine getting an invoice that didn't add up!

What's the solution? Well, one solution is to round the discount amount to 2 decimal places as soon as it's calculated. To do that, you can add a line of code like the last line of code shown in the last figure immediately after the statement that calculates the discount amount.

Another solution is to use BigDecimal objects instead of double values as shown in the third example. Then, you can use the methods of the BigDecimal class to perform the calculations and round the discount amount. This example starts by constructing BigDecimal objects from String objects for the subtotal and discount percent. Then, it uses the multiply method to calculate the discount amount, uses the setScale method to round this decimal number to 2 decimal places, and uses the subtract method to calculate the total before tax.

In this example, only the discount amount needs to be rounded. That's because it's calculated using multiplication, which can result in extra decimal places. In contrast, the total before tax doesn't need to be rounded because it's calculated using subtraction, which can't result in extra decimal places. Once this code performs the calculations and does the rounding, it can safely use the NumberFormat objects to format the decimal values for display.

Isn't this a lot of work just to do simple arithmetic? Relative to some other languages, you would have to say that it is. In fact, it's fair to say that this is a weakness of Java. However, once you get the hang of working with the BigDecimal class, you should be able to fix rounding problems with ease.

If the BigDecimal class solves all problems with decimal numbers, why isn't it the default way to work with decimal numbers? Unfortunately, using the BigDecimal class is extremely slow when compared to the double and float types. That's because the BigDecimal class can't access the processor's FPU. For most applications, this relative slowness isn't noticeable. However, it wouldn't be acceptable for games or scientific applications that need to make thousands of floating-point calculations per second.

Code that uses double values to store monetary values

```
double subtotal = 100.05;                                  // 100.050
double discountPercent = .1;
double discountAmount = subtotal * discountPercent;  //  10.005
double totalBeforeTax = subtotal - discountAmount;   //  90.045
```

Code that causes a rounding error

```
// get the objects for currency and percent formatting
NumberFormat currency = NumberFormat.getCurrencyInstance();
NumberFormat percent = NumberFormat.getPercentInstance();

// format the message and print it to the console
String formattedMessage =
    "Subtotal:         " + currency.format(subtotal) + "\n"
  + "Discount percent: " + percent.format(discountPercent) + "\n"
  + "Discount amount:  " + currency.format(discountAmount) + "\n"
  + "Total before tax: " + currency.format(totalBeforeTax) + "\n";
System.out.println(formattedMessage);
```

The formatted result that contains the rounding error

```
Subtotal:         $100.05
Discount percent: 10%
Discount amount:  $10.01
Total before tax: $90.05
```

Code that uses BigDecimal objects to fix the rounding error

```
BigDecimal subtotal = new BigDecimal("100.05");                          // 100.05
BigDecimal discountPercent = new BigDecimal(".1");
BigDecimal discountAmount = subtotal.multiply(discountPercent);         // 10.005
discountAmount = discountAmount.setScale(2, RoundingMode.HALF_UP); // 10.01
BigDecimal totalBeforeTax = subtotal.subtract(discountAmount);          // 90.04
```

The formatted result

```
Subtotal:         $100.05
Discount percent: 10%
Discount amount:  $10.01
Total before tax: $90.04
```

Description

- With this code, all of the numbers are stored in BigDecimal objects, and all of the results have two decimal places that have been rounded correctly when needed.
- Once the results have been calculated, you can use the NumberFormat methods to format the values in the BigDecimal objects without any fear of rounding problems.

The Invoice application

This chapter ends by presenting the code for an Invoice application. Although this application is simple, it gets input from the user, performs calculations that use this input, and displays the results of the calculations.

The user interface

Figure 7-12 starts by showing the console for the Invoice application. This application begins by getting a subtotal value from the user. Then, it calculates the discount percent, discount amount, total before tax, sales tax, and total. Next, it formats and displays these values. Finally, it asks the user if he or she wants to continue. If the user enters "y", the application performs another calculation like the one shown in this figure. On the other hand, if the user enters "n", the application exits and displays a goodbye message.

The code

Much of the code for the Invoice application works like the code for the Line Item application presented in chapter 3. As a result, the following description focuses on the new skills that were presented in this chapter.

To start, this code imports the BigDecimal class and the RoundingMode enumeration. This allows you to use the BigDecimal class to round numbers that have decimal places as described earlier in this chapter.

Within the while loop, the first statement prompts the user to enter a subtotal. Then, the second statement gets a String object for the text that the user entered. Next, the third statement creates a new BigDecimal object from this String object, calls the setScale method directly from this object, and calls the doubleValue method directly from the setScale method. This returns a double value that's rounded to 2 decimal places and stores it in the variable named subtotal. This is necessary because it's possible that the user might enter a subtotal that had more than 2 decimal places. In that case, this code would prevent a rounding error by rounding the number to 2 decimal places.

After getting a double value for the subtotal, the loop uses an if/else statement to calculate the discount amount based on the value of the subtotal. If, for example, the subtotal is greater than or equal to 200, the discount amount is .2 times the subtotal (a 20% discount). If that condition isn't true and the subtotal is greater than or equal to 100, the discount is .1 times subtotal (a 10% discount). Otherwise, the discount amount is 0.

The console

```
Welcome to the Invoice Total Calculator

Enter subtotal:    100.05

INVOICE
Subtotal:          $100.05
Discount percent: 10%
Discount amount:  $10.01
Total before tax: $90.04
Sales tax:        $4.50
Invoice total:    $94.54

Continue? (y/n): n

Bye!
```

The code

```
package murach.invoice;

import java.util.Scanner;
import java.text.NumberFormat;
import java.math.BigDecimal;
import java.math.RoundingMode;

public class InvoiceApp {

    public static void main(String[] args) {
        // display a welcome message
        System.out.println("Welcome to the Invoice Total Calculator");
        System.out.println();

        // create a Scanner object named sc
        Scanner sc = new Scanner(System.in);

        // perform invoice calculations until choice isn't equal to "y" or "Y"
        String choice = "y";
        while (!choice.equalsIgnoreCase("n")) {
            // get the input from the user
            System.out.print("Enter subtotal:    ");
            String subtotalLine = sc.nextLine();
            double subtotal = new BigDecimal(subtotalLine)
                    .setScale(2, RoundingMode.HALF_UP)
                    .doubleValue();

            // get discount percent based on subtotal
            double discountPercent;
            if (subtotal >= 200) {
                discountPercent = .2;
            } else if (subtotal >= 100) {
                discountPercent = .1;
            } else {
                discountPercent = 0;
            }
```

Figure 7-12 The Invoice application (part 1 of 2)

After the if/else statement, this code calculates the discount amount by multiplying the subtotal by the discount percent. Since this can result in more than 2 decimal places, this code uses the BigDecimal class to round the result to 2 decimal places, and it returns the number as a double value. To do that, this code creates a new BigDecimal object from the double value for the discount amount, uses the setScale method to round the number, and uses the doubleValue method to return the double value. Then, this code calculates the total before tax by subtracting discountAmount from subtotal.

This code continues by declaring a constant named SALES_TAX_PCT that stores the sales tax percent. Here, this constant is set to a value of .05 (5%). Then, this code multiplies this constant by the total before tax to get the sales tax amount. Since this amount might contain more than 2 decimal places, this code uses the BigDecimal class to round this number to 2 decimal places using the same technique that was used earlier in this class.

After this code finishes making all of its calculations, it uses the NumberFormat class to apply currency and percent formatting to the monetary and percent values. Then, it prints a message to the console that includes these values. Since all of the monetary values have been rounded to 2 decimal places before this formatting was applied, the values that are displayed should add up. In other words, this application shouldn't contain any rounding errors.

Unfortunately, this application still doesn't handle the exception that's thrown if the user doesn't enter a valid value for the subtotal. However, you'll learn how to handle this exception in the next chapter.

The code (continued)

```
            // calculate discount amount
            double discountAmount = subtotal * discountPercent;
            discountAmount = new BigDecimal(discountAmount)
                    .setScale(2, RoundingMode.HALF_UP)
                    .doubleValue();

            // calculate total before tax
            double totalBeforeTax = subtotal - discountAmount;

            // calculate sales tax
            final double SALES_TAX_PCT = .05;
            double salesTax = SALES_TAX_PCT * totalBeforeTax;
            salesTax = new BigDecimal(salesTax)
                    .setScale(2, RoundingMode.HALF_UP)
                    .doubleValue();

            // calculate total
            double total = totalBeforeTax + salesTax;

            // get the currency and percent formatter objects
            NumberFormat currency = NumberFormat.getCurrencyInstance();
            NumberFormat percent = NumberFormat.getPercentInstance();

            // display the data
            String message = "\nINVOICE\n" +
                "Subtotal:         " + currency.format(subtotal) + "\n"
              + "Discount percent: " + percent.format(discountPercent) + "\n"
              + "Discount amount:  " + currency.format(discountAmount) + "\n"
              + "Total before tax: " + currency.format(totalBeforeTax) + "\n"
              + "Sales tax:        " + currency.format(salesTax) + "\n"
              + "Invoice total:    " + currency.format(total) + "\n";

            System.out.println(message);

            // see if the user wants to continue
            System.out.print("Continue? (y/n): ");
            choice = sc.nextLine();
            System.out.println();
        }
        System.out.println("Bye!");
    }
}
```

Figure 7-12 The Invoice application (part 2 of 2)

Perspective

If this chapter has succeeded, you should now be able to work with any of the primitive data types you need in your applications. In addition, you should be able to use the Math class whenever you need it. And you should be able to use the BigDecimal class to solve the problems that are associated with floating-point numbers such as rounding errors.

Summary

- Java provides eight *primitive data types* to store *integer*, *floating-point*, *character*, and *boolean* values.
- *Variables* store data that changes as an application runs. *Constants* store data that doesn't change as an application runs. You use *assignment statements* to assign values to variables.
- You can use *arithmetic operators* to form *arithmetic expressions*, and you can use some *assignment operators* as a shorthand for some types of arithmetic expressions.
- Java can *implicitly cast* a less precise data type to a more precise data type. Java also lets you *explicitly cast* a more precise data type to a less precise data type.
- You can use the static methods of the Math class to perform mathematical operations such as calculating the square root of a number.
- You can use the BigDecimal class to create BigDecimal objects that store decimal values that aren't limited to 16 significant digits. In addition, you can use the methods of these objects to perform operations such as addition, subtraction, multiplication, division, and rounding.

Exercise 7-1 Modify the Line Item application

In this exercise, you'll use some of the skills that you learned in this chapter to modify the Line Item application.

1. Open the project named ch07_ex1_LineItem that's in the ex_starts folder. Then, review the code for this project and run it until you understand how it works.
2. Open the Product class. Use the float type instead of the double type for the price. To do that, you need to modify the declaration for the instance variable, the constructor that sets the price, the getPrice method, and the setPrice method.
3. Open the LineItem class. Modify the getTotal method so it returns a float type instead of a double type.
4. Open the ProductDB class. Modify the statements that use the setPrice method so they pass float literals instead of double literals.
5. Run the application to make sure it still works correctly.
6. Before the while loop, declare a counter variable of the byte type. After the code that displays the line item, use the increment operator to increment the counter variable. After the while loop, display the number of line items that the user entered. For example, for 2 line items, display a message like this:

   ```
   Number of line items: 2
   ```

7. Before the while loop, declare a total variable of the float type. After the code that displays the line item, use the compound addition operator to add the total for the line item to the total variable. After the while loop, display the total like this:

   ```
   Invoice total: 287.5
   ```

8. Before the while loop, declare one variable of the float type that stores the largest line item and another variable of the float type that stores the smallest line item. After displaying the line item, use the max and min methods of the Math class to update the values for the largest and smallest line items. After the loop, display the total like this:

   ```
   Largest line item: 172.5
   Smallest line item: 100.0
   ```

   To get this to work correctly, you need to initialize the minimum value to a very large value. Also, within the min and max methods of the Math class, you need to cast the value that's returned by the getTotal method of the LineItem class to a float value.

Exercise 7-2 Modify the Invoice application to use the BigDecimal class

In this exercise, you'll modify the Invoice application that's presented in this chapter so it uses the BigDecimal class to perform calculations.

1. Open the project named ch07_ex2_Invoice that's in the ex_starts folder. Then, review the code for this project.
2. Run the application and test it with a range of subtotal values including a subtotal value of 100.05. Note that the totals all add up correctly.
3. Remove the statement that rounds the sales tax.
4. Run the application and test it by entering a subtotal value of 100.05. Note that the totals don't add up correctly.
5. Modify the code so it uses the methods of the BigDecimal class to perform all of the rounding, multiplication, addition, and subtractions that needs to be done for this application. In other words, don't use the arithmetic operators for multiplication (*), addition (+), or subtraction (-). Make sure to round numbers up to 2 decimal places wherever that's necessary.
6. Run the application and test it by entering a subtotal value of 100.05. The totals should add up correctly.

8

How to code control statements

In chapter 3, you learned how to code simple if/else statements and while loops to control the execution of your applications. Now, you'll learn more about coding these statements. In addition, you'll learn how to code some other control statements such as switch statements, for loops, and try/catch statements.

How to code Boolean expressions 198
How to compare primitive data types 198
How to use the logical operators 200
How to code if/else and switch statements 202
How to code if/else statements 202
How to code switch statements 206
A new if/else statement for the Invoice application 210
How to code loops 212
How to code while loops 212
How to code do-while loops 214
How to code for loops 216
How to code break and continue statements 218
How to code try/catch statements 220
How exceptions work 220
How to catch exceptions 222
The Future Value application 224
The user interface 224
The code 224
Perspective 230

How to code Boolean expressions

A *Boolean expression* is an expression that evaluates to a *Boolean value* of true or false. Boolean expressions are often in control statements like the ones described in this chapter. That's why this chapter begins by showing how to use the relational and logical operators to code Boolean expressions.

How to compare primitive data types

Figure 8-1 shows how to use the six *relational operators* to code a Boolean expression that compares operands that are primitive data types. In a Boolean expression, an operand can be a literal, a variable, an arithmetic expression, or a keyword such as true or false.

The first three expressions in this figure use the equality operator (==) to test if the two operands are equal. To use this operator, you must code two equals signs instead of one. That's because a single equals sign is used for assignment statements. As a result, if you try to code a Boolean expression with a single equals sign, your code doesn't compile.

The fourth expression uses the inequality operator (!=) to test if a variable is not equal to a numeric literal. Here, the expression evaluates to true if the variable named subtotal is not equal to zero.

The fifth and sixth expressions use the greater than operator (>) and the less than operator (<). Then, the seventh and eighth expressions use the greater than or equal operator (>=) and less than or equal operator (<=).

The last two expressions show that you don't need the == or != operator when you use a boolean variable in an expression. That's because, by definition, a boolean variable evaluates to a Boolean value. As a result, if you declare a boolean variable named isValid, then

```
isValid == true
```

is the same as

```
isValid
```

Although the first expression may be easier for a beginning programmer to understand, the second expression is commonly used by professional programmers.

When comparing numeric values, you usually compare values of the same data type. However, if you compare different types of numeric values, Java automatically casts the less precise numeric type to the more precise type. For example, if you compare an int type to a double type, Java casts the int type to the double type before performing the comparison.

Since floating-point numbers don't represent the exact value of a number, you shouldn't use the equals operator (==) to compare them for equality. Instead, you can use the greater than (>) and less than (<) operators to make sure two numbers fall within a range that's close enough to be considered equal.

As you learned in chapter 3, a string is a reference type, not a primitive type. As a result, you shouldn't use the equals operator (==) to test two strings for equality. Instead, you should use the equals or equalsIgnoreCase method of the String class.

Relational operators

Operator	Name	Description
`==`	Equality	Returns a true value if both operands are equal.
`!=`	Inequality	Returns a true value if the left and right operands are not equal.
`>`	Greater Than	Returns a true value if the left operand is greater than the right operand.
`<`	Less Than	Returns a true value if the left operand is less than the right operand.
`>=`	Greater Than Or Equal	Returns a true value if the left operand is greater than or equal to the right operand.
`<=`	Less Than Or Equal	Returns a true value if the left operand is less than or equal to the right operand.

Boolean expressions

```
discountPercent == 2.3      // equal to a numeric literal
letter == 'y'               // equal to a char literal
isValid == true             // equal to a true value

subtotal != 0               // not equal to a numeric literal

years > 0                   // greater than a numeric literal
i < months                  // less than a variable

subtotal >= 500             // greater than or equal to a numeric literal
quantity <= reorderPoint    // less than or equal to a variable

isValid                     // isValid is equal to true
!isValid                    // isValid is equal to false
```

Description

- You can use the relational operators to create a *Boolean expression* that compares two operands and returns a *Boolean value* that is either true or false.
- If you compare two numeric operands that are not of the same type, Java converts the less precise operand to the type of the more precise operand before comparing the operands.
- A variable of the boolean type stores a Boolean value of true or false.
- The floating-point types (double and float) don't always represent the exact value of a number. As a result, you shouldn't use the equals operator (==) to compare them for equality.
- String objects are reference types, not primitive types. As a result, you shouldn't use the equals operator (==) to compare them for equality. Instead, you should use the equals or equalsIgnoreCase methods of the String class as described in chapter 3.

Figure 8-1 How to compare primitive data types

How to use the logical operators

Figure 8-2 shows how to use the *logical operators* to code a Boolean expression that consists of two or more Boolean expressions. For example, the first expression uses the && operator. As a result, it evaluates to true if both the first expression *and* the second expression evaluate to true. Conversely, the second expression uses the || operator. As a result, it evaluates to true if either the first expression *or* the second expression evaluate to true.

When you use the && and || operators, the second expression is only evaluated if necessary. Because of that, these operators are sometimes referred to as the *short-circuit operators*. To illustrate, suppose the value of subtotal in the first example is less than 250. Then, the first expression evaluates to false. That means that the entire expression returns a false value. As a result, Java doesn't evaluate the second expression. Since this is more efficient than always evaluating both expressions, you typically use these operators.

You can also use multiple logical operators in the same expression as shown by the third example. Here, the && and || operators connect three expressions. As a result, the entire expression is true if the first *and* second expressions are true *or* the third expression is true.

When you code this type of expression, the expression is evaluated from left to right based on this order of precedence: arithmetic operations first, followed by relational operations, followed by logical operations. For logical operations, And operations are performed before Or operations. If you need to change this sequence or if there's any doubt about the order of precedence, you can use parentheses to clarify or control this evaluation sequence.

If necessary, you can use the ! operator to reverse the value of an expression. However, this can create code that's difficult to read. As a result, you should avoid using the ! operators whenever possible. For example, instead of coding

```
!(subtotal < 100)
```

you can code

```
subtotal >= 100
```

Both expressions perform the same task, but the second expression is easier to read.

Logical operators

Operator	Name	Description
`&&`	And	Returns a true value if both expressions are true. This operator only evaluates the second expression if necessary.
`||`	Or	Returns a true value if either expression is true. This operator only evaluates the second expression if necessary.
`!`	Not	Reverses the value of the expression.

Boolean expressions that use the logical operators

```
subtotal > 250 && subtotal < 500                  // short-circuit AND
quantity <= 4 || quantity >= 12                   // short-circuit OR

(subtotal > 250 && subtotal < 500) || isValid     // 2 logical operators

!(counter++ >= years)                             // NOT
```

Description

- You can use the *logical operators* to create a Boolean expression that combines two or more Boolean expressions.
- Since the && and || operators only evaluate the second expression if necessary, they're sometimes referred to as *short-circuit operators* and are slightly more efficient than the & and | operators.
- By default, Not operations are performed first, followed by And operations, and then Or operations. These operations are performed after arithmetic operations and relational operations.
- You can use parentheses to change the sequence of operations. In addition, you can use parentheses to clarify the sequence of operations.

Figure 8-2 How to use the logical operators

How to code if/else and switch statements

In chapter 3, you were introduced to the basic skills for working with an if/else statement. Now, this topic reviews those skills and expands on them. In addition, it shows how to code the switch statement, which can be used instead of some types of if/else statements.

How to code if/else statements

Figure 8-3 reviews the use of the *if/else statement* (or just *if statement*). This is Java's implementation of the *selection structure*.

Whenever you code a set of braces in Java, you are explicitly defining a *block* of code that may contain one or more statements. Then, any variables declared within those braces have *block scope*. In other words, they can't be accessed outside of that block. As a result, if you want to access a variable outside of the block, you must declare it before the block.

The first three examples show how block scope works. In these examples, the variable named discountPercent is declared before the if/else statement. As a result, the blocks of code defined by the if/else statement can modify the value of this variable, but this variable is still available after the if/else statement finishes executing.

The first example shows an if/else statement that only contains an if clause. In this example, the statement that declares the discountPercent variable initializes it to a value of .05 (5%). Then, the if clause checks whether the subtotal is greater than or equal to 100. If so, it sets the discountPercent variable to a value of .1 (10%). Otherwise, it leaves the discountPercent variable at its default value of .05 (5%).

The second example shows an if/else statement that contains an if clause and an else clause. This performs the same task as the first example. However, it uses the else clause to set the value of the discountPercent variable.

The advantage of the second example is that the statements that set the value for the discountPercent variable are all coded at the same level. As a result, some programmers find it easier to read and understand this example. The disadvantage of this approach is that it requires three more lines of code. Since the first and second examples work equally well, you can choose the approach that you prefer.

The third example shows an if/else statement that contains multiple else if clauses. When coding a statement like this, it's important to remember that Java evaluates if/else statements from the top down. Once a clause evaluates to true, Java executes the statements for that clause and skips the rest of the if/else statement. As a result, it's most efficient to code the most likely conditions first and the least likely conditions last.

In the third example, for instance, the if clause contains the most likely condition (a subtotal greater than or equal to 100 and less then 200). For this to work, you must use the logical operator to connect two Boolean expressions.

The syntax of the if/else statement

```
if (booleanExpression) {statements}
[else if (booleanExpression) {statements}] ...
[else {statements}]
```

An if statement that only has an if clause

```
double discountPercent = .05;
if (subtotal >= 100) {
    discountPercent = .1;
}
```

With an else clause

```
double discountPercent;
if (subtotal >= 100) {
    discountPercent = .1;
} else {
    discountPercent = .05;
}
```

With multiple else if clauses

```
double discountPercent;
if (subtotal >= 100 && subtotal < 200) {
    discountPercent = .1;
} else if (subtotal >= 200 && subtotal < 300) {
    discountPercent = .2;
} else if (subtotal >= 300) {
    discountPercent = .3;
} else {
    discountPercent = .05;
}
```

Description

- An *if/else statement*, or just *if statement*, always contains an if clause. In addition, it can contain one or more else if clauses, and one else clause.
- A pair of braces defines a *block* of code. Any variables declared within a block have *block scope*. As a result, they can only be used within that block.
- Java evaluates if/else statements from the top down. Once a clause evaluates to true, Java skips the rest of the if/else statement. As a result, it's most efficient to code the most likely conditions first and the least likely conditions last.

Figure 8-3 How to code if/else statements (part 1 of 2)

If efficiency isn't your primary concern, you should code the conditions in a logical sequence. For example, you could start by coding a condition that checks for the highest subtotal and work your way down to the lowest subtotal. This would simplify the condition for each clause by removing the need for the logical operators. As always, the easier your code is to read and understand, the easier it is to test, debug, and maintain.

The fourth example of this figure shows an if/else statement that contains multiple statements within each clause. Here, the first statement sets the variable named discountPercent, and the second statement sets the variable named shippingMethod. Since these clauses contain multiple statements, the braces are required.

If a clause only contains a single statement, the braces are optional. In that case, you can just end the clause with a semicolon as shown in the fifth and sixth examples. Here, the fifth example shows an if/else statement that uses two lines per clause. Then, the sixth example shows an if statement that uses one line. Some programmers prefer the second approach since it clearly shows that the clause should only contain a single statement.

However, it's generally considered a good coding style to use braces for all if/else statements. That's why the first three examples in part 1 of this figure use them. That way, you won't introduce bugs later if you add more statements and forget to add the braces.

When coding if statements, it's a common practice to code one if statement within another if statement. This is known as *nesting* if statements, and it's shown by the third example in this figure. When you nest if statements, it's a good practice to indent the nested statements and their clauses since this allows the programmer to easily identify where each nested statement begins and ends. In this figure, for example, Java only executes the nested statement if the customer type is "r". Otherwise, it executes the statements in the outer else clause.

An if statement with clauses that contain multiple statements

```
double discountPercent;
String shippingMethod = "";
if (subtotal >= 100) {
    discountPercent = .1;
    shippingMethod = "UPS";
} else {
    discountPercent = .05;
    shippingMethod = "USPS";
}
```

An if statement without braces

```
double discountPercent;
if (subtotal >= 100)
    discountPercent = .1;
else
    discountPercent = .05;
```

Another way to code an if statement without braces

```
double discountPercent;
if (subtotal >= 100) discountPercent = .1;
```

Nested if statements

```
double discountPercent;
if (customerType.equals("r")) {
    if (subtotal >= 100) {          // begin nested if
        discountPercent = .2;
    } else {
        discountPercent =.1;
    }                               // end nested if
}
else {
    discountPercent = .4;
}
```

Description

- If a clause in an if/else statement contains just one statement, you don't have to enclose the statement in braces. You can just end the clause with a semicolon.
- It's generally considered a good coding style to use braces for all if/else statements. That way, you won't introduce bugs later if you add more statements and forget to add the braces.
- Whenever necessary, you can *nest* one if statement within another.

Figure 8-3 How to code if/else statements (part 2 of 2)

How to code switch statements

Figure 8-4 shows how to work with the *switch statement*. This is the Java implementation of a control structure known as the *case structure*, which lets you code different actions for different cases. The switch statement can sometimes be used in place of an if statement with else if clauses.

Prior to Java 7, the switch statement could only be used with expressions that evaluate to an integer. As a result, in early versions of Java, the switch statement had limited use. However, with Java 7 and later, the switch statement can also be used with expressions that evaluate to a string.

To code a switch statement, you start by coding the switch keyword followed by a switch expression that evaluates to one of the integer types or to a string. After the switch expression, you can code one or more *case labels* that represent the possible values of the switch expression. Then, when the switch expression matches the value specified by the case label, the statements after the label are executed.

You can code the case labels in any sequence, but you should be sure to follow each label with a colon. Then, if the label contains one or more statements, you can code a *break statement* after them to jump to the end of the switch statement. Otherwise, the execution of the program *falls through* to the next case label and executes the statements in that label. The *default label* is an optional label that identifies the statements to execute if none of the case labels are executed.

The first example shows how to code a switch statement that sets the description for a product based on the value of an int variable named productID. Here, the first case label assigns a value of "Hammer" to the productDescription variable if productID is equal to 1. Then, the break statement exits the switch statement. Similarly, the second case label sets the product description to "Box of Nails" if productID is equal to 2 and then exits the switch statement. If productID is equal to something other than 1 or 2, the default case label is executed. Like the other two case labels, this one sets the value of the productDescription variable and then exits the switch statement.

The second example works like the first example, but the switch statement evaluates the value of a String variable named productCode. Here, the first case label assigns a value of "Hammer" to the productDescription variable if productCode is equal to "hm01". Since the switch statement is case-sensitive, this case label is only executed if the productCode variable stores a string with the exact same capitalization. For example, this case isn't executed if productCode is equal to "HM01". Similarly, the second case label sets the product description to "Box of Nails" if productCode is equal to "bn03".

The syntax of the switch statement

```
switch (switchExpression) {
    case label1:
        statements
        break;
    [case label2:
        statements
        break;] ...
    [default:
        statements
        break;]
}
```

A switch statement that uses an int variable named productID

```
switch (productID) {
    case 1:
        productDescription = "Hammer";
        break;
    case 2:
        productDescription = "Box of Nails";
        break;
    default:
        productDescription = "Product not found";
        break;
}
```

A switch statement that uses a String variable named productCode

```
switch (productCode) {
    case "hm01":
        productDescription = "Hammer";
        break;
    case "bn03":
        productDescription = "Box of Nails";
        break;
    default:
        productDescription = "Product not found";
        break;
}
```

Description

- Prior to Java 7, the switch statement could only be used with an expression that evaluated to one of these integer types: char, byte, short, or int.
- Starting with Java 7, the switch statement can also be used with string expressions. Then, the switch statement uses the equals method of the String object to compare the strings. As a result, the strings in switch statements are case-sensitive.
- The switch statement transfers control to the appropriate *case label*. If control isn't transferred to one of the case labels, the optional *default label* is executed.
- For primitive types, switch statements are generally more efficient than if/else statements.

Figure 8-4 How to code switch statements (part 1 of 2)

The third example shows how to code a switch statement that sets a day variable to “weekday” or “weekend” depending on the value of the integer in the variable named dayOfWeek. Here, the case labels for 1, 2, 3, and 4 don’t contain any statements, so execution falls through to the case label for 5. As a result, day is set to “weekday” for any of those values. Similarly, whenever dayOfWeek equals 6 or 7, day is set to “weekend”.

Although a break statement is coded at the end of the last case label in this example, you should know that it isn’t required. If you omit this break statement, program execution automatically falls through to the statement that follows the switch statement. However, it’s generally considered a good programming practice to code a break statement at the end of the last case label. That way, if you add a new case label after the last case label, your switch statement still works correctly. Similarly, if you move the last case label so it occurs earlier in the switch statement, it still works correctly.

When you code switch statements, you can nest one statement within another. You can also nest if/else statements within switch statements and switch statements within if/else statements. Here again, you should try to code the statements with a logical structure that is relatively easy to understand. If necessary, you can also add comments that clarify the logic of your code.

A switch statement that falls through case labels

```
switch (dayOfWeek)  {
    case 1:
    case 2:
    case 3:
    case 4:
    case 5:
        day = "weekday";
        break;
    case 6:
    case 7:
        day = "weekend";
        break;
}
```

Description

- If a case label doesn't contain a break statement, code execution *falls through* to the next label. Otherwise, the break statement ends the switch statement.
- The case labels can be coded in any sequence.

A new if/else statement for the Invoice application

To give you a better idea of how if/else statements work, figure 8-5 presents an enhanced version of the Invoice application. This time, the console prompts the user for two entries: customer type and subtotal. Then, it uses a nested if/else statement to determine the discount for the user.

If the user enters "r" or "c" for the customer type, the discount percent changes depending on the value of the subtotal. If, for example, the customer type is "r" and the subtotal is less than 100, the discount percent is .1. Or, if the customer type is "c" and the subtotal is less than 250, the discount percent is .2.

This example codes the conditions in a logical order. For instance, the expressions in the nested if statement for customer type "r" go from a subtotal that's less than 100, to a subtotal that's greater than or equal to 100 but less than 250, to a subtotal that's greater than or equal to 250. That covers all of the possible subtotals from the smallest to the largest. Although you could code this statement in other ways, this sequence makes it easy to tell that all possibilities have been covered.

The console

```
Welcome to the Invoice Calculator

Enter customer type (r/c): r
Enter subtotal:    100

INVOICE
Subtotal:          $100.00
Discount percent: 10%
Discount amount:  $10.00
Total before tax: $90.00
Sales tax:         $4.50
Invoice total:     $94.50

Continue? (y/n): n

Bye!
```

The nested if/else statement that determines the discount percent

```
double discountPercent = 0;
if (customerType.equalsIgnoreCase("r")) {
    if (subtotal < 100) {
        discountPercent = 0.0;
    } else if (subtotal >= 100 && subtotal < 250) {
        discountPercent = .1;
    } else if (subtotal >= 250) {
        discountPercent = .2;
    }
}
else if (customerType.equalsIgnoreCase("c"))  {
   if (subtotal < 250) {
        discountPercent = .2;
   } else if (subtotal >= 250) {
        discountPercent = .3;
   }
} else {
    discountPercent = .1;
}
```

Figure 8-5 A new if/else statement for the Invoice application

How to code loops

In chapter 3, you learned how to code while statements and while loops. Now, you'll review the coding for those loops and learn how to code two other Java statements that implement the *iteration structure*.

How to code while loops

Figure 8-6 shows how to use the *while statement* to code a *while loop*. When coding while loops, it's common to use a *counter variable* to execute the statements in the loop a certain number of times. For example, the first loop in this figure uses an int counter variable named i that's initialized to 1. Then, the last statement in the loop increments the counter variable with each iteration of the loop. As a result, the first statement in this loop is executed as long as the counter variable is less than or equal to 36. When working with counter variables, it is a common coding practice to name them with single letters like *i, j,* and *k.*

When you code loops, it's important to remember that the code within a loop has block scope. As a result, any variables that are declared within the loop can't be used outside of the loop. That's why the variables that are needed outside of the loops in this figure have been declared outside of the loop. In the first loop, for example, the variable named futureValue has been declared outside the loop. That way, you can use this variable after the loop has finished executing.

When you code loops, you usually want to avoid *infinite loops*. If, for example, you forget to code a statement that increments the counter variable, the loop never ends. If this happens, in NetBeans, you can stop the loop by clicking on the Stop button that's displayed in the Output window.

However, there are times when you may want to code an infinite loop. For example, you may want a loop to run endlessly until it accomplishes its task. In that case, you can code an infinite loop like the one in the second example. Then, you can end the loop once the task is accomplished. To do that, you can use a break statement as described later in this chapter.

The syntax of the while loop

```
while (booleanExpression) {
    statements
}
```

A while loop that calculates a future value

```
int i = 1;
int months = 36;
while (i <= months) {
    futureValue = (futureValue + monthlyPayment) *
                  (1 + monthlyInterestRate);
    i++;
}
```

An infinite while loop

```
while (true) {
    // run this code endlessly
}
```

Description

- In a *while loop*, the condition is tested before the loop is executed.
- A while loop executes the block of statements within the loop as long as its Boolean expression is true.
- If a loop requires more than one statement, you must enclose the statements in braces. This identifies the block of statements that are executed by the loop, and any variables or constants that are declared in that block have block scope.
- If a loop requires just one statement, you don't have to enclose the statement in braces. However, it's generally considered a good practice to use braces to identify the statements that are executed by the loop.
- If the condition for a loop never becomes false, the loop never ends. This is known as an *infinite loop*. Although infinite loops can be useful at times, beginning programmers often code them accidentally. In NetBeans, you can cancel an infinite loop by clicking on the Stop button in the Output window.

Figure 8-6 How to code while loops

How to code do-while loops

Figure 8-7 shows how to code a *do-while loop*. The difference between a while loop and a do-while loop is that the Boolean expression is evaluated at the beginning of a while loop and at the end of a do-while loop. As a result, the statements in a while loop are executed zero or more times while the statements in a do-while loop are always executed at least once.

Most of the time, you can use either of these two types of loops to accomplish the same task. For example, the first do-while loop in this figure performs the same calculation as the first while loop in the previous figure.

One problem with a do-while loop is that it's possible for the while statement to get separated from the loop if a programmer inserts code between the loop and the while statement. This can introduce a bug that's difficult to find and fix.

As a result, it's generally considered a best practice to use while loops instead of do-while loops. In practice, do-while loops are rarely used.

The syntax of the do-while loop

```
do {
   statements
} while (booleanExpression);
```

A do-while loop that calculates a future value

```
int i = 1;
int months = 36;
do {
    futureValue = (futureValue + monthlyPayment) *
                  (1 + monthlyInterestRate);
    i++;
} while (i <= months);
```

Description

- A *do-while loop* works like a while loop, except that the condition is tested after the loop is executed.
- In general, while loops are preferred over do-while loops. In practice, while loops are commonly used and do-while loops are rarely used.
- One problem with a do-while loop is that it's possible for the while statement to get separated from the loop if a programmer inserts code between the loop and the while statement. This can introduce a bug that's difficult to find and fix.

Figure 8-7 How to code do-while loops

How to code for loops

Figure 8-8 shows how to use the for statement to code *for loops*. This type of loop is useful when you need to increment or decrement a counter that determines how many times the loop is executed.

To code a for loop, you start by coding the for keyword followed by three expressions enclosed in parentheses and separated by semicolons. The first expression is an initialization expression that gives the starting value for the counter variable. This expression can also declare the counter variable, if necessary. The second expression is a Boolean expression that determines when the loop ends. And the third expression is an increment expression that determines how the counter is incremented or decremented each time the loop is executed.

The first example in this figure shows how to use these expressions. First, the initialization expression declares a counter named i that's of the int type and is initialized to a value of 0. Next, a Boolean expression specifies that the loop should be repeated as long as the counter is less than 5. Then, the increment expression increments the counter by 1 at the end of each repetition of the loop. Since this loop stores the counter variable followed by a space in a string, this code stores the numbers 0 to 4 in a string variable with each number followed by a space.

The second example calculates the sum of 8, 6, 4, and 2. Here, the sum variable is declared before the loop so it's available outside of the loop. Within the parentheses of the for loop, the initialization expression initializes the counter variable to 8, the Boolean expression indicates that the loop ends when the counter variable is no longer greater than zero, and the increment expression uses an assignment operator to subtract 2 from the counter variable with each repetition of the loop. Within the loop, the value of the counter variable is added to the value that's already stored in the sum variable. As a result, the final value for the sum variable is 20.

The third example shows how to code a loop that calculates the future value for a series of monthly payments. Here, the loop executes one time for each month. If you compare this for loop with the while loop in figure 8-6, you can see how a for loop improves upon a while loop when a counter variable is required.

The fourth example shows how to code an infinite for loop. Here, the initialization expression, the Boolean expression, and the increment expression are all left blank. In most cases, it's easier to read and understand an infinite while loop like the one shown in figure 8-6. As a result, in practice, for loops are rarely used to code infinite loops.

The fifth example performs the same task as the for loop that's shown in the first example. However, this loop only uses a single statement within the loop. As a result, the braces for the loop are optional. This works the same as it does for the if/else statements. As with that statement, it's generally considered a good coding style to use braces. That's why the first four examples in this figure use them.

The syntax of the for loop

```
for (initializationExpression; booleanExpression; incrementExpression) {
    statements
}
```

A for loop that stores the numbers 0 through 4 in a string

```
String numbers = "";
for (int i = 0; i < 5; i++)  {
    numbers += i;
    numbers += " ";
}
```

The console after the string is printed to it

```
0 1 2 3 4
```

A for loop that adds the numbers 8, 6, 4, and 2

```
int sum = 0;
for (int i = 8; i > 0; i -= 2) {
    sum += i;
}
```

A for loop that calculates a future value

```
for (int i = 1; i <= months; i++) {
    futureValue = (futureValue + monthlyPayment) *
                  (1 + monthlyInterestRate);
}
```

An infinite for loop

```
for ( ; ; ) {
    // continue executing loop until the application ends
}
```

A for loop without braces

```
String numbers = "";
for (int i = 0; i < 5; i++)
    numbers += i + " ";
```

Description

- A *for loop* is useful when you need to increment or decrement a counter that determines how many times the loop is executed.
- Within the parentheses of a for loop, you code an initialization expression that gives the starting value for the counter, a Boolean expression that determines when the loop ends, and an increment expression that increments or decrements the counter.
- The loop ends when the Boolean expression is false.
- If necessary, you can declare the counter variable before the for loop. Then, this variable is in scope after the loop finishes executing.
- Within the parentheses of a for loop, all three expressions are optional. As a result, you can code an infinite for loop by coding the semicolons that separate these expressions but by not coding any of these expressions.

Figure 8-8 How to code for loops

How to code break and continue statements

When you code loops, you usually want them to run to completion. Occasionally, though, you may need to jump to the end of a loop and exit the loop. To do that, you can use the break statement as described in figure 8-9. Conversely, you may need to jump to the top of a loop and continue the loop. To do that, you can use the continue statement.

If you need to exit the current loop, you can code a break statement as shown in the first example. Here, the Boolean expression for the while loop has been set to true. As a result, this loop would execute indefinitely without a statement that explicitly jumps out of the loop.

Within this loop, the first statement generates a random integer ranging in value from 0 to 10. Then, the second statement prints the number to the console. After that, an if statement checks whether this number is equal to 7. If so, this code prints a message to the control and uses a break statement to exit the loop.

If you need to jump to the top of the current loop, you can use the continue statement as shown in the second example. This statement work similarly to a break statement, but it jumps to the beginning of a loop instead of the end of a loop. Here, the for loop uses a counter variable to execute 5 times. Within this loop, the first example generates a random integer ranging in value from 0 to 10. Then, if the random number is greater than 7, the loop prints a message to the console and uses a continue statement to jump to the top of the loop. As a result, the println method that comes after the if statement is only executed if the random number is less than or equal to 7. In other words, random numbers of 8 through 10 aren't printed to the console. Instead, they cause the "invalid value" message to be printed to the console.

When reviewing other programmers code, it's possible that you might come across one loop that's nested within another. In addition, it's possible that the outer loop may have a *label* that allows the code in the inner loop to jump to the top or to jump out of the outer loop. However, using labels with loops often yields code that's difficult to read and maintain. As a result, it's generally considered a best practice to avoid using labels with loops.

The syntax of the break statement

```
break;
```

A break statement that exits the loop

```
while (true) {
    int random = (int) (Math.random() * 10);
    System.out.println(random);
    if (random == 7) {
        System.out.println("value found - exit loop!");
        break;
    }
}
```

The console

```
2
5
7
value found - exit loop!
```

The syntax of the continue statement

```
continue;
```

A continue statement that jumps to the beginning of a loop

```
for (int i = 0; i < 5; i++) {
    int random = (int) (Math.random() * 10);
    if (random > 7) {
        System.out.println("invalid value - continue loop!");
        continue;
    }
    System.out.println(random);
}
```

The console

```
invalid value - continue loop!
0
1
2
invalid value - continue loop!
```

Description

- To jump to the end of the current loop, you can use the break statement.
- To skip the rest of the statements in the current loop and jump to the top of the current loop, you can use the continue statement.

Figure 8-9 How to code break and continue statements

How to code try/catch statements

To prevent your applications from crashing, you can write try/catch statements that handle exceptions when they occur. This is known as *exception handling*, and it plays an important role in most applications.

How exceptions work

When Java can't perform an operation, it *throws* an *exception*. An exception is an object that's created from one of the classes in the Exception hierarchy such as the ones shown in figure 8-10. Exception objects represent errors that have occurred, and they contain information about those errors. One of the most common causes of exceptions is invalid input data.

The Exception class that's at the top of the exception hierarchy defines the most general type of exception. The RuntimeException class is a *subclass* of the Exception class that defines a more specific type of exception. In particular, it defines an exception that occurs at runtime.

The other four exceptions in this figure are subclasses of the RuntimeException class. As a result, they define even more specific types of exceptions that occur at runtime. For example, the NumberFormatException occurs at runtime when the parseInt method of the Integer class can't convert the specified String object to an int value. Similarly, the NumberFormatException occurs at runtime when the parseDouble method of the Double class can't convert the specified String object to a double value.

A well-coded application *catches* any exceptions that are thrown and handles them. Exception handling can be as simple as notifying users that they must enter valid data. Or, it may involve notifying users that the application is being shut down, saving as much data as possible, cleaning up resources, and exiting the application as smoothly as possible.

When you're testing an application, it's common to encounter exceptions that haven't been handled. For a console application, this typically causes information about the exception to be displayed at the console. This information usually includes the name of the exception class, a brief message that describes the cause of the exception, and a *stack trace*. In this figure, for example, you can see the information that's displayed when the user enters an invalid double value.

A stack trace is a list of the methods that were called before the exception occurred. These methods are listed in the reverse order from the order in which they were called. Each method includes a line number, which can help you find the statement that caused the exception in your source code. In this figure, for example, the stack trace indicates that line 18 of the main method of the FutureValueApp class threw an exception when it called the parseDouble method of the Double class.

One common situation where you'll need to handle exceptions is when you convert string data to numeric data. If, for example, the parseDouble method of the Double class can't convert user input to a double type, it throws a NumberFormatException.

Some of the classes in the Exception hierarchy

```
Exception
    RuntimeException
        IllegalArgumentException
            NumberFormatException
        ArithmeticException
        NullPointerException
```

The console after an InputMismatchException has been thrown

```
Enter monthly investment:   $100
Exception in thread "main" java.lang.NumberFormatException: For
input string: "$100"
    at sun.misc.FloatingDecimal.readJavaFormatString(
        FloatingDecimal.java:2043)
    at sun.misc.FloatingDecimal.parseDouble(
        FloatingDecimal.java:110)
    at java.lang.Double.parseDouble(
        Double.java:538)
    at murach.futurevalue.FutureValueApp.main(
        FutureValueApp.java:18)
Java Result: 1
```

Two methods that might throw an exception

Class	Method	Throws
Integer	parseInt(String)	NumberFormatException
Double	parseDouble(String)	NumberFormatException

Description

- An *exception* is an object that contains information about an error that has occurred. When an error occurs in a method, the method *throws* an exception.
- If an exception is thrown when you're testing a console application, some information about the exception, including its name and stack trace, is displayed at the console.
- A *stack trace* is a list of the methods that were called before the exception occurred. The list appears in reverse order, from the last method called to the first method called.
- All exceptions are *subclasses* of the Exception class. The Exception class represents the most general type of exception. Each successive layer of subclasses represents more specific exceptions.
- The RuntimeException class represents exceptions that occur at runtime. All of the exceptions described in this chapter are runtime exceptions.

How to catch exceptions

To catch and handle exceptions, you can use a *try/catch statement* like the one shown in figure 8-11. First, you code a try clause that contains a block of one or more statements that may cause an exception. Then, you code a catch clause immediately after the try clause. This clause contains the block of statements that's executed if an exception is thrown by a statement in the try block. Since this block contains the code that handles the exception, it is known as an *exception handler*.

The example in this figure shows how you can use a try statement in an application that's getting input from a user and attempting to convert it to a double value. Here, the parseDouble method of the Double class is coded within a try clause, and a catch clause is coded for the NumberFormatException. Then, if the user enters a non-numeric value, the parseDouble method throws a NumberFormatException and the code in the catch block is executed.

In this case, the catch block starts by displaying an error message. Then, it uses the continue statement to jump to the beginning of the loop, which causes the application to prompt the user to enter the number again.

The catch block in this example is only executed if the NumberFormatException is thrown. Since this exception is the only exception that's likely to be thrown in the try block, this is the clearest way to catch this exception. If you wanted the catch clause to catch other exceptions as well, however, you could name an exception higher up in the Exception hierarchy. For example, if you wanted to catch any runtime exception, you could code this catch clause:

```
catch (RuntimeException e)
```

Or, if you wanted to catch any exception, you could code this catch clause:

```
catch (Exception e)
```

You'll learn more about how this works in chapter 16.

The syntax for a simple try/catch statement

```
try { statements }
catch (ExceptionClass exceptionName) { statements }
```

Code that catches a NumberFormatException

```
String choice = "y";
while (!choice.equalsIgnoreCase("n")) {
    // get the input from the user
    System.out.print("Enter monthly investment:    ");
    double monthlyInvestment;
    try {
        String line = sc.nextLine();
        monthlyInvestment = Double.parseDouble(line);
    } catch (NumberFormatException e)  {
        System.out.println("Error! Invalid number. Try again.\n");
        continue;       // jump to the top of the loop
    }

    // see if the user wants to continue
    System.out.print("Continue? (y/n): ");
    choice = sc.nextLine();
    System.out.println();
}
```

Console output

```
Enter monthly investment:   $100
Error! Invalid number. Try again.

Enter monthly investment:
```

Description

- In a *try statement* (or *try/catch statement*), you code any statements that may throw an exception in a *try block*. Then, you can code a *catch block* that handles any exceptions that may occur in the try block.
- When an exception occurs, any remaining statements in the try block are skipped and the statements in the catch block are executed.
- Any variables or objects that are used in both the try and catch blocks must be declared before the try and catch blocks so both the try and catch blocks can access them.
- If you use a catch block to catch a specific type of exception, you should also import the package that contains that exception class.

Figure 8-11 How to catch exceptions

The Future Value application

This chapter finishes by presenting a Future Value application that calculates a future value for a series of monthly payments at the specified interest rate. This application shows some of the skills presented in this chapter within the context of an application. In addition, this application uses a Console class that you can use to display data on the console or to get data from the console.

The user interface

Figure 8-12 begins by showing the console for this application. Here, the user starts by entering valid numbers for the monthly investment, the yearly interest rate, and the number of years. Then, the application calculates the future value and displays it on the console.

After the first calculation, the user enters a "y" to continue with a second calculation. For this calculation, the user enters an invalid number ("four") for the number of years. The application handles this by displaying an error message that indicates that the user entered an invalid integer and prompting the user to enter the years again.

Note that this does not restart the application. As a result, the user does not lose the data (monthly investment and yearly interest rate) that he or she has already entered. Also, the error message is specific enough (invalid integer) to be helpful.

The code

Part 1 of this figure shows the Financial class that's stored in the package named murach.calculators. This class contains a single static method named calculateFutureValue. This method accepts three arguments: (1) the monthly investment, (2) the yearly interest rate, and (3) the number of years. From these arguments, this method calculates the future value and returns it.

Within this method, the first two statements convert the yearly values to monthly values. To do that, the first statement divides the yearly interest rate by 12 to convert it to a monthly interest rate, and divides that rate by 100 to convert it to a percent value. Then, the second statement multiples the number of years by 12 to get the number of months.

After this method creates the monthly variables, it uses a for loop to calculate the future value. To do that, it executes the loop once for each month.

Within the loop, the first statement adds the monthly investment to the future value. The second statement calculates the amount of interest for the month. And the third statement adds the interest to the future value. After the loop, the return statement method returns the future value to the calling method.

The console

```
Welcome to the Future Value Calculator

Enter monthly investment:   100
Enter yearly interest rate: 3
Enter number of years:      3
Future value:               $3,771.46

Continue? (y/n): y

Enter monthly investment:   100
Enter yearly interest rate: 3
Enter number of years:      four
Error! Invalid integer. Try again.
Enter number of years:      4
Future value:               $5,105.85

Continue? (y/n): n

Bye!
```

The Financial class

```
package murach.calculators;

public class Financial {

    public static double calculateFutureValue(double monthlyInvestment,
            double yearlyInterestRate, int years) {

        // convert yearly values to monthly values
        double monthlyInterestRate = yearlyInterestRate / 12 / 100;
        int months = years * 12;

        // calculate the future value
        double futureValue = 0;
        for (int i = 1; i <= months; i++) {
            futureValue += monthlyInvestment;
            double monthlyInterestAmount = futureValue * monthlyInterestRate;
            futureValue += monthlyInterestAmount;
        }

        return futureValue;
    }
}
```

Part 2 of this figure shows the Console class that's stored in the package named murach.ui. This class contains static methods that display data on the console and get input from the console.

To start, this class begins with the import statement for the Scanner class. Then, within the class, the first statement declares a static instance variable for a Scanner object named sc and creates this object. As a result, all of the static methods in this class can use that Scanner object.

The two displayLine methods use the println method of the System.out object to display data to the console. Here, the first displayLine method displays a blank line, and the second displayLine method displays the specified string on its own line.

The getString method begins by displaying the specified string to prompt the user to enter data. For example, you could specify a string of "Enter your name:" to prompt the user to enter a string. Then, this method uses the nextLine method of the Scanner object to get a String object for the data that the user enters, and it returns that String object.

The getInt method begins by declaring an int variable named i. This variable stores the int value that's returned by this method. Then, this method uses an infinite while loop to continue prompting the user until he or she enters a valid integer. Within the infinite while loop, the first statement displays the prompt. For example, you specify a string of "Enter years:" to prompt the user to enter an integer for the number of years.

After the prompt, this method uses a try/catch statement. Within the try block, the first statement attempts to convert the data that the user enters to an integer. If this conversion throws a NumberFormatException, the catch block prints an error message that indicates that the user didn't enter a valid integer and the while loop continues. As a result, it prompts the user for the integer again.

However, if this conversion succeeds, the code in the try block stores the integer in the variable named i. Then, the try block calls the break statement. This exits the while loop, which returns the integer stored in the variable named i.

The getDouble method works like the getInt method. However, it works with the double type instead of the int type.

The Console class

```
package murach.ui;

import java.util.Scanner;

public class Console {

    private static Scanner sc = new Scanner(System.in);

    public static void displayLine() {
        System.out.println();
    }

    public static void displayLine(String s) {
        System.out.println(s);
    }

    public static String getString(String prompt) {
        System.out.print(prompt);
        String s = sc.nextLine();
        return s;
    }

    public static int getInt(String prompt) {
        int i = 0;
        while (true) {
            System.out.print(prompt);
            try {
                i = Integer.parseInt(sc.nextLine());
                break;
            } catch (NumberFormatException e) {
                System.out.println("Error! Invalid integer. Try again.");
            }
        }
        return i;
    }

    public static double getDouble(String prompt) {
        double d = 0;
        while (true) {
            System.out.print(prompt);
            try {
                d = Double.parseDouble(sc.nextLine());
                break;
            } catch (NumberFormatException e) {
                System.out.println("Error! Invalid decimal. Try again.");
            }
        }
        return d;
    }
}
```

Part 3 of this figure shows the Main class that's stored in the package named murach.ui. This class contains the main method for the application. Much of the code for this method works like the main method for the Line Item application presented in chapter 3. As a result, the following description focuses on the new skills that were presented in this chapter.

To start, this application begins with import statements that import the NumberFormat class and the Financial class shown in part 1 of this figure. As a result, this application can use the Financial class to calculate the future value, and it can use the NumberFormat class to format the future value.

Within the main method, the first two statements use the Console class to display a welcome message. Then, within the while loop, the first three statements use the getDouble and getInt methods of Console class. These statements get the double and int values that correspond with the monthly investment, the yearly interest rate, and number of years. Here, the Console class converts the string that's entered by the user to the correct numeric type and handles the exception that's thrown if the user enters an invalid number. As a result, it makes it easy to get numeric data from the user.

After getting the numeric data from the user, this code uses the Financial class shown earlier to calculate the future value. Then, this code uses the Console class and the NumberFormat class to display the future value with currency formatting.

After displaying the future value, this code uses the Console class to ask the user if he or she wants to continue. To do that, this code uses the getString method to get the data that's entered by the user.

The Main class

```
package murach.ui;

import java.text.NumberFormat;
import murach.calculators.Financial;

public class Main {

    public static void main(String[] args) {
        // displayLine a welcome message
        Console.displayLine("Welcome to the Future Value Calculator");
        Console.displayLine();

        String choice = "y";
        while (choice.equalsIgnoreCase("y")) {

            // get input from user
            double monthlyInvestment =
                    Console.getDouble("Enter monthly investment:   ");
            double yearlyInterestRate =
                    Console.getDouble("Enter yearly interest rate: ");
            int years =
                    Console.getInt("Enter number of years:      ");

            // call the future value method
            double futureValue = Financial.calculateFutureValue(
                    monthlyInvestment, yearlyInterestRate, years);

            // format and displayLine the result
            Console.displayLine("Future value:               " +
                    NumberFormat.getCurrencyInstance().format(futureValue));
            Console.displayLine();

            // see if the user wants to continue
            choice = Console.getString("Continue? (y/n): ");
            Console.displayLine();
        }
        Console.displayLine("Bye!");
    }
}
```

Figure 8-12 The Future Value application (part 3 of 3)

Perspective

If this chapter has succeeded, you should now be able to use if, switch, while, do-while, and for statements. These are the Java statements that implement the selection, case, and iteration structures, and they provide the logic of an application. You should also be able to code try/catch statements that handle some runtime exceptions that occur when the user enters invalid numbers.

Summary

- You can use the *relational operators* to create *Boolean expressions* that compare primitive data types and return true or false values, and you can use the *logical operators* to connect two or more Boolean expressions.
- To determine whether two strings are equal, you can call the equals or equalsIgnoreCase method from a String object.
- You can use *if/else statements* and *switch statements* to control the logic of an application, and you can *nest* these statements whenever necessary.
- You can use *while*, *do-while*, and *for loops* to repeatedly execute one or more statements until a Boolean expression evaluates to false, and you can nest these statements whenever necessary.
- You can use *break statements* to jump to the end of the current loop, and you can use *continue statements* to jump to the start of the current loop.
- An *exception* is an object that's created from the Exception class or one of its *subclasses*. This object contains information about an error that has occurred.
- The *stack trace* is a list of methods that were called before an exception occurred.
- You can code a *try statement* to create an *exception handler* that *catches* and handles any exceptions that are *thrown*. This is known as *exception handling*.

Exercise 8-1 Modify the Invoice application

In this exercise, you'll modify the Invoice application so it uses more complex control statements.

1. Open the project named ch08_ex1_Invoice that's stored in the ex_starts folder. Then, test it with valid data to make sure it works correctly.
2. Modify the if/else statement so customers of type "r" with a subtotal that is greater than or equal to $250 but less than $500 get a 25% discount and those with a subtotal of $500 or more get a 30% discount. Next, change the if/else statement so customers of type "c" always get a 20% discount. Then, test the application to make sure this works correctly.
3. Add another customer type to the if/else statement so customers of type "t" get a 40% discount for subtotals of less than $500, and a 50% discount for subtotals of $500 or more. Then, test the application.
4. Check your code to make sure that no discount is provided for a customer type code that isn't "r", "c", or "t". Then, fix this if necessary.
5. Use a switch statement for the customer type instead of using an if/else statement.
6. Add a try/catch statement that catches the NumberFormatException that occurs when the user enters an invalid subtotal. In the catch block, add code that prints an error message and jumps to the top of the while loop.
7. Modify the while loop so it is an infinite loop. Then, add code to the end of the loop that breaks out of the loop if the user enters "n" at the "Continue (y/n)" prompt.

Exercise 8-2 Modify the Future Value application

In this exercise, you'll modify the Future Value application presented at the end of this chapter.

Modify a for loop

1. Open the project named ch08_ex2_FutureValue that's stored in the ex_starts folder. Then, run the application to see how it works.
2. Open the Financial class that's in the murach.calculators package. Then, edit the for loop to use a counter variable named month instead of i.
3. Run the application to make sure it works correctly.

Use if statements to check for minimum and maximum values

4. Open the Console class that's in the murach.ui package. Then, review this code.
5. Modify the getDouble method so it accepts three parameters: (1) a String object for the prompt, (2) a double type for a minimum value, and (3) a double type for a maximum value.
6. Within the getDouble method add an if statement that makes sure the user enters a value within the minimum and maximum values. If the user enters a value that's not within the minimum and maximum values, display a user-friendly error message and jump to the top of the loop.
7. Open the Main class and edit it so it uses the getDouble method of the Console class to specify minimum and maximum values for the monthly investment and the monthly interest rate. For example, you might want to specify that the monthly investment should be greater than 0 but less than 100,000. Similarly, you might want to specify that the yearly interest rate should be greater than 0 but less than 20.
8. Run the application to make sure it works correctly.

9

How to work with strings

In section 1 of this book, you learned some basic skills for working with strings. In this chapter, you'll learn more about working with strings. Because you'll use strings in many of the applications that you develop, you should know how to use all of the skills presented in this chapter.

How to work with the String class 234
How to create strings 234
How to join strings 234
How to append data to a string 234
How to compare strings 236
How to work with string indexes 238
How to modify strings 240
How to work with the StringBuilder class 242
How to create a StringBuilder object 242
How to append data to a string 242
How to modify strings 244
The Product Lister application 246
The user interface 246
The StringUtil class 246
The Main class 248
Perspective 250

How to work with the String class

In chapter 2, you learned how to create and join strings. In chapter 3, you learned how to use two methods of the String class to compare strings. Now, you'll review those skills, and you'll learn some new skills for working with strings.

How to create strings

The first example in figure 9-1 shows how to create String variables and initialize them. The first statement creates a String variable named product-Code and assigns it an empty string (""). The second statement creates a String variable named productCode and assigns it a String literal of "Murach's Java Programming". And the third statement creates a String variable named bookTitle and assigns it the String variable named title. As a result, both of these variables refer to the same String object.

How to join strings

The second and third examples show how to *join* strings. This is also known as *concatenating* strings. To do that, you can use the + operator to join String variables and String literals. In the second example, for instance, the second statement creates a String variable named message that refers to a string of "Hi, Bob".

When you join or append other data types to a String variable, Java automatically converts the other data types so they can be used as part of the string. In the fourth example, for instance, the second statement joins a String literal of "Years: " with an int value of 3 and assigns the result to a String variable named message. As a result, this String variable refers to a string of "Years: 3".

How to append data to a string

The fourth and fifth examples show how to append data to a string. This works the same as joining strings except that it adds the new data to the end of the string.

In the fourth example, for instance, the first statement declares a String variable that refers to a first name. Then, the second statement appends a space to that variable, and the third statement appends a last name. Here, the name variable is coded on both sides of the equals sign, and the + operator joins the new String literal to this variable.

The fifth example works the same as the fourth example. However, it uses the += operator to append the data. As a result, it isn't necessary to code the name variable on both sides of the equals sign. Since this is easy to read and requires less code than the previous example, it's more commonly used.

The String class

```
java.lang.String;
```

How to declare and initialize String variables

```
String productCode = "";                          // refers to an empty string
String title = "Murach's Java Programming";      // refers to a String literal
String bookTitle = title;  // refers to the same object as another variable
```

How to join strings

```
String name = "Bob";                         // name is "Bob"
String message = "Hi, " + name;              // message is "Hi, Bob"
```

How to join a string and a number

```
int years = 3;
String message = "Years: " + years;          // message is "Years: 3"
```

How to append one string to another

```
String name = "Bob";              // name is "Bob"
String name = name + " ";         // name is "Bob "
String name = name + "Smith";     // name is "Bob Smith"
```

A more common way to append one string to another

```
String name = "Bob";              // name is "Bob"
String name += " ";               // name is "Bob "
String name += "Smith";           // name is "Bob Smith"
```

Description

- You can initialize a String variable by assigning a String literal or another variable that refers to a String object.
- To *join* (or *concatenate*) one string with another string or another data type, you can use the + operator.
- To *append* a string or another data type to a string, you can use the += operator.
- When you join or append other data types to a String object, Java automatically converts the other data types to String objects so they can be used as part of the string.

Figure 9-1 How to create, join, and append strings

How to compare strings

In chapter 3, you learned how to use the equals and equalsIgnoreCase methods of the String class to compare strings. Now, figure 9-2 reviews those methods and introduces you to more methods that you can use to compare strings.

All of the methods in this figure return a Boolean value of true or false. For example, the equals method compares strings and returns a true value if the strings are equal and have the same capitalization. Similarly, the startsWith method checks whether a string starts with a certain combination of characters and returns a true value if it does.

The first example shows a common mistake that beginners often make when comparing strings. Here, the code uses the equality operator (==) that's used for comparing primitive types to compare strings. But, this doesn't check whether two strings are equal. Instead, it checks whether they refer to the same String object. However, it's possible that two String variables may refer to different String objects and still have the same combination of characters. As a result, this isn't a reliable way to check for equality.

The second example shows how to use the equals method to compare strings. This checks whether two String variables store the same characters with the same capitalization. As a result, it's a reliable way to check for equality.

As you learned in chapter 3, if you don't care about capitalization, you can use the equalsIgnoreCase method to check two strings for equality. This method works the same as the equals method, but it isn't case-sensitive.

The third example shows how to use the equals method to check for an empty string. To do that, you just supply an empty string as the argument of the equals method. Here, the if statement checks whether the String variable named productCode refers to an empty string. If so, it prints a message to the console.

The fourth example shows how to use the isEmpty method that was introduced with Java 6 to check for an empty string. This example works like the equals method in the previous example. However, some programmers consider the isEmtpy method easier to read.

The fifth example shows how to use the startsWith method. Here, the if statement checks whether the String variable named productDescription starts with a string of "Murach". If so, it prints a message to the console.

The sixth example shows how to use the endsWith method. Here, the if statement checks whether the String variable named productDescription ends with a string of "Programming". If so, it prints a message to the console.

Methods for comparing strings

Method	Description
equals(String)	Returns a true value if the specified string is equal to the current string. This comparison is case-sensitive.
equalsIgnoreCase(String)	Returns a true value if the specified string is equal to the current string. This comparison is not case-sensitive.
isEmpty()	Returns a true value if this string contains an empty string. This method was introduced with Java 1.6.
startsWith(String)	Returns a true value if this string starts with the specified string.
endsWith(String)	Returns a true value if this string ends with the specified string.

A common mistake when testing for equality

```
if (productCode == "java"){
    System.out.println("This does not test for equality.");
}
```

How to use the equals method to test for equality

```
if (productCode.equals("java")){
    System.out.println("This tests for equality.");
}
```

How to use the equals method to check for an empty string

```
if (productCode.equals("")){
    System.out.println("You must enter a product code.");
}
```

How to use the isEmpty method (Java 1.6 and later)

```
if (productCode.isEmpty()) {
    System.out.println("You must enter a product code.");
}
```

How to use the startsWith method

```
if (productDescription.startsWith("Murach")) {
    System.out.println("This book is a Murach book.");
}
```

How to use the endsWith method

```
if (productDescription.endsWith("Programming")) {
    System.out.println("This book is about programming.");
}
```

Description

- The String class provides methods that you can use to compare strings.
- The equality operator (==) checks whether two strings refer to the same String object. It's possible for two strings to contain the same characters, but to refer to different String objects. As a result, you should not use this operator to check whether two strings contain the same characters.

Figure 9-2 How to compare strings

How to work with string indexes

Figure 9-3 begins by listing some methods that you can use to work with the indexes of a String object. Here, the indexOf and lastIndexOf methods return a value that represents an *index* within a string. When you work with indexes, you need to remember that the first index is 0, not 1. As a result, the index for the first character is 0, the index for the second character is 1, the index for the third character is 2, and so on.

The first example shows how to use the length method. Here, the length method is called from a String variable named productCode that refers to a string of "java". As a result, the length method returns a value of 4.

The second example shows how to use the length method to check for an empty string. To do that, the if statement checks whether the String variable named productCode has a length of 0. If so, it prints a message to the console.

The third example shows how to use the indexOf method. Here, the first call to the indexOf method returns an index for the first occurrence of the space character in the specified string. Then, the second call to the indexOf method returns an index for the second occurrence of the space character in the specified string. To do that, this code adds a value of 1 to the index for the first space and starts searching at that index. As a result, this code finds the second occurrence of the space character instead of finding the first occurrence again.

The fourth example shows how to use the lastIndexOf method. This works like the third example. However, it begins searching from the end of the string and works toward the beginning of the string. To do that, this code subtracts a value of 1 from the index for the first space that's found.

The fifth example shows another way to use the indexOf method. Here, the indexOf method searches the string for a value of "Van". This shows that you can use the indexOf method to search for a string of characters. In addition, it shows that the index that's returned is for the first character in this string. In other words, this code returns an int value of 7 because that's the index for where "Van" begins in this string.

The sixth example shows how to use the charAt method. This code gets the first three characters in the specified String variable and stores them in variables of the char type. This shows how indexes work. In addition, it shows that a string contains a sequence of char values. In the next figure, you'll learn how to loop through all of the characters in a string and do some processing on them.

Methods for working with string indexes

Method	Description
`length()`	Returns an int value for the number of characters in this string.
`indexOf(String)`	Returns an int value for the index of the first occurrence of the specified string in this string. If the string isn't found, this method returns -1.
`indexOf(String, startIndex)`	Returns an int value for the index of the first occurrence of the specified string starting at the specified index. If the string isn't found, this method returns -1.
`lastIndexOf(String)`	Returns an int value for the index of the last occurrence of the specified string in this string.
`lastIndexOf(String, startIndex)`	Returns an int value for the index of the last occurrence of the specified string in this string starting at the specified index.
`charAt(index)`	Returns the char value at the specified index.

How to get the length of a string

```
String productCode = "java";
int length = productCode.length();                    // length is 4
```

How to use the length method to check for an empty string

```
if (productCode.length() == 0){
    System.out.println("You must enter a product code.");
}
```

Code that gets the index values for the two spaces

```
String name = "Martin Van Buren";
int index1 = name.indexOf(" ");                       // index1 is 6
int index2 = name.indexOf(" ", index1+1);             // index2 is 10
```

Another way to get the index values for the two spaces

```
String name = "Martin Van Buren";
int index1 = name.lastIndexOf(" ");                   // index1 is 10
int index2 = name.lastIndexOf(" ", index1-1);         // index2 is 6
```

Code that gets the index of a string

```
String name = "Martin Van Buren";
int index = name.indexOf("Van");                      // index is 7
```

Code that gets the character at the specified index

```
String name = "Martin Van Buren";
char char1 = name.charAt(0);                          // char1 is 'M'
char char2 = name.charAt(1);                          // char2 is 'a'
char char3 = name.charAt(2);                          // char3 is 'r'
```

Description

- You can use an *index* to refer to each character within a string where 0 is the first character, 1 is the second character, and so on.

Figure 9-3 How to use string indexes

How to modify strings

Figure 9-4 begins by listing some methods that you can use to modify strings. These methods return another String object that occurs within the current String object. This String object that's returned is known as a *substring*.

The first example shows how to use the trim method to remove any spaces from the beginning and end of a String object. As a result, after this code executes the String variable named choice refers to a String literal of "y".

The second example shows how to use the substring method to parse the first name and last name from a string for a full name. Here, the first statement sets the string to a string literal that includes a first and last name. Then, the second statement uses the indexOf method to get the index of the first space in the string, which is the space between the first and last names. Next, the third statement uses the substring method to set the first name variable equal to the string that begins at the first character of the string and ends at the first space character in the string. Finally, the fourth statement uses the substring method to set the last name variable equal to the string that begins one index after the index for the space and continues to the end of the string.

The third example shows how to add dashes to a Visa credit card number. To do that, this example creates four strings, one for each four-digit part of the credit card number. To do that, it uses the substring method to return four String objects from the String object for the credit card number. Then, the last statement joins the four parts of the credit card number adding dashes at the appropriate locations in the string.

The fourth example shows how to remove the dashes from a credit card number that's referred to by a String variable named ccNumber. To do that, this example creates a second String variable named temp. Then, it loops through each index in the credit card number string. Within this loop, an if statement uses the charAt method to check whether the character at the current index is not equal to the dash character. If not, this code appends the character that's returned by the charAt method to the String variable named temp. As a result, this code appends all characters to the temp variable, except the dash character. Later in this chapter, you'll learn an easier way to accomplish this task.

When using methods that require an index, you must be careful to supply a valid index. If you supply an index argument that doesn't exist in the String object, the method will throw a StringIndexOutOfBoundsException. This is a mistake that's often made by beginning programmers. Fortunately, you can prevent this exception by making sure that you use indexes that are greater than or equal to 0 and less than the length of the String object. In the fourth example, for instance, the loop begins at an index of 0 and stops at an index of one less than the length of the String object for the ccNumber variable.

Methods for modifying strings

Method	Description
`trim()`	Returns a String object with any spaces removed from the beginning and end of this string.
`substring(startIndex)`	Returns a String object that starts at the specified index and goes to the end of the string.
`substring(startIndex, endIndex)`	Returns a String object that starts at the specified start index and goes to, but doesn't include, the end index.

Code that removes spaces from the start and end of a string

```
String choice = "  y  ";
choice = choice.trim();                          // choice is "y"
```

Code that parses a first name and last name from a string

```
String name = "Mike Murach";
int index = name.indexOf(" ");                   // index is 4
String firstName = name.substring(0, index);     // firstName is "Mike"
String lastName = name.substring(index + 1);     // lastName is "Murach"
```

Code that adds dashes to a credit card number

```
String ccNumber = "4012888888881881";
String part1 = ccNumber.substring(0,4);
String part2 = ccNumber.substring(4,8);
String part3 = ccNumber.substring(8,12);
String part4 = ccNumber.substring(12,16);
ccNumber = part1 + "-" + part2 + "-" + part3 + "-" + part4;
```

Code that removes dashes from a credit card number

```
String ccNumber = "4012-8888-8888-1881";
String temp = "";
for(int i = 0; i < ccNumber.length(); i++) {
   if (ccNumber.charAt(i) != '-') {
      temp += ccNumber.charAt(i);
   }
}
ccNumber = temp;
```

Figure 9-4 How to modify strings

How to work with the StringBuilder class

When you use a String variable to work with strings, each String object has a fixed length, and you can't edit the characters that make up the String object. In other words, the String objects are *immutable*. As a result, if you want to change the String object that's referred to by the String variable, you must create a new String object and assign it to that String variable.

If you want more flexibility when working with strings, you can use the StringBuilder class. When you use this class, you create strings that are *mutable*. Then, you can edit the characters that are stored in the StringBuilder object without creating a new StringBuilder object. For example, you can append characters to the end of the string, insert characters into the middle of the string, or delete characters from the string. This makes it easier to write code that works with strings, and it can improve the efficiency of your code.

The StringBuilder class was introduced with Java 5. It's designed to be a more efficient replacement for the StringBuffer class that was used prior to Java 5. Because the API for the StringBuffer class is identical to the API for the StringBuilder class, you can easily switch between the StringBuffer and StringBuilder classes. However, the StringBuilder class is not thread-safe. As a result, if you need your code to be thread-safe, you should use the StringBuffer class.

How to create a StringBuilder object

Figure 9-5 shows three constructors and three methods of the StringBuilder class. The first constructor creates an empty StringBuilder object with an initial capacity of 16 characters. Then, if you add more than 16 characters to this StringBuilder object, Java automatically increases the capacity. To do that, it doubles the current capacity and adds 2.

Whenever possible, you should set the capacity to an appropriate value by using the second or third constructor. Otherwise, Java has to allocate memory each time the capacity is exceeded, and that can cause your code to run less efficiently. On the other hand, if you set a large capacity and use a small percentage of it, you waste memory.

How to append data to a string

Once you create a StringBuilder object, you can use the methods of the StringBuilder class to work with the object. For instance, the first example shows how to use the append method of the StringBuilder class. Here, the first statement creates an empty StringBuilder object with the default capacity of 16 characters. Then, the next four statements use the append method to add 16 characters to the string. As a result, the length of the string is 16 and the capacity of the StringBuilder object is 16.

The StringBuilder class

```
java.lang.StringBuilder;
```

Constructors of the StringBuilder class

Constructor	Description
`StringBuilder()`	Creates an empty StringBuilder object with an initial capacity of 16 characters.
`StringBuilder(capacity)`	Creates an empty StringBuilder object with an initial capacity of the specified number of characters.
`StringBuilder(String)`	Creates a StringBuilder object that contains the specified string plus an additional capacity of 16 characters.

Some starting methods of the StringBuilder class

Methods	Description
`append(data)`	Adds a string for the specified primitive type or object to the end of the string.
`capacity()`	Returns an int value for the capacity of this StringBuilder object.
`length()`	Returns an int value for the number of characters in this StringBuilder object.

Code that creates a credit card number

```
StringBuilder ccNumber = new StringBuilder();
ccNumber.append("4012");
ccNumber.append("8888");
ccNumber.append("8888");
ccNumber.append("1881");
```

Code that shows how capacity automatically increases

```
StringBuilder name = new StringBuilder(8);
int capacity1 = name.capacity();      // capacity1 is 8
name.append("Raymond R. Thomas");
int length = name.length();           // length is 17
int capacity2 = name.capacity();      // capacity2 is 18 (2 * capacity1 + 2)
```

Description

- String objects are *immutable*. As a result, they can't grow or shrink.
- StringBuilder objects are *mutable*, which means you can modify the characters in the string. The capacity of a StringBuilder object is automatically increased if necessary.
- The StringBuilder class was introduced with Java 5. It's designed to replace the older StringBuffer class.
- The StringBuffer class has identical constructors and methods as the StringBuilder class. As a result, you can use it to accomplish the same tasks.
- The StringBuffer class isn't as efficient as the StringBuilder class, but it is thread-safe. As a result, you can use it instead of the StringBuilder class whenever you need to make sure your code is thread-safe.

Figure 9-5 How to create a StringBuilder object and append data to it

As you learned earlier in this chapter, you can accomplish the same task by using the String class and the += operator. However, if you do that, Java must create a new String object for each statement. In contrast, when you use the append method of the StringBuilder class, Java doesn't create a new StringBuilder object. Instead, it increases the length of the StringBuilder object. If necessary, it also increases the capacity of the StringBuilder object. As a result, the StringBuilder object usually works more efficiently than the String object.

The second example in figure 9-5 shows how a StringBuilder object automatically increases its capacity as the length of the string increases. Here, the first statement creates an empty StringBuilder object with a capacity of 8 characters. The second statement uses the capacity method to verify that the capacity is 8. The third statement appends a string of 17 characters to the empty string. Since this exceeds the capacity of the StringBuilder object, Java automatically increases the capacity by doubling the current capacity and adding 2. As a result, this code increases the capacity from 8 to 18 characters. Then, the last two statements verify the new length and capacity.

How to modify strings

Figure 9-6 shows some more methods of the StringBuilder class. Some of these methods provide additional functionality that isn't available from the String class. For example, you can use the methods of the StringBuilder class to insert, replace, or delete strings or characters. However, the StringBuilder class also provides methods that work the same as the methods of the String class. For example, the charAt and substring methods work the same for the StringBuilder class as they do for the String class. As a result, you shouldn't have any trouble using these methods.

The first example adds dashes to the Visa credit card number string created in the previous figure. Here, the first statement uses the insert method to insert a dash after the first four characters. This pushes the remaining numbers back one index. Then, the second statement uses the insert method to insert a dash after the ninth character in the string, which was the eighth character in the original string. This pushes the remaining eight numbers in the string back one index. And so on. Note that this task is easier to accomplish with a mutable StringBuilder object than it was with an immutable String object.

The second example shows how to remove dashes from a credit card number. Here, a loop cycles through each character, using the charAt method to check if the current character is a dash. If so, the deleteCharAt method deletes that character. Since this causes all characters to the right of the dash to move forward one index, the next statement decrements the counter. That way, the loop doesn't skip any characters. Again, note that this task is easier to accomplish with a mutable StringBuilder object than it was with an immutable String object.

The third example shows how to use the substring method of the StringBuilder class to separate the four parts of a credit card number. This shows that the substring method works the same for the String class as it does for the StringBuilder class.

More methods of the StringBuilder class

Methods	Description
`insert(index, data)`	Inserts a string for the specified primitive type or object at the specified index pushing the rest of the string back.
`replace(startIndex, endIndex, String)`	Replaces the characters from the start index to, but not including, the end index with the specified string.
`delete(startIndex, endIndex)`	Removes the substring from the start index to, but not including, the end index. This moves the rest of the string forward.
`deleteCharAt(index)`	Removes the character at the specified index.
`setCharAt(index, character)`	Replaces the character at the specified index with the specified character.
`charAt(index)`	Returns a char value for the character at the specified index.
`substring(index)`	Returns a String object for the characters starting at the specified index to the end of the string.
`substring(startIndex, endIndex)`	Returns a String object for the characters from the start index to, but not including, the end index.
`toString()`	Returns a String object for the string that's stored in the StringBuilder object.

Code that adds dashes to a credit card number

```
ccNumber.insert(4, "-");
ccNumber.insert(9, "-");
ccNumber.insert(14, "-");
```

Code that removes dashes from a credit card number

```
for(int i = 0; i < ccNumber.length(); i++) {
    if (ccNumber.charAt(i) == '-') {
        ccNumber.deleteCharAt(i);
        i--;
    }
}
```

Code that parses a credit card number

```
String part1 = ccNumber.substring(0,4);
String part2 = ccNumber.substring(4,8);
String part3 = ccNumber.substring(8, 12);
String part4 = ccNumber.substring(12);
```

Description

- The StringBuilder class provides many of the same methods as the String class. In addition, it contains some methods that make it easier to modify strings.

Figure 9-6 How to modify a StringBuilder object

The Product Lister application

This chapter finishes by presenting a Product Lister application that allows the user to print a list of one or more products. This application shows some of the skills presented in this chapter within the context of an application. In addition, this application uses a StringUtil class that contains a static method that makes it easier to work with strings.

The user interface

Figure 9-7 begins by showing the console for this application. Here, the user starts by entering the product code for the first product and "y" to continue entering product codes. Then, the user enters a second product code and "n" to stop entering product codes. At this point, the application displays the list of products.

The list shown here consists of three columns. The top of the list is a header row that displays the names of the columns. The bottom of the list displays the code, description, and price for each product in the list.

The StringUtil class

This figure also shows the StringUtil class. This class contains a single static method, the pad method. You can use this method to add spaces to the end of the string until it is a specified length. This is known as *padding* a string.

The pad method specifies two parameters. The first parameter is the String object that you want to pad. The second is the length that you want the String to be.

Within the method, an if/else statement begins by checking whether the length of the String parameter is less than the length parameter. If so, this code adds spaces to the string until it's the specified length and returns that string. Otherwise, this code truncates the string and returns it. Either way, the String object that's returned has a length that's equal to the length parameter.

Within the if clause, the first statement creates a StringBuilder object that starts with the String parameter. To do that, this code passes the String parameter to the constructor of the StringBuilder class. Then, this code uses a while loop to append spaces to the StringBuilder object until the length of this object is equal to the length parameter. Finally, it converts the StringBuilder object to a String object and returns that object.

The console

```
Welcome to the Product Lister

Enter product code: java
Another product? (y/n): y

Enter product code: mysql
Another product? (y/n): n

Code      Description                      Price
========= ================================ =========
java      Murach's Java Programming        $57.50
mysql     Murach's MySQL                   $54.50
```

The StringUtil class

```
package murach.ui;

public class StringUtil {

    public static String pad(String s, int length) {
        if (s.length() < length) {
            // append spaces until the string is the specified length
            StringBuilder sb = new StringBuilder(s);
            while (sb.length() < length) {
                sb.append(" ");
            }
            return sb.toString();
        } else {
            // truncate the string to the specified length
            return s.substring(0, length);
        }
    }
}
```

The Main class

Part 2 of figure 9-7 shows the code for the Main class of the Product Lister application. This code begins by declaring three constants that specify the width in characters for the code, description, and price columns.

After declaring the constants, this code creates a StringBuilder object for the list. Then, it appends the heading row to this string. To do that, it uses the static pad method of the StringUtil class to append spaces to the column so it's the correct width.

After setting up the header row, this code uses a while loop to allow the user to enter product codes. Within this loop, the first statement gets the product code from the user. To do that, it uses the static getString method of the Console class described in the previous chapter. Then, it gets a Product object for the specified code. To do that, it uses the static getProduct method of the ProductDB class.

After getting the Product object for the specified code, this code appends a row for the product to the list. To do that, it uses the static pad method of the StringUtil class.

The three constants defined at the beginning of this method are used in three places. First, they are used to specify the width of the three columns in the heading row. Second, they are used to specify the width of the three columns that create a separator between the heading row and the rest of the rows. Third, they are used to specify the width of the three columns for the data for each product.

As a result, if you want to change the width of a column, you only need to change the value of the constant. For example, if you want to make the description column 50 characters wide, you just need to change the value of the constant named DESC_WIDTH to 50.

The Main class

```
package murach.ui;

import murach.db.ProductDB;
import murach.business.Product;

public class Main {

    public static void main(String args[]) {
        System.out.println("Welcome to the Product Lister\n");

        final int CODE_WIDTH = 10;
        final int DESC_WIDTH = 34;
        final int PRICE_WIDTH = 10;

        // set up display string
        StringBuilder list = new StringBuilder();
        list.append(StringUtil.pad("Code", CODE_WIDTH));
        list.append(StringUtil.pad("Description", DESC_WIDTH));
        list.append(StringUtil.pad("Price", PRICE_WIDTH));
        list.append("\n");

        list.append(
            StringUtil.pad("=========", CODE_WIDTH));
        list.append(
            StringUtil.pad("=================================", DESC_WIDTH));
        list.append(
            StringUtil.pad("=========", PRICE_WIDTH));
        list.append("\n");

        // perform 1 or more calculations
        String choice = "y";
        while (choice.equalsIgnoreCase("y")) {
            // get the input from the user
            String productCode = Console.getString("Enter product code: ");

            Product product = ProductDB.getProduct(productCode);

            list.append(
                StringUtil.pad(product.getCode(), CODE_WIDTH));
            list.append(
                StringUtil.pad(product.getDescription(), DESC_WIDTH));
            list.append(
                StringUtil.pad(product.getPriceFormatted(), PRICE_WIDTH));
            list.append("\n");

            // see if the user wants to continue
            choice = Console.getString("Another product? (y/n): ");
            System.out.println();
        }
        System.out.println(list);
    }
}
```

Perspective

Now that you've finished this chapter, you should be able to use the String and StringBuilder classes to work with strings. These skills are fundamental to developing Java applications. Keep in mind that this chapter has only covered some of the most useful methods of these classes. As a result, if you want to learn about the other methods of these classes, you can look them up in the documentation for the Java API.

Summary

- You can use methods of the String class to compare all or part of a string, locate a string within another string, and return parts of a string.
- When working with strings, you often need to use an *index* to refer to the characters that make up the string. In a string, the first character has an index of 0, the second character has an index of 1, and so on.
- String objects are *immutable*. As a result, you can't add, delete, or modify individual characters in a string.
- StringBuilder objects are *mutable*. As a result, you can use the methods of the StringBuilder class to append, insert, delete, or replace characters in a StringBuilder object.
- StringBuilder objects are more efficient than String objects, especially if you need to modify the string that you're working with.

Exercise 9-1 Parse a name

In this exercise, you'll write an application that parses full names into first and last name or first, middle, and last name, depending on whether the user enters a string consisting of two or three words. The output for the application should look something like this:

```
Enter a name: Joel Murach

First name:  Joel
Last name:   Murach
```

Or this:

```
Enter a name: Joel Ray Murach

First name:  Joel
Middle name: Ray
Last name:   Murach
```

1. Open the project named ch9_ex1_NameParser that's in the ex_starts folder. Then, review the code in the NameParserApp class.
2. Add code that separates the name into two or three strings depending on whether the user entered a name with two words or three.
3. Display each word of the name on a separate line.
4. If the user enters fewer than two words or more than three words, display an error message.
5. Make sure the application works even if the user enters one or more spaces before or after the name.
6. Test the application to make sure it works correctly.

Exercise 9-2 Improve the Future Value application

In this exercise, you'll improve the Future Value application by allowing the user to enter dollar signs ($) and percent signs (%) when they enter numbers for monetary and percent values like this:

```
Welcome to the Future Value Calculator

Enter monthly investment:    $100
Enter yearly interest rate: 3%
Enter number of years:       3
Future value:                $3,771.46
```

1. Open the project named ch9_ex2_FutureValue that's in the ex_starts folder. Then, open the Main and Console classes and review the code.
2. Open the Console class and modify the getDouble method so it removes any dollar ($) or percent (%) signs from the string that's entered by the user.
3. Run the application and test it to make sure it works correctly. You should be able to enter dollar signs and percent signs.

10

How to work with arrays

In this chapter, you'll learn how to work with arrays, which are important in many types of Java applications. For example, you can use a sales array to hold the sales amounts for each of the 12 months of the year. Then, you can use that array to perform calculations on those amounts. In this chapter, you'll learn the basic concepts and techniques for working with arrays.

Essential skills for working with arrays 254

How to create an array 254

How to assign values to the elements of an array 256

How to use for loops with arrays 258

How to use enhanced for loops with arrays 260

How to work with two-dimensional arrays 262

How to use the Arrays class 264

How to fill an array 264

How to sort an array 264

How to search an array 264

How to create a reference to an array 264

How to copy an array 266

How to compare two arrays 266

The Month Selector application 268

The user interface 268

The Main class 268

Perspective 270

Essential skills for working with arrays

This chapter begins by showing how to use the Java language to create and work with arrays.

How to create an array

An *array* is an object that contains one or more items called *elements*. Each element within an array can be a primitive type such as an int value or a reference type such as a String object or a Product object. As you'll see later in this chapter, an array itself is a reference type.

In Java, all of the elements in an array must be of the same type. As a result, an array of the int type can only contain int values, and an array of the String type can only contain String objects. However, an array can contain elements that are derived from the array's base type. As a result, if you declare an array of the Product type, the array can contain any object that inherits the Product class. You'll learn more about how this works in the next chapter.

The *length* (or *size*) of an array indicates the number of elements it contains. In Java, arrays have a fixed length. As a result, once you create an array, you can't change its length. If you need to change the length of an array, you should consider using a collection instead of an array. For example, you may want to use the ArrayList class described in chapter 14 instead of an array. Then, the collection automatically adjusts its length to fit the array.

Figure 10-1 shows several ways to create an array. To start, you must declare a variable that refers to the array object. Then, you create an array object and assign it to the variable. To create a new array object, you code the new keyword, followed by the data type, followed a pair of brackets. Within the brackets, you code the length of the array.

You can use separate statements to declare the array variable and create the array object as shown in the first example. Or, you can declare the variable and instantiate the array object in a single statement as shown in the second example. Both of these examples create an array that holds four double values.

When you declare the array variable, you use an empty set of brackets to indicate that the variable is an array. Most programmers prefer to code the empty brackets after the data type to indicate that the array is an array of a particular type. However, if you prefer, you can code these brackets after the variable name as shown in the third example.

The fourth and fifth examples create arrays of objects. More specifically, the fourth example creates an array of three String objects, and the fifth example creates an array of five Product objects.

If you know the size of an array at compile time, you can code the length of the array as a literal value as shown in the first five examples. Or, you can code the length as a constant as shown in the sixth example. However, if you don't know the size of the array until runtime, you can use a variable to specify its size as shown in the seventh example.

The syntax for declaring and instantiating an array

With two statements

```
type[] arrayName;
arrayName = new type[length];
```

With one statement

```
type[] arrayName = new type[length];
```

With one statement and brackets after the variable name

```
type arrayName[] = new type[length];
```

An example that declares and instantiates an array of double values

With two statements

```
double[] prices;
prices = new double[4];
```

With one statement

```
double[] prices = new double[4];
```

With one statement and brackets after the variable name

```
double prices[] = new double[4];
```

Other examples

An array of String objects

```
String[] titles = new String[3];
```

An array of Product objects

```
Product[] products = new Product[5];
```

Code that uses a constant to specify the array length

```
final int TITLE_COUNT = 100;
String[] titles = new String[TITLE_COUNT];
```

Code that uses a variable to specify the array length

```
System.out.print("Enter number of titles: ");
int titleCount = Integer.parseInt(sc.nextLine());
String[] titles = new String[titleCount];
```

Description

- An *array* can store multiple primitive types such as int values or multiple reference types such as String objects. An *element* is one of the items in an array.
- To create an array, you must declare a variable of the correct type and instantiate an array object that the variable refers to. You can declare and instantiate the array in separate statements, or you can combine the declaration and instantiation into a single statement.
- To declare an array variable, you code a set of empty brackets after the type or the variable name.
- To instantiate an array, you use the new keyword and specify the *length*, or *size*, of the array in brackets following the array type.
- When you instantiate an array of primitive types, numeric types are set to zeros and boolean types to false. When you create an array of reference types, they are set to nulls.

Figure 10-1 How to create an array

How to assign values to the elements of an array

Figure 10-2 shows how to assign values to the elements of an array. As the syntax at the top of this figure shows, you refer to an element in an array by coding the array name followed by an *index* in brackets. The index must be an int value starting at 0 and ending at one less than the size of the array. In other words, 0 refers to the first element in the array, 1 refers to the second element, 2 refers to the third element, and so on.

The first example in this figure shows how to assign values to the elements in an array by coding one statement per element. The first example creates an array of 4 double values. Then, it assigns a literal value to each element. In this example, the first element holds the value 14.95, the second holds 12.95, the third holds 11.95, and the fourth holds 9.95.

If you specify an index that's outside of the range of the array, Java throws an ArrayIndexOutOfBoundsException. For instance, the commented out line at the end of the first example refers to the element with index number 4. Since this array only has four elements, this statement throws this exception. Although you can catch this exception, it's better to write your code so it avoids using indexes that are out of bounds. To do that, you can check the length of the array as shown in the next figure.

The second and third examples work similarly to the first example. However, the second example creates an array that holds 3 String objects and initializes those strings. Similarly, the third example creates an array that holds 2 Product objects and initializes those objects. To do that, this code uses the getProduct method of the ProductDB class to return a Product object that corresponds with the specified product code.

After the third example, this figure shows how to create an array and assign values to the elements of the array in one statement. Here, you declare the array variable as usual. Then, you use the special assignment syntax to assign the initial values. With this syntax, you simply list the values you want assigned to the array within braces following the equals sign. Then, the number of values you list within the braces determines the size of the array that's created. The last three examples show how to use this special syntax to create the same arrays that were created by the first three examples in this figure.

The syntax for referring to an element of an array

```
arrayName[index]
```

Examples that assign values by accessing each element

Code that assigns values to an array of double types

```
double[] prices = new double[4];
prices[0] = 14.95;
prices[1] = 12.95;
prices[2] = 11.95;
prices[3] = 9.95;
//prices[4] = 8.95;     // this would throw ArrayIndexOutOfBoundsException
```

Code that assigns values to an array of String types

```
String[] names = new String[3];
names[0] = "Ted Lewis";
names[1] = "Sue Jones";
names[2] = "Ray Thomas";
```

Code that assigns objects to an array of Product objects

```
Product[] products = new Product[2];
products[0] = ProductDB.getProduct("java");
products[1] = ProductDB.getProduct("jsp");
```

The syntax for creating an array and assigning values in one statement

```
type[] arrayName = {value1, value2, value3, ...};
```

Examples that create an array and assign values in one statement

```
double[] prices = {14.95, 12.95, 11.95, 9.95};
String[] names = {"Ted Lewis", "Sue Jones", "Ray Thomas"};
Product[] products = {
        ProductDB.getProduct("java"),
        ProductDB.getProduct("jsp")
};
```

Description

- To refer to the elements in an array, you use an *index* that ranges from zero (the first element in the array) to one less than the number of elements in the array.
- If you specify an index that's less than zero or greater than the upper bound of the array, Java throws an ArrayIndexOutOfBoundsException.
- You can instantiate an array and provide initial values in a single statement by listing the values in braces. The number of values you provide determines the size of the array.

Figure 10-2 How to assign values to the elements of an array

How to use for loops with arrays

For loops are commonly used to process the elements in an array one at a time by incrementing an index variable. Figure 10-3 shows how to process an array using a for loop.

The syntax at the top of this figure shows how to use the length field to return the length of an array. Since length is a field rather than a method, you don't need to include parentheses after it. The length field returns an int value that represents the length of the array. Typically, you use this value to stop a for loop after it gets the last element but before the loop attempts to use an index that's out of bounds.

The first example in this figure shows how to create an array of 10 int values and fill it with the numbers 0 through 9. Here, the loop uses an int variable named i to index the array and to assign a value to each element in the array. As a result, each element stores a value that's equal to its index.

The second example shows how you can use a for loop to print the contents of an array to the console. Here, the first statement creates an array of double values named prices and initializes its values. Then, the for loop cycles through each element of the array. Within the loop, a statement prints the value of the current element to the console.

The third example shows how you can use a for loop to calculate the average of the prices array. Here, the first statement creates an array of double values named prices and initializes its values. Then, the second statement declares a double variable named sum to store the sum total of the values. Next, the for loop cycles through each element of the array and adds the value of each element to a variable named sum. When the for loop finishes, the sum variable contains the total of all the prices in the array. Then, the average is calculated by dividing the sum by the number of elements in the array.

The syntax for getting the length of an array

```
arrayName.length
```

Code that puts the numbers 0 through 9 in an array

```
int[] values = new int[10];
for (int i = 0; i < values.length; i++) {
   values[i] = i;
}
```

Code that prints an array of prices to the console

```
double[] prices = {14.95, 12.95, 11.95, 9.95};
for (int i = 0; i < prices.length; i++) {
   System.out.println(prices[i]);
}
```

The console output

```
14.95
12.95
11.95
9.95
```

Code that computes the average of the array of prices

```
double[] prices = {14.95, 12.95, 11.95, 9.95};
double sum = 0.0;
for (int i = 0; i < prices.length; i++) {
   sum += prices[i];
}
double average = sum/prices.length;
```

Description

- You can use for loops to process each element in an array.
- You can use the length field of an array to determine the number of elements in the array.

Figure 10-3 How to use for loops with arrays

How to use enhanced for loops with arrays

Figure 10-4 shows how to use the *enhanced for loop* that was introduced with Java 5. Since this loop was designed to make it easy to process each element in an array or a collection, it's sometimes called a *foreach loop*.

Unlike a regular for loop, the enhanced for loop doesn't use separate expressions to initialize, test, and increment a counter variable. Instead, it declares a variable that's used to refer to each element of the array. Within the loop, you can use this variable to access each element of the array.

The first example in this figure shows how you can use an enhanced for loop to print the elements of an array of doubles. This example performs the same function as the second example in figure 10-3. However, in the enhanced for loop version, a variable named price is used to access each element in the prices array. Then, the statement within the for loop simply prints the price variable to the console. Since the enhanced for loop gets the current element automatically, you don't need to use an index to get each element of the array, and you don't need to use the length field of the array to keep the index within the bounds of the array.

The second example shows how to use an enhanced for loop to calculate the average value in the prices array. This example performs the same function as the third example in figure 10-3. Again, since the enhanced for loop automatically indexes the array, no indexing is required.

The syntax of the enhanced for loop

```
for (type variableName : arrayName) {
    statements
}
```

Code that prints an array of prices to the console

```
double[] prices = {14.95, 12.95, 11.95, 9.95};
for (double price : prices) {
   System.out.println(price);
}
```

The console output

```
14.95
12.95
11.95
9.95
```

Code that computes the average of the array of prices

```
double[] prices = {14.95, 12.95, 11.95, 9.95};
double sum = 0.0;
for (double price : prices) {
   sum += price;
}
double average = sum / prices.length;
```

Description

- Java 5 introduced the *enhanced for loop*. This loop simplifies the code required to loop through arrays. The enhanced for loop is sometimes called a *foreach loop* because it lets you process each element of an array.
- Within the parentheses of an enhanced for loop, you declare a variable with the same type as the array followed by a colon and the name of the array.
- With each iteration of the loop, the variable that's declared by the for loop is assigned the value of the next element in the array.
- You can also use enhanced for loops to work with collections as described in chapter 14.

Figure 10-4 How to use enhanced for loops with arrays

How to work with two-dimensional arrays

So far, this chapter has shown how to work with an array that uses one index to store a single set of elements. This is known as a *one-dimensional array*, and you can think of it as a column of values.

Now, figure 10-5 shows how to work with an array that uses two indexes to store data. This is known as a *two-dimensional array*, and you can think of it as a table made up of rows and columns. Here, each element in the array is at the intersection of a row and column.

Java implements a two-dimensional array as an *array of arrays* where each element of the first array is itself an array. This figure shows how to create and use a two-dimensional array. To start, you specify two sets of empty brackets following the array type. Then, you specify the number of rows and columns when you instantiate the array. Thus, the code example shown here declares and instantiates an array with three rows and two columns.

To refer to an element in a two-dimensional array, you specify two index values in separate sets of brackets. The first value refers to the row index, and the second value refers to the column index. Thus, numbers[1][0] refers to row 2, column 1 of the numbers array. Remember, 0 refers to the first element of an array, 1 refers to the second element, and so on.

You can also create a two-dimensional array and assign values to its elements using a single statement. To do that, you can use the same shorthand notation that's available for one-dimensional arrays. However, you code each element of the array as a separate array as shown in this figure. Here, the numbers array is assigned three elements, each of which is a two-element array with the values {1, 2}, {3, 4}, and {5, 6}.

The last example uses two enhanced for loops to cycle through the elements of a two-dimensional array. To do that, it nests one enhanced for loop within the other. Here, the outer for loop cycles through the rows of the array to get each row. However, each row is an array that contains multiple columns. As a result, the inner for loop cycles through each column of the current row. This gets the element from the current column of the current row.

The arrays in this figure are the most common type of two-dimensional array, a *rectangular array*. In this type of array, each row has the same number of columns. However, it's possible to create a *jagged array*. In this type of array, the rows may contain unequal numbers of columns. That's possible because each row of a two-dimensional array is a separate one-dimensional array, and Java doesn't require that each of these arrays be the same size.

If necessary, you can create a three-dimensional array to represent things such as object positions within 3D space on an x, y, and z axis. In theory, it's possible use Java to create arrays that have more than three dimensions. However, using more than three dimensions is very rare because humans don't visualize more than three dimensions very well.

How to create a rectangular array

The syntax for creating a rectangular array

```
type[][] arrayName = new type[rowCount][columnCount];
```

A statement that creates a 3x2 array

```
int[][] numbersTable = new int[3][2];
```

How to assign values to a rectangular array

The syntax for referring to an element of a rectangular array

```
arrayName[rowIndex][columnIndex]
```

The indexes for a 3x2 array

```
[0][0]              [0][1]
[1][0]              [1][1]
[2][0]              [2][1]
```

Code that assigns values to the array

```
numbersTable[0][0] = 1;
numbersTable[0][1] = 2;
numbersTable[1][0] = 3;
numbersTable[1][1] = 4;
numbersTable[2][0] = 5;
numbersTable[2][1] = 6;
```

Code that creates a 3x2 array and initializes it in one statement

```
int[][]numbersTable = { {1,2} {3,4} {5,6} };
```

How to use nested for loops to process a rectangular array

Code that processes a rectangular array with nested for loops

```
int[][] numbersTable = { {1,2}, {3,4}, {5,6} };
for (int[] row : numbersTable) {
    for (int column : row) {
        System.out.print(column + "  ");
    }
    System.out.print("\n");
}
```

The console output

```
1  2
3  4
5  6
```

Description

- *Two-dimensional arrays* use two indexes and allow data to be stored in a table that consists of rows and columns. This can also be thought of as an *array of arrays* where each row is a separate array of columns.
- Most two-dimensional arrays are *rectangular arrays* where each row has the same number of columns. However, it's also possible to create *jagged arrays* where each row may have a different number of columns.
- If necessary, you can extend this two-dimensional syntax to work with arrays that have more than two dimensions.

Figure 10-5 How to work with rectangular arrays

How to use the Arrays class

Now that you know the basic language skills for creating and using arrays, you're ready to learn how to use the Arrays class of the java.util package to perform some additional operations on arrays. This class contains static methods that you can use to fill, sort, search, copy, and compare arrays. Figure 10-6 presents three of these methods, and figure 10-7 presents two more.

When you work with these methods, you can supply any type of one-dimensional array as the array argument. Similarly, you can supply a primitive value or an object as the value argument. However, you must make sure that the value or object type matches the array type.

How to fill an array

The first example shows how to use the fill method to assign a value to all of the elements in an array. Here, the first statement creates an array of 5 int values. By default, this statement automatically initializes each element to 0. Then, the second statement uses the fill method of the Arrays class to set all five elements to a value of 1.

How to sort an array

The second example shows how to use the sort method to sort an array of 10 int values. Here, the first statement creates an unsorted array of int values from 0 to 9. Then, the second statement uses the sort method to sort these values. After that, this code uses an enhanced for loop to print the contents of the array to the console. This shows that the sort method successfully sorted the array.

How to search an array

The third example shows how to use the binarySearch method. This method searches for an element with a specific value and returns its index. However, before you can use this method, you must use the sort method to sort the array. In this example, the first statement creates an array of unsorted strings. Then, the second statement uses the sort method to sort this array. For strings, this sorts the array alphabetically from A to Z. In other words, it sorts the strings of this array like this: "java", "jsp", and "mysql". As a result, the binarySearch method that's called in the third statement returns a value of 2, which means that the string is the third element of the array.

How to create a reference to an array

Like a string, an array is a *reference type*. As a result, it works a little differently than primitive types. To start, when you use the assignment operator (=) to assign a variable to an array, the variable doesn't store a copy of the array. Instead, it *refers* to the array object. As a result, it's possible for multiple variables to refer to the same array object.

The Arrays class

```
java.util.Arrays
```

Some static methods of the Arrays class

Method	Description
`fill(array, value)`	Fills all elements of the specified array with the specified value.
`sort(array)`	Sorts the elements of an array into ascending order.
`binarySearch(array, value)`	Returns an int value for the index of the specified value in the specified array. Returns -1 if the specified value is not found in the array. For this method to work correctly, the array must first be sorted by the sort method.

How to fill an array

```
int[] quantities = new int[5];        // all elements are set to 0
Arrays.fill(quantities, 1);           // all elements are set to 1
```

How to sort an array

```
int[] numbers = {2,6,4,1,8,5,9,3,7,0};
Arrays.sort(numbers);
for (int number : numbers) {
    System.out.print(number + " ");
}
```

The console output

```
0 1 2 3 4 5 6 7 8 9
```

How to search an array

```
String[] productCodes = {"mysql", "jsp", "java"};
Arrays.sort(productCodes);
int index = Arrays.binarySearch(productCodes, "mysql");  // sets index to 2
```

Description

- All of these methods accept arrays of primitive data types and arrays of objects for the array argument, and they all accept primitive types and objects for the value argument.
- For the sort method to work correctly with an array of objects created from a user-defined class, such as the Product class, the class must implement the Comparable interface. For more information about implementing interfaces, see chapter 12.

Figure 10-6 How to fill, compare, sort, and search arrays

The first example in figure 10-7 shows how this works. Here, the code creates two variables that refer to the same array. More specifically, the grades variable and the percentages variable both refer to the same array. As a result, any change to the grades variable is reflected by the percentages variable and vice versa. In this example, for instance, the third statement sets percentages[1] to 70.2. As a result, this change is reflected by grades[1]. This is shown by the statement that prints grades[1]. Since the percentages and grades variables both refer to the same array, this statement prints the value 70.2.

How to copy an array

If you want a copy of an array instead of another reference to the array, you can use the copyOf method to copy all of the elements of one array into another array. The easiest way to do that is to use the static copyOf method as shown in the second example. Then, each array variable points to its own copy of the array, and any changes that are made to one array aren't reflected in the other arrays.

In this example, the length argument is set to the length of the grades array. As a result, this example copies all of the elements of the grades array into the percentages array. However, if you specified a larger number for the length argument, the percentages array would be padded with extra elements with a default value of zero. Or, if you specified a smaller number for the length argument, the extra elements in the percentages array would be truncated.

The copyOf method was introduced with Java 6. As a result it doesn't work with earlier versions of Java. If you need to use an earlier version of Java, you can create a copy of an array by using the arraycopy method of the System class. This method is a little more difficult to use than the copyOf method of the Arrays class. However, you should be able to figure out how to use it if you refer to the documentation for the Java API.

When you use the copyOf method with an array of reference types, you need to know that it produces a *shallow copy*, not a *deep copy*. That means that it creates a new array with copies of the references to the objects in the original array. As a result, if you change a value in one of the objects from one array, the object in the other array also changes.

How to compare two arrays

If you want to check whether two variables refer to the same array object, you can use the equality operator (==) as shown in the third example. However, this only checks whether the two variables refer to the same array object, not whether the two arrays store the same number of elements with the same values for each element. To do that, you need to use the equals method of the Arrays class as shown in the fourth example. When you use this method with an array of reference types, you may need to implement the equals method for the reference type as described in the next chapter.

More static methods of the Arrays class

Method	Description
`copyOf(array, length)`	Copies the specified array, truncating or padding with default values as necessary so the copy has the specified length.
`equals(array1, array2)`	Returns a boolean true value if both arrays are of the same type and all of the elements within the arrays are equal to each other.

How to create a reference to an array

```
double[] grades = {92.3, 88.0, 95.2, 90.5};
double[] percentages = grades;
percentages[1] = 70.2;                          // changes grades[1] too
System.out.println("grades[1]=" + grades[1]);   // prints 70.2
```

How to create a shallow copy of an array (Java 6 or later)

```
double[] grades = {92.3, 88.0, 95.2, 90.5};
double[] percentages = Arrays.copyOf(grades, grades.length);
percentages[1] = 70.2;                          // doesn't change grades[1]
System.out.println("grades[1]=" + grades[1]);   // prints 88.0
```

How to determine if two variables refer to the same array

```
if (grades == percentages) {
    System.out.println("Both variables refer to the same array.");
}
else {
    System.out.println("Each variable refers to a different array.");
    System.out.println("However, these arrays may contain the same data.");
}
```

How to determine if two variables contain the same data

```
if (Arrays.equals(grades, percentages)) {
    System.out.println("Both variables refer to the same data.");
}
else {
    System.out.println("Both variables do not refer to the same data.");
}
```

Description

- Like a string, an array is a *reference type*.
- To create a *reference* to an existing array, you can use the assignment operator (=) to assign a variable that points to an existing array to another variable. Then, both variables point to the same array.
- To check if two array variables refer to the same array, you can use the equality operator (==).
- The copyOf method was introduced with Java 6. As a result, it only works with Java 6 and later. Prior to Java 6, you can use the arraycopy method of the System class.
- When you copy an array, the new array must be the same type as the source array.

Figure 10-7 How to refer to and copy arrays

The Month Selector application

This chapter finishes by presenting a Month Selector application that allows the user to select the text for a month by entering its number. This application shows some of the skills presented in this chapter within the context of an application.

The user interface

Figure 10-8 begins by showing the console for this application. Here, the user starts by entering 1 to select January and "y" to continue. Then, the user enters 12 to select December and "n" to exit the application.

The Main class

This figure also shows the code for the Main class of the Month Selector application. This code begins by declaring an array of 12 String objects that contains the names of the 12 months.

After declaring the array, this code uses a while loop to allow the user to select one or more months. Within this loop, the first statement gets the number of the month from the user. To do that, it uses the static getInt method of the Console class described in chapter 8.

After getting the number of the month, this code uses an if statement to check whether this number is a valid number for a month. To do that, this code checks whether this number is less than 1 or greater than the length of the array, which is 12. If so, this code uses the Console class to display an error message to the console, and it uses a continue statement to jump to the top of the while loop.

If the number of the month is valid, this code continues by subtracting 1 from the month number that was entered by the user. That way, this code can use the new int value as the index to access the correct String object from the array of month names. As you should know by now, this is necessary because the index for an array starts with 0, not 1. As a result, the indexes for this array range from 0 to 11, not from 1 to 12.

The console

```
Welcome to the Month Selector

Enter month number: 1
You selected:       January

Continue? (y/n): y

Enter month number: 12
You selected:       December

Continue? (y/n): n
```

The Main class

```
package murach.ui;

public class Main {

    public static void main(String[] args) {
        System.out.println("Welcome to the Month Selector\n");

        String[] monthName = {"January", "February", "March", "April", "May",
            "June", "July", "August", "September", "October", "November",
            "December"};

        // select 1 or more months
        String choice = "y";
        while (choice.equalsIgnoreCase("y")) {
            // get the input from the user
            int monthNumber = Console.getInt("Enter month number: ");

            // validate input
            if (monthNumber < 1 || monthNumber > monthName.length) {
                Console.displayLine("Invalid month number. Try again.");
                continue;
            }

            // display output
            int monthIndex = monthNumber - 1;
            Console.displayLine("You selected:       "
                    + monthName[monthIndex] + "\n");

            // check if the user wants to continue
            choice = Console.getString("Continue? (y/n): ");
            System.out.println();
        }
    }
}
```

Perspective

Now that you've finished this chapter, you should know how to work with one-dimensional and two-dimensional arrays. Although arrays are a core part of Java, they may not always provide the functionality you need. In many cases, it's preferable to use a more advanced data structure called a collection. For example, instead of using an array as shown in this chapter, you may want to use an ArrayList object as shown in chapter 14.

Summary

- An *array* is a special type of object that can store multiple *elements* of the same type.
- When working with arrays, you can use an *index* to identify any element in the array. An index of 0 refers to the first element, 1 refers to the second element, and so on.
- The *length* (or *size*) of an array is the number of elements that are in the array.
- For loops are often used to process arrays. Java 5 introduced a new type of for loop, called an *enhanced for loop* or a *foreach loop*, that lets you process each element of an array without using indexes.
- A *one-dimensional array* provides for a single column of elements. In contrast, a *two-dimensional array*, or an *array of arrays*, provides for a table of elements that has rows and columns.
- A two-dimensional array can be *rectangular,* where each row has the same number of columns, or *jagged,* where each row may have a different number of columns.
- You can use the Arrays class to fill, sort, search, copy, and compare arrays.
- Like a string, an array is a *reference type*. As a result, you should use the copy method of the Arrays class if you want to copy the data of an array, and you should use the equals method of the Arrays object if you want to check whether two arrays store the same data.

Exercise 10-1 Use a one-dimensional array

In this exercise, you can get some practice using one-dimensional arrays.

1. Open the project named ch10_ex1_ArrayTest in the ex_starts directory. Then, open the Main class.
2. Create a one-dimensional array of 99 double values. Then, use a for loop to add a random number from 0 to 100 to each element in the array. To do that, you can call the random method of the Math class and multiply it by 100 like this:

```
Math.random() * 100
```

3. Use an enhanced for loop to sum the values in the array. Then, calculate the average value and print that value to the console like this:

```
Average: 50.9526671843517
```

4. Use the sort method of the Arrays class to sort the values in the array, and print the median value (the 50th value) to the console like this:

```
Median:  52.18369291650803
```

5. Print the 9th value of the array to the console and every 9th value after that like this:

```
Position: 9   8.927702403161032
Position: 18   14.053128749806076
...
Position: 99   22.471670293184822
```

Exercise 10-2 Use a two-dimensional array

This exercise guides you through the process of adding a two-dimensional, rectangular array to the Future Value application. This array stores the values for up to ten of the calculations. When the application ends, it prints a summary of those calculations to the console like this:

```
Future Value Calculations

Inv/Mo. Rate    Years   Future Value
$100.00 8.0%    10      $18,416.57
$125.00 8.0%    10      $23,020.71
$150.00 8.0%    10      $27,624.85
```

1. Open the project named ch10_ex2_FutureValue in the ex_starts directory. Then, review the code and run the application to make sure it works correctly.
2. Declare variables at the beginning of the main method for a row counter and a rectangular array of strings that provides for 10 rows and 4 columns.
3. After the code that displays the results for each calculation, add code that formats all values for the calculation and converts them to strings. Then, store these String values in the next row of the array. (Hint: You can use the toString method of the Integer class to convert the years value to a string.)
4. Add code to display the elements on the console when the user exits the application. The output should be formatted as shown above and should only include the rows that contain data.
5. Test the application by making up to 10 future value calculations.

Section 3

Object-oriented programming skills

In the first section of this book, you learned how to create your own classes and use them to create a well-structured, object-oriented application. That's a great start to object-oriented programming. Now, the chapters in this section teach the rest of the skills for object-oriented programming that you should know. Chapter 11 shows you how to use inheritance, an important object-oriented skill. Chapter 12 shows you how to use interfaces, another important object-oriented skill. And chapter 13 shows several more skills including how to work with inner classes, how to work with enumerations, and how to add API documentation to the classes that you create.

Because each of the chapters in this section builds on the previous chapters, we recommend reading these chapters in sequence. In addition, we recommend reading all of the chapters in this section before going on to section 4 or 5. That's because most of the chapters in sections 4 and 5 expect you to understand how inheritance, interfaces, inner classes, and enumerations work.

11

How to work with inheritance

Inheritance is one of the key concepts of object-oriented programming. It lets you create a class that's based on another class. When used correctly, inheritance can reduce code duplication and simplify the overall design of an application.

An introduction to inheritance 276
How inheritance works 276
How the Object class works 278
Basic skills for working with inheritance 280
How to create a superclass 280
How to create a subclass 282
How polymorphism works 284
The Product application 286
The console 286
The Product, Book, and Software classes 288
The ProductDB class 288
The ProductApp class 292
More skills for working with inheritance 294
How to cast objects 294
How to compare objects 296
How to work with the abstract and final keywords 298
How to work with the abstract keyword 298
How to work with the final keyword 300
Perspective 302

An introduction to inheritance

Inheritance allows you to create a class that's based on another class. The next two figures introduce some of the basic concepts of inheritance.

How inheritance works

Figure 11-1 illustrates how inheritance works. When inheritance is used, a *subclass* inherits the fields and methods of a *superclass*. Then, when you create an object from the subclass, that subclass can use these fields and methods. The subclass can also provide its own fields and methods that *extend* the superclass, and it can *override* fields and methods of the superclass by providing new code for them.

The three classes presented in this figure show how this works. Here, the superclass is the Product class. This class has eight public methods. By now, you should already be familiar with the first seven methods. And the next two figures show how to work the eighth method, the toString method.

In this figure, there are two subclasses: the Book and Software classes. These classes inherit the first eight methods from the superclass, the Product class. Then, they both extend the Product class by providing two new methods. In particular, the Book class adds the setAuthor and getAuthor methods, and the Software class adds the setVersion and getVersion methods.

In this book, we'll primarily use superclass to refer to a class that another class inherits and subclass to refer to a class that inherits another class. However, a superclass can also be called a *base* or *parent class*, and a subclass can also be called a *derived* or *child class*.

Business classes for a Product Maintenance application

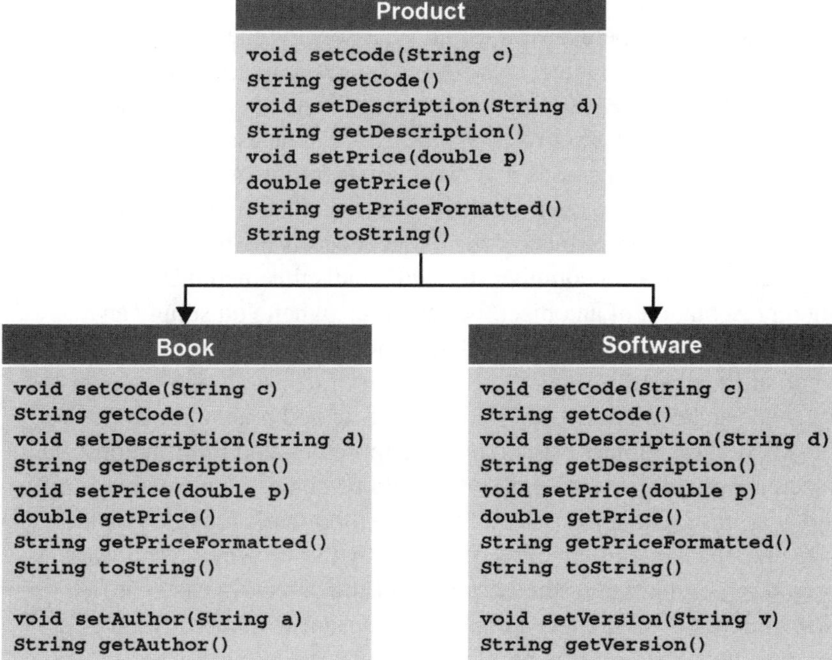

Description

- *Inheritance* lets you create a new class based on an existing class. Then, the new class *inherits* the fields and methods of the existing class.
- A class that inherits from an existing class is called a *derived class, child class,* or *subclass.* A class that another class inherits is called a *base class, parent class,* or *superclass.*
- A subclass can *extend* the superclass by adding new fields and methods to the superclass. It can also *override* a method from the superclass with its own version of the method.

Figure 11-1 How to use inheritance in your applications

How the Object class works

The Object class is the superclass for all Java classes. In other words, every class automatically inherits the Object class. As a result, the methods of the Object class are available from every object. Some of the most common methods of the Object class are summarized in figure 11-2. Since subclasses often override these methods, these methods may work differently from class to class. For example, you'll learn how to override the toString method in the next figure.

Perhaps the most common method of the Object class is the toString method. That's because the Java compiler implicitly calls this method when it needs a string representation of an object. For example, when you supply an object as the argument of the println method, this method implicitly calls the toString method of the object.

When you code a class, it's generally considered a good practice to override the toString method of the Object class to provide more detailed information about the object. If possible, this information should be concise, informative, and easy for a person to read. Otherwise, the toString method that's provided by the Object class returns the name of the class, followed by the @ symbol, followed by a hexadecimal representation of the *hash code* of the object. In case you aren't familiar with hexadecimal, it is a numbering system with a base of 16. To represent the 16 values, Java uses the numbers 0–9 plus the letters a-f.

In contrast, the hashCode method returns an int value that represents the hash code of the object in base 10. If necessary, other code can use the hash code of an object when storing or manipulating the object.

If you need to compare objects of a class for equality, you can override the equals method of the class so it compares two objects to check whether their instance variables are equal as shown later in this chapter. Otherwise, the equals method of the Object class returns true only if the two variables refer to the same object. In other words, it might return false, even if the two variables refer to objects that store the same data.

The Object class

```
java.lang.Object
```

Methods of the Object class

Method	Description
toString()	Returns a String object containing the class name, followed by the @ symbol, followed by a hexadecimal representation of the hash code for this object. If that's not what you want, you can override this method as shown in the next figure.
equals(Object**)**	Returns true if this variable refers to the same object as the specified variable. Otherwise, it returns false, even if both variables refer to objects that contain the same data. If that's not what you want, you can override the equals method as shown later in this chapter.
getClass()	Returns a Class object that represents the type of this object.
clone()	Returns a copy of this object as an Object object. Before you can use this method, the class must implement the Cloneable interface.
hashCode()	Returns an int value that represents the hash code for this object.

A typical value returned by a Product object's toString method

```
murach.business.Product@15db9742
```

A typical value returned by a Product object's hashCode method

```
366712642
```

Description

- The Object class in the java.lang package is the superclass for all classes. In other words, every class inherits the Object class or some other class that ultimately inherits the Object class. As a result, the methods defined by the Object class are available to all classes.
- When coding classes, it's recommended to override the toString method so that it returns a string that's concise, informative, and easy for a person to read.

Figure 11-2 How the Object class works

Basic skills for working with inheritance

Now that you've been introduced to the basic concepts of inheritance, you're ready to learn the details for coding superclasses and subclasses. In addition, you'll learn how to work with one of the major features of inheritance, polymorphism.

How to create a superclass

Figure 11-3 shows how to create a class that can be used as a superclass for one or more subclasses. To do that, you define the fields, constructors, and methods of the class just as you would for any other class.

The table in this figure lists several *access modifiers* you can use to indicate whether members of a superclass are accessible to other classes. By now, you should be familiar with the private and public access modifiers. To review, you use the private keyword for any fields or methods that you want only to be available within the current class. In contrast, you use the public keyword for any fields or methods that you want to be available to all other classes.

Beyond that, you may occasionally want to use the protected keyword to code *protected members*. A protected member is a member that can be accessed within the defining class, any class in the same package, and any class that inherits the defining class, but not by any other class. This lets subclasses access certain parts of the superclass without exposing those parts to other classes. For example, the Product class in this figure includes a static field named count that has protected access. As a result, any subclass of the Product class can access this field, regardless of whether the subclass is in the same package as the Product class.

You can also code a field or method without an access modifier. Then, the classes in the same package are able to access the field or method, but classes in other packages aren't able to do that.

The Product class shown in this figure includes a toString method that overrides the toString method of the java.lang.Object class. This method returns the description for the product, which is a concise and easy-to-read representation of this object. As a result, any subclasses of this class can use this toString method. Or, they can override the toString method to provide their own code for that method.

When you override a method, it's generally considered a good practice to add an *annotation* to the method in the subclass to clearly indicate that the method in the subclass overrides the method in the superclass. An annotation is a standard way to provide information about your code that can be used by the compiler, the JRE, and other software development tools. In this figure, for example, an @Override annotation is coded above the toString method.

Although this annotation isn't required, it's helpful for two reasons. First, the compiler can use this information to make sure that the toString method correctly overrides the toString method in the superclass. If it doesn't, the compiler can generate an error. Second, this makes it easy for other programmers to see that this method overrides a method in the superclass.

Access modifiers

Keyword	Description
`private`	Available within the current class.
`public`	Available to classes in all packages.
`protected`	Available to classes in the same package and to subclasses.
no keyword coded	Available to classes in the same package.

An annotation for overriding a method

```
@Override
// method declaration goes here
```

The code for the Product superclass

```
package murach.business;

import java.text.NumberFormat;

public class Product {

    private String code;
    private String description;
    private double price;
    protected static int count = 0;

    public Product() {
    }

    // get and set accessors for the code, description, and price
    // instance variables

    @Override
    public String toString() {
        return description;
    }

    public static int getCount()  {    // create public access for the
                                       // count variable
        return count;
    }
}
```

Description

- *Access modifiers* specify the accessibility of the members declared by a class.
- *Protected members* are accessible to the current class, to other classes in the same package, and to subclasses.
- An *annotation* is a standard way to provide information about your code. When you override a method, you can add the @Override annotation to the method.

How to create a subclass

Figure 11-4 shows how to create a subclass. To indicate that a class is a subclass, you follow the class name on the class declaration with the extends keyword and the name of the superclass that the subclass inherits. For example, the code for the Book class shown in this figure specifies that the Book class extends the Product class. In other words, the Book class is a subclass of the Product class.

After you declare the subclass, you can extend the functionality of the superclass by adding fields, constructors, and methods. In this figure, for example, the Book class adds a new instance variable and a new constructor. It also adds new setAuthor and getAuthor methods, and it overrides the toString method defined by the Product class.

The constructor for the Book subclass starts by using the super keyword to call the default constructor of the Product class. This initializes the code, description, and price fields. Next, this constructor assigns a default value of an empty string to the author field. Finally, this constructor increments the count field. This constructor can access this field because the superclass declared it with protected access.

To override a method of the superclass, you just code a method with the same signature as the method in the superclass. In this case, the toString method of the Book class overrides the toString method of the Product class. This method accepts no parameters and returns a string. The code within this method uses the super keyword to call the toString method of the Product class. This method returns a string representation of the Product object. Then, this code appends the author's name to this string. Finally, it returns the string. Note that the toString method of the Book class is clearly marked with the @Override annotation.

The syntax for creating subclasses

To declare a subclass

```
public class SubclassName extends SuperClassName{}
```

To call a superclass constructor

```
super(argumentList)
```

To call a superclass method

```
super.methodName(argumentList)
```

The code for a Book subclass

```
package murach.business;

public class Book extends Product {

    private String author;

    public Book() {
        super();  // call constructor of Product superclass
        author = "";
        count++;
    }

    public void setAuthor(String author) {
        this.author = author;
    }

    public String getAuthor() {
        return author;
    }

    @Override
    public String toString() {       // override the toString method
        return super.toString() +    // call method of Product superclass
            " by " + author;
    }
}
```

Description

- You can directly access fields that have public or protected access in the superclass from the subclass.
- You can extend the superclass by adding new fields and methods to the subclass.
- You can override the public and protected methods in the superclass by coding methods in the subclass that have the same signatures as methods in the superclass. However, you can't override private methods in the superclass because they aren't available to the subclass.
- You use the super keyword to call a constructor or method of the superclass. If you call a constructor of the superclass, it must be the first statement in the constructor of the subclass.

Figure 11-4 How to create a subclass

How polymorphism works

Polymorphism is one of the most important features of object-oriented programming and inheritance. As figure 11-5 shows, polymorphism lets you treat objects of different types as if they were the same type by referring to a superclass that's common to both objects. For example, the Book class presented in figure 11-4 inherits the Product class. As a result, you can treat a Book object as if it is a Product object.

One benefit of polymorphism is that you can write generic code that's designed to work with a superclass. Then, you can use that code with instances of any class that's derived from the superclass. For example, suppose you have a method named getDiscountPercent that accepts a Product object as a parameter. Because the Book and Software classes both inherit the Product class, the getDiscountPercent method also works with Book and Software objects.

The examples in this figure show how polymorphism works. To start, the first three examples show the toString methods for the Product, Book, and Software classes. The Book version of the toString method adds the author's name to the end of the string that's returned by the toString method of the Product class. Similarly, the Software version adds the version number to the end of the string that's returned by the toString method of the Product class.

The fourth example shows how polymorphism works with these classes. This code begins by creating an instance of the Book class, assigning it to a variable named b, and assigning values to its instance variables. After that, it creates an instance of the Software class, assigns it to a variable named s, and assigns values to its instance variables.

Next, a variable named p of type Product is declared, and the Book object is assigned to it. Then, the toString method of the Product class is called. When the JRE sees that the p variable refers to a Book object and that this object contains an overridden version of the toString method, it calls the overridden version of this method.

This example finishes by doing the same thing with the Software object. First, this Software object is assigned to the Product variable. Then, the toString method defined by the Product class is called, which causes the toString method of the Software class to be executed.

The key to polymorphism is that the decision on what method to call is based on the inheritance hierarchy at runtime. This can be referred to as *late binding*. At compile time, the compiler recognizes that a method with the specified signature exists.

Three versions of the toString method

The toString method in the Product superclass

```
public String toString() {
    return description;
}
```

The toString method in the Book class

```
public String toString() {
    return super.toString() + " by " + author;
}
```

The toString method in the Software class

```
public String toString() {
    return super.toString() + " " + version;
}
```

Code that uses the overridden methods

```
Book b = new Book();
b.setCode("java");
b.setDescription("Murach's Java Programming");
b.setPrice(57.50);
b.setAuthor("Joel Murach");

Software s = new Software();
s.setCode("netbeans");
s.setDescription("NetBeans");
s.setPrice(0.00);
s.setVersion("8.0");

Product p;
p = b;
System.out.println(p.toString());  // calls toString from the Book class
p = s;
System.out.println(p.toString());  // calls toString from the Software class
```

Description

- *Polymorphism* is a feature of inheritance that lets you treat objects of different subclasses that are derived from the same superclass as if they had the type of the superclass. If, for example, Book is a subclass of Product, you can treat a Book object as if it were a Product object.
- If you access a method of a superclass object and the method is overridden in the subclasses of that class, polymorphism determines which method is executed based on the object's type. For example, if you call the toString method of a Product object, the toString method of the Book class is executed if the object is a Book object.

Figure 11-5 How polymorphism works

The Product application

Now that you've learned how to code superclasses and subclasses, the following topics present a version of the Product application that uses inheritance. This version of the application uses the Book and Software classes that were described in figure 11-4. In addition, it uses a ProductDB class that can return two distinct types of products: books and software.

The console

Figure 11-6 shows the console for the Product application. This application works much like the Product application presented in chapter 4. However, there are three main differences. First, this application displays an additional piece of information about each product, which varies depending on whether the product is a book or software. In particular, it displays an author for a book and a version number for software. Second, this application displays a count of the total number of objects it has created. Third, if the user enters an invalid product code, the application displays an appropriate error message.

The console for the Product application

```
Welcome to the Product Viewer

Enter product code: java

Description: Murach's Java Programming by Joel Murach
Price:       $57.50

Product count: 1

Continue? (y/n): y

Enter product code: netbeans

Description: NetBeans 8.0
Price:       $0.00

Product count: 2

Continue? (y/n): y

Enter product code: xxxx

No product matches this product code.

Continue? (y/n):
```

Description

- This version of the Product application handles two types of products: books and software.
- If you enter the product code for a book, the information about the product includes an author.
- If you enter the product code for software, the information about the product includes a version number.

The Product, Book, and Software classes

Figures 11-7 and 11-8 show the code for the Product superclass and its two subclasses, Book and Software. Since most of the code for the Product and Book classes was presented earlier in this chapter, you shouldn't have much trouble understanding how they work.

In addition, the Software class works like the Book class. As a result, you shouldn't have much trouble understanding it either. After it extends the Product class, it declares a private instance variable named version. Next, it provides a constructor that has no parameters that creates a new Software object with default values. This constructor also increments the count variable defined by the Product class. Finally, the Software class provides setVersion, getVersion, and toString methods.

The toString method of the Software class overrides the toString method of the Product class. However, it uses the super keyword to call the toString method of the Product class, which returns a string for the description of the product. Then, it appends information about the software version to the end of this string.

The ProductDB class

Figure 11-9 shows the code for the getProduct method of the ProductDB class, which returns the Book and Software objects used by the Product application. Here, the return type for the getProduct method is a Product object. Since the Book and Software classes are subclasses of the Product class, this method can return both Book and Software objects.

Within the getProduct method, the first statement declares a Product variable named p and assigns a null value to it. Then, if the user doesn't enter a product code that matches a product, this null value is returned.

If the product code that's passed to this method matches one of the valid book codes, a new Book object is created. Then, the instance variables for that object are set depending on the book code. Finally, that Book object is assigned to the Product variable.

If, on the other hand, the product code that's passed to this method matches the code for a software product, a new Software object is created and its instance variables are set. Then, that Software object is assigned to the Product variable.

The last statement in this method returns the Product variable to the calling method. Here, the Product variable can contain a Book object, a Software object, or a null. As a result, the calling method can check whether the product code is valid by checking whether the Product variable is null.

This chapter presents the ProductDB class as part of an application that shows how inheritance works. However, this class is not a realistic way to get an object and fill it with data since adding any new data would require updating and recompiling the source code. Typically, the data for an object is stored in a database as shown later in this book. Then, a class such as the ProductDB class can read the data from the database and return one or more objects that contain this data.

The code for the Product class

```
package murach.business;

import java.text.NumberFormat;

public class Product  {

    private String code;
    private String description;
    private double price;
    protected static int count = 0;

    public Product() {}

    public void setCode(String code) {
        this.code = code;
    }
    public String getCode(){
        return code;
    }

    public void setDescription(String description) {
        this.description = description;
    }

    public String getDescription()  {
        return description;
    }

    public void setPrice(double price) {
        this.price = price;
    }

    public double getPrice() {
        return price;
    }

    public String getPriceFormatted() {
        NumberFormat currency = NumberFormat.getCurrencyInstance();
        return currency.format(price);
    }

    @Override
    public String toString() {
        return description;
    }

    public static int getCount() {
        return count;
    }
}
```

Figure 11-7 The code for the Product class

The code for the Book class

```
package murach.business;

public class Book extends Product  {

    private String author;

    public Book() {
        super();
        author = "";
        count++;
    }

    public void setAuthor(String author) {
        this.author = author;
    }

    public String getAuthor() {
        return author;
    }

    @Override
    public String toString() {
        return super.toString() + " by " + author;
    }
}
```

The code for the Software class

```
package murach.business;

public class Software extends Product {

    private String version;

    public Software()  {
        super();
        version = "";
        count++;
    }

    public void setVersion(String version) {
        this.version = version;
    }

    public String getVersion() {
        return version;
    }

    @Override
    public String toString() {
        return super.toString() + " " + version;
    }
}
```

Figure 11-8 The code for the Book and Software classes

The code for the ProductDB class

```
package murach.db;

import murach.business.Book;
import murach.business.Product;
import murach.business.Software;

public class ProductDB {

    public static Product getProduct(String productCode) {
        // In a more realistic application, this code would
        // get the data for the product from a file or database
        // For now, this code just uses if/else statements
        // to return the correct product data

        Product p = null;

        if (productCode.equalsIgnoreCase("java")
                || productCode.equalsIgnoreCase("jsp")
                || productCode.equalsIgnoreCase("mysql")) {
            Book b = new Book();
            if (productCode.equalsIgnoreCase("java")) {
                b.setCode(productCode);
                b.setDescription("Murach's Java Programming");
                b.setPrice(57.50);
                b.setAuthor("Joel Murach");
            } else if (productCode.equalsIgnoreCase("jsp")) {
                b.setCode(productCode);
                b.setDescription("Murach's Java Servlets and JSP");
                b.setPrice(57.50);
                b.setAuthor("Mike Urban");
            } else if (productCode.equalsIgnoreCase("mysql")) {
                b.setCode(productCode);
                b.setDescription("Murach's MySQL");
                b.setPrice(54.50);
                b.setAuthor("Joel Murach");
            }
            p = b; // set Product object equal to the Book object
        } else if (productCode.equalsIgnoreCase("netbeans")) {
            Software s = new Software();
            s.setCode("netbeans");
            s.setDescription("NetBeans");
            s.setPrice(0.00);
            s.setVersion("8.0");
            p = s; // set Product object equal to the Software object
        }
        return p;
    }
}
```

Figure 11-9 The code for the ProductDB class

The ProductApp class

Figure 11-10 shows the code for this version of the ProductApp class. This code is similar to the code for the ProductApp class presented in chapter 4. However, in this version of the application, the getProduct method of the ProductDB class returns a null if the product code is invald. Otherwise, it returns a Product variable that refers to a Book or Software object that corresponds to the product code.

Within the loop, this class uses an if/else statement to test whether the Product variable contains a null. If so, this code displays an error message. Otherwise, this code calls the toString method of the object that the Product variable refers to. If the object is a book, this calls the toString method of the Book class. If the object is software, it calls the toString method of the Software class. In other words, this statement uses polymorphism to determine which method to call.

In this application, the product code that's entered by the user determines whether a Book object or a Software object is created. As a result, at compile time, the application doesn't know which version of the toString method to call. At runtime, however, the JRE determines what type of object the Product variable refers to, and it calls the appropriate method.

The code for the ProductApp class

```
package murach.ui;

import java.util.Scanner;
import murach.db.ProductDB;
import murach.business.Product;

public class ProductApp {

    public static void main(String args[]) {
        // display a welcome message
        System.out.println("Welcome to the Product Viewer");
        System.out.println();

        // perform 1 or more selections
        Scanner sc = new Scanner(System.in);
        String choice = "y";
        while (choice.equalsIgnoreCase("y")) {
            System.out.print("Enter product code: ");
            String productCode = sc.nextLine();    // read the product code

            // get the Product object
            Product p = ProductDB.getProduct(productCode);

            // display the output
            System.out.println();
            if (p != null) {
                System.out.println("Description: " + p.toString());
                System.out.println("Price:       " + p.getPriceFormatted());
            } else {
                System.out.println("No product matches this product code.\n");
            }

            System.out.println();
            System.out.println("Product count: " + Product.getCount() + "\n");

            // see if the user wants to continue
            System.out.print("Continue? (y/n): ");
            choice = sc.nextLine();
            System.out.println();
        }
    }
}
```

Figure 11-10 The code for the ProductApp class

More skills for working with inheritance

Now that you've learned the basic skills for working with inheritance and polymorphism, you're ready to learn some additional skills for working with inheritance. You might not need to use these skills often, but they provide useful information about how Java works, and they are necessary for some types of applications.

How to cast objects

One potentially confusing aspect of using inheritance is knowing when to cast inherited objects explicitly. The basic rule is that Java can implicitly cast a subclass to its superclass, but you must use explicit casting if you want to treat a superclass object as one of its subclasses.

The first example in figure 11-11 shows how this works. To start, the first group of statements creates a Book object, assigns this object to a Book variable named b, and assigns values to the object's instance variables.

The second group of statements shows how you can cast a subclass to its superclass without explicitly coding a cast. The first statement in this group casts the Book object to a Product variable named p. Since this cast goes up the inheritance hierarchy (from more data to less), you don't need to explicitly code the cast. Once you perform a cast like this, you can't call methods that are specific to the subclass. For example, once you cast a Book object to a Product object, you can't call the setAuthor method of the Book object. However, you can call methods of the Product class such as the setDescription method.

The third group of statements shows how to explicitly cast a superclass to a subclass. Since this cast goes down the inheritance hierarchy (from less data to more), you need to code the class name within parentheses in the assignment statement before you code the name of the object you're casting. Here, the first statement casts a Product object to a Book object. This works because the Product object is actually the Book object that was created in the first group of statements. This makes all methods of the Book object available again and doesn't cause any of the data in the original Book object to be lost.

The fourth group of statements shows a cast that causes a ClassCastException to be thrown. Here, the first statement creates a Product object. Then, the second statement attempts to cast this object to the Book type. Since the Product variable named p2 refers to an instance of the Product class, not an instance of the Book class, an exception is thrown when this statement is executed.

The second example shows how you can check an object's type. This code uses the instanceof operator to check whether the variable named p is an instance of the Book object. You can use code like this to avoid a ClassCastException like the one shown by the last statement in the first example.

Code that casts Product and Book objects

```
Book b = new Book();
b.setCode("java");
b.setDescription("Murach's Beginning Java");
b.setAuthor("Andrea Steelman");
b.setPrice(49.50);

Product p = b;                // cast Book object to a Product object
p.setDescription("Test"); // OK - method in Product class
//p.setAuthor("Test");        // not OK - method not in Product class

Book b2 = (Book) p;           // cast the Product object back to a Book object
b2.setAuthor("Test");         // OK - method in Book class

Product p2 = new Product();
Book b3 = (Book) p2;          // throws a ClassCastException because
                              // p2 is a Product object not a Book object
```

Code that checks an object's type

```
Product p = new Book();    // create a Book object
if (p instanceof Book) {
    System.out.println("This is a Book object");
}
```

The console

```
This is a Book object
```

Description

- Java can implicitly cast a subclass to a superclass. As a result, you can use a subclass whenever a reference to its superclass is called for. For example, you can specify a Book object whenever a Product object is expected because Book is a subclass of Product.
- You must explicitly cast a superclass object when a reference to one of its subclasses is required. For example, you must explicitly cast a Product object to Book if a Book object is expected. This only works if the Product object is a valid Book object. Otherwise, this throws a ClassCastException.
- Casting affects the methods that are available from an object. For example, if you store a Book object in a Product variable, you can't call the setAuthor method because it's defined by the Book class, not the Product class.
- You can use the instanceof operator to check if an object is an instance of a particular class.

Figure 11-11 How to cast objects and check an object's type

How to compare objects

Figure 11-11 shows how the equals method of the Object class works. In short, this method checks whether two variables refer to the same object, not whether two variables hold the same data. Since that's not usually the behavior you want when comparing objects for equality, many classes in the API, such as the String class, override this method. When you code your own classes, you'll often want to override this method too.

The first two examples in this figure show how the equals method of the Object class works when the Book class doesn't override the equals method. In the first example, the first two statements create two variables that refer to the same object. Since both variables point to the same object, the expression that uses the equals method to compare these variables evaluates to true.

In the second example, though, the first two statements create two objects that contain the same data. However, since the two variables in this example don't refer to the same object, the expression that uses the equals method to compare these variables evaluates to false. But that's usually not what you want.

The third example shows how to code an equals method in the Product class that overrides the equals method of the Object class. To start, this method uses the same signature as the equals method of the Object class, which returns a boolean value and accepts a parameter of the Object type. Then, an if statement uses the instanceof operator to make sure that the passed object is an instance of the Product class. If so, it casts the Object parameter to a Product object. Then, an if statement compares the three instance variables stored in the Product object with the instance variables stored in the current object. If all instance variables are equal, this statement returns true. Otherwise, it returns false. As a result, the first two examples in this figure return a true value if the Product class contains this method.

The fourth example shows how to code an equals method in the LineItem class you saw in the previous chapter. The code for this method works the same as the code for the equals method of the Product class. However, because a LineItem object contains a Product object, the equals method of the LineItem class uses the equals method of the Product class. As a result, you must code an equals method for the Product class for this method to work correctly.

How the equals method of the Object class works

Both variables refer to the same object

```
Product product1 = new Product();
Product product2 = product1;
if (product1.equals(product2))              // expression returns true
```

Both variables refer to different objects that store the same data

```
Product product1 = new Product();
Product product2 = new Product();
if (product1.equals(product2))              // expression returns false
```

How to override the equals method of the Object class

The equals method of the Product class

```
@Override
public boolean equals(Object object) {
    if (object instanceof Product)  {
        Product product2 = (Product) object;
        if (code.equals(product2.getCode()) &&
            description.equals(product2.getDescription()) &&
            price == product2.getPrice()) {
                return true;
        }
    }
    return false;
}
```

The equals method of the LineItem class

```
@Override
public boolean equals(Object object) {
    if (object instanceof LineItem) {
        LineItem li = (LineItem) object;
        if (product.equals(li.getProduct()) &&
            quantity == li.getQuantity()) {
                return true;
        }
    }
    return false;
}
```

Description

- To test if two objects variables refer to the same object, you can use the equals method of the Object class.
- To test if two objects store the same data, you can override the equals method in the subclass so it tests whether all instance variables in the two objects are equal.
- Many classes from the Java API (such as the String class) already override the equals method to test for equality.

Figure 11-12 How to override the equals method

How to work with the abstract and final keywords

The last two figures in this chapter show how you can require or restrict the use of inheritance in the classes you create by using the abstract and final keywords.

How to work with the abstract keyword

An *abstract class* is a class that can't be instantiated. In other words, you can't create an object directly from an abstract class. Instead, you can code a class that inherits an abstract class, and you can create an object from that class.

Figure 11-12 shows how to work with abstract classes. To declare an abstract class, you include the abstract keyword in the class declaration as shown in the Product class at the top of this figure. Within an abstract class, you can use the abstract keyword to code *abstract methods*. For example, the Product class shown here includes an abstract method named getDisplayText that returns a string. The declaration for this method includes the abstract keyword, it ends with a semicolon, and no method body is coded.

When you include abstract methods in an abstract class, you must override them in any class that inherits the abstract class. This is illustrated in the second example in this figure. Here, a class named Book that inherits the Product class overrides the abstract getDisplayText method that's defined by that class.

When you work with an abstract class, you can still declare a variable of the abstract type. However, you can't use the new keyword create an instance of the abstract type. In this figure, for example, you can still declare a Product variable. However, you can't use the new keyword to create a Product object to store in this variable. Instead, you must store a Book or Software object in the Product variable.

So, why you would use abstract classes? Well, one common use is to implement most, but not all, of the functionality of a class as a convenience to the programmer. This leaves only a few abstract methods that are specific to the subclass. In chapter 21, for example, the AbstractTableModel class implements most of the methods common to all table models, but it leaves a few abstract methods that are specific to the table that the subclass defines.

An abstract Product class

```
package murach.business;

public abstract class Product {
    private String code;
    private String description;
    private double price;

    // regular constructors and methods for instance variables

    @Override
    public String toString() {
        return description;
    }

    public abstract String getDisplayText();  // an abstract method
}
```

A class that inherits the abstract Product class

```
package murach.business;

public class Book extends Product {
    private String author;

    // regular constructor and methods for the Book class

    @Override
    public String getDisplayText()  {  // implement the abstract method
        return super.toString() + " by " + author;
    }
}
```

Description

- An *abstract class* is a class that can be inherited by other classes but that you can't use to create an object. To declare an abstract class, code the abstract keyword in the class declaration.
- An abstract class can contain fields, constructors, and methods just like other superclasses. In addition, an abstract class can contain abstract methods.
- To create an *abstract method*, you code the abstract keyword in the method declaration and you omit the method body. Abstract methods cannot have private access. However, they may have protected or default access (no access modifier).
- When a subclass inherits an abstract class, all abstract methods in the abstract class must be overridden in the subclass. Otherwise, the subclass must also be abstract.
- An abstract class doesn't have to contain abstract methods. However, any class that contains an abstract method must be declared as abstract.

Figure 11-13 How to work with the abstract keyword

How to work with the final keyword

Figure 11-13 shows how to use the final keyword to declare *final classes, final methods*, and *final parameters*. You can use this keyword whenever you want to make sure that no one can override or change your classes, methods, or parameters. When you declare a final class, other programmers won't be able to create a subclass from your class. When you declare a final method, other programmers won't be able to override that method. And when you declare a final parameter, other programmers won't be able to assign a new value to that parameter.

In early versions of Java, using final methods sometimes resulted in a significant performance gain. However, with modern versions of Java, the performance gain is almost nonexistent.

So, why would you want to use final classes, methods, or parameters? The main reason is because you may not want other programmers to be able to change the behavior of a method or a class. For example, you may need to make a method public so other programmers can use it. However, changing that method in a subclass might cause the method to not work properly. In that case, you can declare the method as final.

The first example shows how to declare a final class. This example declares the Book class that inherits the Product class as final. When you declare a final class like this, all methods in the class automatically become final methods.

The second example shows how to declare a final method. Since this method is in the Software class, which hasn't been declared as final, the class can still be inherited by other classes. However, any class that inherits the Software class won't be able to override the getVersion method.

The third example shows how you can declare a final parameter when you're coding a method. In most cases, there's no reason to declare a parameter as final. However, in some rare cases, you may need to declare a parameter as final to guarantee that the parameter cannot change. In these cases, the compiler usually gives a warning that the variable must be final or effectively final. Then, you can add the final keyword to the declaration of the parameter.

In most cases, you'll declare an entire class as final rather than declaring specific methods as final. Because of that, you typically don't need to worry about whether individual methods of a class are final. However, if you encounter final methods, you should now understand how they work.

A final class

```
public final class Book extends Product {
    // all methods in the class are automatically final
}
```

A final method

```
public final String getVersion() {
    return version;
}
```

A final parameter

```
public void setVersion(final String version)  {

    // version = "new value"; // not allowed
    this.version = version;
}
```

Description

- To prevent a class from being inherited, you can create a *final class* by coding the final keyword in the class declaration.
- To prevent subclasses from overriding a method of a superclass, you can create a *final method* by coding the final keyword in the method declaration. In addition, all methods in a final class are automatically final methods.
- To prevent a method from assigning a new value to a parameter, you can code the final keyword in the parameter declaration to create a *final parameter*. Then, if a statement in the method tries to assign a new value to the parameter, the compiler reports an error.

Figure 11-14 How to work with the final keyword

Perspective

Conceptually, this is one of the most difficult chapters in this book. Although the basic idea of inheritance isn't that difficult to understand, the complications of polymorphism, overriding, and casting make inheritance a difficult topic. So if you find yourself a bit confused right now, don't be disheartened. It will become clearer as you actually use the techniques you've learned here and see them used in the Java API.

The good news is that you don't have to understand every nuance of how inheritance works to use it. In fact, since all classes automatically inherit the Object class, you've already been using inheritance without even knowing it. Now that you've completed this chapter, you should have a better understanding of how the Java API works. In addition, you should have a better idea of how you can use inheritance to improve the design of your own classes.

Summary

- *Inheritance* lets you create a new class based on an existing class. The existing class is called the *superclass*, *base class*, or *parent class*, and the new class is called the *subclass*, *derived class*, or *child class*.
- A subclass inherits all of the fields and methods of its superclass that aren't private. The subclass can *extend* the superclass by adding its own fields and methods, and it can *override* a method with a new version of the method.
- All classes inherit the java.lang.Object class. This class provides methods, such as the toString and equals methods, that are available to all classes.
- You can use *access modifiers* to limit the accessibility of the fields and methods declared by a class. *Protected members* can be accessed only by classes in the same package or by subclasses.
- An *annotation* is a standard way to provide information about your code to other software tools and developers. When you override a method, it's generally considered a good practice to add the @Override annotation to the method.
- In a subclass, you can use the super keyword to access the fields, constructors, and methods of the superclass.
- *Polymorphism* is a feature of inheritance that lets you treat subclasses as though they were their superclass.
- Java can implicitly cast a subclass type to its superclass type, but you must use explicit casting to cast a superclass type to a subclass type.
- You can use the instanceof operator to check if an object is an instance of a particular class.
- *Abstract classes* can be inherited by other classes but can't be used to create an object. Abstract classes can include *abstract methods*.

- If you extend an abstract class, you must implement all abstract methods. Otherwise, you must also declare your class as abstract.
- You can use the final keyword to declare *final classes*, *final methods*, and *final parameters*. No class can inherit a final class, no method can override a final method, and no statement can assign a new value to a final parameter.

Exercise 11-1 Use inheritance with the Product application

In this exercise, you'll modify the Product application shown in this chapter so it provides for an additional kind of product: a music album. When you enter the code for a music album, it should look like this:

```
Enter product code: sgtp

Description: Sgt. Peppers (The Beatles)
Price:       $14.99

Product count: 1
```

Create a new subclass named Album

1. Open the project named ch11_ex1_Product that's in the ex_starts folder. Then, review the code.
2. In the murach.business package, create a new class named Album that inherits the Product class. This new class should store data about the artist of the album. In addition, its toString method should append the name of the artist to the end of the string.

Modify the ProductDB class so it returns an Album object

3. Modify the ProductDB class so it creates at least one Album object.
4. Run the application to make sure that it works correctly.

Modify the protected variable

5. Open the Product class and delete the protected access modifier for the count variable. This restricts the availability of this variable even further, making it only available to the other classes in the current package.
6. Run the application to make sure that the count is maintained properly.

Exercise 11-2 Use the abstract and final keywords

In this exercise, you'll experiment with the abstract and final keywords to see how they work.

Use an abstract class with an abstract method

1. Open the project named ch11_ex2_Product that's in the ex_starts folder. Then, review the code.
2. Open the Product class. Then, add the abstract keyword to the class declaration.
3. In the Product class, add an abstract method named getDisplayText. This method should accept no parameters, and it should return a String object.
4. Attempt to compile the application. This should display an error message that indicates that the Book and Software classes must override the getDisplayText method.
5. Open the Book and Software classes. Then, add a getDisplayText method to these classes that overrides the abstract getDisplayText method of the Product class. One easy way to do that is to rename the toString method to getDisplayText.
6. Open the ProductApp class. Then, modify it so it calls the getDisplayText method of a product object instead of the toString method.
7. Run the application to make sure it works correctly.

Use a final class

8. In the Book class, add the final keyword to its class declaration.
9. Create a new class named UsedBook that inherits the Book class. You don't need to include any code in the body of this class. This should display an error message that indicates that the Book class can't be inherited because it is final.
10. In the Book class, remove the final keyword from its class declaration.
11. Run the application to make sure it works correctly.

Use a final method

12. In the Book class, add the final keyword to the getDisplayText method.
13. Add a getDisplayText method to the UsedBook class to override the getDisplayText method of the Book class. This method can return an empty string. This should display an error message that indicates that the getDisplayText method can't be overridden because it is final.
14. In the Book class, remove the final keyword from the getDisplayText method.
15. Run the application to make sure it works correctly.

Exercise 11-3 Code an equals method

In this exercise, you'll add an equals method to the Product and LineItem classes that you can use to compare the instance variables of two objects.

1. Open the project named ch11_ex3_EqualsTest in the ex_starts folder. This application creates and compares two Product objects and two LineItem objects using the equals method. Review this code to see how it works.
2. Run the project. Since the equals method isn't overridden in the Product or LineItem class, the output from this application should indicate that the comparisons are based on object references and not the data the objects contain like this:

```
The Product class is comparing references.
The LineItem class is comparing references.
```

3. Open the Product class, and add an equals method as shown in this chapter. Then, run the project again. This time, the output should indicate that the products are being compared based on their data like this:

```
The Product class is comparing data.
The LineItem class is comparing references.
```

4. Repeat step 3 for the LineItem class. This time, the comparisons for both the products and line items should be based on their data like this:

```
The Product class is comparing data.
The LineItem class is comparing data.
```

12

How to work with interfaces

Interfaces are similar to abstract classes. However, they have several advantages that make them easier to create and more flexible to use.

The Java API defines hundreds of interfaces. Many classes in the Java API use these interfaces. You can use interfaces from the Java API in your own applications. In addition, you can create and use your own interfaces.

An introduction to interfaces ... 308

A simple interface ... 308

Interfaces compared to abstract classes ... 310

Basic skills for working with interfaces ... 312

How to code an interface ... 312

How to implement an interface ... 314

How to inherit a class and implement an interface ... 316

How to use an interface as a parameter ... 318

How to use inheritance with interfaces ... 320

New features for working with interfaces ... 322

How to work with default methods ... 322

How to work with static methods ... 324

The Product Viewer application ... 326

The console ... 326

The ProductReader interface ... 326

The ProductDB class ... 326

The ProductApp class ... 328

Perspective ... 330

An introduction to interfaces

In some object-oriented programming languages, such as C++, a class can inherit more than one class. This is known as *multiple inheritance*. Although Java doesn't support multiple inheritance, it does support a special type of coding element known as an *interface*. An interface provides many of the advantages of multiple inheritance without some of the problems that are associated with it.

A simple interface

Figure 12-1 illustrates how you create and use an interface. Here, the first example shows the code for a simple interface named Printable. This code is similar to the code that defines a class and is stored in a file named Printable.java. However, the code for an interface uses the interface keyword instead of the class keyword. In addition, all of the methods in an interface are automatically public and abstract. As a result, you don't need to code the public or abstract keywords for the methods in an interface.

The second example shows a Product class that *implements* the Printable interface. To implement the Printable interface, the declaration for the Product class uses the implements keyword followed by the name of the interface. Then, the body of the Product class implements the print method that's specified by the Printable interface.

The third example shows that a Product object that implements the Printable interface can be stored in a variable of the Printable type. In other words, an object created from the Product class shown in this figure is both a Product object and a Printable object. As a result, you can use this object anywhere a Printable object is expected as shown later in this chapter.

A Printable interface that defines an abstract print method

```
package murach.business;

public interface Printable {
    void print();      // this method is automatically public and abstract
}
```

A Product class that implements the Printable interface

```
package murach.business;

import java.text.NumberFormat;

public class Product implements Printable {
    private String code;
    private String description;
    private double price;

    public Product(String code, String description, double price) {
        this.code = code;
        this.description = description;
        this.price = price;
    }

    // get and set methods for the fields

    public void print()       // implement the Printable interface
        System.out.println(description);
    }
}
```

Code that uses the print method of the Product class

```
Printable p = ProductDB.getProduct("java");
p.print();
```

Resulting output

```
Murach's Java Programming
```

Description

- An *interface* can define one or more methods. These methods are automatically public and abstract. As a result, the interface only specifies the method signatures, not any code that implements the methods.
- A class that *implements* an interface can use any constants defined by the interface. In addition, it must provide an implementation for each abstract method defined by the interface. If it doesn't, it must be declared as abstract.

Figure 12-1 A simple interface

Interfaces compared to abstract classes

So, how does an interface compare to an abstract class like the abstract class shown in the last figure? Figure 12-2 shows the similarities and differences and lists some of the advantages of each.

Abstract classes and interfaces are similar in some ways. To start, with all versions of Java, both abstract classes and interfaces can define abstract methods and static constants. In addition, you can't create an object from an abstract class or an interface.

Abstract classes and interface also have some important differences. To start, with all versions of Java, an abstract class can also define and use other types of fields such as instance variables, and it can define regular methods and static methods. However, interfaces can't.

Java 8 introduced two new features that make interfaces more powerful. First, they can define *default methods*, which work much like regular methods in a class. Second, they can define static methods. As a result, with Java 8 and later, abstract classes have fewer advantages over interfaces. In addition, interfaces have always had one important advantage over abstract classes: a class can implement multiple interfaces, but it can only inherit one class.

To illustrate, suppose you want to create several types of products, such as books, software, and music albums, and you want each type of product to have a print method that prints information about the product that's appropriate for the product type. You could implement this hierarchy using inheritance, with an abstract Product class at the top of the hierarchy and Book, Software, and Album classes that extend the Product class. Then, the Product class would provide features common to all products, such as a product code, description, and price. In addition, the Product class would declare an abstract print method, and the Book, Software, and Album classes would provide their own implementations of this method.

The drawback of this approach is that there are undoubtedly other objects in the applications that use these classes that can be printed as well. For example, objects such as invoices and customers have information that can be printed. Obviously, these objects wouldn't inherit the abstract Product class, so they'd have to define their own print methods.

In contrast, if you created a Printable interface like the one in this figure, it could be implemented by any class that represents an object that can be printed. One advantage of this is that it enforces consistency within the application by guaranteeing that any Printable object will be printed using a method named print. Without the interface, some printable objects might use a method called print, while others might use methods with names like display or show.

More importantly, an interface defines a Java type, so any object that implements an interface is marked as that interface type. As a result, an object that's created from a Book class that extends the Product class and implements the Printable interface is not only an object of the Book type and of the Product type, but also an object of the Printable type. That means you can use the object, or any other object that implements the Printable interface, wherever a Printable type is called for. You'll see examples of this later in this chapter.

An abstract class compared to an interface

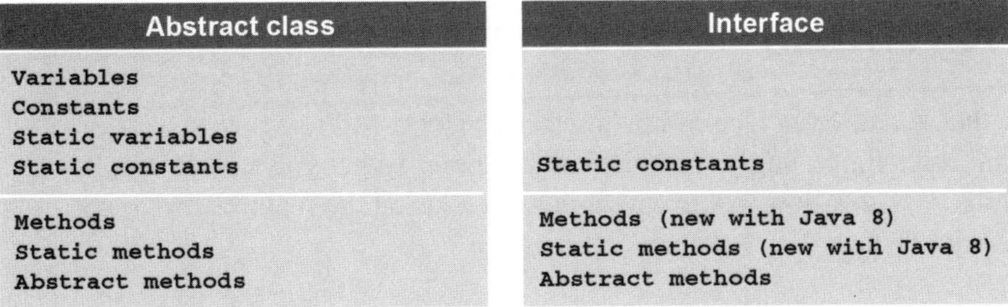

Abstract class	Interface
Variables Constants Static variables Static constants	Static constants
Methods Static methods Abstract methods	Methods (new with Java 8) Static methods (new with Java 8) Abstract methods

A Printable interface

```
public interface Printable {
    void print();
}
```

A Printable abstract class

```
public abstract class Printable {
    public abstract void print();
}
```

Advantages of an abstract class

- An abstract class can use instance variables and constants as well as static variables and constants. Interfaces can only use static constants.
- An abstract class can define regular methods that contain code. Prior to Java 8, an interface can't define regular methods.
- An abstract class can define static methods. Prior to Java 8, an interface can't define static methods.

Advantages of an interface

- A class can only directly inherit one other class, but a class can implement multiple interfaces.

Description

- A *default method* of an interface works much like a regular (non-static) method of a class.

Figure 12-2 Interfaces compared to abstract classes

Basic skills for working with interfaces

Now that you have an idea of how interfaces work, you're ready to learn some basic skills for coding and implementing them. To get you started, the next five figures show how to work with interfaces using the features that were available prior to Java 8.

How to code an interface

Figure 12-3 shows how to code an interface. To start, you code the public keyword, followed by the interface keyword, followed by the name of the interface. When you name an interface, it's common to end the name with a suffix of "able" or "er". For example, the Java API uses names like Cloneable, Comparable, EventListener, ActionListener, and so on. Another common naming strategy is to prefix the name of an interface with "I". For example, some programmers use names such as IProduct.

The first example in this figure shows the code for the Printable interface. This interface contains a single abstract method named print that doesn't accept any arguments or return any data. As with all abstract methods, you don't code braces at the end of the method. Instead, you code a semicolon immediately after the parentheses.

The second example shows the code for an interface named ProductWriter. This interface contains three abstract methods: add, update, and delete. All three of these methods accept a Product object as an argument and return a boolean value that indicates whether the operation was successful.

The third example shows how to code an interface that defines constants. In this case, an interface named DepartmentConstants defines three constants that map departments to integer values. You'll see how you can use constants like these in the next figure.

When you code an abstract method in an interface, you don't have to use the public and abstract keywords. That's because Java automatically supplies these keywords for all methods. Similarly, Java automatically supplies the public, static, and final keywords for constants. As a result, most programmers typically don't code these keywords in their interfaces. However, you can code these keywords if you think that they help clarify the code.

The fourth example shows the code for an interface named Serializable. This interface is available from the java.io package of the Java API, and it's designed to let programmers identify objects that can be stored (serialized) and then later reconstructed (unserialized) for reuse. For example, you might use this interface if you want to transport an object over a network or save an object to disk. Since this interface contains no constants or methods, it is known as a *tagging interface*. To code a tagging interface, you code an interface that doesn't contain any constants or methods.

The syntax for declaring an interface

```
public interface InterfaceName {
    type CONSTANT_NAME = value;                  // static constant
    returnType methodName([parameterList]);      // abstract method
}
```

An interface that defines one abstract method

```
public interface Printable {
    void print();
}
```

An interface that defines three abstract methods

```
public interface ProductWriter {
    boolean add(Product p);
    boolean update(Product p);
    boolean delete(Product p);
}
```

An interface that defines three static constants

```
public interface DepartmentConstants {
    int ADMIN = 1;
    int EDITORIAL = 2;
    int MARKETING = 3;
}
```

A tagging interface with no members

```
public interface Serializable {
}
```

Description

- Declaring an interface is similar to declaring a class except that you use the interface keyword instead of the class keyword.
- In an interface, all methods are automatically declared public and abstract.
- In an interface, all fields are automatically declared public, static, and final.
- When working with an interface, you can code the public, abstract, and final keywords. However, they're optional.
- An interface that doesn't contain any methods is known as a *tagging interface*. This type of interface is typically used to identify that an object is safe for a certain type of operation such as cloning or serializing.

Figure 12-3 How to code an interface

How to implement an interface

Figure 12-4 shows how to code a class that implements an interface. To do that, you code the implements keyword after the name of the class followed by the names of one or more interfaces separated by commas. For example, this figure shows a class named Employee that implements both the Printable and DepartmentConstants interfaces.

A class that implements an interface must implement all of the abstract methods defined by that interface. For example, the Employee class implements the Printable interface. As a result, it must implement the print method declared by that interface. If this method isn't implemented, the class must be declared as abstract, or it won't compile.

When a class implements an interface, you can use any of the constants defined by that interface. To do that, you can code the name of the constant without any qualification as shown in this figure. Here, the Employee class implements the DepartmentConstants interface. As a result, this class can use the ADMIN, EDITORIAL, and MARKETING constants defined by that interface. In this example, the print method includes an if/else statement that uses these constants to determine the department name to include in the output.

If you want, you can qualify the constant with the name of the interface. To do that, code the name of the interface, followed by the dot operator, followed by the name of the constant. For example, you can qualify the ADMIN constant like this:

```
DepartmentConstants.ADMIN
```

Although this makes it clear where the constant is stored, it also takes more code. As a result, most programmers typically omit the interface name when referring to constants.

Even if a class doesn't implement an interface, you can still use any of the constants defined by that interface. However, in that case, you must qualify the constant with the name of the interface as shown above.

The syntax for implementing an interface

```
public class ClassName implements Interface1[, Interface2]...{}
```

A class that implements two interfaces

```
package murach.business;

public class Employee implements Printable, DepartmentConstants {

    private int department;
    private String firstName;
    private String lastName;

    public Employee(int department, String lastName, String firstName) {
        this.department = department;
        this.lastName = lastName;
        this.firstName = firstName;
    }

    @Override
    public void print() {
        String dept = "Unknown";
        if (department == ADMIN) {
            dept = "Administration";
        } else if (department == EDITORIAL) {
            dept = "Editorial";
        } else if (department == MARKETING) {
            dept = "Marketing";
        }

        System.out.println(firstName + " " + lastName + " (" + dept + ")");
    }
}
```

Description

- To declare a class that implements an interface, you use the implements keyword. Then, you provide an implementation for each method defined by the interface.
- If you forget to implement a method that's defined by an interface that you're implementing, the compiler will issue an error message.
- A class that implements an interface can use any constant defined by that interface.

How to inherit a class and implement an interface

Figure 12-5 shows how to code a class that inherits another class and implements an interface. In particular, this figure shows how the Book class that you learned about in the previous chapter can inherit the Product class and implement the Printable interface. To do that, the declaration for the Book class uses the extends keyword to indicate that it inherits the Product class. Then, it uses the implements keyword to indicate that it implements the Printable interface. Finally, the Book class implements the print method specified by the Printable interface. As a result, an object created from the Book class can be used anywhere a Book, Product, or Printable object is required.

In figure 12-1, you saw a Product class that implements the Printable interface. If the Book class inherits this version of the Product class, it automatically implements the Printable interface, and it can use the print method implemented by the Product class. If you want, however, you can include the implements keyword on the declaration for the Book class to clearly show that this class implements the Printable interface. In that case, though, you don't need to implement the print method since it's already implemented in the Product class. However, if you want, you can override this method. In this figure, for example, the Book class overrides the print method to provide code that's different than the code provided by the print method of the Product class.

The syntax for inheriting a class and implementing an interface

```
public class SubclassName extends SuperclassName implements Interface1
    [, Interface2]...{}
```

A Book class that inherits Product and implements Printable

```
package murach.business;

public class Book extends Product implements Printable {

    private String author;

    public Book(String code, String description, double price,
            String author) {
        super(code, description, price);
        this.author = author;
    }

    public void setAuthor(String author) {
        this.author = author;
    }

    public String getAuthor() {
        return author;
    }

    @Override
    public void print() {     // implement the Printable interface
        System.out.println(super.getDescription() + " by " + author);
    }
}
```

Description

- A class can inherit another class and also implement one or more interfaces.
- If a class inherits another class that implements an interface, the subclass automatically implements the interface. However, you can code the implements keyword in the subclass for clarity.
- If a class inherits another class that implements an interface, the subclass has access to any methods of the interface that are implemented by the superclass and can override those methods.

How to use an interface as a parameter

Figure 12-6 shows how to code a method that uses an interface as the type for one of its parameters. When you do that, the statement that calls the method can pass any object that implements the interface to the method. Then, the method can call any of the methods that are defined by the interface and implemented by the object. You can use this type of code to create a flexible design that provides for processing objects created from different classes.

The first example in this figure shows a method named printMultiple that accepts two parameters. The first parameter is an object that implements the Printable interface, and the second parameter is an integer value that specifies the number of times to print the first parameter. Since the first parameter specifies Printable as the type, the printMultiple method doesn't know the type of the object. However, it does know that the object contains a print method. As a result, the code in the body of the method can call the print method.

In the second example, the code uses the printMultiple method to print two copies of a Product object to the console. This works because the Product class implements the Printable interface. Here, the first statement creates the Product object and assigns it to a variable of the Product type. Then, the second statement uses the printMultiple method to print two copies of the Product object.

The third example works like the second example. The only difference is that it declares the variable using an interface as the type. In other words, it declares the variable as being of the Printable type. Then, you can assign any object that implements the interface to the variable, and you can pass the variable to any method that accepts the interface as a parameter. This code yields the same result as the second example, but it clearly shows that the Product object implements the Printable interface.

The fourth example also works like the second example. However, it prints one copy of an Employee object to the console. This is another way of showing that the printMultiple method accepts any object that implements the Printable interface.

A method that accepts a Printable object

```
private static void printMultiple(Printable p, int count) {
    for (int i = 0; i < count; i++) {
        p.print();
    }
}
```

Code that passes a Product object to the method

```
Product product = new Product("java", "Murach's Java Programming", 57.50);
printMultiple(product, 2);
```

Resulting output

```
Murach's Java Programming
Murach's Java Programming
```

Another way to pass a Product object to the method

```
Printable product = new Product("java", "Murach's Java Programming", 57.50);
printMultiple(product, 2);
```

Code that passes an Employee object to the method

```
Employee employee = new Employee(
        DepartmentConstants.EDITORIAL, "Murach", "Joel");
printMultiple(employee, 1);
```

Resulting output

```
Joel Murach (Editorial)
```

Description

- You can declare a parameter that's used by a method as an interface type. Then, you can pass any object that implements the interface to the parameter.
- You can also declare a variable as an interface type. Then, you can assign an instance of any object that implements the interface to the variable, and you can pass the variable as an argument to a method that accepts the interface type.

Figure 12-6 How to use an interface as a parameter

How to use inheritance with interfaces

Figure 12-7 shows how one interface can inherit other interfaces. To start, this figure presents three interfaces: ProductReader, ProductWriter, and ProductConstants. Then, it presents a ProductDAO interface that inherits the first three interfaces. This interface is named ProductDAO because it defines an object that provides data access for products. In other words, DAO stands for "Data Access Object."

When an interface inherits other interfaces, any class that implements that interface must implement all of the abstract methods declared by that interface and the inherited interfaces. For example, if a class implements the ProductDAO class, it must implement all of the methods defined by the ProductReader and ProductWriter interfaces. If it doesn't, the class must be declared as abstract so that no objects can be created from it.

When a class implements an interface that inherits other interfaces, it can use any of the constants stored in the interface or any of its inherited interfaces. For example, any class that implements the ProductDAO interface can use any of the constants in the ProductConstants interface.

When a class implements an interface that inherits other interfaces, you can use an object created from that class anywhere any of interfaces in the inheritance hierarchy are expected. If a class implements the ProductDAO interface, for example, an object created from that class can be passed to a method that accepts the ProductReader type as a parameter. Similarly, the object can be passed to a method that accepts the ProductWriter type as a parameter. That's because any class that implements the ProductDAO interface must also implement the ProductReader and ProductWriter interfaces.

The syntax for declaring an interface that inherits other interfaces

```
public interface InterfaceName
    extends InterfaceName1[, InterfaceName2]... {
    // the constants and methods of the interface
}
```

A ProductReader interface

```
public interface ProductReader {
    Product getProduct(String code);
    String getProducts();
}
```

A ProductWriter interface

```
public interface ProductWriter {
    boolean add(Product p);
    boolean update(Product p);
    boolean delete(Product p);
}
```

A ProductConstants interface

```
public interface ProductConstants {
    int CODE_SIZE = 10;
    int DESCRIPTION_SIZE = 34;
    int PRICE_SIZE = 10;
}
```

A ProductDAO interface that inherits these three interfaces

```
public interface ProductDAO extends ProductReader, ProductWriter,
        ProductConstants {
    // all methods and constants are inherited
}
```

Description

- An interface can inherit one or more other interfaces by specifying the inherited interfaces in an extends clause.
- An interface can't inherit a class.
- A class that implements an interface must implement all abstract methods declared by the interface as well as all abstract methods declared by any inherited interfaces unless the class is defined as abstract.
- A class that implements an interface can use any of the constants declared in the interface as well as any constants declared by any inherited interfaces.

Figure 12-7 How to use inheritance with interfaces

New features for working with interfaces

Now that you know how to work with interfaces using the features available prior to Java 8, you're ready to learn how to use the new features for interfaces available with Java 8 and later.

How to work with default methods

Prior to Java 8, interfaces could only contain abstract methods. This was a significant limitation and sometimes resulted in a lot of code duplication. For example, the print method in the Printable interface may be virtually identical for most classes. However, using the techniques you've seen up until now, you'd still need to implement the print method for every class that implements the Printable interface.

Fortunately, Java 8 provides a new feature that allows you to include regular (non-abstract) methods in interfaces. These methods are known as *default methods*. If a class implements an interface, it doesn't have to override the default methods of the interface. Instead, it can use these default methods. However, whenever necessary, a class can override a default method to change its functionality.

The first example in figure 12-8 shows an interface that declares a default method named print. This method calls the toString method from the object that implements the interface to get a String object that represents the object. Then, it prints that String object to the console.

The second example shows a class that implements this interface and uses the default print method. Since this method is included in the interface, this class does not need to implement the print method. Instead, it can use the functionality that's provided by the default method in the interface. This works as if the class had inherited the method from another class.

The third example shows a class that implements the interface in the first example and overrides the print method. This allows the class to change the functionality that's provided by the default method. Again, this works as if the class had overridden a method in another class.

The syntax for declaring a default method (Java 8 and later)

```
default returnType methodName([parameterList]);
```

An interface that defines a default method

```
package murach.business;

public interface Printable {
    default void print() {
        System.out.println(toString());
    }
}
```

A class that uses the default method

```
package murach.business;

public class Product implements Printable {
    // This class doesn't override the print method.
    // As a result, it uses the print method defined by the interface.
}
```

A class that overrides the default method

```
package murach.business;

public class Product implements Printable {
    @Override
    public void print() {
        System.out.println(getDescription() + "|" + getPriceFormatted());
    }
}
```

Description

- With Java 8 and later, you can add regular (non-abstract) methods to an interface. These methods are known as *default methods*.
- To add a regular method to an interface, you can begin the declaration for the method with the default keyword.
- When you code a class that implements an interface, you don't need to implement its default methods. Instead, you can use the default methods defined in the interface in your class. However, if you want to change the functionality of a default method, you can override it.

How to work with static methods

With Java 8 and later, you can also code static methods in interfaces. Since this works similarly to coding static methods in classes, you shouldn't have much trouble understanding how this works.

The first example in figure 12-9 shows an interface named Printer that includes a static print method. This static method accepts a parameter of the Printable type. This method contains a single statement that calls the print method of the Printable object.

The second example shows code that uses the Printer interface. To start, the first statement creates a Printable object named product. Then, the second statement passes this object to the static print method of the Printer interface. As you can see, this works much like calling a static method from a class.

The syntax for declaring a static method (Java 8 and later)

```
static returnType methodName([parameterList]);
```

An interface that implements a static method

```
package murach.business;

public interface Printer {
    static void print(Printable p) {
        p.print();
    }
}
```

Code that calls a static method from an interface

```
Printable product = new Product("java", "Murach's Java Programming", 57.50);
Printer.print(product);
```

Description

- With Java 8 and later, you can include static methods in interfaces.
- To call a static method from an interface, prefix the static method with the name of the interface.

Figure 12-9 How to work with static methods

The Product Viewer application

This chapter finishes by presenting a Product Viewer application. This application works like the Product Viewer application presented in chapter 4. However, it uses the ProductReader interface presented earlier in this chapter.

When you use interfaces like this, you can minimize the linkage between the presentation layer of the application and the database layer. That's because the presentation layer can use the methods of a ProductReader object to access the database layer. Then, any class that implements the ProductReader object can supply the code for the specified methods.

The console

Figure 12-10 shows the console for the Product Viewer application. From the user's perspective, this application works the same as earlier versions of the Product Viewer application. In short, it allows the user to enter a product code. Then, it displays the details of the product with the specified code.

The ProductReader interface

The ProductReader interface specifies the methods of the database layer for reading products: getProduct and getProducts. As a result, it is stored in the murach.db package with the ProductDB class that's also shown in this figure. Otherwise, it works like the ProductReader interface described earlier in this chapter.

The ProductDB class

The ProductDB class in this figure is similar to the ProductDB class that's presented throughout this book. However, this ProductDB class implements the ProductReader interface. To do that, it includes a regular getProduct method that implements the abstract getProduct method specified by the ProductReader interface.

In addition, this ProductDB class implements the abstract getProducts method specified by the ProductReader interface. To do that, it just returns a String literal that indicates that the operation isn't supported yet. When you're developing classes that implement interfaces, it's common to start methods with code like this. Then, you can provide better implementations of these methods later as you develop the application. In this case, the Product Viewer application only needs the getProduct method, not the getProducts method. As a result, this version of the ProductDB class doesn't need to provide a better implementation of the getProducts method.

The console

```
Welcome to the Product Viewer

Enter product code: java

PRODUCT
Code:        java
Description: Murach's Java Programming
Price:       $57.50

Continue? (y/n): n
```

The ProductReader interface

```
package murach.db;

import murach.business.Product;

public interface ProductReader {
    Product getProduct(String code);
    String getProducts();
}
```

The ProductDB class

```
package murach.db;

import murach.business.Product;

public class ProductDB implements ProductReader {

    @Override
    public Product getProduct(String productCode) {
        Product product = new Product();
        product.setCode(productCode);
        if (productCode.equalsIgnoreCase("java")) {
            product.setDescription("Murach's Java Programming");
            product.setPrice(57.50);
        } else if (productCode.equalsIgnoreCase("jsp")) {
            product.setDescription("Murach's Java Servlets and JSP");
            product.setPrice(57.50);
        } else if (productCode.equalsIgnoreCase("mysql")) {
            product.setDescription("Murach's MySQL");
            product.setPrice(54.50);
        } else {
            product.setDescription("Unknown");
        }
        return product;
    }

    @Override
    public String getProducts() {
        return "This method hasn't been implemented yet.";
    }
}
```

Figure 12-10 The console, ProductReader interface, and ProductDB class

The ProductApp class

Figure 12-11 shows the code for the ProductApp class. This code is similar to versions of the ProductApp class that have been presented earlier in this book. However, it declares a ProductReader variable named reader and assigns a new ProductDB object to that variable. Then, it calls the getProduct method from the ProductReader object to get a Product object.

Note that this code only uses the name of the ProductDB class once. In other words, this is the only linkage between the ProductApp class and the ProductDB class. As a result, if necessary, it would be easy to swap in any other class that implements the ProductReader interface and use it instead of the ProductDB class.

The ProductApp class

```
package murach.ui;

import java.util.Scanner;
import murach.business.Product;
import murach.db.ProductDB;
import murach.db.ProductReader;

public class ProductApp {

    public static void main(String args[]) {
        // display a welcome message
        System.out.println("Welcome to the Product Viewer");
        System.out.println();

        // create 1 or more line items
        Scanner sc = new Scanner(System.in);
        String choice = "y";
        while (choice.equalsIgnoreCase("y")) {
            // get input from user
            System.out.print("Enter product code: ");
            String productCode = sc.nextLine();

            // Use a ProductReader object to get the Product object
            ProductReader reader = new ProductDB();
            Product product = reader.getProduct(productCode);

            // display the output
            String message = "\nPRODUCT\n" +
                "Code:        " + product.getCode() + "\n" +
                "Description: " + product.getDescription() + "\n" +
                "Price:       " + product.getPriceFormatted() + "\n";
            System.out.println(message);

            // see if the user wants to continue
            System.out.print("Continue? (y/n): ");
            choice = sc.nextLine();
            System.out.println();
        }
        System.out.println("Bye!");
    }
}
```

Figure 12-11 The ProductApp class

Perspective

In this chapter, you've learned how to use interfaces and how they can be used to improve the design of an application. That means that you should now be able to implement all types of classes that are commonly used in business applications. In the next chapter, though, you'll learn some additional object-oriented skills that will round out your knowledge of object-oriented programming.

Summary

- An *interface* is a special type of coding element that can contain static constants and abstract methods.
- With Java 8 and later, an interface can also contain regular methods, known as *default methods*, and static methods.
- A class can only inherit one other class, but it can *implement* more than one interface.
- To implement an interface, a class must implement all the abstract methods defined by the interface.
- An interface can inherit other interfaces. Then, the implementing class must also implement all the abstract methods of the inherited interfaces.
- An interface defines a Java type. As a result, you can use an object that's created from a class that implements an interface anywhere that interface is expected.
- A class does not have to implement default methods provided by the interface, but it can override them.

Exercise 12-1 Create and work with interfaces

In this exercise, you'll create the DepartmentConstants interface presented in this chapter. In addition, you'll implement an interface named Displayable that's similar to the Printable interface presented in this chapter.

Create the interfaces

1. Open the project named ch12_ex1_DisplayableTest in the ex_starts folder. Then, review the code.
2. Note that this code includes an interface named Displayable that contains a single method named getDisplayText that returns a String.
3. Open the DisplayableTestApp class. Then, note that it includes a method named display that accepts a Displayable object as an argument.
4. Add an interface named DepartmentConstants that contains the three constants: ADMIN, EDITORIAL, and MARKETING.

Implement the interfaces

5. Open the Product class. Then, edit it so it implements the Displayable interface. To do that, add a getDisplayText method that returns a description of the product.
6. Open the Employee class. Then, edit it so it implements the DepartmentConstants and Displayable interfaces. To do that add a getDisplayText method that uses the constants in the DepartmentConstants interface to include the department name and the employee's name in the string that it returns.

Use the classes that implement the interfaces

7. Open the DisplayableTestApp class. Then, modify the variable that stores the Employee object so it is of the Displayable type.
8. Add code that passes the Displayable object to the static display method that's coded at the end of this class.
9. Run the application to make sure that it displays the employee information.
10. Repeat the previous three steps for a Product object. When you're done, the console should look like this:

```
Welcome to the Displayable Test application

John Smith (Editorial)
Murach's Java Programming
```

Use a default method

11. In the Employee and Product classes, rename the getDisplayText methods to toString methods so that they override the toString method of the Object class. This should prevent the class from compiling and display an error message that indicates that the classes don't implement the getDisplayText method.
12. In the Displayable interface, modify the getDisplayText method so it's a default method. The code for this method should return the String object that's returned by the toString method. This should allow the Employeee and Product classes to compile since they can now use the default method.
13. Run the application to make sure it works as before.

13

How to work with inner classes, enumerations, and documentation

In this chapter, you'll learn some other skills that are related to object-oriented programming. In particular, you'll learn how to work with inner classes, which are often used in GUI programming. Then, you'll learn how to work with enumerations. Finally, you'll learn how to generate API documentation for your classes that looks and works like the documentation for the Java API.

How to work with inner classes **334**
An introduction to GUI programming 334
How to code an inner class 336
How to code an anonymous class 338
How to work with enumerations **340**
How to declare an enumeration 340
How to use an enumeration 340
How to enhance an enumeration 342
How to work with static imports 342
How to document a class **344**
How to add javadoc comments to a class 344
How to use HTML and javadoc tags in javadoc comments 346
How to use NetBeans to generate documentation 348
How to view the documentation 348
Perspective **350**

How to work with inner classes

So far, all of the applications in this book have declared one class per file. Most of the time, that's how you want to code your classes. However, in some situations, one class only makes sense within the context of another class. For example, when coding a *GUI* (*graphical user interface*), it's common to code one class within another class. When you do that, the class that's coded within the other class is known as an *inner class*.

An introduction to GUI programming

Since inner classes are commonly used when coding graphical user interfaces (GUIs), figure 13-1 briefly introduces GUI programming. However, don't worry if you don't understand all of the details of the GUI programming presented in this figure and the next two. You'll learn more about GUI programming later in this book. Instead, focus on the code that's related to inner classes.

This figure begins by showing the GUI that's used in the next two figures. From the user's point of view, this GUI consists of a window named Test Frame that contains a button named Test Button.

To create this GUI, the next two figures use *Swing*, which is the most common Java library for creating GUIs. Its classes are stored in the javax.swing package. With Swing, a window like the one shown in this figure is also known as a *frame*.

When you write code for a GUI, you also write code that handles *events* that occur on the components of the GUI. For example, you can handle the event that occurs when a user clicks on a button. To do that, the next two figures use interfaces and classes from another Java library, the *AWT* (*Abstract Window Toolkit*). This library is stored in the java.awt package.

When you develop a GUI with Swing, you typically begin by displaying a frame that acts as the main window for the application. Then, you add components such as buttons to the frame. Finally, you handle the events that occur when the user interacts with these components.

When handling events, you typically code a class known as an *event listener* that listens for the events. In Swing, you can do that by coding a class that implements the ActionListener interface. This class implements the actionPerformed method that contains the code that's executed when the event occurs. Since the action listener only makes sense within the context of the class that defines the frame, it's common to code this class within the class that defines the frame. In other words, it's common to code the class for an event listener as an inner class as shown in the next two figures.

A GUI that displays a button

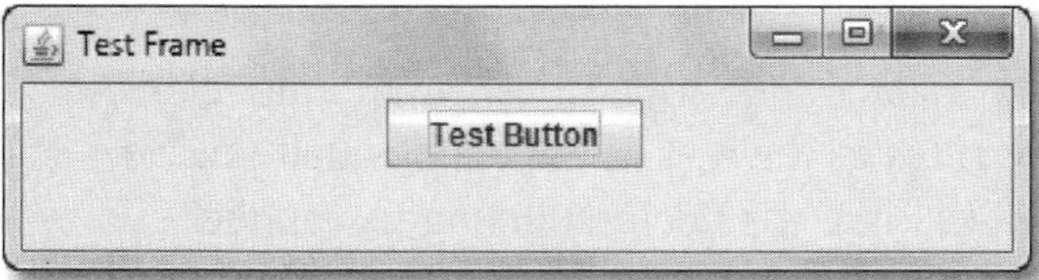

Three Swing classes that you can use to display a button

Class	Description
`javax.swing.JFrame`	A class that defines the window that contains the other components.
`javax.swing.JPanel`	A class that defines an invisible component that contains other components.
`javax.swing.JButton`	A class that defines a button that the user can click.

Two AWT classes that you can use to handle a button click

Interface/Class	Description
`java.awt.event.ActionListener`	An interface that defines the method that contains the code that's executed when a user clicks a button.
`java.awt.event.ActionEvent`	A class that defines an object that contains information about an event such as the event that occurs when a user clicks a button.

The method that's defined by the ActionListener interface

```
void actionPerformed(ActionEvent e);
```

Description

- Most modern applications use a *GUI* (*graphical user interface*) that displays windows and components, such as buttons, to interact with the user.
- *Swing* is the most common Java library for creating GUIs. Its classes are stored in the javax.swing package.
- With Swing, a window is also known as a *frame*.
- When you write code for a GUI, you can handle *events* that occur on it. For example, you can handle the event that occurs when a user clicks on a button. To do that, you typically code an *event listener* that contains the code that's executed when an event occurs.
- To handle events, Swing uses interfaces and classes from another Java library, the *AWT* (*Abstract Window Toolkit*). This library is stored in the java.awt package.

Figure 13-1 An introduction to GUI programming

How to code an inner class

Figure 13-2 begins by showing the syntax and scope rules for an inner class. Here, the outer class follows the same rules as the rest of the classes that you've been working with throughout this book. First, it's declared using the public keyword. Second, it can contain instance variables, static variables, methods, and static methods.

The inner class, on the other hand, follows slightly different rules. First, an inner class can't be declared as public. Second, an inner class has direct access to all private variables and methods of the outer class. Third, an inner class can declare its own instance variables and methods. Fourth, an inner class can't contain any static variables or methods.

The code example in this figure shows a class named TestFrame that contains an inner class named ClickListener. The TestFrame class defines a window that displays a button. The ClickListener class definers a listener that contains the code that's executed when the user clicks on that button.

The TestFrame class starts by importing some classes from the java.awt and javax.swing packages. Then, it extends the JFrame class.

The constructor for this class begins with some statements that set up the frame. The first three statements set the title, size, and location of the frame. The fourth statement sets the operation that's executed when the user clicks the Close button of the frame. The fifth and sixth statements create a panel and add it to the frame.

The seventh statement creates a button. Then, the eighth statement creates an object from the inner ClickListener class and assigns it to an ActionListner variable. This is possible because the ClickListener class implements the ActionListener interface and its actionPerformed method. Then, the ninth statement passes the ActionListener object to the addActionListener method of the button. As a result, the code within the inner class is executed if the user clicks on this button. For now, this code just prints a message to the console. However, later in this book, you can learn how to perform other operations.

The last two statements of the constructor add the button to the panel and display the frame to the user. Without the last statement, the code would create the frame, but it would not be visible to the user.

An introduction to inner classes

```
public class ClassName {
    // can contain instance variables and methods
    // can contain static variables and methods

    class InnerClassName {
        // can access all variables and methods of OuterClass
        // can contain instance variables and methods
        // can't contain static variables or methods
    }
}
```

A class that contains and uses an inner class

```
package murach.test;

import java.awt.event.ActionEvent;
import java.awt.event.ActionListener;
import javax.swing.JButton;
import javax.swing.JFrame;
import javax.swing.JPanel;

public class TestFrame extends JFrame {

    public TestFrame() {
        // code that sets up the frame
        this.setTitle("Test Frame");
        this.setSize(400, 100);
        this.setLocationByPlatform(true);
        this.setDefaultCloseOperation(JFrame.EXIT_ON_CLOSE);

        JPanel panel = new JPanel();
        this.add(panel);


        // code that creates the button and adds the listener
        JButton button1 = new JButton("Test Button");
        ActionListener listener = new ClickListener();
        button1.addActionListener(listener);

        // code that displays the frame
        panel.add(button1);
        this.setVisible(true);
    }

    // the inner class that implements the listener
    class ClickListener implements ActionListener {
        @Override
        public void actionPerformed(ActionEvent e) {
            System.out.println("The button was clicked!");
        }
    }
} // the end of the outer class
```

Description

- An *inner class* is a class that's coded within another class.

Figure 13-2 How to code and use an inner class

How to code an anonymous class

In the previous figure, the inner class that implemented the ActionListener interface had a name. However, if you want, you can create an inner class that implements this interface without specifying a name for the class as shown in figure 13-3. When you do that, the inner class is known as an *anonymous class*.

The first example shows how to implement the ActionListener interface without specifying a name for the class that implements the interface. Here, the code defines a variable for an ActionListener object named listener. Then, it creates a new ActionListener object, and it supplies all code for the class that implements the interface within the braces ({}). Next, it calls the addActionListener method of the button and passes the listener variable to it. This adds the listener to the button.

The second example shows how to implement the ActionListener interface without assigning the listener object to an instance variable. To do that, this code calls the addActionListener method of the button. Within the parentheses of this method, this code creates a new ActionListener object and supplies all code for the class that implements this interface within the braces ({}).

If you want to use the object that's created from the anonymous class more than once, you can assign the object to a variable as shown in the first example. In this figure, for example, you might want to use the same anonymous class for more than one button. However, if you only want to use the object that's created from the inner class once, you don't need to assign it to a variable. This results in concise code and saves you the trouble of naming the variable.

A class that contains and uses an anonymous class

```
public class TestFrame extends JFrame {

    public TestFrame() {
        // code that starts setting up the frame

        // code that creates the button and adds the listener
        JButton button1 = new JButton("Test Button");
        ActionListener listener = new ActionListener() {
            @Override
            public void actionPerformed(ActionEvent e) {
                System.out.println("The button was clicked!");
            }
        };
        button1.addActionListener(listener);

        // code that finishes setting up the frame
    }
}
```

Another way to use an anonymous class

```
public class TestFrame extends JFrame {

    public TestFrame() {
        // code that starts setting up the frame

        // code that creates the button and adds the listener
        JButton button1 = new JButton("Test Button");
        button1.addActionListener(new ActionListener() {
            @Override
            public void actionPerformed(ActionEvent e) {
                System.out.println("Button 1 clicked! ");
            }
        });

        // code that finishes setting up the frame
    }
}
```

Description

- An *anonymous class* is a type of inner class that doesn't have a name.
- You can code the braces for an anonymous class immediately after the parentheses that attempt to create an object from an interface.
- Within the braces for an anonymous class, you can supply the code that implements the interface.
- If you want to use the object that's created from the inner class more than once, you can assign that object to a variable.

Figure 13-3 How to code and use an anonymous class

How to work with enumerations

If you need to define a set of related constants, it's typically considered a best practice to use an *enumeration*. Enumerations have been available since Java 5, and they have several advantages over storing related constants in a class or interface. In chapter 7, you learned how to use the RoundingMode enumeration of the Java API to set the rounding mode for a BigDecimal object. Now, you'll learn how to create and use your own enumerations.

How to declare an enumeration

Figure 13-4 shows how to declare an enumeration. To do that, you code the public keyword, followed by the enum keyword, followed by the name of the enumeration. Then, within the enumeration, you code the names of one or more constants, separating each name with a comma.

Internally, each constant within the enumeration is assigned an integer value beginning with zero. For instance, in the ShippingType enumeration shown in the first example in this figure, the UPS_NEXT_DAY constant has a value of zero, the UPS_SECOND_DAY constant has a value of one, and so on. In most cases, though, you won't use these integer values.

When coding your own enumerations, it's common to store them in a separate file. That way, the enumeration is available to all classes within the application. To do that, you can add a file for a new class. Then, you can edit the code for that file so it defines an enumeration instead.

How to use an enumeration

The next three examples in figure 13-4 show how you can use an enumeration. The second example shows that you can declare a variable as an enumeration type. Then, you can assign a constant in that enumeration to the variable. In this case, the UPS_SECOND_DAY constant is assigned to a ShippingType variable named secondDay.

The third example shows a getShippingAmount method that accepts a ShippingType enumeration as a parameter. Then, the code within the method compares the constant that's passed to the method with two of the constants in the enumeration to determine the shipping amount.

The fourth example shows a statement that calls the getShippingAmount method. This statement passes the UPS_SECOND_DAY constant of the ShippingType enumeration to the getShippingAmount method.

The statement that's commented out in the fourth example illustrates that you can't use an integer, or any other type, in place of an enumeration even though the constants in the enumeration are assigned integer values. In other words, enumerations are *type-safe*. In contrast, if you didn't code the constants in an enumeration, you could use the constant name or its value wherever the constant is expected. This is one of several reasons that enumerations are generally preferred to constants.

The syntax for declaring an enumeration

```
public enum EnumerationName {
    CONSTANT_NAME1[,
    CONSTANT_NAME2]...
}
```

An enumeration that defines three shipping types

```
public enum ShippingType {
    UPS_NEXT_DAY,
    UPS_SECOND_DAY,
    UPS_GROUND
}
```

A statement that uses the enumeration and one of its constants

```
ShippingType secondDay = ShippingType.UPS_SECOND_DAY;
```

A method that uses the enumeration as a parameter type

```
public static double getShippingAmount(ShippingType st) {
    double shippingAmount = 2.99;
    if (st == ShippingType.UPS_NEXT_DAY) {
        shippingAmount = 10.99;
    } else if (st == ShippingType.UPS_SECOND_DAY) {
        shippingAmount = 5.99;
    }
    return shippingAmount;
}
```

A statement that calls the method

```
double shippingAmount = getShippingAmount(ShippingType.UPS_SECOND_DAY);
// double shippingAmount2 = getShippingAmount(1); // Wrong type, not allowed
```

Description

- An *enumeration* contains a set of related constants. The constants are defined with the int type and are assigned values from 0 to the number of constants in the enumeration minus 1.
- An enumeration defines a type. Because of that, you can't specify another type where an enumeration type is expected. That means that enumerations are *type-safe*.

Figure 13-4 How to declare and work with enumerations

How to enhance an enumeration

Most of the time, the skills presented in figure 13-4 are the only ones you'll need for working with enumerations. However, whenever necessary, you can override methods that an enumeration inherits from the java.lang.Object and java.lang.Enum classes. In addition, you can add your own methods. When you do that, you may want to use methods of the enumeration constants. Two of those methods are shown at the top of figure 13-5.

This figure also shows an enhanced version of the ShippingType enumeration. This enumeration includes a toString method that overrides the toString method of the Enum class. Without this method, the toString method of the Enum class would return the name of the constant.

In this example, a semicolon is coded following the constants of the enumeration. This semicolon lets the compiler know that there are no more constants. Then, the toString method uses a series of if/else statements to return an appropriate string for each constant in the enumeration. To do that, it begins by using the ordinal method to return an int value for the constant. Then, it compares that value to integer values and returns a string that's appropriate for the current constant.

How to work with static imports

In addition to enumerations, Java 5 introduced a new feature known as *static imports*. This feature lets you simplify references to the constants in an enumeration.

To use the static import feature, you begin by coding a static import statement. This statement is similar to a regular import statement, but you code the static keyword after the import keyword, and you typically use the wildcard character (*) to import all of the constants of an enumeration. In this figure, for example, the static import statement specifies that all of the constants in the ShippingType enumeration in the murach.business package should be imported. (This assumes that the ShippingType enumeration has been stored in the murach.business package.)

Once you code a static import statement, you no longer need to code the name of the enumeration that contains the constants. In this figure, for instance, the last example shows how to import the constants in the ShippingType enumeration. Then, it shows a statement that refers to the UPS_GROUND constant without coding the name of this enumeration.

In addition to using static imports to import enumerations, you can use them to import the static fields and methods of a class. For example, you could use a static import to import all the static fields and methods of the java.lang.Math class. Then, you could refer to those fields and methods without qualification.

Although you can save some typing by using static imports, they often result in code that's more difficult to read. That's because it may not be obvious where the constants, fields, and methods that an application refers to are stored. Worse, using static imports can result in name collisions. As a result, you should use static imports only when they don't cause confusion or name collisions.

Two methods of an enumeration constant

Method	Description
`name()`	Returns a String for the enumeration constant's name.
`ordinal()`	Returns an int value that corresponds to the enumeration constant's position.

How to add a method to an enumeration

An enumeration that overrides the toString method

```
public enum ShippingType {
    UPS_NEXT_DAY,
    UPS_SECOND_DAY,
    UPS_GROUND;

    @Override
    public String toString() {
        String s = "";
        if (ordinal() == 0) {
            s = "UPS Next Day (1 business day)";
        } else if (this.ordinal() == 1) {
            s = "UPS Second Day (2 business days)";
        } else if (this.ordinal() == 2) {
            s = "UPS Ground (5 to 7 business days)";
        }
        return s;
    }
}
```

How to use an enumeration

```
ShippingType ground = ShippingType.UPS_GROUND;
System.out.println("Shipping type: " + ground.toString());
```

Resulting output

```
Shipping type: UPS Ground (5 to 7 business days)
```

How to use an enumeration with static imports

How to code a static import statement

```
import static murach.business.ShippingType.*;
```

How to use an enumeration after a static import

```
ShippingType ground = UPS_GROUND;
System.out.println("Shipping type: " + ground.toString());
```

Description

- All enumerations inherit the java.lang.Object and java.lang.Enum classes and can use or override the methods of those classes or add new methods.
- By default, the toString method of an enumeration constant returns the same string as the name method.
- You can use a *static import* to import all of the constants of an enumeration or all of the static fields and methods of a class.

Figure 13-5 How to enhance an enumeration and work with static imports

How to document a class

If you develop classes that are used by other programmers, you'll typically want to provide some documentation for them. That way, other programmers can learn how to use the fields, constructors, and methods that are provided by your classes. Fortunately, the JDK includes a utility named javadoc that makes it easy to generate HTML-based documentation for your classes. This documentation looks and works like the documentation for the Java API.

How to add javadoc comments to a class

Figure 13-6 shows how to add simple *javadoc comments* to a class. A javadoc comment begins with /** and ends with */. Within a javadoc comment, any additional asterisks are ignored. Because of that, asterisks are commonly used as shown here to set the comments off from the rest of the code. For these comments to work, though, they must be coded directly above the class, field, constructor, or method that they describe.

If you're using NetBeans, you'll find that it makes it easy to enter javadoc comments. To do that, you enter a slash (/) followed by two or more asterisks on a blank line before the code for a class, field, constructor, or method. Then, when you press the Enter key, NetBeans generates the starting comment for the class or its member. That includes one line with a single asterisk where you can start entering the comment, followed by a line with the */ characters that end the comment. It can also include one or more of the javadoc tags you'll learn about in the next figure.

The Product class with javadoc comments

```
package murach.business;

import java.text.NumberFormat;

/**
 * The Product class represents a product and is used by
 * the LineItem and ProductDB classes.
 */
public class Product {

    private String code;
    private String description;
    private double price;

    /**
     * Creates a new Product with default values.
     */
    public Product() {
        code = "";
        description = "";
        price = 0;
    }

    /**
     * Sets the product code to the specified String.
     */
    public void setCode(String code) {
        this.code = code;
    }

    /**
     * Returns a String that represents the product code.
     */
    public String getCode() {
        return code;
    }

    ...
```

Description

- A *javadoc comment* begins with /** and ends with */, and asterisks within the comment are ignored. You can use javadoc comments to describe a class and its public and protected fields, constructors, and methods.
- A comment should be placed immediately above the class or member it describes. For a class, that means that the comment must be placed after any import statements.
- If you enter a slash (/) followed by two or more asterisks on a blank line before the code for a class, field, constructor, or method in NetBeans, NetBeans generates beginning javadoc comments. That includes comments with some of the javadoc tags you'll learn about in the next figure.

How to use HTML and javadoc tags in javadoc comments

To help format the information that's displayed in the documentation for a class, you can include HTML and javadoc tags in your javadoc comments as shown in figure 13-7. The *HTML tag* you're most likely to use is the <code> tag. This tag can be used to display text in a monospaced font. In the Product class in this figure, for example, this tag is used to format the name of each class that's referred to in the class comment, and it's used to format the name of any object that's referred to in the other comments. Although it's not shown here, this tag is also commonly used to format references to primitive types.

The four *javadoc tags* shown here should be self-explanatory. You typically use the @author and @version tags in the class comment to document the author and current version of the class. Note that by default, this information isn't displayed in the documentation that's generated. Although you can specify that you want to include this information when you generate the documentation, that's usually not necessary.

You use the @param tag to describe a parameter that's accepted by a constructor or public method. In this figure, for example, you can see that a @param tag is used to document the code parameter used by the setCode method. Similarly, if a method returns a value, you can use the @return tag to describe that value. In this figure, the @return tag is used to document the String that's returned by the getCode method.

In addition to the tags shown here, you should realize that additional HTML and javadoc tags are available. For example, you can use the <i> tag to italicize text, and you can use the <b> tag to boldface text. To create a hyperlink, you can use the javadoc @see tag. For more information on this tag and other javadoc tags, see the online documentation for the javadoc utility.

Common HTML tag used to format javadoc comments

HTML tag	Description
`<code></code>`	Displays the text between these tags with a monospaced font.

Common javadoc tags

Javadoc tag	Description
`@author`	Identifies the author of the class. Not displayed by default.
`@version`	Describes the current version of the class. Not displayed by default.
`@param`	Describes a parameter of a constructor or method.
`@return`	Describes the value that's returned by a method.

The Product class with comments that use HTML and javadoc tags

```
package murach.business;

/**
 * The <code>Product</code> class defines a product and is used
 * by the <code>LineItem</code> and <code>ProductDB</code> classes.
 * @author Joel Murach
 * @version 1.0.0
 */
public class Product {
    private String code;
    private String description;
    private double price;

    /**
     * Creates a <code>Product</code> with default values.
     */
    public Product() {
        code = "";
        description = "";
        price = 0;
    }

    /**
     * Sets the product code.
     * @param code A <code>String</code> for the product code.
     */
    public void setCode(String code) {
        this.code = code;
    }

    /**
     * Gets the product code.
     * @return A <code>String</code> for the product code.
     */
    public String getCode() {
        return code;
    }

    ...
```

Figure 13-7 How to use HTML and javadoc tags in javadoc comments

How to use NetBeans to generate documentation

After you add javadoc comments to the classes of a project, you can use NetBeans to generate the documentation for those classes as described in figure 13-8. After it generates the documentation, NetBeans displays it in your default web browser as shown here. Then, you can review this documentation to be sure that it contains all the necessary information.

By default, NetBeans stores the documentation for a project in the dist/javadoc subfolder of the project's root folder. This documentation consists of multiple files and subfolders. Note that if you generate documentation for a project and the dist/javadoc folder already contains documentation, NetBeans overwrites the old files with the new ones, which is usually what you want.

How to view the documentation

You can use a web browser to view the documentation for user-defined classes the same way that you view the documentation for the Java API. The main difference is that the index.html file for user-defined classes is stored somewhere on your hard drive. In figure 13-8, for example, the documentation is stored in this folder:

```
/murach/java_netbeans/book_apps/ch13_LineItem/dist/javadoc
```

Here, I selected the murach.business package from the upper left frame. When I did that, the two classes in that package were listed in the lower left frame. Then, when I selected the Product class, the documentation for that class was displayed in the right frame.

The documentation for the Product class indicates that the Product class is in the murach.business package. It also includes a brief description of the Product class, which was generated from the javadoc comment for the class. Next, it provides a summary of the constructors and methods of the class that are available to other classes, along with the descriptions I provided. If this class contained public or protected fields, the documentation would also include a summary of those fields. Finally, the documentation includes details of all the fields, constructors, and methods in the summaries. This is where you'll see any information provided with @param and @return tags.

Note that the documentation doesn't expose the code that is encapsulated within the class. As a result, the documentation makes it easy for other programmers to use your classes without knowing the details of how they're coded.

The API documentation that's generated for the Product class

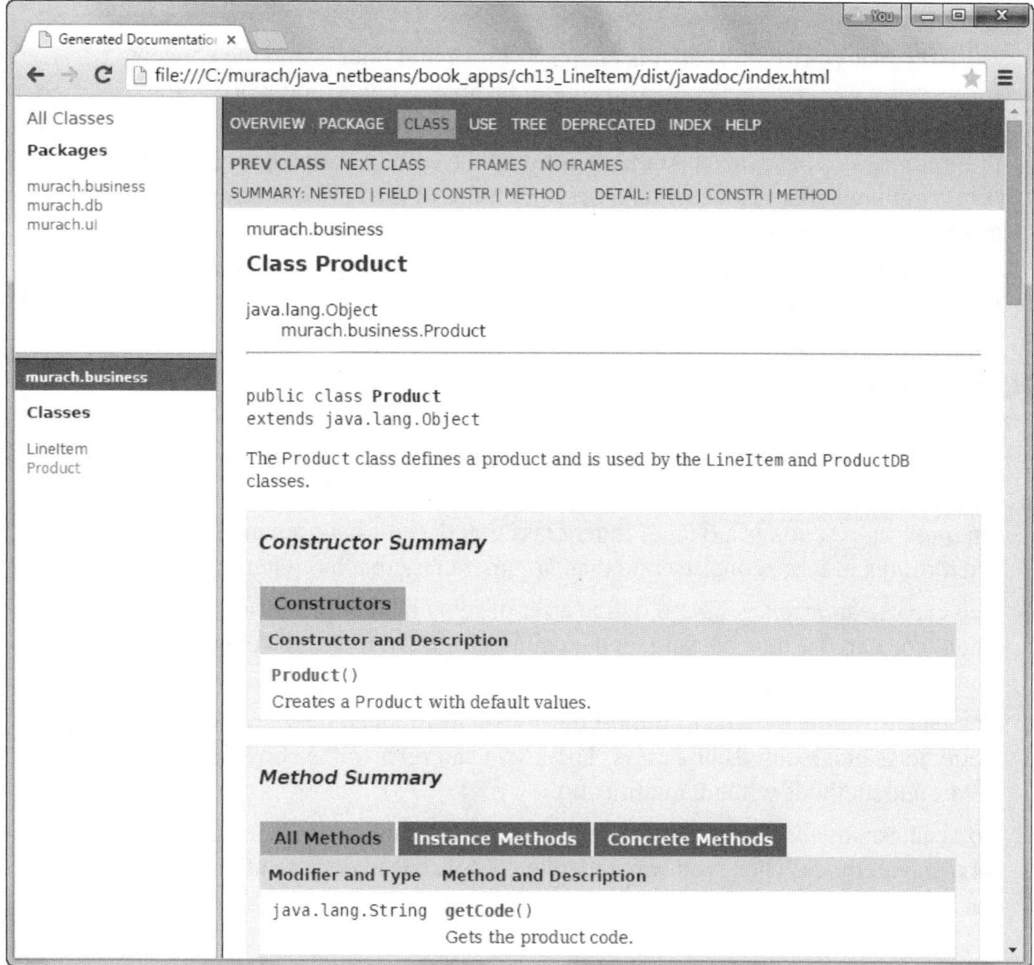

Description

- To generate or view the documentation for a project from NetBeans, you can right-click on the project in the Projects window and select the "Generate Javadoc" command. When you do, NetBeans generates the Java documentation for the project and displays it in the default web browser.
- By default, NetBeans stores the documentation for a project in a subfolder named dist/javadoc that's in the project's root folder. This folder contains an index.html file that you can double-click to view the documentation.
- If the project already contains documentation, NetBeans overwrites existing files without any warning.

Perspective

Now that you've finished this chapter, you should understand the concepts for working with inner classes. You should be able to create and work with enumerations. And you should be able to document your classes so other programmers can use them. At this point, you have all of the object-oriented programming skills you need to learn about more of the classes that are available from the Java API such as the collection classes described in the next chapter. In addition, you have a solid foundation for working with GUI programming as described at the end of this book.

Summary

- An *inner class* is a class that's coded within another class. This is useful when a class only makes sense within the context of another class.
- An *anonymous class* is a type of inner class that doesn't have a name. This often results in more concise code than an inner class that has a name.
- You can use an *enumeration* to define a set of related constants as a type. Then, you can use the constants in the enumeration anywhere the enumeration is allowed.
- You can use *static imports* to import the constants of an enumeration or the static fields and methods of a class. Then, you can refer to the constants, fields, and methods without qualification.
- You can use *javadoc comments* to document a class and its fields, constructors, and methods. Then, you can generate HTML-based documentation for your class.

Exercise 13-1 Test an inner class

In this exercise, you'll experiment with inner and anonymous classes.

Review the application

1. Open the project named ch13_ex1_InnerClassTester that's stored in the ex_starts folder. Review the code for the TestFrame class and the code for the ClickListener class. Note that these classes are stored in separate files.
2. Run the application. It should display the Test Frame window. Then, click on the button in this window. It should display a message to the console.

Create an inner class

3. Open the TestFrame and ClickListener classes and make the ClickListener class an inner class of the TestFrame class. To do that, you can cut most of the code from the ClickListener class and paste it into the TestFrame class.
4. Delete the public modifier from the declaration of the ClickListener class, add the import statement for the ActionEvent class, and make any other modifications to this code that are necessary.
5. Delete the ClickListener.java file. At this point, the project should only contain the TestFrame.java file and the Main.java file.
6. Run the application and click on the button. It should work as it did before.

Create an anonymous class

7. Open the TestFrame class and make the ClickListener class an anonymous inner class. To do that, you can begin by cutting the code from the ClickListener class starting with the opening brace and ending with the closing brace.
8. Delete the declaration of the ClickListener class, modify the code so it creates an object from the anonymous ActionListener class, and make any other modifications to this code that are necessary.
9. Run the application and click on the button. It should work as it did before.

Exercise 13-2 Create and use an enumeration

In this exercise, you'll create an enumeration and use it in a test application.

Create an enumeration

1. Open the project named ch13_ex2_Enumeration that's in the ex_starts folder.
2. Create an enumeration named CustomerType. This enumeration should contain constants that represent three types of customers: retail, trade, and college.

Use an enumeration

3. Open the CustomerTypeApp class. Then, add a method to this class that returns a discount percent (.10 for retail, .30 for trade, and .20 for college) depending on the CustomerType variable that's passed to it.
4. Add code to the main method that declares a CustomerType variable, assigns one of the customer types to it, gets the discount percent for that customer type, and displays the discount percent. It should display a message like this to the console:

```
discountPercent: 0.3
```

5. Run the application to be sure that it works correctly.

Modify the toString method of an enumeration

6. Add a statement to the main method that displays the string returned by the toString method of the customer type. Then, run the application again to see the result of this method. Depending on the customer type, it should display the name of the constant like this:

```
toString: TRADE
```

7. Add a toString method to the CustomerType enumeration. Depending on the customer type, this method should return a string that contains "Retail," "Trade," or "College" like this:

```
toString: Trade
```

8. Run the application again to view the results of the toString method.

Exercise 13-3 Work with API documenation

This exercise guides you through the process of adding javadoc comments to the classes in the murach.business package of the Line Item application. Then, it shows you how to generate the API documentation for this application.

Review the existing javadoc comments for two business classes

1. Open the project named ch13_ex3_LineItem that's stored in the ex_starts folder.
2. Open the Product class that's in the murach.business package. Then, view the javadoc comments for this class. Note that this class contains javadoc comments that don't include the @param or @return tags.
3. Open the LineItem class that's in the murach.business package. Note that this class only includes a single javadoc comment at the beginning of this class.

Generate and view the API documentation

4. Generate the documentation for the project. This should automatically open the documentation in a web browser. If it doesn't, open the documentation in a browser by navigating to the dist/javadoc folder for the project and opening the index.html page.
5. View the documentation for the Product class. To do that, click on the link for the murach.business package. Then, click on the link for the Product class. Note that it includes descriptions of its constructors and methods.
6. View the details for the getCode and setCode methods. To do that, click on the links for these methods. Note that these methods don't include information about the parameters and return values.
7. View the documention for the LineItem class by clicking on the link for the LineItem class. Note that it doesn't include descriptions of its constructors and methods.

Improve the javadoc comments

8. Open the Product class. Modify the javadoc comments for this class so they include @param and @return tags wherever those tags are appropriate.
9. Open the LineItem class. Add javadoc comments to all public constructors and methods using the @param and @return tags wherever those tags are appropriate.

Generate and view the improved API documentation

10. Generate the documentation for the project again.
11. View the documentation for the Product and LineItem classes again. This time, this documentation should include descriptions for all of the constructors and methods as well as information about all parameters and return values. For example, the second constructor of the LineItem class should include information about both of its parameters.

Section 4

More essential skills as you need them

The five chapters in this section show you how to use more of the core Java features. Chapter 14 shows how to work with collections, the generics feature introduced with Java 5, and the lambdas feature introduced with Java 8. Chapter 15 shows how to work with the new date/time API introduced with Java 8. Chapter 16 shows how to work with exceptions. Chapter 17 shows how to work with file input and output, which is also known as file I/O. And chapter 18 shows the most important concepts and skills for working with threads.

Once you've read chapters 14 and 16, which present skills that are critical to most Java applications, you can skip ahead to section 5. The chapters in this section show how to develop a desktop application that uses a graphical user interface to work with a database. Conversely, as you read section 5, you can skip back to the chapters in this section whenever necessary.

14

How to work with collections, generics, and lambdas

In this chapter, you'll learn how to work with collections. As you'll see, collections are similar to arrays but provide more advanced features. Along with collections, you'll be introduced to generics, a feature that has been available since Java 5. Finally, you'll learn how to use lambdas, a feature that was introduced with Java 8.

This chapter assumes that you already know how to work with arrays. As a result, you should read chapter 10 before reading this chapter.

An introduction to Java collections 358
A comparison of arrays and collections 358
An overview of the Java collection framework 360
An introduction to generics 362
How to use the ArrayList class 364
How to create an array list 364
How to add and get elements 366
How to replace, remove, and search for elements 368
How to store primitive types in an array list 370
The Invoice application 372
The user interface 372
The Invoice class 374
The InvoiceApp class 376
How to work with lambda expressions 378
An introduction to lambdas 378
A method that doesn't use a lambda expression 380
A method that uses a lambda expressions 382
How to use the Predicate interface 384
Perspective 386

An introduction to Java collections

Like an array, a *collection* is an object that can hold one or more elements. However, unlike arrays, collections aren't a part of the Java language itself. Instead, collections are classes that are available from the Java API.

A comparison of arrays and collections

Figure 14-1 presents a brief comparison of arrays and collections. This shows that you can use arrays or collections to store multiple elements of the specified type. In fact, some collection classes—most notably the ArrayList class—actually use an array internally to store elements. However, this is transparent to the programmer.

Although arrays and collections have some similarities, they also have many differences. One important difference is that arrays are fixed in size. That means that if you initially create an array with 100 elements and then need to add another element, you must create a new array large enough to hold 101 elements, copy the 100 elements from the first array to the new array, add the new element, and discard the old array.

In contrast, a collection automatically increases its size when necessary. Behind the scenes, a collection may copy elements between arrays, but this is transparent to the programmer. As a result, when you create a collection, you don't need to specify the maximum size of the collection. Instead, you add as many elements to the collection as you want. Then, if necessary, the collection expands automatically to hold the new elements.

A second difference between arrays and collections is that arrays can store primitive types such as int and double values, but collections must use wrapper classes to store primitive types. Fortunately, with Java 5 and later, collections automatically add and remove the wrapper classes whenever necessary using a feature known as *autoboxing*.

A third difference is that you typically use the methods of a collection to set and get the elements of a collection. Since you can't call methods from an array, you typically use its indexes to set and get its elements. The two code examples in this figure show how this works. Here, the first example uses indexes to set three values in an array, but the second example uses the add method of the ArrayList class to set the elements in the collection. Then, both examples use an enhanced for loop to get the elements and print them to the console.

By the way, don't worry if you don't understand all of the code in the second example. You'll learn the details of working with the ArrayList class later in this chapter. This example is only meant to illustrate some of the differences between working with arrays and collections.

How arrays and collections are similar

- Both can store multiple elements of the same type.

How arrays and collections differ

- Arrays are fixed in size and require the programmer to increase the size if necessary. Collections automatically increase their size if necessary.
- Arrays can store primitive types without using wrapper classes. Collections must use wrapper classes to store primitive types.
- Arrays don't provide methods for operations such as adding, replacing, and removing elements. Collections often provide methods that perform these operations.

Code that uses an array

```
String[] codes = new String[3];
codes[0] = "java";
codes[1] = "jsp";
codes[2] = "mysql";
for (String s : codes) {
    System.out.println(s);
}
```

Code that uses a collection

```
ArrayList<String> codes = new ArrayList<>();
codes.add("java");
codes.add("jsp");
codes.add("mysql");
for (String s : codes) {
    System.out.println(s);
}
```

Description

- A *collection* is an object that can hold other objects. Collections are similar to arrays, but are more flexible to use.
- With Java 5 and later, collections use a feature known as *autoboxing* to automatically add and remove the wrapper classes for primitive types whenever necessary.

Figure 14-1 A comparison of arrays and collections

An overview of the Java collection framework

Figure 14-2 shows a simplified diagram of the Java *collection framework*. This framework consists of a hierarchy of interfaces and classes. Here, the boxes with darker shading (Collection, Set, List, and Map) represent interfaces that define the basic collection types, and the boxes with lighter shading (ArrayList, LinkedList, HashSet, HashMap, and TreeMap) represent classes that implement these interfaces.

The collection framework provides two main types of collections represented by two distinct class hierarchies. The first hierarchy begins with an interface named Collection. A *collection* is an object that can hold one or more objects. The Set and List interfaces inherit the Collection interface and define two distinct types of collections. A *set* is a collection of unique objects. In most cases, sets are also unordered. That means that sets don't retain information about the order of elements added to the set.

On the other hand, a *list* is an ordered collection of objects. A list always maintains some sort of order for the objects it contains. Depending on the type of list, the order might be the order in which the items were added to the list, or it might be a sorted order based on a key value. In addition, lists allow duplicate elements.

The second main type of collection is called a *map*, and it's defined by the Map interface. A map is similar to a collection, but its elements consist of *key-value pairs* in which each value element is associated with a unique key element. Each key must be associated with one and only one value. For example, a map might be used to store Customer objects mapped to customer numbers. In that case, the customer numbers are the keys and the Customer objects are the values. Even though the Map interface doesn't inherit the Collection interface, the term *collection* is often used to refer to both collections and maps.

Although Java provides more than 30 classes that implement the List, Set, or Map interfaces, you don't need to know how to use them all. The second table in this figure lists five collection classes that are commonly used. However, to get started, you can begin by learning how to use the ArrayList class as shown in this chapter. This is the only collection that you need to be able to work with all of the applications presented in this book. Once you learn how to use this class, you shouldn't have much trouble learning how to use other collection classes if the need arises. If necessary, you can learn more about the other collection classes by searching the Internet.

The ArrayList class is an implementation of the List interface. This class defines an *array list* that works much like a standard array. In fact, the ArrayList class uses an array internally to store the elements of the list. The ArrayList class provides efficient access to the elements in the list. However, inserting an element into the middle of a list can be inefficient because all of the elements after the insertion point must be moved to accommodate the inserted element.

The LinkedList class is another implementation of the List interface. This class uses a special structure called a *linked list* to store the list's elements. The LinkedList class provides an efficient way to insert elements into the middle of a list. However, a linked list is less efficient when accessing elements.

The collection framework

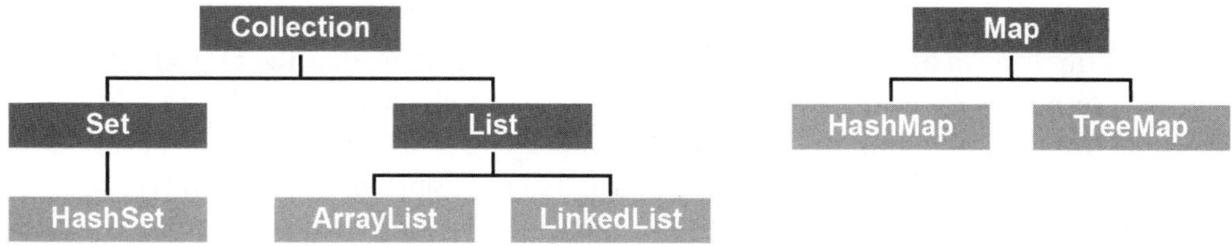

Collection interfaces

Interface	Description
`Collection`	Defines the basic methods available for all collections.
`Set`	Defines a collection that does not allow duplicate elements.
`List`	Defines a collection that maintains the sequence of elements in the list. It accesses elements by their integer index and typically allows duplicate elements.
`Map`	Defines a map. A map is similar to a collection. However, it holds one or more key-value pairs instead of storing only values (elements). Each key-value pair consists of a key that uniquely identifies the value, and a value that stores the data.

Common collection classes

Class	Description
`ArrayList`	More efficient than a linked list for accessing individual elements randomly. However, less efficient than a linked list when inserting elements into the middle of the list.
`LinkedList`	Less efficient than an array list for accessing elements randomly. However, more efficient than an array list when inserting items into the middle of the list.
`HashSet`	Stores a set of unique elements. In other words, it does not allow duplicates elements.
`HashMap`	Stores key-value pairs where each key must be unique. In other words, it does not allow duplicate keys, but it does allow duplicate values.
`TreeMap`	Stores key-value pairs in a hierarchical data structure known as a *tree*. In addition, it automatically sequences elements by key.

Description

- The Java *collection framework* is interface based, which means that each class in the collection framework implements one of the interfaces defined by the framework.
- The collection framework consists of two class hierarchies: Collection and Map. A *collection* stores individual objects as elements. A *map* stores key-value pairs where you can use a key to retrieve a value (element).

Figure 14-2 The Java collection framework and classes

An introduction to generics

Prior to Java 5, the elements of a collection were defined as the Object type. As a result, you could store any type of object as an element in a collection. At first, this flexibility might seem like an advantage. But with it comes two disadvantages. First, there's no way to guarantee that only objects of a certain type are added to a collection. For example, you can't limit an ArrayList so it can hold only Product objects. Second, you must use casting whenever you retrieve an object from a collection. That's because an element can be any type of object. For example, to retrieve a Product object from a collection, you must cast the object to the Product type.

Java 5 introduced a new feature called *generics* that addresses these two problems. The generics feature lets you specify the element type for a collection. Then, Java can make sure that it only adds objects of the specified type to the collection. Conversely, Java can automatically cast any objects you retrieve from the collection to the correct type.

Figure 14-3 shows how the generics feature works. To specify a type when you declare a collection, you code the type in angle brackets immediately following the name of the collection class (such as ArrayList or LinkedList). Prior to Java 7, you had to do this twice: once when you use the collection class to declare the collection, and again when you use the constructor of the collection class to create an instance of the collection. However, Java 7 introduced a feature that lets you simplify this code as shown by the last example in this figure.

The first example shows a statement that declares and instantiates an instance of an array list collection named codes that holds String objects. Here, <String> is specified following the ArrayList class name to indicate that the elements of the array list must be String objects.

The second and third examples are similar, but they create collections that can hold integers and Product objects. Here, the second example uses a *wrapper class* (the Integer class) instead of the primitive type (the int type). This allows the collection to store an array of integer values. That's necessary because it's illegal to declare a collection with a primitive type like this:

```
ArrayList<int> numbers = new ArrayList<int>();   // illegal!
```

If you're using Java 7 or later, you can omit the type from the brackets that follow the constructor as long as the compiler can infer the type from the context. The fourth example shows how this works. Here, the code accomplishes the same task as the first example but without duplicating the collection type. Since this feature results in shorter and simpler code, it's used throughout the rest of this chapter.

The syntax for specifying the type of elements in a collection

```
CollectionClass<Type> collectionName = new CollectionClass<Type>();
```

A statement that creates an array list of String objects

```
ArrayList<String> codes = new ArrayList<String>();
```

A statement that creates an array list of integers

```
ArrayList<Integer> numbers = new ArrayList<Integer>();
```

A statement that creates an array list of Product objects

```
ArrayList<Product> products = new ArrayList<Product>();
```

The syntax for using type inference with Java 7 or later

```
CollectionClass<Type> collectionName = new CollectionClass<>();
```

A statement that creates an array list of String objects

```
ArrayList<String> codes = new ArrayList<>();
```

Description

- *Generics* refers to a feature that lets you create typed collections. A *typed collection* is a collection that can hold only objects of a certain type. This feature was introduced with Java 5.
- To declare a variable that refers to a typed collection, you list the type in angle brackets (<>) following the name of the collection class.
- When you use a constructor for a typed collection, you can specify the type variable in angle brackets following the constructor name. The type variable can't be a primitive type such as int or double, but it can be a wrapper class such as Integer or Double. It can also be a user-defined class such as Product.
- Beginning with Java 7, you can omit the type from within the brackets that follow the constructor if the compiler can infer the type from the context. This empty set of brackets is known as the *diamond operator*.
- If you do not specify a type for a collection, the collection can hold any type of object. However, the Java compiler will issue warning messages whenever you access the collection to warn you that type checking can't be performed for the collection.

Figure 14-3 An introduction to generics

How to use the ArrayList class

The ArrayList class is one of the most commonly used collections in Java. You can use this class to create a type of collection called an *array list*. An array list uses an array internally to store list elements. As a result, an array list is similar to an array in many ways. However, unlike an array, an array list automatically adjusts its size as you add elements to it. As a result, you don't have to write any special code to make sure that you don't exceed the capacity of an array list.

How to create an array list

Figure 14-4 shows two constructors that you can use to create an array list. These constructors use a capital letter E to indicate that you must specify the type of element that you want to store in the collection within the angle brackets.

The first example in this figure creates an array list named codes that can store String objects. Since this code uses the default constructor for the ArrayList class, this example creates an array list that has an initial capacity of 10 elements. Then, if necessary, the array list automatically increases capacity to be able to store more elements.

Unfortunately, increasing the capacity of an array list is not an efficient operation, especially if the array list is large. First, the ArrayList class must create a new array of the expanded size. Then, the elements of the old array must be copied to the new array. Next, the new element must be added to the new array. Finally, the old array must be removed from memory.

As a result, if you know the number of elements that you're going to need to store, it's more efficient to create an array list that has an initial capacity that's slightly larger than the number of elements. To do that, you can use code like the code shown in the second example. This code creates an array list that has an initial capacity of 200 elements.

The ArrayList class

```
java.util.ArrayList
```

Common constructors of the ArrayList class

Constructor	Description
`ArrayList<E>()`	Creates an empty array list of the specified type with the default capacity of 10 elements.
`ArrayList<E>(intCapacity)`	Creates an empty array list of the specified type with the specified capacity.

Code that creates an array list of String objects

With the default starting capacity of 10 elements

```
ArrayList<String> codes = new ArrayList<>();
```

With a specified starting capacity of 200 elements

```
ArrayList<String> codes = new ArrayList<>(200);
```

Description

- The ArrayList class uses an array internally to store the elements in the list.
- The capacity of an array list automatically increases whenever necessary.
- When you create an array list, you can use the default starting capacity of 10 elements, or you can specify the starting capacity.
- If you know the number of elements that your list needs to be able to store, you can improve the performance of the ArrayList class by specifying a starting capacity that's just over that number of elements.

Figure 14-4 How to create an array list

How to add and get elements

The first example of figure 14-5 shows how to add elements to an array list. More specifically, it adds three String objects to the array list named codes. To do that, it uses the add method of the ArrayList class. Here, the third statement specifies an index of 0. As a result, this statement adds the string ("java") as the first element in the array list. Then, the array list automatically moves the other strings in the list ("jsp" and "mysql") back by one index.

The second example gets an element from the array list named codes. More specifically, it gets the last element in the list. To do that, it calculates the index for the last element by subtracting a value of 1 from the size. Then, it uses this index to get the last element in the array list.

Although you may need to get one element from an array list, it's more common to need to process all elements of an array list. To do that, it's common to use an enhanced for loop as shown in the third example. This example prints each element in the array list to the console. However, if necessary, you could perform more complex processing on each element.

The fourth example shows another way to get and display the values in a collection. To do that, you specify the name of the collection in the println method. This implicitly calls the collection's toString method, which returns a string that lists the value of each element. Since this displays all elements on the same line and enclosed in brackets, this technique is useful only for small collections. However, this technique is often useful when developing and debugging applications.

Common methods of the ArrayList class

Method	Description
`add(object)`	Adds the specified object to the end of the list.
`add(index, object)`	Adds the specified object at the specified index position.
`get(index)`	Returns the object at the specified index position.
`size()`	Returns the number of elements in the list.

Code that adds three elements to an array list

```
codes.add("jsp");
codes.add("mysql");
codes.add(0, "java");
```

Code that gets the last element

```
int lastIndex = codes.size() - 1;
String lastCode = codes.get(lastIndex);   // "mysql"
```

Code that gets and displays each element of an array list

```
for (String code : codes) {
    System.out.println(code);
}
```

Resulting output

```
java
jsp
mysql
```

An easy way to display the contents of a collection

```
System.out.println(codes);
```

Resulting output

```
[java, jsp, mysql]
```

Description

- You can use the methods of the ArrayList class to add elements to an array list and to get elements from an array list.

Figure 14-5 How to add and get the elements of an array list

How to replace, remove, and search for elements

The first example in figure 14-6 shows how to replace an element in an array list. To do that, the first statement calls the set method to replace the element that's stored at the index of 2 with "android." In other words, it changes the third element of the array list to "android".

The second example shows how to remove an element from an array list. To do that, this code calls the remove method and specifies an index of 1. As a result, this code removes the second element from the array list and stores it in the String variable named code.

The output for this example shows that second element ("jsp") was removed and all elements after it have shifted forward. In other words, the third element ("android") shifted forward and is now the second element.

The third example shows how to search for an element in an array list. To do that, this code calls the contains method and specifies the object that it's searching for. If this object exists, the code in this example prints a message to the console that indicates that the object exists. However, once you know an object exists in the array list, you can perform any type of processing on it.

More methods of the ArrayList class

Method	Description
clear()	Removes all elements from the list.
contains(object)	Returns true if the specified object is in the list.
indexOf(object)	Returns the index position of the specified object.
isEmpty()	Returns true if the list is empty.
remove(index)	Removes the object at the specified index position and returns that object.
remove(object)	Removes the specified object and returns a boolean value that indicates whether the operation was successful.
set(index, object)	Sets the element at the specified index to the specified object.
toArray()	Returns an array containing the elements of the list.

Code that replaces an element

```
codes.set(2, "android");
System.out.println(codes);
```

Resulting output

```
[java, jsp, android]
```

Code that removes an element

```
String code = codes.remove(1);    // removes "jsp"
System.out.println("'" + code + "' was removed.");
System.out.println(codes);
```

Resulting output

```
'jsp' was removed.
[java, android]
```

Code that searches for an element

```
String searchCode = "android";
if (codes.contains(searchCode)) {
    System.out.println("This list contains: '" + searchCode + "'");
}
```

Resulting output

```
This list contains: 'android'
```

Description

- You can use the methods of the ArrayList class to replace, remove, and search the elements of an array list.

Figure 14-6 How to replace, remove, and search the elements of an array list

How to store primitive types in an array list

Figure 14-7 shows how to store primitive types such as int values in an array list. To do that, you can use a *wrapper class* to specify the type of element that can be stored by the array list.

In this figure, for instance, the first example creates an array list of Integer objects. Then, it adds int values such as 1, 2, and 3 to the array list. This works because the compiler automatically converts the int values to Integer objects before it stores them in the array list.

Conversely, the second and third examples get int values such as 1, 2, and 3 from the array list, even though this list stores Integer objects. Again, that's possible because the compiler automatically converts the Integer objects to int values.

This feature is known as *autoboxing*, and it is available with Java 5 and later. Prior to Java 5, it was necessary to write extra code to store primitive types in their wrapper classes and to get them out of their wrapper classes. Fortunately, that's not necessary with recent versions of Java.

Code that stores primitive types in an array list

```
ArrayList<Integer> numbers = new ArrayList<>();
numbers.add(1);
numbers.add(2);
numbers.add(3);
System.out.println(numbers);
```

Resulting output

```
[1, 2, 3]
```

Code that gets a primitive type from an array list

```
int firstNumber = numbers.get(0);   // 1
```

Code that gets a primitive type from an array list

```
for (int number : numbers) {
    System.out.println(number);
}
```

Resulting output

```
1
2
3
```

Description

- All primitive types have corresponding *wrapper classes*. For example, the Integer class is the wrapper class for the int type, the Double class is the wrapper class for the double type, and so on.
- To store a primitive type in a collection, you can specify its wrapper class as the type for the collection. Then, the compiler automatically converts the primitive value to its wrapper type when adding values to the collection. This feature is known as *autoboxing*.
- To get a primitive type from a collection, you don't need to do anything because the compiler automatically gets the primitive value from the wrapper class for you.

Figure 14-7 How to store primitive types in an array list

The Invoice application

Now that you know how to work with an array list, this chapter shows how to use an array list within the context of the Invoice application that's presented in the next few figures.

The user interface

Figure 14-8 presents the console for the Invoice application. This console works much like the Line Item application presented in earlier chapters. However, it adds each line item to the invoice. Then, when the user finishes adding line items, the Invoice application displays each line item and the total for the invoice. To do that, it uses the Invoice class presented in figure 14-9.

The console

```
Welcome to the Invoice application

Enter product code: java
Enter quantity:     2
Another line item? (y/n): y

Enter product code: jsp
Enter quantity:     1
Another line item? (y/n): n

Description                        Price     Qty  Total
Murach's Java Programming          $57.50    2    $115.00
Murach's Java Servlets and JSP     $57.50    1    $57.50

Invoice total: $172.50
```

Description

- This application allows you to enter one or more line items for the invoice. When you're done, it displays all of the line items that you entered. In addition, it displays the total amount for the invoice.
- To enter a line item, enter the product code and quantity for the line item. Then, you can enter "y" to enter another line item, or you and enter "n" to complete the invoice.

Figure 14-8 The console for the Invoice application

The Invoice class

The Invoice class begins by defining one instance variable, an array list of LineItem objects named lineItems. This array list stores the line items for the invoice. The default constructor for the Invoice class creates this array list but doesn't add any line items to it. However, the addItem method provides a way to add line items to the invoice. This method defines a LineItem object as a parameter. Then, it calls the add method of the lineItems array list and adds the LineItem object to the array list.

The getLineItems method provides a way to get the lineItems array list. The return type for this method (ArrayList<LineItem>) uses generics to specify that the array list can only store LineItem objects, which is what you want.

The getTotal method uses an enhanced for loop to process each LineItem element in the lineItems array list. Within this loop, the code calls the getTotal method of the current line item and adds that total to the invoiceTotal variable. After this loop, the getTotal method returns the invoiceTotal variable.

The getTotalFormatted method formats the invoice total as a currency string. To do that, this method calls the getTotal method of the invoice. That way, the getTotalFormatted method doesn't duplicate any code in the getTotal method.

The Invoice class

```
package murach.business;

import java.text.NumberFormat;
import java.util.ArrayList;

public class Invoice {

    // the instance variable
    private ArrayList<LineItem> lineItems;

    // the constructor
    public Invoice() {
        lineItems = new ArrayList<>();
    }

    // a method that adds a line item
    public void addItem(LineItem lineItem) {
        lineItems.add(lineItem);
    }

    // the get accessor for the line item collection
    public ArrayList<LineItem> getLineItems() {
        return lineItems;
    }

    // a method that gets the invoice total
    public double getTotal() {
        double invoiceTotal = 0;
        for (LineItem lineItem : lineItems) {
            invoiceTotal += lineItem.getTotal();
        }
        return invoiceTotal;
    }

    // a method that returns the invoice total in currency format
    public String getTotalFormatted() {
        NumberFormat currency = NumberFormat.getCurrencyInstance();
        return currency.format(getTotal());
    }
}
```

Figure 14-9 The Invoice class

The InvoiceApp class

Figure 14-10 shows the code for the InvoiceApp class. This class contains a main method that begins by declaring a variable that stores an Invoice object. Then, it passes this object to the other two static methods in this class.

The static getLineItems method contains the code that prompts the user to enter the product code and quantity for the line item. To do that, it uses the Console class presented earlier in this book. Then, this method creates a new LineItem object from the user input and adds that object to the Invoice object.

The displayInvoice method contains the code that displays the Invoice object after the user has finished entering line items. This code uses the StringUtil class described earlier in this book to pad the strings used by the application to create columns that are the specified number of characters wide.

The InvoiceApp class

```
package murach.ui;

import murach.db.ProductDB;
import murach.business.Invoice;
import murach.business.LineItem;
import murach.business.Product;

public class InvoiceApp {

    public static void main(String args[]) {
        System.out.println("Welcome to the Invoice application\n");
        Invoice invoice = new Invoice();
        getLineItems(invoice);
        displayInvoice(invoice);
    }

    public static void getLineItems(Invoice invoice) {
        String choice = "y";
        while (choice.equalsIgnoreCase("y")) {
            String productCode = Console.getString("Enter product code: ");
            int quantity = Console.getInt("Enter quantity:     ");

            Product product = ProductDB.getProduct(productCode);
            invoice.addItem(new LineItem(product, quantity));

            choice = Console.getString("Another line item? (y/n): ");
            System.out.println();
        }
    }

    public static void displayInvoice(Invoice invoice) {
        StringBuilder sb = new StringBuilder();
        sb.append(StringUtil.pad("Description", 34));
        sb.append(StringUtil.pad("Price", 10));
        sb.append(StringUtil.pad("Qty", 5));
        sb.append(StringUtil.pad("Total", 10));
        sb.append("\n");

        for (LineItem lineItem : invoice.getLineItems()) {
            Product product = lineItem.getProduct();
            sb.append(StringUtil.pad(product.getDescription(), 34));
            sb.append(StringUtil.pad(product.getPriceFormatted(), 10));
            sb.append(StringUtil.pad(lineItem.getQuantityFormatted(), 5));
            sb.append(StringUtil.pad(lineItem.getTotalFormatted(), 10));
            sb.append("\n");
        }
        sb.append("\nInvoice total: ");
        sb.append(invoice.getTotalFormatted());
        sb.append("\n");
        System.out.println(sb);
    }
}
```

Figure 14-10 The InvoiceApp class

How to work with lambda expressions

Lambda expressions are the most important new feature of Java 8. They are similar in some ways to a method in an anonymous class. However, they allow you to eliminate the enclosing method and the anonymous class. In other words, lambda expressions allow you to pass the functionality of a method as a parameter. As a result, they are sometimes called *anonymous functions*.

An introduction to lambdas

In the previous chapter, you learned how to use an anonymous class to implement a method that contains the code that's executed when an event occurs. Then, you learned how to pass this anonymous class to another method as a parameter. Lambda expressions allow you to do something similar, but with a much cleaner syntax. In particular, lambda expressions allow you to specify the code that's executed without having to create the anonymous class and its method to store this code. In other words, lambda expressions allow you to store functionality of a method and pass it to another method as a parameter.

This ability to treat functionality as if it were data can result in the benefits listed in figure 14-11. It can allow you to write methods that are more flexible. This can greatly reduce code duplication, which can make your code easier to maintain.

However, lambda expressions do have some drawbacks as summarized in this figure. As a result, you might not always want to use them. Most of these drawbacks stem from the fact that the Java virtual machine doesn't support lambdas. Instead, the Java compiler rewrites lambdas into "normal" Java code.

This rewriting by the compiler results in three drawbacks. First, lambda expressions can be difficult to debug because you can't step through them with the debugger like normal methods. Second, when a lambda throws an exception, the stack trace can be difficult to understand. Third, methods that use lambdas can sometimes be inefficient compared to methods that accomplish the same task without using lambdas.

A fourth drawback is that lambda expressions can result in code that's confusing and difficult to maintain. This is especially true if you use lambda expressions in situations where they aren't necessary.

So, when should you avoid using a lambda expression? If you find yourself needing to perform the same task more than once, you probably want to avoid using a lambda expression. In that case, you probably want to store the code in a normal method so that it is reusable.

Lambdas expressions...

- Are anonymous functions that can be passed as arguments to methods.
- Allow you to treat functions like data.

Some benefits of lambda expressions

- They can reduce code duplication.
- They can allow you to write methods that are more flexible and easier to maintain.

Some drawbacks of lambda expressions

- They don't work well with the integrated debugger.
- They can be inefficient.
- They can result in stack traces that are very difficult to understand.
- They can result in code that's difficult to understand.
- They can result in code duplication for commonly used functionality.

Description

- Like a method, a *function* has parameters and returns a value. An *anonymous function* is a function that doesn't have a name.

Figure 14-11 An introduction to lambda expressions

A method that doesn't use a lambda expression

To understand how lambdas can be helpful, figure 14-12 shows a method that doesn't use a lambda expression that could benefit from the use of a lambda expression. This method accepts a list of Contact objects as a parameter, and returns a new list of Contact objects consisting only of the people from the original list who have a null phone number.

To accomplish this task, the code within this method creates a new list of Contact objects to store the Contact objects that have null phone numbers. Then it, uses a loop to check each Contact in the list that's passed in as a parameter. Within this loop, an if statement checks whether the Contact object's phone number is null. If so, this code adds the Contact object to the new list. After the loop, this code returns the new list.

This method has several advantages. First, there's nothing tricky about this code. As a result, it's easy to read and understand. Second, since this method is easy to read and understand, it should be easy to maintain.

However, this method also has several drawbacks. First, it's inflexible. For example, suppose you wanted to find all of the people who had a null email address instead of a null phone number? This method can't do it. To do that, you'd have to write a new method that checks for a null email address instead. However, most of the code in the new method would be duplicate code. You'd only need to change the condition inside the if statement.

And what if you wanted to find a list of people who had a null phone number and a null email address? To do that, you'd have to write a third method. Once again, the code in the third method would be almost identical to the code in the first two methods.

At this point, the code duplication begins to make it difficult to maintain these methods. For example, if you need to change the Contact class, you might need to change the code in all three methods to reflect that change. In this situation, it makes sense to use a lambda expression because it can make the method more flexible, which reduces code duplication and makes your code easier to maintain.

The Contact class

```
public class Contact {
    private String name;
    private String email;
    private String phone;

    // constructor and get / set methods here ...
}
```

Code that creates a list of contacts

```
List<Contact> contacts = new ArrayList<>();
contacts.add(new Contact("John Doe", "john_doe@foo.com", "555-1212"));
contacts.add(new Contact("Jane Doe", null, null));
contacts.add(new Contact("George Doe", "george_doe@foo.com", null));
```

A method that returns contacts that don't have phone numbers

```
public List<Contact> filterContactsWithoutPhone(List<Contact> contacts) {
    List<Contact> contactsWithoutPhone = new ArrayList<>();
    for (Contact c : contacts) {
        if (c.getPhone() == null) {
            contactsWithoutPhone.add(c);
        }
    }
    return contactsWithoutPhone;
}
```

Code that gets contacts that don't have phone numbers

```
List<Contact> contactsWithoutPhone = filterContactsWithoutPhone(contacts);
```

Code that prints contacts to the console

```
for (Contact p : contactsWithoutPhone) {
    System.out.println(p.getName());
}
```

The output

```
Jane Doe
George Doe
```

Description

- The filterContactsWithoutPhone method accepts a list of Contact objects, finds all the contacts in the list that have a null phone number, adds these contacts to a new list, and returns this list to the caller.
- In the filterContactsWithoutPhone method, the code that filters the list is hard-coded. As a result, this method is inflexible and fragile.

Figure 14-12 A method that doesn't use lambda expressions

A method that uses a lambda expressions

Figure 14-13 shows how to perform the same task as the previous figure with a method that uses a lambda expression. This results in a flexible method that you can use to filter the list of Contact objects in multiple ways.

Before you can code a lambda expression, you need to define the parameters and return type for the lambda expression. To do that, you can use a *functional interface.* A functional interface works like a normal interface except that it can only contain one method.

The first example in this figure shows a functional interface named TestContact that contains one method. This method accepts a Contact object as its only parameter and returns a boolean value.

The second example shows a method named filterContacts that accepts the functional interface as its second parameter. This works the same as coding a method that accepts any other type of interface as a parameter. So, this method accepts a list of Contact objects as its first parameter and a TestContact object as its second parameter.

Within this method, most of the code is similar to the code in the previous figure. However, the condition for the if statement checks whether the Contact object should be added to the list by calling the test method of the TestContact object. This is the key. In other words, this method doesn't include the test condition, nor does it care what the test condition is. All it cares about is that the test method of the TestContact object returns a boolean value.

The third example shows how to call the filterContacts method and pass it a lambda expression that specifies the test condition. To start, the first argument that's passed to the filterContacts method is the list of Contact objects. The second argument is the *lambda expression*, which is also known as an *anonymous function*. To define the lambda expression, you begin with a placeholder variable, followed by the *lambda operator* (->), followed by the functionality of the lambda. Here, the lambda operator (->) is a new operator that's available from Java 8 and later. In this example, the method call passes a lambda expression that checks whether the contact's phone number is null.

The fourth example shows how to pass a lambda expression that checks whether the contact's email list is null. This shows that the method in this figure is more flexible than the method in the previous figure. If you want, you could code more complex lambda expressions to filter the list in other ways. For example, you could check for Contact objects that have a null or empty phone number by using this lambda expression:

```
c -> c.getPhone() == null || c.getPhone().isEmpty()
```

Although this figure presents a simple example of lambda expressions, it should already be clear how lambdas can make methods more flexible, reduce code duplication, and make code easier to maintain by replacing multiple methods that perform almost identical functions with a single method that allows the functionality to be passed in at runtime as a lambda expression.

A functional interface

```
public interface TestContact {
    boolean test(Contact c);
}
```

A method that uses a functional interface to specify the filter condition

```
public List<Contact> filterContacts(List<Contact> contacts,
        TestContact condition) {
    List<Contact> filteredContacts = new ArrayList<>();
    for (Contact c : contacts) {
        if (condition.test(c)) {
            filteredContacts.add(c);
        }
    }
    return filteredContacts;
}
```

Code that gets contacts that don't have phone numbers

```
List<Contact> contactsWithoutPhone = filterContacts(contacts,
        c -> c.getPhone() == null);
```

The list after it's printed to the console

Code that gets contacts that don't have email addresses

```
List<Contact> contactsWithoutEmail = filterContacts(contacts,
        c -> c.getEmail() == null);
```

The list after it's printed to the console

Description

- A *functional interface* can only contain one method.
- A method can specify a functional interface as the type for a parameter. Then, within the method, you can call the method of the functional interface from the parameter.
- You can pass a *lambda expression* to a method that accepts a functional interface as a parameter. To code a lambda expression, you code the variable name, followed by the *lambda operator* (->), followed by an anonymous function. The anonymous function can use the variable name to call methods from the object type that's used by the method.

Figure 14-13 A method that uses lambda expressions

How to use the Predicate interface

Figure 14-14 shows how to perform the same task as the previous figure with a method that uses the Predicate interface, a functional interface that's available from the java.util.function package. This interface defines a method named test that works much like the test method in the TestContact functional interface that's presented in the previous figure.

However, the Predicate interface has two advantages over the TestContact interface. First, it's already available from the Java API. As a result, you don't need to write the code to define this interface. Second, the Predicate interface uses generics to specify the type of object that's passed to its test method. As a result, its test method can accept an object of any type. By contrast, the test method of the TestContact interface can only accept a Contact object.

In this figure, the second parameter of the filterContacts method defines a parameter of the Predicate<Contact> type. As a result, the lambda expressions that are passed to this method can call methods of the Contact object.

The Predicate interface that's available from the java.util.function package

```
public interface Predicate<T> {
    boolean test(T t);
}
```

A method that uses the Predicate interface to specify the condition

```
public static List<Contact> filterContacts(List<Contact> contacts,
        Predicate<Contact> condition) {
    List<Contact> filteredContacts = new ArrayList<>();
    for (Contact c : contacts) {
        if (condition.test(c)) {
            filteredContacts.add(c);
        }
    }
    return filteredContacts;
}
```

Description

- The Predicate interface is a functional interface that's available from the java.util.function package.
- The Predicate interface uses generics to specify the type of object that's passed to its test method.

Figure 14-14 How to use the Predicate interface

Perspective

Now that you've finished this chapter, you should know how to work with array lists, one of the most commonly used Java collections. This includes knowing how to use generics to specify the type of object that's stored by a collection. This is a good foundation for learning how to work with other collections.

You should also understand that many collections are available from the Java API. Each of these collections provides functionality that's useful in certain situations. As a result, if the collections presented in this chapter don't provide the functionality that your application requires, there's a good chance that the Java API already includes a collection that does provide this functionality. To find that collection and to learn how it works, you can start by looking in the documentation for the java.util package or by searching the Internet.

Finally, you should have a general idea of how lambda expressions work. As you might expect, there's plenty more to learn about lambda expressions. To do that, you can search the Internet for a tutorial or get a more advanced book about Java programming.

Summary

- A *collection* is an object that's designed to store other objects.
- The most commonly used collection class is the ArrayList class. An *array list* uses an array internally to store its data.
- The *generics* feature, which became available with Java 5, lets you specify the type of elements a collection can store. This feature also lets you create *generic classes* that work with variable data types.
- The *diamond operator*, which became available with Java 7, allows you to code an empty set of brackets (<>) in the constructor of a typed collection instead of having to code the type within those brackets.
- A *functional interface* is an interface that only contains one method.
- A *lambda expression* (also known as an *anonymous function*) can be passed as an argument to a method that accepts a functional interface as a parameter. This allows you to treat functions like data.

Exercise 14-1 Use an array list

This exercise guides you through the process of adding an array list to the Future Value application. This array list stores the values for each calculation that the user makes. When the application ends, it prints a summary of those calculations to the console. This summary should that looks something like this:

```
Future Value Calculations

Inv/Mo. Rate     Years    Future Value
$100.00 8.0%     10       $18,416.57
$125.00 8.0%     10       $23,020.71
$150.00 8.0%     10       $27,624.85
```

1. Open the project named ch14_ex1_FutureValue in the ex_starts folder. Then, review the code for this application and run it to make sure it works correctly.
2. Declare a variable at the beginning of the main method for an array list that stores strings.
3. After the code that calculates, formats, and displays the results for each calculation, add code that formats a string with the results of the calculation and then stores the string in the array list.
4. Add code to print the elements in the array list to the console when the user exits the application. Then, test the application by making at least 3 future value calculations.

Exercise 14-2 Use a lambda expression

In this exercise, you'll use a lambda expression to reduce code duplication when searching a book catalog for certain types of books

1. Open the project named ch14_ex2_BookCatalog in the ex_starts folder. Then, review the code for this application and run it to make sure it works correctly. It should print lists of books filtered by title, category, and format like this:

```
BOOKS BY TITLE:
[Java Programming, Java, Paperback]
[Java Programming, Java, Electronic]

BOOKS BY CATEGORY:
[Java Servlets and JSP, Java, Paperback]
[Java Servlets and JSP, Java, Electronic]
[Java Programming, Java, Paperback]
[Java Programming, Java, Electronic]

BOOKS BY FORMAT:
[MySQL, Database, Paperback]
[Java Servlets and JSP, Java, Paperback]
[Java Programming, Java, Paperback]
[Android Programming, Mobile, Paperback]
```

2. Open the BookManager class and examine these three methods: getBooksByTitle, getBooksByTech, and getBooksByFormat. Note that the code for these methods is almost identical, except for the condition at the beginning of the if statement.
3. Add a functional interface named TestBook that includes a method named test that accepts a Book object as a parameter and returns a boolean value.
4. In the BookManager class, add a single method named getBooksByLambda that accepts a TestBook object as a parameter and uses its test method in the condition at the beginning of the if statement.
5. Open the Main class and replace the old calls to the methods of the BookManager class with three calls to the new getBooksByLambda method. To do that, you'll need to pass a lambda expression as an argument to this method. For example, here's the lambda expression to test the title of a book:

```
b -> b.getTitle().equals("Java Programming")
```

6. In the BookManager class, delete the getBooksByTitle, getBooksByTech, and getBooksByFormat methods. Note how this reduces code duplication and increases the flexibility of your code.
7. Run the application and test it to make sure it works correctly. It should print the same list to the console as in step 1.

15

How to work with dates and times

In this chapter, you'll learn how to work with dates and times, which are necessary for many types of Java applications. To start, this chapter introduces you to the date/time API that was available prior to Java 8 as well as the new date/time API that's available with Java 8 and later.

Oracle recommends the new date/time API for new development. As a result, this chapter only shows how to use the new date/time API. However, if you need to use the older date/time API, you can learn more about it by searching the Internet or by consulting a more comprehensive book such as *Murach's Java Programming*.

An introduction to date/time APIs 390
The date/time API prior to Java 8 390
The date/time API for Java 8 and later 390
How to use the new date/time API 392
How to create date and time objects 392
How to get date and time parts 394
How to compare dates and times 396
How to adjust date/time objects 398
How to add or subtract a period of time 400
How to format dates and times 402
An Invoice class that includes an invoice date 404
Perspective 406

An introduction to date/time APIs

Figure 15-1 summarizes the two date/time APIs that are available with Java 8. The first was available prior to Java 8 and is included with Java 8 for backwards compatibility. The second is a new and improved date/time API that was added to Java 8. Oracle recommends this date/time API for new development.

The date/time API prior to Java 8

If you need your application to work with older versions of Java, you can use the Date, Calendar, and GregorianCalendar classes of the java.util package to work with dates and times. These classes are available to all modern versions of Java. To format these dates and times, you can use the DateFormat or SimpleDateFormat classes of the java.text package. These classes are also available to all modern versions of Java.

However, these classes have some design flaws. To start, they are not thread-safe. In addition, most programmers consider the design of these classes to be unintuitive. For example, in the Date class, years start at 1900, months start at 1, and days start at 0. Finally, these classes don't make it easy to localize your application for parts of the world that don't use the Gregorian calendar. For example, when using these classes, it isn't easy to write code that supports the Lunar calendar.

The date/time API for Java 8 and later

To fix these problems, Java 8 introduced a new date/time API. All of the classes and enumerations for this new API are stored in the java.time package.

This API is thread-safe because all of the classes are immutable. In other words, the methods of these objects always return a new object instead of modifying the existing one. In addition, most programmers consider the design to be more intuitive than the old API. Finally, the new API supports separate calendars, which makes it easier to localize your application for parts of the world that don't use the Gregorian calendar.

The date/time API prior to Java 8

Package	Description
`java.util`	An older package that contains the Date, Calendar, and GregorianCalendar classes. Prior to Java 8, programmers commonly used these classes to work with dates and times.
`java.text`	An older package that contains the DateFormat and SimpleDateFormat classes. Prior to Java 8, programmers used these classes to format dates and times.

Pros

- Works with older versions of Java.

Cons

- Not thread-safe.
- Not intuitive.
- Not easy to localize for parts of the world that don't use the Gregorian calendar.

The date/time API with Java 8 and later

Package	Description
`java.time`	A newer package that contains the LocalDate, LocalTime, LocalDateTime, and DateTimeFormatter classes as well as the Month and DayOfWeek enumerations. With Java 8 and later, you can use these classes and enumerations to work with dates and times.

Pros

- Thread-safe.
- Intuitive.
- Easier to localize for parts of the world that don't use the Gregorian calendar.

Cons

- Doesn't work with versions of Java prior to Java 8.

Description

- Java 8 introduces a new date/time API that fixes some of the problems with the old date/time API that was used prior to Java 8.

Figure 15-1 A summary of Java date/time APIs

How to use the new date/time API

The rest of this chapter shows how to use the new date/time API that was introduced with Java 8. As a result, this code only works with Java 8 and later. For new development, this is usually fine. However, if you need your application to work with older versions of Java, or if you need to modify code for an old application, you may want to use the old date/time API.

How to create date and time objects

With the new date and time API, you typically begin by using one of these three classes: LocalDate, LocalTime, or LocalDateTime. As the name implies, the LocalDate class stores a date but not the time. Conversely, the LocalTime class stores the time but not the date. And the LocalDateTime class stores both the date and time.

All three of these classes work from the observer's perspective. In other words, they use time zone and location information from the system the application is running on and work with the local date and time.

Figure 15-2 shows how you can create date and time objects using these classes. All of these classes use static methods that return dates and times.

The now method works the same for all three classes. It returns the current local time, date, or date and time. In this figure, for example, the first statement returns the current local date, the second returns the current local time, and the third returns the current local date and time.

The of method takes different parameters depending on whether it's called from a LocalDate, LocalTime, or LocalDateTime class. To create a LocalDate object, you can call the of method from the LocalDate class and pass it the year, month, and day as parameters. To specify the month, you can use the constants from JANUARY through DECEMBER that are available from the Month enumeration. Or, you can specify an int value for the month where January is 1, February is 2, and so on.

To create a LocalTime object, you can call the of method from the LocalTime class and pass it integer values for the hours, minutes, seconds, and nanoseconds. These parameters are in 24-hour format. This means they start at 00:00, which is midnight, and go to 23:59, which is 11:59 PM. Of these parameters, the hours and minutes are required. However, you can specify seconds and nanoseconds if you need to as shown in this figure. For most applications, you don't need to specify seconds and nanoseconds, but the new date/time API supports them if necessary.

To create a LocalDateTime object, you can call the of method of the LocalDateTime class and pass it values for the year, month, day, hour, minute, second, and nanosecond. This works like a combination of the LocalDate and LocalTime classes.

The parse method allows you to create a date, time, or date/time from a string. For a LocalDate object, you specify the date in this format YYYY-MM-DD. For a LocalTime object, you specify the time in this format HH:MM:SS.NNNNNNNNN. Here, the seconds and nanoseconds are optional.

The java.time package

Class	Description
`LocalDate`	A class for working with dates but not times.
`LocalTime`	A class for working with times but not dates.
`LocalDateTime`	A class for working with dates and times.
Enumeration	**Description**
`Month`	An enumeration that contains the months in the year (JANUARY through DECEMBER).
`DayOfWeek`	An enumeration that contains the days of the week (MONDAY through SUNDAY).

Static methods of the LocalDate, LocalTime, and LocalDateTime classes

Method	Description
`now()`	Returns an appropriate object for the current local date, time, or date/time.
`of(parameters)`	Return an appropriate object for the specified date, time, or date/time parameters. For a date, you can specify the year, month, and day parameters. For a time, you can specify the hour, minute, second, and nanosecond parameters. However, the second and nanosecond parameters are optional and default to 0. For a date/time, you can specify all of the parameters.
`parse(string)`	Returns an appropriate object for the specified string. For a date, you specify a string in the form of YYYY-MM-DD. For a time, you specify a string in the form of HH:MM:SS.NNNNNNNNN. However, the seconds and nanoseconds are optional and default to 0. For a date/time, the date and time are separated by a "T".

Code that creates date/time objects

```
LocalDate currentDate = LocalDate.now();
LocalTime currentTime = LocalTime.now();
LocalDateTime currentDateTime = LocalDateTime.now();

LocalDate halloween1 = LocalDate.of(2015, Month.OCTOBER, 31);
LocalDate halloween2 = LocalDate.of(2015, 10, 31);
LocalTime startTime1 = LocalTime.of(14, 32);                 // minutes
LocalTime startTime2 = LocalTime.of(14, 32, 45);             // seconds
LocalTime startTime3 = LocalTime.of(14, 32, 45, 123456789);  // nanoseconds
LocalDateTime startDateTime = LocalDateTime.of(2015, 10, 31, 14, 32);

LocalDate halloween3 = LocalDate.parse("2015-10-31");
LocalTime startTime4 = LocalTime.parse("02:32:45");
LocalDateTime startDateTime2 =
        LocalDateTime.parse("2015-10-31T02:32:45.123456789");
```

Description

- These classes represent the local date and time from the observer's perspective.
- The LocalDateTime class is a combination of the LocalDate and LocalTime classes.

Figure 15-2 How to create LocalDate, LocalTime, and LocalDateTime objects

For a LocalDateTime object, you separate the strings for the date and time with a T. This indicates the start of the time part of the string.

If any of the values are out of range, these methods typically throw a DateTimeException. For example, if you specify a day of 32, these methods throw this exception since no month has 32 days. Similarly, if you specify 25 hours or 61 seconds, these methods throw this exception.

All of these classes have several more static methods for creating dates and times, but the ones presented in figure 15-2 are the most common. For more information, you can look at the API documentation for these classes.

How to get date and time parts

Figure 15-3 shows several methods you can use to access the various parts of the date and time. The getMonth and getMonthValue methods return the same information, but in different formats. For example, if the date is set to October 31, 2015, the getMonth method returns the OCTOBER constant of the Month enumeration. On the other hand, the getMonthValue method returns an int value of 10. This value corresponds with the OCTOBER constant of the Month enumeration.

The toString method of the Month enumeration returns the name of the constant in all caps. As a result, if you print a constant of the Month enumeration to the console, it displays the name of the month in all caps.

The LocalDateTime class supports all of the methods shown in this figure. However, the LocalDate class only supports the methods for getting date parts, and the LocalTime class only supports the methods for getting time parts. This is logical since it doesn't make sense to call the getHour method on a LocalDate object because that object doesn't store the time. Similarly, it doesn't make sense to call the getYear method on a LocalTime object because that object doesn't store the date.

Unlike most classes, these get methods do not have corresponding set methods. That's because, as mentioned previously, the objects of these classes are immutable. In other words, you can't change them once they have been constructed.

Methods for getting parts of date and time objects

Method	Description
`getYear()`	Returns the current year as an in integer.
`getMonth()`	Returns the current month as a Month object.
`getMonthValue()`	Returns the current month as an integer between 1 and 12.
`getDayOfMonth()`	Returns the current day of the month as an integer.
`getDayOfYear()`	Returns the current day of the year as an integer.
`getDayOfWeek()`	Returns the current day of the week as a DayOfWeek object.
`getHour()`	Returns the current hour of the day as an integer in 24-hour format.
`getMinute()`	Returns the current minute of the hour as an integer.
`getSecond()`	Returns the current second of the minute as an integer.
`getNano()`	Returns the current nanosecond of the second as an integer.

Code that gets the parts of a LocalDateTime object

```
// Assume a current date/time of October 31, 2015 14:32:45.898000000

int year = currentDateTime.getYear();                        // 2015
Month month = currentDateTime.getMonth();                    // OCTOBER
int monthValue = currentDateTime.getMonthValue();            // 10
int day = currentDateTime.getDayOfMonth();                   // 31

int dayOfYear = currentDateTime.getDayOfYear();              // 304
DayOfWeek dayOfWeek = currentDateTime.getDayOfWeek();        // SATURDAY

int hour = currentDateTime.getHour();                        // 14
int minute = currentDateTime.getMinute();                    // 32
int second = currentDateTime.getSecond();                    // 45
int nano = currentDateTime.getNano();                        // 898000000
```

Description

- The LocalDateTime class supports all of the get methods.
- The LocalDate class only supports the get methods relevant to getting dates.
- The LocalTime class only supports the get methods relevant to getting times.
- LocalDate, LocalTime, and LocalDateTime objects are immutable. As a result, these get methods do not have corresponding set methods.

Figure 15-3 How to get date and time parts

How to compare dates and times

Figure 15-4 shows several ways that you can compare dates and times. To determine whether a date or time is before another date or time, you can use the isBefore method. In this figure, for instance, the first example checks whether the current date is before October 31, 2015. If so, it prints an appropriate message to the console.

To do that, this code compares two LocalDate objects. However, you could use similar techniques with two LocalDateTime objects or two LocalTime objects. When you compare date/time objects, you can only compare objects of the same type. For example, you can't compare a date to a time.

Conversely, you can use the isAfter method to determine whether a date or time object is after another date or time. In this figure, for instance, the second example checks whether the current time is after 15:30, which is 3:30PM. If so, it prints an appropriate message to the console. To do that, this code compares two LocalTime objects.

In most cases, you only need to use the isBefore or isAfter methods to compare dates. However, in some cases, you may need to use the compareTo method to determine whether a date/time is before, after, or equal to another date/time. This works because the compareTo method returns a negative value if a date/time is before another date/time, a positive value if a date/time object is after another date/time object, and 0 if the two date/time objects are equal. In this figure, for instance, the third example checks whether the current date is before, after, or equal to October 31, 2015.

Methods for comparing dates and times

Method	Description
`isBefore(dateTime)`	Returns true if the date or time is before the other specified date or time. Otherwise, this method returns false.
`isAfter(dateTime)`	Returns true if date or time is after the other specified date or time. Otherwise, this method returns false.
`compareTo(dateTime)`	Returns a negative value if the date or time is before the other specified date or time, a positive value if the date or time is after, and 0 if they are equal.

Code that uses the isBefore method

```
LocalDate currentDate = LocalDate.now();
LocalDate halloween = LocalDate.of(2015, Month.OCTOBER, 31);
if (currentDate.isBefore(halloween)) {
    System.out.println("Current date is before Halloween.");
}
```

Code that uses the isAfter method

```
LocalTime currentTime = LocalTime.now();
LocalTime startTime = LocalTime.of(15, 30);
if (currentTime.isAfter(startTime)) {
    System.out.println("Current time is after start time.");
}
```

Code that uses the compareTo method

```
LocalDate currentDate = LocalDate.now();
LocalDate halloween = LocalDate.of(2015, Month.OCTOBER, 31);
if (currentDate.compareTo(halloween) < 0) {
    System.out.println("Current date is BEFORE Halloween.");
}
else if (currentDate.compareTo(halloween) > 0) {
    System.out.println("Current date is AFTER Halloween.");
}
else if (currentDate.compareTo(halloween) == 0) {
    System.out.println("Current date is Halloween.");
}
```

Description

- You can use these methods to compare LocalTime, LocalDate, and LocalDateTime objects.

Figure 15-4 How to compare dates and times

How to adjust date/time objects

Sometimes you might need to create a new date time object by adjusting an existing date time object. To do this, you can use the methods shown in figure 15-5.

In the first example, for instance, the first statement creates a LocalDate object that's set to October 20, 2015. Then, the second statement creates a new LocalDate object set to October 31, 2015. To do that, this statement calls the withDayofMonth method on the first LocalDate object to change the day of the month from 20 to 31.

As usual, the LocalDateTime class supports all of these methods. However, the LocalDate and LocalTime classes only support the methods that are relevant to them. For example, the LocalTime class doesn't support the withMonth method, which makes sense.

When you use these methods, there are some potential inconsistent behaviors to be aware of. To start, if you a call a method and pass it an invalid value, the method typically throws a DateTimeException. For instance, the second example calls the withDayOfMonth method and passes it a value of 29. However, in this case, the month is February, and the year is 2015, which is not a leap year. As a result, February 2015 only has 28 days. So, this code throws a DateTimeException. This is what most programmers would expect.

However, what happens if you set the date to October 31, 2015 and then call the withMonth method to set the month to February as shown in the third example? This time, the class quietly adjusts the day to the last day of February. In other words, it sets the day to February 28. This might not be what most programmers would expect. As you develop applications, it's important to keep this in mind. If you don't, it could cause bugs in your application.

Methods for adjusting dates and times

Method	Description
`withDayOfMonth(day)`	Returns a new object based on the original with the day of month changed to day.
`withDayOfYear(dayOfYear)`	Returns a new object based on the original with the month and day set to dayOfYear (1 to 365).
`withMonth(month)`	Returns a new object based on the original with the month changed to month.
`withYear(year)`	Returns a new object based on the original with the year changed to year.
`withHour(hour)`	Returns a new object based on the original with the hour changed to hour.
`withMinute(minute)`	Returns a new object based on the original with the minute changed to minute.

An example that changes the month to December

```
LocalDate date = LocalDate.of(2015, 10, 20);
LocalDate newDate = date.withDayOfMonth(31);
```

An example that throws an exception due to an invalid day of month

```
LocalDateTime dateTime1 = LocalDateTime.parse("2015-02-28T15:30");
LocalDateTime newDateTime1 = dateTime.withDayOfMonth(29);
// Throws a DateTimeException because 2015 is not a leap year.
// As a result, February only has 28 days
```

An example that quietly changes the day of month

```
LocalDateTime dateTime2 = LocalDateTime.parse("2015-10-31T15:30");
LocalDateTime newDateTime2 = dateTime.withMonth(2);
// Does not throw an exception, but quietly changes the day to 28
// because there are only 28 days in February 2015.
```

Description

- To adjust a date/time object, you can use the with methods.
- These methods create a new object from the existing date/time object. In other words, they don't alter the existing date/time object.
- The LocalDateTime class supports all of the methods in the table.
- The LocalDate class only supports the methods relevant to dates.
- The LocalTime class only support the methods relevant to times.
- These methods can throw a DateTimeException for arguments that are out of range.
- The withMonth method may change the day if the current day stored in the object is out of range for the new month.

Figure 15-5 How to adjust dates and times

How to add or subtract a period of time

Figure 15-6 shows another way you can create new date and time objects using a concept called *adjusters*. Unlike the with methods shown in the previous figure, adjusters return a new date or time based on the current one, after it has been adjusted by the specified time period. For example, you can create a new date by adding or subtracting a specified time period from an existing date.

The most general way to add or subtract a period of time from an existing date or time is to use the plus or minus methods. These methods take two parameters. The second parameter uses a ChronoUnit constant to specify the unit of time. The first parameter specifies the number of units. For instance, the first example in this figure creates a new date/time by using the plus method to add 3 weeks to the current date. Conversely, the second example creates a new date/time by using the minus method to subtract 3 weeks from the current date. To do that, these examples use the WEEKS constant of the ChronoUnit enumeration.

The third example creates a new LocalTime object by using the plus method to add 3 hours to the current time. To do that, this example uses the HOURS constant of the ChronoUnit enumeration.

All of the ChronoUnit constants shown in this figure also have shortcut methods. For example, you can call the plusWeeks or minusWeeks methods to adjust the date by the specified number of weeks as shown in this figure. Similarly, you can call the plusHours or minusHours methods to adjust a time by the specified number of hours.

The last example in this figure shows how you can use method chaining when adjusting dates and times. Here, the code creates a new LocalDateTime object that is three weeks and three hours after the current date and time.

As you may have guessed, the LocalDate class doesn't support the ChronoUnit constants or shortcut methods that work with times. Conversely, the LocalTime class doesn't support the ChronoUnit constants or shortcut methods that work with dates.

A common mistake among new programmers, especially since these methods are called adjusters, is to assume that these methods change the date or time stored in the existing object. However, like all of the methods in the new date/time API, these methods return new objects and don't change the existing objects. As a result, using these methods in loops can be inefficient since it can result in a very large number of objects being created and destroyed.

This figure only lists the most commonly used ChronoUnit constants. There are others available. However, you probably won't need them unless you are working in scientific fields that need to deal with very small or large units of time.

Methods for adding or subtracting time

Method	Description
plus(long, chronoUnit)	Returns a new object after adding the specified amount of time.
minus(long, chronoUnit)	Returns a new object after subtracting the specified amount of time.

Common constants of the ChronoUnit enumeration

```
ChronoUnit.YEARS
ChronoUnit.MONTHS
ChronoUnit.WEEKS
ChronoUnit.DAYS
ChronoUnit.HOURS
ChronoUnit.MINUTES
ChronoUnit.SECONDS
```

Code that adds three weeks to the current date/time

```
LocalDateTime newDateTime = currentDateTime.plus(3, ChronoUnit.WEEKS);
```

Code that subtracts three weeks from the current date/time

```
LocalDateTime newDateTime = currentDateTime.minus(3, ChronoUnit.WEEKS);
```

Code that adds three hours to the current time

```
LocalTime newTime = currentTime.plus(3, ChronoUnit.HOURS);
```

Shortcut methods for adding or subtracting weeks

Method	Description
plusWeeks(long)	Returns a new object after adding the specified number of weeks.
minusWeeks(long)	Returns a new object after subtracting the specified number of weeks.

Shortcut methods for the previous three examples

```
LocalDateTime newDateTime = currentDateTime.plusWeeks(3);
LocalDateTime newDateTime = currentDateTime.minusWeeks(3);
LocalTime newTime = currentTime.plusHours(3);
```

Code that uses method chaining

```
LocalDateTime newDateTime = currentDateTime.plusWeeks(3).plusHours(3);
```

Description

- To adjust the date or time forward or backward, you can use the plus and minus methods with the ChronoUnit enumeration to specify a period of time. However, it's usually easier to use the shortcut methods such as the plusWeeks or minusWeeks methods.
- Shortcut methods exist for all of the ChronoUnit constants shown in this figure.
- The LocalDateTime class supports all of the methods and ChronoUnit constants. The LocalDate and LocalTime classes only support the methods and constants that are relevant to them.
- All of the plus and minus methods return new objects of the same type. In other words, they do not alter the existing objects.
- You can use method chaining to perform multiple calculations in a single statement.

Figure 15-6 How to add or subtract a period of time

How to format dates and times

If necessary, you could format dates and times by using the get methods presented earlier to build a string containing the date and time formatted the way you want. However, this approach has one major disadvantage: It doesn't account for local formatting preferences. Fortunately, the new date/time API includes a DateTimeFormatter class that accounts for local formatting preferences.

Figure 15-7 shows several static methods you can call on the DateTimeFormatter class to get different format styles for dates and times. These formatters automatically present the date in a format that's appropriate for the current locale. So, depending on your locale, the format might look different than the format shown in this figure.

For example, suppose you have a LocalDate object set to October 31, 2015, and you use the SHORT format style to format it. In the United States, it's customary to start with the month, followed by the day. As a result, in the United States this formats the date as:

```
10/31/15
```

However, in many European countries, it is customary to start with the day, followed by the month. As a result, in those countries, the same formatter formats the date as:

```
31/10/15
```

The same is true with the time formatter. For example, suppose you have a LocalTime object set to 14:30, and you use the SHORT format style to format it. In the United States, the 12-hour AM/PM clock is the norm. As a result, in the United States, this formats that time as:

```
2:30 PM
```

However, in countries where the 24-hour clock is the norm, this formats the time as:

```
14:30
```

The FormatStyle enumeration provides for four format styles: SHORT, MEDIUM, LONG, and FULL. Dates support all four of these format styles. However, times only support the SHORT and MEDIUM styles. As a result, if you want to use the same format style for both the date and time as shown in the first example, you must use the SHORT or MEDIUM styles. Otherwise, the compiler throws a DateTimeException. However, if you want, you can specify one format style for the date and another style for the time as shown in the second example.

There are several other formatters available, but they are beyond the scope of this chapter. Also, if you can't find a formatter that does what you need, you can write your own. For more information on how to do this, see the API documentation for the DateTimeFormatter class.

A class and an enumeration for formatting dates and times

```
java.time.format.DateTimeFormatter
java.time.format.FormatStyle
```

Common static methods of the DateTimeFormatter class

Method	Description
ofLocalizedDate(dateStyle)	Returns a DateTimeFormatter object for the date, but not time.
ofLocalizedTime(timeStyle)	Returns a DateTimeFormatter object for the time, but not date.
ofLocalizedDateTime(dateTimeStyle)	Returns a DateTimeFormatter object for the date and time.
ofLocalizedDateTime(dateStyle, timeStyle)	Returns a DateTimeFormatter object for the date and time, but with different formatting styles used for each.

A common method of the DateTimeFormatter class

Method	Description
format(dateTime)	Returns a String object for the formatted date/time.

Constants of the FormatStyle enumeration

Constant	Date example	Time example
FormatStyle.SHORT	10/31/15	6:30 PM
FormatStyle.MEDIUM	Oct 31, 2015	6:30:00 PM
FormatStyle.LONG	October 31, 2015	DateTimeException
FormatStyle.FULL	Saturday, October 31, 2015	DateTimeException

Code that uses the same style to format both the date and time

```
DateTimeFormatter dtf = DateTimeFormatter.ofLocalizedDateTime(
        FormatStyle.MEDIUM);
String currentDateTimeFormatted = dtf.format(currentDateTime);
```

Code that uses a separate style for the date and time

```
DateTimeFormatter dtf = DateTimeFormatter.ofLocalizedDateTime(
        FormatStyle.LONG, FormatStyle.SHORT);
String currentDateTimeFormatted = dtf.format(currentDateTime);
```

Description

- You can use the ofLocalized methods to format a date and time for the locale of the system that the application is running on.
- You can use the FormatStyle constants to specify the format style for the date and time.
- If you attempt to use the LONG or FULL style to format a time, the compiler throws a DateTimeException.
- If none of the formats included with the API meets your needs, you can write your own custom formatters.

Figure 15-7 How to format dates and times

An Invoice class that includes an invoice date

Figure 15-8 shows how to add a date to the Invoice class that was presented in the previous chapter. To start, this class declares a LocalDateTime instance variable to store the invoice date. As a result, the invoice date includes both a date and a time.

The constructor for this class sets the invoice date to the current date and time. To do that, it uses the now method of the LocalDateTime class.

If you don't want to store the time, you can use a LocalDate object to store the date. In this figure, for example, you could use a LocalDate object to store the invoice date. However, it's entirely possible that you may also want to know what time an invoice was created. As a result, in most cases, it makes sense to store the extra data as shown by the class in this figure.

This class includes three methods that provide access to the invoice date. First, the setInvoiceDate method provides a method that allows you to set the invoice date. For example, if you get the data for an Invoice object from a database, you can use this method to set the invoice date. Second, the getInvoiceDate method returns the invoice date as a LocalDateTime object.

Third, the getInvoiceDateFormatted method returns a String object for the invoice date after the code has applied formatting to the LocalDateTime object for the invoice date. Within this method, the first statement creates a formatter for the date only that uses the SHORT format style. Then, the second statement uses this formatter to format the invoice date and return the resulting String object. As a result, this method only displays the date the invoice was created, even though the Invoice object also stores the time the invoice was created. If that's not what you want, you can add more methods to this class that get the date and time in other formats.

An Invoice class that includes a date

```
package murach.business;

import java.text.NumberFormat;
import java.time.LocalDateTime;
import java.time.format.DateTimeFormatter;
import java.time.format.FormatStyle;
import java.util.ArrayList;

public class Invoice {

    private ArrayList<LineItem> lineItems;
    private LocalDateTime invoiceDate;

    public Invoice() {
        lineItems = new ArrayList<>();
        invoiceDate = LocalDateTime.now();
    }

    public void addItem(LineItem lineItem) {
        lineItems.add(lineItem);
    }

    public ArrayList<LineItem> getLineItems() {
        return lineItems;
    }

    public double getTotal() {
        double invoiceTotal = 0;
        for (LineItem lineItem : lineItems) {
            invoiceTotal += lineItem.getTotal();
        }
        return invoiceTotal;
    }

    public String getTotalFormatted() {
        NumberFormat currency = NumberFormat.getCurrencyInstance();
        return currency.format(getTotal());
    }

    public void setInvoiceDate(LocalDateTime invoiceDate) {
        this.invoiceDate = invoiceDate;
    }

    public LocalDateTime getInvoiceDate() {
        return invoiceDate;
    }

    public String getInvoiceDateFormatted() {
        DateTimeFormatter dtf = DateTimeFormatter.ofLocalizedDate(
                FormatStyle.SHORT);
        return dtf.format(invoiceDate);
    }
}
```

Figure 15-8 An Invoice class that includes an invoice date

Perspective

Now that you've finished this chapter, you should understand some of the differences between the old date/time API that was available prior to Java 8 and the new date/time API that's available with Java 8 and later. In addition, you should be able to use the classes provided by the new date/time API to work with dates and times.

Summary

- Prior to Java 8, it was common to use classes in the java.util and java.text packages to work with and format dates and times.
- With Java 8 or later, you can use the classes in the java.time package to work with and format dates and times. This package has several advantages over the older classes for working with dates and times.

Exercise 15-1 Add a due date to the Invoice application

For this exercise, you'll modify the Invoice class that's shown at the end of this chapter so it contains methods that return a due date, calculated as 30 days after the invoice date.

1. Open the project named ch15_ex1_Invoice that's in the ex_starts folder. Then, review the code in the Invoice and InvoiceApp classes.
2. In the Invoice class, modify the getInvoiceDateFormatted method so it returns the due date using the MEDIUM format style.
3. In the Invoice class, add a method named getDueDate. This method should calculate and return a LocalDateTime object that's 30 days after the invoice date.
4. In the Invoice class, add a method named getDueDateFormatted. This method should return the due date using the MEDIUM format style.
5. In the InvoiceApp class, modify the displayInvoice method so it displays the invoice date and the due date before it displays the line items like this:

```
Invoice date:     Jul 1, 2015
Invoice due date: Jul 31, 2015

Description                        Price    Qty  Total
Murach's Java Programming          $57.50   2    $115.00

Invoice total: $115.00
```

6. Run the application to make sure it works correctly.

Exercise 15-2 Calculate the user's age

In this exercise, you'll write an application that gets the user's date of birth, calculates the user's age in years, and displays the user's age. When you're done, the console should look something like this:

```
Welcome to the Age Calculator

Enter your date of birth (YYYY-MM-DD): 1968-02-04

Your date of birth is Feb 4, 1968
The current date is Apr 8, 2015
Your age is 47
```

1. Open the project named ch15_ex2_AgeCalculator that's in the ex_starts folder. Then, review the code in the AgeCalculatorApp class.
2. Add code to this class that parses the string entered by the user to create a LocalDate object.
3. Add code to format and print the user's date of birth.
4. Add code to format and print the current date.
5. Add code to calculate and print the user's age in years.
6. Run the application and test it to make sure it works correctly for a date in the correct format.
7. Run the application and test it with a date in an invalid format such as "Feb 4, 1968". This should cause an exception to occur.
8. Run the application and test it with a date that's after the current date. This date doesn't make sense, but that's OK for now. If necessary, you can add data validation code to prevent the user from entering such a date later.

16

How to handle exceptions

In chapter 8, you learned how to use a try statement to catch exceptions. However, there's more to exceptions than what was covered in that chapter. In this chapter, you'll learn the rest of what you need to know to develop professional applications that handle all kinds of exceptions.

An introduction to exceptions 410
The exception hierarchy 410
How exceptions are propagated 412
How to work with exceptions 414
How to use the try statement 414
How to use the try-with-resources statement 416
How to use the methods of an exception 418
How to use a multi-catch block 420
How to use the throws clause 422
How to use the throw statement 424
How to work with custom exception classes 426
How to create your own exception class 426
How to use exception chaining 428
Perspective 430

An introduction to exceptions

All applications can encounter errors when they run. For example, a user may enter data that's not appropriate, or a file that your application needs may get moved or deleted. These types of errors may cause a poorly-coded application to crash and cause the user to lose data. In contrast, when an error occurs in a well-coded application, the application notifies the user and attempts to recover from the error. If it can't recover, it saves as much data as possible, cleans up resources, and exits the application as smoothly as possible.

In the old days of programming, this was rather difficult to do because programming languages had no easy way to check for errors. Even worse, they had no easy way to communicate those errors to other parts of the application that might need to know about them. To address this problem, most modern programming languages, including Java, support an error handling mechanism known as *exceptions*. Exceptions allow you to write robust code that can handle errors more easily and reliably. Before you learn how to handle errors, though, you need to learn about the exception hierarchy and the exception handling mechanism.

The exception hierarchy

In Java, an *exception* is an object that's created from the Exception class or one of its subclasses. An exception represents an error that has occurred, and it contains information about the error. All exception classes are derived from the Throwable class as shown by the diagram in figure 16-1.

As this diagram shows, two classes directly inherit the Throwable class: Error and Exception. The classes that inherit the Error class represent internal errors that you usually can't do anything about, such as problems with the Java runtime environment. As a result, you can ignore these errors most of the time (or in some cases, file a bug report with the JVM vendor). In contrast, you need to handle most of the exceptions that are derived from the Exception class.

The classes in the Exception hierarchy are divided into two categories: (1) exceptions that are derived from the RuntimeException class and (2) all other exceptions. The exceptions that are derived from the RuntimeException class are called *unchecked exceptions* because the compiler doesn't force you to explicitly handle them. On the other hand, the compiler requires that you explicitly handle all the other exceptions that are derived from the Exception class. As a result, these exceptions are known as *checked exceptions*.

Unchecked exceptions often occur because of coding errors. For example, if an application attempts to access an array with an invalid index, Java throws an ArrayIndexOutOfBoundsException, which is a type of IndexOutOfBoundsException. If you're careful when you write your code, you can usually prevent these types of exceptions from being thrown.

Checked exceptions, on the other hand, usually occur due to circumstances that are beyond the programmer's control, such as a missing file or a bad network connection. Although you can't avoid these exceptions, you can write code that handles them when they occur.

The Throwable hierarchy

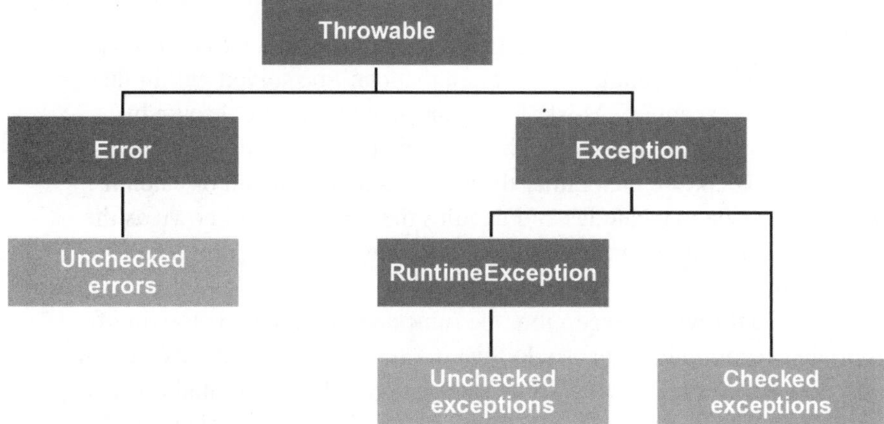

Common checked exceptions

```
ClassNotFoundException
IOException
    EOFException
    FileNotFoundException
```

Common unchecked exceptions

```
ArithmeticException
IllegalArgumentException
    NumberFormatException
IndexOutOfBoundsException
    ArrayIndexOutOfBoundsException
    StringIndexOutOfBoundsException
NullPointerException
```

Description

- An *exception* is an object of the Exception class or any of its subclasses. It represents a condition that prevents a method from successfully completing.
- The Exception class is derived from a class named Throwable. Two types of exceptions are derived from the Exception class: checked exceptions and unchecked exceptions.
- *Checked exceptions* are checked by the compiler. As a result, you must write code that handles all checked exceptions before you can compile your code.
- *Unchecked exceptions* are not checked by the compiler, but they can occur at runtime. It's generally considered a good practice to write code that handles unchecked exceptions. If an unchecked exception occurs and isn't handled by your code, your application terminates.
- Like the Exception class, the Error class is also derived from the Throwable class. However, the Error class identifies internal errors that are rare and can't usually be recovered from. As a result, you can usually ignore the Error class.

Figure 16-1 The exception hierarchy

How exceptions are propagated

Figure 16-2 shows how the exception handling mechanism works in Java. To start, when a method encounters a problem that can't be solved within that method, it *throws* an exception. Most of the time, exceptions are thrown by methods from classes in the Java API. Then, any method that calls a method that throws a checked exception must either throw the exception again or catch it and handle it. The code that catches and handles the exception is known as the *exception handler*. You'll learn the details of throwing, catching, and handling exceptions in this chapter.

Once a method throws an exception, the runtime system begins looking for the appropriate exception handler. To do this, it searches through the execution *stack trace,* also called the *call stack*. The stack trace is the list of methods that have been called in the reverse order that they were called. In this diagram, for example, the stack trace when the code in MethodD executes is: MethodD, MethodC, MethodB, and MethodA.

This figure shows how MethodA calls MethodB, which calls MethodC, which calls MethodD. Here, MethodD may throw an exception. If it does, MethodD throws the exception up to MethodC, which throws it to MethodB, which throws it to MethodA, which catches it in a catch clause.

If you throw a checked exception all the way out of the application by coding a throws clause on each method in the call stack, including the main method, the application terminates when the exception occurs. Then, Java displays information about the exception at the console.

Note that unchecked exceptions work the same way, except that you don't have to explicitly list unchecked exceptions in the throws clause of a method declaration. For example, suppose the try statement in MethodA also includes a catch clause that catches a runtime exception such as ArithmethicException. Then, if the code in MethodD throws ArithmeticException, the exception propagates up through MethodC and MethodB and is handled by the exception handler in MethodA, even though none of the method declarations include a throws clause that lists ArithmeticException.

How Java propagates exceptions

```
MethodA() {
    try {
        MethodB();
    } catch(ExceptionOne e) {
        // handle exception here
    }
}

MethodB() throws ExceptionOne {
    MethodC();
}

MethodC() throws ExceptionOne {
    MethodD();
}

MethodD() throws ExceptionOne {
    throw new ExceptionOne();
}
```

Two ways to handle checked exceptions

- Throw the exception to the calling method
- Catch the exception and handle it

Description

- When a method encounters a condition it can't handle, that method should throw an exception. This allows users of the method to handle the exception in a way that's appropriate for their applications. Many methods in the Java API throw exceptions.
- When a method calls another method that throws a checked exception, the method must either throw the exception to its caller or catch the exception and handle it directly. Code that catches an exception is known as an *exception handler*.
- When an exception occurs, the runtime system looks for the appropriate exception handler. To do that, it looks through the *stack trace*, or *call stack*, which lists the methods that have been called until it finds a method that catches the exception.

Figure 16-2 How exceptions are propagated

How to work with exceptions

In the topics that follow, you'll learn some additional techniques for using the try statement. You'll also learn how to throw an exception and how to use some of the constructors and methods of the Throwable class.

How to use the try statement

Figure 16-3 starts by showing the syntax for coding a try statement that catches exceptions. This syntax shows that a *try statement* begins with a *try block* that's coded around any statements that may throw an exception. The try block is followed by a *catch block* for each type of exception that may be thrown in the try block.

When you add catch blocks, you should be sure to code them in sequence from the most specific class in the Throwable hierarchy to the least specific class. For example, the FileNotFoundException inherits IOException, so FileNotFoundException must be coded before IOException. Otherwise, the code won't compile. For exceptions that are at the same level in the exception hierarchy, such as FileNotFoundException and EOFException, the order doesn't matter.

After the catch blocks, you can code a *finally block* to free any system resources that are used by the try statement. For example, you might close files or release database connections in a finally block. The finally block is optional, but if you code it, it is always executed. This is true whether or not an exception has been thrown, and it's true even if a return statement has been executed.

The code example shows a method named readFirstLine that contains a try statement that includes two catch blocks and a finally block. This method accepts a String that specifies the path to a file, and it returns a String for the first line of the file. Within the body of the method, the first statement initializes a variable that can store a BufferedReader object. This object lets you read data from a file in an efficient way.

Within the try block, the first statement creates a BufferedReader object by passing it a new FileReader object for the file at the specified path. If the file doesn't exist, this constructor throws a FileNotFoundException, and code execution jumps into the first catch block. However, if the file exists, the second statement calls the readLine method of the BufferedReader object to read the first line of the file. If this method isn't able to read the first line, it throws an IOException and code execution jumps into the second catch block. Otherwise, the return statement in the try block returns a String object for the first line to the calling method.

Both catch blocks work similarly. To start, the first statement prints a message to the console that briefly describes the error. Then, the second statement returns a null to the calling method. This return value is appropriate since the method was unable to read the first line of the file.

Within the finally block, the code attempts to close the BufferedReader object by calling its close method. Unfortunately, if the code in the try block doesn't execute successfully, the BufferedReader object may be null. As a result,

The syntax of the try statement

```
try {statements}
[catch (MostSpecificExceptionType e) {statements}] ...
[catch (LeastSpecificExceptionType e) {statements}]
[finally {statements}]
```

A method that catches two types of exceptions and uses a finally clause

```
public static String readFirstLine(String path) {
    BufferedReader in = null;
    try {
        in = new BufferedReader(
             new FileReader(path));      // may throw FileNotFoundException
        String line = in.readLine();     // may throw IOException
        return line;
    } catch (FileNotFoundException e) {
        System.out.println("File not found.");
        return null;
    } catch(IOException e) {
        System.out.println("I/O error occurred.");
        return null;
    } finally {
        try {
            if (in != null) {
                in.close();              // may throw IOException
            }
        } catch (Exception e) {
            System.out.println("Unable to close file.");
        }
    }
}
```

Description

- You can code a *try block* around any statements that may throw an exception.
- You can code one *catch block* for each type of exception that may be thrown in the try block. You should code the catch clauses in sequence from the most specific class in the Throwable hierarchy to the least specific class.
- You can code a *finally block* to free any system resources that are used by objects created in the try block. The code in the finally block is always executed.

Figure 16-3 How to use the try statement

this code checks that this object is not null before it calls its close method. In addition, the close method may throw an IOException, so you need to code a try statement within the finally block that catches this exception.

When you code try statements, it's often tempting to create empty catch clauses for checked exceptions just to get your code to compile. However, this can make debugging difficult because if an exception is thrown, you never find out about it. Instead, your code doesn't work correctly and gives no indication of what went wrong. Furthermore, it's all too easy to forget to code the exception handler later. In that case, the exception never gets handled. Instead, the empty catch clause catches the exception and ignores it. This is sometimes called *swallowing an exception*, or *eating an exception*, and it's rarely an acceptable coding practice.

How to use the try-with-resources statement

Prior to Java 7, you had to use a finally block to release system resources as you saw in the previous figure. That required including additional exception handling code in case the code in the finally block threw exceptions. Unfortunately, the length of this exception handling code can make it difficult to read and maintain your code.

That's why Java 7 introduced the *try-with-resources* statement that's described in figure 16-4. This is a special type of try statement that declares and instantiates one or more objects that use system resources and automatically closes those objects and releases the resources after the try statement finishes executing. This allows you to write less error handling code and to focus on the logic of your code. For example, the readFirstLine method in this figure accomplishes the same task as the method in the previous figure, but without the unwieldy finally clause. As a result, the code is easier to read and to maintain.

To use the try-with-resources statement, you begin by coding a set of parentheses after the try keyword but before the braces for the try block. Then, within the parentheses, you can code one or more statements that declare and instantiate objects that use system resources. In this figure, for example, the statement that creates the BufferedReader object is coded within these parentheses. To create multiple objects, you just separate the statements that declare and instantiate them with a semicolon.

Note that you can only use the try-with-resources statement with objects that implement the java.lang.AutoCloseable interface. However, as of Java 7, most of the classes in the Java API that work with system resources have been retrofitted to implement this interface. That includes all of the classes for working with files and databases that are described in this book.

The syntax of the try-with-resources statement

```
try (statement[;statement] ...) {statements}
[catch (MostSpecificExceptionType e) {statements}] ...
[catch (LeastSpecificExceptionType e) {statements}]
```

A method that catches two types of exceptions and automatically closes the specified resource

```
public static String readFirstLine(String path) {
    try (BufferedReader in = new BufferedReader(
                                  new FileReader(path))) {
        String line = in.readLine();
        return line;
    } catch (FileNotFoundException e) {
        System.err.println("File not found.");
        return null;
    } catch (IOException e) {
        System.err.println("I/O error occurred.");
        return null;
    }
}
```

Description

- The *try-with-resources* statement is a special type of try statement that declares and instantiates one or more objects that use system resources and automatically closes those objects and releases the resources after the try statement finishes executing.
- The try-with-resources statement was introduced with Java 7.
- Any object that implements the java.lang.AutoCloseable interface can be created using the try-with-resources statement.
- As of Java 7, most of the classes in the Java API that use system resources have been retrofitted to implement the AutoCloseable interface.
- If an object doesn't implement the AutoClosable interface, NetBeans warns you if you attempt to use try-with-resources with it. It also causes a compile-time error.

Figure 16-4 How to use the try-with-resources statement

How to use the methods of an exception

Figure 16-5 shows how to use the methods of an exception to get more information about the exception. Since the Throwable class provides these methods, they are available to all exception objects.

The first example uses the first three methods in the table to print increasing amounts of information about an exception. In this case, the catch block catches an IOException object and assigns it to a variable named e. Within the catch block, the first statement uses the getMessage method to get the exception's message, and it prints this message to the console. Then, the second statement uses the toString method to get the exception's class and message, and it prints this data to the console. Next, the third statement uses the printStackTrace method to print the exception's class, message, and stack trace to the console.

When you write code that handles exceptions, you need to decide how much information is the right amount to display. For example, in some cases, you only want to use the getMessage method to display the exception's message. However, not all exceptions include messages. Because of that, it's often helpful to use the toString method to display the exception's class name and message. Other times, you may want to use the printStackTrace method to display a complete stack trace for the exception. This can help you debug your applications when you're testing them. However, it's generally considered a good practice to remove the printStackTrace method from production applications or replace it with a better way of logging exceptions.

In the first example, the statements in the catch block use the System.err object to print data to the standard error output stream. This works the same as using the System.out object to print data to the standard output stream. In NetBeans, for example, both of these objects print data to the Output window. However, the error output stream is displayed in red, which is consistent with how NetBeans displays exceptions. As a result, it's common to use the error output stream for displaying information about exceptions. You can also direct the standard output stream to one source (such as the console) and the standard error output stream to another source (such as a log file).

If you don't supply an argument for the printStackTrace method, it prints its data to the error output stream (System.err). However, if you want to print this data to another output stream such as the standard output stream (System.out), you can specify that output stream as an argument of the method. In this figure, for example, all of the statements in the second example print data to the standard output stream.

Four methods available from all exceptions

Method	Description
`getMessage()`	Returns the exception's message, if one is available.
`toString()`	Returns the exception's class name and message, if one is available.
`printStackTrace()`	Prints the exception's class name, message, and stack trace to the standard error output stream (System.err).
`printStackTrace(outputStream)`	Prints the exception's class name, message, and stack trace to the specified output stream.

How to print exception data to the error output stream

```
catch(IOException e) {
    System.err.println(e.getMessage() + "\n");
    System.err.println(e.toString() + "\n");
    e.printStackTrace();
    return null;
}
```

Resulting output for a FileNotFoundException

```
c:\murach\java_netbeans\produx.txt (The system cannot find the
file specified)

java.io.FileNotFoundException:
c:\murach\java_netbeans\produx.txt (The system cannot find the
file specified)

java.io.FileNotFoundException:
c:\murach\java_netbeans\produx.txt (The system cannot find the
file specified)
  at java.io.FileInputStream.open(Native Method)
  at java.io.FileInputStream.<init>(FileInputStream.java:131)
  at java.io.FileInputStream.<init>(FileInputStream.java:87)
  at java.io.FileReader.<init>(FileReader.java:58)
  at ProductApp.readFirstLine(ProductApp.java:70)
  at ProductApp.main(ProductApp.java:10)
```

How to print exception data to the standard output stream

```
catch(IOException e) {
    System.out.println(e.getMessage() + "\n");
    System.out.println(e.toString() + "\n");
    e.printStackTrace(System.out);
    return null;
}
```

Description

- The Throwable class provides methods that are available to all exceptions.
- The System.err object works like the System.out object, but it prints data to the standard error stream instead of the standard output stream.
- It's generally considered a good practice to remove the printStackTrace method from production applications or replace it with a better way of logging exceptions.

Figure 16-5 How to use the methods of an exception

How to use a multi-catch block

Figure 16-6 shows how to use the *multi-catch block* feature that was introduced with Java 7. This feature allows you to use a single catch block for multiple exceptions that are at the same level in the inheritance hierarchy. To do that, you separate the exceptions with a pipe character (|) as shown in the syntax at the top of this figure.

To illustrate how the multi-catch block works, the first example in this figure shows how you would catch both the FileNotFoundException and the EOFException prior to Java 7. Here, a separate catch clause is coded for each exception. Because these exceptions are at the same level in the inheritance hierarchy, though, and because the code in the catch blocks for these exceptions are identical, you can catch them in a multi-catch block as shown in the second example.

On a related note, both FileNotFoundException and EOFException are subclasses of IOException. As a result, if you want to execute the same code for all three exceptions, you only need to code a catch block for the IOException like this:

```
try (BufferedReader in = new BufferedReader(new FileReader(path))) {
    String line = in.readLine();    // may throw IOException
    return line;
} catch(IOException e) {
    System.err.println(e.toString());
    return null;
}
```

In this case, the same code is executed for IOException and all of its subclasses, including the FileNotFoundException and EOFException. Although this technique doesn't provide as much flexibility as the multi-catch block feature, it's commonly used and works for all versions of Java.

The syntax of the multi-catch block

```
catch (ExceptionType | ExceptionType [| ExceptionType]... e) {statements}
```

A method that does not use a multi-catch block

```
public static String readFirstLine(String path) {
    try (BufferedReader in = new BufferedReader(
                             new FileReader(path))) {
        String line = in.readLine();          // may throw IOException
        return line;
    } catch (FileNotFoundException e) {
        System.err.println(e.toString());
        return null;
    } catch (EOFException e) {
        System.err.println(e.toString());
        return null;
    } catch(IOException e) {
        e.printStackTrace();
        return null;
    }
}
```

A method that uses a multi-catch block

```
public static String readFirstLine(String path) {
    try (BufferedReader in = new BufferedReader(
                             new FileReader(path))) {
        String line = in.readLine();          // may throw IOException
        return line;
    } catch (FileNotFoundException | EOFException e) {
        System.err.println(e.toString());
        return null;
    } catch(IOException e) {
        e.printStackTrace();
        return null;
    }
}
```

Description

- The *multi-catch block* allows you to use a single catch block for multiple exceptions that are at the same level in the inheritance hierarchy.
- The multi-catch block was introduced with Java 7.

Figure 16-6 How to use a multi-catch block

How to use the throws clause

When you call a method from the Java API that throws a checked exception, you must either rethrow the exception or catch it. If you decide that you can't handle the exception properly in the method that you're coding, you can code a throws clause on the method declaration as shown in figure 16-7. This throws the exception up to the calling method, which can handle it with an exception handler or throw it up to its calling method.

The first example shows a readFirstLine method that's similar to the other readFirstLine methods that you've seen in this chapter. However, this method throws the exception instead of catching it. Here, the first statement in this method calls the constructor of the FileReader class, which may throw a FileNotFoundException. Then, the next statement calls the readLine method of the BufferedReader object, which may throw an IOException. Since the FileNotFoundException class inherits the IOException class, this method can throw both types of exceptions by using a throws clause to throw an IOException.

If the first example throws a FileNotFoundException, that exception is implicitly cast to an IOException. As a result, the calling method can catch or throw either exception. That's true even though the throws clause of the readLine method doesn't explicitly throw the FileNotFoundException.

The second example shows how to explicitly throw both exceptions. To do that, you use commas to separate the exceptions in the throws clause. The advantage of this approach is that it clearly identifies all exceptions that can be thrown by the method. The disadvantage of this approach is that it requires more code for the same functionality that's provided by the first example.

This figure also shows an example of an error message that the compiler generates if you don't catch or throw a checked exception. More specifically, the compiler generates an error message like this if you call the readLine method and don't catch or throw the IOException.

At this point, you may be wondering when you should throw an exception and when you should handle an exception. In general, you should throw exceptions early and catch them late. In other words, if you are at a low level in your application where you aren't able to handle the exception, you should throw it. Then, the exception propagates up to a higher level where you can catch the exception and handle it in a way that makes sense for your application. For example, you can ask the user how to handle the exception. You can display a user-friendly error message. Or, if necessary, you can save data, close resources, and exit the application as gracefully as possible.

The syntax for the declaration of a method that throws exceptions

```
modifiers returnType methodName([parameterList]) throws exceptionList {}
```

A method that throws an IOException

```
public static String readFirstLine(String path) throws IOException {
    BufferedReader in = new BufferedReader(
                        new FileReader(path));
    String line = in.readLine();
    return line;
}
```

A method that throws two exceptions

```
public static String readFirstLine(String path)
       throws FileNotFoundException, IOException {
    BufferedReader in = new BufferedReader(
                        new FileReader(path));
    String line = in.readLine();
    return line;
}
```

Compiler error if you don't catch or throw a checked exception

```
error: unreported exception IOException; must be caught or
declared to be thrown
```

Description

- Any method that calls a method that throws a checked exception must either catch the exception or throw the exception. Otherwise, the application won't compile.
- To throw a checked exception, you code a throws clause in the method declaration. The throws clause must name each checked exception that's thrown up to the calling method. If you list multiple exceptions, you can separate each exception with a comma.
- Although you can specify unchecked exceptions in the throws clause, the compiler doesn't force you to handle unchecked exceptions.

Figure 16-7 How to use the throws clause

How to use the throw statement

When you're coding a method, you may sometimes need to throw an exception. For example, you may need to throw an exception when a method encounters a problem that prevents it from completing its task, such as when the method is passed unacceptable argument values. You may also need to throw an exception to test an exception handler. Finally, you may need to throw an exception when you want to catch an exception, perform some processing, and then throw the exception again so it can be handled by the calling method.

Figure 16-8 shows how to throw an exception. To do that, you code a throw statement that throws an object of an exception class. To do that, you usually use the new keyword to create an object from the exception class. Since all exception classes inherit the Throwable class, you can use either of the constructors shown in this figure to create an exception. If you use the first constructor, no message is assigned to the exception. If you use the second constructor, the message you specify is assigned to the exception.

The first example in this figure shows a method named calculateFutureValue that accepts three parameters and throws an IllegalArgumentException if any of these parameters are less than or equal to zero. In general, it's a good coding practice for any public method to throw an IllegalArgumentException if the method is passed any parameters that have unacceptable values.

The second example shows how you might throw an exception to test an exception handler. This technique is useful for exceptions that are difficult to force otherwise. For example, you can easily test a handler for FileNotFoundException by providing a file name that doesn't exist. But testing a handler for IOException can be difficult. Sometimes, the easiest way is to explicitly throw the exception at the point you would expect it to occur.

When you throw an exception for testing, the throw statement must be the last statement of the try clause, or it must be coded within an if statement. Otherwise, the code won't compile, and the compiler will display a message that indicates that the code contains unreachable statements. In the second example, because a statement is coded after the throw statement, the throw statement is coded within an if statement. Notice that this if statement is coded so its condition is always true, so the exception is always thrown. However, this if statement allows the code to compile.

The third example shows code that rethrows an exception after processing it. Here, the exception handler prints an error message that indicates an exception has occurred. Then, it rethrows the exception so the calling method can handle it. To do that, the throw statement throws the IOException object named e that was declared in the catch clause.

The syntax of the throw statement

```
throw throwableObject;
```

Common constructors of the Throwable class

Constructor	Description
`Throwable()`	Creates a new exception with a null message.
`Throwable(message)`	Creates a new exception with the specified message.

A method that throws an unchecked exception

```
public double calculateFutureValue(double monthlyPayment,
        double monthlyInterestRate, int months) {
    if (monthlyPayment <= 0) {
        throw new IllegalArgumentException("Monthly payment must be > 0");
    }
    if (monthlyInterestRate <= 0) {
        throw new IllegalArgumentException("Interest rate must be > 0");
    }
    if (months <= 0) {
        throw new IllegalArgumentException("Months must be > 0");
    }

    // code to calculate and return future value goes here
}
```

Code that throws an IOException for testing purposes

```
try {
    // code that reads the first line of a file

    if (true) {
        throw new IOException("I/O exception test");
    }
    return firstLine;
} catch (IOException e) {
   // code to handle IOException goes here
}
```

Code that rethrows an exception

```
try {
    // code that throws IOException goes here
} catch (IOException e) {
   System.out.println("IOException thrown in readFirstLine method.");
   throw e;
}
```

Description

- You use the throw statement to throw an exception. You can throw any object that's created from a subclass of the Throwable class.
- You can use the constructors of the Throwable class to create a new exception. Then, you can throw that exception. To throw an existing exception, you must first catch it.

Figure 16-8 How to use the throw statement

How to work with custom exception classes

Although the Java API contains a wide range of exceptions, you may encounter a situation where none of those exceptions describes your exception accurately. In other cases, you may want to wrap an exception with a different exception in order to make code more abstract. In either case, you can code a class that defines a custom exception as described in the following topics. Then, you can throw your exception just as you would throw any other exception.

How to create your own exception class

Figure 16-9 shows how to create your own custom exception class. To do that, you inherit the Exception class or one of its subclasses to create a checked exception. To illustrate, the first example in this figure shows an exception class named DBException that inherits the Exception class. As a result, DBException is a checked exception. However, you can also code a class that defines an unchecked exception by inheriting the RuntimeException class or one of its subclasses.

By convention, all exception classes should have a default constructor that doesn't accept any arguments and another constructor that accepts a string argument. As a result, if you code these constructors for your exception classes, they will behave like the rest of the exception classes in the Java API. The first example shows how to code these two constructors. Here, the second constructor uses the super keyword to call the constructor of the Exception class and passes the message parameter to it.

The second example shows code that throws the custom DBException. This example defines a method named getProduct, which calls a method named readProduct to retrieve a Product object for a specified product code. The readProduct method throws an IOException, which is caught by the catch clause. The catch clause then throws a DBException.

The third example shows code that catches the custom exception. Here, the getProduct method is called in a try statement and the DBException is caught by the catch clause. In the exception handler for the DBException, an error message is displayed at the console.

At first glance, it might seem that the custom exception defined by these examples isn't necessary. After all, couldn't the getProduct method simply throw an IOException if an IO error occurs? Although it could, that would result in a poor design because it would expose too many details of the getProduct method's operation. An IOException can occur only when file I/O operations are used. As a result, throwing IOException would reveal that the getProduct method uses file I/O to access the product data.

What if the application is changed so the product data is kept in a database instead of a file? In that case, the getProduct method would throw some type of database exception instead of an IOException. Then, any methods that call the

Code for the DBException class

```
public class DBException extends Exception {
    public DBException() {}

    public DBException(String message) {
        super(message);
    }
}
```

A method that throws the DBException

```
public static Product getProduct(String productCode) throws DBException {
    try {
        Product p = readProduct(productCode);     // may throw IOException
        return p;
    } catch (IOException e) {
        throw new DBException(
            "An error occurred while reading the product.");
    }
}
```

Code that catches the DBException

```
try {
    Product p = getProduct("1234");
} catch (DBException e) {
    System.out.println(e.getMessage());
}
```

When to define your own exceptions

- When a method requires an exception that isn't provided by any of Java's exception types.
- When using a built-in Java exception would inappropriately expose details of a method's operation.

Description

- To define a checked exception, inherit the Exception class or any of its subclasses.
- To define an unchecked exception, inherit the RuntimeException class or any of its subclasses.
- By convention, each exception class should contain a default constructor that doesn't accept any arguments and another constructor that accepts a string argument.

Figure 16-9 How to create your own exception class

getProduct method would have to be changed to handle the new exception. By creating a custom DBException for the getProduct method, you can hide the details of how the getProduct method works from methods that call it. So even if the application is changed to use a database, the getProduct method can still throw DBException if an error occurs while retrieving a product object.

How to use exception chaining

You'll often throw custom exceptions in response to other exceptions that occur. For example, in the previous figure, DBException was thrown in response to IOException. Unfortunately, in that figure, information about the underlying error that led to the DBException was lost. And that information might prove invaluable to determining what caused the DBException to occur.

Figure 16-10 shows how you can throw a custom exception without losing the details of the original exception that was thrown. This feature is called *exception chaining* because it lets you chain exceptions together. Whenever you create a custom exception type, it's a good practice to use exception chaining to avoid losing valuable debugging information.

To use exception chaining, you use an exception constructor that lets you specify an exception object as the cause for the new exception you're creating. In the first example, for instance, the DBException class lets you specify a cause via the constructor. Here, the second constructor accepts a Throwable object as a parameter. Then, it passes this parameter on to the Exception constructor.

The second example shows code that throws a DBException in response to an IOException. Here, the IOException object is passed to the DBException constructor as an argument. That way, all of the information contained in the original IOException is saved as part of the DBException object.

The third example shows code that catches a DBException and displays information about the exception. Here, an error message is displayed that indicates that a DBException has occurred, that the DBException was caused by a FileNotFoundException, and it includes the message that's stored in the FileNotFoundException. In most cases, that should be all the information you need to determine the cause of this exception.

A constructor of the Throwable class for exception chaining

Constructor	Description
`Throwable(cause)`	Creates a new exception with the specified exception object as its cause.

A custom exception class that uses exception chaining

```
public class DBException extends Exception {
    public DBException() {}

    public DBException(Exception cause) {
        super(cause);
    }
}
```

Code that throws a DBException with chaining

```
catch (IOException e) {
    throw new DBException(e);
}
```

Code that catches a DBException

```
catch (DBException e) {
    System.err.println(e);
}
```

Resulting output

```
DBException: java.io.FileNotFoundException:
c:\murach\produx.txt (The system cannot find the file specified)
```

Description

- *Exception chaining* lets you maintain exception information for exceptions that are caught when new exceptions are thrown. Exception chaining uses the cause field, which represents the original exception that caused the current exception to be thrown.

Perspective

In this chapter, you learned the most important techniques for handling exceptions in Java. Exceptions can help you write more robust, more error free code by allowing an error to be propagated up the call stack where it can be handled better than at the low level where the error occurred. For example, a getProduct method that retrieves Product objects probably has no idea what should be done if an error occurs. So this low-level method throws an exception that's handled by a higher-level method, which can write the exception to an error log, display an error message, or even terminate the application. In short, exception handling usually affects every level of an application's design.

Summary

- In Java, an *exception* is an object that's created from a class that's derived from the Exception class or one of its subclasses. When an exception occurs, a well-coded application notifies its users of the exception and minimizes any disruptions or data loss that may result from the exception.
- Exceptions derived from the RuntimeException class and its subclasses are *unchecked exceptions* because they aren't checked by the compiler. All other exceptions are *checked exceptions*.
- Any method that calls a method that *throws* a checked exception must either throw the exception by coding a throws clause or *catch* it by coding *try/catch/finally blocks* as an *exception handler*.
- The *try-with-resources* statement is a special type of try statement that declares and instantiates one or more objects that use system resources and automatically closes the objects and releases the resources after the try statement finishes executing.
- The *multi-catch block* allows you to use a single catch block for multiple exceptions that are at the same level in the inheritance hierarchy.
- When coding your own methods, if you encounter a potential error that can't be handled within that method, you can code a *throw statement* that throws the exception to another method. If you can't find an appropriate exception class in the Java API, you can code your own exception class.
- You can create custom exception classes to represent exceptions your methods might throw. This is often useful to hide the details of how a method is implemented.
- When you create custom exceptions, you can use *exception chaining* to save information about the cause of an exception.

Exercise 16-1 Throw and catch exceptions

In this exercise, you'll experiment with ways to throw and catch exceptions.

1. Open the project named ch16_ex1_ExceptionTester in the ex_starts folder. Then, open the Main class and review its code. Run this class to get a feel for how it works.
2. Add code to Method3 that throws an unchecked exception by attempting to divide an integer by zero. Compile and run the application and note where the exception is thrown.
3. Delete the code you just added to Method3. Then, add a statement to this method like the one in figure 16-7 that creates an object from the BufferedReader class, but use the string "products.ran" in place of the path variable. The constructor for this class throws a checked exception named FileNotFoundException. Note the error message that indicates that you haven't handled the exception. If this error message isn't shown, compile the class to display the error message.
4. Add throws clauses to all of the methods including the main method. Then, run the application to see how a checked exception can propagate all the way out of an application.
5. Add the code necessary to handle the FileNotFoundException in Method1. To do that, you'll need to remove the throws clauses from the main method and Method1, and you'll need to add a try statement to Method1 that catches the exception. The catch block should display an appropriate error message. Run the application to make sure the exception handler works.

Exercise 16-2 Release system resources

In this exercise, you'll get a chance to use try and a try-with-resources statements to release the system resources used by an object.

1. Open the project named ch16_ex2_ResourcesTester in the ex_starts folder. Then, open the Main class. Note that the main method calls two other methods that open a BufferedReader object but don't close it.
2. Modify the method named readLineWithResources so it uses a try-with-resources statement to close the BufferedReader object. Run the application to make sure it works correctly. If it does, the try-with-resources statement is working correctly too.
3. Modify the method named readLineWithFinally so it uses a finally block to close the BufferedReader object. To do that, you'll need to declare this object outside the try block. Add statements to the finally block that print information to the console to indicate whether the file was closed (this is typical for normal operations), never opened (which happens if the file can't be found), or unable to close (which happens only in rare cases).

4. Run the application to make sure the finally clause works as expected. To test what happens if the file is never opened, you can change the name of the file to cause a FileNotFoundException. To test what happens if the close method doesn't work, you can throw an IOException just before the statement that closes the resource.

Exercise 16-3 Create a custom class

In this exercise, you'll experiment with custom classes and chained exceptions.

1. Open the project named ch16_ex3_CustomTester in the ex_starts folder. Then, create a custom checked exception class named TestException that contains two constructors: one that accepts no parameters and one that accepts a message.
2. Open the Main class. Then, add a statement to Method3 that throws a TestException without a message. Add the code necessary to catch this exception in Method2. The catch block should print a message of your choice at the console. Run the application to make sure it works correctly.
3. Modify your solution so that a custom message of your choice is passed to the TestException and is then displayed in the catch block. Run the application to make sure the custom message is displayed correctly.
4. Add another constructor to the TestException class that accepts a Throwable object as a parameter.
5. Add a try statement to Method3 of the Main class. The try clause should throw an IOException, and the catch clause should throw a TestException, passing the IOException to its constructor.
6. Modify the catch block in Method2 that catches the TestException so it prints a message that gives information about the exception and its underlying cause. Run the application to make sure it works correctly.

17

How to work with file I/O

In this chapter, you'll be introduced to two types of files: text files and binary files. Although binary files are required for some applications, text files are preferred whenever possible because they are more portable and less platform dependent. That's why this chapter only shows how to work with text files. However, many of the same skills and concepts apply to working with binary files. As a result, if you need to work with binary files, you can learn more about them by searching the Internet or by getting a more comprehensive book such as *Murach's Java Programming*.

When you work with files, you frequently use arrays or collections (chapters 10 and 14). You need to be able to handle the exceptions thrown by I/O operations (chapter 16). And you may need to parse strings (chapter 9). As a result, you may want to review those chapters as you progress through this chapter.

An introduction to directories and files 434
A package for working with directories and files 434
Code examples that work with directories and files 436
An introduction to file input and output 438
How files and streams work 438
A file I/O example 440
How to work with I/O exceptions 442
How to work with text files 444
How to connect a character output stream to a file 444
How to write to a text file 446
How to connect a character input stream to a file 448
How to read from a text file 450
A class that works with a text file 452
The Product Manager application 456
The console 456
The Main class 456
Perspective 460

An introduction to directories and files

Prior to Java 7, it was common to use the File class from the java.io package to perform some basic operations on directories and files. However, this class has many limitations. That's why Java 7 introduced the java.nio.file package (also known as NIO.2). This package provides an improved way to access the default file system. As a result, it's generally considered a best practice to use the classes and interfaces of this package to work with directories and files.

A package for working with directories and files

Figure 17-1 begins by presenting the static get method of the Paths class in the java.nio.file package. You can pass one or more strings to this method to return a Path object that represents a path to a directory or a file. A Path object includes *name elements* that represent the directories and file in the path. For example, here's a typical path on a Windows system:

```
c:\murach\java_netbeans\files\products.txt
```

This path includes name elements for three directories (murach, java_netbeans, and files) and one file (products.txt). In addition, it includes the root component (the C drive).

Once you have a Path object, you can use the methods of the Path interface to get information about the path. For example, you can use the getName method to get a Path object for the name element at the specified index. The index refers to the position of the name element in the path, where the first element is at index 0.

You can also use the static methods of the Files class to get information about a path. For example, you can use the first four methods to check whether a path exists and whether you can read from or write to a path. Similarly, you can use the next two methods to test whether the path refers to a directory or a file. Finally, if the path refers to a file, you can use the size method to return the number of bytes in the file.

To display the contents of a directory, you can use the newDirectoryStream method with a Path object. This method returns a DirectoryStream<Path> object. Then, you can use this object to loop through all of the subdirectories and files within that directory. You'll see an example of how this works in the next figure.

Finally, you can use the last four methods of the Files class to create and delete directories and files. If these methods aren't able to create or delete a file or directory, they throw exceptions that should give you a good idea of why they failed. For example, if you try to create a file that already exists, Java throws a FileAlreadyExistsException. Similarly, if you try to delete a directory that contains files, Java throws a DirectoryNotEmptyException.

As you review these methods, you should know that they're only some of the most commonly used methods of the java.nio.file package. So, if you need to perform other file-handling tasks, you can consult the Java API documentation for this package.

A package for working with directories and files

`java.nio.file`

A static method of the Paths class

Method	Description
get(String[, String]...)	Returns a Path object for the string or series of strings that specify the path.

Methods of the Path interface

Method	Description
getFileName()	Returns a Path object for the name of the file or directory.
getName(int)	Returns a Path object for the element at the specified index.
getNameCount()	Returns an int value for the number of name elements in the path.
getParent()	Returns a Path object for the parent path if one exists. Returns a null value if a parent does not exist.
getRoot()	Returns a Path object for the root component of the path. Returns a null value if a root does not exist.
toAbsolutePath()	Returns a Path object for the absolute path to the file or directory.
toFile()	Returns a File object for the path to the file.

Static methods of the Files class

Method	Description
exists(Path)	Returns a true value if the path exists.
notExists(Path)	Returns a true value if the path does not exist.
isReadable(Path)	Returns a true value if the path exists and is readable.
isWritable(Path)	Returns a true value if the path exists and is writable.
isDirectory(Path)	Returns a true value if the path exists and refers to a directory.
isRegularFile(Path)	Returns a true value if the path exists and refers to a regular file.
size(Path)	Returns a long value for the number of bytes in the file.
newDirectoryStream(Path)	Returns a DirectoryStream<Path> object that you can use to loop through all files and subdirectories of the directory.
createFile(Path)	Creates a new file for the specified Path object if one doesn't already exist. Returns a Path object for the file.
createDirectory(Path)	Creates a new directory for the specified Path object if the directory doesn't already exist and all parent directories do exist. Returns a Path object for the directory.
createDirectories(Path)	Creates a new directory represented by the specified Path object including any necessary but non-existent parent directories. Returns a Path object for the directory.
delete(Path)	Deletes the file or directory represented by the Path object. A directory can only be deleted if it's empty.

Description

- To work with a directory or file, you use a Path object. A Path object can include a root component as well as directory names and a file name.

Figure 17-1 How to work with directories and files (part 1 of 2)

Code examples that work with directories and files

The first example in part 2 of figure 17-1 shows how to create a new directory. To do this, the first statement creates a string that refers to a directory. In this case, the directory is the murach/java_netbeans/files directory on the C drive. Then, the second statement uses the Paths class to get a Path object for this directory. Finally, an if statement checks whether this directory already exists. If it doesn't, the last statement calls the static createDirectories method of the Files class to create the directory and any necessary parent directories.

The second example shows how to create a new file. To do this, the first statement creates a string that contains the name of the file. Then, the second statement gets a Path object that refers to the directory and file. In this case, the file is named products.txt and the directory is c:\murach\java_netbeans\files. If the file doesn't already exist, the last statement calls the static createFile method of the Files class to create the file.

Notice that the get method of the Paths class in this example includes two arguments: one for the directory and one for the file. When you code the get method like this, the arguments are joined together and separated by a separator character. In most cases, the separator character is the same as the character that's used to separate the name elements in the arguments. In this case, the separator character is a front slash.

In this example, the Path object contains an *absolute path name*. In other words, this example specifies the entire path and file name for the file. However, if you want to create a Path object contains a *relative path name*, you can do that too. Then, the path is relative to the *current working directory* (*CWD*). For example, if you just specify the name of the file, the file is stored in the current working directory. This directory is usually the directory that the application was started from, which may or may not be the same directory where the application is located. In addition, on some operating systems, such as Windows, it's possible to set the working directory in the application's shortcut icon.

The third example shows how to get information about the Path object that was created in the previous example. First, the getFileName method returns the name of the file. Then, the toAbsolutePath method returns a Path object for the full path. Finally, the static isWritable method of the Files class returns a true value to show that the file is not read-only, which is the default.

The fourth example shows how to list the names of the files in a directory. To start, an if statement checks whether the path exists and whether it is a directory. If both are true, the first statement in the if block prints the name of the directory, and the second statement prints a string. Then, the static newDirectoryStream method of the Files class returns a DirectoryStream<Path> object. Finally, this code loops through all of the Path objects in this stream, checks if the Path object is a file, and prints the file name if it is.

If you're used to working with Windows, you may be surprised to find that you use a front slash (/) instead of a backslash (\) to separate the parts of a path. That's because Java uses the backslash to identify escape characters. This makes it cumbersome to use backslashes when specifying paths.

Code that creates a directory if it doesn't already exist

```
String dirString = "c:/murach/java_netbeans/files";
Path dirPath = Paths.get(dirString);
if (Files.notExists(dirPath)) {
    Files.createDirectories(dirPath);
}
```

Code that creates a file if it doesn't already exist

```
String fileString = "products.txt";
Path filePath = Paths.get(dirString, fileString);
if (Files.notExists(filePath)) {
    Files.createFile(filePath);
}
```

Code that displays information about a file

```
System.out.println("File name:       " + filePath.getFileName());
System.out.println("Absolute path:   " + filePath.toAbsolutePath());
System.out.println("Is writable:     " + Files.isWritable(filePath));
```

Resulting output

```
File name:       products.txt
Absolute path:   c:\murach\java_netbeans\files\products.txt
Is writable:     true
```

Code that displays the files in a directory

```
if (Files.exists(dirPath) && Files.isDirectory(dirPath)) {
    System.out.println("Directory: " + dirPath.toAbsolutePath());
    System.out.println("Files: ");
    DirectoryStream<Path> dirStream = Files.newDirectoryStream(dirPath);
    for (Path p: dirStream) {
        if (Files.isRegularFile(p))
            System.out.println("    " + p.getFileName());
    }
}
```

Description

- Java 7 introduced the java.nio.file package (also known as NIO.2). This package provides an improved way to access the default file system and is designed to replace the functionality that was available from the java.io.File class.
- The java.nio.file package provides support for many features that aren't provided by the java.io.File class.
- When coding paths, you can use a front slash to separate directory names. This works equally well for Windows and other operating systems.
- To identify the name and location of a file, you can use an *absolute path name* to specify the entire path for a file. You can also use a *relative path name* to specify the path of the file relative to the *current working directory* (*CWD*). This is usually but not always the directory that the application was started from.
- Although the java.nio.file package was introduced with Java 7, the java.nio package was introduced with Java 4.

Figure 17-1 How to work with directories and files (part 2 of 2)

An introduction to file input and output

This topic introduces the types of files and streams that you can use for file input and output. Then, it presents an example that introduces the code that's needed to perform input and output operations on a file. Finally, it shows how to handle the exceptions that occur most frequently when you perform input and output operations.

How files and streams work

Figure 17-2 presents the two types of files and the two types of streams that you use when you perform *I/O operations* (or *file I/O*). In a *text file*, all of the data is stored as *Unicode* characters on disk. Often, the fields and records in this type of file are separated by delimiters like tabs and new line characters. In this figure, for example, the fields in the text file are separated by tabs and the records by new line characters. Other types of text files include XML and HTML files. An XML file uses special tags to structure the data that's stored in the file. And an HTML file uses special tags to tell a web browser how to format text, display images, and so on.

In contrast, the data in a *binary file* is stored in a different format that can read and write the primitive data types. In this figure, for example, some of the bytes in this format can't be read by a text editor. Here, two non-character bytes are written before the code and description fields of each product record, and the price field is written in a non-character format that isn't readable by a text editor. Also, since the records in a binary file don't end with new line characters, all records are displayed on a single line when a binary file is opened by a text editor. Other types of binary files include image, audio, video, and application files.

To handle I/O operations, Java uses *streams*. You can think of a stream as the flow of data from one location to another. For instance, an *output stream* can flow from the internal memory of an application to a disk file, and an *input stream* can flow from a disk file to internal memory. When you work with a text file, you use a *character stream*. When you work with a binary file, you use a *binary stream*.

Although this chapter shows you how to use streams with disk files, Java also uses streams with other types of devices. For instance, you can use an output stream to send data to the console or to a network connection. In fact, the System.out and System.err objects are the standard output streams that are used for printing data to the console. Similarly, you can use an input stream to read data from a source like a keyboard or a network connection. In fact, the System.in object that's used by the Scanner class is a standard input stream that is used for reading data from the keyboard.

When you save a text or binary file, you can use any extension for the file name. In this book, we have used *txt* as the extension for all text files and *bin* for all binary files. For instance, the text file in this figure is named products.txt, and the binary file is named products.bin.

A text file that's opened by a text editor

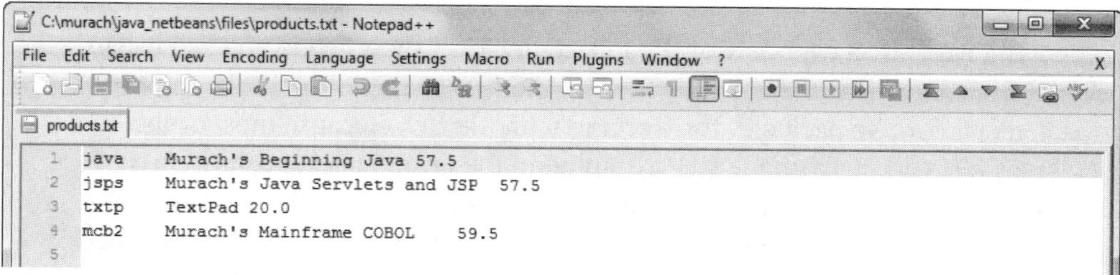

A binary file that's opened by a text editor

Two types of files

File	Description
Text	A file that contains characters. The fields and records in this type of file are often delimited by special characters like tab and new line characters. Web pages are also plain text files that use a special markup language known as HTML.
Binary	A file that may contain characters as well as other non-character data types that can't be read by a text editor. Common binary file types include images, movies, and applications.

Two types of streams

Stream	Description
Character	Used to transfer text data to or from an I/O device.
Binary	Used to transfer binary data to or from an I/O device.

Description

- An *input file* is a file that is read by an application. An *output file* is a file that is written by an application. Input and output operations are often referred to as *I/O operations* or *file I/O*.
- A *stream* is the flow of data from one location to another. To write data to a file from internal storage, you use an *output stream*. To read from a file into internal storage, you use an *input stream*.
- To read and write *text files*, you use *character streams*. To read and write *binary files*, you use *binary streams*.
- Streams are not only used with disk devices, but also with input devices like keyboards and network connections and output devices like PC monitors and network connections.

Figure 17-2 How files and streams work

A file I/O example

To give you an overview of file I/O, figure 17-3 shows code you can use to read from and write to a text file. To start, the first example shows the import statements for two packages for working with file I/O. Because most of the classes for working with file I/O are stored in the java.io package, any class that works with file I/O typically imports all of the classes in this package. In addition, the import statement for the java.nio.file package is typically included to make it easy to work with the classes (Paths and Files) and interfaces (Path) described in the previous figures.

The second example shows how to create a File object that refers to a file named products.txt. To start, the first statement creates a Path object that refers to the file. Since no directory is specified for the file, the Path object refers to a file that's stored in the working directory, which is usually, but not always, the directory the application was started from. Then, the second statement calls the toFile method of the Path object to convert it to a File object. This is necessary because many of the classes in the file.io package were created before the Path object was introduced. As a result, they are designed to work with a File object and don't work directly with a Path object.

The third example shows how to write data to a file. To start, you create an output stream. In this example, the output stream is created in the try clause of a try-with-resources statement.

To create a stream that has all the functionality that you need for an application, you can *layer* two or more streams into a single stream. To layer streams in Java, you use an object of one class as the argument for the constructor of another class. In this example, a BufferedWriter object is used as the argument of the PrintWriter constructor, and a FileWriter object is used as the argument of the BufferedWriter constructor.

The BufferedWriter object adds a block of internal memory known as a *buffer* to the stream. This causes the data in the stream to be stored in a buffer before it is written to the output device. Then, when the buffer is full or the stream is closed, all of the data in the buffer is *flushed* to the disk file in a single I/O operation. Similarly, when you use a buffer for input, a full buffer of data is read in a single I/O operation.

After creating the output stream, the statement in the try block uses the println method of the output stream to write the data to a file. Then, when the try block finishes executing, the try-with-resources statement automatically closes the stream and flushes any data that's in the buffer to the file.

The fourth example reads the data that was written by the third example. To start, it uses the try clause of a try-with-resources statement to create a buffered input stream for the products file. Within the try block, the two statements read the first line of that file and print that line to the console. Finally, once the try-with-resources statement finishes executing, it automatically closes the input stream, which flushes the buffer and frees all system resources associated with the input stream.

The benefit of buffering is that it reduces the number of I/O operations that are done by a disk device. If, for example, a buffer can hold 4000 bytes of data,

Import all necessary packages

```
import java.io.*;
import java.nio.file.*;
```

Get a Path object for the file

```
Path productsPath = Paths.get("products.txt");
File productsFile = productsPath.toFile();
```

Write data to the file

```
try (PrintWriter out = new PrintWriter(
                       new BufferedWriter(
                       new FileWriter(productsFile)))) {
    out.println("java\tMurach's Beginning Java\t57.50");
}
catch (IOException e) {
    System.out.println(e);
}
```

Read data from the file

```
try (BufferedReader in = new BufferedReader(
                         new FileReader(productsFile))) {
    String line = in.readLine();
    System.out.println(line);
}
catch (IOException e) {
    System.out.println(e);
}
```

Resulting output

```
java    Murach's Beginning Java         57.50
```

Description

- The java.io package contains dozens of classes that can be used to work with different types of streams that have different functionality.
- To get the functionality you need for a stream, you often need to combine, or *layer*, two or more streams.
- To make disk processing more efficient, you can use a *buffered stream* that adds a block of internal memory called a *buffer* to the stream.
- When working with buffers, you often need to *flush* the buffer. This sends all data in the buffer to the I/O device. One way to do that is to use a try-with-resources statement to automatically close the I/O stream after you use it.

Figure 17-3 A file I/O example

only one write or read operation is required to flush or fill the buffer. In contrast, if the data is written or read one field at a time, 4000 bytes might require hundreds of I/O operations. For each I/O operation, the disk has to rotate to the starting disk location. Since this rotation is extremely slow relative to internal operations, buffering dramatically improves the performance of I/O operations.

Because this figure is only intended to give you an idea of how file I/O works, you shouldn't worry if you don't understand it completely. As you progress through this chapter, you'll learn about all of the classes and methods shown here in more detail.

How to work with I/O exceptions

If you read the previous chapter, you are familiar with the basic skills for handling exceptions. In fact, you have already been introduced to some of the exceptions that are thrown by I/O operations.

Now, figure 17-4 summarizes three types of checked exceptions that must be handled when you're working with file I/O. To start, all exceptions that are thrown by classes that perform file I/O operations inherit the IOException class. In particular, an EOFException may be thrown when code attempts to read beyond the end of a file, and a FileNotFoundException is thrown when code attempts to open a file that doesn't exist.

The code in this figure prevents a FileNotFoundException. To do that, this code gets a Path object for a file. Then, it uses the exists method of the Files class to check if a file exists for that path. If so, the code within the if block executes. Otherwise, this code prints an error message to the console.

This code also handles the IOException that might occur while reading the file. To do that, the code within the if block begins by converting the Path object to a File object. Then, it uses a try-with-resources statement to create an input stream for the file, and it uses the corresponding catch block to handle any I/O exceptions that might occur while reading that input stream. To do that, this code prints the exception it to the console.

Finally, this code prevents the EOFException. To do that, the while loop within the try block checks if the end of the file has been reached. If so, it exits the loop. To do that, the first statement within the try block declares a string variable named line and uses the readLine method to read a line from the input stream. Then, the while loop checks whether this line is null. If not, the code within the loop displays the line and uses the readLine method to read the next line. This continues as long as the line isn't null. If the line is null, it indicates that the end of the file has been reached and the loop ends.

The last code example shows another way to code the loop that prevents the EOFException. Here, the condition in while loop reads the line and checks whether the line is null. To do that, it uses parentheses to make sure this code reads the line before it checks if it is null. If the line is not null, the loop continues. Otherwise, the loop ends. The advantage of this approach is that it is easier to maintain since it doesn't duplicate the readLine call. The disadvantage is that it is more difficult to read. When you review other programmer's code, you may encounter either approach, so you should be familiar with both.

A subset of the IOException hierarchy

```
IOException
    EOFException
    FileNotFoundException
```

Common I/O exceptions

Exception	Description
IOException	Thrown when an error occurs in I/O processing.
EOFException	Thrown when code attempts to read beyond the end of a file.
FileNotFoundException	Thrown when code attempts to open a file that doesn't exist.

Code that handles I/O exceptions

```
Path productsPath = Paths.get("products.txt");
if (Files.exists(productsPath)) {       // prevent the FileNotFoundException
    File productsFile = productsPath.toFile();
    try (BufferedReader in = new BufferedReader(
                             new FileReader(productsFile))) {
            String line = in.readLine();
            while(line != null) {       // prevent the EOFException
                System.out.println(line);
                line = in.readLine();
            }
    }
    catch (IOException e) {             // catch the IOException
        System.out.println(e);
    }
}
else {
    System.out.println(
        productsPath.toAbsolutePath() + " doesn't exist");
}
```

The loop that prevents the EOFException

```
String line = in.readLine();
while(line != null) {
    System.out.println(line);
    line = in.readLine();
}
```

Another way to code this loop

```
String line;
while((line = in.readLine()) != null) {
    System.out.println(line);
}
```

Figure 17-4 How to work with I/O exceptions

How to work with text files

When working with text files, you need to layer two or more classes to create a character input or output stream. You'll learn how to do that in the topics that follow. In addition, you'll learn how to use the methods of these classes to work with text files. Then, you'll see a complete class that you can use to read and write Product objects to a text file.

How to connect a character output stream to a file

Before you can write to a text file, you need to create a character output stream, and you need to connect that stream to a file. To do that, you must layer two or more of the classes in the Writer hierarchy as shown in figure 17-5. Then, you use the methods of the PrintWriter class to write data to the output stream, you use the BufferedWriter class to create a buffer for the output stream, and you use the FileWriter class to connect the stream to a file.

Although it's typically a good coding practice to use a buffer, the first example in this figure shows how to connect to a file without using a buffer. Here, the first statement creates a FileWriter object by passing a String object for a path name to the constructor of the FileWriter class. Alternately, this statement could pass a File object for a file to this constructor. Either way, the second statement creates a PrintWriter object by passing the FileWriter object to the constructor of the PrintWriter class.

The second example shows a more concise way to write the first example. Here, you don't assign the FileWriter object to a named variable. Instead, you nest the call to the constructor of the FileWriter class within the constructor of the PrintWriter class. You can align these nested constructor calls any way you like. In this example, the whole statement is coded on one line, but it's often easier to read if each constructor call is coded on a separate line as shown in the next three examples.

The third example shows how to include a buffer in the output stream. To do that, you use a BufferedWriter object in addition to a FileWriter and PrintWriter object.

The fourth example shows how to append data to an existing file. To do that, you set the second argument of the FileWriter constructor to true. If you don't code a value for this argument, the existing data in the file is overwritten.

By default, the data in an output stream is flushed from the buffer to the disk when the buffer is full. However, if you set the second argument of the PrintWriter constructor to true, the *autoflush feature* is turned on. Then, the buffer is flushed each time the println method is executed.

The constructors in this figure should help you understand how to layer output streams. Here, the PrintWriter constructor accepts any class derived from the Writer class. As a result, you can supply a BufferedWriter object or a FileWriter object as an argument of the PrintWriter constructor. Similarly, since the BufferedWriter constructor also accepts any Writer object, you can supply a FileWriter object as an argument of the BufferedWriter constructor.

A subset of the Writer hierarchy

```
Writer <<abstract>>
    BufferedWriter
    PrintWriter
    OutputStreamWriter
        FileWriter
```

Classes used to connect a character output stream to a file

PrintWriter contains the methods for writing data to a text stream

→BufferedWriter creates a buffer for the stream

→FileWriter connects the stream to a file

Constructors of these classes

Constructor	Throws
PrintWriter(Writer[, booleanFlush])	None
BufferedWriter(Writer)	None
FileWriter(File[, booleanAppend])	IOException
FileWriter(StringPathName[, booleanAppend])	IOException

How to connect without a buffer (not recommended)

```
FileWriter fileWriter = new FileWriter("products.txt");
PrintWriter out = new PrintWriter(fileWriter);
```

A more concise way to code the previous example

```
PrintWriter out = new PrintWriter(new FileWriter("products.txt"));
```

How to connect to a file with a buffer

```
PrintWriter out = new PrintWriter(
                  new BufferedWriter(
                  new FileWriter("products.txt")));
```

How to connect for an append operation

```
PrintWriter out = new PrintWriter(
                  new BufferedWriter(
                  new FileWriter("products.txt", true)));
```

How to connect with the autoflush feature turned on

```
PrintWriter out = new PrintWriter(
                  new BufferedWriter(
                  new FileWriter("products.txt")), true);
```

Description

- The Writer class is an abstract class that's inherited by all of the classes in the Writer hierarchy. To learn more about the Writer hierarchy, see the Java API documentation.
- If the output file doesn't exist when the FileWriter object is created, it's created automatically. If it does exist, it's overwritten by default. If that's not what you want, you can specify true for the second argument of the constructor to append data to the file.
- If you specify true for the second argument of the PrintWriter constructor, the *autoflush feature* flushes the buffer each time the println method is called.

Figure 17-5 How to connect a character output stream to a file

How to write to a text file

Figure 17-6 shows how to write to a text file. To do that, you use the print and println methods of a PrintWriter object to print data to the file. These methods work like the print and println methods of the System.out object. However, they print data to a file instead of printing data to the console.

As you saw earlier in this chapter, you can use a try-with-resources statement to create a stream. Then, the stream is automatically flushed and closed when the try statement ends. If you don't use a try-with-resources statement, though, you can use the close method to manually close the output stream. This flushes the buffer and frees any system resources that are being used by the output stream. Or, if you want to keep the output stream open, you can use the flush method to flush all the data in the stream to the file. Either way, you need to throw or catch the IOException that can be thrown by these methods.

The first example in this figure shows how to append a string and an object to a text file named log.txt. To start, the FileWriter constructor creates a FileWriter object that can append data to the file. If no file named log.txt exists in the current directory, this statement creates the file. Then, the print method prints a string, and the println method prints a LocalDateTime object that represents the current date and time. For this to work, the toString method of the LocalDateTime object is called automatically to convert the date to a string.

The second example in this figure shows how to write the data that's stored in a Product object to a *delimited text file*. In this type of file, one type of *delimiter* is used to separate the *fields* (or *columns*) that are written to the file, and another type of delimiter is used to separate the *records* (or *rows*). In this example, the tab character (\t) is used as the delimiter for the fields, and the new line character is used as the delimiter for the records. That way, the code, description, and price for one product are stored in the same record separated by tabs. Then, the new line character ends the data for that product, and the data for the next product can be stored in the next record.

Common methods of the PrintWriter class

Method	Throws	Description
`print(argument)`	None	Writes the character representation of the argument type to the file.
`println(argument)`	None	Writes the character representation of the argument type to the file followed by the new line character. If the autoflush feature is turned on, this also flushes the buffer.
`flush()`	IOException	Flushes any data that's in the buffer to the file.
`close()`	IOException	Flushes any data that's in the buffer to the file and closes the stream.

Code that appends a string and an object to a text file

```
// open an output stream for appending to the text file
PrintWriter out = new PrintWriter(
                  new BufferedWriter(
                  new FileWriter("log.txt", true)));

// write a string and an object to the file
out.print("This application was run on ");
LocalDateTime currentDateTime = LocalDateTime.now();
out.println(currentDateTime);

// flush data to the file and close the output stream
out.close();
```

Code that writes a Product object to a delimited text file

```
// open an output stream for overwriting a text file
PrintWriter out = new PrintWriter(
                  new BufferedWriter(
                  new FileWriter(productsFile)));

// write the Product object to the file
out.print(product.getCode() + "\t");
out.print(product.getDescription() + "\t");
out.println(product.getPrice());

// flush data to the file and close the output stream
out.close();
```

Description

- To write a character representation of a data type to an output stream, you use the print and println methods of the PrintWriter class. If you supply an object as an argument, these methods call the toString method of the object.
- To create a *delimited text file*, you delimit the *records* or *rows* in the file with one *delimiter*, such as a new line character, and you delimit the *fields* or *columns* of each record with another delimiter, such as a tab character.
- To flush all data to the file, you can use a try-with-resources statement to automatically close the stream when you're done using it. You can also use the flush or close methods of the stream to manually flush all data to the file.

Figure 17-6 How to write to a text file

How to connect a character input stream to a file

Before you can read characters from a text file, you must connect the character input stream to a file. Figure 17-7 shows how to do that with a buffer and a File object. As you can see in the example in this figure, you supply the FileReader class as the argument of the constructor of the BufferedReader class. This creates a stream that uses a buffer and has methods that you can use to read data.

If you look at the constructors for the BufferedReader and FileReader classes, you can see why this code works. Since the constructor for the BufferedReader object accepts any object in the Reader hierarchy, it can accept a FileReader object that connects the stream to a file. However, the BufferedReader object can also accept an InputStreamReader object, which can be used to connect the character input stream to the keyboard or to a network connection rather than to a file.

A subset of the Reader hierarchy

```
Reader <<abstract>>
    BufferedReader
    InputStreamReader
        FileReader
```

Classes used to connect to a file with a buffer

BufferedReader contains the methods for reading data from the stream

→**FileReader** connects the stream to a file

Constructors of these classes

Constructor	Throws
`BufferedReader(Reader)`	None
`FileReader(File)`	FileNotFoundException
`FileReader(StringPathName)`	FileNotFoundException

How to connect a character input stream to a file

```
BufferedReader in = new BufferedReader(
                    new FileReader("products.txt"));
```

Description

- The Reader class is an abstract class that's inherited by all of the classes in the Reader hierarchy. To learn more about the Reader hierarchy, check the documentation for the Java API. All classes in the java.io package that end with Reader are members of the Reader hierarchy.
- Although you can read files with the FileReader class alone, the BufferedReader class improves efficiency and provides better methods for reading character input streams.

Figure 17-7 How to connect a character input stream to a file

How to read from a text file

The two examples in figure 17-8 show how to read the two text files that are written by the examples in figure 17-6. In the first example, a while loop reads each line and then prints it to the console. When the readLine method attempts to read past the end of the file, it returns a null, which causes the while loop to end. Then, the close method is called to flush the buffer and close the input stream.

The second example shows how to read a row from the products file. To do that, it uses the readLine method. Then, because this file is a delimited text file, it parses the string into its individual columns. To do that, it uses the split method of the String class to split the string into an array of strings. In this example, the tab character is supplied as the argument of the split method since this is the character that's used to divide the columns in the row.

This example continues by creating a Product object from the data in the columns array. Since the product code and description are strings, the columns that contain these values can be passed directly to the constructor of the Product object. However, the price column must be converted from a String object to a double value. In this example, the parseDouble method of the Double class is used to do that.

The last statement in this example calls the close method. That flushes the buffer and frees any system resources.

Common methods of the BufferedReader class

Method	Throws	Description
`readLine()`	IOException	Reads a line of text and returns it as a string.
`close()`	IOException	Closes the input stream and flushes the buffer.

Code that reads the records in a text file

```
// read the records of the file
String line;
while((line = in.readLine()) != null) {
    System.out.println(line);
}

// close the input stream
in.close();
```

Sample output

```
This application was run on 2015-05-28T12:06:55.084
This application was run on 2015-05-28T12:07:28.041
```

A method of the String class

Method	Description
`split(delimiter)`	Splits the current String object on the specified delimiter and returns an array of String objects.

Code that reads a Product object from a delimited text file

```
// read the next line of the file
String line = in.readLine();

// parse the line into its columns
String[] columns = line.split("\t");
String code = columns[0];
String description = columns[1];
String price = columns[2];

// create a Product object from the data in the columns
Product p = new Product(code, description, Double.parseDouble(price));

// print some Product object data
System.out.println(p.getDescription() + " (" + p.getPriceFormatted() + ")");

// close the input stream
in.close();
```

Sample output

```
Murach's Beginning Java ($57.50)
```

Figure 17-8 How to read from a text file

A class that works with a text file

Figure 17-9 shows a complete class named ProductIO that you can use to read and write products to a text file. To start, the static constant named productsPath stores the Path object for the text file named products.txt that's stored in the current working directory. Then, the static constant named productsFile stores the File object that corresponds with that path. Next, the static constant named FIELD_SEP specifies that the tab character is used to separate the fields in the file. Finally, the static variable named products stores a List of Product objects for the products in the file. To do that, this statement calls the static getAll method that's defined later in the class.

The private constructor for the ProductIO class prevents anyone from creating an object form this class. That's a good practice since this class only contains static methods.

The getAll method returns a List of Product objects for all products in the file. This method starts by checking whether the products list has been created. If so, it returns that list. This increases efficiency by reading the file only when necessary.

If the products list hasn't been created, this code creates it. To do that, it begins by creating an empty ArrayList of Product objects. Then, it checks if the products file exists. If so, it uses a try-with-resources statement to create a buffered input stream. To create the Product objects, this method uses a while loop to read and process the lines in the file until the end of the file is reached. As you learned earlier in this chapter, you can test for an end-of-file condition by checking the string that's returned by the readLine method for a null.

Within the while loop, the first statement uses the FIELD_SEP constant to split the line into its three columns (code, description, and price). Then, this loop creates a Product object, sets its data from the values in these columns, and adds the Product object to the products list. Then, control returns to the top of the loop and the next line is read.

If an IOException is thrown somewhere in the getAll method, this method returns a null. That way, any method that calls the getAll method can test whether it executed successfully by checking the whether list it returns is null. Whether or not an exception is thrown, the try-with-resources statement automatically closes the input stream.

In this class, the catch clauses print the exception to the console. This is useful when you're testing and debugging an application, but it might not be appropriate when you put an application into production. As a result, before putting a class like this into a production environment, you might want to change the way that exceptions are handled. For example, you might want to write an error message to a log file. Or, you might want to throw a custom exception that indicates that a generic access error has occurred. For more information on how to create a custom exception, see chapter 16.

The code for the ProductIO class

Page 1

```
package murach.io;

import java.util.*;
import java.io.*;
import java.nio.file.*;
import murach.business.Product;

public class ProductIO {
    private static final Path productsPath = Paths.get("products.txt");
    private static final File productsFile = productsPath.toFile();
    private static final String FIELD_SEP = "\t";
    private static List<Product> products = getAll();

    // prevent instantiation of class
    private ProductIO() {}

    public static List<Product> getAll() {
        // if the products file has already been read, don't read it again
        if (products != null) {
            return products;
        }

        products = new ArrayList<>();
        if (Files.exists(productsPath)) {
            try (BufferedReader in = new BufferedReader(
                                     new FileReader(productsFile))) {
                // read all products stored in the file into the array list
                String line = in.readLine();
                while(line != null) {
                    String[] columns = line.split(FIELD_SEP);
                    String code = columns[0];
                    String description = columns[1];
                    String price = columns[2];

                    Product p = new Product();
                    p.setCode(code);
                    p.setDescription(description);
                    p.setPrice(Double.parseDouble(price));
                    products.add(p);

                    line = in.readLine();
                }
            }
            catch(IOException e) {
                System.out.println(e);
                return null;
            }
        }
        return products;
    }
```

Figure 17-9 A class that works with a text file (part 1 of 2)

The get method returns a Product object for a product that matches the specified product code. To search for the product, this method loops through each product in the products list until it finds one with the specified product code. Finally, it returns that product. If no product has the specified code, this method returns a null.

The saveAll method accesses the list of products and writes all of the Product objects to the file. If this operation is successful, it returns a true value. If an IOException is thrown, this method returns a false value. This indicates that the save operation wasn't successful.

The saveAll method starts by creating a buffered output stream that connects to the products file. Then, this method uses a loop to write each product in the list to the file. To do that, it uses the FIELD_SEP constant to separate each field in a product record, and it uses the println method to insert a new line character at the end of each product record.

The add method starts by calling the add method of the List interface to add the product to the list of products. Then, it calls the saveAll method to save the modified list to the products file so that the list and the file contain the same data. Here, the add method returns the boolean value that's returned by the saveAll method. That way, if the saveAll method returns a true value, the add method also returns a true value.

The delete method works similarly. It starts by calling the getAll method to return a products list. Then, it calls the remove method of the List interface to remove the product from the list. Finally, it calls the saveAll method to save the list to the products file, and it returns the boolean value that's returned by that method.

The update method works a little differently. This method updates the data for an existing product with the data in a new Product object. To start, this method uses the get method to get the old Product object with the same product code as the new Product object. Then, it gets the index for the old product and removes that product from the list. Next, it inserts the new product into the list where the old product used to be. Finally, it calls the saveAll method to save the list to the products file, and it returns a value that indicates whether the save operation was successful.

It's important to note that this class won't work correctly for multiple users. For example, suppose user A and user B read the products file, and user A modifies that file. Then, suppose user B also modifies the file. At this point, user B's changes overwrite user A's changes. This is known as a *concurrency problem*.

One way to reduce concurrency problems would be to read the data from the file each time the getAll, get, add, update, and delete methods are called. That way, the data is more likely to be current. However, this would be inefficient, particularly if the file contained thousands of records, and it still wouldn't be thread-safe. The easiest and most professional way to solve this problem is to use a database as described in chapters 19 and 20.

The code for the ProductIO class

Page 2

```
    public static Product get(String code) {
        for (Product p : products) {
            if (p.getCode().equals(code))
                return p;
        }
        return null;
    }

    private static boolean saveAll() {
        try (PrintWriter out = new PrintWriter(
                               new BufferedWriter(
                               new FileWriter(productsFile)))) {
            // write all products in the array list to the file
            for (Product p : products) {
                out.print(p.getCode() + FIELD_SEP);
                out.print(p.getDescription() + FIELD_SEP);
                out.println(p.getPrice());
            }
        }
        catch(IOException e) {
            System.out.println(e);
            return false;
        }

        return true;
    }

    public static boolean add(Product p) {
        products.add(p);
        return saveAll();
    }

    public static boolean delete(Product p) {
        products.remove(p);
        return saveAll();
    }

    public static boolean update(Product newProduct) {
        // get the old product and remove it
        Product oldProduct = get(newProduct.getCode());
        int i = products.indexOf(oldProduct);
        products.remove(i);

        // add the updated product
        products.add(i, newProduct);

        return saveAll();
    }
}
```

The Product Manager application

This chapter finishes by showing the Product Manager application. This application uses the ProductIO class described in the previous figure to work with the product data that's stored in a text file. In addition, it uses the Product, Console, and StringUtil classes described earlier in this book.

The console

Figure 17-10 shows the console for the Product Manager application. When it starts, this application displays a welcome message and a menu of commands. Then, it prompts the user to enter one of those commands. In this figure, for example, the user started by entering the list command. This displayed a list of the products that are stored in the text file.

After displaying the products, the user used the add command to add a new product to the text file. Then, the user used the del command to delete that product. Finally, the user entered the exit command to end the application.

The Main class

Figure 17-11 shows the code for the Main class. This class contains the main method that's executed when the application starts. To start, this method displays a welcome message. Then, it calls the displayMenu method to display the menu of commands for working with this application. After that, the main method enters a loop that continues until the user enters the exit command.

Within this loop, the first statement prompts the user for a command. If the user enters "list", this code calls the displayAllProducts method shown in part 2 of figure 17-11. This method displays a list of products. To do that, it calls the getAll method of the ProductIO class to get a list of Product objects. Then, it loops through these Product objects and builds a string that displays them. To do that, this code uses the StringUtil class presented earlier in this book to align the columns with the specified number of spaces.

If the user enters "add", this code calls the addProduct method shown in part 2 of figure 17-11 to add a product to the text file. To do that, this method creates a Product object from the data that's entered by the user and passes this object to the add method of the ProductIO class.

If the user enters "del" or "delete", this code calls the deleteProduct method shown in part 2 to delete the product with the specified code from the text file. To do that, this method calls the get method of the ProductIO class to get a Product object that corresponds with the specified code. Then, it calls the delete method of the ProductIO class to delete this product from the text file.

The console

```
Welcome to the Product Manager

COMMAND MENU
list     - List all products
add      - Add a product
del      - Delete a product
help     - Show this menu
exit     - Exit this application

Enter a command: list

PRODUCT LIST
java         Murach's Java Programming          $57.50
jsp          Murach's Java Servlets and JSP     $57.50
mysql        Murach's MySQL                     $54.50
android      Murach's Android Programming       $57.50
html5        Murach's HTML5 and CSS3            $54.50
oracle       Murach's Oracle and PL/SQL         $54.50
javascript   Murach's JavaScript and jQuery     $54.50

Enter a command: add

Enter product code: bjava
Enter product description: Murach's Beginning Java
Enter price: 54.50

Murach's Beginning Java was added to the database.

Enter a command: del

Enter product code to delete: bjava

Murach's Beginning Java was deleted from the database.

Enter a command: exit

Bye.
```

Description

- This application allows you to manage the products that are stored in a text file. When it starts, it displays a list of commands that you can use. Then, it prompts you to enter one of these commands.
- To view the products, you can use the list command.
- To add or delete a product, you can use the add or del commands.
- To display the list of commands again, you can use the help command.
- To exit the application, you can type the exit command.

Figure 17-10 The console for the Product Manager application

The Main class

```
package murach.ui;

import java.util.List;
import murach.business.Product;
import murach.io.ProductIO;

public class Main {

    public static void main(String args[]) {

        // display a welcome message
        System.out.println("Welcome to the Product Manager\n");

        // display the command menu
        displayMenu();

        // perform 1 or more actions
        String action = "";
        while (!action.equalsIgnoreCase("exit")) {
            // get the input from the user
            action = Console.getString("Enter a command: ");
            System.out.println();

            if (action.equalsIgnoreCase("list")) {
                displayAllProducts();
            } else if (action.equalsIgnoreCase("add")) {
                addProduct();
            } else if (action.equalsIgnoreCase("del") ||
                       action.equalsIgnoreCase("delete")) {
                deleteProduct();
            } else if (action.equalsIgnoreCase("help") ||
                       action.equalsIgnoreCase("menu")) {
                displayMenu();
            } else if (action.equalsIgnoreCase("exit")) {
                System.out.println("Bye.\n");
            } else {
                System.out.println("Error! Not a valid command.\n");
            }
        }
    }

    public static void displayMenu() {
        System.out.println("COMMAND MENU");
        System.out.println("list    - List all products");
        System.out.println("add     - Add a product");
        System.out.println("del     - Delete a product");
        System.out.println("help    - Show this menu");
        System.out.println("exit    - Exit this application\n");
    }
```

Figure 17-11 The Main class (part 1 of 2)

The Main class (continued)

```
    public static void displayAllProducts() {
        System.out.println("PRODUCT LIST");

        List<Product> products = ProductIO.getAll();

        if (products == null) {
            System.out.println("\nError! Unable to get products.\n");
        } else {
            Product p;
            StringBuilder sb = new StringBuilder();
            for (Product product : products) {
                p = product;
                sb.append(StringUtil.padWithSpaces(
                        p.getCode(), 12));
                sb.append(StringUtil.padWithSpaces(
                        p.getDescription(), 34));
                sb.append(p.getPriceFormatted());
                sb.append("\n");
            }
            System.out.println(sb.toString());
        }
    }

    public static void addProduct() {
        String code = Console.getString("Enter product code: ");
        String description = Console.getString("Enter product description: ");
        double price = Console.getDouble("Enter price: ");

        Product product = new Product();
        product.setCode(code);
        product.setDescription(description);
        product.setPrice(price);

        ProductIO.add(product);
        System.out.println("\n" + description
                + " was added to the database.\n");
    }

    public static void deleteProduct() {
        String code = Console.getString("Enter product code to delete: ");

        Product product = ProductIO.get(code);
        if (product == null) {
            System.out.println("\nError! Unable to get product.");
        }
        else {
            ProductIO.delete(product);
            System.out.println("\n" + product.getDescription() +
                    " was deleted from the database.\n");
        }
    }
}
```

Figure 17-11 The Main class (part 2 of 2)

Perspective

In this chapter, you learned how to read and write text files. In addition, you learned how you can use a class such as the ProductIO class to store the data for business objects such as Product objects in a text file. This should help you see how the presentation, business, and database layers of an application can work together.

As you work with text files, remember that they are only one option for storing data. Another option is to store data in a database. Because databases provide sophisticated features for organizing and managing data, they're used for most serious applications. You'll learn how to work with databases in chapters 19 and 20.

If you need to read and write objects to a binary file, you may want to consider using a Java feature known as object *serialization*. This feature automates the process of reading and writing objects to a binary file. Most programmers don't need to write code that performs serialization unless they are writing low-level code. For example, a programmer who is writing a Java EE application server might use serialization to read and write objects to a binary file. However, an application programmer who is using the application server doesn't need to write this code. Instead, the application programmer only needs to provide objects that implement the Serializable interface.

Summary

- A *text file* stores data as characters. A *binary file* stores data in a binary format.
- In a *delimited text file*, *delimiters* are used to separate the *fields* and *records* of the file.
- You use *character streams* to read and write text files. To get the functionality you need, you can *layer* two or more streams.
- A *buffer* is a block of memory that is used to store the data in a stream before it is written to or after it is read from an I/O device. When an output buffer is full, its data is *flushed* to the I/O device.
- When you work with I/O operations, you'll need to catch or throw three types of checked exceptions: IOException, FileNotFoundException, and EOFException.
- To identify a file when you create a File object, you can use an *absolute path name* or a *relative path name*.
- The java.nio.file package provides classes and interfaces that you can use to check whether a file or directory exists, to get information about a path, to create or delete directories and files, and to create a File object.
- You can use the classes in the Writer and Reader hierarchies to work with a text file.

Exercise 17-1 Work with a text file

In this exercise, you'll add code to a Customer Manager application for reading and writing data from a text file named customers.txt. Each record in this file contains three fields with the customer's first name, last name, and email. The fields are separated by a tab character, and the records are separated by a new line character.

Review the code for the application

1. Open the project named ch17_ex1_CustomerManager that's in the ex_starts folder.
2. Open the Customer class and review its code.

Add the I/O code to the application

3. Open the CustomerTextFile class, and notice the three static variables that store the list of Customer objects, a Path object for the file, and a File object for the file. Add code to initialize these variables.
4. Add code to the getCustomers method that loads the list variable with the Customer objects that are created from the data in the customers.txt file. Be sure to check that this file exists, and if it does, use a try-with-resources statement to open the input stream. If an IOException occurs when the input stream is opened, print the exception to the console and return a null to the calling method.
5. Add code to the saveCustomers method that writes the data in each Customer object in the list to a record in the customer file. Be sure to delimit the fields and records with the appropriate character. If an IOException occurs when the output stream is opened, print the exception to the console and return false to the calling method.
6. Run the application, and test the list, add, and delete functions to be sure they work correctly.

Exercise 17-2 Modify the exception handling

In this exercise, you'll modify the way that exceptions are handled by the ProductIO and Main classes of the Product Manager application.

Open the application and review its code

1. Open the project named ch17_ex2_ProductManager that's in the ex_starts folder.
2. Open the ProductIO class. Note that the getAll and saveAll methods handle all I/O exceptions. Note also that all methods besides the getAll method begin by calling the getAll method.
3. Open the Main class. Note that it doesn't contain any exception handling code.
4. Run the application to make sure it works correctly.

Modify the exception handling code

5. In the ProductIO class, modify the getAll method so it throws an IOException. Since all other methods call this method, you'll also need to modify all other methods in the class so they throw an IOException.
6. Modify the getAll method so it doesn't use a try-with-resources statement to catch any exceptions.
7. Modify the saveAll method so it doesn't use a try-with-resources statement to catch any exceptions. At this point, the ProductIO class should throw exceptions but not handle any of them.
8. In the Main class, add code that handles the exceptions that are thrown by the ProductIO class. To do that, you can add try/catch statements that have a catch block that prints two lines to the console like this:

```
Error! Unable to get products.
java.io.IOException: Test
```

   Here, the first line is a user-friendly message, and the second line contains details about the exception that was thrown.
9. Run the application to make sure it works correctly.

Test the new exception handling code

10. In the ProductIO class, add the following code to the beginning of the getAll method:

```
if (true) {
    throw new IOException("Test");
}
```

11. Run the application and test the exception handling. At this point, you should be able to test the exception handling for the list, add, and delete commands.
12. In the ProductIO class, comment out the statement that throws the IOException. Then, run the application to make sure it still works correctly.

18

How to work with threads

When you run an application in Java, the application runs in one or more threads. So far in this book, all of the applications have executed within a single thread. In this chapter, you'll learn how to develop applications that run in two or more threads that perform separate tasks. For example, you can use one thread to retrieve data from a database while another thread makes a complicated calculation. Then, the application can alternate between the two tasks so it runs more efficiently.

An introduction to threads 464
How threads work 464
Typical uses for threads 464
Classes and interfaces for working with threads.. 466
The life cycle of a thread 468
Two ways to create threads 470
Constructors and methods of the Thread class 470
How to extend the Thread class..472
How to implement the Runnable interface 474
How to synchronize threads 476
How to use synchronized methods 476
When to use synchronized methods 476
Perspective 478

An introduction to threads

Before you learn how to develop applications that use two or more threads, you need to understand how threads work and when you would typically use them. You also need to be familiar with the classes and interfaces you use when you work with threads, and you need to understand the life cycle of a thread. That's what you'll learn in the topics that follow.

How threads work

As figure 18-1 explains, a *thread* is a single flow of execution through an application. By default, Java applications use a single thread, called the *main thread*. This thread begins executing with the first statement of an application's main method and continues executing statements in sequence until the main method exits. The application may create additional objects and call additional methods, but the flow of control is always sequential, one statement at a time.

In some cases, single-threaded execution can be inefficient. For example, imagine an application that performs two independent tasks. To accomplish the first task, the application must read data from a file, and this task spends most of its time waiting for file I/O operations to complete. As a result, the second task must wait too, even though it doesn't require any I/O operations.

The first diagram in this figure shows how this application might work when executed as a single thread. First, the application performs the first task. In this case, the CPU (central processing unit) is idle while it waits for the I/O operations required by this task. When the first task is complete, the application runs the second task.

The second diagram shows how this application could benefit from being split into two threads, one to perform each task. Here, using two threads allows the two tasks to overlap, so the second task is executed while the first task waits on I/O operations. The result is that the two tasks finish sooner than they would if they were executed as a single thread.

Applications that perform several tasks that aren't dependent on one another benefit the most from *multithreading*. For example, the second task shown in this figure can only be overlapped with the first task if the second task doesn't depend on the results of the first task. If the second task depends on the results of the first task, some overlap may still be possible, but the two tasks must communicate with each other so they can coordinate their operations.

Typical uses for threads

In addition to showing the basics of how threads work, figure 18-1 lists three of the most common uses for threads. The first is to improve the performance of I/O operations. Any application that performs extensive I/O can benefit from multithreading. That's because I/O operations are thousands of times slower than CPU operations. So any application that reads data from a disk spends almost all of its time waiting for that information to be retrieved.

How using threads can improve performance

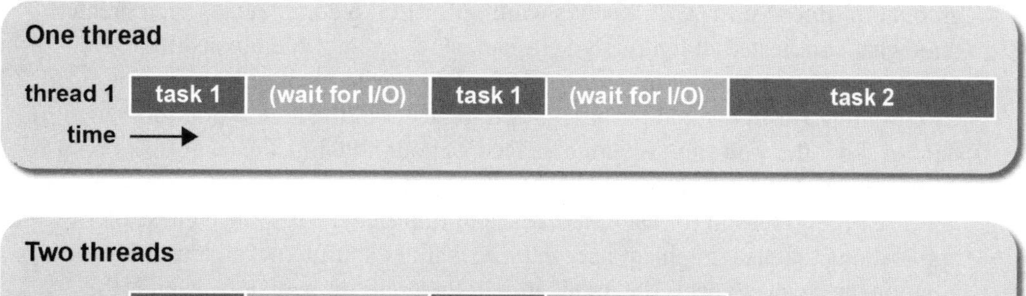

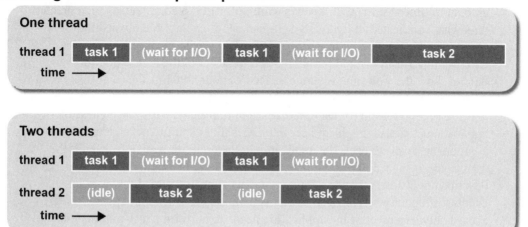

Typical uses for threads

- To improve the performance of applications with extensive I/O operations
- To improve the responsiveness of GUI applications
- To allow two or more users to run server-based applications simultaneously

Description

- A *thread* is a single sequential flow of control within an application. A thread often completes a specific task.
- By default, a Java application uses a single thread, called the *main thread.* However, some applications can benefit by using two or more threads to allow different parts of the application to execute simultaneously.
- On a computer that has just one *CPU (central processing unit) core*, the threads don't actually execute simultaneously. Instead, a part of the operating system called the *thread scheduler* alternately lets each thread execute. This happens faster than humans are able to realize, thus giving the appearance that all of the tasks are running at the same time. As a result, this can make an application work more efficiently.
- Most modern CPUs have multiple cores and can run multiple threads at the same time, even though there is only one CPU.

Figure 18-1 How threads work

To give you some perspective on this, you should realize that the actual amount of time that the CPU spends waiting for I/O to complete is much greater than what's indicated in figure 18-1. In fact, since each of the blocks that show task 1 executing are about one half of an inch long, the blocks that show the CPU waiting for I/O would probably need to be about the length of a football field to show the wait time accurately. That's about how much slower disk operations are than CPU operations.

The second reason for using threads is to improve the responsiveness of applications that use graphical user interfaces. For example, when a user clicks a button, he or she expects the application to respond immediately, even if the application is busy doing something else. A GUI application that uses Swing as described in chapters 21 and 22 automatically runs in a thread that handles the events that occur when the user interacts with the GUI. Then, it updates the GUI accordingly. However, if the application needs to perform a task that may take a long time, this task should be performed in a second thread.

The final reason for using multithreading is to allow two or more users to run server-based applications simultaneously. For example, Java *servlets* automatically create one thread for each user. (To learn more about web programming in Java, you can read, *Murach's Java Servlets and JSP*. For now, you should just realize that each person who uses a servlet runs it in a separate thread. As a result, when you write servlet code, you must make sure that the code is thread-safe.)

Classes and interfaces for working with threads

Figure 18-2 presents a class and an interface that you can use to create and work with threads and summarizes the key methods they provide. To start, the Thread class inherits the Object class, which means it has access to all of its public and protected methods. In addition, the Thread class implements the Runnable interface. Because the Runnable interface declares a single method named run, that means that the Thread class must implement this method.

To create a thread, you can use one of two techniques. First, you can define a class that inherits the Thread class. This class should override the run method so it contains the code to be executed by the thread. Then, you can instantiate this class to create a thread.

Second, you can define a class that implements the Runnable interface. To do that, this class must implement the run method. Then, you pass an instance of this class to a constructor of the Thread class. This creates a thread that executes the Runnable object by calling its run method.

If these two techniques seem confusing right now, don't worry. They should become clearer when you see examples later in this chapter. For now, you just need to know that the Thread class defines a thread, but the code that's executed by the thread can be provided by any class that implements the Runnable interface.

An interface and a class that are used to create threads

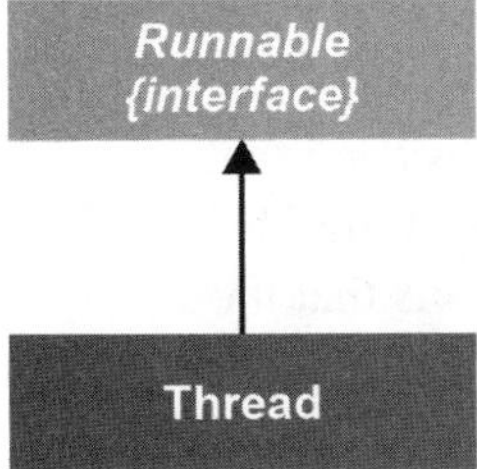

Summary of these classes and interfaces

Class/Interface	Description
`Thread`	A class that defines a thread. This class implements the Runnable interface.
`Runnable`	An interface that must be implemented by any class whose objects are going to be executed by a thread. The only method in this interface is the run method.

Key methods of the Thread class and Runnable interface

Method	Class/Interface	Description
`start`	`Thread`	Registers this thread with the thread scheduler so it's available for execution.
`run`	`Runnable, Thread`	An abstract method that's declared by the Runnable interface and implemented by the Thread class. The thread scheduler calls this method to run the thread.
`sleep`	`Thread`	Causes the current thread to wait (sleep) for a specified period of time so the CPU can run other threads.
`stop`	`Thread`	This method should never be used and only exists for compatibility reasons. It is inherently unsafe and can leave the data it was using in an inconsistent state.

Two ways to create a thread

- Inherit the Thread class.
- Implement the Runnable interface. Then, pass a reference to the Runnable object to the constructor of the Thread class.

Description

- After you create a Thread object, you can call its start method so the thread scheduler can run the thread. Then, you can use the other methods shown above to manage the thread.
- The advantage of implementing the Runnable interface is that it allows the thread to inherit a class other than the Thread class.

Figure 18-2 Classes and interfaces for working with threads

The life cycle of a thread

Figure 18-3 shows the life cycle of a thread and explains each of the five states a thread can be in. To create a thread, the programmer writes code that defines a class for the thread and instantiates a Thread object. When the Thread object is first instantiated, it is placed in the New state, which means that the thread has been created but is not yet ready to be run.

When the application is ready for the thread to be run, it calls the thread's start method. Although you might think that this causes the thread to begin execution, all it really does is change the state of the thread from New to Runnable. Once it's in the Runnable state, the thread joins a list of any other threads that are also in the Runnable state. Then, a component of the operating system called the *thread scheduler* selects one of the Runnable threads to be executed.

Note that there isn't a separate state for the thread that's running. The thread that's running is in the Runnable state, as well as all other threads that are eligible to be running. Also, the thread scheduler may at any time decide that the thread that's currently running has been running long enough. Then, the thread scheduler interrupts that thread and lets one of the other threads in the Runnable state run. This doesn't change the state of either thread.

A thread enters the Blocked state if a condition occurs that makes the thread temporarily not runnable. For example, a thread enters the Blocked state when it is waiting for an I/O operation to complete. The thread automatically returns to the Runnable state when the I/O operation completes. A thread that's in Blocked state can't be selected for execution by the thread scheduler.

The Waiting state comes into play when threads need to coordinate their activities. For example, if a thread can't continue what it's doing until another thread completes, it can enter the Waiting state. Then, when the other thread it is waiting on completes its task, it can notify the waiting thread to stop waiting and enter the Runnable state again.

Finally, when the run method of a thread finishes execution, the thread enters the Terminated state. Once a thread has entered the Terminated state, it remains there until the application ends.

The life cycle of a thread

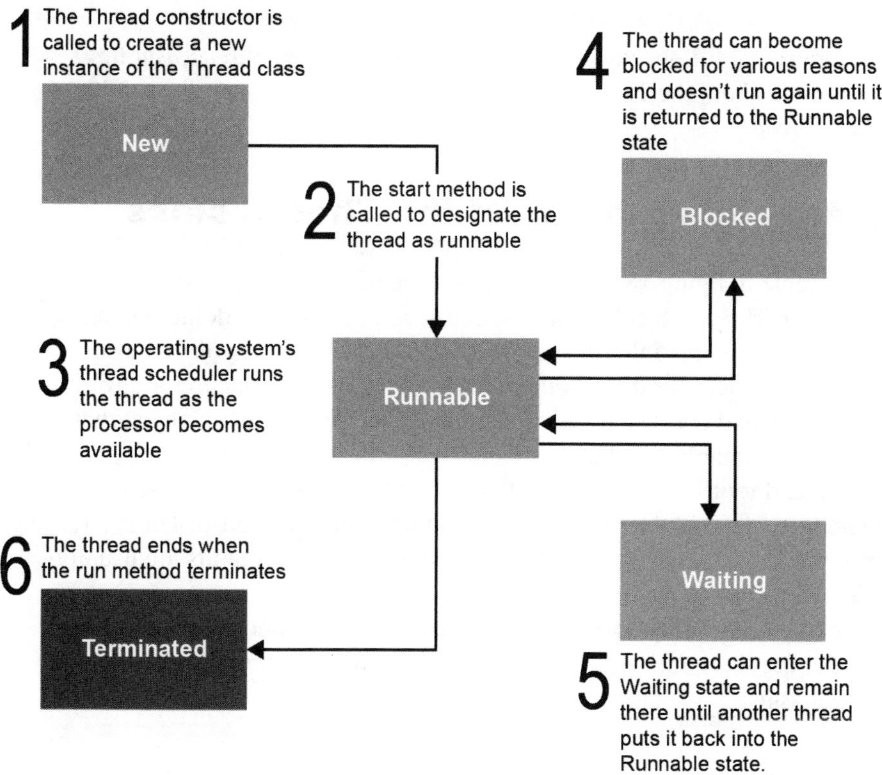
1 The Thread constructor is called to create a new instance of the Thread class
New
2 The start method is called to designate the thread as runnable
4 The thread can become blocked for various reasons and doesn't run again until it is returned to the Runnable state
Blocked
3 The operating system's thread scheduler runs the thread as the processor becomes available
Runnable
6 The thread ends when the run method terminates
Terminated
Waiting
5 The thread can enter the Waiting state and remain there until another thread puts it back into the Runnable state.

Thread states

State	Description
`New`	The thread has been created (its constructor has been called), but not yet started.
`Runnable`	The thread's start method has been called and the thread is available to be run by the thread scheduler. A thread in Runnable state may actually be running, or it may be waiting in the thread queue for an opportunity to run.
`Blocked`	The thread has been temporarily removed from the Runnable state so it can't be executed. This can happen if the thread's sleep method is called, if the thread is waiting on I/O, or if the thread requests a lock on an object that's already locked. When the condition changes (for example, the I/O operation completes), the thread is returned to the Runnable state.
`Waiting`	The thread is waiting and allowing other threads to access the object. It remains in the waiting state until another thread notifies it to stop waiting and re-enter the Runnable state.
`Terminated`	The thread's run method has ended.

Description

- All threads have a life cycle that can include five states: New, Runnable, Blocked, Waiting, and Terminated.

Figure 18-3 The life cycle of a thread

Two ways to create threads

In the topics that follow, you'll learn two ways to create a thread. But first, you'll learn more about the Thread class, which you must use regardless of how you create a thread.

Constructors and methods of the Thread class

The first table in figure 18-4 summarizes some of the constructors you can use to create Thread objects. The first constructor is used by default when you instantiate a class that inherits the Thread class. (Of course, you can also overload this constructor or define other constructors just as you can for any subclass.) The second constructor is used to create a thread from an object that implements the Runnable interface.

The third and fourth constructors let you specify the name of the thread that's created. By default, threads are named numerically (Thread-0, Thread-1, etc.). Since you don't typically refer to threads by name, the defaults are usually acceptable.

The second table in this figure presents some of the methods of the Thread class. You can use these methods to get information about a thread and to control when a thread runs.

The Thread class

`java.lang.Thread;`

Common constructors of the Thread class

Constructor	Description
`Thread()`	Creates a default Thread object.
`Thread(Runnable)`	Creates a Thread object from any object that implements the Runnable interface.
`Thread(String)`	Creates a Thread object with the specified name.
`Thread(Runnable, String)`	Creates a Thread object with the specified name from any object that implements the Runnable interface.

Common methods of the Thread class

Method	Description
`run()`	Implements the run method of the Runnable interface. This method should be overridden in all subclasses to provide the code that's executed by a thread.
`start()`	Places a thread in the Runnable state so it can be run by the thread scheduler.
`getName()`	Returns the name of a thread.
`currentThread()`	A static method that returns a reference to the currently executing thread.
`sleep(long)`	A static method that places the currently executing thread in the Blocked state for the specified number of milliseconds so other threads can run.
`isInterrupted()`	Returns a true value if a thread has been interrupted.

Description

- By default, the threads that you create explicitly are named numerically. If that's not what you want, you can specify the name on the constructor of the thread.
- The sleep method throws an InterruptedException. Because this is a checked exception, you must throw or catch this exception when you use the sleep method.

Figure 18-4 Constructors and methods of the Thread class

How to extend the Thread class

Figure 18-5 shows how to create a thread by extending the Thread class. Here, the IOThread class defines a thread that simulates an I/O operation, and the Main class contains the main method that's run when the application starts.

The IOThread class starts by inheriting the Thread class. Then, it overrides the run method to provide the code that's executed when the thread is run. Within this method, the first statement prints the name of the thread. Then, the run method uses the static sleep method to place the thread in Blocked state for 2000 milliseconds (2 seconds). After 2 seconds, the thread is returned to Runnable state so the thread scheduler can resume its execution.

Because the sleep method can throw an InterruptedException, that exception must be either caught or thrown. This exception indicates that some other thread is attempting to interrupt the current thread while it is sleeping. How you deal with this exception depends on the application. In this case, the application simply ignores any attempts to interrupt the thread by catching the exception but not providing any code to process it. Normally, "swallowing" an exception like this is not a good programming practice. In this case, however, it's appropriate.

If you use the sleep method, you should also realize that it doesn't guarantee that the thread will start running after the amount of time you specify. Instead, it simply guarantees that the thread will be returned to the Runnable state after that amount of time. It's up to the thread scheduler to decide when the thread will resume execution. Because of that, you shouldn't use the sleep method for applications that require precise timing.

The Main class contains the main method for the application. Within this method, the first statement calls the currentThread method of the Thread class and assigns the Thread object that's returned to a variable named t1. Then, the second statement uses the println method to display a message that indicates that the thread has started. To include the name of the thread in this message, this code uses the getName method to get the name of the current thread.

The third statement creates the IOThread object and assigns it to a Thread variable named t2. Then, the fourth statement starts the thread by calling its start method. This places the thread in the Runnable state so the thread scheduler can run it. The fifth statement prints a message indicating that the main thread has started the second thread. And the sixth statement prints a message indicating that the main thread has finished.

The first three lines of the output shown at the bottom of this figure are printed by the main method, which runs in a thread named "main". Then, the next two lines are printed by the thread that's created from the IOThread class, named "Thread-0". The first line is printed at the beginning of the run method to indicate that the thread has started, and the second line is printed at the end of the run method to indicate that the thread has finished. This output shows that the main thread can continue executing while the code in the second thread executes. In other words, the statements in the main method don't have to wait for the statements in the run method of the second thread to finish.

A procedure for creating a thread from the Thread class

1. Create a class that inherits the Thread class.
2. Override the run method to perform the desired task.
3. Create the thread by instantiating an object from the class.
4. Call the start method of the thread object.

A class named IOThread that defines a thread

```
public class IOThread extends Thread {
    @Override
    public void run() {
        System.out.println(this.getName() + " started.");
        try {
            Thread.sleep(2000);         // Sleep for 2 seconds to simulate
                                        // an IO task that takes a long time
        }
        catch(InterruptedException e) {}
        System.out.println(this.getName() + " finished.");
    }
}
```

A Main class that starts a thread

```
public class Main {
    public static void main(String[] args) {
        Thread t1 = Thread.currentThread();
        System.out.println(t1.getName() + " started.");

        Thread t2 = new IOThread();     // create the IO thread
        t2.start();                     // start the IO thread
        System.out.println(t1.getName() + " starts " + t2.getName() + ".");

        System.out.println(t1.getName() + " finished.");
    }
}
```

Sample output

```
main started.
main starts Thread-0.
main finished.
Thread-0 started.
Thread-0 finished.
```

Figure 18-5 How to extend the Thread class

How to implement the Runnable interface

Figure 18-6 shows how to create a thread by implementing the Runnable interface. Although this method of creating threads requires a little more code, it's also more flexible because it lets you define a thread that inherits a class other than the Thread class.

If you compare this code to the code in the previous figure, you'll notice that the IOTask class differs in several ways from the IOThread class. To start, the IOTask class implements the Runnable interface rather than extending the Thread class. Then, within the run method of the IOTask class, the first statement calls the static currentThread method of the Thread class to get a reference to the thread that's currently executing. That way, the getName method can be used to get the name of this thread.

In the main method, you can't create a Thread object directly from the IOTask class. Instead, you have to create a Runnable object from this class and pass it to the constructor of the Thread class. That's shown in the third statement of the main method.

A procedure for creating a thread using the Runnable interface

1. Create a class that implements the Runnable interface.
2. Implement the run method to perform the desired task.
3. Create the thread by supplying an instance of the Runnable class to the Thread constructor.
4. Call the start method of the thread object.

An IOTask class that implements the Runnable interface

```
public class IOTask implements Runnable {
    @Override
    public void run() {
        Thread ct = Thread.currentThread();
        System.out.println(ct.getName() + " started.");
        try {
            Thread.sleep(2000);     // Sleep for 2 seconds to simulate
                                    // an IO task that takes a long time
        }
        catch(InterruptedException e) {}

        System.out.println(ct.getName() + " finished.");
    }
}
```

A Main class that starts a thread using the Runnable interface

```
public class Main {
    public static void main(String[] args) {
        Thread t1 = Thread.currentThread();
        System.out.println(t1.getName() + " started.");

        Thread t2 = new Thread(new IOTask());      // create the new thread
        t2.start();                                // start the new thread
        System.out.println(t1.getName() + " starts " + t2.getName() + ".");

        System.out.println(t1.getName() + " finished.");
    }
}
```

Sample output

```
main started.
main starts Thread-0.
main finished.
Thread-0 started.
Thread-0 finished.
```

Figure 18-6 How to create a thread by implementing the Runnable interface

How to synchronize threads

So far, the threads in this chapter execute independently of each other. These types of threads are known as *asynchronous threads*. However, in some cases, multiple threads need to use the same fields within a class or object. These types of threads are known as *synchronous threads*, and they need to be coordinated so they can work together without causing any problems.

Concurrency refers to a situation where multiple threads are using the same class or object at the same time. Whenever this happens, concurrency problems such as lost updates can result.

When you design classes that might be used by multiple threads, you need to make sure that they are *thread-safe*. This means that multiple threads can safely use them without causing concurrency problems.

How to use synchronized methods

One common way to create a thread-safe class is to add the synchronized keyword to any methods that aren't thread-safe as shown in figure 18-7. Here, the InvoiceQueue class defines an object that allows a thread to add or remove an invoice from a list of invoices.

Within this class, the declaration for the add method includes the synchronized keyword. As a result, when a thread calls this method, the Java virtual machine *locks* the object until this method finishes executing.

When an object is locked, the entire object is locked, not just the synchronized method. In other words, when a thread calls one synchronized method, all of the synchronized methods are locked. In this figure, for example, if a thread calls the add method, both the add and remove methods are locked until the add method finishes executing.

However, when an object is locked, unsynchronized methods are not locked. In this figure, for example, the print method doesn't include the synchronized keyword. As a result, the Java virtual machine doesn't lock this method.

When to use synchronized methods

So far, most of the applications in this book only use a single thread, the main thread. As a result, the classes in these applications don't need to use synchronized methods. However, if multiple threads may access a class, you may need to use synchronized methods.

As a general rule, any methods that access the instance variables of an object should be synchronized. This prevents two threads from accessing the same instance variables at the same time. In this figure, both the add and remove methods work with the instance variable named invoiceQueue that stores the list of invoices. As a result, both of these methods should be synchronized. However, the print method doesn't access any instance variables. As a result, it doesn't need to be synchronized.

The syntax for creating a synchronized method

```
public|private synchronized returnType methodName([parameterList]) {
    statements
}
```

A class that contains two synchronized methods

```
public class InvoiceQueue {
    private ArrayList<Invoice> invoiceQueue = new ArrayList<>();

    public synchronized void add(Invoice invoice) {
        invoiceQueue.add(invoice);
    }

    public synchronized Invoice remove() {
        if (invoiceQueue.size() > 1) {
            return invoiceQueue.remove(0);
        } else {
            return null;
        }
    }

    public void print() {
        System.out.println("This method doesn't need to be synchronized.");
    }
}
```

Description

- *Asynchronous threads* execute independently of each other. *Synchronous threads* need to be coordinated if they could access the same field within a class or object at the same time.
- *Concurrency* refers to a state when multiple threads use the same class or object at the same time. Whenever this happens, concurrency problems such as lost updates may occur.
- When you code a class that multiple threads may use, you need to make sure that the class is *thread-safe*. This means that multiple threads can use it safely without causing concurrency problems.
- The synchronized keyword *locks* the class or object and guarantees that only one thread at a time can execute any of its synchronized methods. Any other thread that attempts to run any synchronized method for the class or object is blocked until the first thread releases the lock by exiting the synchronized method.
- A thread can run an unsynchronized method even if the class or object is locked by a synchronized method. This can potentially cause problems if the unsynchronized method accesses the same field that's used by a synchronized method.
- It's a best practice to use synchronized methods whenever two or more threads might execute the same method, and the method accesses instance variables of the class or object. This is true even if the method only contains one line of code.

Figure 18-7 How to synchronize threads

Perspective

In this chapter, you learned the basic skills for working with threads. Threads are a complex topic, so this chapter could only provide a very brief introduction. Frankly, threading is one of the most challenging topics in this book. So don't be too worried if you don't understand every detail of how it works. As you learn more about different types of Java programming, such as web programming or Android programming, you'll learn more about working with threads in those environments.

On that note, there's more to learn about working with threads when programming applications that use graphical user interfaces (GUIs). One important concept is described later in this book at the end of chapter 22.

Summary

- A *thread* is a single sequential flow of control within an application that often completes a specific task.
- A *multithreaded application* consists of two or more threads whose execution can overlap.
- A single core processor can only execute one thread at a time, and the *thread scheduler* determines which thread to execute.
- Most modern processors have multiple cores and can run more than one thread at the same time. In this case, the thread scheduler determines which threads to run, and which core to run them on.
- *Multithreading* is typically used to improve the performance of applications with I/O operations, to improve the responsiveness of GUI operations, and to allow two or more users to run server-based applications simultaneously.
- You can create a thread by extending the Thread class and then instantiating the new class. Or, you can implement the Runnable interface and then pass a reference to the Runnable object to the constructor of the Thread class.
- You can use the methods of the Thread class to start a thread and to control when a thread runs.
- The *synchronized* keyword on a method ensures that two or more threads cannot run the method at the same time.
- *Asynchronous threads* execute independently of each other.
- *Synchronized methods* can be used to ensure that two threads don't run the same method of an object simultaneously. When a thread calls a synchronized method, the object that contains that method is *locked* so other threads can't access it.
- It's generally considered a best practice to synchronize any methods where there's potential for two threads to access the same field of a class or object at the same time.

Exercise 18-1 Extend the Thread class

In this exercise, you'll create an application that extends the Thread class to create one thread that prints odd numbers from 1 to 10 and another thread that prints even numbers from 1 to 10. The output from this application should look something like this:

```
main started.
Thread-0 started.
Thread-1 started.
main finished.
1
3
5
2
4
7
9
Thread-0 finished.
6
8
10
Thread-1 finished.
```

1. Open the project named ch18_ex1_Counter in the ex_starts folder. Review the code for the Main class and note that it prints a message to the console that indicates when the main thread starts and finishes.
2. Add a class named CounterThread that extends the Thread class.
3. Add an instance variable for a starting value and a constructor that sets that starting value like this:

```
private final int startingValue;

public CounterThread(int startingValue) {
    this.startingValue = startingValue;
}
```

4. In the CounterThread class, add a run method that prints every other number from the starting value to 10 to the console and displays an appropriate message when it's finished.
5. In the Main class, add code to create and start two instances of the CounterThread class. The first should use the ODD constant to specify the starting value, and the second should use the EVEN constant to specify the starting value.
6. Run the application two or more times to make sure it works correctly. The output may vary each time you run the application.
7. Depending on the speed of your system, it's possible that one thread will finish running before the thread scheduler switches threads. In that case, it may look like the two threads are running in sequence rather than in parallel.

8. Add a Thread.sleep call to CounterThread to make the thread sleep for one second between each number. See if this changes the order of the output when you run the application.
9. Run the application two or more times to make sure it works correctly. The output may vary each time you run the application.

Exercise 18-2 Implement the Runnable interface

In this exercise, you'll create an application that's similar to the one that you created in exercise 18-1. However, in this exercise, you implement the Runnable interface instead of extending the Thread class.

1. Open the project named ch18_ex2_Counter in the ex_starts folder. Review the code for the Main class and note that it prints a message to the console that indicates when the main thread starts and finishes.
2. Add a class named CounterThread to the project that implements the Runnable interface.
3. Follow steps 3 through 9 from the previous exercise.

Section 5

Real-world skills

For most Java applications in the real world, the critical data is stored in a database. In most cases, this provides many advantages over storing the data in a file as described in chapter 17. That's why the first two chapters in this section present the essential database skills that you need for developing Java applications. In particular, they describe the essential database skills that you need to develop the Product Manager application that's presented throughout this section.

In addition, most desktop Java applications use a graphical user interface (GUI) to interact with the user. That's why the third and fourth chapters in this section show how to create a GUI. In particular, they describe the essential skills you need to create the GUI for the Product Manager application.

19

How to work with a MySQL database

You can use Java to work with almost any type of database. For desktop or web applications, it's common to use an Oracle or MySQL database. For Android apps, it's common to use a SQLite database. The database you end up using depends on many factors.

Of these databases, MySQL is one of the most popular for Java applications. In addition, there's an open-source version that's free, easy to install, and easy to use. As a result, this chapter shows how to create a MySQL database that can store the data for the Product Manager application that's described in the next few chapters. As you learn this, you will also learn some basic concepts and SQL (Structured Query Language) skills that apply to all databases.

How a relational database is organized 484

How a table is organized 484

How the tables in a database are related 486

How the columns in a table are defined 488

An introduction to MySQL 490

What MySQL provides 490

Ways to interact with MySQL 492

How to open a database connection 494

How to enter and execute a SQL statement 494

A SQL script that creates a database 496

How to drop, create, and select a database 496

How to create a table and insert data 496

How to create a user and grant privileges 496

The SQL statements for data manipulation 498

How to select data from a table 498

How to insert, update, and delete rows 500

Perspective 502

How a relational database is organized

In 1970, Dr. E. F. Codd developed a model for a new type of *database* called a *relational database*. This type of database eliminated some of the problems that were associated with earlier types of databases like hierarchical databases. By using the relational model, you can reduce data redundancy, which saves disk storage and leads to more efficient data retrieval. You can also view and manipulate data in a way that is both intuitive and efficient. Today, relational databases are the de facto standard for database applications.

How a table is organized

A relational database stores data in *tables*. Each table contains *rows* and *columns* as shown in figure 19-1. In practice, rows and columns are often referred to by the traditional terms, *records* and *fields*. That's why this book uses these terms interchangeably.

In a relational database, a table has one column that's defined as the *primary key*. The primary key uniquely identifies each row in a table. That way, the rows in one table can easily be related to the rows in another table. In this table, the ProductID column is the primary key.

The software that manages a relational database is called the *database management system* (*DBMS*) or *relational database management system* (*RDBMS*). The DBMS provides features that let you design the database. After that, the DBMS manages all changes, additions, and deletions to the database. Four of the most popular database management systems are Oracle, Microsoft SQL Server, IBM's DB2, and MySQL.

The Product table

Primary key **Columns**

ProductID	Code	Description	ListPrice
1	java	Murach's Java Programming	57.50
2	jsp	Murach's Java Servlets and JSP	57.50
3	mysql	Murach's MySQL	54.50
4	android	Murach's Android Programming	57.50
5	html5	Murach's HTML5 and CSS3	54.50
6	oracle	Murach's Oracle and PL/SQL	54.50
7	javascript	Murach's JavaScript and jQuery	54.50

Rows

Description

- A *relational database* uses *tables* to store and manipulate data. Each table contains one or more *records*, or *rows*, that contain the data for a single entry. Each row contains one or more *fields*, or *columns*, with each column representing a single item of data.
- Most tables contain a *primary key* that uniquely identifies each row in the table.
- The software that manages a relational database is called a *database management system* (*DBMS*). Four popular database management systems today are Oracle, Microsoft SQL Server, IBM's DB2, and MySQL.

Figure 19-1 How a table is organized

How the tables in a database are related

Figure 19-2 shows how a relational database uses the values in the primary key column to relate one table to another. Here, each ProductID column in the LineItem table contains a value that identifies one row in the Product table. Since the ProductID column in the LineItem table points to a primary key in another table, it's called a *foreign key*. Often, a table has several foreign keys.

In this figure, each row in the Product table relates to one or more rows in the LineItem table. As a result, the Product table has a *one-to-many relationship* with the LineItem table. Although a one-to-many relationship is the most common type of relationship between tables, you can also have a *one-to-one relationship* or a *many-to-many relationship*. However, a one-to-one relationship between two tables is rare since the data can be stored in a single table. In contrast, a many-to-many relationship between two tables is typically implemented by using a third table that has a one-to-many relationship with both of the original tables.

Incidentally, the primary key in the LineItem table is the LineItemID column. It is automatically generated by the DBMS when a new row is added to the database. This works like the ProductID column of the Product table. In general, it's a common practice for the database to automatically generate the value for the primary key.

The relationship between the Product and LineItem tables

Primary key

ProductID	Code	Description	ListPrice
1	java	Murach's Java Programming	57.50
2	jsp	Murach's Java Servlets and JSP	57.50
3	mysql	Murach's MySQL	54.50
4	android	Murach's Android Programming	57.50
5	html5	Murach's HTML5 and CSS3	54.50
6	oracle	Murach's Oracle and PL/SQL	54.50
7	javascript	Murach's JavaScript and jQuery	54.50

LineItemID	InvoiceID	ProductID	Quantity
1	1	3	5
2	1	2	5
3	2	4	1
4	3	5	1
5	3	6	2
6	4	7	1
7	4	3	1
8	5	2	5

Foreign key

Description

- The tables in a relational database are related to each other through their key columns. For example, the ProductID column is used to relate the Product and LineItem tables. The ProductID column in the LineItem table is called a *foreign key* because it identifies a related row in the Product table.
- Three types of relationships can exist between tables. The most common type is a *one-to-many relationship* as illustrated above. However, two tables can also have a *one-to-one relationship* or a *many-to-many relationship*.

Figure 19-2 How the tables in a database are related

How the columns in a table are defined

Figure 19-3 shows how a DBMS defines a column in a database. In particular, it shows how the DBMS defines a name and data type for each column, which are required by all relational databases. In addition, most modern relational databases let you set other attributes for each column in the database such as whether the column is the primary key, whether the values in the column must be unique, whether the column can contain nulls, and so on.

This figure shows the names and data types for the columns in the Product table. Here, the ProductID column is defined with the INT data type, which maps to the int type in Java. The Code and Description columns are defined with the VARCHAR data type, which maps to the String type in Java. Here, the Code column can store a maximum of 10 characters, while the Description column can store a maximum of 255 characters. In contrast, the ListPrice column is defined with the DECIMAL data type, which maps to the double type in Java.

You can define a column so it can store a *null*. Then, you can store a null in the column to indicate that that value for the column is unknown. However, you can also define a column so it can't store a null. In that case, you must provide a value for the column when you attempt to add a row to the table.

For the Product table, the Code, Description, and ListPrice columns use the NOT NULL attribute to specify that they can't store a null. In addition, the ProductID column uses the PRIMARY KEY attribute to specify that it's a primary key. As a result, this column can't store a null. In addition, each row must contain a unique value. Similarly, the Code column uses the UNIQUE attribute to specify that each row must contain a unique value.

The design of the Product table

Column name	Data type	Attribute
`ProductID`	`INT`	`PRIMARY KEY`
`Code`	`VARCHAR(10)`	`NOT NULL UNIQUE`
`Description`	`VARCHAR(255)`	`NOT NULL`
`ListPrice`	`DECIMAL(10, 2)`	`NOT NULL`

Description

- A database management system requires a name and data type for each column in a table. Depending on the data type, the column definition can include other properties such as the column's size.
- Each column definition also specifies whether or not the column can contain a *null*. A null indicates that the value of the column is not known.
- A column definition can specify that the column is the primary key. A primary key column can't be null.
- A column definition can specify that the column must contain a unique value. A unique column can be null. However, if this column is not null, it must contain a unique value.

Figure 19-3 How the columns in a table are defined

An introduction to MySQL

MySQL is an open-source database management system (DBMS) that you can download for free from the MySQL website (www.mysql.com) as described in the appendixes. It is also available as part of a hosting package from many Internet Service Providers (ISPs). MySQL Workbench is a free graphical tool that makes it easy to work with MySQL. As of press time for this book, the current version of MySQL Workbench is version 6.3, so that's the version presented in this chapter. However, with some minor variations, the skills presented in this chapter should work for earlier and later versions as well.

What MySQL provides

Figure 19-4 begins by listing some of the reasons that MySQL enjoys such popularity. To start, it's inexpensive and easy to use when compared with products like Oracle Database or Microsoft SQL Server. It runs fast when compared to those products, especially when you consider the costs. And it runs on most modern operating systems, while Microsoft SQL Server runs only on Windows.

Even though it's free for most uses, MySQL provides most of the features that you would expect from a modern relational database management system (RDBMS). In particular, it provides support for *Structured Query Language* (*SQL*), which is the industry standard. It provides support for multiple clients. And it provides for connectivity and security.

That means you can write Java applications that use SQL statements to access and update the data in a MySQL database. You can connect a Java application to a MySQL database. And you can secure your data by restricting access to it.

With MySQL 5.5 and later, MySQL provides referential integrity and transaction processing by default. When you use these powerful features correctly, they reduce the chance that your data will become corrupted. That's why commercial databases such as Oracle Database and Microsoft SQL Server provide these features.

Prior to MySQL 5.0, MySQL didn't provide referential integrity or transaction processing. As a result, each application that was using MySQL had to provide for these features. In the early days of web programming, this was adequate for many types of web applications. These days, it usually makes sense to have MySQL implement these features.

MySQL is...

- **Inexpensive.** MySQL is free for most uses and relatively inexpensive for other uses.
- **Fast.** By many accounts, MySQL is one of the fastest relational databases that's currently available.
- **Easy to use.** Compared to other database management systems, MySQL is easy to install and use.
- **Portable.** MySQL runs on most modern operating systems including Windows, OS X, and Linux.

MySQL provides...

- **Support for SQL.** Like any modern database product, MySQL supports SQL, which is the standard language for working with data that's stored in relational databases.
- **Support for multiple clients.** MySQL supports access from multiple clients from a variety of interfaces and programming languages including Java, PHP, Python, Perl, and C.
- **Connectivity.** MySQL can provide access to data via an intranet or the Internet.
- **Security.** MySQL can protect access to your data so only authorized users can view the data.
- **Referential integrity.** With MySQL 5.5 and later, InnoDB tables are used by default. These tables support referential integrity, which reduces the chance of data corruption. Most commercial databases also provide this feature.
- **Transaction processing.** With version 5.5, MySQL uses InnoDB tables by default. These tables provide support for transaction processing, which reduces the chance of data corruption. Most commercial databases also provide this feature.

Figure 19-4 An introduction to MySQL

Ways to interact with MySQL

Figure 19-5 shows two ways that you can interact with MySQL. When you install MySQL, it includes a command-line tool like the one at the top of this figure. Although this shows the command-line for the Windows operating system, MySQL's command-line tool works similarly on all operating systems. In this example, the user has started the command-line tool, selected a database named mma, and displayed seven rows from the Product table in that database.

If you install MySQL Workbench as described in the appendixes, you can use it to work with a database as shown in this chapter. To do that, you can enter a SQL statement in the SQL tab at the top of the tool and click on the Execute button to run the SQL statement. Then, the results for the statement are displayed in the Output window. You can also use the Schemas section of the Navigator window to view and work with the databases that are running on the current server. In this figure, for example, the Schemas section shows the columns for the Product table of the mma database.

When you work with MySQL, you may notice that the terms *database* and *schema* are often used interchangeably. For example, the mma database is sometimes referred to as the mma schema.

In general, it's easier to use MySQL Workbench than a command-line tool to work with databases. That's why this chapter shows you how to use MySQL Workbench.

The MySQL command line

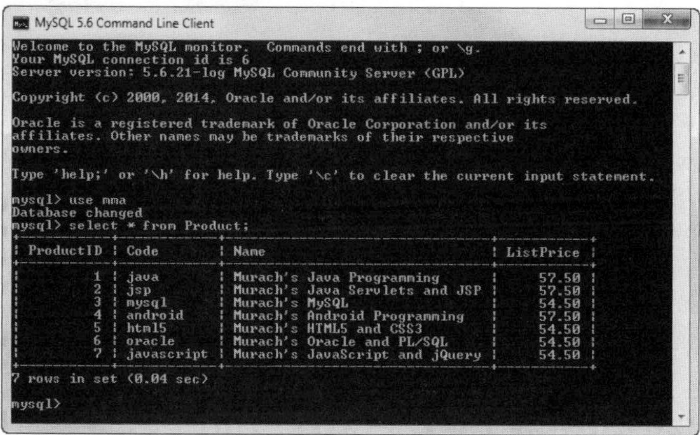

MySQL Workbench

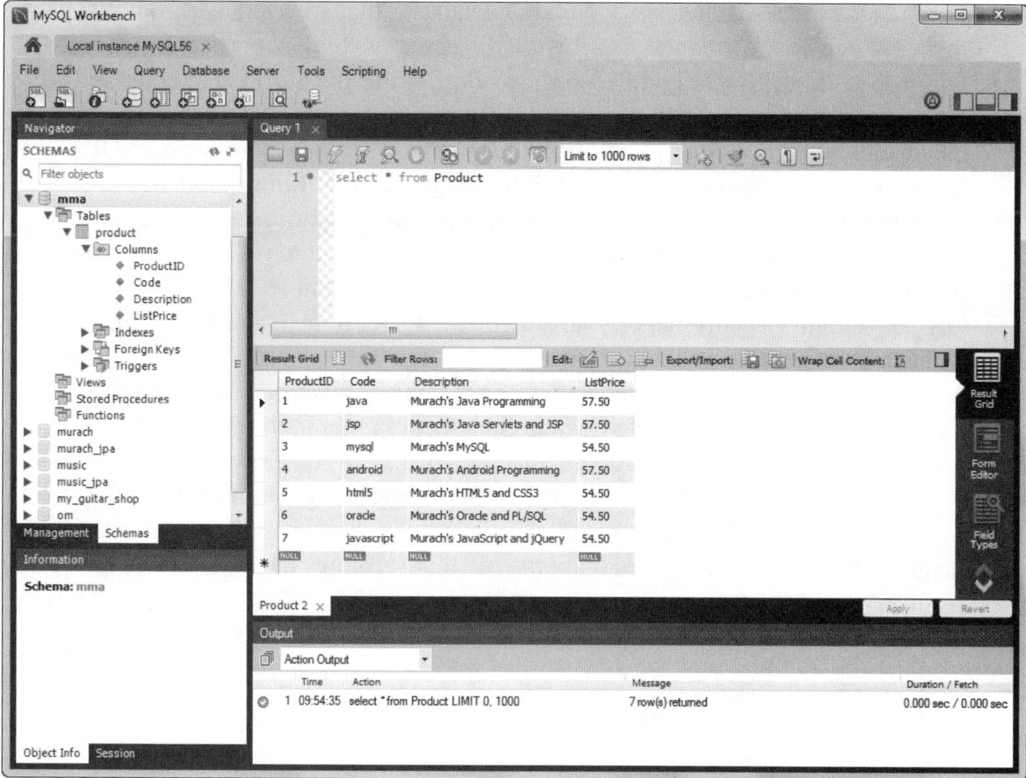

Description

- When working with a desktop application, it's common to use a GUI application such as MySQL Workbench to work with a MySQL database.

Figure 19-5 Ways to work with MySQL

How to open a database connection

Whenever you use MySQL, its *database server* must be running. Usually, this server starts automatically whenever you start your system. If it doesn't, you should be able to start it as described in the appendixes.

Before you can work with a database, you need to connect to the database server. When you start MySQL Workbench, the MySQL Connections section displays a list of saved connections.

By default, MySQL Workbench has one saved connection named "Local instance MySQL56", assuming you installed MySQL 5.6. To connect, click the connection and enter the password for the root user if you're prompted for it.

How to enter and execute a SQL statement

Once MySQL Workbench is connected to a database server, you can use it to run *SQL statements* that work with the databases that are available from that server. When you first connect to a MySQL server, MySQL Workbench automatically opens a SQL tab. Figure 19-6 shows how to use the SQL tab to enter and execute a SQL statement. In this figure, only one SQL tab is open. However, you can open several SQL tabs at a time if you want. One easy way to open a SQL tab is to click the Create New SQL Tab button in the SQL Editor toolbar.

Once you open a SQL tab, you can use standard techniques to enter or edit a SQL statement. As you enter statements, you'll notice that MySQL Workbench automatically applies colors to various elements. For example, it displays keywords in green. This makes your statements easier to read and understand and can help you identify coding errors.

To execute a single SQL statement like the one in this figure, you can press Ctrl+Enter or click the Execute Current Statement button in the SQL Editor toolbar. If the statement returns data, that data is displayed below the SQL Editor window in a corresponding Result grid. In this figure, for example, the result set returned by the SELECT statement is displayed. If necessary, you can adjust the height of the Result grid by dragging the bar that separates the SQL Editor tab from the Result grid.

A SELECT statement and its results

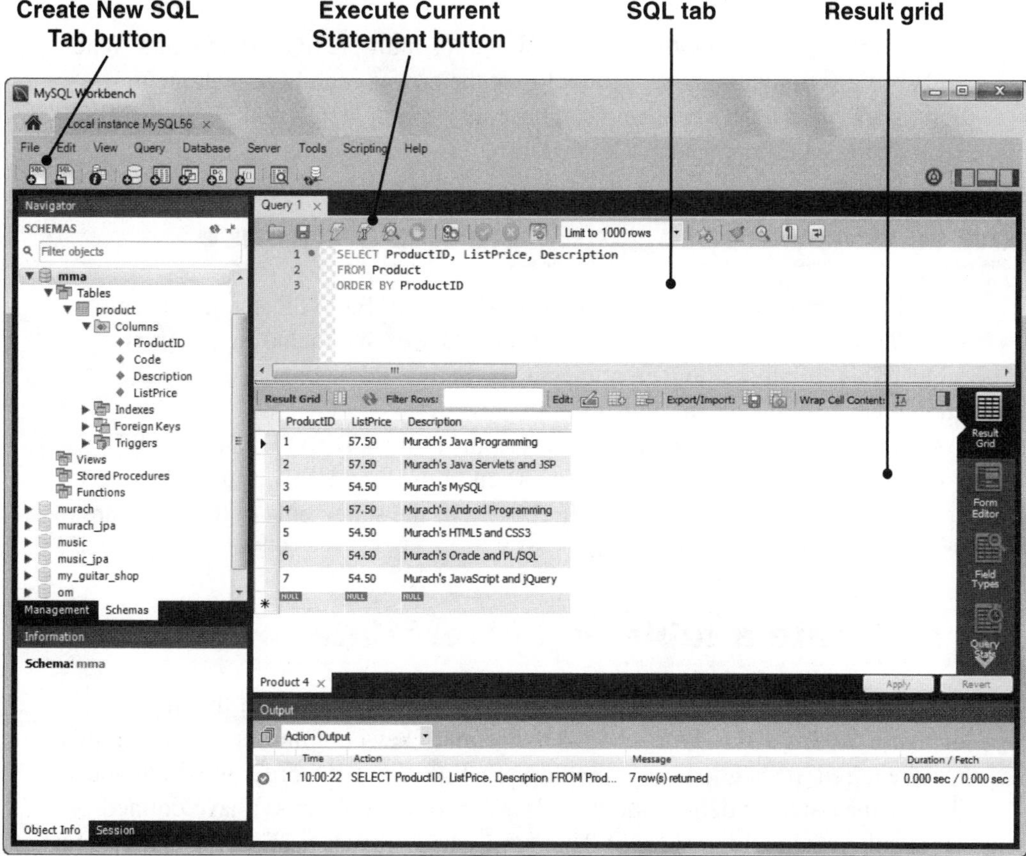

Description

- To open a new SQL tab, press Ctrl+T or click the Create New SQL Tab button in the SQL editor toolbar.
- To select the current database, double-click it in the Schemas section of the Navigator window. This displays the selected database in bold.
- To enter a SQL statement, type it into the SQL tab.
- As you enter the text for a statement, the SQL tab applies color to various elements, such as SQL keywords, to make them easy to identify.
- To execute a SQL statement, press Ctrl+Enter, or click the Execute Current Statement button in the SQL editor toolbar. If the statement retrieves data, the data is displayed in a Result grid below the SQL tab.

Figure 19-6 How to execute a SQL statement with MySQL Workbench

A SQL script that creates a database

A *SQL script* is a file that typically contains multiple SQL statements. When you code a script, you code a semicolon at the end of each SQL statement. Scripts are often used to create a database. For example, figure 19-7 shows a script that creates the database named mma.

How to drop, create, and select a database

This script begins with a DROP DATABASE IF EXISTS statement. This script drops the entire mma database if it already exists, including all of its tables. This suppresses any error messages that would be displayed if you attempted to drop a database that didn't exist.

After dropping this database, this script uses the CREATE DATABASE command to create the mma database. Then, it uses the USE command to select the mma database. As a result, the rest of the statements in the script are executed against the mma database.

How to create a table and insert data

The CREATE TABLE statement creates the Product table of the mma database. In this script, I have coded the primary key column first. Although this isn't required, it's a good programming practice. Since the order in which you declare the columns defines the default order for the columns, I have defined these columns in a logical order. That way, when you use a SELECT * statement to retrieve all of the columns, they're returned in this order.

The INSERT INTO statement inserts seven rows into the Product table. The VALUES clause supplies the data for each row. Here, the number of values supplied for each row must match the number of columns for this table.

How to create a user and grant privileges

The GRANT statement at the end of the script creates a user named mma_user on the local computer with a password of sesame. In addition, it grants this user the SELECT, INSERT, UPDATE, and DELETE privileges on all tables in the mma database. As a result, if you connect to MySQL from the local computer as the user named mma_user, you can work with any of the data that's stored in the database named mma. However, you can't change the structure of this database.

The SQL script that creates the database named mma

```
-- create and select the database
DROP DATABASE IF EXISTS mma;
CREATE DATABASE mma;
USE mma;

-- create the Product table
CREATE TABLE Product (
  ProductID      INT             PRIMARY KEY  AUTO_INCREMENT,
  Code           VARCHAR(10)     NOT NULL     UNIQUE,
  Description    VARCHAR(255)    NOT NULL,
  ListPrice      DECIMAL(10,2)   NOT NULL
);

-- insert some rows into the Product table
INSERT INTO Product VALUES
(1, 'java', 'Murach''s Java Programming', '57.50'),
(2, 'jsp', 'Murach''s Java Servlets and JSP', '57.50'),
(3, 'mysql', 'Murach''s MySQL', '54.50'),
(4, 'android', 'Murach''s Android Programming', '57.50'),
(5, 'html5', 'Murach''s HTML5 and CSS3', '54.50'),
(6, 'oracle', 'Murach''s Oracle and PL/SQL', '54.50'),
(7, 'javascript', 'Murach''s JavaScript and jQuery', '54.50');

-- create a user and grant privileges to that user
GRANT SELECT, INSERT, DELETE, UPDATE
ON mma.*
TO mma_user@localhost
IDENTIFIED BY 'sesame';
```

Description

- You can use the CREATE DATABASE statement to create a database and the DROP DATABASE statement to delete a database. These are *SQL statements*.
- You can use the USE command to select the database that you want to work with.
- You can use the CREATE TABLE statement to create a table. When you create a table, you define each of its columns and you identify its primary key. To define a column, you must supply the name and the data type, whether it's automatically generated for new rows, and so on.
- When you use MySQL, the INSERT statement lets you insert one or more rows into one table of a database. When you code it, you need to include data for all columns that aren't defined with default values or aren't automatically generated.
- You can use the GRANT statement to create a user, specify a password for that user, and grant privileges to the user.

Figure 19-7 The script that creates the database named mma

The SQL statements for data manipulation

With the exception of the INSERT statement, most of the SQL statements that you've seen thus far have been part of SQL's *Data Definition Language (DDL)*. These statements let you create databases, drop databases, create tables, create users, and so on. However, they don't let you work with the data in the tables.

In contrast, the statements that make up SQL's *Data Manipulation Language (DML)* let you work with the data in a database. As a result, they are the statements that you typically use in your Java applications. These statements include the SELECT, INSERT, UPDATE, and DELETE statements.

How to select data from a table

The SELECT statement is the most commonly used SQL statement. When you run a SELECT statement, it is commonly referred to as a *query*. The result of this query is known as a *result set*, or a *result table*.

In figure 19-8, the first example shows how to use this statement to retrieve all rows and columns from the Product table. Here, the SELECT clause uses the asterisk wildcard to indicate that all of the columns in the table should be retrieved. Then, the FROM clause identifies the Product table. This query returns four columns and seven rows.

The second example shows how to use this statement to retrieve two columns and seven rows from the Product table. Here, the SELECT clause identifies the two columns, and the FROM clause identifies the table. Last, the ORDER BY clause indicates that the retrieved rows should be sorted by the Description column.

The third example uses the WHERE clause to limit the number of rows that are retrieved. To do that, it specifies that the statement should only retrieve rows where the value in the ListPrice column is less than 56. Last, the ORDER BY clause indicates that the retrieved rows should be sorted by the Description column.

The result set is a logical table that's created temporarily within the database. Then, the *current row pointer*, or *cursor*, keeps track of the current row. You can use this pointer from your Java applications.

As you might guess, queries can have a significant effect on the performance of a database application. In general, the more columns and rows that a query returns, the more traffic the network has to bear. As a result, when you design queries for your application, you should try to keep the number of columns and rows to a minimum.

A SELECT statement that gets all columns

```
SELECT * FROM Product
```

Result set

ProductID	Code	Description	ListPrice
1	java	Murach's Java Programming	57.50
2	jsp	Murach's Java Servlets and JSP	57.50
3	mysql	Murach's MySQL	54.50
4	android	Murach's Android Programming	57.50
5	html5	Murach's HTML5 and CSS3	54.50
6	oracle	Murach's Oracle and PL/SQL	54.50
7	javascript	Murach's JavaScript and jQuery	54.50

A SELECT statement that gets selected columns

```
SELECT Description, ListPrice
FROM Product
ORDER BY Description
```

Result set

Description	ListPrice
Murach's Android Programming	57.50
Murach's HTML5 and CSS3	54.50
Murach's Java Programming	57.50
Murach's Java Servlets and JSP	57.50
Murach's JavaScript and jQuery	54.50
Murach's MySQL	54.50
Murach's Oracle and PL/SQL	54.50

A SELECT statement that gets selected columns and selected rows

```
SELECT Description, ListPrice
FROM Product
WHERE ListPrice < 56
ORDER BY Description
```

Result set

Description	ListPrice
Murach's HTML5 and CSS3	54.50
Murach's JavaScript and jQuery	54.50
Murach's MySQL	54.50
Murach's Oracle and PL/SQL	54.50

Description

- A SELECT statement is a SQL DML statement that returns a *result set* (or *result table*) that consists of the specified rows and columns.
- To specify the columns, you use the SELECT clause.
- To specify the table that the data should be retrieved from, you use the FROM clause.
- To specify the rows, you use the WHERE clause.
- To specify how the result set should be sorted, you use the ORDER BY clause.

Figure 19-8 How to select data from a single table

How to insert, update, and delete rows

Figure 19-9 shows how to use the INSERT, UPDATE, and DELETE statements to add, update, or delete one or more rows in a database.

The two examples for the INSERT statement show two ways to add the same row to a database. Here, the first INSERT statement doesn't specify a column list after the name of the table. As a result, the VALUES clause must supply values for all columns of the table.

However, the second INSERT statement supplies a column list after the name of the table. As a result, the VALUES clause only needs to supply values for the columns specified in the column list. This works because the Product table has been defined so it automatically generates a value for the ProductID column if this column isn't specified in the column list.

Both of these INSERT statements use single quotes to identify the start and end of numeric and string literals. As a result, to include a single quote within a string literal, these statements must use two single quotes. This is necessary to be able to insert an apostrophe into a string like "Murach's PHP".

The three examples for the UPDATE statement show how to update rows. In the first example, the UPDATE statement updates the ListPrice column of the Product table for the row where the Code column is equal to 'javascript'. Since each row contains a unique value in the Code column, this only updates one row. In the second example, the UPDATE statement updates the ListPrice and Description columns for the same row. In the third example, the UPDATE statement updates the ListPrice column to 55.50 for all rows that have a ListPrice of 54.50.

The two examples for the DELETE statement show how to delete rows. In the first example, the DELETE statement deletes one row from the Product table, the row where the Code column equals 'php'. In the second example, this code doesn't include a WHERE clause. As a result, it deletes all rows from the Product table.

When you issue an INSERT, UPDATE, or DELETE statement from a Java application, you usually work with one row at a time as shown in the next chapter by the ProductDB class. SQL statements that affect more than one row are typically issued by database administrators. Still, an application programmer should understand how these statements work.

When you develop SQL statements, you need to know that the names of the tables and columns are not case-sensitive on Windows. However, these names are case-sensitive on Unix. As a result, if you use Windows to develop an application and you don't use the same case for these names, the application will work fine until you try to run it on a Unix server. Then, the SQL statements will fail. That's why it's a best practice to always use the same case for table and column names even when you're using Windows.

An INSERT statement

That doesn't use a column list

```
INSERT INTO Product
VALUES ('8', 'php', 'Murach''s PHP', '54.50')
```

That uses a column list

```
INSERT INTO Product (Code, Description, ListPrice)
VALUES ('php', 'Murach''s PHP', '54.50')
```

An UPDATE statement

That updates the ListPrice column in one row

```
UPDATE Product
SET ListPrice = '57.50'
WHERE Code = 'javascript'
```

That updates the ListPrice and Description columns in one row

```
UPDATE Product
SET ListPrice = '57.50', Description = 'Murach''s Beginning JavaScript'
WHERE Code = 'javascript'
```

That updates the ListPrice column in selected rows

```
UPDATE Product
SET ListPrice = '55.50'
WHERE ListPrice = '54.50'
```

A DELETE statement

That deletes one row from the Product table

```
DELETE FROM Product
WHERE Code = 'php'
```

That deletes all rows from the Product table

```
DELETE FROM Product
```

Description

- The INSERT, UPDATE, and DELETE statements modify the data that's stored in a database. These statements don't return a result set. Instead, they return the number of rows that were affected by the query.
- To identify a numeric or string literal in a SQL statement, you can enclose the literal in single quotes ('). To include a single quote within a string literal that's enclosed in single quotes, you can enter two single quotes.
- On Unix systems, the table and column names are case-sensitive.

Figure 19-9 How to insert, update, and delete data

Perspective

The primary goal of this chapter is to introduce you to the database concepts and SQL statements that you'll need to develop database applications with Java. The secondary goal of this chapter is to present the basic skills that you need to use MySQL. If this chapter has succeeded, you should now understand the SQL statements presented in this chapter, and you should be able to use MySQL Workbench to run them.

Keep in mind, though, that this chapter has presented just a small subset of SQL skills. In particular, it has only presented the SQL statements you need to understand the Java code presented in the next chapter. For a complete mastery of SQL, you'll probably want to get a book about SQL for the database that you're using. If, for example, you're using MySQL, *Murach's MySQL* presents all of the SQL statements that you'll need for your applications.

Summary

- MySQL is a *relational database management system* (*RDBMS*) that can manage one or more *databases*.
- To retrieve and modify the data in one of its databases, MySQL provides support for *Structured Query Language* (*SQL*), which is the standard language for working with databases.
- Whenever you use MySQL, its *database server* must be running. Usually, this server starts automatically whenever you start your system.
- To work with a MySQL database, you can use a graphical tool called MySQL Workbench. It makes it easy to enter and run *SQL statements*.
- A *SQL script* is a file that stores multiple SQL statements.
- The SQL statements that you use for creating and deleting databases and tables are part of the *Data Definition Language* (*DDL*).
- The SQL statements that you use for retrieving and modifying the data in a database make up the *Data Manipulation Language* (*DML*). These are the SELECT, INSERT, UPDATE, and DELETE statements.
- The SELECT statement can get data from one or more tables and put it in a *result set*, or *result table*. This is commonly referred to as a *query*.
- The INSERT, UPDATE, and DELETE statements are used to add one or more rows to a table, update the data in one or more rows, and delete one or more rows.

Before you do the exercises for this chapter

If you haven't already done so, you should install MySQL and MySQL Workbench as described in the appendixes.

Exercise 19-1 Run a SQL script

1. Start MySQL Workbench.
2. In the MySQL Connections section, click on the "Local instance MySQL" connection. If prompted, enter the password for the root user. This should connect you to the local MySQL server as the root user.
3. Use MySQL Workbench to open the create_databases.sql file that's in the java_netbeans/db folder.
4. Note that this script contains the statements that create the mma database, create its tables, insert rows into some tables, and create a user that has limited privileges.
5. Note that this script uses the DROP DATABASE command to delete the database before creating it.
6. Run this script. It should execute without displaying any errors. If it displays any errors, read the error message and troubleshoot the problem.

Exercise 19-2 Run some SQL statements

1. Start MySQL Workbench.
2. In the MySQL Connections section, click on the "Local instance MySQL" item. If prompted, enter the password for the root user. This should connect you to the local MySQL server as the root user.
3. Use the Navigator window to view the Schemas section and note which databases are installed on your system.
4. View the columns of the Product table by expanding the mma node, the Tables node, the Product node, and the Columns node.
5. Select the mma database by double-clicking on it in the Schemas section. This should display the database name in bold.
6. Run the first SELECT statement in figure 19-8 to view the data stored in the Product table of the mma database.
7. Run the third SELECT statement in figure 19-8 to view a subset of the data in the previous step.
8. Run the first UPDATE statement in figure 19-9. Then, run the first SELECT statement in figure 19-8 again to view the updated data.

20

How to use JDBC to work with databases

This chapter shows how to use Java to work with a database. In particular, it shows the JDBC skills needed to create the classes for the database tier of the Product Manager application. Then, the next two chapters show how to create the classes for the presentation tier.

How to work with JDBC 506
An introduction to database drivers 506
How to connect to a database 508
How to return a result set and move the cursor through it 510
How to get data from a result set 512
How to insert, update, and delete data 514
How to work with prepared statements 516
Two classes for working with databases 518
The DBUtil class 518
The ProductDB class 520
Code that uses the ProductDB class 526
Perspective 528

How to work with JDBC

To write Java code that works with a database, you can use *JDBC*, which is sometimes referred to as *Java Database Connectivity*. The core JDBC API is stored in the java.sql package, which comes as part of Java SE.

An introduction to database drivers

Before you can connect to a database, you must make a *database driver* available to your application. Figure 20-1 lists the four types of JDBC database drivers that you can use. Then, it shows how to download a database driver and make it available to your application. For most applications, you'll want to use a type-4 driver. The other three driver types are generally considered less preferable, with the type-1 driver being the least preferable. As a result, you'll only want to use these drivers if a type-4 driver isn't available for the database that you're using.

For a MySQL database, you can use the type-4 driver named Connector/J that's available for free from the MySQL website. For other types of databases, you can usually download a type-4 driver from the website for that database. The documentation for these drivers typically shows how to install and configure the driver.

To use the database driver in an application, you can add the JAR file that contains the database driver to the application's classpath. The easiest way to do that is to use your IDE to add the JAR file for the database driver to your application. To add a MySQL driver to a NetBeans project, you can right-click on the project's Library folder, select the Add Library command, and use the resulting dialog box to select the MySQL JDBC Driver library.

The four types of JDBC database drivers

Type 1	A *JDBC-ODBC bridge driver* converts JDBC calls into ODBC calls that access the DBMS protocol. For this data access method, an ODBC driver must be installed on the client machine. A JDBC-ODBC bridge driver was included as part of the JDK prior to Java 8 but is not included or supported with Java 8 and later.
Type 2	A *native protocol partly Java driver* converts JDBC calls into the native DBMS protocol. Since this conversion takes place on the client, the database client library must be installed on the client machine.
Type 3	A *net protocol all Java driver* converts JDBC calls into a net protocol that's independent of any native DBMS protocol. Then, middleware software running on a server converts the net protocol to the native DBMS protocol. Since this conversion takes place on the server side, the database client library isn't required on the client machine.
Type 4	A *native protocol all Java driver* converts JDBC calls into the native DBMS protocol. Since this conversion takes place on the server, the database client library isn't required on the client machine.

How to download a database driver

- For MySQL databases, you can download a JDBC driver named Connector/J from the MySQL website. This driver is an open-source, type-4 driver that's available for free.
- For other databases, you can usually download a type-4 JDBC driver from the database's website.
- The Connector/J driver for MySQL databases is included with NetBeans. As a result, if you're using NetBeans, you don't need to download this driver.

How to make a database driver available to an application

- Before you can use a database driver, you must make it available to your application. The easiest way to do this is to use your IDE to add the JAR file for the driver to your application.
- To add the MySQL JDBC driver to a NetBeans project, right-click on the Libraries folder, select the Add Library command, and use the resulting dialog box to select the MySQL JDBC Driver library.
- To add any JDBC driver to a NetBeans project, right-click on the Libraries folder, select the Add JAR/Folder command, and use the resulting dialog box to select the JAR file for the driver.

Figure 20-1 An introduction to database drivers

How to connect to a database

Before you can access or modify the data in a database, you must connect to the database as shown in figure 20-2. To start, this figure shows the syntax for a database URL. You can use this syntax within the code that gets the connection.

The first example shows how to use a type-4 MySQL driver to get a connection to a database. To start, you use the getConnection method of the DriverManager class to return a Connection object. This method requires three arguments: the URL for the database, a username, and a password. In the first example, the URL consists of the API (jdbc), the subprotocol for MySQL drivers (mysql), the host machine (localhost), the port for the database service (3306), and the name of the database (mma).

For security reasons, it's considered a best practice to connect to the database with a username that only has the privileges that the application needs. That's why the script that creates the mma database creates a user named mma_user that only has limited privileges to work with the data of the mma database, not to modify its structure. As a result, the user named mma_user is appropriate for the sample applications presented in this book.

The second example shows how to connect to an Oracle database. Here again, you provide the URL for the database, a username, and a password. This is true no matter what type of database you're using with JDBC.

In practice, connecting to the database is often frustrating because it's hard to figure out what the URL, username, and password need to be. So if your colleagues have already made a connection to the database that you need to use, you can start by asking them for this information.

Since the getConnection method of the DriverManager class throws a SQLException, you need to handle this exception whenever you connect to a database. With JDBC 4.0 (Java 6) and later, you can use an enhanced for statement to loop through any exceptions that are nested within the SQLException object. In this figure, the catch block in the first example loops through all the exceptions that are nested in the SQLException object.

To do that, this loop retrieves a Throwable object named t for each nested exception. Then, it prints the exception to the console. This works because the Throwable class is the superclass for all exceptions, and a Throwable object is returned by the iterator for the SQLException class.

The first two examples present a new feature of JDBC 4.0 called *automatic driver loading*. This feature loads the database driver automatically based on the URL for the database.

If you're working with an older version of Java, though, you need to use the forName method of the Class class to explicitly load the driver before you call the getConnection method as shown by the third example. Since this method throws a ClassNotFoundException, you also have to handle this exception.

Even with JDBC 4.0 and later, you might get a message that says, "No suitable driver found." In that case, you can use the forName method of the Class class to explicitly load the driver. However, if automatic driver loading works, it usually makes sense to remove this method call from your code. That way, you can connect to the database with less code, and you don't have to hard code the name of the database driver.

Database URL syntax

```
jdbc:subprotocolName:databaseURL
```

How to connect to a MySQL database with automatic driver loading

```
try {
    // set the db url, username, and password
    String dbURL = "jdbc:mysql://localhost:3306/mma";
    String username = "mma_user";
    String password = "sesame";

    // get connection
    Connection connection =
            DriverManager.getConnection(dbURL, username, password);
} catch(SQLException e) {
    for (Throwable t : e) {
        System.out.println(t);
    }
}
```

How to connect to an Oracle database with automatic driver loading

```
    Connection connection = DriverManager.getConnection(
        "jdbc:oracle:thin@localhost/mma", "mma_user", "sesame");
```

How to load a MySQL database driver prior to JDBC 4.0

```
try {
    Class.forName("com.mysql.jdbc.Driver");
} catch(ClassNotFoundException e) {
    System.out.println(e);
}
```

Description

- Before you can get or modify the data in a database, you need to connect to it. To do that, you use the getConnection method of the DriverManager class to return a Connection object.
- When you use the getConnection method of the DriverManager class, you must supply a URL for the database. In addition, you usually supply a username and a password, though you might not for an embedded database. This method throws a SQLException.
- With JDBC 4.0 and later, the SQLException class implements the Iterable interface. As a result, you can use an enhanced for statement to loop through any nested exceptions.
- With JDBC 4.0 and later, the database driver is loaded automatically. This feature is known as *automatic driver loading*.
- Prior to JDBC 4.0, you needed to use the forName method of the Class class to load the driver. This method throws a ClassNotFoundException.
- Although the connection string for each driver is different, the documentation for the driver should explain how to write a connection string for that driver.
- Typically, you only need to connect to one database for an application. However, it's possible to load multiple database drivers and establish connections to multiple types of databases.

Figure 20-2 How to connect to a database

How to return a result set and move the cursor through it

Once you connect to a database, you're ready to retrieve data from it as shown in figure 20-3. Here, the first two examples show how to use Statement objects to create a *result set*, or *result table*. Then, the next two examples show how to move the *row pointer*, or *cursor*, through the result set.

Both of the result sets in this figure are read-only, forward-only result sets. This means that you can only move the cursor forward through the result set, and that you can read but not write rows in the result set. Although JDBC supports other types of scrollable, updateable result sets, these features require some additional overhead, and they aren't necessary for most applications.

The first example calls the createStatement method from a Connection object to return a Statement object. Then, it calls the executeQuery method from the Statement object to execute a SELECT statement that's coded as a string. This returns a ResultSet object that contains the result set for the SELECT statement. In this case, the SELECT statement only retrieves a single column from a single row (the product code for a specific product ID) so that's what the ResultSet object contains. You can use this object to check whether a row exists.

The second example works like the first example. However, it returns all of the rows and columns for the Product table and puts this result set in a ResultSet object named products. You can use this object to display all products.

The third example shows how to use the next method of the ResultSet object to move the cursor to the first row of the result set that's created by the first example. When you create a result set, the cursor is positioned before the first row in the result set. As a result, the first use of the next method attempts to move the cursor to the first row in the result set. If the row exists, the cursor moves to that row and the next method returns a true value. Otherwise, the next method returns a false value. In the next figure, you'll learn how to retrieve values from the row that the cursor is on.

The fourth example shows how to use the next method to loop through all of the rows in the result set that's created in the second example. Here, the while loop calls the next method. Then, if the next row is a valid row, the next method moves the cursor to the row and returns a true value. As a result, the code within the while loop is executed. Otherwise, the next method returns a false value and the code within the while loop isn't executed.

Since all of the methods described in this figure throw a SQLException, you either need to throw or catch this exception when you're working with these methods. The ProductDB class presented later in this chapter shows how this works.

Although there are other ResultSet methods, the one you'll use the most with a forward-only, read-only result set is the next method. However, this figure summarizes two other methods (last and close) that you may occasionally want to use for this type of result set.

How to create a result set that contains 1 row and 1 column

```
Statement statement = connection.createStatement();
ResultSet product = statement.executeQuery(
    "SELECT ProductCode FROM Product " +
    "WHERE ProductID = '1'");
```

How to create a result set that contains multiple columns and rows

```
Statement statement = connection.createStatement();
ResultSet products = statement.executeQuery(
    "SELECT * FROM Product ");
```

How to move the cursor to the first row in the result set

```
boolean productExists = product.next();
```

How to loop through a result set

```
while (products.next()) {
    // statements that process each row
}
```

ResultSet methods for forward-only, read-only result sets

Method	Description
`next()`	Moves the cursor to the next row in the result set.
`last()`	Moves the cursor to the last row in the result set.
`close()`	Releases the result set's resources.

Description

- To return a *result set*, you use the createStatement method of a Connection object to create a Statement object. Then, you use the executeQuery method of the Statement object to execute a SELECT statement that returns a ResultSet object.
- By default, the createStatement method creates a forward-only, read-only result set. This means that you can only move the *cursor* through it from the first row to the last and that you can't update it. Although you can pass arguments to the createStatement method that create other types of result sets, the default is appropriate for most applications.
- When a result set is created, the cursor is positioned before the first row. Then, you can use the methods of the ResultSet object to move the cursor. To move the cursor to the next row, for example, you call the next method. If the row is valid, this method moves the cursor to the next row and returns a true value. Otherwise, it returns a false value.
- The createStatement, executeQuery, and next methods throw a SQLException. As a result, any code that uses these methods needs to catch or throw this exception.

Figure 20-3 How to return a result set and move the cursor through it

How to get data from a result set

When the cursor is positioned on the row that you want to get data from, you can use the methods in figure 20-4 to get that data. The examples show how to use the getInt, getString, and getDouble methods of the ResultSet object to return int, String, and double values. However, you can use similar get methods to return other types of data.

The methods in this figure show the two types of arguments accepted by the get methods. The first method accepts an int value that specifies the index number of the column in the result set, where 1 is the first column, 2 is the second column, and so on. The second method accepts a String object that specifies the name of the column in the result set. Although the get methods with column indexes require less typing, the get methods with column names lead to code that's easier to read and understand.

The first example shows how to use column indexes to return data from a result set named products. Here, the first statement uses the getInt method to return the ID for the product, the next two statements use the getString method to return the code and description, and the third statement uses the getDouble method to return the list price. Since these methods use the column index, the first column in the result set must contain the product ID, the second column must contain the product code, and so on.

The second example shows how to use column names to return data from the products result set. Since this code uses the column names, the order of the columns in the result set doesn't matter. However, the column names must exist in the result set or a SQLException is thrown that indicates that a column wasn't found.

The third example shows how you can use the get methods to create a Product object. Here, the first statement creates a new Product object. Then, the next four statements store the data that was retrieved from the ResultSet object in the Product object. Since objects are often created from data that's stored in a database, code like this is commonly used when you use the JDBC API. However, this code is handled automatically by some other database APIs such as JPA (Java Persistence API).

If you look up the ResultSet interface in the documentation for the JDBC API, you'll see that get methods exist for all of the primitive types as well as for other types of data. For example, get methods exist for the Date, Time, and Timestamp classes that are a part of the java.sql package. In addition, they exist for *BLOB objects* (*Binary Large Objects*) and *CLOB objects* (*Character Large Objects*). You can use these types of objects to store large objects such as images, audio, and video in databases.

Methods of a ResultSet object that return data from a result set

Method	Description
`getXXX(columnIndex)`	Returns data from the specified column number.
`getXXX(columnName)`	Returns data from the specified column name.

Code that uses indexes to return columns from the products result set

```
int productID = products.getInt(1);
String code = products.getString(2);
String description = products.getString(3);
double price = products.getDouble(4);
```

Code that uses names to return the same columns

```
int productID = products.getInt("ProductID");
String code = products.getString("Code");
String description = products.getString("Description");
double price = products.getDouble("ListPrice");
```

Code that creates a Product object from the products result set

```
Product p = new Product();
p.setId(productID);
p.setCode(code);
p.setDescription(description);
p.setPrice(price);
```

Description

- The getXXX methods can be used to return all eight primitive types. For example, the getInt method returns the int type and the getLong method returns the long type.
- The getXXX methods can also be used to return strings, dates, and times. For example, the getString method returns an object of the String class, and the getDate, getTime, and getTimestamp methods return objects of the Date, Time, and Timestamp classes of the java.sql package.

Figure 20-4 How to retrieve data from a result set

How to insert, update, and delete data

Figure 20-5 shows how to use JDBC to modify the data in a database. To do that, you use the executeUpdate method of a Statement object to execute SQL statements that add, update, and delete data.

When you work with the executeUpdate method, you just pass a SQL statement to the database. In these examples, the code adds, updates, and deletes a product in the Product table. To do that, the code combines data from a Product object with the appropriate SQL statement. For the UPDATE and DELETE statements, the SQL statement uses the product's code in the WHERE clause to select a single product.

Unfortunately, if you build a SQL statement from user input and use a method of the Statement object to execute that SQL statement, you are susceptible to a security vulnerability known as a SQL injection attack. A *SQL injection attack* allows a hacker to execute SQL statements against your database to read sensitive data or to delete or modify data. For the Product Manager application, for instance, the user might be able to execute a DROP TABLE statement by entering the following code:

```
test'); DROP TABLE Product; --
```

Here, the first semicolon ends the first SQL statement. Then, the database might execute the second SQL statement. To prevent most types of SQL injection attacks, you can use a prepared statement as described in the next figure.

How to use the executeUpdate method to modify data

How to add a row

```
String query =
    "INSERT INTO Product (ProductCode, ProductDescription, ProductPrice) " +
    "VALUES ('" + product.getCode() + "', " +
            "'" + product.getDescription() + "', " +
            "'" + product.getPrice() + "')";
Statement statement = connection.createStatement();
int rowCount = statement.executeUpdate(query);
```

How to update a row

```
String query = "UPDATE Product SET " +
    "ProductCode = '" + product.getCode() + "', " +
    "ProductDescription = '" + product.getDescription() + "', " +
    "ProductPrice = '" + product.getPrice() + "' " +
    "WHERE ProductCode = '" + product.getCode() + "'";
Statement statement = connection.createStatement();
int rowCount = statement.executeUpdate(query);
```

How to delete a row

```
String query = "DELETE FROM Product " +
               "WHERE ProductCode = '" + productCode + "'";
Statement statement = connection.createStatement();
int rowCount = statement.executeUpdate(query);
```

Description

- The executeUpdate method is an older method that works with most JDBC drivers. Although there are some newer methods that require less SQL code, they may not work properly with all JDBC drivers.
- The executeUpdate method returns an int value that identifies the number of rows that were affected by the SQL statement.

Warning

- If you build a SQL statement from user input and use a method of the Statement object to execute that SQL statement, you may be susceptible to a security vulnerability known as a SQL injection attack.
- A *SQL injection attack* allows a hacker to bypass authentication or to execute SQL statements against your database that can read sensitive data, modify data, or delete data.
- To prevent most types of SQL injection attacks, you can use prepared statements as described in the next figure.

Figure 20-5 How to insert, update, and delete data

How to work with prepared statements

Each time a Java application sends a new SQL statement to the database server, the server checks the statement for syntax errors, prepares a plan for executing the statement, and executes the statement. If the same statement is sent again, though, the database server checks to see whether it has already received one exactly like it. If so, the server doesn't have to check its syntax and prepare an execution plan for it so the server just executes it. This improves the performance of the database operations.

To take advantage of this database feature, Java provides for the use of *prepared statements* as shown in figure 20-6. This feature lets you send statements to the database server that get executed repeatedly by accepting the parameter values that are sent to it. That improves the database performance because the database server only has to check the syntax and prepare the execution plan once for each statement.

In addition, prepared statements automatically check their parameter values to prevent most types of SQL injection attacks. As a result, it's generally considered a best practice to use prepared statements whenever possible.

The first example uses a prepared statement to create a result set that contains a single product. Here, the first statement uses a question mark (?) to identify the parameter for the SELECT statement, which is the product code for the book, and the second statement uses the prepareStatement method of the Connection object to return a PreparedStatement object. Then, the third statement uses a set method (the setString method) of the PreparedStatement object to set a value for the parameter, and the fourth statement uses the executeQuery method of the PreparedStatement object to return a ResultSet object.

The second example shows how to use a prepared statement to execute an UPDATE query that requires four parameters. Here, the first statement uses four question marks to identify the four parameters of the UPDATE statement, and the second statement creates the PreparedStatement object. Then, the next four statements use set methods to set the four parameters in the order that they appear in the UPDATE statement. The last statement uses the executeUpdate method of the PreparedStatement object to execute the UPDATE statement.

The third and fourth examples show how to insert and delete rows with prepared statements. This works similarly to the second example.

In this figure, the type of SQL statement that you're using determines whether you use the executeQuery method or the executeUpdate method. If you're using a SELECT statement to return a result set, you use the executeQuery method. However, if you're using an INSERT, UPDATE, or DELETE statement, you use the executeUpdate method. In other words, this works the same for a PreparedStatement object as it does for a Statement object.

How to use a prepared statement

To return a result set

```
String sql = "SELECT ProductCode, ProductDescription, ProductPrice "
           + "FROM Product WHERE ProductCode = ?";
PreparedStatement ps = connection.prepareStatement(sql);
ps.setString(1, productCode);
ResultSet product = ps.executeQuery();
```

To modify a row

```
String sql = "UPDATE Product SET "
           + "    ProductCode = ?, "
           + "    ProductDescription = ?, "
           + "    ProductPrice = ?"
           + "WHERE ProductCode = ?";
PreparedStatement ps = connection.prepareStatement(sql);
ps.setString(1, product.getCode());
ps.setString(2, product.getDescription());
ps.setDouble(3, product.getPrice());
ps.setString(4, product.getCode());
ps.executeUpdate();
```

To insert a row

```
String sql =
      "INSERT INTO Product (ProductCode, ProductDescription, ProductPrice) "
    + "VALUES (?, ?, ?)";
PreparedStatement ps = connection.prepareStatement(sql);
ps.setString(1, product.getCode());
ps.setString(2, product.getDescription());
ps.setDouble(3, product.getPrice());
ps.executeUpdate();
```

To delete a row

```
String sql = "DELETE FROM Product "
           + "WHERE ProductCode = ?";
PreparedStatement ps = connection.prepareStatement(sql);
ps.setString(1, product.getCode());
ps.executeUpdate();
```

Description

- When you use *prepared statements* in your Java applications, the database server only has to check the syntax and prepare an execution plan once for each SQL statement. This improves the efficiency of the database operations. In addition, it prevents most types of SQL injection attacks.
- To specify a parameter for a prepared statement, type a question mark (?) in the SQL statement.
- To supply values for the parameters in a prepared statement, use the set methods of the PreparedStatement interface. For a complete list of set methods, look up the PreparedStatement interface of the java.sql package in the documentation for the Java API.
- To execute a SELECT statement, use the executeQuery method. To execute an INSERT , UPDATE, or DELETE statement, use the executeUpdate method.

Figure 20-6 How to work with prepared statements

Two classes for working with databases

Now that you know how to use JDBC to work with a database, you're ready to learn how to code a class that allows you to map an object to a table in a database. In particular, you're ready to learn how to map the Product object to the Product table in the mma database. But first, you'll be introduced to a utility class that you can use to get a connection to a database.

The DBUtil class

Figure 20-7 shows a class named DBUtil. This class begins by declaring a static variable for the Connection object. Then, it provides a private constructor that prevents other classes from creating an object from the DBUtil class. That's a good practice since the DBUtil class only provides two static methods.

The first static method, the getConnection method, returns a Connection object that provides a connection to the database. This method begins by checking whether the connection has already been opened. If so, it returns that connection. As a result, this method only opens one connection to the database. This helps the application run efficiently after it opens the first connection to the database.

However, if the connection hasn't been opened, this code opens a connection by creating a Connection object. To do that, this code specifies the URL, username, and password for the database. Here, the code connects to the mma database as the user named mma_user. This works as described earlier in this chapter.

After specifying the URL, username, and password for the database, the getConnection method uses the static getConnection method of the DriverManager class to automatically load the appropriate database driver and connect to the database. If this method is successful, this method returns the Connection object to the calling method. Otherwise, this method throws a SQLException. Then, the catch block catches this exception, wraps it in the custom DBException class presented in chapter 16, and throws that exception.

The second static method, the closeConnection method, closes the one connection that's opened by this class. Typically, you call this method when the application exits. In other words, you close the connection to the database when you close the application. This prevents resource leaks.

Both of the static methods include the synchronized keyword. As a result, each method must finish before you can call another method, which is what you want. For example, if you call the getConnection method, you want it to finish executing before the close method can begin executing.

The DBUtil class

```
package murach.db;

import java.sql.Connection;
import java.sql.DriverManager;
import java.sql.SQLException;

public class DBUtil {

    private static Connection connection;

    private DBUtil() {}

    public static synchronized Connection getConnection() throws DBException {
        if (connection != null) {
            return connection;
        }
        else {
            try {
                // set the db url, username, and password
                String url = "jdbc:mysql://localhost:3306/mma";
                String username = "mma_user";
                String password = "sesame";

                // get and return connection
                connection = DriverManager.getConnection(
                        url, username, password);
                return connection;
            } catch (SQLException e) {
                throw new DBException(e);
            }
        }
    }

    public static synchronized void closeConnection() throws DBException {
        if (connection != null) {
            try {
                connection.close();
            } catch (SQLException e) {
                throw new DBException(e);
            } finally {
                connection = null;
            }
        }
    }
}
```

Description

- To make it easier to get and close a connection to a database, you can use a utility class like the one shown in this figure.

Figure 20-7 The DBUtil class

The ProductDB class

Figure 20-8 presents the complete code for the ProductDB class. This class maps the Product object to the Product table of the mma database.

The getAll method returns a List object that contains all of the Product objects that are stored in the Product table of the mma database. Here, the first statement creates a string that contains a SQL statement that selects all columns from the Product table and sorts them in ascending order by the ProductID column. The second statement creates an ArrayList object that can store Product objects. And the third statement uses the static getConnection method of the DBUtil class to get a connection to the database.

After getting the connection, this code uses a try-with-resources statement to create the PreparedStatement and ResultSet objects that are needed by this method. That way, these objects are automatically closed when the try block ends.

Once the ResultSet object has been created, the getAll method uses a loop to read each row in the result set. Within the loop, the first statement uses the getInt method of the ResultSet object to get the int value for the ProductID column of the result set. The next two statements use the getString method to return strings for the Code and Description columns. And the fourth statement uses the getDouble method to return a double value for the ListPrice column. Then, this loop creates the Product object, stores the data in it, and adds it to the products array list.

If this code executes successfully, the getAll method returns the products array list. However, if a SQLException is thrown anywhere in the try block, the catch block creates a new DBException that stores the SQLException and throws this exception to the calling method. That way, the calling method can throw or handle this exception. Ultimately, this should lead to the exception being handled at a level that's appropriate for the application, often by having the user interface display an appropriate user-friendly message to the user.

The ProductDB class

Page 1

```
package murach.db;

import java.sql.Connection;
import java.sql.PreparedStatement;
import java.sql.ResultSet;
import java.sql.SQLException;
import java.util.ArrayList;
import java.util.List;

import murach.business.Product;

public class ProductDB {

    public static List<Product> getAll() throws DBException {
        String sql = "SELECT * FROM Product ORDER BY ProductID";
        List<Product> products = new ArrayList<>();
        Connection connection = DBUtil.getConnection();
        try (PreparedStatement ps = connection.prepareStatement(sql);
             ResultSet rs = ps.executeQuery()) {
            while (rs.next()) {
                int productID = rs.getInt("ProductID");
                String code = rs.getString("Code");
                String name  = rs.getString("Description");
                double price = rs.getDouble("ListPrice");

                Product p = new Product();
                p.setId(productID);
                p.setCode(code);
                p.setDescription(name);
                p.setPrice(price);
                products.add(p);
            }
            return products;
        } catch (SQLException e) {
            throw new DBException(e);
        }
    }
```

Figure 20-8 The ProductDB class (part 1 of 3)

The get method returns a Product object for a product that matches the specified product code. To do that, it uses a prepared SQL statement to return a result set. Then, it calls the next method of the result set to attempt to move the cursor to the first row in the result set. If successful, this method continues by reading the columns from the row, closing the result set, creating a Product object from this data, and returning the Product object.

Unlike the getAll method, the result set used by the get method can't be created in the try-with-resources statement. That's because before the result set can be opened, the value of the parameter in the prepared statement must be set. However, the prepared statement can still be created in the try-with-resources statement, which means that it doesn't have to be closed explicitly.

If no product row contains a product code that matches the specified code, this method closes the result set and returns a null to indicate that the product couldn't be found. In addition, if a SQLException is thrown anywhere in this method, this method creates a new exception from the DBException class and throws this exception to the calling method. That way, the method that calls the get method can throw or handle this exception.

As you review the get method, note that if the try block throws a SQLException, the result set isn't explicitly closed. In most cases, that's not a problem because the result set is automatically closed when the prepared statement that was used to create the result set is closed. If you wanted to close the result set explicitly, though, you could do that by adding a finally clause to the try statement.

The add method begins by creating a prepared statement that can be used to insert values into three columns of the Product table. Then, it sets the values of the three parameters in the prepared statement to the values stored in the Product object that's passed to it. Finally, it calls the executeUpdate method of the prepared statement. If a SQLException is thrown anywhere in this method, this code stores that exception in a DBException and throws it to the calling method.

The ProductDB class

Page 2

```
public static Product get(String productCode) throws DBException {
    String sql = "SELECT * FROM Product WHERE Code = ?";
    Connection connection = DBUtil.getConnection();
    try (PreparedStatement ps = connection.prepareStatement(sql)) {
        ps.setString(1, productCode);
        ResultSet rs = ps.executeQuery();
        if (rs.next()) {
            long productId = rs.getLong("ProductID");
            String name = rs.getString("Description");
            double price = rs.getDouble("ListPrice");
            rs.close();

            Product p = new Product();
            p.setId(productId);
            p.setCode(productCode);
            p.setDescription(name);
            p.setPrice(price);

            return p;
        } else {
            rs.close();
            return null;
        }
    } catch (SQLException e) {
        throw new DBException(e);
    }
}

public static void add(Product product) throws DBException {
    String sql
            = "INSERT INTO Product (Code, Description, ListPrice) "
            + "VALUES (?, ?, ?)";
    Connection connection = DBUtil.getConnection();
    try (PreparedStatement ps = connection.prepareStatement(sql)) {
        ps.setString(1, product.getCode());
        ps.setString(2, product.getDescription());
        ps.setDouble(3, product.getPrice());
        ps.executeUpdate();
    } catch (SQLException e) {
        throw new DBException(e);
    }
}
```

Figure 20-8 The database class for the Email List application (part 2 of 3)

The update method uses a prepared SQL statement to update an existing product in the Product table with the data that's stored in the Product object that's passed to it. Note that this method only works if the Product object has a product ID that exists in the Product table. Like the add method, this method throws a DBException if it isn't able to execute successfully.

The deleteProduct method uses a prepared SQL statement to delete the product row that has the same product code as the Product object that's passed to it. Like the add and update methods, the delete method throws a DBException if it isn't able to execute successfully.

The code for this class only uses methods from JDBC 1.0. That's because this is still the most common way to use JDBC to work with databases. The disadvantage of this technique is that you must understand SQL. However, SQL is easy to learn, and most programmers who work with databases already know how to use it. In fact, some programmers prefer using SQL so they have direct control over the SQL statement that's sent to the database.

Each method in this class that needs a connection uses the DBUtil class to get a connection. As a result, the first method call opens a connection to the database. Then, subsequent method calls use this connection until it is closed. Typically, the application closes this connection when the user exits. Since opening a database connection can be a relatively time-consuming process, this works much more efficiently than opening and closing a connection for each method call.

The ProductDB class Page 3

```
    public static void update(Product product) throws DBException {
        String sql = "UPDATE Product SET "
                + "Code = ?, "
                + "Description = ?, "
                + "ListPrice = ? "
                + "WHERE ProductID = ?";
        Connection connection = DBUtil.getConnection();
        try (PreparedStatement ps = connection.prepareStatement(sql)) {
            ps.setString(1, product.getCode());
            ps.setString(2, product.getDescription());
            ps.setDouble(3, product.getPrice());
            ps.setLong(4, product.getId());
            ps.executeUpdate();
        } catch (SQLException e) {
            throw new DBException(e);
        }
    }

    public static void delete(Product product) throws DBException {
        String sql = "DELETE FROM Product "
                   + "WHERE ProductID = ?";
        Connection connection = DBUtil.getConnection();
        try (PreparedStatement ps = connection.prepareStatement(sql)) {
            ps.setLong(1, product.getId());
            ps.executeUpdate();
        } catch (SQLException e) {
            throw new DBException(e);
        }
    }
}
```

Figure 20-8 The database class for the Email List application (part 3 of 3)

Code that uses the ProductDB class

Figure 20-9 shows some code that uses the ProductDB class. You can use code like this in the user interface for a console application.

The ProductDB, DBException, and DBUtil classes are stored in the mma.db package. If you're calling this code from a different package, you need to include import statements for these classes as shown in the first example. In addition, you need to include an import statement for the Product class that's stored in the mma.business package.

The second example shows how to get all products. To do that, you begin by declaring a List<Product> object to store the products. Then, you call the static getAll method from the ProductDB class. Since this code throws a DBException, you need to handle this exception. In this case, the code handles the exception by printing some information to the console. To start, it prints a user-friendly message to the console. This should give the user a good idea of what went wrong. Then, it prints the exception to the console. This should provide more detailed technical information that may help a programmer or administrator resolve the problem.

The third example shows how to get a single product. This works much like the first example. However, it uses the static get method of the ProductDB class to get a Product object for the specified code. This code assumes that the variable named code stores a product code.

The fourth example shows how to add a product. This works much like the previous two examples. However, it uses the static add method of the ProductDB class to add a Product object to the database. If successful, this code prints a message to the console to indicate that it worked. This code assumes that the variable named product stores a Product object.

The fifth example shows how to delete a product. This works much like the fourth example. However, it uses the ProductDB class to delete rows in the database. Like the fourth example, this example assumes that the product variable stores a Product object.

The sixth example shows how to close a connection. To do that, this code calls the closeConnection method of the DBUtil class. Then, it handles the DBException that's thrown by this method by printing some information to the console. Typically, you execute code like this when your application exits.

How to import the business and database classes

```
import mma.business.Product;
import mma.db.ProductDB;
import mma.db.DBException;
import mma.db.DBUtil;
```

How to get all products

```
List<Product> products;
try {
    products = ProductDB.getAll();
} catch (DBException e) {
    System.out.println("Error! Unable to get products");
    System.out.println(e + "\n");
}
```

How to get a product with the specified product code

```
Product product;
try {
    product = ProductDB.get(code);
} catch (DBException e) {
    System.out.println("Error! Unable to get product for code: " + code);
    System.out.println(e + "\n");
}
```

How to add a product

```
try {
    ProductDB.add(product);
    System.out.println(product.getDescription() + " was added.\n");
} catch (DBException e) {
    System.out.println("Error! Unable to add product.");
    System.out.println(e + "\n");
}
```

How to delete a product

```
try {
    ProductDB.delete(product);
    System.out.println(product.getDescription() + " was deleted.\n");
} catch (DBException e) {
    System.out.println("Error! Unable to delete product.");
    System.out.println(e + "\n");
}
```

How to close a connection

```
try {
    DBUtil.closeConnection();
} catch (DBException e) {
    Console.display("Error! Unable to close connection.");
    Console.display(e + "\n");
}
```

Description

- You can use the static methods of the ProductDB class to map Product objects to the rows of the Product table.
- You can use the DBUtil class to close the database connection when the application exits.

Figure 20-9 Code that uses the ProductDB class

Perspective

Now that you've finished this chapter, you should understand how to use JDBC to store data in a database and to retrieve data from a database. Although there's much more to learn about working with databases, those are the essential skills. To enhance your database skills, you can learn more about database management systems like MySQL or Oracle and the SQL that works with them.

You should also understand that the JDBC API requires the developer to write a significant amount of low-level code. This provides a good conceptual background if you are new to Java and databases. In addition, many legacy applications use JDBC. As a result, you may need to use it when working on old applications.

However, for new development, you might prefer to use another data access API such as JPA (Java Persistence API). This API handles much of the object to database mapping automatically. As a result, it doesn't require the developer to write as much code, and the code that the developer does need to write is often easier to maintain.

Summary

- With JDBC 4.0 (Java 6) and later, the *database driver* that's used to connect the application to a database is loaded automatically. This is known as *automatic driver loading*.
- With JDBC 4.0 and later, you can loop through any exceptions that are nested within the SQLException object.
- A Java application can use one of four driver types to access a database. It's considered a best practice to use a type-4 driver if one is available for that database.
- You can use JDBC to execute SQL statements that select, add, update, or delete one or more rows in a database. You can also control the location of the *cursor* in the result set.
- You can use *prepared statements* to supply parameters to SQL statements. Since prepared statements provide better performance and security than regular statements, you should use them whenever possible.

Exercise 20-1 Work with JDBC

In this exercise, you'll write JDBC code that works with the MySQL database named mma that was described in the previous chapter.

Review the code and test the application

1. Open the project named ch20_ex1_DBTester that's in the ex_starts folder.
2. Expand the Libraries folder for this project and note that it includes a JAR file for the MySQL database driver.
3. Make sure the MySQL server is running.
4. Review the code in the source files and run the project. It should print all of the rows in the Product table to the console three times with some additional messages.

Write and test code that uses JDBC

5. Write the code for the printFirstProduct method. This method should print the first product in the list of products to the console. Use column names to retrieve the column values.
6. Run this application to make sure it's working correctly.
7. Write the code for the printProductByCode method. This method should print the product with the specified code to the console. Use a prepared statement to create the result set, and use indexes to retrieve the column values.
8. Run this application to make sure it's working correctly.
9. Write the code for the insertProduct method. This method should add the product to the database and print that product to the console.
10. Run this application to make sure it's working correctly. If you run this application multiple times, it should display an error message that indicates that the product can't be added because of a duplicate key.
11. Write the code for the deleteProduct method. This method should delete the product that was added by the insertProduct method.
12. Run this application to make sure it's working correctly. You should be able to run this application multiple times without displaying any error messages.

Exercise 20-2 Modify the Product Manager application

In this exercise, you'll modify a Product Manager application that works with the MySQL database named mma that was described the previous chapter.

Review the code and test the application

1. Open the project named ch20_ex2_ProductManager that's in the ex_starts folder.
2. Expand the Libraries folder for this project and note that it includes a JAR file for the MySQL database driver.
3. Open the ProductDB class and review its code. Note that it provides all of the methods presented in this chapter, including an update method.
4. Open the Main class and review its code. Then, run this application. It should let you view and store product data in a database.

Modify the JDBC code

5. In the ProductDB class, modify the getAll method so it uses column numbers instead of column names to get the data for the row.
6. Run this application to make sure this code works correctly.
7. In the ProductDB class, add a private method that can create a Product object from the current row in the result set like this:
   ```
   private static Product getProductFromRow(ResultSet rs)
   throws SQLException {
   ```
8. In the ProductDB class, modify the getAll and get methods so they use the getProductFromRow method to get Product object from the current row. Note how this reduces code duplication and makes your code easier to maintain.
9. Run this application to make sure this code works correctly.

Add an update command

10. In the Main class, modify the code so it includes an update command. This command should prompt the user for the product code to update. Then, it should prompt the user for a new description and price like this:
    ```
    Enter product code to update: java
    Enter product description: Murach's Beginning Java
    Enter price: 54.50
    ```
11. In the Main class, add code that gets the specified product from the database, sets the new data in that product, and updates the database with the new data. If successful, this should display a message like this:
    ```
    Murach's Beginning Java was updated in the database.
    ```
12. Run this application to make sure this code works correctly.

21

How to develop a GUI with Swing (part 1)

Up until now, all of the code you've been working with in this book has used a console interface. However, most modern applications—such as word processors, spreadsheets, web browsers, and so on—use a graphical user interface, often abbreviated as GUI. In this chapter and the next, you'll learn the basics of developing GUI applications with Swing, which is the most popular library for developing GUI applications with Java.

An introduction to GUI programming 532
A summary of GUI toolkits 532
The inheritance hierarchy for Swing components 534
How to create a GUI that handles events 536
How to display a frame 536
How to add a panel to a frame 538
How to add buttons to a panel 538
How to handle a button event 540
How to work with layout managers 542
A summary of layout managers 542
How to use the FlowLayout manager 544
How to use the BorderLayout manager 546
How to work with tables 548
How to create a model for a table 548
The ProductTableModel class 550
How to create a table 554
How to get the selected row or rows 554
How to add scrollbars to a table 556
How to work with built-in dialog boxes 558
How to display a message 558
How to confirm an operation 560
The Product Manager frame 564
The user interface 564
The ProductManagerFrame class 566
Perspective 570

An introduction to GUI programming

Up until the late 1980s (and even into the 90s), most computer applications used text-based user interfaces. The introduction of the Apple Macintosh, followed shortly after by Microsoft Windows, changed all that. By the mid 1990s, most major applications used graphical user interfaces, also called *GUIs*.

In the early days, programming GUIs was very complicated because the APIs for doing so were extremely low level. Thankfully, that situation has changed, and modern APIs make writing good looking GUIs much easier.

A summary of GUI toolkits

If you want to use Java to develop a GUI, you can choose from several APIs, which are often called *toolkits*. Figure 21-1 shows the most common ones, though there are others available as well.

AWT (*Abstract Window Toolkit*) was the first GUI toolkit for Java. AWT allows you to create native operating system *components* (commonly called *widgets*). However, this approach has several limitations. Since it's operating system dependent, widgets take up different amounts of space on different operating systems. As a result, a GUI that looks perfect on one operating system might look terrible on another. In addition, because AWT can only use the native components of an operating system, it lacks advanced widgets.

To address the shortcomings of AWT, Java 2 included a new toolkit named Swing. Swing is built on top of AWT, but creates its own widgets instead of using the ones provided by the operating system. This has the advantage of ensuring that GUIs look the same on all platforms that Java runs on. In addition, it allows the toolkit to have more advanced widgets.

Unfortunately, in the early days, Swing was slow and inefficient. In addition, the early Swing widgets were relatively ugly and didn't look like native widgets. Fortunately, these problems with Swing no longer exist today. Today, Swing performs much better, and, modern themes provided with Java can make Swing applications look like native applications.

To compete with early versions of Swing, IBM created *SWT* (*Standard Widget Toolkit*). Unlike Swing, SWT uses native widgets. As a result, SWT widgets look like native widgets. In addition, in the early days, SWT had a speed advantage over Swing.

However, SWT also has two drawbacks. First, because it relies on native widgets, you are required to ship a native library for each operating system you want to support. Second, the core SWT widget set is primitive. As a result, it's difficult to create advanced user interfaces with it.

JavaFX is a newer framework for developing *rich Internet applications* (*RIAs*). However, since JavaFX completes with Adobe's already popular Flash plugin, it was late to the game. In addition, the introduction of HTML 5 is making proprietary browser plugins such as Adobe Flash, Oracle Java, and Microsoft Silverlight, obsolete. As a result, JavaFX has been virtually ignored by developers.

Common Java GUI libraries

Library	Description
AWT	Abstract Window Toolkit. This is the oldest Java GUI library. It uses the native widgets from the operating system. This library is not recommended for modern application development due to problems with cross-platform portability.
Swing	Created to replace AWT and fix the cross-platform portability problems. Swing widgets are not native, but can use themes to look identical to native widgets. Most modern Java GUIs are written using Swing.
SWT	Standard Widget Toolkit. This library was created by IBM to fix performance problems and the non-native look and feel of earlier versions of Swing. This library uses native widgets. However, it's not as powerful as Swing without adding additional libraries.
JavaFX	Designed to replace the aging Swing library and make it easier to develop rich Internet applications (RIAs). However, it has been slow to catch on.
Pivot	An open-source Apache project that allows you to create modern looking GUIs that work with Internet resources. Like JavaFX, this library has been slow to catch on.

Description

- When creating GUIs with Java, you have several possible libraries that you can use. Of these libraries, Swing is the most widely used.

Figure 21-1 A summary of Java GUI toolkits

Pivot is an open-source Apache project that was intended primarily to compete with JavaFX. Although it was initially designed for producing rich Internet applications that run in a browser, it works just as well for developing desktop applications.

Although JavaFX and Pivot are newer than Swing, they are not nearly as popular as Swing. Instead, Swing dominates the world of GUI programming with Java and is what you are most likely to encounter in the real world. As a result, this book covers Swing instead of JavaFX or Pivot. However, if you need to write an application that works extensively with Internet resources, you might want to investigate JavaFX or Pivot.

The inheritance hierarchy for Swing components

Like all Java APIs, Swing is object oriented, and the Swing classes exist in a hierarchy. Figure 21-2 shows a partial diagram of this hierarchy, along with some of the most commonly used classes.

As mentioned in the previous figure, Swing builds on the older AWT framework. As a result, all Swing components ultimately inherit the abstract AWT Container class, which itself inherits the abstract AWT Component class. In this diagram, all Swing classes begin with the letter J (for Java). This distinguishes them from AWT components with the same name. For example, Frame is an AWT component, and JFrame is a Swing component.

As this diagram shows, most Swing components inherit from the JComponent class. As a result, any method that accepts a JComponent object as a parameter, accepts most Swing widgets. In this diagram, the exception is a JFrame widget. This widget is commonly called a *top-level widget* because it inherits from the Window class and holds other widgets. Typically, a JFrame widget is used as the main window for the application.

A *container* is a type of component that can hold other components. The diagram in this figure shows that all Swing widgets inherit from the Container class. As a result, all Swing widgets can act as a container to hold other widgets. That means, it's possible for a JButton widget to hold another JButton widget. However, it's more common to use a container widget such as a JFrame widget to hold other widgets. Later in this chapter and the next, you'll learn about some other container widgets including the JPanel, JScrollPane, and JDialog widgets.

As a general rule, you should not mix AWT and Swing components. This typically results in bugs and display problems. For example, you should not put a JButton widget inside a Frame object. Instead, you should put a JButton widget inside a JFrame.

The Swing inheritance hierarchy

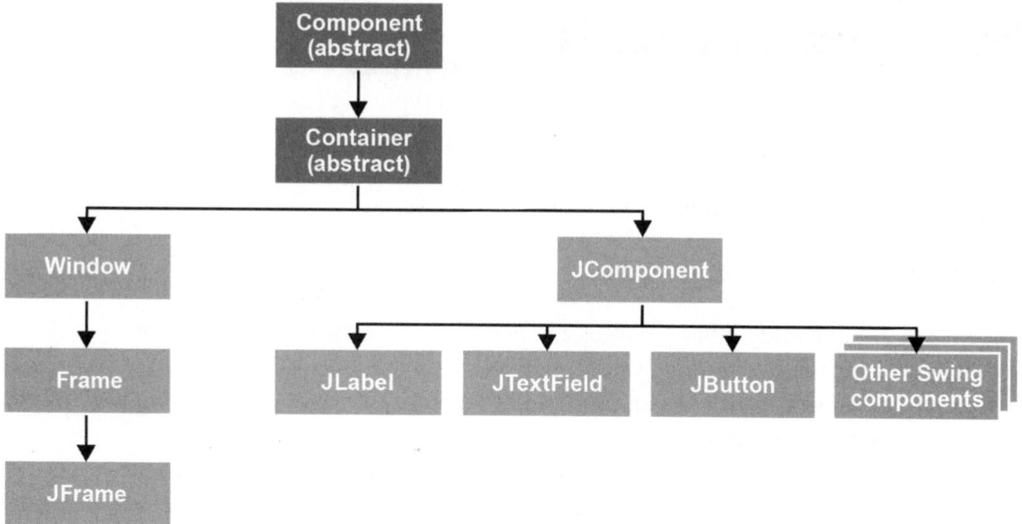

A summary of these classes

Class	Description
`Component`	An abstract AWT class that defines any object that can be displayed. For instance, frames, panels, buttons, labels, and text fields are derived from this class.
`Container`	An abstract AWT class that defines any component that can contain other components.
`Window`	The AWT class that defines a window without a title bar or border.
`Frame`	The AWT class that defines a window with a title bar and border.
`JFrame`	The Swing class that defines a window with a title bar and border.
`JComponent`	A base class for Swing components such as JPanel, JButton, JLabel, and JTextField.
`JPanel`	The Swing class that defines a panel, which is used to hold other components.
`JButton`	The Swing class that defines a button.
`JLabel`	The Swing class that defines a label.
`JTextField`	The Swing class that defines a text field.

Description

- The Swing library is built upon the AWT library. In other words, Swing classes often inherit AWT classes.
- Most Swing classes begin with the letter J (for Java).

Figure 21-2 The inheritance hierarchy for Swing components

How to create a GUI that handles events

When you develop a GUI with Swing, you typically begin by displaying a frame that acts as the main window for the application. Then, you add components such as panels and buttons to the frame. Finally, you handle the events that occur when the user interacts with these components.

How to display a frame

A JFrame widget has a border and contains all of the normal window controls for your operating system such as minimize, maximize, and close buttons. Figure 21-3 shows an example of an empty JFrame widget along with the code that displays it.

To set the title of the frame, you can either pass it as a parameter to the JFrame constructor, or you can create a JFrame object and then use the setTitle method.

To set the size of the frame, you can use the setSize method. This method takes two integers which represent the width and height in pixels. In this figure, for example, the frame is set to a width of 600 pixels and a height of 400 pixels. Another way to size a frame is to use the pack method. This method takes no parameters and sizes the frame just large enough to hold all of the components it contains. If you don't set the size, the frame has a width and height of zero, and you can't see any of the components it contains. As a result, you typically want to set the size of the frame.

To set the location of the frame, you can pass a true value to the setLocationByPlatform method. Then, the operating system determines the location of the frame, which is usually what you want.

When the user clicks on the close button of a frame, you typically want to close the frame and exit the application. The easiest way to do this is to call the setDefaultCloseOperation method and pass it the EXIT_ON_CLOSE value as show in the figure. Although there are other possible values that you can use with this method, the EXIT_ON_CLOSE value is a quick and easy way to close a frame. If you don't include this code and the user clicks the close button, the frame closes, but the application continues running. That's because, the close button only closes the frame by default, but doesn't end the application.

Before you display a frame, you can set the look and feel to any look and feel that's available from Swing. To do that, you can use the UIManager class that's available from the javax.swing package as shown in this figure. In this figure, the code sets the look and feel for the Swing components to the current operating system. As result, this application looks like a Windows application on Windows, a Mac application on Mac OS X, and a Linux application on Linux. In practice, you typically have to do some more work to get the application to act exactly like a native Mac application. However, that's beyond the scope of this book.

Finally, to display the frame, you can pass a true value to the setVisible method.

The package that contains the Swing classes

```
javax.swing
```

An empty frame

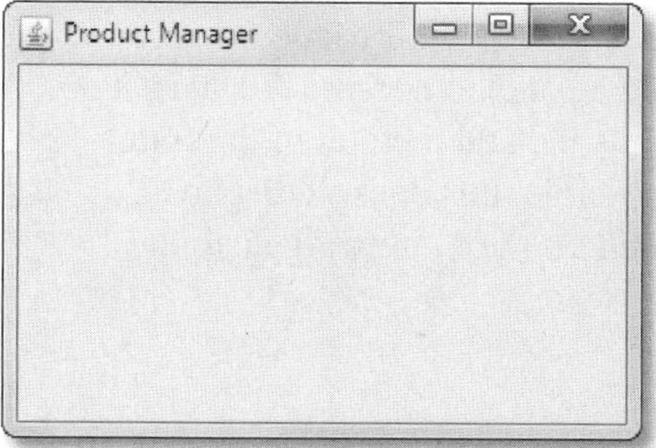

A main method that creates and displays a frame

```
public static void main(String[] args) {
    JFrame frame = new JFrame("Product Manager");
    frame.setSize(600, 400);
    frame.setLocationByPlatform(true);

    frame.setDefaultCloseOperation(JFrame.EXIT_ON_CLOSE);

    try {
        UIManager.setLookAndFeel(
                UIManager.getSystemLookAndFeelClassName());
    } catch (ClassNotFoundException | IllegalAccessException |
             InstantiationException | UnsupportedLookAndFeelException e) {
        System.err.println("Unsupported look and feel.");
    }

    frame.setVisible(true);
}
```

Description

- A *frame* typically defines the main window of an application.
- To set the title of a frame, you can use the constructor of the JFrame class. Or, you can call the setTitle method of the JFrame object.
- To set the size of a frame, you call the setSize method and send it the height and width in pixels. Or, you can call the pack method to automatically size the window so it is just large enough to hold all of its components.
- To let the operating system set the location of a frame, you can call the setLocation-ByPlatfrom method and send it a true value.
- To exit the application when the user selects the close button, you can set the default close operation. If you don't, the application may keep running after the window closes.
- To set the look and feel to use the default platform look and feel, you call the setLookAndFeel method of the UIManager class inside a try-catch block.
- To make the frame visible, you call the setVisible method and pass it a true value.

Figure 21-3 How to work with frames

How to add a panel to a frame

Usually, the easiest way to build a GUI application is to use an invisible container known as a *panel* to group components. To do that with Swing, you can use the JPanel class. Then, you can add one or more panels to the frame.

Figure 21-4 shows an example of how to add a panel to a frame. To start, it creates a JPanel widget named panel. Then, it calls the add method of the frame to add the panel to the frame. Since a panel is invisible, this doesn't display anything on the frame. To do that, you need to add one or more widgets to the panel.

How to add buttons to a panel

The second example adds two buttons to the panel. To do that, it creates two buttons from the JButton class. Then, it uses the add method of the panel to add the buttons to the panel.

To set the text of the button, you can use the constructor of the JButton class. Or, you can create the JButton widget and call its setText method. In this figure, for example, the text for both buttons is set by the constructor for the JButton widget.

The JButton widget provides some other methods that are commonly used. For example, you can use the setEnabled method to disable a button and gray it out. If you want to disable an OK button until the user has filled in the required data, for instance, you can use this method. Or, you may want to display a *tooltip*, which is a common graphical user interface element that's displayed when the user hovers the pointer over an item for about one second. To do that, you can use the setToolTipText method.

A common method of the JFrame and JPanel objects

Method	Description
add(Component)	Adds the specified component to the frame or panel.

Code that adds a panel to a frame

```
JPanel panel = new JPanel();
frame.add(panel);
```

Code that adds two buttons to a panel

```
JButton button1 = new JButton("Click me!");
JButton button2 = new JButton("No, click me!");
panel.add(button1);
panel.add(button2);
```

Two buttons in a panel

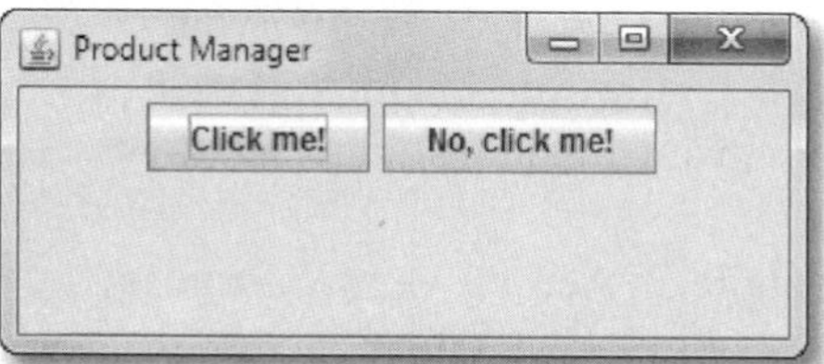

Common constructors and methods of the JButton object

Constructor	Description
JButton(String)	Sets the text displayed by the button.
Method	**Description**
setText(String)	Sets the text displayed by the button.
setEnabled(boolean)	Sets whether the button is enabled or disabled and grayed out.
setToolTipText(String)	Sets the text for the tooltip. If the user hovers the mouse over the button for about one second, the tooltip is displayed.

Description

- A *panel* is an invisible container that's used to group other components.
- To create a panel, you can create a JPanel object. Then, you can add it to a frame.
- To create a button, you can create a JButton object. Then, you can add it to a frame or a panel.
- You should add all of the panels and components to the frame before calling its setVisible method. Otherwise, the user interface may flicker when it's first displayed.

Figure 21-4 How to work with buttons

How to handle a button event

The buttons displayed by the code in the previous figure don't do anything when you click on them. That's because there is nothing to handle the *event* that's generated by the button when it's clicked.

Each time the user interacts with your GUI, an event is fired. For example, when the user clicks on a button, an event is fired notifying your code that the button was clicked. An event is also fired each time the user presses a key on the keyboard, or moves the mouse.

If you want to respond to the event that is fired when the button is clicked, you need to register something that listens for the event. This is referred to as an *action listener* or *event listener*.

Figure 21-5 shows how you can use the addActionListener method of the button to register a method that handles the event when the button is clicked. This method is known as an *event handler*. When the button is clicked, an ActionEvent object is created and sent to the event handler. This ActionEvent object contains a lot of information about the event. However, in simple cases like this, you don't need any of that information. Instead, you just need to know that the button fired an ActionEvent.

Prior to Java 8, the most common way to handle an ActionEvent was to use an anonymous inner class as shown in the first example. Here, an anonymous class is coded within the parentheses of the addActionListener method. This code begins by creating a new ActionListener object that contains a method named actionPerformed that accepts an ActionEvent argument. Then, the code within the actionPerformed method is executed when the user clicks the button. In this case, this method just prints a message of "Button 1 clicked!" to the console. However, this method could contain more complex code such as code that updates a database.

With Java 8 and later, you can use a lambda instead of an anonymous class as shown in the second example. In this case, the lambda is cleaner, more concise, and easier to understand than an anonymous inner class would be. As a result, if you're using Java 8 or later, you'll probably want to use lambdas. However, if you plan to distribute your application to users who might be using Java 7 or earlier, you'll probably want to use anonymous methods.

Although this figure shows how to handle the event that occurs when a user clicks a button, other Swing components also generate events that you can handle. For example, when a user changes the contents of a text box, it generates an event that you can handle. Handling those types of events is outside the scope of this book. However, you can use the concepts presented in this figure to get started with them, and you can use the API documentation to get more information about them.

The package that contains the events

```
java.awt.event
```

A common method of most components

Method	Description
addActionListener(ActionEvent)	Adds an event listener to a component such as a button so it can listen for and respond to events such as click events.

Code that adds an event handler to a button

With an anonymous class (prior to Java 8)

```
button1.addActionListener(new ActionListener() {
    @Override
    public void actionPerformed(ActionEvent e) {
        System.out.println("Button 1 clicked! ");
    }
});
```

With a lambda expression (Java 8 and later)

```
button1.addActionListener((ActionEvent e) -> {
    System.out.println("Button 1 clicked!");
});
```

Description

- To make a button do something when clicked, you add an action listener by calling its addActionListener method.
- The addActionListener method accepts an ActionListener object that includes an actionPerformed method that accepts an ActionEvent object. Within the actionPerformed method, you write the code that's executed when the button is clicked.
- Prior to Java 8, it was common to write anonymous inner classes to handle actions. However, with Java 8 or later, you can use a lambda expression, which is cleaner and more concise.

Figure 21-5 How to handle the event that occurs when a button is clicked

How to work with layout managers

In the old days of GUI design, it was common to place non-resizable components wherever you wanted them. This type of layout is known as *fixed width layout*. Although fixed width layout is quick and easy, it causes several problems. For example, if the window is resized, the components inside don't resize with it, which means it's possible for components to disappear outside the boundaries of the window. Furthermore, if the user's operating system uses a different font size, it's possible for components to end up on top of each other or hidden underneath other components. To address this problem, most modern GUI toolkits, including Swing, use a concept known as a *layout manager*.

A summary of layout managers

Java provides several built-in layout managers such as the ones summarized in figure 21-6. Some are easy to use, but are not flexible. Others are harder to use, but are flexible and can produce complex layouts. Still others are intended primarily for use by GUI tools that generate GUI code for programmers rather than for use by programmers who are coding by hand. In addition, there are several third-party layout managers that are available for free that might be easier to use for some tasks.

This chapter shows how to use two of the most common layout managers included with Java: FlowLayout and BorderLayout. The next chapter shows how to use the GridBagLayout manager. The Product Manager application presented in this chapter and the next uses all three of these layout managers. Once you are familiar with the basics of using these layout managers, you can search the Internet for information about the other layout managers, which might be easier to use for certain types of tasks.

By default, a JFrame widget uses the BorderLayout manager, and a JPanel widget uses the FlowLayout manager. If the default layout manager provided by a container doesn't suit your needs, you can change it to a different one by calling the container's setLayout method, as shown in this figure. This code changes the layout manager of the frame from its default of BorderLayout to FlowLayout instead.

The package that contains the layout managers

```
java.awt
```

A summary of layout managers

Manager	Description
`BorderLayout`	Lays out components by providing five areas that can each hold one component. The five areas are north, south, east, west, and center.
`FlowLayout`	Lays out components by flowing them from left to right, or right to left, similar to words on a page.
`GridBagLayout`	Lays out components in a rectangular grid as shown in the next chapter.
`GridLayout`	Lays out components in a rectangular grid of cells where each cell is the same size.
`CardLayout`	Lays out components on a card where only one card is visible at a time. This layout is rarely used, but can be useful for creating wizard dialogs that guide the user through a step-by-step procedure.
`BoxLayout`	Lays out components in a horizontal or vertical row of cells. This layout is rarely used, but it can be useful for producing rows of buttons.

A common method of most container components

Method	Description
`setLayout(layout)`	Sets the layout to the specified layout manager.

To change a container's layout manager

```
JFrame frame = new JFrame();
frame.setLayout(new FlowLayout());
```

Description

- A *layout manager* determines how your components are placed in the container and how they behave if the container is resized or if the font size changes.
- By default, a JFrame uses the BorderLayout manager.
- By default, a JPanel uses the FlowLayout manager.

Figure 21-6 A summary of layout managers

How to use the FlowLayout manager

Of the three layout managers presented in this book, the FlowLayout manager is the easiest to use. It adds components in a row and aligns the components according to the alignment parameter. By default, the FlowLayout manager centers components.

The first example in figure 21-7 begins by creating a new JFrame widget with a title of "Product Manager". Then, this code sets the size to a width of 600 pixels and a height of 400 pixels. Next, this code calls the frame's setLayout method and passes it a new instance of the FlowLayout manager. Since this statement doesn't specify an alignment for the FlowLayout manager, it uses the default alignment of center.

After setting the layout manager, this code adds four buttons to the frame labeled Button 1, Button 2, Button 3, and Button 4. As a result, the layout manager arranges these buttons from left to right in the same order that the code added them to the frame.

If there isn't enough space in the container to hold all of the components, FlowLayout wraps the components to the next row. This is similar to how a word processor wraps text when it reaches the right margin. Once again, the layout manager arranges the components according to the alignment we specified, which in this case, is center.

To change the default alignment, you can supply an alignment parameter to the constructor of the FlowLayout class. In the second example, for instance, the alignment parameter tells FlowLayout that it should align the components with the left edge of the frame, similar to left aligning text in a word processor. It's also possible to right align the components.

Code that creates a FlowLayout and adds four buttons to it

```
JFrame frame = new JFrame("Product Manager");
frame.setSize(600, 400);
frame.setLayout(new FlowLayout());
frame.add(new JButton("Button 1"));
frame.add(new JButton("Button 2"));
frame.add(new JButton("Button 3"));
frame.add(new JButton("Button 4"));
```

The FlowLayout when all components fit on one line

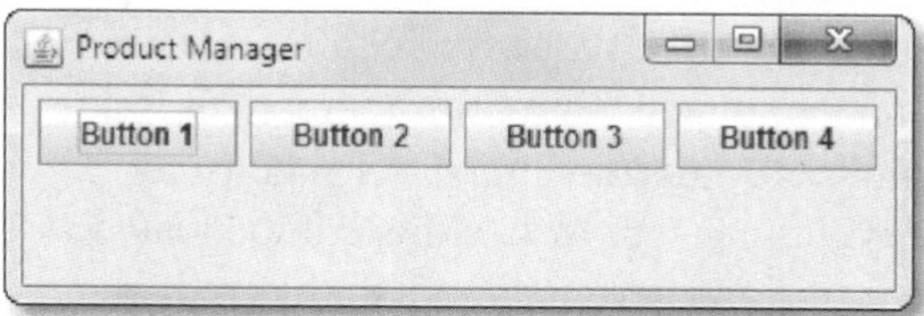

The FlowLayout when components wrap to the next line

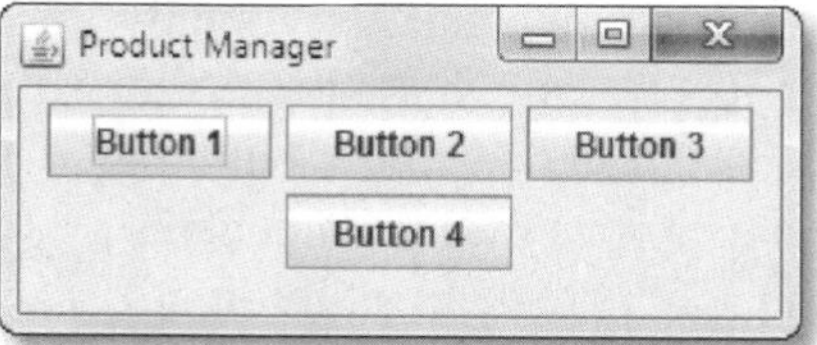

A common constructor of the FlowLayout class

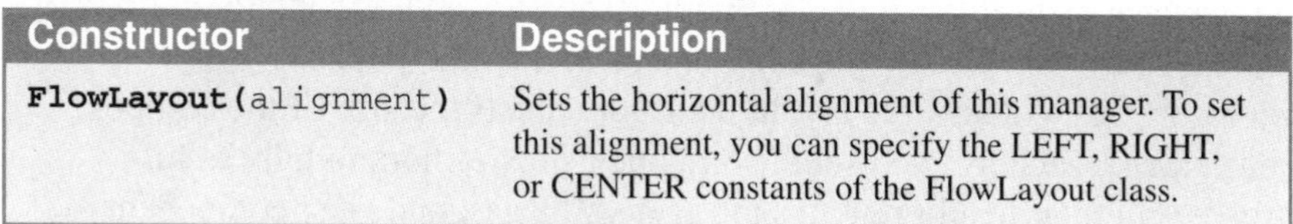

Constructor	Description
FlowLayout(alignment)	Sets the horizontal alignment of this manager. To set this alignment, you can specify the LEFT, RIGHT, or CENTER constants of the FlowLayout class.

How to change the default layout

```
frame.setLayout(new FlowLayout(FlowLayout.LEFT));
```

Description

- If the components don't fit on one line, the FlowLayout manager wraps the components to a new line.
- The FlowLayout manager can align components to the left, right, or center. The default is center.

Figure 21-7 How to work with the FlowLayout manager

How to use the BorderLayout manager

The BorderLayout manager has five areas: north, south, east, west, and center. Each of these areas can hold a single component.

Figure 21-8 shows a frame that uses the BorderLayout manager to display one button in each of the five areas. This code begins by creating a frame like the one in the previous figure. However, since BorderLayout is the default layout manager for a frame, this code doesn't set the layout manager.

After creating the frame, this code adds a new button to the north area of the frame by calling the add method of the frame. Then, it passes the component as the first argument and the area as the second argument. Here, the component is a new JButton widget that says "North", and the BorderLayout.NORTH constant specifies the north area. This causes the layout manager to size this component horizontally to fill the entire width of the frame and vertically to its preferred height, which is the height of the button.

In a similar fashion, this code adds a new button to the south area of the frame. Like the north area, the layout manager sizes the component horizontally to fill the entire width of the frame and vertically to its preferred height.

After adding a button to the north and sound areas, this code adds a button to the east and west areas. In this case, the layout manager sizes these components to fill all of the vertical space between the north and south areas. In addition, it sizes these components to their preferred width, which is the width of the button.

Finally, the code adds a button to the center area of the frame. In this case, the layout manager sizes this component both vertically and horizontally to fill any remaining space not used by the components in the other areas.

If you resize this window, the layout manager adjusts the size of the components in each area. The north and south components resize horizontally to fill the new space, but their height remains the same. The east and west components resize vertically to fill the new space but their width remains the same. And the center component resizes to fill any remaining space.

If you don't provide a component for one or more of the areas in the BorderLayout, that area has a size of zero. For example, if you remove the button from the east area, the east area has a size of 0. As a result, the component in the center expands to the right edge of the frame.

The BorderLayout manager is often used to lay out the main screen of an application. For example, suppose you were writing an email client. You might use the north area as a toolbar, the west area to hold a list of folders, the center area to hold the list of emails, and the south area to hold a status bar. In this case, you might not use the east area.

When working with the BorderLayout manager, it's important to remember that each area can only hold one component. As a result, if you want to add multiple components, you need to group those buttons into a panel before you add them. For example, if you want to add a toolbar with multiple buttons, you need to group those buttons into a panel (probably using FlowLayout for that panel) and then add the panel to the north area of the BorderLayout.

A common method of the BorderLayout class

Method	Description
`add(component, area)`	Adds the specified component to the specified area. To set the area, you can specify the NORTH, SOUTH, EAST, WEST, or CENTER constants of the BorderLayout class.

Code that adds five buttons to each area of a BorderLayout

```
JFrame frame = new JFrame("Product Manager");
frame.setSize(600, 400);
frame.add(new JButton("North"), BorderLayout.NORTH);
frame.add(new JButton("South"), BorderLayout.SOUTH);
frame.add(new JButton("East"), BorderLayout.EAST);
frame.add(new JButton("West"), BorderLayout.WEST);
frame.add(new JButton("Center"), BorderLayout.CENTER);
```

The JFrame produced by the above code

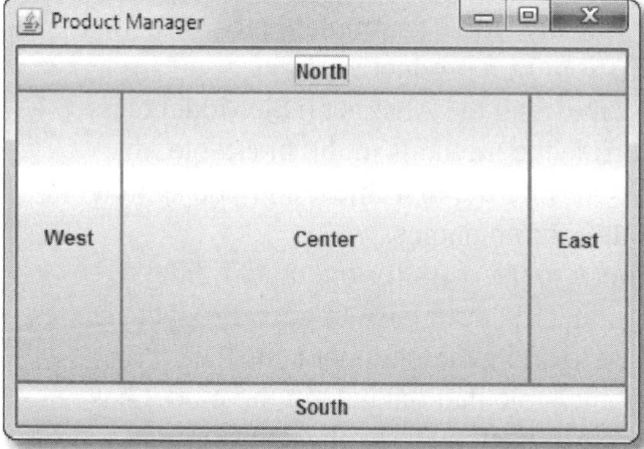

Description

- A BorderLayout has five areas: NORTH, SOUTH, EAST, WEST, and CENTER.
- The default area is CENTER. As a result, if you don't specify the area, the component is added to the center.
- The NORTH and SOUTH areas get their preferred height, which usually means they are tall enough to hold whatever is placed in them. The preferred width is ignored.
- The WEST and EAST areas get their preferred width, which usually means they are wide enough to hold whatever is placed in them. The preferred height is ignored.
- The CENTER area gets whatever space is left over and expands or contracts as the window is resized.
- Each area of a BorderLayout can only hold one component. If you need to add multiple components to an area, you can add them to a panel and then add the panel to the area.

Figure 21-8 How to work with the BorderLayout manger

How to work with tables

Many applications, especially applications that work with a database, need to display rows of data in a table. To do that, you can use a JTable widget. But first, you typically begin by creating a model for the table. A table model holds the data for the table and determines how the data is displayed in the table.

How to create a model for a table

Figure 21-9 begins by showing a JTable widget along with some terminology that's necessary to work with the table and its model. The first row of the table, commonly referred to as the table header, contains a column name for each column of the table. In this figure, the column names are "Code", "Description", and "Price". A column usually stores a certain type of data. In this figure, the first column stores product codes, the second column stores descriptions, and the third column stores prices. And a row typically stores a complete record. In this figure, each row stores all of the information for a product.

To create a model for a table, you can extend the AbstractTableModel class that's part of Swing. Then, you can override the methods in the first table of this figure. Of these methods, you must override the first three, and you should override the fourth if you want to include column names.

In addition, you can add other methods to the class for the model. For example, you may want to add a method that makes it easy to get a Product object from the model. Or, you may need to add a method that calls the fireTableDataChanged method to notify the table that the data in the model has been updated. That way, the table can refresh itself so it displays the current data. You'll see how this works in the next figure.

JTable terminology

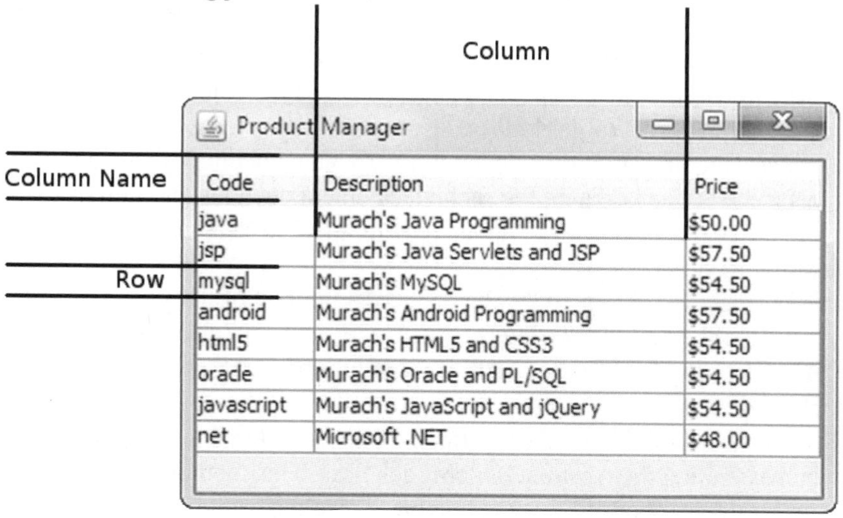

Column

Column Name

Row

Product Manager

Code	Description	Price
java	Murach's Java Programming	$50.00
jsp	Murach's Java Servlets and JSP	$57.50
mysql	Murach's MySQL	$54.50
android	Murach's Android Programming	$57.50
html5	Murach's HTML5 and CSS3	$54.50
oracle	Murach's Oracle and PL/SQL	$54.50
javascript	Murach's JavaScript and jQuery	$54.50
net	Microsoft .NET	$48.00

AbstractTableModel methods that you typically override

Method	Description
getRowCount()	Returns an integer for the number of rows in the table.
getColumnCount()	Returns an integer for the number of columns in the table.
getValueAt(row, column)	Returns an object for the value at the given row and column index of the table.
getColumnName(column)	Returns a string representing the name of the column at the specified column index. This value is used as the column label in the table header.

An AbstractTableModel method that you can call

Method	Description
fireTableDataChanged()	Notifies all listeners that all cell values in the table's rows may have changed.

Description

- The easiest way to create a custom table model is to extend the AbstractTableModel class.
- At a minimum, you need to override the getRowCount, getColumnCount, and getValueAt methods. In addition, it's common to override the getColumnName method.
- When you update the database, you can call the fireTableDataChanged method to refresh all data that's displayed in the table.
- The AbstractTableModel class contains other methods, such as fireTableCellUpdated and fireTableRowsInserted, that you can call to update part of a table. These methods can be much more efficient, especially for a large table. See the API documentation for more information.

Figure 21-9 How to create a table model

The ProductTableModel class

Figure 21-10 shows the code for the class that defines the model that's used by the table in the previous figure. This class is named ProductTableModel, and it begins by extending AbstractTableModel.

Within the class, the first statement declares a variable named products that stores a List of Product objects. Then, the second statement declares and initializes an array of strings for the names of the three columns. These column names are Code, Description, and Price.

The constructor for the table model calls the getAll method of the ProductDB class described in the previous chapter to retrieve a List of Product objects from the database. Then, it assigns this list of products to the variable named products.

The getRowCount method is the first of three methods that you are required to override when extending the AbstractTableModel class. This method returns an integer value for the number of rows in the table. Since this value is equal to the number of products in the products list, this code returns the value of the size method of the products list.

The getColumnCount method is the second method you are required to override. This method returns an integer value for the number of columns. To do that, this returns the length of the COLUMN_NAMES array, which is the same as the number of columns.

The getColumnName method isn't required, but it's necessary if you want to display column names. This method takes a column index value and returns the name of the column for the specified index. To do that, this method returns the string at that index of the COLUMN_NAMES array.

The getValueAt method is the third method you are required to override. This method defines a row index and a column index as parameters. Then, it returns the value at the specified row and column. To do that, this method uses a switch statement to determine the column to display. For a column index of 0, this code calls the get method of the products list to return a Product object at the specified row index. Then, it uses method chaining to call the getCode method of that Product object. For a column index of 1, this code calls the getDescription method of the Product object at the specified row index. And for a column index of 2, this code calls the object's getPriceFormatted method.

One thing that can cause some confusion for new programmers is that you define these four methods, but you never call them anywhere. That's because the JTable widget calls these methods whenever it needs information about how to display the table. For example, when the JTable widget needs to know what value to display for the description column in the first row of the table, it calls the getValueAt method with a row index of 0, and a column index of 1. Then, the getValueAt method gets the Product object from the first row of the product list (remember that list indexes start at 0) and calls its getDescription method to return the description.

The ProductTableModel class

```
package mma.ui;

import java.util.List;
import javax.swing.table.AbstractTableModel;

import mma.business.Product;
import mma.db.ProductDB;
import mma.db.DBException;

public class ProductTableModel extends AbstractTableModel {
    private List<Product> products;
    private final String[] COLUMN_NAMES = { "Code", "Description", "Price" };

    public ProductTableModel() {
        try {
            products = ProductDB.getAll();
        } catch (DBException e) {
            System.out.println(e);
        }
    }

    @Override
    public int getRowCount() {
        return products.size();
    }

    @Override
    public int getColumnCount() {
        return COLUMN_NAMES.length;
    }

    @Override
    public String getColumnName(int columnIndex) {
        return COLUMN_NAMES[columnIndex];
    }

    @Override
    public Object getValueAt(int rowIndex, int columnIndex) {
        switch (columnIndex) {
            case 0:
                return products.get(rowIndex).getCode();
            case 1:
                return products.get(rowIndex).getDescription();
            case 2:
                return products.get(rowIndex).getPriceFormatted();
            default:
                return null;
        }
    }
```

Figure 21-10 The ProductTableModel class (part 1 of 2)

Part 2 of figure 21-10 shows two more methods of the table model. When you write the code for an application, you can call these methods to work with the data in the table. You'll see how this works later in this chapter.

The getProduct method returns a Product object for the row at the specified index. This lets you get the Product object for the row that's selected by the user, which is useful if you want to update or delete this product in the database.

The databaseUpdated method updates the old data in the table model with new data from the database. Then, it calls the fireTableDataChanged method of the table model. This notifies the JTable widget that the data in the model has changed. This allows the JTable widget to display the new data. If you modify the underlying data in the database, you can call this method to synchronize the data that's displayed in the table with the data that's in the database.

The ProductTableModel class (continued)

```
        Product getProduct(int rowIndex) {
            return products.get(rowIndex);
        }

        void databaseUpdated() {
            try {
                products = ProductDB.getAll();
                fireTableDataChanged();
            } catch (DBException e) {
                System.out.println(e);
            }
        }
    }
```

Description

- When a row represents a business object such as a Product object, you can include a method that returns an object for the specified row index.
- To synchronize the data in the table with the data in the database, you can include a method that updates the model with the data from the database and then calls the fireTableDataChanged method. This causes the table to display the new data that's stored in the model.

Figure 21-10 The ProductTableModel class (part 2 of 2)

How to create a table

Once you create a model for a table, you can create a JTable widget to display the data that's stored in that model. The first example of figure 21-11 shows how.

This code begins by creating a ProductTableModel object from the class shown in the previous figure. Then, it creates a new JTable widget by passing the model to the constructor of the JTable class. Alternately, this code could call the empty constructor of the JTable class and then use the setModel method to set the model.

After setting the model for the table, this code sets the selection mode of the table to SINGLE_SELECTION mode. As a result, users can only select one row at a time. However, you can use two other values to set the selection mode.

First, you can use the SINGLE_INTERVAL_SELECTION mode to allow the user to select multiple rows by holding the Control or Shift keys. However, this only works if those rows are contiguous. In other words, it only works if the selected rows are next to each other.

Second, if you want to allow more possibilities, you can use the MULTIPLE_INTERVAL_SELECTION mode to allow the user to select multiple rows by holding the Control or Shift keys. However, in this mode, those rows don't have to be contiguous.

After setting the selection mode, this code calls the setBorder method of the table and passes a null value to that method. As a result, this table doesn't include a border. If you plan to add scrollbars to a table as shown in the next figure, this makes sure that the GUI doesn't display two borders: one for the table and one for the scrollbar. This is a best practice whenever the component is going to take up the entire space of the container.

How to get the selected row or rows

The second example shows how to get the selected row or rows from a table after it's displayed. This code starts by calling the getSelectedRow method of the table. This gets the index for the first row that the user selected.

After getting the row index, this code checks to make sure that the user selected a row. If so, it passes the row index to the getProduct method of the model for the table. This gets the Product object that corresponds with the selected row.

It makes sense for this example to use the getSelectedRow method because the first example only allows the user to select a single row. However, if the first example had allowed the user to select multiple rows, it would make sense for this example to use the getSelectedRows method to get the indexes for all selected rows.

Some common constructors and methods of the JTable class

Constructor	Description
`JTable(model)`	Constructs a new JTable and sets the model for the table to the specified TableModel object.
Method	**Description**
`setModel(model)`	Sets the model for the table to the specified TableModel object.
`setSelectionMode(mode)`	Sets the selection mode to one of the ListSelectionModel values. This determines how the user can select items from the table.
`setBorder(border)`	If you enclose the table in a scroll pane, setting the border to null may improve the appearance.
`getSelectedRow()`	Returns an int value for the index of the first selected row or -1 if no rows are selected.
`getSelectedRows()`	Returns an array of int values for the indexes of the selected rows.

ListSelectionModel values

Value	Description
`SINGLE_SELECTION`	Allows selecting only one row at a time.
`SINGLE_INTERVAL_SELECTION`	Allows selecting multiple rows, but only if they are contiguous.
`MULTIPLE_INTERVAL_SELECTION`	Allows for selection of multiple rows at the same time, even if they are not contiguous

Code that creates a table

```
ProductTableModel productTableModel = new ProductTableModel();
JTable productTable = new JTable(productTableModel);
productTable.setSelectionMode(ListSelectionModel.SINGLE_SELECTION);
productTable.setBorder(null);
```

Code that gets data from the table

```
int rowIndex = productTable.getSelectedRow();
if (rowIndex != -1) {
    Product product = productTableModel.getProduct(rowIndex);
}
```

Description

- Once you have created a model for a table, you can create the table and set the model in the table. Then, you can use the methods of the table to work with it.

Figure 21-11 How to create a table

How to add scrollbars to a table

It's common for a table to contain so many rows or columns that it doesn't fit on one screen. Fortunately, Swing provides a container called JScrollPane that you can use to add scrollbars to a table. Of course, JScrollPane also works with any other component, such as text areas, where the content of the component is too large to fit on one screen.

The first example in figure 21-12 shows how to create a scroll pane and add a table to it. To do that, this code passes the table to the constructor of the JScrollPane class. Then, it adds the JScrollPane object to the frame.

The second code example shows an alternate and common method of adding a component to a scroll pane and adding the scroll pane to the frame. Since this example doesn't maintain a reference to the JScrollPane object, you can't call any of its methods later. However, this is usually fine as long as you don't need to change the default scroll pane policy.

If you need to change the scroll pane policy, you can use the setHorizontalScrollBarPolicy and setVerticalScrollBarPolicy methods of the scroll pane as shown in the third example. These methods determine when the scrollbars are visible to the user. The default for both scrollbars is AS_NEEDED. As a result, if all the content fits in the container, the scrollbars are hidden. However, if the content doesn't fit, the scrollbars are displayed. This could happen, for example, if you resize the window to make the container smaller.

If you want to make it so the scrollbars are always visible, even if they are not needed, you can set the policy to ALWAYS. In this case, the scrollbars are displayed even when they are not needed, but they don't do anything if you try to use them.

If you want to make it so the scrollbars are never visible, you can set the policy to NEVER. This hides the scrollbars. However, the user can still scroll the component by using the arrow keys and the Page Up and Page Down keys.

To add a component to a scroll pane

```
JScrollPane scrollPane = new JScrollPane(productTable);
frame.add(scrollPane);
```

An alternate way of adding a scroll pane

```
frame.add(new JScrollPane(productTable));
```

A constructor and two methods of the JScrollPane class

Constructor	Description
`JScrollPane(component)`	Adds the component to the scroll pane.
Method	**Description**
`setHorizontalScrollBarPolicy(policy)`	Controls when the horizontal scrollbar is visible using one of the constants from the next table.
`setVerticalScrollBarPolicy(policy)`	Controls when the vertical scrollbar is visible using one of the constants from the next table.

ScrollPaneConstants

Value	Description
`HORIZONTAL_SCROLLBAR_AS_NEEDED`	Display the horizontal scrollbar only if the content is wider than the view port and can't all be displayed at the same time. This is the default.
`HORIZONTAL_SCROLLBAR_NEVER`	Never display the horizontal scrollbar. It's still possible to scroll left and right using the left and right arrow keys on the keyboard.
`HORIZONTAL_SCROLLBAR_ALWAYS`	Always display the horizontal scrollbar, whether it is needed or not.
`VERTICAL_SCROLLBAR_AS_NEEDED`	Display the vertical scrollbar only if the content is longer than the viewport and can't all be displayed at the same time. This is the default.
`VERTICAL_SCROLLBAR_NEVER`	Never display the vertical scrollbar. It's still possible to scroll the content up and down using the up and down arrow keys and the page up / page down keys on the keyboard.
`VERTICAL_SCROLLBAR_ALWAYS`	Always display the vertical scrollbar, whether it is needed or not.

To make the scrollbars always visible

```
scrollPane.setHoizontalScrollBarPolicy(
        ScrollPaneConstants.HORIZONATAL_SCROLLBAR_ALWAYS);

scrollPane.setVerticalScrollBarPolicy(
        ScrollPaneConstants.VERTICAL_SCROLLBAR_ALWAYS);
```

Description

- You can use a *scroll pane* to add scrollbars to any component that might not fit in a window.
- By default, scroll panes only display the scrollbars if they are needed.

Figure 21-12 How to work with scroll panes

How to work with built-in dialog boxes

If you work with GUIs, you may sometimes need to use a dialog box to display a message to the user. For example, you may need to display a notification or a warning. Other times, you may need to use a dialog box to confirm an operation. For example, you may need to ask a simple question to determine whether it's ok to delete a file.

Manually writing GUI code for common dialog boxes like these would be tedious. Fortunately, Swing provides built-in dialog boxes, and you can use the JOptionPane class to work with them.

A dialog box created from the JOptionPane class is always displayed on top of the parent container. It is always *modal*, which means that the user cannot interact with any other part of the application until they have responded to the dialog. And it is always *blocking*, which means that the dialog halts the currently running thread and prevents it from resuming until the user has responded to the dialog.

How to display a message

Figure 21-13 shows how to use the JOptionPane class to display a message to the user. To do that, you can call the static showMessageDialog method. This method takes four parameters: (1) the parent container, (2) the message, (3) the title, and (4) the type of message.

Typically, the parent for a dialog box is one of the frames of the application. However, it can also be a custom dialog box like the one described in the next chapter.

The JOptionPane can display the five message types listed in this figure. In most cases, the main difference between these types is the icon that's displayed by the message box. This icon may vary between operating systems and different look and feel settings. In addition, some operating systems may play a sound for certain types of messages.

The first example displays an information message. As a result, it uses the information icon. Since the purpose of this dialog box is to display a message, it only contains one button labeled "OK". After reading the message, the user can click this button to close the dialog and continue with the application.

The second example displays an error message. This example works like the first example. However, since it's an error message, it uses the error icon.

Again note that these icons may look different depending on the operating system and look and feel. These examples both use the default Swing look and feel.

JOptionPane message types

Type	Description
ERROR_MESSAGE	An error icon.
WARNING_MESSAGE	A warning icon.
INFORMATION_MESSAGE	An information icon.
QUESTION_MESSAGE	A question icon.
PLAIN_MESSAGE	No icon.

To display an information message

```
JOptionPane.showMessageDialog(frame, "The software has been updated.",
    "Updated", JOptionPane.INFORMATION_MESSAGE);
```

The dialog box that's displayed

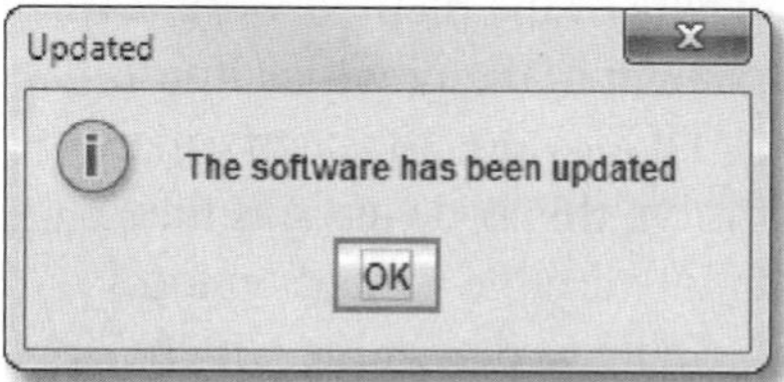

To display an error message

```
JOptionPane.showMessageDialog(frame,
    "The internet could not be accessed because it doesn't exist.",
    "Resource doesn't exist", JOptionPane.ERROR_MESSAGE);
```

The dialog box that's displayed

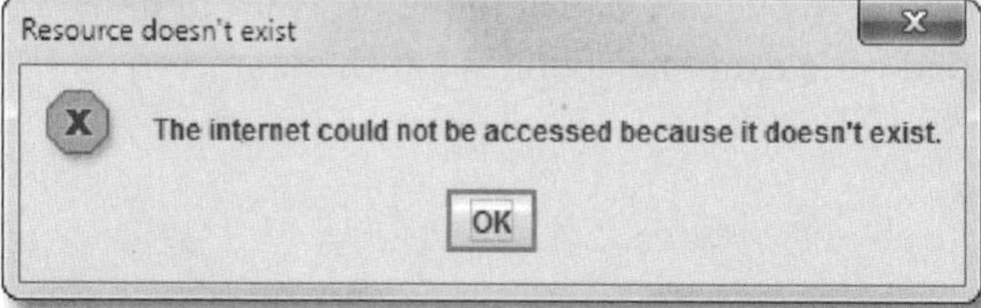

Description

- To show a dialog box that displays a message, you use the static showMessage-Dialog method of the JOptionPane class. This method has four parameters: (1) the parent container, (2) the message, (3) the title, and (4) the type of dialog.
- Java uses the parent container parameter to determine where to display the dialog. On Windows, Java typically centers the dialog box on the parent container.
- By default, the dialog box has a single OK button.
- The dialog box is *modal*. This means that it is always on top of the rest of the application. As a result, users can't continue until they have responded to the dialog.
- The appearance of the icons displayed by the dialogs varies depending on the look and feel that the application is using. In addition, these icons may vary depending on the locale.

Figure 21-13 How to display a message

How to confirm an operation

Figure 21-14 shows how to use the JOptionPane class to display a message that confirms an operation by asking the user a question. To do that, you can call the showConfirmDialog method. This method works similarly to the showMessageDialog method described in the previous figure. However, the fourth parameter of the showConfirmDialog method determines which buttons the dialog should display. In addition, this method returns a value that indicates which button the user selected.

The showConfirmDialog can display a dialog box with the button options listed in this figure. Of these, the YES_NO_OPTION type and the OK_CANCEL_OPTION type are the most commonly used.

The first example displays a dialog box that asks the user whether he or she wants to create a new file. Here, the first three parameters of the method work the same as the first three parameters of the method shown in the previous figure. However, the fourth parameter uses the YES_NO_OPTION value to specify that the dialog should display Yes and No buttons. In addition, this code assigns the return value of the showConfirmDialog method to an int variable named option. In part 2 of this figure, you'll learn how to use this variable to determine which button the user selected.

By default, the showConfirmDialog uses the QUESTION_MESSAGE type. This message type displays a question mark method as shown in the first example. However, you may want to use an icon that gives a stronger warning if the action the user is performing is going to delete a file, change data, or perform an operation that can't be undone. To do that, you can supply an optional fifth parameter that uses one of the message type values shown in the previous figure. In this figure, for instance, the second code example supplies a fifth parameter that specifies the WARNING_MESSAGE type.

JOptionPane option types

Type	Buttons
DEFAULT_OPTION	OK
YES_NO_OPTION	Yes and No
YES_NO_CANCEL_OPTION	Yes, No, and Cancel
OK_CANCEL_OPTION	OK and Cancel

To display a question dialog with Yes and No buttons

```
int option = JOptionPane.showConfirmDialog(frame,
        "Do you want to create a new file?", "New file",
         JOptionPane.YES_NO_OPTION);
```

The dialog box that's displayed

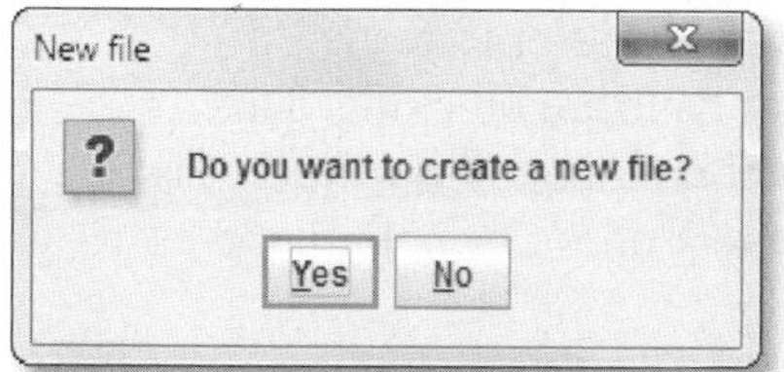

To display a question dialog with a warning icon

```
int option = JOptionPane.showConfirmDialog(frame,
        "Are you sure you want to to delete the Internet?\n"
               + "This operation cannot be undone.", "Are you sure?",
               JOptionPane.YES_NO_OPTION, JOptionPane.WARNING_MESSAGE);
```

The dialog box that's displayed

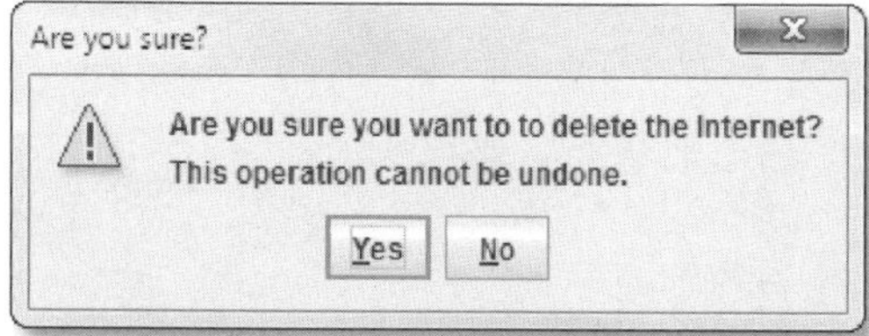

Description

- To display a dialog box that lets the user confirm or cancel an operation, you can use the static showConfirmDialog method of the JOptionPane class.
- The first three parameters of the showConfirmDialog method work the same as the showMessageDialog method shown in the previous figure.
- The fourth parameter determines the buttons that are displayed.
- By default, the showConfirmDialog method displays a question icon. However, you can specify another type of icon by supplying the fifth parameter.
- To wrap a long message to a second line, you can use the line break character (\n).

Figure 21-14 How to confirm an operation (part 1 of 2)

Part 2 of figure 21-14 shows how to use the return value of the showConfirmDialog method to determine which button the user selected. This method can return any of the values listed in this figure. Of course, the possible return values depend on the type of dialog. For example, a dialog box of the YES_NO_OPTION returns the YES_OPTION or the NO_OPTION. In other words, it never returns the CANCEL_OPTION or the OK_OPTION. However, all dialog types can return the CLOSED_OPTION that indicates that the user closed the dialog box without selecting any of the buttons.

The code example uses a switch statement to determine which button the user selected. To do that, this switch statement provides one case for each possible return value: the YES_OPTION, the NO_OPTION, and the CLOSE_OPTION. Then, it prints a different message to the console depending on which option the user selected. Alternately, it's possible to use an if/else statement instead of a switch statement. However, as a general rule, switch statements are more efficient. In addition, for code like this, they're easier to read.

Remember that the dialogs produced by JOptionPane are blocking. This means that they halt the thread and prevent it from continuing until the user has responded to the dialog. As result, the switch statement doesn't run until the user selects one of the dialog buttons or closes the dialog.

JOptionPane return values

Value	Description
YES_OPTION	The Yes button was selected.
NO_OPTION	The No button was selected.
CANCEL_OPTION	The Cancel button was selected.
OK_OPTION	The OK button was selected.
CLOSED_OPTION	The message box was closed without making any selection.

A switch statement that determines which button was selected

```
int option = JOptionPane.showConfirmDialog(frame,
        "Are you sure you want to to delete the Internet?\n"
                + "This operation cannot be undone.", "Are you sure?",
                JOptionPane.YES_NO_OPTION, JOptionPane.WARNING_MESSAGE);

switch (option) {
    case JOptionPane.YES_OPTION:
        System.out.println("You clicked the Yes button.");
        break;
    case JOptionPane.NO_OPTION:
        System.out.println("You clicked the No button.");
        break;
    case JOptionPane.CLOSED_OPTION:
        System.out.println("You closed the dialog.");
        break;
}
```

Description

- When the user selects an option from a dialog box, the showConfirmDialog method closes the dialog box and returns an int value for the option.
- To determine the option selected by the user, it's common to use a switch statement. However, it's also possible to use an if/else statement.

Figure 21-14 How to confirm an operation (part 2 of 2)

The Product Manager frame

This chapter finishes by presenting the complete code for the main window of the Product Manager application. This code uses most of the concepts and components you learned about in this chapter.

The user interface

Figure 21-15 shows the user interface for the Product Manager application. The main window of the application is a JFrame widget that uses the BorderLayout manager. This frame displays two components.

The first is a JPanel widget that uses the FlowLayout manager to display three JButton widgets. The frame displays this panel in the NORTH area of its layout.

The second is a JScrollPane widget that contains a JTable widget. This table displays the data for the products that are stored in the database. The frame displays this scroll pane in the CENTER area of its layout.

To delete a product, the user can select the row for the product and click the Delete button. This displays the Confirm Delete dialog box shown in this figure. If the user selects the Yes button to confirm the deletion, this deletes the product from the database and updates the data that's displayed in the JTable widget.

At this point, the Add and Edit buttons haven't been implemented. As a result, if the user clicks on either of these buttons, the application displays a dialog box that indicates that the feature hasn't been implemented yet. In the next chapter, you'll learn how to implement these buttons so they can be used to add a new product or update an existing product.

The Product Manager frame

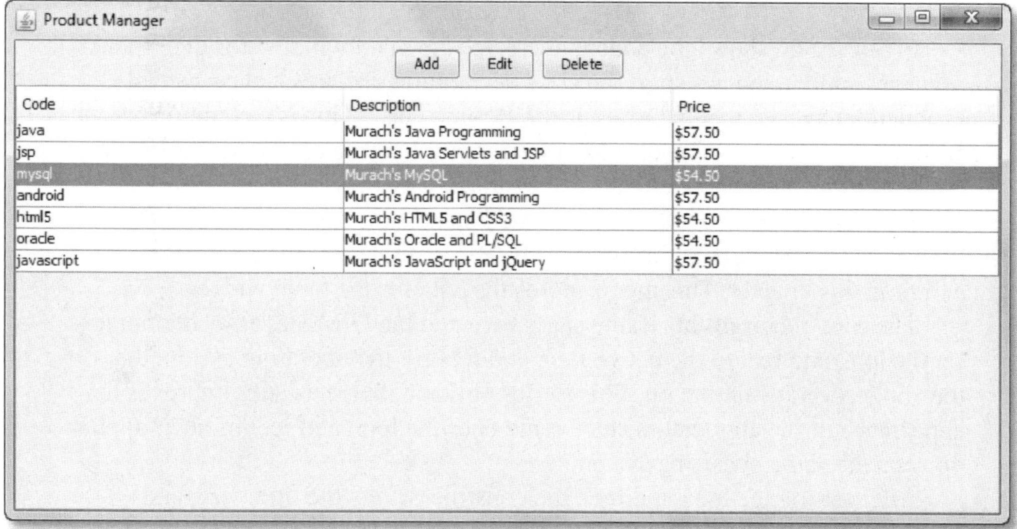

The dialog box for the Delete button

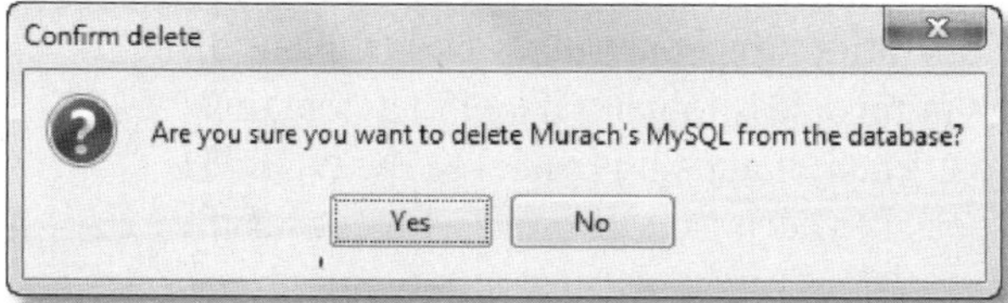

The dialog box for the Add and Edit buttons

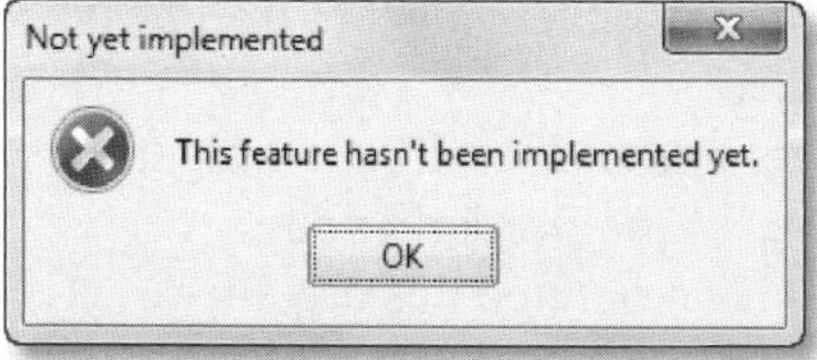

Description

- The main window for the Product Manager application is a frame that displays a panel that contains three buttons, as well as a table that contains the data for several products.
- If the user selects the row for a product and clicks the Delete button, the application displays a dialog box that allows the user to confirm the deletion.
- If the user selects the Add or Edit buttons, the application displays a dialog box that indicates that these features haven't been implemented yet. You'll learn how to implement these features in the next chapter.

Figure 21-15 The user interface for the Product Manager application

The ProductManagerFrame class

Figure 21-16 shows the code that creates the main window for the Product Manager application. To start, the class declaration declares a class named ProductManagerFrame that extends the JFrame class. This is a common practice since it allows you to store all code that defines this frame within a single class.

This class begins by defining two instance variables. First, it defines a JTable widget named productTable. This widget displays the table of products to the user. Second, it defines an instance of the ProductTableModel class described earlier in this chapter. This model stores the data for the table widget.

The constructor of this frame starts by using the UIManager to attempt to set the look and feel to the native look and feel for the operating system that the application is running on. This step is optional, but it usually improves the appearance of the application since it matches the look and feel of other applications on the same operating system.

After setting the look and feel, the constructor sets the title, size, and location of the frame. Then, it sets the default close operation so the application exits if the user closes the window. If you don't include this line of code, the window closes, but the application continues to run in the background.

After setting the default close operation, the constructor calls the buildButtonPanel method that's shown later in this class to get a panel that contains the three buttons for this application. Then, it adds this panel to the NORTH area of the BorderLayout. This is possible because a JFrame widget uses the BorderLayout manager by default.

After adding the button panel to the NORTH area, the constructor calls the buildProductTable method that's shown later in this class to get the JTable widget for the product table. In addition, it assigns this JTable widget to the productTable variable.

After creating the JTable widget, the constructor adds a JScrollPane widget that contains the JTable widget to the CENTER area of the BorderLayout. Since CENTER is the default area, this code could have omitted this argument. However, including this argument clearly identifies the area of the BorderLayout.

Finally, the constructor calls the setVisible method to display the user interface to the user. This statement is coded last because coding it earlier in the constructor can sometimes cause the user interface to flicker when it's first displayed.

The buildButtonPanel method begins by creating a JPanel object named panel. By default, a JPanel object uses the FlowLayout manager. Since that's what we want in this case, this code doesn't set a layout.

This method continues by creating the Add, Edit, and Delete buttons. Then, it sets a tooltip for some of these buttons. For example, it sets a tooltip of "Edit selected product" for the Edit button. Next, it uses lambda expressions to add action listeners to each button. Each of these listeners call an appropriately named method. For example, the action listener for the Add method calls the doAddButton method that's coded later in this class.

The ProductManagerFrame class

```
package mma.ui;

import java.awt.BorderLayout;
import javax.swing.JButton;
import javax.swing.JFrame;
import javax.swing.JOptionPane;
import javax.swing.JPanel;
import javax.swing.JScrollPane;
import javax.swing.JTable;
import javax.swing.ListSelectionModel;
import javax.swing.UIManager;
import javax.swing.UnsupportedLookAndFeelException;

import mma.business.Product;
import mma.db.ProductDB;
import mma.db.DBException;

public class ProductManagerFrame extends JFrame {
    private JTable productTable;
    private ProductTableModel productTableModel;

    public ProductManagerFrame() {
        try {
            UIManager.setLookAndFeel(
                    UIManager.getSystemLookAndFeelClassName());
        } catch (ClassNotFoundException | InstantiationException |
                 IllegalAccessException | UnsupportedLookAndFeelException e) {
            System.out.println(e);
        }
        setTitle("Product Manager");
        setSize(768, 384);
        setLocationByPlatform(true);
        setDefaultCloseOperation(JFrame.EXIT_ON_CLOSE);

        add(buildButtonPanel(), BorderLayout.NORTH);
        productTable = buildProductTable();
        add(new JScrollPane(productTable), BorderLayout.CENTER);
        setVisible(true);
    }

    private JPanel buildButtonPanel() {
        JPanel panel = new JPanel();

        JButton addButton = new JButton("Add");
        addButton.addActionListener((ActionEvent) -> {
            doAddButton();
        });
        panel.add(addButton);

        JButton editButton = new JButton("Edit");
        editButton.setToolTipText("Edit selected product");
        editButton.addActionListener((ActionEvent) -> {
            doEditButton();
        });
        panel.add(editButton);
```

Figure 21-16 The code for ProductManagerFrame (part 1 of 2)

After creating these three buttons, this code adds these three buttons to the panel. Finally, the last statement in the buildButtonPanel method returns the panel.

The next three methods are the event handler methods for the action listeners. For now, the methods for the Add and Edit buttons just display a dialog box with a message indicating the feature hasn't been implemented yet. In the next chapter, you'll learn how to add code to these methods so the Add and Edit buttons can be used to add new products or to edit existing products.

However, the method for the Delete button contains code that deletes the selected product from the database. To start, this code uses the getSelectedRow method of the JTable widget to get the index for the selected row. Then, this code checks whether this index is equal to -1. If so, it displays a message dialog that indicates that the user must select a product before clicking the Delete button. Otherwise, it displays a dialog that contains Yes and No buttons that allow the user to confirm the operation. If the user clicks the Yes button, this code uses the delete method of the ProductDB class described in the previous chapter to delete the product. Then, it calls the fireDatabaseUpdatedEvent method that's coded later in this class. In turn, this method calls the databaseUpdated method of the table model to update the data that's displayed by the JTable widget.

The code that calls the methods of the JOptionPane class specifies the keyword named *this* as the first argument of the method. This tells the JOptionPane class that the current object (the ProductManagerFrame object) is the parent for the dialog box.

The buildProductTable method creates a ProductTableModel object and assigns it to the productTableModel instance variable. Remember that the constructor for ProductTableModel class makes a call to the ProductDB class to get all of the records. As a result, this creates a model that contains a list of products that corresponds with the products in the database.

After creating the model, this code creates a new JTable widget and sets its model. To do that, it passes the productTableModel variable to the constructor of the JTable class.

After creating the JTable widget, the next line of code sets the selection mode of the table to a value of SINGLE_SELECTION. As a result, the user can only select one row at a time.

Because this table is displayed in a JScrollPane widget, this code also sets the border of the table to null. This makes sure that the Product Manager application doesn't display two borders: one for the table and one for the scroll pane.

Finally, this code returns the table. Remember that the constructor of this class calls the buildProductTable method to get this table. Then, it adds this table to a scroll pane, and it adds the scroll pane to the center area of the frame.

The ProductManagerFrame class

```
        JButton deleteButton = new JButton("Delete");
        deleteButton.setToolTipText("Delete selected product");
        deleteButton.addActionListener((ActionEvent) -> {
            doDeleteButton();
        });
        panel.add(deleteButton);

        return panel;
    }

    private void doAddButton() {
        JOptionPane.showMessageDialog(this,
            "This feature hasn't been implemented yet.",
            "Not yet implemented", JOptionPane.ERROR_MESSAGE);
    }

    private void doEditButton() {
        doAddButton();
    }

    private void doDeleteButton() {
        int selectedRow = productTable.getSelectedRow();
        if (selectedRow == -1) {
            JOptionPane.showMessageDialog(this,
                    "No product is currently selected.",
                    "No product selected", JOptionPane.ERROR_MESSAGE);
        } else {
            Product product = productTableModel.getProduct(selectedRow);
            int ask = JOptionPane.showConfirmDialog(this,
                    "Are you sure you want to delete " +
                        product.getDescription() + " from the database?",
                    "Confirm delete", JOptionPane.YES_NO_OPTION);
            if (ask == JOptionPane.YES_OPTION) {
                try {
                    ProductDB.delete(product);
                    fireDatabaseUpdatedEvent();
                } catch (DBException e) {
                    System.out.println(e);
                }
            }
        }
    }

    public void fireDatabaseUpdatedEvent() {
        productTableModel.databaseUpdated();
    }

    private JTable buildProductTable() {
        productTableModel = new ProductTableModel();
        JTable table = new JTable(productTableModel);
        table.setSelectionMode(ListSelectionModel.SINGLE_SELECTION);
        table.setBorder(null);
        return table;
    }
}
```

Figure 21-16 The code for ProductManagerFrame (part 2 of 2)

Perspective

In this chapter, you learned some essential skills for developing a GUI with Swing, the most widely used GUI toolkit for Java. In particular, you learned how to create the main window of an application. You learned how to add buttons. You learned how to handle the events that occur when these buttons are clicked. You learned how to work with a table that displays data from a database. And you learned how to work with built-in dialog boxes. In the next chapter, you'll learn how to create data entry forms that allow you to add and update data in a database.

Summary

- *Swing* is the most commonly used GUI toolkit for Java.
- An element of a GUI is called a *component* or a *widget*.
- Swing provides pluggable look and feels that you can change.
- A component that can contain other components is called a *container*. Three commonly used containers are frames, panels, and scroll panes.
- A JFrame widget usually serves as the main window of your application.
- A JPanel widget is an invisible component that you can use to group other components.
- A JButton widget displays a button.
- To handle the *event* that occurs when the user clicks a JButton widget, you can use the addActionListener method to add an *action listener*, or *event listener*.
- An *event handler* is a method that responds to GUI events such as a button click.
- A *layout manager* lays out the components in a container and controls how they respond to events such as resizing the window.
- The BorderLayout and FlowLayout managers are two of the most commonly used layout managers.
- A JTable widget displays tabular data, such as tables from a database.
- A *table model* provides tabular data for a JTable widget. The easiest way to create a table model is to extend the AbstractTableModel class.
- A JScrollPane adds scrollbars to a component such as a JTable widget so that the user can scroll through the component if it doesn't all fit in the container.
- You can use the methods of the JOptionPane class to displays a dialog box that contains an informational message or a dialog box that confirms an operation.

Exercise 21-1 Modify an existing GUI

In this exercise, you'll modify the GUI for the Product Manager window that's described in this chapter.

1. Open the project named ch21_ex1_ProductManager that's in the ex_starts folder.
2. Run the application and test the GUI. Select one of the rows and verify that you can delete it with the Delete button. Then click the Add and Edit buttons and verify that they display the dialog informing the user that the functionality hasn't been implemented yet.
3. Add a Print button that displays a dialog that tells the user that the product has been sent to the printer. To do this, add another JButton to the buildButtonPanel method, add an action listener, and create a method (you can name it doPrintButton) to handle the action.
4. Modify the code that's executed by the Print button so that it displays an error message if no row is currently selected in the product table. To do this, you can use the code for the doDeleteButton method as a reference.
5. Modify the code so the button panel is displayed in the SOUTH area of the frame's BorderLayout. To do this, you'll need to modify the part of the constructor that calls the buildButtonPanel method.

22

How to develop a GUI with Swing (part 2)

In the last chapter, you learned how to create the main window for the Product Manager application, including the table that displays the products that are stored in the database. In this chapter, you'll learn how to create a data entry form that allows you to add new products to the database or to edit existing ones.

How to work with labels and text fields 574
How to work with labels 574
How to work with text fields 576

How to use the GridBagLayout manager 578
An introduction to the GridBagLayout manager 578
How to lay out components in a grid 580
How to add padding 582
How to avoid a common pitfall 584

How to code a data entry form 586
How to create a custom dialog 586
How to pass data between a dialog and its parent 588

The Product form 590
The user interface 590
The ProductForm class 592
Two methods that use the ProductForm class 600

How to use threads with Swing 602
A common problem 602
How to solve the problem 602

Perspective 604

How to work with labels and text fields

Most applications use one or more *text fields*, also known as *text boxes*, to allow the user to enter data. In addition, most applications use one or more *labels* to display text that labels the text boxes for the user. In figure 22-1, for example, the Add Product window contains three labels and three text fields.

How to work with labels

You can use the JLabel class to create a label. For example, the first label in this figure displays "Code:" to label the text field that contains the product code.

The first example creates a label and adds it to a panel. Here, the first statement uses the constructor of the JLabel class to create a label and set its text. However, it's also possible to use the setText method to set the text of a label. Then, the second statement adds the label to the panel.

The second example shows how to create a label and add it to a panel in a single statement. Here, the code doesn't create a variable that refers to the JLabel object. As a result, you can't call any methods of the JLabel class later. However, this is usually fine since you rarely need to call methods from a label.

Although the labels in this figure display text, a label can also display an image. For example, you can use a label to display an icon that identifies a text field, or to display a photograph of a product. However, using images in labels is not covered in this book.

A window that contains labels and text fields

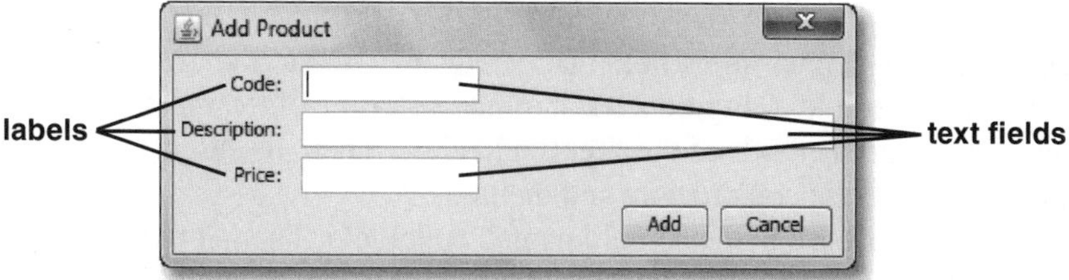

A common constructor and method of the JLabel class

Constructor	Description
`JLabel(String)`	Constructs a new JLabel and sets the text displayed by the label to the specified string.
Method	**Description**
`setText(String)`	Sets the text displayed by the label to the specified string.

How to create a JLabel object and add it to a container

```
JLabel codeLabel = new JLabel("Code:");
panel.add(codeLabel)
```

A common way of adding a JLabel to a container

```
panel.add(new JLabel("Code:"));
```

Description

- A JLabel component defines a *label*, which is a non-editable widget that typically displays text that labels other components such as text fields.
- Since you rarely need to call any methods from a JLabel object, it's a common practice to call the constructor of the JLabel class from within an add method. This does not create a variable that refers to the JLabel object.
- A JLabel object can also display an image. However, that's not covered in this book.

Figure 22-1 How to work with labels

How to work with text fields

The JTextField class defines a text field that can display text to the user and allows the user enter or edit text. Figure 22-2 summarizes some of the most common constructors and methods of the JTextField class. Then, it presents some examples that use these constructors and methods.

The first example creates a new text field named codeField. Then, it uses the setColumns method to set the width of this text field to approximately 20 characters. This means that the width of the text field depends on the font size for the text field. However, some layout managers ignore this setting. As a result, you can't always count on it to work correctly. In that case, you can use the setPreferredSize and setMinimumSize methods as described later in this chapter.

The second example shows how to create the same text field as the first example. However, this example uses the constructor to set the number of characters.

The third and fourth examples show how to get and set the text that's stored in a text field. Here, the third example uses the getText method of the text field to get the string that's stored in the text field and assign it to a String variable. Conversely, the fourth example uses the setText method of the text field to store the specified string in the text field.

By default, a text field is editable. As a result, the user can enter text into it or edit the text that's already in it. However, if you want to create a read-only text field, you can pass a false value to its setEditable method as shown in the fifth example. Then, the user can't enter text into it.

So, why wouldn't you use a label if you want to display text that the user can't edit? One reason is that the user can select and copy text from a read-only text field. This is useful if you want to display some text to the user that they can copy to the clipboard and paste somewhere else, but you don't want them to be able to edit the text. For example, you might want to allow the user to copy and paste an exception stack trace into an email to help the programmer debug a problem.

The setEnabled method works similarly to the setEditable method as shown in the sixth example. However, it also grays out the text box and doesn't allow selecting or copying text from the field. This is useful if you want to prevent users from entering data into a text field until after they have completed other steps.

The setPreferredSize and setMinimumSize methods provide another way besides the setColumns method to set the width of the text field. Like the setColumns method, some layout managers ignore these methods. As a result, you can't always count on them to work correctly. Unlike the setColumns method, these methods set the width in pixels, and they are common to all components. Later in this chapter, you'll see an example of how to use these methods to fix a common problem with Swing layout.

Common constructors and methods of the JTextField class

Constructor	Description
`JTextField(columns)`	Creates a text field with the specified number of columns (characters).
`JTextField(text)`	Creates a text field containing the specified text.
`JTextField(text, columns)`	Creates a text field that starts with the specified text and contains the specified number of columns (characters).

Method	Description
`getText(text)`	Gets the text contained by the text field.
`setText(text)`	Sets the text displayed by the text field.
`setColumns(int)`	Sets the width of the text field in columns (characters). Many layout managers ignore this setting.
`setEditable(boolean)`	Sets whether the user can edit the text or not.
`setEnabled(boolean)`	Sets whether the text field is enabled. If set to false, the text field is disabled, which means that it is grayed out and the user can't change the text in it.

How to create a text box for approximately 20 characters

```
JTextField codeField = new JTextField();
codeField.setColumns(20);
```

Another way to create the same text box

```
JTextField codeField = new JTextField(20);
```

How to get text from a text box

```
String productCode = codeField.getText();
```

How to set text in a text box

```
codeField.setText("java");
```

How to create a read-only text box

```
codeField.setEditable(false);
```

How to disable a text box

```
codeField.setEnabled(false);
```

Description

- A JTextField component defines a *text field* that displays text to the user and allows the user to enter text. This type of component is also known as a *text box*.

Figure 22-2 How to work with text fields

How to use the GridBagLayout manager

The GridBagLayout manager is more complicated than the layout managers described in the previous chapter. However, it's also more powerful and more flexible.

An introduction to the GridBagLayout manager

Using the GridBagLayout manager, you can lay out components in a grid like the one shown in in figure 22-3. Of course, the heavy black lines don't appear in the application when it's run. We added them to help you visualize the six cells of this grid. Here, the grid has two columns and three rows. As a result, the grid has six cells, and each cell holds a component.

With the GridBagLayout manager, you can create layouts that resize properly to fit the window size, and automatically look right if the user is using a font size other than the default. However, it can often require a fair amount of tweaking and testing to get a layout to look exactly right.

Using the GridBagLayout manager typically involves using the three classes described in this figure. These classes are stored in the java.awt package and are designed to work together.

First, the GridBagLayout class defines the layout manager that you provide to the container's setLayout method. This works the same as it does for the BorderLayout and FlowLayout managers described in the previous chapter.

Second, the GridBagConstraints class contains multiple fields that control how components are laid out within the grid. This includes how much padding they have, how they resize if the window is resized, and so on. You'll learn more about using this class in the next figure.

Third, the Insets class defines the amount of space between components in the grid, as well as the amount of space between components and the edge of the container. This space is often referred to as *padding*.

Six components in a grid of two columns and three rows

The package that contains the layout manager classes

```
java.awt
```

Three classes for working with the GridBagLayout manager

Class	Description
`GridBagLayout`	Creates a layout manager that can lay out components in a grid.
`GridBagConstraints`	Specifies how the GridBagLayout manager lays out its components. This object controls horizontal and vertical space, whether components resize or not, how they resize, and several other aspects of component behavior.
`Insets`	Specifies the amount of padding that the GridBagConstraints object applies between a component and the edge of the container.

Description

- The GridBagLayout manager is more complicated than the layout managers presented in the previous chapter. However, it's also the most powerful and flexible layout manager in Swing.
- To lay out components in a grid, you can use the GridBagConstraints class with the GridBagLayout class as shown in the next figure.
- To specify the padding between components, you can use the Insets class with the GridBagConstraints class as shown in figure 22-5.

Figure 22-3 An introduction to the GridBagLayout manager

How to lay out components in a grid

Figure 22-4 shows how to use a GridBagConstraints object to control the layout of components inside a container that uses the GridBagLayout manager. This figure starts by showing some fields of the GridBagConstraints class.

To start the gridx and gridy fields control the position on the grid where the component is placed. In this figure, for example, both the gridx and gridy fields are set to a value of 0 for the "Code:" label. As a result, the layout manager places this label in the cell at the top left corner of the grid. Here, the coordinates represent cells, not pixels.

The first text field has a gridx value of 1 and a gridy value of 0. As a result, the layout manager places this text field in the cell that's at the intersection of the second column and the first row. The second text field has a gridx value of 1 and a gridy value of 1. As a result, the layout manager places this label in the cell at the intersection of the second row and the second column. And so on.

The anchor field controls where the layout manager places the component within the cell if the cell is larger than the component. By default, the layout manager places the component in the center of the cell. However, you can specify an anchor value of LINE_END to align the component with the right side of the cell. In this figure, for example, the first three labels have an anchor field that's set to this value. Similarly, you can use an anchor value of LINE_START to align the component with the left side of the cell. In this figure, for example, all of the text fields have an anchor field that's set to this value.

Although LINE_START and LINE_END are two of the most common values for the anchor field, many other possible values exist. To view a complete list, see the API documentation for the anchor field.

The LINE_START and LINE_END values are relatively new to Java. Prior to their introduction, developers commonly used the WEST and EAST values instead of the LINE_START and LINE_END values. However, for new development, it's recommended that you use the newer LINE_START and LINE_END values because they are more portable across regions.

The gridwidth and gridheight fields determine how many cells the component takes up. As a result, setting the gridwidth field to 2 causes the component to take up two horizontal cells rather than one. In this figure, for example, the fourth label takes up two horizontal cells rather than one.

The code example begins by creating a JPanel object. By default, a JPanel object uses the FlowLayout manager. That's why the second statement uses the setLayout method to set the layout manager to the GridBagLayout manager.

After setting the layout manager, this code creates a new GridBagConstraints object. In practice, it's common to use the variable named c for this, so that's what this code does.

After creating the GridBagConstraints object, this codes sets the gridx, gridy, and anchor fields of the GridBagConstraints object. Then, it adds the components to the panel, and passes the GridBagConstraints object as the second parameter.

This code resets the gridx, gridy, and anchor fields before adding every label. Reusing a GridBagConstraints object as shown in this figure makes it easy to view and edit the coordinates and alignment of each component. However, if

Some common fields of the GridBagConstraints class

Field	Description
`gridx, gridy`	Sets the x and y coordinates of the component in the grid where 0, 0 is the top left cell of the grid.
`anchor`	Sets where the component is displayed if the component is smaller than the cell that is its display area. The most commonly used are LINE_START and LINE_END. In older versions of Java, these were called WEST and EAST.
`gridwidth, gridheight`	Sets the number of horizontal and vertical cells that the component occupies.

Code that uses a GridBagConstraints object

```
JPanel panel = new JPanel();
panel.setLayout(new GridBagLayout());

GridBagConstraints c = new GridBagConstraints();

c.gridx = 0; c.gridy = 0; c.anchor = GridBagConstraints.LINE_END;
panel.add(new JLabel("Code:"), c);
c.gridx = 1; c.gridy = 0; c.anchor = GridBagConstraints.LINE_START;
panel.add(codeField, c);
c.gridx = 0; c.gridy = 1; c.anchor = GridBagConstraints.LINE_END;
panel.add(new JLabel("Description:"), c);
c.gridx = 1; c.gridy = 1; c.anchor = GridBagConstraints.LINE_START;
panel.add(descriptionField, c);
c.gridx = 0; c.gridy = 2; c.anchor = GridBagConstraints.LINE_END;
panel.add(new JLabel("Price:"), c);
c.gridx = 1; c.gridy = 2; c.anchor = GridBagConstraints.LINE_START;
panel.add(priceField, c);
c.gridx = 0; c.gridy = 3; c.anchor = GridBagConstraints.LINE_START;
c.gridwidth = 2;
panel.add(new JLabel ("This label spans both columns."), c);
```

The resulting layout

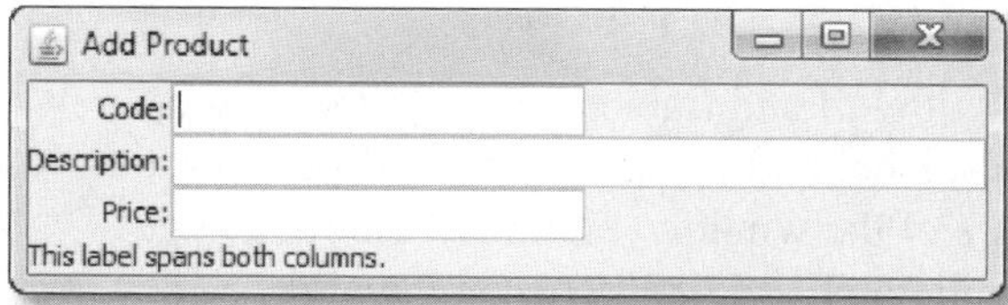

Description

- You can reuse the same GridBagConstraints object for multiple widgets. However, you must reset any values you don't want to use in the next widget.

Figure 22-4 How to lay out components in a grid

you don't reset values, you may end up accidentally reusing the values that were set for a previous component, which may cause strange layout behavior. As a result, you need to make sure to reset all values, or you need to create a new GridBagConstraint object for each component.

How to add padding

By default, a GridBagConstraints object doesn't provide any padding between components or between components and the edge of the container. That's why the components displayed in the previous figure don't have any padding between them. And that's why there's no padding between the components and the edge of the container.

To make this layout more visually appealing, you can use the insets field of the GridBagConstraints object to apply some padding as shown in figure 22-5. This field uses an Inserts object to determine the amount of padding around a component. Here, the four parameters of the Insets object are the top, left, bottom, and right padding in pixels. If you think of a clock, these values are in a counterclockwise direction, starting at the top of the clock.

In this figure, the insets field of the GridBagConstraints object is set to an Insets object that specifies 5 pixels of padding for the top, left, and right of the component and no padding for the bottom of the component. Since this code uses the same Insets object for all components in the container, the label at the bottom of the layout touches the bottom edge of the container. However, the rest of the components are separated by 5 pixels of padding. This padding makes this layout more visually appealing than the layout in the previous figure.

When working with an Insets object, there are two important things to remember. First, unlike a GridBagConstraints object, you can't change the values of an Insets object and then reuse it. If you do, your layout will behave strangely. Second, if you set 5 pixels of top spacing and 5 pixels of bottom spacing, the spacing between components is actually 10 pixels. In other words, the layout uses five pixels of space at the bottom of one component and five pixels of space at the top of the component in the next row for a total of 10 pixels.

Of course, the same thing is true with left and right spacing. In this figure, for example, the left side of the longest label has a small amount of padding between its first letter and the left edge of the window. Similarly, the right edge of the longest text field has a small amount of padding between it and the right edge of the window. However, there is twice the padding between the end of the labels and the beginning of the text fields. That's because this area uses the padding from the right side of the label and the padding from the left side of the text box.

Most of the time, you only need to use the insets field of the GridBagConstraints object to specify external padding. However, if you need to specify internal padding, you can use the ipadx and ipady fields shown in this figure. These fields determine how much padding is placed inside the component. For example, if you set the ipadx and ipady values of a JButton component to 10, the layout displays 10 pixels of padding between the text of the JButton component and the edges of the button.

More common fields of the GridBagConstraints class

Field	Description
`insets`	Uses an Insets object to specify how much external padding should be applied to the component.
`ipadx, ipady`	Sets how much internal padding to add to the width and height of the component. The value applies to both sides.

The Insets class

Constructor	Description
`Insets(top, left, bottom, right)`	Specifies the top, left, bottom, and right padding in pixels.

To create an Insets object and add it to a GridBagConstraints object

```
GridBagConstraints c = new GridBagConstraints();
c.insets = new Insets(5, 5, 0, 5);

c.gridx = 0; c.gridy = 0; c.anchor = GridBagConstraints.LINE_END;
panel.add(new JLabel("Code:"), c);
c.gridx = 1; c.gridy = 0; c.anchor = GridBagConstraints.LINE_START;
panel.add(codeField, c);

// the rest of the code that adds the labels and text boxes
```

The example from the previous figure with insets

Description

- If you forget the order of the parameters for the constructor of the Insets class, it may help to remember that they start at the top and go counterclockwise.

How to avoid a common pitfall

Figure 22-6 demonstrates a common pitfall with GUI layout and shows how to avoid it. To start, this figure shows the same form shown in the previous figure after a user resized it by shrinking its horizontal width slightly. This caused all of the text fields to collapse. What's going on here?

Basically, if the container isn't wide enough to display the component at its specified size, the GridBagLayout manager assigns the minimum size to the component instead. By default, a component has a minimum size of 0. As a result, this causes the width of the text fields to completely collapse.

One common way to solve this problem is to use the setMinimumSize method on the text fields to set the preferred and minimum sizes to the same value as shown in this figure. Here, the first statement creates a new Dimension object that's 100 pixels wide and 20 pixels tall. Then, the next four statements set the preferred and minimum sizes of the text fields for the product code and price to that Dimension object.

After that, the sixth statement creates a second new Dimension object with a width of 250 and a height of 20. Then, the next two statements sets the preferred and minimum sizes of text field for the product description to that Dimension object. As a result, the code and price text fields are 100 pixels wide and the description text field is 250 pixels wide.

If you run this code now and shrink the width of the window, the text fields don't collapse. However, the labels begin to collapse as the GridBagLayout manager tries to give the text fields their minimum size and still stay within the window. If you continue to press the issue by shrinking the window even further, the edges of the text fields eventually disappear outside the window.

Because the labels start collapsing, you might say that we solved one problem, but created another. In some sense, that's true. And this shows that the GridBagLayout manager is complex and often requires a lot of tweaking to get a layout to behave exactly as intended.

For the Product Manager application, the user is unlikely to have any need to resize this window. As a result, the solution described in this figure is probably adequate.

Another possible solution to this problem is to make it so the user can't resize the window. To do that, you can call the setResizable method of the window and pass it a value of false. Again, for the Product Manager application, this solution is acceptable. However, you should use this technique with caution as most users expect to be able to resize a window, especially if it helps the window fit better on their display.

There is a third possible solution that's more elegant but also more difficult to code. This solution involves using the weightx, weighty, and fill fields of the GridBagConstraints object to control how the components are resized when the user resizes a window. The weightx and weighty fields control how to distribute any extra horizontal or vertical space among the components. This allows you to specify a percentage for each component. In addition, the fill field determines whether the component resizes if the container is resized. A component can be set to resize either horizontally, vertically, both, or not at all.

A common problem that occurs after horizontal resizing

A constructor of the Dimension class

Constructor	Description
Dimension(width, height)	Specifies the width and height of a component in pixels.

Two methods you can use to fix this problem

Method	Description
setMinimumSize(Dimension)	Specifies the minimum width and height of a component in pixels.
setPreferredSize(Dimension)	Specifies the preferred width and height of a component in pixels.

Code that sets the preferred and maximum sizes

```
Dimension dim1 = new Dimension(100, 20);
codeField.setPreferredSize(dim1);
codeField.setMinimumSize(dim1);
priceField.setPreferredSize(dim1);
priceField.setMinimumSize(dim1);

Dimension dim2 = new Dimension(250, 20);
descriptionField.setPreferredSize(dim2);
descriptionField.setMinimumSize(dim2);
```

The improved example after horizontal resizing

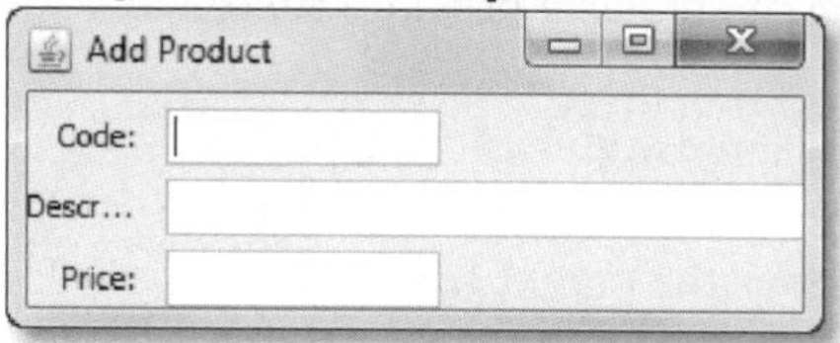

Three ways to fix this problem

1. Use the window's setResizable method to prevent the user from resizing the window. However, you should use this technique sparingly since users often expect to be able to resize a window.
2. Use the component's setPreferredSize and setMinimumSize methods. This isn't a perfect solution, but it's acceptable for most applications.
3. Use the weightx, weighty, and fill fields of the GridBagConstraints class to control how the components are resized. This technique can yield the best results, but it also requires the most tweaking.

Description

- When a window is resized horizontally, components (especially text fields) can sometimes collapse to a size of zero. This is a common problem.

Figure 22-6 How to avoid a common pitfall

How to code a data entry form

Most applications need to get input from the user. For example, it's common for an application to need a user to enter or edit the data that's stored in a database. To do this, most applications use a special type of window known as a *form*.

Often, you want to use a special type of window known as a *dialog*, or *dialog box*, to display a form. To do that in Swing, you can use the JDialog component. This allows you to create custom dialogs that work similarly to the built-in dialogs that are available from the JOptionPane class.

How to create a custom dialog

Figure 22-7 begins by showing one of the most common JDialog constructors. This constructor takes three parameters. The first parameter specifies the *owner*, or *parent*, of the dialog. Typically, the parent of a dialog is the JFrame component for the main window of the application.

The second parameter specifies the title of the dialog. This works the same as setting the title for a JFrame component.

The third parameter determines whether the dialog is *modal*. If a dialog is modal, Java prevents the user from interacting with any other part of the application until the user has responded to the dialog. You should use modal dialogs with caution as they can annoy users if they aren't necessary. As a general rule, you should only use a modal dialog when the application can't continue the current operation until the user responds to the dialog.

The code example creates a NameDialog class that defines a dialog. This class begins by extending the JDialog class. Then, it creates a private JTextField component named dialogNameField.

The constructor of the NameDialog class takes one argument: the parent frame. Within this constructor, the first statement uses the super keyword to call the constructor of the JDialog class and it passes the parent frame, a title of "Name Dialog", and a boolean value of true. As a result, the NameDialog component is a modal dialog. The second statement in the constructor continues by setting the default close operation to DISPOSE_ON_CLOSE. As a result, the dialog is closed and its resources are released if the user closes it with the window's close button. Without this code, Java would hide the dialog but not free its resources. And the third statement sets the layout of the dialog to the FlowLayout manager.

The constructor continues by creating the components for the dialog and adding them to the dialog. First, it creates a text field and sets its width to 20 characters. Then, it creates two buttons and adds action listeners to them. Here, the code for the action listener of the Okay button is shown in the next figure, and the code for action listener of the Cancel button just calls the dialog's dispose method. This closes the dialog and releases any resources it was using.

After adding components to the dialog, this code calls the pack method to set the size of the dialog to the minimum size needed to hold the components. Finally, this code calls the setVisible method to make the dialog visible.

A commonly used JDialog constructor

Constructor	Description
`JDialog(parent, title, isModal)`	Specifies the parent frame of the dialog, the title of the dialog, and whether the dialog is modal.

A class for a custom dialog

```
public class NameDialog extends JDialog {

    private JTextField dialogNameField;

    public NameDialog(java.awt.Frame parent) {
        super(parent, "Name Dialog", true);
        this.setDefaultCloseOperation(WindowConstants.DISPOSE_ON_CLOSE);
        this.setLayout(new FlowLayout());

        dialogNameField = new JTextField();
        dialogNameField.setColumns(20);

        JButton okayButton = new JButton("Okay");
        okayButton.addActionListener((ActionEvent) -> {
            // TODO: Add code here
        });

        JButton cancelButton = new JButton("Cancel");
        cancelButton.addActionListener((ActionEvent) -> {
            dispose();
        });

        this.add(new JLabel("Name:"));
        this.add(dialogNameField);
        this.add(okayButton);
        this.add(cancelButton);
        this.pack();

        this.setVisible(true);
    }
}
```

A statement that displays this dialog

```
new NameDialog(this);
```

The dialog produced by the above code

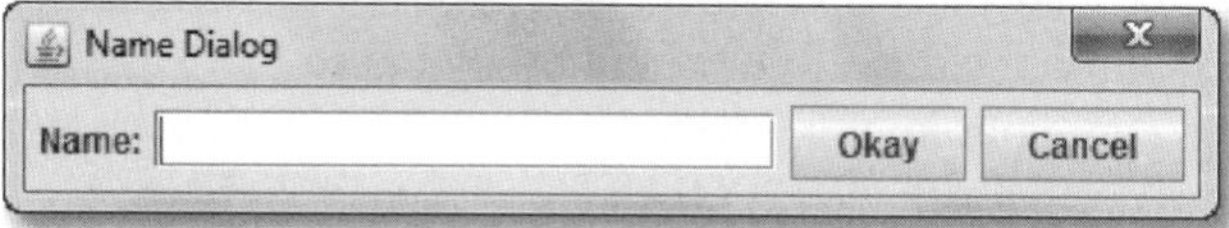

Description

- A *modal* dialog prevents the user from interacting with other parts of the application until they have responded to the dialog.
- On most operating systems, a JDialog component is displayed on top of its parent frame, has fewer window controls than a JFrame (for example, no maximize or minimize buttons), and does not get its own entry in the taskbar.

Figure 22-7 How to create a custom dialog

At first glance, it might seem there aren't that many differences between a JFrame component and a JDialog component. However, on closer inspection, there are few important differences. First, a dialog is designed to have a parent window. As a result, a dialog is displayed on top of its parent window, even if the dialog is not the active window. Second, on most operating systems, a dialog has fewer window controls. On Windows, for example, a dialog has a close button but no minimize, maximize, or restore buttons. Third, on most operating systems, a dialog doesn't get an entry in the taskbar or window list. As a result, you can't switch directly to the dialog using window switch commands. Instead, you need to switch to the window that owns the dialog. Fourth, as described earlier, a dialog can be modal.

How to pass data between a dialog and its parent

Figure 22-8 shows how to get and set the data contained in a dialog. In this figure, the dialog only works with the data that's stored in a single text field. However, it's possible for a dialog to work with the data that's stored in multiple components. For example, the Product form shown later in this chapter works with the data that's stored in three text fields.

The first two examples show how to set data in a dialog. Here, the first example shows a modified version of the constructor from the previous figure. However, it includes an additional parameter for a String object that specifies the name that's stored in the dialog. This parameter provides a way to pass data to the dialog. Then, the code in the constructor can set the data on the components in the dialog. In this figure, for example, the constructor calls the setText method of the text field to set it to the name parameter.

The second example shows code that calls the constructor of the dialog. This code is stored in the parent frame. It begins by passing the keyword named *this* to refer to the object itself. In this case, this means that this code is passing the frame itself to the NameDialog constructor. Next, it gets the value from a text field in the frame by calling its getText method and passing the String object that's returned as the second parameter. As a result, the text field in the dialog displays the same text as the text field in the frame.

The third and fourth examples show how to get data from a dialog. To do that, the third example adds a public method named setNameText to the frame that the dialog can call. This method takes a String object as a parameter. Within this method, the code sets the text on the text field in the frame by calling its setText method and passing it the name parameter.

The fourth example shows the code for the action listener of the dialog's Okay button. Within this action listener, the first statement gets a reference to the NameFrame object by calling the getOwner method and casting the Window object that's returned to the NameFrame type. This cast is necessary because the Window type doesn't include the setNameText method. Then, the second line of code calls the setNameText method on the frame, and passes it the text that's stored in the text field of the dialog. Finally, the third line of code calls the dispose method of the dialog. This closes the dialog and frees any resources it was using.

How to set data in a dialog

A constructor of the dialog class that allows you to set data

```
public NameDialog(java.awt.Frame parent, String name) {
    super(parent, "Name Dialog", true);
    this.setDefaultCloseOperation(WindowConstants.DISPOSE_ON_CLOSE);
    this.setLayout(new FlowLayout());

    dialogNameField = new JTextField();
    dialogNameField.setColumns(20);
    dialogNameField.setText(name);
```

Code from the frame that calls this constructor

```
new NameDialog(this, frameNameField.getText());
```

A method of the Window class

Method	Description
`getOwner()`	Returns a Window object for the owner or parent of a dialog. You typically cast this Window object to a more specific type.

How to get data from a dialog

A method in the frame class that the dialog can call

```
public void setNameText(String name) {
    frameNameField.setText(name);
}
```

Code in the dialog that calls this method

```
okayButton.addActionListener((ActionEvent) -> {
    NameFrame frame = (NameFrame) getOwner();
    frame.setNameText(dialogNameField.getText());
    dispose();
});
```

Description

- Within the dialog class, you can code a constructor that allows the main window to set data in the dialog.
- Within the class for the main window, you can code a method that allows the dialog to return set data to the main window.
- To close a dialog, you can call its dispose method. This closes the dialog object and frees any resources that it's using.

Figure 22-8 How to pass data between a dialog and its parent frame

The Product form

This chapter finishes by presenting the code for the Product form. This form is the data entry form used by the main window of the Product Manager application described in the previous chapter.

The user interface

Figure 22-9 shows the user interface for the data entry form. To start, if the user clicks on the Add button in the main window, this form has a title of Add Product, doesn't display any text in its three text fields, and has an Add button. However, if the user clicks on the Edit button in the main window, this form has a title of Edit Product, displays the text for the selected product in its text fields, and has a Save button.

If the user doesn't enter valid data for a product, the application uses the JOptionPane class to display a built-in dialog that asks the user to enter valid data. In this figure, for example, the last dialog displays the message that's displayed if the user leaves one of the text fields blank. However, this application would display a different message if the user had entered an invalid number for the product price.

The Product form inherits the JDialog class. As a result, it is a custom dialog. On Windows, a dialog only includes a close button in its upper-right corner. In other words, it doesn't include minimize, maximize, or restore buttons like the main window for the Product Manager application. However, this is specific to the Windows operating system. These buttons may vary depending on the operating system.

The Product form uses the BorderLayout manager. Within this layout, it contains two panels.

The first panel contains the three labels and their corresponding text fields. This panel uses the GridBagLayout manager to lay out these labels and text fields. Then, this panel is added to the center of the border layout. As a result, it gets all available space that isn't taken up by any other components.

The second panel uses a right-aligned FlowLayout manager. This panel lays out the two buttons for the form. Then, this panel is added to the south area of the border layout. As a result, this panel gets its preferred height, and the width expands to take up the entire horizontal space of the container. In this case, that means that the panel's height is just tall enough to hold the buttons, and the panel's width is the entire width of the window.

The Add Product dialog

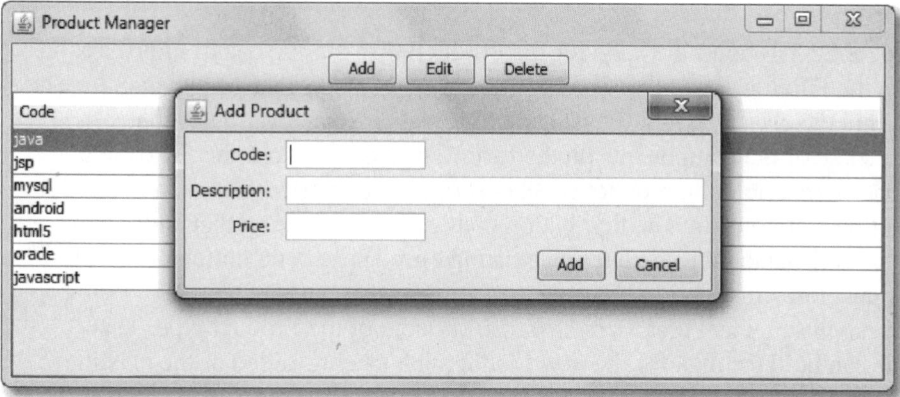

The Edit Product dialog

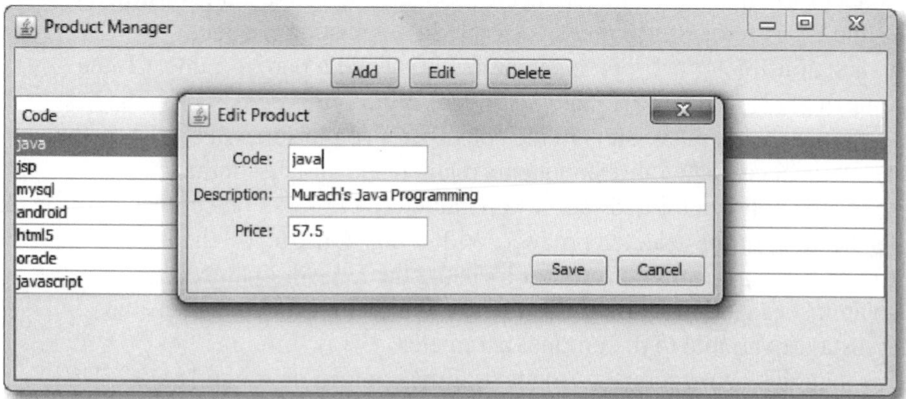

One of the data validation dialogs

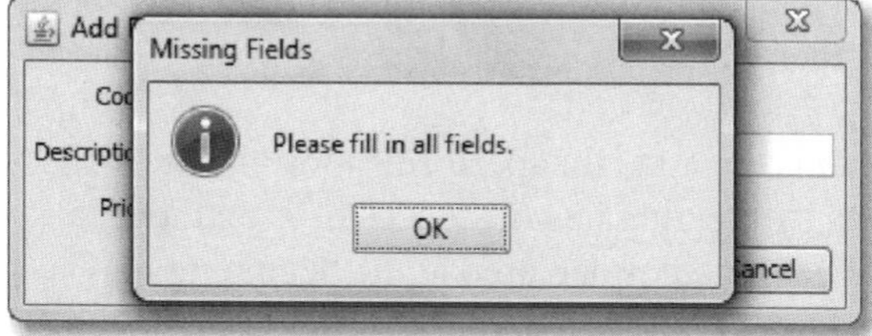

Description

- The Product Manager application uses the same dialog to add a new product or to edit an existing product. The only difference in appearance is the title of the dialog and the text that's displayed on the first button.
- When you add or edit a product, the Product form uses built-in dialogs to display validation messages if the fields for the product are missing or not valid.

Figure 22-9 The user interface for the Product form

The ProductForm class

Figure 22-10 shows the code for the ProductForm class. To start, this class extends the JDialog class. This is a common way to create a custom dialog.

Within the class, the first five statements create instance variables that refer to some of the components on the form. The first three are the JTextField components that hold the product code, description, and price. The next two are the JButton components. The first button confirms the operation that adds a new product to the database or updates an existing one. The second button cancels the dialog and closes it.

The sixth statement creates an instance variable of the Product type. This variable can hold the data for the new product that's being added or the existing product that's being edited.

This class defines two constructors. Here, the first constructor displays the Add Product form that's used to add a new product, and the second constructor displays the Edit Product form that's used to edit an existing product.

The first constructor accepts three parameters: (1) the parent frame, (2) the dialog title, and (3) whether the dialog is modal. Within this constructor, the first statement passes these parameters to the constructor of the super class. Then, the second statement calls the initComponents method shown later in this class.

The second constructor adds a fourth parameter: a Product object that contains the data for the selected product. Within this constructor, the first statement calls the previous constructor by using the keyword named *this*, which refers to an instance of the current class. Then, the second statement sets the product instance variable to the product parameter.

After that, this constructor sets the text of the confirm button to "Save". That way, the button on the Edit Product form is labeled "Save" instead of "Add". This is necessary because the initComponents method shown later in this class sets the text of this button to "Add". In addition, this constructor uses the setText methods on the three text fields to set their values to reflect the appropriate values stored in the Product object.

The initComponents method contains the code that performs most of the setup of the dialog. The method begins by creating new instances of JTextField and JButton components for the instance variables declared at the beginning of the class. Next, the code sets the default close operation of the dialog to DISPOSE_ON_CLOSE. As a result, Java disposes the dialog and frees its resources when the user clicks on the close button of the dialog.

The ProductForm class

```
package mma.ui;

import java.awt.BorderLayout;
import java.awt.Dimension;
import java.awt.FlowLayout;
import java.awt.GridBagConstraints;
import java.awt.GridBagLayout;
import java.awt.Insets;
import javax.swing.JButton;
import javax.swing.JDialog;
import javax.swing.JLabel;
import javax.swing.JOptionPane;
import javax.swing.JPanel;
import javax.swing.JTextField;
import javax.swing.WindowConstants;

import mma.business.Product;
import mma.db.DBException;
import mma.db.ProductDB;

public class ProductForm extends JDialog {
    private JTextField codeField;
    private JTextField descriptionField;
    private JTextField priceField;
    private JButton confirmButton;
    private JButton cancelButton;

    private Product product = new Product();

    public ProductForm(java.awt.Frame parent, String title, boolean modal) {
        super(parent, title, modal);
        initComponents();
    }

    public ProductForm(java.awt.Frame parent, String title,
            boolean modal, Product product) {
        this(parent, title, modal);
        this.product = product;
        confirmButton.setText("Save");
        codeField.setText(product.getCode());
        descriptionField.setText(product.getDescription());
        priceField.setText(Double.toString(product.getPrice()));
    }

    private void initComponents() {
        codeField = new JTextField();
        descriptionField = new JTextField();
        priceField = new JTextField();
        cancelButton = new JButton();
        confirmButton = new JButton();

        setDefaultCloseOperation(WindowConstants.DISPOSE_ON_CLOSE);
```

Figure 22-10 The ProductForm class (part 1 of 4)

The next two lines of code create Dimension objects and assign them a width of 100 pixels and 300 pixels respectively, with both having a height of 20 pixels. Then, the code sets the preferred size and minimum size of the code and price text fields to the shorter Dimension object. It also sets the preferred and minimum size of the description text field to the longer Dimension object. In both cases, this prevents the pitfall described earlier in this chapter where the text fields collapse to a width of zero if the user resizes the dialog.

The next section of the initComponents method creates the two buttons. To start, it sets the text of the first button to "Cancel" and adds an action listener to it that calls a method named cancelButtonActionPerformed that's shown later in this class. Then, it sets the text of the second button to "Add" and adds an action listener to it that calls a method named confirmButtonActionPerformed. However, if the user is editing an existing product instead of adding one, the setText method call here is overridden by the setText method call in the second constructor as discussed on the previous page.

The next section creates a new JPanel to store the text fields and their corresponding labels. To start, this code sets the layout manager for the panel to the GridBagLayout manager. Then, it adds the text fields and labels for the form to the panel. To make working with the GridBagConstraints object easier, the calls to the panel's add method use a helper method called getConstraints that's shown later in this class. This method takes three parameters: An x coordinate for the grid row, a y coordinate for the grid column, and an anchor value.

The next section creates another JPanel for the buttons. To start, this code sets the layout manager to a FlowLayout manager with right alignment. Then, it adds the confirm and cancel buttons to the layout.

The last section adds the panel that contains the labels and text fields to the center area of the dialog's BorderLayout manager. Then, it adds the panel that contains the buttons to the south area of the dialog's BorderLayout manager. Like a JFrame component, a JDialog component uses the BorderLayout manager by default. As a result, it isn't necessary to explicitly set the layout. Finally, the last statement uses the pack method to size the dialog by packing it so it's just large enough to hold all of the components.

Note that none of this code sets the location of this form or makes this form visible. As a result, the parent frame must do that. For example, the main frame of the Product Manager application could display the Add Product form like this:

```
ProductForm productForm = new ProductForm(this, "Add Product", true);
productForm.setLocationRelativeTo(this);
productForm.setVisible(true);
```

This displays a modal version of this form in the middle of the main window.

The getConstraints method creates and returns a GridBagConstraints object with the specified parameters. This method begins by creating a new GridBagConstraints object. Then, it sets the insets field to a new Insets object that has five pixels of spacing on the top, left, and right, but no spacing on the bottom. Next, it sets the gridx, gridy, and anchor fields of the GridBagConstraints object to the corresponding parameters. Finally, it returns the new GridBagConstraints object.

The ProductForm class (continued)

```
        Dimension shortField = new Dimension(100, 20);
        Dimension longField = new Dimension(300, 20);
        codeField.setPreferredSize(shortField);
        codeField.setMinimumSize(shortField);
        priceField.setPreferredSize(shortField);
        priceField.setMinimumSize(shortField);
        descriptionField.setPreferredSize(longField);
        descriptionField.setMinimumSize(longField);

        cancelButton.setText("Cancel");
        cancelButton.addActionListener((ActionEvent) -> {
            cancelButtonActionPerformed();
        });

        confirmButton.setText("Add");
        confirmButton.addActionListener((ActionEvent) -> {
            confirmButtonActionPerformed();
        });

        // JLabel and JTextField panel
        JPanel productPanel = new JPanel();
        productPanel.setLayout(new GridBagLayout());
        productPanel.add(new JLabel("Code:"),
                getConstraints(0, 0, GridBagConstraints.LINE_END));
        productPanel.add(codeField,
                getConstraints(1, 0, GridBagConstraints.LINE_START));
        productPanel.add(new JLabel("Description:"),
                getConstraints(0, 1, GridBagConstraints.LINE_END));
        productPanel.add(descriptionField,
                getConstraints(1, 1, GridBagConstraints.LINE_START));
        productPanel.add(new JLabel("Price:"),
                getConstraints(0, 2, GridBagConstraints.LINE_END));
        productPanel.add(priceField,
                getConstraints(1, 2, GridBagConstraints.LINE_START));

        // JButton panel
        JPanel buttonPanel = new JPanel();
        buttonPanel.setLayout(new FlowLayout(FlowLayout.RIGHT));
        buttonPanel.add(confirmButton);
        buttonPanel.add(cancelButton);

        // add panels to main panel
        setLayout(new BorderLayout());
        add(productPanel, BorderLayout.CENTER);
        add(buttonPanel, BorderLayout.SOUTH);
        pack();
    }

    private GridBagConstraints getConstraints(int x, int y, int anchor) {
        GridBagConstraints c = new GridBagConstraints();
        c.insets = new Insets(5, 5, 0, 5);
        c.gridx = x; c.gridy = y; c.anchor = anchor;
        return c;
    }
```

Figure 22-10 The ProductForm class (part 2 of 4)

The next two methods in the class are the event handlers for the buttons. The first event handler is called if the user presses the cancel button. The statement within this method calls the dispose method of the dialog to close the dialog and free its resources.

The second event handler is called if the user presses the confirm button. To start, it uses an if statement that calls the validateData method shown later in this class. This method makes sure the user entered all required data and that all of the data is valid. If so, the event handler continues by calling the setData method shown later in this class. This method gets the data from the form and sets that data in the product instance variable.

The second if statement in the event handler checks whether the application is editing an existing product or adding a new one. To do that, it checks the text of the confirm button. If the text of the confirm button is “Add”, this code calls the doAdd method shown later in this class. This method adds a new product to the database. However, if the text of the button is not “Add”, this code calls the doEdit method shown later in this class. This method updates an existing product in the database.

The validateData method makes sure that the user has entered data for all three text fields and that the user has entered a valid number for the product price. To start, this code gets String objects for the product code, description, and price variables by calling the getText methods on the corresponding text fields. Then, this code uses an if statement to check whether all three fields in the form contain values. If they don’t, the variables defined earlier are null or empty. In that case, the code uses the JOptionPane class to display a dialog that contains a message that asks the user to fill in all fields. Then, it returns a value of false.

This code also verifies that the price the user entered is a valid number. To do this, it codes a statement that attempts to convert the price string to a double value within a try statement. If this statement isn’t able to convert the string to a double value, it throws a NumberFormatException, which causes the catch block to be executed.

The catch block uses the JOptionPane class to display a dialog that contains a message that informs the user that the data entered in the price field is not a valid price. Then, it attempts to move the focus to the text field for the price. However, this statement might not be able to move the focus. As a result, you shouldn’t count on it working. Finally, the catch block returns a value of false.

If the user has entered data for all three fields, and the price is a valid number, the validateData method returns a value of true. This indicates that the data in the form is valid.

The setData method begins by getting the data contained in the form’s text fields by calling their getText methods. Once again, to get a double value for the price, this code needs to convert the String object returned by the getText method to a double value. Then, this method sets this data in the instance variable for the Product object by using its set methods.

For this method, the code doesn’t catch the NumberFormatException that may be thrown by the parseDouble method because the validateData method shown earlier has already made sure that the user has entered a valid number for the price.

The ProductForm class (continued)

```
private void cancelButtonActionPerformed() {
    dispose();
}

private void confirmButtonActionPerformed() {
    if (validateData()) {
        setData();
        if (confirmButton.getText().equals("Add")) {
            doAdd();
        } else {
            doEdit();
        }
    }
}

private boolean validateData() {
    String code = codeField.getText();
    String name = descriptionField.getText();
    String priceString = priceField.getText();
    double price;
    if (code == null || name == null || priceString == null ||
            code.isEmpty() || name.isEmpty() || priceString.isEmpty()) {
        JOptionPane.showMessageDialog(this, "Please fill in all fields.",
                "Missing Fields", JOptionPane.INFORMATION_MESSAGE);
        return false;
    } else {
        try {
            price = Double.parseDouble(priceString);
        } catch (NumberFormatException e) {
            JOptionPane.showMessageDialog(this,
                    "The data entered in the price field is invalid",
                    "Invalid Price",
                    JOptionPane.INFORMATION_MESSAGE);
            priceField.requestFocusInWindow();
            return false;
        }
    }
    return true;
}

private void setData() {
    String code = codeField.getText();
    String name = descriptionField.getText();
    String priceString = priceField.getText();
    double price = Double.parseDouble(priceString);
    product.setCode(code);
    product.setDescription(name);
    product.setPrice(price);
}
```

Figure 22-10 The ProductForm class (part 3 of 4)

The next two methods, doEdit and doAdd, are almost identical, except that the doEdit method calls the update method of the ProductDB class, and the doAdd method calls the add method of the ProductDB class. Then, these methods both call the dispose method to close the dialog and free its resources. Next, they call the fireDataBaseUpdatedEvent method.

The fireDatabaseUpdatedEvent notifies the main window that a new record has been added to the database or that an existing record has been updated. In turn, the main window notifies the table model that the table data needs to be updated to reflect the changes made to the database as shown in the previous chapter. To do this, the code begins by getting a reference to the parent window of the dialog by calling the getOwner method. However, this method returns a Window object. As a result, this code must cast it to the ProductManagerFrame type before it can call its fireDatabaseUpdatedEvent method.

The ProductForm class (continued)

```
    private void doEdit() {
        try {
            ProductDB.update(product);
            dispose();
            fireDatabaseUpdatedEvent();
        } catch (DBException e) {
            System.out.println(e);
        }
    }

    private void doAdd() {
        try {
            ProductDB.add(product);
            dispose();
            fireDatabaseUpdatedEvent();
        } catch(DBException e) {
            System.out.println(e);
        }
    }

    private void fireDatabaseUpdatedEvent() {
        ProductManagerFrame mainWindow = (ProductManagerFrame) getOwner();
        mainWindow.fireDatabaseUpdatedEvent();
    }
}
```

Figure 22-10 The ProductForm class (part 4 of 4)

Two methods that use the ProductForm class

Figure 22-11 shows the two methods of the ProductManagerFrame class that use the ProductForm class. These methods weren't implemented in the previous chapter, but now you can see how they work. In short, they contain the code that's executed when the user clicks on the Add or Edit button in the main window of the Product Manager application.

The code for the Add button begins by creating a modal Add Product dialog. Then, it attempts to set the location of that dialog so it's relative to the current window. In this case, the current window is the Product Manager window. On Windows, this centers the dialog on the current window. However, this is platform specific, and some operating systems may ignore this method completely.

After attempting to set the location of the dialog, this code uses the setVisible method to display the dialog to the user. As a result, this code displays an Add Product dialog like the one shown earlier in this chapter.

The code for the Edit button begins by getting an index for the selected row from the table of products. If the index is -1, this code uses the JOptionPane class to displays a dialog that contains a message that indicates that no product has been selected. Otherwise, this code gets a Product object that corresponds with the selected row in the table.

After getting a Product object, this code creates a modal Edit Product dialog and passes this Product object to the dialog. This allows the dialog to display the data for the selected product. Then, it attempts to set the location of the dialog relative to the Product Manager window. Finally, it displays the dialog to the user. As a result, this code displays an Edit Product dialog like the one shown earlier in this chapter.

Two methods that use the ProductForm class

```
private void doAddButton() {
    ProductForm productForm = new ProductForm(this, "Add Product", true);
    productForm.setLocationRelativeTo(this);
    productForm.setVisible(true);
}

private void doEditButton() {
    int selectedRow = productTable.getSelectedRow();
    if (selectedRow == -1) {
        JOptionPane.showMessageDialog(this,
                "No product is currently selected.",
                "No product selected",
                JOptionPane.ERROR_MESSAGE);
    } else {
        Product product = productTableModel.getProduct(selectedRow);
        ProductForm productForm =
                new ProductForm(this, "Edit Product", true, product);
        productForm.setLocationRelativeTo(this);
        productForm.setVisible(true);
    }
}
```

Figure 22-11 Two methods that use the ProductForm class

How to use threads with Swing

At this point, you should understand how to code an application like the Product Manager application. However, if you need to perform a long running operation in response to a GUI event, you may run into a problem similar to the one shown in figure 12-12.

A common problem

The first code example calls a method that could potentially take a long time to complete. Because this method was called in response to the user pressing a print button in the GUI, it runs on a special thread known as the *event dispatch thread*, or *EDT*. All actions that are a result of an event run on the EDT, as do all Swing operations that update the display, and respond to events.

Unfortunately, this means that the printProductList method also runs on the EDT, which results in it becoming blocked until the method returns. As a result, it can't process other events, or redraw the screen if required. This causes the application to become unresponsive to any other user events. In addition, the display can become corrupt if it needs to be repainted, such as if it is resized, or minimized and then restored.

At first, you might think you can solve this problem by running the printProductList method on a new thread using the techniques shown in the second code example. Unfortunately, it's unsafe to perform any GUI operations outside of the EDT, so this code causes a new problem, which is that this code runs the JOptionPane dialog on a new thread rather than on the EDT, which can result in display corruption.

How to solve the problem

The solution to this problem is to run the printProductList method on another thread, but perform the GUI updates on the EDT. Fortunately, Swing provides the SwingWorker class for doing just that.

The last code sample in the figure uses the SwingWorker class to solve this problem. To start, this code begins by creating a SwingWorker object using an inner class. Within the inner class, the code overrides the doInBackground method, and calls the printProductList method from it. This method runs on a worker thread, which allows the EDT to continue to process events. Although this method can return an object, this example doesn't need to do that, so it returns a null instead.

The inner class also includes a done method that's called when the doInBackground method finishes. The done method runs on the EDT. As a result, you can safely update the GUI from this method.

The SwingWorker class has other methods as well, including ones that allow you to safely update the GUI before the long running operation has finished. However, these methods aren't covered in this book. For more information, you can view the API documentation for this class or search the Internet.

Code that may cause the GUI to become unresponsive

```
private void doPrintButton() {
    printProductList();    // This method may take a long time to run.
    JOptionPane.showMessageDialog(ProductManagerFrame.this,
        "Product list has been printed.");  // This code updates the GUI.
}
```

Code that keeps the GUI responsive but shouldn't update the GUI

```
private void doPrintButton() {
    Thread printThread = new Thread() {
       // This method runs on a background thread (not the EDT).
       // As a result, the GUI remains responsive.
       // However, it isn't safe to update the GUI from this thread.
       @Override
       public void run() {
            printProductList();  // This method may take a long time to run.
            JOptionPane.showMessageDialog(ProductManagerFrame.this,
                "Product list has been printed.");    // NOT safe!
       }
    };
    printThread.start();
}
```

Code that keeps the GUI responsive and can update the GUI

```
private void doPrintButton() {
    SwingWorker worker = new SwingWorker() {
       // This method runs on a background thread (not the EDT).
       // As a result, the GUI remains responsive.
       @Override
       protected Object doInBackground() throws Exception {
           printProductList();  // This method may take a long time to run.
           return null;
       }

        @Override
        // This method runs on the EDT after the background thread finishes.
        // As a result, it's safe to update the GUI from this method.
        protected void done() {
            JOptionPane.showMessageDialog(ProductManagerFrame.this,
                "Product list has been printed.");    // Safe!
        }
    };
    worker.execute();
}
```

Description

- Any code that runs in response to a Swing event runs on a special thread called the *event dispatch thread* or *EDT*. All code that updates the GUI should run on this thread.
- If you run a task that takes a long time on the EDT, the GUI becomes unresponsive.
- If you use the techniques shown in chapter 18 to start a new thread, the GUI remains responsive. However, you can't safely update the GUI from this new thread.
- To allow the GUI to remain responsive while a long-running task runs and to be able to update the GUI when that task finishes, you can use the SwingWorker class.

Figure 22-12 How to use threads with Swing

Perspective

In this chapter, you learned all of the remaining skills you need to know to complete the Product Manager application. You learned how to use the JLabel and JTextField classes to create labels and text fields for data entry forms. You learned how to work with the GridBagLayout manager to create professional looking forms. You learned how to use the JDialog class to create a modal data entry form. And you learned how to pass data back and forth between two windows in an application.

There's still plenty more to learn about working with Swing. For example, you may want to learn about other types of controls such as check boxes, radio buttons, combo boxes, and lists. You may want to learn how to display photographs or other graphics in Swing. You may want to learn about other layout managers. You may want to learn more about using the SwingWorker class to create threads in Swing. Or, you may want to learn how to use a GUI builder tool that's available from your IDE. Whatever you decide to learn next about Swing, the skills presented in the last two chapters are a solid foundation that you can build on.

Summary

- You can use the JLabel class to create *labels* that label other components on a form.
- You can use the JTextField class to create *text fields*, also known as *text boxes* that allow a user to enter data.
- You can use the GridBagLayout manager to create professional looking form layouts that lay out the components in a grid. This class has two helper classes: GridBagConstraints and Insets.
- You can use the JDialog class to create a *dialog* that stays on top of its parent window.
- A dialog can be *modal*, which means it prevents users from interacting with any other part of the application until they have responded to the dialog. However, you should only use modal dialogs when the application cannot complete an operation until the user responds to the dialog.
- Any code that runs in response to a Swing event runs on a special thread called the *event dispatch thread* or *EDT*.
- To prevent the GUI from becoming unresponsive during long running tasks, as well as make sure GUI updates happen safely on the EDT, you can use the SwingWorker class.

Exercise 22-1 Create a new GUI

In this exercise, you'll create a GUI application that calculates the area and perimeter of a rectangle based on its length and width. When you're done, the application should look like this:

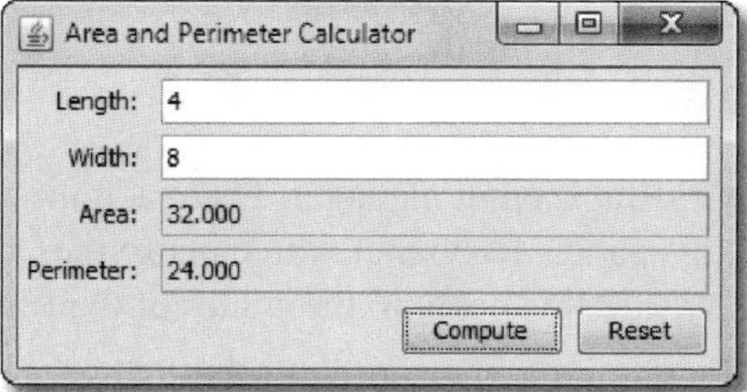

Review the existing code for the application

1. Open the project named ch22_ex1_AreaAndPerimeter_start that's in the ex_starts folder.
2. Open the Rectangle class in the murach.business package and review its fields and methods.
3. Open the AreaAndPerimeterFrame class and examine the existing code. Note that:
   - This class extends the JFrame class.
   - This class has a constructor that sets up the frame and calls the initComponents method.
   - This class contains several methods such as the initComponents method that haven't been implemented.
   - This class contains a getConstraints method that has been implemented. This method works like the getConstraints method shown in this chapter.
4. Open the Main class and note that it creates a new instance of AreaAndPerimeterFrame class.
5. Run the application. This should display a frame that doesn't contain any components. Then, resize the frame to make it larger so you can see its title.

Add the components to the frame

6. Add instance variables for the four text fields and two buttons.

7. Add code to the initComponents method that initializes the frame and its components. This method should:
   - Create the four text fields.
   - Modify the text fields for the area and perimeter so the user can't edit them.
   - Set the minimum and preferred dimension for all four fields.
   - Create the two buttons.
   - Create a panel that uses the GridBagLayout manager. Then, add the four labels and text fields to this panel. To do that, you can use the getConstraints method. Finally, add this panel to the center of the frame.
   - Create a panel that uses the FlowLayout manager with right alignment. Then, add the two buttons to this panel. Finally, add this panel to the bottom of the frame.
   - Pack the frame to set its size.
8. Run the application. This should display a frame that looks like the frame shown above. However, if you click on one of the buttons, it should not perform an action.

Handle the events that occur when the user clicks the buttons

9. Add action listeners to both of the buttons. These action listeners should call the computeButtonClicked and resetButtonClicked methods.
10. Implement the computeButtonClicked method. This method should get the text that the user entered into the text fields for the length and width and attempt to convert this text to double values.
    - If the user enters an invalid length or width, this method should use a dialog to display a user-friendly error message. Then, the user can try again.
    - If the user enters a valid length and width, this method should calculate the area and perimeter and set the corresponding text fields. To do that, you can use the Rectangle class.
11. Implement the resetButtonClicked method. This method should set all four text fields to empty strings.

Appendix A

How to set up Windows for this book

This appendix shows how to install and configure the software that we recommend for developing Java applications on a Windows system. For the first 18 chapters of this book, you only need to install the Java Development Kit (JDK), the NetBeans IDE, and the source code for this book. However, for the last four chapters in this book, you need to install MySQL and MySQL Workbench, and you need to create the database for this book.

As you read this appendix, please remember that most websites are updated constantly. As a result, some of the procedures in this appendix may have changed since this book was published. Nevertheless, these procedures should still be good guides to installing the software. And if there are significant changes, we will post updates on our website (www.murach.com).

How to install the JDK and NetBeans 608
How to install the source code for this book 610
How to install MySQL and MySQL Workbench 612
How to create the database for this book 614
How to restore the database for this book 614

How to install the JDK and NetBeans

Figure A-1 shows how to install the Java Development Kit (JDK) and the NetBeans IDE. To make this easy, the Oracle website provides a single installer program that installs them both.

If you want, you can install these products separately. To do that, you can start by searching the Internet for the download for "Java SE" or "NetBeans". Then, you can find the download for the most current version of the JDK and NetBeans for your operating system.

The code in this book has been tested against Java 8. However, Java is backwards compatible. As a result, the code in this book should work equally well with later versions of Java.

The URL for the JDK and NetBeans download

```
http://www.oracle.com/technetwork/java/javase/downloads
```

Procedure

1. Go to the download page for Java SE. If necessary, you can search the Internet to find this page.
2. Click the Download button for "NetBeans with JDK 8".
3. Follow the instructions for downloading the installer program for your operating system.
4. Save the installer program to your hard disk.
5. Run the installer program by double-clicking on it.
6. Respond to the resulting dialog boxes. When you're prompted for the JDK folder, use the default folder.

The default folder for the JDK for Java SE 8

```
C:\Program Files\Java\jdk1.8.0_45
```

Notes

- For more information about installing the JDK, you can refer to the Oracle website.
- For more information about installing NetBeans, you can refer to the NetBeans website.

Figure A-1 How to install the JDK and NetBeans

How to install the source code for this book

Figure A-2 shows how to download and install the source code for this book. This includes the source code for the applications presented in this book as well the starting points and solutions for the exercises that are at the end of each chapter. When you finish this procedure, you can review the applications presented in this book and you can do the exercises.

The Murach website

www.murach.com

The folders for the book applications and exercises

```
C:\murach\java_netbeans\book_apps
C:\murach\java_netbeans\ex_starts
C:\murach\java_netbeans\ex_solutions
```

Procedure

1. Go to www.murach.com.
2. Find the page for *Murach's Beginning Java with NetBeans*.
3. Click the "FREE Downloads" tab.
4. Click the link to download the exe file for the book applications and exercises. Then, respond to the resulting pages and dialog boxes. This should download an installer file named bjwn_allfiles.exe to your hard drive.
5. Use Windows Explorer to find the exe file on your C drive.
6. Double-click this file and respond to the dialog boxes that follow. This should install the files for this book in folders that start with C:\murach\java_netbeans.

How to use a zip file instead of a self-extracting zip file

- Although we recommend using the self-extracting zip file (bjn1_allfiles.exe) to install the downloadable files as described above, some systems won't allow self-extracting zip files to run. In that case, you can download a regular zip file (bjn1_allfiles.zip) from our website. Then, you can unzip the files stored in this zip file into the C:\murach folder. If the C:\murach folder doesn't already exist, you will need to create it.

Notes for other versions of the JDK

- This source code should work with JDK 1.8 (Java SE 8) or later.
- If you're using an earlier version of the JDK, you can still view the source code, but you won't be able to compile and run applications that use the features of Java introduced with later versions of the JDK.

Figure A-2 How to install the source code for this book

How to install MySQL and MySQL Workbench

Figure A-3 shows how to install all of the software that you'll need to work with a MySQL database. This includes the MySQL Community Server and MySQL Workbench. This software is available for free from the MySQL website. We tested the procedure in this figure against MySQL 5.6 and MySQL Workbench 6.3. However, you should be able to use similar procedures to install earlier and later versions of these products.

When you install MySQL on your computer, you need to specify a password for the root user. When you do, *make sure to remember the password that you enter.* If security isn't a concern for you as you're learning, *we recommend using "sesame" as the password*. That way, the password will be easy to remember.

If you get a "status: failed" message at the end of this installation, you may need to install the Visual C++ 2013 Redistributable Package. To do that, you can go to the MySQL Workbench Prerequisites page shown in this figure and follow the directions there.

MySQL is a database server that's free and easy to use. Since it's designed to run on most modern computers, it's ideal for developers who want to install it on their own computer so they can learn how to work with MySQL databases. That's why the last four chapters of this book assume that you have installed the MySQL server on your computer as shown in this figure.

MySQL Workbench is a free graphical tool that makes it easy to work with MySQL databases. Since MySQL Workbench is an ideal tool for working with MySQL, it is bundled with the Community Server in one convenient installation package.

However, if you want to install MySQL or MySQL Workbench separately, you can do that too. For example, if you want to install the latest version of MySQL Workbench, you can do that by searching the Internet for "MySQL Workbench" to find the download for the latest version. Then, you can download it and install it.

All of the skills for working with MySQL Workbench that are presented in this book were tested against version 6.3. As a result, if you're using this version of MySQL Workbench, these skills should work exactly as described. However, MySQL Workbench is being actively developed and is changing quickly. As a result, if you're using a later version of MySQL Workbench, these skills may not work exactly as described, but they should work similarly.

The URL for the MySQL Installer download

```
http://dev.mysql.com/downloads/installer/
```

Procedure

1. Find the download page for the MySQL Installer for Windows. This page is currently available at the URL shown above. If necessary, you can search the Internet for "MySQL Installer for Windows".
2. Follow the instructions provided on that web page to download the installer file to your hard drive.
3. Find the installer file on your hard drive and run it.
4. Respond to the resulting dialog boxes. You can accept most of the default options, but you should specify a password for the root user. *Make sure to remember the password that you enter.* If security isn't a concern for you as you're learning, *we recommend using "sesame" as the password.*
5. To make sure that the database has been installed correctly, start MySQL Workbench when the installation is finished. Then, use the password you entered in the previous step to log in to the database server as the root user.

The default installation folder for MySQL 5.6

```
C:\Program Files\MySQL\MySQL Server 5.6
```

Recommended username and password

Username: root
Password: sesame

The URL for the MySQL Workbench Prerequisites

```
http://dev.mysql.com/resources/wb62_prerequisites.html
```

How to install the MySQL Workbench Prerequisites

1. Find the download page for the MySQL Workbench Prerequisites. This page is currently available at the URL shown above. If necessary, you can search the Internet for "MySQL Workbench Prerequisites".
2. Follow the instructions provided on that web page to download the installer file to your hard drive.
3. Find the installer file on your hard drive and run it.

Notes

- If you get a "status: failed" message when trying to install or upgrade to MySQL Workbench 6.3 using the MySQL installer, you may need to install the Visual C++ 2013 Redistributable Package. The MySQL Workbench Prerequisites page has directions and links for doing that.
- You can also install MySQL Server and MySQL Workbench separately. For more information about that, you can visit the Downloads page of the MySQL website.
- To make it easy to start MySQL Workbench, you may want to pin the program to your taskbar or add a shortcut to your desktop.

Figure A-3 How to install MySQL and MySQL Workbench

How to create the database for this book

If an application uses a database, you must create the database before the application can work correctly. For example, the application at the end of this book uses a database named mma. The easiest way to create this database is to use MySQL Workbench to run the SQL script shown in figure A-4. If you downloaded the source code for this book as described earlier in this appendix, this script should be in the folder shown in this figure.

To determine if the SQL script ran successfully, you can review the results in the Output window. In this figure, for example, the Output window shows as a series of statements that have executed successfully. In addition, the Navigator window shows that the database named mma has been created.

However, if the script encounters problems, MySQL Workbench displays one or more errors in the Output window. Then, you can read these errors to figure out why the script isn't executing correctly.

Before you can run the create_database.sql script, the database server must be running. When you install MySQL on most systems, the MySQL database server starts every time you start your computer, which is usually what you want. However, if it isn't running on your system, you can use the Server Administration tab of MySQL Workbench to start it. To do that, click on the Home tab, click on the Startup / Shutdown item, and use the resulting screen to start the server. Or, if SQL Notifier is available on your system, you can use that to start the MySQL server.

How to restore the database for this book

As you work with the applications that are presented in this book, you may make changes to the database or its tables that you didn't intend to make. In that case, you may want to restore the database to its original state so your results match the results shown in this book. To do that, you can run the create_database.sql file again. This drops the database described in this figure and recreates it.

The script that creates the database

```
C:\murach\java_netbeans\db\create_database.sql
```

MySQL Workbench after executing the create_database.sql file

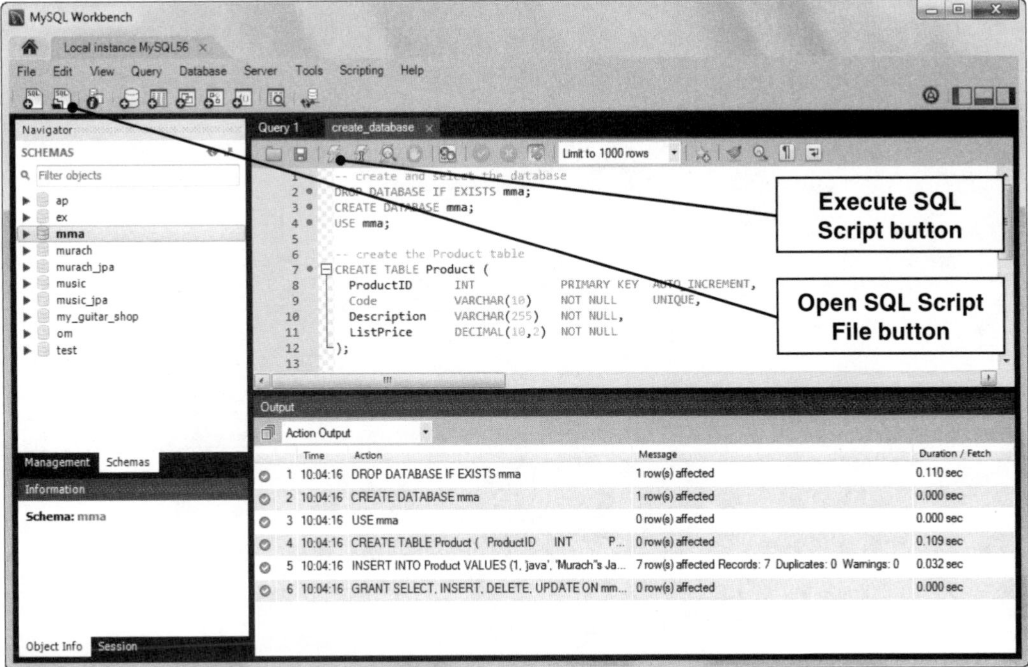

How to create the database

1. Start MySQL Workbench.
2. Connect as the root user to an instance of MySQL that's running on the localhost computer. To do that, double-click on the stored connection named "Local instance MySQL56" and enter the password for the root user if prompted.
3. Open the script file by clicking the Open SQL Script File button in the SQL Editor toolbar. Then, use the resulting dialog box to locate and open the create_database.sql file. When you do, MySQL Workbench displays this script in a code editor tab.
4. Execute the script by clicking the Execute SQL Script button in the code editor toolbar. When you do, the Output window displays messages that indicate whether the script executed successfully.

How to restore the database

- Run the create_database.sql script again to drop the database and recreate it.

Description

- For the create_database.sql file to run, the database server must be running. By default, the database server is automatically started when your start your computer. If it isn't running on your system, you can use MySQL Notifier to start it.

Figure A-4 How to create and restore the database for this book

Appendix B

How to set up Mac OS X for this book

This appendix shows how to install and configure the software that we recommend for developing Java applications on a Mac OS X system. For the first 18 chapters of this book, you only need to install the Java Development Kit (JDK), the NetBeans IDE, and the source code for this book. However, for the last four chapters in this book, you need to install MySQL and MySQL Workbench, and you need to create the database for this book.

As you read this appendix, please remember that most websites are updated constantly. As a result, some of the procedures in this appendix may have changed since this book was published. Nevertheless, these procedures should still be good guides to installing the software. And if there are significant changes, we will post updates on our website (www.murach.com).

How to install the JDK and Netbeans 618
How to install the source code for this book 620
How to install the MySQL Community Server 622
How to install MySQL Workbench 624
How to create the databases for this book 626
How to restore the databases 626
How to update the password for the root user 628

How to install the JDK and Netbeans

Figure B-1 shows how to install the Java Development Kit (JDK) and the NetBeans IDE. For convenience, you can install them as one package. To start, click on the "NetBeans with JDK 8" button to download the dmg file for the installer program. Then, run the installer program, and respond to the resulting dialog boxes.

By the way, all of the examples in this book have been tested against Java 8. Since Java has a good track record of being backwards compatible, these examples should work equally well with later versions of the JDK.

The URL for the JDK and NetBeans download

```
http://www.oracle.com/technetwork/java/javase/downloads/index.html
```

Procedure

1. Go to the download page for Java SE. If necessary, you can search the Internet to find this page.
2. Click on the Download button for "NetBeans with JDK 8".
3. Follow the instructions for downloading the installer program for your operating system.
4. Save the installer program to your hard disk.
5. Run the installer program by double-clicking on it.
6. Respond to the resulting dialog boxes. When you're prompted for the JDK folder, use the default folder.

The default folder for the JDK for Java SE 8

```
/Library/Java/JavaVirtualMachines/jdk1.8.0_45
```

Notes

- For more information about installing the JDK, you can refer to the Oracle website.
- For more information about installing NetBeans, you can refer to the NetBeans website.

Figure B-1 How to install the JDK and NetBeans

How to install the source code for this book

Figure B-2 shows how to download and install the source code for this book. This includes the source code for the applications that are presented in this book as well as the source code for the starting points and solutions for the exercises that are presented at the end of each chapter.

When you finish this procedure, the book applications, exercise starts, and exercise solutions should be in the folders that are shown in this figure. Then, you can review the applications that are presented in this book, and you'll be ready to do the exercises in this book.

As you read this book, you'll notice that it often instructs you to right-click, which is a common technique on PCs. On a Mac, right-clicking is not enabled by default. Instead, you can use the Ctrl-click instead of the right-click. Or, if you prefer, you can enable right-clicking by editing the system preferences for your mouse. Then, you can follow the instructions in this book more closely.

The Murach website

www.murach.com

The folders for the book applications and exercises

```
/murach/java_netbeans/book_apps
/murach/java_netbeans/ex_starts
/murach/java_netbeans/ex_solutions
```

Procedure

1. Go to www.murach.com.
2. Find the page for *Murach's Beginning Java with NetBeans.*
3. Click the "FREE Downloads" tab.
4. Click on the link to download the zip file for the book applications and exercises. Then, respond to the resulting pages and dialog boxes. This should download a zip file named bjwn_allfiles.zip to your hard drive.
5. Use the Finder to locate the zip file on your hard drive, and double-click on it to unzip it. This creates the java_netbeans folder and its subfolders.
6. If necessary, use the Finder to create the murach folder directly on your hard drive.
7. Use the Finder to move the java_netbeans folder into the murach folder.

A note about right-clicking

- This book often instructs you to right-click, because that's common in Windows. On a Mac, right-clicking is not enabled by default. However, you can enable right-clicking by editing the system preferences for your mouse.

Notes for other versions of the JDK

- This source code should work with JDK 1.8 (Java SE 8) or later.
- If you're using an earlier version of the JDK, you can still view the source code, but you won't be able to compile and run applications that use the features of Java introduced with later versions of the JDK.

Figure B-2 How to install the source code for this book

How to install the MySQL Community Server

MySQL Community Server is a database server that's free and easy to use. Since it's designed to run on most modern computers, it's ideal for developers who want to install it on their own computer so they can learn how to work with a MySQL database. That's why this book assumes that you have installed the Community Server on your computer as shown in figure B-3.

When you install the Community Server on your computer, the root user is created automatically so you can log in to the server. However, a password isn't assigned to this user by default. In other words, the server is not secure. If you want to secure the server, you can assign a password to the root user as described later in this appendix.

In addition to the server itself, the download for MySQL Community Server includes the MySQL preference pane. You can use the MySQL preference pane shown in this figure to start and stop the server and to control whether the MySQL server starts automatically when you start your computer.

All of the SQL statements presented in this book have been tested against the MySQL Community Server 5.6. As a result, you can use the statements presented in this book to work with this version of the database. Since MySQL is backwards compatible, these statements should also work with future versions of MySQL. In addition, most statements presented in this book work with earlier versions of MySQL, and we have done our best to identify any statements that don't.

The URL for downloading the MySQL Community Server

```
http://dev.mysql.com/downloads/mysql/
```

How to download and install the MySQL Community Server

1. Find the download page for the MySQL Community Server. This page is currently available at the URL shown above. If necessary, you can search the Internet for "MySQL Community Server download".
2. Follow the instructions provided on that web page to download the appropriate disk image (DMG) file for your operating system to your hard drive.
3. Find the DMG file on your hard drive and double-click it. This opens a window with a package (PKG) file in it with a filename like mysql-5.6.25-osx10.9-x86_64.pkg.
4. Double-click the PKG file for MySQL, and respond to the resulting dialog boxes to install it.
5. Make sure MySQL has been installed correctly by going to System Preferences under the Apple menu and clicking on the MySQL icon. If the MySQL preference pane indicates that the server is running or if you can start the server, MySQL is installed correctly.

The MySQL preference pane

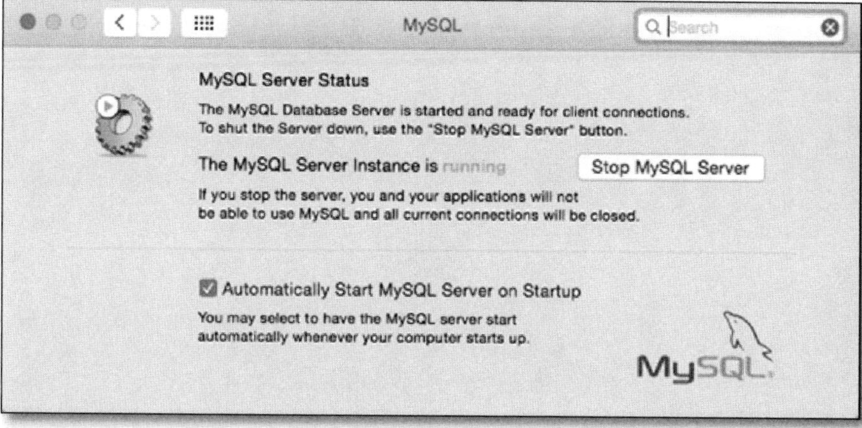

Description

- You can use the MySQL preference pane to start and stop MySQL and to control whether MySQL starts automatically when you start your computer.
- To display the MySQL preference pane, use the Apple menu to display the System Preferences dialog box. Then, click the MySQL icon.

Figure B-3 How to install the MySQL Community Server

How to install MySQL Workbench

MySQL Workbench is a free graphical tool that makes it easier to work with MySQL databases. To install MySQL Workbench, you can use the first procedure in figure B-4.

After you install MySQL Workbench, you should make sure that it's configured for use with this book. To do that, you may need to add a connection as described in the second procedure in this figure.

All of the skills for working with MySQL Workbench that are presented in this book were tested against version 6.3. As a result, if you're using this version of MySQL Workbench, these skills should work exactly as described. However, MySQL Workbench is being actively developed and is changing quickly. As a result, if you're using a later version of MySQL Workbench, these skills may not work exactly as described, but they should work similarly.

The URL for downloading MySQL Workbench

```
http://dev.mysql.com/downloads/workbench/
```

How to download and install MySQL Workbench

1. Find the download page for MySQL Workbench. This page is currently available at the URL shown above. If necessary, you can search the Internet for "MySQL Workbench download".
2. Follow the instructions provided on that web page to download the disk image (DMG) file for MySQL Workbench.
3. Find the DMG file on your hard drive and double-click on it. Then, respond to the resulting dialog boxes.

How to configure MySQL Workbench for this book

1. Start MySQL Workbench.
2. If the MySQL Connection section of the Home tab contains a connection named "localhost", you can use that connection to code and run SQL statements.
3. If the MySQL Connections section doesn't include a connection, you'll need to create one so you can use it to code and run SQL statements. To do that, click the + icon to the right of MySQL Connections section. Then, enter "Local instance MySQL56" for the connection name in the resulting dialog box and click the OK button.

Notes

- Although you can use any names you want for the connections you create in MySQL Workbench, "Local instance MySQL56" is the name of the default connection that is created on a Windows system for MySQL version 5.6, and that's the name we use in this book.
- To make it easy to start MySQL Workbench, you may want to keep this application in your dock.

Figure B-4 How to install MySQL Workbench

How to create the databases for this book

Before you can run the SQL statements presented in this book, you need to create the three databases described in the previous figure. The easiest way to do that is to use MySQL Workbench to run the SQL script that's stored in the create_databases.sql file. The procedure for doing this is described in figure B-5.

To determine if the SQL script ran successfully, you can review the results in the Output window. In this figure, for example, the Output window shows a series of statements that have executed successfully. In addition, the Object Browser window shows that the three databases have been created. The other database, named Test, is a database that comes with MySQL.

If the script encounters problems, MySQL Workbench displays one or more errors in the Output window. Then, you can read these errors to figure out why the script isn't executing correctly.

Before you can run the create_databases.sql script, the database server must be running. By default, the database server is automatically started when you start your computer, so this usually isn't a problem. However, if it isn't running on your system, you can start it as described in figure B-3.

How to restore the databases

As you work with the code that's presented in this book, you may make changes to the databases or tables that you don't intend to make. In that case, you may want to restore the databases to their original state so your results match the results shown in this book. To do that, you can run the create_databases.sql file again. This drops the three databases described in this appendix and recreates them.

The script that creates the database

/murach/java_netbeans/db/create_database.sql

MySQL Workbench after executing the create_database.sql file

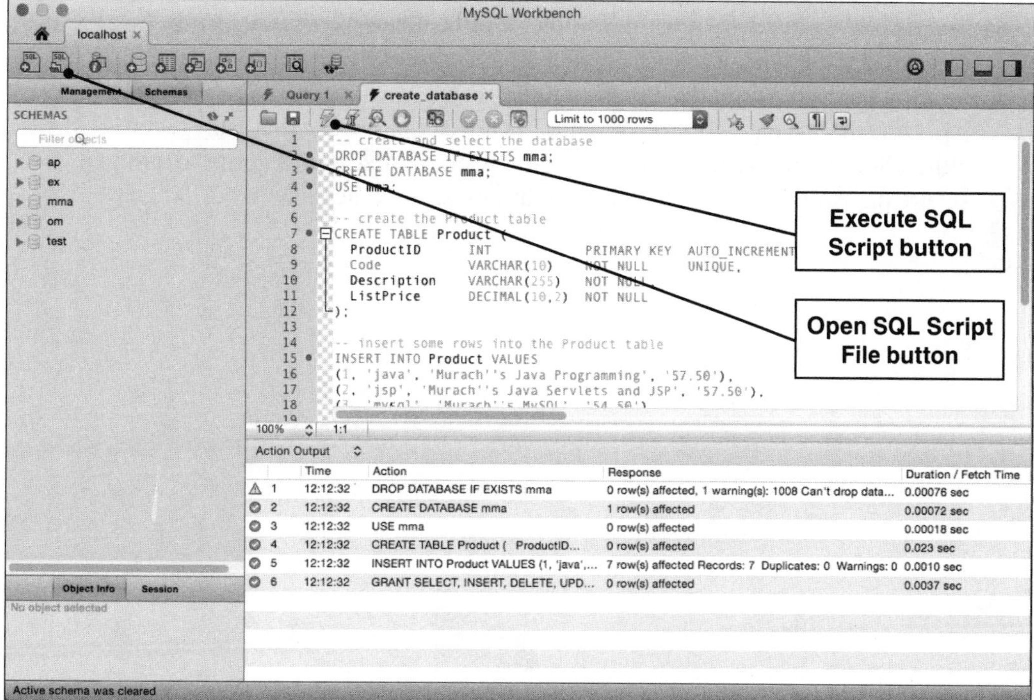

How to create the database

1. Start MySQL Workbench.
2. Connect as the root user to an instance of MySQL that's running on the localhost computer. To do that, double-click on the stored connection named "Local instance MySQL56" and enter the password for the root user if prompted.
3. Open the script file by clicking the Open SQL Script File button in the SQL Editor toolbar. Then, use the resulting dialog box to locate and open the create_database.sql file. When you do, MySQL Workbench displays this script in a code editor tab.
4. Execute the script by clicking the Execute SQL Script button in the code editor toolbar. When you do, the Output window displays messages that indicate whether the script executed successfully.

How to restore the database

- Run the create_database.sql script again to drop the database and recreate it.

Description

- For the create_database.sql file to run, the database server must be running. By default, the database server is automatically started when your start your computer. If it isn't running on your system, you start it as described in figure B-3.

Figure B-5 How to create and restore the database for this book

How to update the password for the root user

When you install the Community Server on your computer, the root user is created automatically so you can log in to the server. However, a password isn't assigned to this user by default. In other words, the server is not secure. As a result, we recommend that you assign a password of "sesame" to the root user by running the SQL script described in figure B-6.

Of course, a password of "sesame" is a weak password that isn't secure either. So, for a production system, you'd want to modify this script to assign a secure password to the root user that can't be easily cracked.

The script that updates the password

```
/murach/java_netbeans/db/update_root_password.sql
```

Procedure

1. Start MySQL Workbench.
2. Connect as the root user to an instance of MySQL that's running on the localhost computer. To do that, click on the stored connection for the root user. Since a password hasn't been assigned to the root user, you don't need to enter a password.
3. Open the update_root_password.sql file by clicking the Open SQL Script File button in the SQL Editor toolbar and navigating to the /murach/java_netbeans/db folder.
4. Click the Execute SQL Script button. This should update the root password to "sesame".
5. Use the MySQL preference pane shown earlier in this appendix to stop and start the MySQL server.

Description

- By default, the root user doesn't have a password. This is not secure.
- For this book, you can run a script like the one shown in this figure to change the password for the root user to "sesame".
- For a production system, you can modify the script shown in this figure to make the password for the root user more secure.

Figure B-6 How to update the password for the root user

Index

- operator, 174-177
-- operator, 176, 177
! operator, 200, 201
!= operator, 79, 198, 199
% operator, 174, 175
%= operator, 178, 179
& operator, 200, 201
&& operator, 200, 201
* operator, 174, 175
*= operator, 178, 179
/ operator, 174, 175
/= operator, 178, 179
@author tag (javadoc), 346, 347
@Override annotation, 280, 281
@param tag (javadoc), 346, 347
@return tag (javadoc), 346, 347
@version tag (javadoc), 346, 347
| operator, 200, 201
|| operator, 200, 201
+ operator
    numbers, 174-177
    strings, 52, 53
++ operator, 176, 177
+= operator, 178, 179
< operator, 79, 198, 199
<= operator, 79, 198, 199
<> operator (generics), 362, 363
<code> tag (HTML), 346, 347
-= operator, 178, 179
-> operator (lambda), 382, 383
== operator, 79, 198, 199
> operator, 79, 198, 199
>= operator, 79, 198, 199

A

Absolute path name, 436, 437
abstract class, 298, 299
    advantages, 310, 311
    compared to interfaces, 310, 311
abstract keyword, 298, 299
abstract method, 298, 299
Abstract Window Toolkit (AWT), 334, 335, 532-535
AbstractTableModel class, 548, 549
Access modifier, 32, 33, 100, 101, 108, 109, 280, 281
Accessors (set and get), 108, 109
Action listener, 540, 541
ActionListener interface, 338, 339
actionPerformed method, 540, 541
add method (ArrayList), 366, 367
add method (BigDecimal), 186, 187
add method (BorderLayout), 546, 547
add method (JFrame, JPanel), 538, 539
addActionListener method, 540, 541
Adding records to tables, 500, 501
Addition operator, 174, 175
    compound, 178, 179
Adjuster (date/time), 400, 401
anchor field (GridBagConstraints), 580, 581
And operator, 200, 201
Android app, 12, 13
Android Studio IDE, 18, 19
Annotation (@Override), 280, 281
Anonymous class, 338, 339
Anonymous functions (lambda), 378, 379
API documentation, 66, 67
Append
    data to a file, 446, 447
    data to a string, 52, 53, 234, 235
append method (StringBuilder), 242, 243
Applet, 10, 11
Application, 8, 9
Argument, 36, 37, 64, 65
    sending to method, 112, 113
Arithmetic expression, 50, 51, 174, 175
Arithmetic operators, 50, 51, 174, 175
Array
    assigning values to, 256, 257
    comparing, 266, 267
    compared to a collection, 358, 359
    copying, 266, 267
    creating, 254, 255
    creating references to, 266, 267
    referring to elements, 256, 257
Array list, 360, 361, 364, 365
Array of arrays, 262, 263
ArrayIndexOutOfBoundsException, 256, 257
ArrayList class (java.util), 360, 361, 364-369
    constructor, 364, 365
Arrays class, 264, 265
ASCII character set, 168, 169
Assign
    value to variable, 170, 171
    values to array elements, 256, 257
Assignment operator, 170, 171
Assignment statement, 46-49, 120, 121
Asynchronous thread, 476, 477
Augmented assignment operator, 178, 179
Autoboxing, 358, 359, 370, 371
AutoCloseable interface (java.lang), 416, 417
Autoflush feature, 444, 445
Automatic driver loading, 508, 509
AWT (Abstract Window Toolkit), 334, 335, 532-535

B

Base class, 276, 277
BigDecimal class, 186-189
Binary file, 438, 439
Binary operator, 174, 175
Binary stream, 438, 439
binarySearch method (Arrays class), 264, 265
Bit, 168, 169
BLOB objects (Binary Large Objects), 512, 513
Block comment, 34, 35
Block of code, 32, 33, 202, 203
Block scope, 80-83, 202, 203
Blocked state (thread), 468, 469
Blocking (dialog box), 558, 559
Boolean
  expression, 78, 79, 198-201
  type, 168, 169
  value, 78, 79, 198, 199
  variable, 198, 199
BorderLayout manager, 542, 543, 546, 547
BoxLayout manager, 542, 543
break statement, 206-208
  with loops, 218, 219
Breakpoints (debugging), 156, 157
Buffer, 440, 441
Buffered
  input stream, 448, 449
  output stream, 444, 445
  stream, 440, 441
BufferedReader class (java.io), 448-451
BufferedWriter class (java.io), 444, 445
Built-in dialog box, 558, 559
Business classes, 132, 133
Business objects, 132, 133
Business tier, 132, 133
Button
  add to panel, 538, 539
  handle event, 540, 541
byte type, 168, 169
Bytecodes, 16, 17

C

C# (compared to Java), 6, 7
C++ (compared to Java), 6, 7
Call stack, 412, 413
  debugging, 160, 161
Calling
  methods, 64, 65, 112, 113
  static fields, 122, 123
  static methods, 122, 123
Camel case, 170, 171
Camel notation, 46
CANCEL_OPTION (JOptionPane), 562, 563
capacity method (StringBuilder class), 242, 243
CardLayout manager, 542, 543
Case label (switch statement), 206-208
Case structure, 206, 207
Case-sensitive language, 48, 49
Casting, 50, 51, 182, 183
  objects, 294, 295
catch block, 222, 223
catch clause (try statement), 414, 415
Catching an exception, 70, 71, 220-223, 414, 415
Central processing unit (CPU), 464, 465
char type, 168, 169
Character
  input stream, 448, 449
  output stream, 444, 445
  stream, 438, 439
charAt method (String), 236, 237
charAt method (StringBuilder), 244, 245
Checked exception, 410, 411, 426, 427
  throwing, 422, 423
Child class, 276, 277
ChronoUnit enumeration, 400, 401
Class, 14-17, 32, 33
  declaration, 32, 33
  diagram, 96, 97, 138, 139
  documentation, 344, 345
  field, 116, 117
  importing, 62, 63
  instance of, 64, 65
  method, 116, 117
  storing in packages, 134-137
  structuring an app with, 132, 133
Class class, 508, 509
ClassCastException (java.lang), 294, 295
clear method (ArrayList class), 368, 369
CLOB (Character Large Object), 512, 513
clone method (Object class), 278, 279
Close a project (NetBeans), 26, 27
close method (BufferedReader class), 450, 451
close method (PrintWriter class), 446, 447
close method (ResultSet), 510, 511
CLOSED_OPTION (JOptionPane), 562, 563
Code completion feature, 42, 43
Code editor, 22, 23, 38-41
Code execution (tracing), 154, 155
code tag (HTML), 346, 347
Coding error, 150, 151
Collection, 358-361
  compared to an array, 358, 359
Collection framework, 360, 361
Collection interface (java.util), 360, 361
Column
  database, 484, 485, 488, 489
  file, 446, 447
Command prompt, 8, 9

Comment
  end-of-line, 34, 35
  single-line, 34, 35
  coding, 34, 35
  javadoc, 344, 345
Comparable interface, 264, 265
compareTo method, 396, 397
Comparing
  objects, 296, 297
  primitive types, 198, 199
  variables, 78, 79
Compile a project (NetBeans), 24, 25
Compiler (Java), 16, 17
Compile-time error, 148, 149
Component, 532, 533
  hierarchy, 534, 535
  grid, 580, 581
Component class (java.awt), 534, 535
Compound assignment operator, 178, 179
Concatenate strings, 52, 53, 234, 235
Concurrency (threads), 476, 477
Confirm an operation (JOptionPane), 560, 561
Connect to a database, 508, 509
Connector/J driver, 506, 507
Console, 8, 9
  input, 68, 69
  output, 36, 37
Console application, 8, 9, 532, 533
Constant, 172, 173
  in an enumeration, 340, 341
  in an interface, 309
Constructor, 64, 65, 102, 103
  coding, 106, 107
Container class (java.awt), 534, 535
contains method (ArrayList class), 368, 369
continue statement (with loops), 218, 219
Control statements, 78-83
Convert
  numbers to strings, 74, 75
  strings to numbers, 70, 71
copyOf method (Arrays class), 266, 267
Counter variable, 212, 213
  while loop, 80
CPU (central processing unit), 464, 465
CREATE DATABASE statement (SQL), 496, 497
CREATE TABLE statement (SQL), 496, 497
Create user (SQL), 496, 497
createDirectories method (Files class), 434, 435
createDirectory method (Files class), 434, 435
createFile method (Files class), 434, 435
Current row pointer (SQL), 498, 499
Current working directory (CWD), 436, 437
currentThread method (Thread class), 471, 474, 475
Cursor, 510, 511
  result set (SQL), 498, 499
Custom exception classes, 426-429

D

Data
  append to file, 446, 447
  delete from table, 514, 515
  get from a result set, 512, 513
  insert into table, 496, 497, 514, 515
  pass between form and dialog, 588, 589
  update table, 514, 515
Data Definition Language (DDL), 498
Data entry form, 586, 587
Data hiding, 96
Data Manipulation Language (DML), 498
Data type (declaring), 46, 47
Database (SQL)
  create on Mac, 626, 627
  create on Windows, 614, 615
  restore on Mac, 626, 627
  restore on Windows, 614, 615
Database, 484, 485, 492, 493
  connecting to, 508, 509
  create (SQL), 496, 497
  drop (SQL), 496, 497
  select (SQL), 496, 497
Database connection, 494, 495
Database drivers, 506, 507
Database management system (DBMS), 484, 485
Database server, 494, 495
Database tier, 132, 133
Date/time APIs, 390-403
Date/time objects, 392, 393
  adjust, 398, 399
  compare, 396, 397
  format, 402, 403
DayOfWeek enumeration, 392, 393
DB2, 484, 485
DBMS (database management system), 484, 485
DDL (Data Definition Language), 498
Debugger, 156-161
Debugging applications, 148, 149
Declare
  array, 254, 255
  classes, 32, 33
  enumerations, 340, 341
  typed collection, 362, 363
  variable, 46, 47, 170, 171
Decrement operator, 176, 177
Deep copy (array), 266, 267
Default constructor, 106, 107
Default label (switch statement), 206, 207
Default methods (interface), 322, 323
Default value (database), 488, 489
DEFAULT_OPTION (JOptionPane), 560, 561

Delete
  files, 434, 435
  projects from NetBeans, 26, 27
  records from tables, 500, 501, 514, 515
delete method (Files class), 434, 435
delete method (StringBuilder class), 244, 245
DELETE statement (SQL), 500, 501, 514, 515
deleteCharAt method (StringBuilder class), 244, 245
Delimited text file, 446, 447
Delimiter, 446, 447
Derived class, 276, 277
Desktop application, 8, 9
Diagram (class), 96, 97
Dialog box, 586, 587
  built-in, 558, 559
  passing data to form, 588, 589
Diamond operator, 362, 363
Dimension, 584, 585
Directories (working with), 434-437
divide method (BigDecimal class), 186, 187
Division operator, 174, 175
  compound, 178, 179
DML (Data Manipulation Language), 498
Documentation
  API, 66, 67
  class, 344, 345
  generating, 348, 349
  viewing, 348, 349
Double class, 70, 71
double data type, 46, 47, 168, 169
Double-precision number, 168, 169
doubleValue method (BigDecimal class), 186, 187
do-while loop, 214, 215
DriverManager class, 508, 509
Drivers (database), 506, 507
DROP DATABASE statement (SQL), 496, 497

E

Eating exceptions, 416
Eclipse IDE, 18, 19
EDT (event dispatch thread), 602, 603
EE (Enterprise Edition), 4, 5
Elements
  array, 254, 255
  assigning values, 256, 257
Empty string, 52, 53
Encapsulation, 96, 97
End-of-line comment, 34, 35
endsWith method (String), 236, 237
Enhanced for loop (array), 260, 261
Enum class (java.lang), 342, 343
enum keyword, 340, 341
Enumeration, 340, 341
Enumeration type, 342, 343
EOFException (java.io), 442, 443
Equality operator, 79, 198, 199
equals method (Arrays class), 266, 267
equals method (Object class), 278, 279, 296, 297
equals method (String class), 78, 79, 236, 237
equals method (overriding), 296, 297
equalsIgnoreCase method (String class), 78, 79, 236, 237
Error
  coding, 150, 151
  compile-time, 152, 153
  determining cause of, 152, 153
  Java, 150, 151
  logic, 152, 153
  runtime, 152, 153
  syntax, 150, 151
Error class (java.lang), 410, 411
ERROR_MESSAGE (JOptionPane), 558, 559
Escape sequences, 54, 55
Event, 334, 335
  handler, 540, 541
  listener, 540, 541
Event dispatch thread (EDT), 602, 603
Exception, 70, 71, 220, 221, 410, 411
  catching, 70, 71, 414, 415, 220-223
  chaining, 428, 429
  checked, 426, 427
  custom, 426-429
  eating, 416
  handling, 70, 71
  hierarchy, 220, 221
  multi-catch, 420, 421
  propagation, 412, 413
  swallowing, 416
  throwing, 70, 71, 412, 413, 422, 423
  try-with-resources, 416, 417
  unchecked, 426, 427
  when to throw, 424, 425
Exception class (java.lang), 410, 411
  creating, 426-429
Exception handler, 220- 222, 410- 413
  testing, 424, 425
executeUpdate method, 514, 515
Execution (tracing), 154, 155
exists method (Files class), 434, 435
EXIT_ON_CLOSE value, 536, 537
Explicit cast, 182, 183
Extend a class, 276, 277, 282, 283
extends keyword, 282, 283, 316, 317

F

Falls through (switch statement), 208, 209
Field,
  class, 96, 97, 102-105
  database, 484, 485
  file, 446, 447, 574, 575
File I/O, 438, 439
FileNotFoundException (java.io), 442, 443
FileReader class (java.io), 448, 449
Files (working with), 434-437
Files class (java.nio.file), 434-437
FileWriter class (java.io), 444, 445
fill method (Arrays class), 264, 265
final class, 300, 301
final keyword, 172, 173, 300, 301
final method, 300, 301
final parameter, 300, 301
final variable, 172, 173
finally clause (try statement), 414, 415
fireTableDataChanged method, 548, 549
Fixed-width layout, 542, 543
float type, 168, 169
Floating-point number, 168, 169
FlowLayout manager, 542-545
  constructor, 544, 545
flush method (PrintWriter class), 446, 447
flushing the buffer, 440, 441
Folders (working with), 434-437
for loop, 216, 217
  array, 258, 259
for statement, 216, 217
  array, 258, 259
foreach loop, 260, 261
Foreign key, 486, 487
Form, 534, 535, 586, 587
  data entry, 586, 587
format method (DateTimeFormatter), 402, 403
format method (NumberFormat), 74, 75
formatStyle.FULL constant, 402, 403
formatStyle.LONG constant, 402, 403
formatStyle.MEDIUM constant, 402, 403
formatStyle.SHORT constant, 402, 403
forName method (Class class), 508, 509
Forward-only result set, 510, 511
Frame class (java.awt), 534, 535
Frame, 334, 335, 534-537
  add panel, 538, 539
  how to display, 536, 537
FROM clause (SELECT statement), 498, 499
Function (lambda), 378, 379
Functional interface (lambda), 382, 383

G

Generics, 362, 363
get accessor, 108, 109
get method, 102, 103, 108, 109
  ArrayList class, 366, 367
  Paths class, 434-437
getClass method (Object), 278, 279
getColumnCount method, 548, 549
getColumnName method, 548, 549
getConnection method, 508, 509
getCurrencyInstance method (NumberFormat), 74, 75
getDayOfMonth method, 394, 395
getDayOfWeek method, 394, 395
getDayOfYear method, 394, 395
getFileName method (Path), 435
getHour method, 394, 395
getMessage method (Throwable), 418, 419
getMinute method, 394, 395
getMonth method, 394, 395
getMonthValue method, 394, 395
getName method (Path), 435
getName method (Thread), 471
getNameCount method (Path), 435
getNano method, 394, 395
getNumberInstance method (NumberFormat), 74, 75
getOwner method (Window), 588, 589
getParent method (Path), 435
getPercentInstance method (NumberFormat),74, 75
getRoot method (Path), 435
getRowCount method (AbstractTableModel), 548, 549
getSecond method, 394, 395
getSelectedRow method (JTable), 554, 555
getSelectedRows method (JTable), 554, 555
getText method (JTextField), 576, 577
getValueAt method (AbstractTableModel), 548, 549
getYear method, 394, 395
Grant privileges (SQL), 496, 497
GRANT statement (SQL), 496, 497
Graphical user interface (GUI), 334, 335, 532, 533
Greater Than operator, 79, 198, 199
Greater Than Or Equal operator, 79, 198, 199
GridBagConstraints, 578-581
GridBagLayout, 542, 543, 578, 579
gridheight field (GridBagConstraints), 580, 581
GridLayout manager, 542, 543
gridwidth field (GridBagConstraints), 580, 581
gridx field (GridBagConstraints), 580, 581
gridy field (GridBagConstraints), 580, 581
GUI (graphical user interface), 8, 9, 334, 335, 532, 533
  unresponsive problem, 602, 603

H

HALF_DOWN (RoundingMode), 186, 187
HALF_EVEN (RoundingMode), 186, 187
HALF_UP (RoundingMode), 186, 187
Handle exception, 70, 71
Hash code, 278, 279
hashCode method (Object class), 278, 279
HashMap class (java.util), 360, 361
HashSet class (java.util), 360, 361
Horizontal resizing problem, 584, 585
HORIZONTAL_SCROLLBAR_ALWAYS, 556, 557
HORIZONTAL_SCROLLBAR_AS_NEEDED, 556, 557
HORIZONTAL_SCROLLBAR_NEVER, 556, 557
HTML documentation
  generating, 348, 349
  viewing, 348, 349
HTML tags (in javadoc), 346, 347

I

I/O exceptions, 442, 443
I/O operations, 438, 439
IDE (Integrated Development Environment), 18, 19
Identifier, 150, 151
Identity of an object, 98, 99
if/else statement, 82, 83, 202-205
  nested, 82, 83, 204, 205
IllegalArgumentException (java.lang), 424, 425
Immutable strings, 242, 243
Implementing interfaces, 308, 309, 314-316
implements keyword, 314, 315
Implicit cast, 182, 183
import statement, 62, 63
  static, 342, 343
Increment operator, 176, 177
Index
  array, 256, 257
  string, 238, 239
indexOf method (ArrayList class), 368, 369
indexOf method (String), 236, 237
Inequality operator, 79, 198, 199
Infinite loop, 80, 81, 212, 213
INFORMATION_MESSAGE (JOptionPane), 558, 559
Inherit a class, 316, 317
Inheritance, 276, 277
  using with interfaces, 320, 321
Initializing
  constants, 172, 173
  variables, 46, 47, 170, 171
Injection attack (SQL), 514, 515
Inner class, 334-337
Input file, 438, 439
Input stream, 438, 439, 448, 449
InputStreamReader class (java.io), 448, 449
insert method (StringBuilder class), 244, 245
INSERT statement (SQL), 496, 497, 500, 501, 514, 515
Insets class (GridBagLayout), 578, 579, 582, 583
insets field (GridBagConstraints), 582, 583
Inspect variables (debugging), 158, 159
Instance of a class, 64, 65, 98, 99
Instance variable, 102-105
instanceof keyword, 294, 295
Instantiation
  object, 64, 65
  array, 254, 255
int data type, 46, 47, 168, 169
Integer, 168, 169
Integer class, 70, 71
Integrated Development Environment (IDE), 18, 19
IntelliJ IDE, 18, 19
interface keyword, 312, 313
Interface, 308, 309
  advantages, 310, 311
  coding, 312, 313
  compared to abstract class, 310, 311
  implementing, 314, 315
  inheriting, 320, 321
  using as type, 318, 319
Interpreter (Java),16, 17
InterruptedException (java.lang), 470-473
IOException (java.io), 442, 443
ipadx field (GridBagConstraints), 582, 583
ipady field (GridBagConstraints), 582, 583
isAfter method, 396, 397
isBefore method, 396, 397
isDirectory method (Files), 434, 435
isEmpty method (ArrayList), 368, 369
isEmpty method (String), 236, 237
isInterrupted method (Thread), 471
isReadable method (Files), 434, 435
isRegularFile method (Files), 434, 435
isWritable method (Files), 434, 435
Iteration structure, 80

J

J2EE (Java 2 Platform, Enterprise Edition), 4
J2SE (Java 2 Platform, Standard Edition), 4
Jagged array, 262, 263
Java API (Application Programming Interface), 53
Java classes (importing), 62, 63
Java collection framework, 360, 361
Java compiler, 16, 17
Java Database Connectivity (JDBC), 506

Java Development Kit (JDK), 4, 5
Java driver
  native protocol all, 506, 507
  native protocol partly, 506, 507
  net protocol all, 506, 507
Java EE, 4, 5
Java errors (common), 150, 151
Java interpreter, 16, 17
Java ME, 4, 5
Java plug-in, 16, 17
Java runtime environment (JRE), 16, 17
Java SE, 4, 5
Java source code, 40, 41
Java virtual machine (JVM), 16, 17
java.awt package, 542, 543, 578, 579
java.io package, 434, 435, 440, 441
java.lang package, 62, 63
java.math.BigDecimal class, 186, 187
java.math.RoundingMode enumeration, 186, 187
java.nio package, 440, 441
java.nio.file package, 436, 437
java.text package, 390, 391
java.time package, 390, 391
java.util package, 390, 391
javadoc
  comments, 344, 345
  tags, 346, 347
  viewing, 348, 349
JavaFX 532-534
javax.swing package, 536, 537
JButton class (javax.swing), 534, 535, 538, 539
  constructor, 538, 539
JComponent class (javax.swing), 534, 535
JDBC (Java Database Connectivity), 506
JDBC driver manager, 506, 507
JDBC-ODBC bridge driver, 506, 507
JDialog constructor, 586, 587
JDK (Java Development Kit), 4, 5
  install on Mac, 618, 619
  install on Windows, 608, 609
JFrame class (javax.swing), 534-527
JIT (Just-in-time compiler), 16, 17
JLabel class (javax.swing), 534, 535
  constructor, 574, 575
Join strings, 52, 53, 234, 235
JOptionPane message, 558, 559
JPanel class (javax.swing), 534, 535, 538, 539
JRE (Java runtime environment), 16, 17
JScrollPane, 556, 557
JSP (Java Server Page), 10
JTable
  constructor, 554, 555
  terminology, 548, 549
  widget, 548, 549
JTextField class (javax.swing), 534, 535
  constructor, 576, 577
Just-in-time compiler (JIT compiler), 16, 17
JVM (Java virtual machine), 16, 17

K

Key-value pair, 360, 361
Keywords (Java), 46-48

L

Label, 574, 575
Lambda expression, 378-383, 540, 541
lambda operator, 382, 383
last method (ResultSet), 510, 511
lastIndexOf method (String), 236, 237
Late binding, 284
Layering
  input streams, 448, 449
  output streams, 444, 445
  streams, 440, 441
Layout manager, 542, 543, 578, 579
Length (array), 254, 255
length field (array), 258, 259
length method (String), 238, 239
length method (StringBuilder), 242, 243
Less Than operator, 79, 198, 199
Less Than Or Equal operator, 79, 198, 199
Libraries, 22, 23
Life cycle of a thread, 468, 469
Linked list, 360, 361
LinkedList class (java.util), 360, 361
List interface (java.util), 360, 361
Literal value, 48, 49
LocalDate class, 392-401
LocalDateTime class, 392-401
LocalTime class, 392-401
Locking objects, 476, 477
Locks (synchronized keyword), 476, 477
Logic error, 148, 149, 152, 153
Logical operators, 200, 201
long type, 168, 169
Loops, 212-219
  array, 258-261

M

Main class, 22, 23, 32, 33
main method, 14, 15, 32, 33
  declaration, 32, 33
Main thread, 464, 465
Main window, 536, 537
Many-to-many relationship, 486, 487

Map interface (java.util), 360, 361
Math class, 184, 185
max method (Math class), 184, 185
ME (Micro Edition), 4, 5
Members of a class, 102, 103
Method, 14, 15, 32, 33, 96, 97
  calling, 64, 65, 112, 113
  calls, 120, 121
  chaining, 74, 75
  coding, 108, 109
  in an interface, 309
  naming, 108, 109
  overloading, 122, 123
  overriding, 282, 283
  signature, 122, 123
  static, 64, 65
Microsoft SQL Server, 484, 485
Middle tier, 132, 133
min method (Math), 184, 185
minus method (LocalDateTime), 400, 401
minusWeeks method, 400, 401
Mobile app, 12, 13
Modal dialog box, 558, 559, 586, 587
Model (for table), 548, 549
Modulus operator, 174, 175
  compound, 178, 179
Month enumeration, 392, 393
Multi-catch block, 420, 421
Multi-layered architecture, 132
Multiple inheritance, 308
MULTIPLE_INTERVAL_SELECTION, 554, 555
Multiplication operator, 174, 175
  compound, 178, 179
multiply method (BigDecimal class), 186, 187
Multithreading, 464, 465
Multi-tier architecture, 132
Mutable strings, 242, 243
MySQL preference pane (Mac), 622, 623
MySQL Workbench, 490-501
  install on Mac, 624, 625
  install on Windows, 612, 613
MySQL, 484, 485, 490-501
  install on Windows, 612, 613
  install on Mac, 622, 623
  update password on Mac, 626, 627

N

Name elements (of a path), 434, 435
name method (enumeration), 342, 343
Naming conventions
  constants, 172, 173
  classes, 32, 33
  variables, 46, 47, 170, 171
Narrowing conversion, 182, 183
Native protocol all Java driver, 506, 507
Native protocol partly Java driver, 506, 507
Negative sign operator, 176, 177
Nested
  if statement, 82, 83, 204, 205
  loop, 262, 263
Net protocol all Java driver, 506, 507
NetBeans, 18-27
  code editor, 38, 39
  create class, 100, 101
  install on Mac, 619 619
  install on Windows, 608, 609
  Java source code, 40, 41
  new project, 38, 39
  packages, 136, 137
  project, 20, 21
  syntax error, 44, 45
  two or more projects, 26, 27
new keyword, 110, 111
New state (thread), 468, 469
newDirectoryStream method (Files class), 434, 435
next method (ResultSet), 510, 511
nextLine method (Scanner class), 68, 69
NIO.2, 436, 437
NO_OPTION (JOptionPane), 562, 563
Not operator, 200, 201
notExists method (Files class), 434, 435
now method (LocalDateTime), 392, 393
Null, 52, 53
  database, 488, 489
NumberFormat class, 74, 75
Numbers to strings (converting), 74, 75
Numeric variables, 46, 47
  comparing, 78, 79

O

Object, 98, 99
  casting, 294, 295
  comparing, 296, 297
  creating, 64, 65, 110, 111
  identity of, 98, 99
  state of, 98, 99
Object class, 278, 279, 342, 343, 466, 467
Object diagram, 98, 99
Object reference, 110, 111
ODBC (Open Database Connectivity), 506, 507
of method (LocalDateTime), 392, 393
ofLocalized methods, 402, 403
ofLocalizedDate method, 402, 403
ofLocalizedDateTime method, 402, 403
ofLocalizedTime method, 402, 403
OK_CANCEL_OPTION (JOptionPane), 560, 561

OK_OPTION (JOptionPane), 562, 563
One-dimensional array, 262, 263
One-to-many relationship, 486, 487
One-to-one relationship, 486, 487
Operand, 50, 51, 174, 175
  in a Boolean expression, 198, 199
Or operator, 200, 201
Oracle, 484, 485
ORDER BY clause (SELECT statement), 498, 499
Order of precedence, 180, 181
ordinal method (enumeration), 342, 343
Output file, 438, 439
Output stream, 438, 439
  character, 444, 445
Output window (NetBeans), 24, 25
Overloading
  constructors, 106, 107
  methods, 122, 123
Overriding
  annotation for, 280, 281
  methods, 276, 277, 282, 283
  equals method, 296, 297
Owner, 586, 587

P

Package, 14, 15, 22, 23, 32, 33, 134, 135
  Java, 62, 63
  NetBeans, 136, 137
  storing classes in, 134-137
Package naming, 134, 135
Padding components
  GridBagConstraints, 582, 583
  GridBagLayout, 578, 579
Padding strings, 246, 247
Panel
  add buttons, 538, 539
  add to frame, 538, 539
Parameter, 96, 97, 120, 121
  of an interface type, 318, 319
Parameter list (of a method), 108
Parent class, 276, 277
Parent form, 586, 587
  passing data to child form, 588, 589
parse method (LocalDateTime), 392, 393
parseDouble method (Double), 70, 71
parseInt method (Integer), 70, 71
Parsing strings, 234, 235
Passing argument
  by reference, 120, 121
  by value, 120, 121
Password for root user (update), 626, 627
Path interface (java.nio.file), 434-437
Path name
  absolute, 436, 437
  relative, 436, 437
Paths class (java.nio.file), 434-437
Pivot, 532-534
PLAIN_MESSAGE (JOptionPane), 558, 559
Platform independence, 16, 17
Plug-in (Java), 16, 17
plus method (date/time), 400, 401
plusWeeks method (date/time), 400, 401
Polymorphism, 284, 285
Positive sign operator, 176, 177
Postfix an operand, 176, 177
pow method (Math class), 184, 185
Predicate interface (java.util), 384, 385
Prefix an operand, 176, 177
Prepared statements (JDBC), 516, 517
Presentation tier, 132, 133
Primary key, 484, 485
Primitive data types, 46, 47, 168, 169
  comparing to each other, 198, 199
  compared to reference types, 120, 121
print method (PrintWriter class), 446, 447
print method (System.out object), 36, 37
Printing output to the console, 36, 37
println method (PrintWriter class), 446, 447
println method (System.out object), 36, 37
printStackTrace method (Throwable class), 418, 419
PrintWriter class (java.io), 444-447
Private (fields and methods), 96, 97
private keyword, 108, 109
  class declaration, 32, 33
  superclass, 280, 281
Public (fields and methods), 96, 97
public keyword, 108, 109
  class declaration, 32, 33
  superclass, 280, 281

Q

Query (SQL), 498-501
Querying tables (SQL), 498, 499
QUESTION_MESSAGE (JOptionPane), 558, 559

R

random method (Math class), 184, 185
RDBMS (relational database management system), 484
Reader class hierarchy (java.io), 448, 449
Reading
  from console, 68, 69
  from text files, 450, 451

readLine method (BufferedReader class), 450, 451
Read-only result set, 510, 511
Record
  database, 484, 485
  file, 446, 447
Rectangular array, 262, 263
Refactor, 136, 137
Reference type, 110, 111
  array, 266, 267
  compared to primitive type, 120, 121
Referential integrity (MySQL), 490, 491
Relational database, 484, 485
Relational operators, 78, 79, 198, 199
Relationships (between tables), 486, 487
Relative path name, 436, 437
remove method (ArrayList), 368, 369
replace method (StringBuilder), 244, 245
Resizing problem, 584, 585
Result set (SQL), 498-501, 510, 511
  get data from, 512, 513
ResultSet methods, 510, 511
return statement, 108, 109
Return type, 108, 109
Return value (of a method), 112, 113
RIAs (rich Internet applications), 532, 533
Rich Internet applications (RIAs), 532, 533
root user (update password), 626, 627
round method (Math class), 184, 185
Rounding errors (fixing), 188, 189
RoundingMode enumeration, 186, 187
Row,
  database, 484, 485
  file, 446, 447
Row pointer, 510, 511
Run a project (NetBeans), 24, 25
run method (Runnable interface), 466, 467
run method (Thread class), 466, 467, 471
Runnable interface (java.lang), 466, 467
  implementing, 474, 475
Runnable state (thread), 468, 469
Runtime error, 148, 149, 152, 153
Runtime exception, 148, 149
RuntimeException class (java.lang), 220, 221, 410, 411

S

Scale, 186, 187
Scanner class, 68, 69
Schema, 492, 493
Scientific notation, 168, 169
Scope of a class, 32, 33
Scroll pane, 556, 557
Scrollbar, 556, 557
ScrollPaneConstants, 556, 557
SDK (Software Development Kit), 4, 5
SE (Standard Edition), 4, 5
Select database (MySQL), 496, 497
SELECT statement (SQL), 496-501
Selection structure, 82, 202, 203
Servlet, 10, 11
set accessor, 108, 109
Set interface (java.util), 360, 361
set method, 102, 103, 108, 109
  ArrayList class, 368, 369
setBorder method (JTable), 554, 555
setCharAt method (StringBuilder), 244, 245
setColumns method (JTextField), 576, 577
setDefaultCloseOperation method, 536, 537
setEditable method (JTextField), 576, 577
setEnabled method, 538, 539
setHorizontalScrollBarPolicy, 556, 557
setLayout method, 542, 543
setLookAndFeel method, 536, 537
setMaximumFractionDigits method, 74, 75
setMaximumSize method, 584, 585
setMinimumFractionDigits method, 74, 75
setMinimumSize method (JTextField), 576, 577
setModel method (JTable), 554, 555
setPreferredSize method, 576, 577, 584, 585
setResizable method, 584, 585
setScale method (BigDecimal class), 186, 187
setSelectionMode method (JTable), 554, 555
setText method, 538, 539
  JLabel, 574, 575
  JTextField, 576, 577
setToolTipText method, 538, 539
setVerticalScrollBarPolicy, 556, 557
setVisible method, 538, 539
Shallow copy (array), 266, 267
short type, 168, 169
Short-circuit operators, 202, 203
showConfirmDialog method (JOptionPane), 560-563
showMessageDialog method (JOptionPane), 558, 559
Signature
  constructor, 106, 107
  method, 122, 123
Significant digits, 168, 169
SINGLE_INTERVAL_SELECTION, 554, 555
SINGLE_SELECTION, 554, 555
Single-line comment, 34, 35
Single-precision number, 168, 169
Size (array), 254, 255
size method
  ArrayList class, 366, 367
  Files class, 434, 435
sleep method (Thread class), 466, 467, 471-475
Software Development Kit (SDK), 4, 5
sort method (Arrays class), 264, 265

Source code, 16, 17
install on Mac, 620, 621
install on Windows, 610, 611
Special characters, 54, 55
split method (String class), 450, 451
SQL (Structured Query Language), 490
SQL injection attack, 514, 515
SQL script, 496, 497
SQL Server, 484, 485
SQL statement, 494, 495
enter and execute, 494, 495
sqrt method (Math class), 184, 185
Stack trace, 160, 161, 220, 221, 412, 413
Standard Widget Toolkit (SWT), 532-535
start method (Thread class), 466-473
startsWith method (String), 236, 237
State of an object, 98, 99
Statements, 34, 35
static field, 116, 117
calling, 122, 123
coding, 114, 115
importing, 342, 343
when to use, 116
static import, 342, 343
static keyword, 114, 115
static method, 64, 65, 116, 117
calling, 122, 123
coding, 114, 115
interface, 322, 323
importing, 342, 343
when to use, 116
Step through code (debugging), 158, 159
stop method (Thread class), 466- 469
Storing classes in packages, 134-137
Stream, 438, 439
buffered, 440, 441
layering, 440, 441
String, 36, 37, 52, 53
appending, 52, 53, 234, 235
comparing, 78, 79, 236, 237
concatenating, 52, 53, 234, 235
converting to number, 70, 71
escape sequences, 54, 55
index, 238, 239
joining, 52, 53, 234, 235
modifying, 240, 241, 244, 245
padding, 246, 247
parsing, 234, 235
special characters, 54, 55
String class, 234, 235
String literal, 52, 53
String object, 52, 53
StringBuffer class, 242, 243
StringBuilder class, 242, 243
StringUtil class, 246, 247
Structured Query Language (SQL), 490
Subclass, 220, 221, 276, 277
casting to superclass, 294, 295
creating, 282, 283
substring method (String), 240, 241
substring method (StringBuilder), 244, 245
subtract method (BigDecimal), 186, 187
Subtraction operator, 174, 175
compound, 178, 179
super keyword, 282, 283
Superclass, 276, 277
casting to subclass, 294, 295
creating, 280, 281
Swallowing exceptions, 416
Swing, 334, 335, 532-535
inheritance hierarchy, 534, 535
threads, 602, 603
switch statement, 202, 206, 207
SWT (Standard Widget Toolkit), 532-535
synchronized keyword, 476, 477
Synchronous threads, 476, 477
Syntax error, 44, 45, 148-151
common, 150, 151
System.err object, 438
System.in object, 68, 69, 438
System.out object, 36, 37, 438

T

Table (database), 484, 485
adding records, 500, 501
deleting records, 500, 501
querying (SQL), 498, 499
relationships between, 486, 487
updating records, 500, 501
Table (JTable), 548, 549
adding a scrollbar to, 556, 557
creating, 554, 555
creating a model for, 548, 549
Terminated state (thread), 468, 469
Testing
applications, 148, 149
exception handlers, 424, 425
Text box, 574-577
Text field, 574-577
Text file, 438, 439, 444-455
delimited, 446, 447
reading, 450, 451
writing, 446, 447
this keyword, 106, 107, 124, 125
Thread, 464- 473
concurrency, 476, 477
creating, 470-475

Thread (cont.)
  life cycle, 468, 469
  putting to sleep, 471-475
  synchronizing, 476, 477
  with Swing, 602, 603
Thread class (java.lang), 466, 467, 470-473
Thread scheduler, 464, 465, 468, 469
Thread states, 468, 469
Thread-safe, 476, 477
Three-tier architecture, 132, 133
Throw an exception, 70, 71, 220, 221, 412, 413, 422, 423
throw statement, 424, 425
Throwable class (java.lang), 410, 411, 418, 419
  constructor, 424, 425, 428, 429
Throwable hierarchy, 410, 411
throws clause, 422, 423
Times, 392, 393
  comparing, 396, 397
  formatting, 402, 403
toAbsolutePath method (Path), 435
toArray method (ArrayList), 368, 369
toFile method (Path), 435
Toolkit, 532, 533
Tooltip, 538, 539
Top-level widget, 534, 535
toString method
  BigDecimal class, 186, 187
  Object class, 278, 279
  StringBuilder class, 244, 245
  Throwable class, 418, 419
Trace execution, 154, 155
Transaction processing (MySQL), 490, 491
TreeMap class (java.util), 360, 361
trim method (String), 240, 241
try block, 222, 223
try/catch statement, 222, 223, 414, 415
try-with-resources statement, 416, 417
Two-dimensional array, 262, 263
Type variable, 362, 363
Typed collection, 362, 363
Type-safe enumerations, 340, 341

U

UIManager class, 536, 537
UML (Unified Modeling Language), 96, 97
Unary operator, 176, 177
Unchecked exception, 410, 411, 426, 427
Unicode character set, 168, 169
Unicode characters, 438, 439
Unified Modeling Language (UML), 96, 97
UPDATE statement (SQL), 500, 501, 514, 515
User thread, 470, 471

VALUES clause (SQL), 496, 497
Variable, 46, 47, 170, 171
  array, 254, 255
  initializing, 46, 47, 170, 171
  numeric, 46, 47
  string, 52-55
VERTICAL_SCROLLBAR_ALWAYS, 556, 557
VERTICAL_SCROLLBAR_AS_NEEDED, 556, 557
VERTICAL_SCROLLBAR_NEVER, 556, 557
void keyword, 108, 109

W

Waiting state (thread), 468, 469
WARNING_MESSAGE (JOptionPane), 558, 559
WHERE clause (SELECT statement), 498, 499
while loop, 80, 81, 212, 213
while statement, 80, 81, 212, 213
Widening conversion, 182, 183
Widget, 532, 533
  top-level, 534, 535
Window (main), 536, 537
Window class (java.awt), 534, 535
withDayOfMonth method, 398, 399
withDayOfYear method, 398, 399
withHour method, 398, 399
withMinute method, 398, 399
withMonth method, 398, 399
withYear method, 398, 399
Workbench (MySQL)
  install on Mac, 624, 625
  install on Windows, 612, 613
Wrapper class, 70, 71, 362, 363, 370, 371
Writer hierarchy, 444, 445
Writing text files, 446, 447

YES_NO_CANCEL_OPTION (JOptionPane), 560, 561
YES_NO_OPTION (JOptionPane), 560, 561
YES_OPTION (JOptionPane), 562, 563

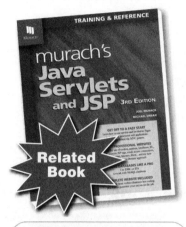

What software you need for this book

- Java SE 8 (JDK 1.8) or later.
- NetBeans IDE 8.0 or later.
- MySQL 5.6 or later.
- MySQL Workbench 6.3 or later.
- You can download this software for free and install it as described in appendix A (Windows) or appendix B (Mac OS X).

The downloadable files for this book

- Complete source code for the applications presented in this book, so you can view the source code and run the applications as you read each chapter.
- Starting points for the exercises presented at the end of each chapter, so you can get more practice in less time.
- Solutions to the exercises, so you can check your work.

How to install the source code for this book

1. Go to murach.com.
2. Go to the page for ***Murach's Beginning Java with NetBeans.***
3. Follow the instructions there to download the zip file that contains the source code for the applications and exercises for this book.
4. Unzip all files. This creates the java_netbeans folder that contains these subfolders: book_apps, ex_starts, ex_solutions, and db.
5. If necessary, create the murach folder on your hard drive.
6. Copy the java_netbeans folder into the murach folder.

- For more information, please see appendix A (Windows) or B (Mac OS X).

How to set up the database for this book

1. Install the source code for this book as described above.
2. Use MySQL Workbench to run the create_database.sql script that's in the db folder. This creates the database described in this book.
3. If a password hasn't been assigned to the root user, which is common on new installations of MySQL on Mac OS X, run the update_root_user.sql script that's in the db folder. This sets a password for the root user.

- For more information, please see appendix A (Windows) or B (Mac OS X).